Martial Art of Horary Astrology

J. Lee Lehman, Ph.D.

A Division of Schiffer Publishing, Ltd.
4880 Lower Valley Road, Atglen, PA 19310
USA

Dedication

To my mother, Kathryn Elizabeth Kennedy Lehman (1916-1998), who may not always have believed in what I was doing, but *always* believed in me.

To my father, Alan D. Lehman, who still provides daily inspiration through his encouragement, intellect, and scholarship.

Library of Congress Card Number: 2001098062

Layout and cover design by Douglas Congdon-Martin
Chart design by the author using Solar Fire v.5 by Esoteric Technologies, Pty. Ltd.
Type set in Korinna BT

ISBN: 0-924608-25-0
Printed in the U.S.A

Published by Whitford
A Division of Schiffer Publishing
4880 Lower Valley Road
Atglen, PA 19310
Phone: (610) 593-1777; Fax: (610) 593-2002
E-mail: Schifferbk@aol.com
Please visit our web site catalog at **www.schifferbooks.com**
We are always looking for people to write books on new and related subjects. If you have an idea for a book please contact us at the above address.

This book may be purchased from the publisher.
Include $3.95 for shipping.
Please try your bookstore first.
You may write for a free catalog.

Contents

Acknowledgments

There are always far more people who should be thanked than one actually manages to thank. Every client I ever had taught me something. The same with every student. And yet, it always seems easiest to thank the teachers.

I have been mostly self-taught, and so my teachers have been the authors of books. Sometimes it's not always clear which teaches more: the sources that one agrees with, or the sources that one doesn't. The formal teacher that I had for the longest time in astrology was Olivia Barclay (1919-2001). Olivia and I managed to put up with each other despite differences of nationality, viewpoint, education, values, and even sometimes language for long enough for me to complete her diploma course in horary. If afterwards I felt the need to set out on my own, it does not negate the fact that for a time, we walked the path together.

I am grateful to Don Weiser and the late Betty Lundsted for pointing me to books I never knew existed. A good book dealer is as great a gift as a good reference librarian, and Don and Betty became friends as well. And I am grateful to my Kepler colleagues, Nick Campion, and Demetra George, for pushing me to excel even more than I would on my own. I can only hope that I have provided them as much as they have given me.

Also thanks to Graham Dawson and Stephanie Johnson of Esoteric Technologies Pty. Ltd. for permission to use Solar Fire chart formats in this book.

Helping me through every step of the way these past seventeen years has been Margaret Meister. Maggie has also contributed countless hours to editing cajoling, and arguing with me over passages in this book: this represents her passion as much as mine.

And I am especially grateful to my student and graduate, Sandy Curran, for reading the entire manuscript. Not only did Sandy catch a number of errors that Maggie and I missed, she provided valuable feedback and suggestions. Judy Curtiss, friend in T'ai Chi and all-around smart lady, helped.

All errors remaining are mine.

Table of Examples

First House Questions

Second House Questions:

Third House Questions

Fourth House Questions

Fifth House Questions

Sixth House Questions

Seventh House Questions

Eighth House Questions

Ninth House Questions

Tenth House Questions

Eleventh House Questions

Twelfth House Questions

Chapter 13 Questions

White Belt.
Why this Book?– and Why the Title?

Astrology is both Art and Technique. To fully grasp these two simple words, we must engage both the historical and a cross-cultural context. The English word "technique" is derived from the Greek word *techne*, which has a much broader meaning. *Techne* is what the Medieval guilds taught. This was the vocational system in which an apprentice was adopted into a master's workshop where he – unfortunately, it always seemed to be *he* – went from seemingly meaningless manual labor, to a gradual acquisition of the tools and the practices of the craft. As his skills began to reach a certain acceptable level, he was sent out into the world as a journeyman, where he began with small or lesser projects, and possibly with training from other masters. Finally, when his technique had truly blossomed, he would create and submit a "master piece" – a work demonstrating mastery of the craft.

While this system has virtually disappeared as a form of vocational training, it remains the training method for traditional Asian style martial arts. While we call them traditional, in fact the modern style of training in the martial arts as a sport is only a relatively recent phenomenon,[1] although particular punches, throws or kicks may be thousands of years old. Martial arts training teaches a combination of method and intuition. The beginner is taught a series of moves or positions – much as the various *asana* in yoga. At first, this makes little sense. The positions are so specific that it's difficult to envision an attacker approaching from a direction and posture that would allow a response! But the ultimate answer is that these "positions" are there to form a meditation in movement – one that the student doesn't even recognize as being a meditation. At first, the student simply *goes through* the motions. At some point, the student *becomes* the motions. This is the process of Mastery. Once this happens, the student goes beyond the positions in a completely *creative* response to the stimuli of the moment. Now here is the vital point. *Mastery cannot be taught, but it can be transmitted.* How do we understand this riddle?

The "technique" portion of *techne* can be taught. This is the easy part. Technique applied over and over becomes embedded in Consciousness. Eventually, technique metamorphoses into "Art." *How* this happens is different for every individual. *Whether* it will happen is mostly a function of the equation: **good technique applied to lots of examples ultimately allows Mastery to manifest.**

And this is what the martial arts allow. Each student practices "forms" (a choreographed sequence of moves) literally hundreds of times before being permitted to advance to a higher level – and then the student receives a new form to practice again. Watch students progressing through the ranks of the martial arts, and you will see a gradual transition from a very rigid and tentative movement, to movement more fluid, confident and powerful. Watch the same form as practiced by a white belt (beginning) practitioner and a black belt (senior) practitioner and you will almost believe that it is a different form. And yet, there is something very Zen about the difference. A white belt practices from the position of beginner body and beginner mind. The black belt has a body trained to act instinctively in ways the beginner can only intuit – and yet the truly great martial artist can operate from trained body and beginner mind, as each move is practiced, but so fresh it is as if it were newly invented today.

I believe that Horary Astrology functions exactly like a martial art. Repetitive practice results not merely in good technique, but ultimately in Art that goes beyond all technique. The reason? Horary Astrology is the only branch of Astrology that deals with matters exclusively *in the moment* – and insight, *satori*, or *samadi* – whatever word you choose to express that out-of-time experience of immediate and immanent Reality also is *in the moment*. Horary Astrology is the astrological manifestation of that same encapsulation of instant and eternity – because in a Question, there is *only* the moment. When we examine birth charts, there is the birth, and in each subsequent moment, there are the transits, progressions, profections, dasas, solar returns, lunations, eclipses – all sorts of accretions and accumulations that take us out of the birth moment. The Horary has only the eternally elusive *Now* – and this makes all the difference in interpretation and delineation. Considered to its fullest potential, a Horary is like a Zen *koan* – a question whose "answer" actually produces a *satori*, or flash of insight.

The purpose of this work is to present the *techne* of Horary, viewed through the lens of Western Classical Astrology. By the time you finish reading this, you will have a good understanding of how Classical Astrology works, how Horary works, the kinds of Questions that Horary can answer, and the approaches that are available to answering those questions.

The next step is up to you. Without your own examples, this book is useless to you. The charts you examine, study and wrestle with are the alchemical ingredients for that mysterious process by which **you** are being worked as you *appear* to be working the charts. Horary, like any true art, cannot be taught only through lecturing or reading to the otherwise passive listener or reader. The student must wrestle with the teaching by bringing it into his or her own being. Once you let the teaching into your being, you can become the ground within which the process germinates. But all growth requires water, and often fertilizer, not to mention care. The charts you study are the raw materials for this process. So don't hesitate to dig in!

Yellow Belt
What is Horary Astrology?
Where and When?
Asking & Negotiating the Question.

> *"For as the* Nativity *is the time of the Birth of the Body, the* Horary Question *is the time of the Birth of the Minde..."*
>
> - John Gadbury[2]

Horary Astrology is the process of examining questions that are asked in Sacred Time. Horary shares this with virtually all other divinatory techniques, whether Tarot, *I Ching*, runes, geomancy, or the examination of chicken bones. And so, to a very large extent, the difference between divinatory methods is primarily a consideration of tools and technologies.

The essential question is: what constitutes sacred time? Consider the Oracle at Delphi. Odysseus didn't just saunter up to the Oracle with a question! In fact, the **Querent** (person asking the question) had better be *very* sure that she or he wanted to ask the Oracle anything at all, because the consequences of frivolity were grave. At the very least, you might not be allowed near the Oracle. But you might also be cursed by the Oracle, and that was equivalent of being cursed by the Divine! The Oracle (actually a person in an altered state of consciousness, whether through meditation or drugs) was located in a building or natural grotto at the center of a complex. The aspirant walked along a sacred path that took hours to complete. Jogging was not allowed! This in effect represented a walking or moving meditation. By the time that the petitioner actually arrived at the Oracle, s/he had had plenty of time to consider the question. As a result, by this stage the Question was anything but casual.

The issue of creating a meditation around a Question is the essence of entering sacred space. We ask questions constantly. We watch the news, and ask our companions, "Is he for real?" as we hear a politician's speech. We ask when the car repair will be finished or what we should have for dinner. We ask questions when we teach and ask more of them when we study. We ask questions on the job. But how many of these questions really *mean* anything? For the most part, they are simple curiosities of the moment, gone from consciousness ten minutes later. These are not Horary Questions, nor Tarot, nor *I Ching* Questions, for that matter.

Any proper divinatory Question is not casual. It is heartfelt. The Querent *must* be more concerned with getting *any* answer at all, rather than being completely committed to the *desired* answer. Let's consider an example scenario.

Karen has been dating Emilio for two months. Karen wonders if she and Emilio will get married. You are friends with Karen, and so she asks you what you think. Is this a Horary Question?

- No, if Karen has been asking this question about Emilio with the same degree of urgency (which is to say, probably little) every time she has talked to you for the last month. This is merely a device to get the conversation going with you about Emilio. Karen is engaging in two Divinatory Taboos: her question isn't really that serious, and she's repeating the same question over and over.

- No, if five minutes earlier she asked the same question about Hans, whom she met last night!

- Probably, if you can see that Karen is really agonizing over this question, losing sleep, or she woke up in the middle of the night last night with this question blazing forth in her mind, and you either haven't heard the question before, or you haven't heard it with any depth or conviction before.

Okay, let's take this a step further. Suppose you and Karen are also friends with Angela, and you're talking to Angela, not Karen. Angela is telling you about her conversation with Karen about Emilio, and now Angela asks, "Will Karen and Emilio get married?" Is this a Horary Question?

This is great gossip, but probably bad Horary. Not to insult Angela, but the real issue is whether she can really get her own emotions embroiled over what Karen will do. If Angela had just broken up with Emilio, and Emilio had gotten into a bounce-back relationship with Karen, then probably Angela *would* have enough emotional steam built up to ask the question! Short of a jealousy or a supreme loathing subplot, or perhaps some arcane economic or business incentive, the fact is that friends are not usually that emotionally attached to ask questions about the potential marriage partners of their friends.

Consider, however, the different emotional dynamic for Angela in asking about her other friend Mary, who had just been diagnosed with colon cancer. Now, Angela is probably absolutely emotionally devastated, and so she asks if Mary will be able to recover. There may be an issue here about whether you would choose to delineate this question, but there's probably no doubt that this is a *very* viable Horary Question.

Back to Angela. Suppose Angela is not Karen's friend, but Karen's mother. The possibility of Karen's marriage raises all sorts of issues for Angela: grandchildren, is Emilio good enough for her daughter, where will they live, etc. Here the issue of Karen's marriage has a much clearer and immediate emotional impact on Angela, so this is likely to be a good Horary Question.

What we see in these different examples is that we have a simple question – marriage – but a complex environment surrounding the question. A True Horary is not a matter of simple curiosity, but one of passionate concern. The measure of a Horary Question is the level of intent of the Querent, and unfortunately, this is something we never know, except when we ask our own questions. All we can do is to look for clues, and try to eliminate the cases where the Querent really is too distant from the action to be that engaged.

So if we filter out the "non-passionate" horaries, is everything left a proper Horary? I don't think so.

Consider George, a passionate fan of the Denver Broncos. George wants to know if the Broncos are going to win the game this Sunday. Not only does George eat, drink and sleep football, but he's bet $2,000 on the Broncos in Vegas, so he *really* cares about whether they win. So can George ask the Horary Question, "Will the Broncos win?"

He may be able to ask the Question, but I wouldn't answer it. Why? Because there's already a better chart to look at, namely the chart for the game itself. There is a question of priority in selecting which chart to read. This idea was expressed as early as 200 C.E. by Dorotheus of Sidon in his work on **Interrogations.** Interrogatory Astrology is composed of the three sisters: Horary, Electional, and Event Interpretation. Dorotheus showed that the three of them are interpreted through extremely similar rules. However, whenever there is an actual event – or perhaps we should say an event with a known time – then the event takes precedence over a horary *about* the event.

The example Dorotheus gave was a question of theft. If you know when an object was stolen, then you don't need to ask a question about the theft. If this seems a little strange, consider that I have gotten questions from people who have been mugged on the street, and know *exactly* when the item was stolen. Attempting to add a horary question as a supplement usually just confuses, rather than clarifies, the issue. If your interrogatory/horary method is sound, then you don't need to pile up additional charts or techniques to support your original thesis.

To return to the Broncos game, the time of a football match is known months in advance if it is a regular season game, and at least a week in advance if it is a post-season game. Therefore, it's better to consider the game chart than the horary chart. However, I should admit that my point of view is controversial, and that many horary astrologers insist on interpreting questions about games, or presidential elections for that matter. I believe there are two reasons for this:

1. Most horary astrologers have never studied gaming astrology, and in the absence of any specific knowledge of the subject, default to known horary rules, or

2. Virtually everyone who studies Interrogatory Astrology gets there via horary, and so it's just more comfortable.

I am far less concerned about comfort than about accuracy. It strains my imagination to realize that 200 million Americans could ask who will win the next election, and that all 200 million would ask at the right time! If they don't, then the astrologer is thrown back upon trying to decide whether the Querent cares *enough* to ask the question, or has enough invested – either emotionally or materially. That in turn is a difficult judgment call – one that the Astrologer really should not have to make.

Unless the event is scheduled, such as an election or a sporting match, the vast majority of the time, the event has already happened. Whether you happen to know the time is another issue, but horary is not meant to substitute for the laziness of not wanting to bother finding out when the event occurred. If, however, the time *cannot* be known, as in a theft which *could* have occurred anytime between when you left the house and returned from work last Thursday, then of course a Horary is completely appropriate.

It's important to remember that the issue of which chart to use – an event or a horary – does not obscure the issue of *how* to read the chart once it has been obtained. The only major difference in focus of the two is that, in the case of horary, the 1st House is the Querent, while in event interpretation, the 1st House is given to the event itself or the subject of the event.

What other kinds of questions are not Horaries? Questions that do not have answers! The question must be *answerable*. "Answerable" is a little broader than its initial meaning may suggest. Consider the question, "Does God exist?" This question may be "answerable" in the sense that one can envision that the response could be either "yes" or "no;" that is; it is possible to frame an appropriate-appearing response. However, this is *not* answerable by reason of lack of verification: how could we possibly tell whether we were right or wrong? If I cannot study the answer to the question, how can I learn to do a better job? This criterion would apply to questions about karma and past lives, theology, philosophy, and speculative history. (e.g., did Lee Harvey Oswald *really* kill John F. Kennedy?)

Here's another variant on the theme. I'm writing this in 1999, the year before the Christian/ Common Era Second Millennium. Many people have been expressing concern about whether we will survive. If you are reading this, we did! Since roughly 1980, I noticed people asking questions like: "Will we survive the Millennium as a species?" (Or if you are New Age in outlook, it was probably, survive as the *same* species!) Okay. Here we have an answerable question, and even one where we can check the result, because either we are still here by the end of the year 2000 or we are not.

There's still a problem. What does Armageddon look like in a chart? I'm serious. First: what is the cause? Would the End of the World by war look different than by environmental disaster? What if the reason was because the Sun's radiation decreased or increased, resulting in a climate change that kills everything on the Earth? What would intervention by a Messiah look like? Exactly how bad does it have to get to be the Point of No Return? Without an answer to this question, we actually have no basis for prediction and, hence, for reading such a chart as a Horary. This is also a good justification for staying away from historically speculative natal charts, such as Jesus, Buddha, or the beginning of the world, for that matter. How can we pretend to have any knowledge of what those charts would look like?

What we have seen so far is that for a question to be a proper Horary Question, the following must be true:

1. The person asking the Question must be emotionally or mentally involved in the question.

2. The question can only be asked once or, at least, answered once. (Sometimes, for technical reasons[3], the question cannot be answered. If that is the case, the Querent may try again later.)

3. The question must have a meaningful, verifiable answer.

What else? I shall be taking up some issues of wording and syntax shortly, but before we get there, just one more caution. Horary is not very good at psychologically or spiritually based questions. Thus, the question, "Is my karma complete in San Francisco so that I can move to Denver?" is much inferior from a Horary perspective than, "Will I move to Denver within the next six months?" The problem with karma is that there is no independent measure of it, and the other problem is that the question implies that the move to Denver will *only* be possible if the San Francisco karma is complete. Suppose it is your karma to move to Denver *without* completing your karma in San Francisco? What then?

There are appropriate questions of a spiritual or psychological nature in Horary, but they must have some basis in physical reality for a good result. You could ask, "Would it be a good idea to travel to India to study with my guru?" Here, the 9th House can be used to evaluate both the trip and the guru. Or you could ask, "Would group therapy be beneficial to my self-understanding?" If we identify self-understanding as being akin to spiritual growth, then we at least have a house that we can use to evaluate an answer. Any answerable horary question requires some method to select a house or planet to represent the outcome or other party.

Where and When to Place the Question

A Horary Question is taken for the time when the astrologer "understands" the question. However, like most of life, understanding occurs as part of a stream of events. Let's consider the actual steps which could lead to a Horary Question.

- The Querent ponders the question for some time, mulling over the issues. Finally: ah ha! I could ask a Horary question! Now, where did I put that astrologer's business card?

- The Querent now writes/calls/faxes/e-mails/sees the astrologer.

- The Querent and Astrologer "negotiate" a question.

Which of these events actually constitutes the Question? I would argue that, at least for a beginning Querent, only the third step in the sequence qualifies. In a sense, a Formal Question (which is what a Horary is – a question that has become embedded in a ritual matrix by the very act of taking it so seriously) is like a legal contract: it takes two parties. In this case, the two parties are the questioner and the questioned. Until both parties are engaged, neither the contract nor the question is "legal." Steps 1 and 2 are like the preliminary steps leading to a contract: someone has to do them, but without the agreement of the two sides, there still is no contract yet.

On Location:

Unfortunately, a complication to placing the Question was added by Ivy Goldstein-Jacobson.[4] That complication involved where geographically to place the question if the question was asked by letter or over the phone. The issue is this. I may not live in the same city as the Querent. So whose location should be used? Jacobson decided to always use the Querent's. I think this borders on silly, because it violates all rules of event-based astrology. Consider the following scenario.

Suppose the Querent lives in Denver, I live in Florida. So the Querent sends me a letter asking a Question; I read it and take down the time. What is happening in Denver at the time that I am taking down the time? Nothing! What is happening in my location in Florida? The Question!

Until Jacobson modified this idea, there was never an issue of where to locate the Question. When William Lilly was living in Diseworth, England, he did the chart for Diseworth. Although most of his examples don't mention the means of getting the Question, I can tell you this: Diseworth is not on anybody's normal route, unless they happen to live there! Which tells me that he was getting his questions by a traveler, messenger or courier.

A horary represents an actual event, namely, the time a question is asked in a divinatory context. If the astrologer determines the time of the question, then what is going on in the location of the Querent? Nothing! Because when the astrologer is pondering the question, the Querent has no idea that this is taking place, unless the Querent is also the Astrologer! Similarly, when the Querent is writing the letter, the astrologer has absolutely no idea what is taking place!

In fact, we know that Jacobson's idea violates tradition. Why? Because in all the examples of horary by letter in sources such as Lilly, Sibly, and even the horary examples from Alan Leo's *Modern Astrology* series, there is no evidence that any astrologer ever used anything but his own location at the time of the question.

Some of the most obvious examples of "astrologer at a distance" were medical. The tradition that evolved was that a sick person would send a messenger – a family member or servant – to notify the doctor/astrologer of his/her illness. It was customary to send a sample of a bodily fluid (usually urine), along with a detailed description of the symptoms. The health care worker (to use our modern designation!) would then cast a chart in his own location for the time of receiving the sample – hence, the old job description of urine caster, for the person who casts horoscopes for medical diagnosis.

Would you redo a natal horoscope if you discovered that the father was absent at the time of birth, and then use the father's location as the standard chart in order to give him some sense of participation? Of course you wouldn't! The father has already contributed to the birth by providing his DNA, just as the Querent has contributed to the question by posing it in the first place! So I believe that we must adhere to the idea that there has to be an event in a particular time and place if that is the chart used.

Many astrologers date and time their letters when they send them. And if a Querent specifies a time when they are asking the Question, then that time may constitute a valid Horary time – in *their* location. It would be just as silly to take their time and my location! The issue to be grasped here is that understanding a Horary Question is an actual event. And while you can relocate an event, I don't think any astrologer would read a relocated chart in preference to the radix coordinates.

If I (the astrologer) must read and understand the question to make it a Horary Question, then it isn't real until I say so – until real understanding happens in me, so of course it is taking place in my location. However, there are still some possible scenarios that are not entirely covered by what we have said so far.

The above holds for mail, e-mail, fax, written correspondence, or any other means of transmission. For a question asked in person, there's no conflict anyway. The one area *not* addressed by classical astrology is the phone call. In this case, I examine both charts, and read the one that *looks* like the background circumstances described. The reason that I make an exception for this particular scenario is that sometimes, a true Horary Question is asked in the absence of an Astrologer, and this could be one of those cases – as it appears to be, maybe about 30% of the time.

To recap, **use the time and place where you understand the question**. If you are curious about what the Querent was thinking, then do a chart for the time and place that the Querent *sent the mail*, if you have it – from e-mail, for example. Either of those are real charts. But horary is like a legal contract – it doesn't take effect until the final signature is on the page!

Going Solo

Can a Horary Question be asked without the intercession of an Astrologer? Yes, of course, but only if the Querent has successfully achieved Sacred Space without support or guidance. The most common instance of this is waking up in the middle of the night with a fully-formed question. If I get a call the next day from a Querent who describes this, I never even bother to take down the current time – I *always* use the Querent's time and location. I also have what I call Experienced Querents – those who have been trained to the Horary process and know a Horary Moment when they experience it. This Querent has become the equivalent of an Astrologer who asks her/his own Horary Question, but in the absence of the ability to delineate the chart.

The important issue, as I've said from the start, is that the Querent arrives at Sacred Space, because then the Question is truly aligned with the Heavens. We as Astrologers act as the agent of that process when we take Horary Questions. However, an Astrologer can act as this agent without being able to delineate a Horary! I delineate questions as referrals from other Astrologers, either when they have the client call me directly, or if they take the Question from the client and then call me with the time and date in *their* (i.e., the Astrologers') location. I take this Question as developed by another Astrologer *exactly* as if I had spoken directly to the client. I then delineate the Question to the Astrologer, who then passes it on to the Querent.

Let's clarify this by example. Suppose that Susan is the Querent, and Jane is her regular astrologer. They both live in Cleveland. Susan is in the midst of a consultation with Jane, and says, "Do you suppose that I'll ever marry Sam?" Jane tells Susan, "That's a Horary question. I'm not trained in Horary." At this point, one of two pathways occurs.

- Jane says, "You should talk to Lee because she can answer your question. Here's her card. Susan calls me up, and asks the question, and we proceed using the time she asks me and my location in Florida.

- Jane says, "Let me take down your question. I'll get back to you with an answer once I've consulted with Lee." Jane takes down the time that Susan asked the question and calls me. I then read the question for that time, in Cleveland, as having been the moment of the question. This option also includes Jane not admitting to Susan that she doesn't do Horary, but saying instead, "Let me get back to you!" and then calling me for the delineation, which then gets relayed to Susan.

Negotiating the Question

Very frequently, the initial attempt at a question is not really the Question. This is often because the Querent is so involved in the emotional ramifications of the question that clarity is not that easy. Let's sort out some of the issues we need to address before moving on to actually figuring out how to answer the Question.

The first consideration lies in the vagaries of language itself. The Question may seem completely obvious to the Querent, but this does not translate to another party. Take the following Question: Should I leave my job? This is perfectly obvious in normal syntax, but as a Horary, it doesn't work. What does "should" mean? "Should could mean any of the following:

- Do I need to get out before I murder my boss?

- Would I be better off working for the company across the street?

- Is this a dead-end job for me?

- Will I get passed up for promotion because I insulted my boss's boss last week?

- Am I about to be fired?

- Is the company about to go bankrupt?

- Are they going to take away my raise?

- Am I about to be transferred to another department?

Each of the items above represents a legitimate Horary Question embedded in the vague "Should I leave my job" question. But notice: you cannot tell which version the Querent actually means, and the delineation of each of these alternative questions is not necessarily the same.

Seldom does the word "should" belong in a Horary Question, although occasionally its meaning is obvious, as in, "Should I marry Dave?" In that case, we normally don't concern ourselves with secondary agendas as we do with jobs, and the Question that is then addressed is either, "Will I marry Dave?" or "Would Dave and I have a good marriage?"

While we're on the topic of marriage, we can proceed to the next item of negotiation: euphemisms. Consider the question: "Is he my soul mate?" What does this question mean? In one sense, this fits into our category of unanswerable questions, because, frankly, Horary doesn't work on the Astral Plane anyway! But beyond that unfortunate shortcoming of Horary, what would the Querent do with the information anyway, even if it were forthcoming?

I have observed that the question is asked in this fashion when you have a Querent with a level of New Age or other religious point-of-view, who gets caught up in a whirlwind romance, generally with a significant 5th House influence! The Querent is not used to such an intensely sexual dynamic, and then tries to understand/rationalize it by assuming that the two of them have clearly done this before, so that's why it's so fast now.

So suppose he *is* your soul mate. So what? Does that mean that you *have* to have a (sexual) relationship with that person *this* time? Could it be that in the past you were parent-child, and you're actually committing karmic incest here? Being soul mates doesn't necessarily change anything – it doesn't guarantee that it will be a wonderful relationship, it doesn't mean you won't get hurt, and it doesn't guarantee that it will last for the rest of this life. Chances are, if you've spent time with this person before, you've also made some serious mistakes before, since most of us manage to do *that* without a whole lot of prompting.

As a result, I simply won't take this question without insisting on going further. My usual approach is to say, if I were able to tell you that you and he *are* soul mates, how would that make the relationship different? That question is usually enough to get the Querent thinking about what the real issue here is, which is usually that the Querent is feeling very vulnerable, and trying to get some reassurance that it's okay. If that's the case, then the real Question is generally, "Will I have a committed relationship with this person," which is a perfectly answerable Horary Question.

This negotiation phase is the time when you get the background information related to the Question. The Querent is usually only too happy to provide it. If he wants to know if it would be a good idea to leave his job *today*, then the obvious follow-up question is, what's so bad about your job that you might want to do this? This background information can be very useful in the stage where you are testing the Question; that is, making sure that you feel comfortable going ahead and answering.

So suppose he says, "I have the boss from hell, who's out to get me. Just this week, this creep lied about me to his boss and he's determined to prevent me from ever getting promoted." So you take the time, do the chart, and now the boss comes out in the chart to be Venus in Pisces. What's wrong with this picture? Clearly, the astrological signature for the boss doesn't match up with the Querent's description. This could mean several things:

- The Querent has completely over dramatized the situation to the point that the premise about the scenario is incorrect.
- The Querent has already asked this question of somebody else, and so this isn't sacred time and space anyway, so the description of the boss is random, so to speak.
- This is one of those cases of a simultaneous conversation in two places (e.g., I'm in Florida and my client is in France), and you've used the wrong place!
- The Querent is lying to you.
- The Querent is delusional.
- This just simply isn't the time of the question.

In any of these cases, would *you* want to answer the Question? I wouldn't! My position is that if I cannot see the *known* scenario behind a question through the chart, how can I use the chart to bring *unknown* information to light? There are other methods that we will cover shortly for examining the chart in more detail for the background surrounding the Question, but this is perhaps the most basic. The chart should look like the Question. If it doesn't, then you may not want to delineate it.

If we could always be sure that the Querent hasn't already asked the question, that the Querent is asking the right question, and that the Querent is really in sacred space, then we wouldn't have to bother with this negotiation phase. And of course, if we would just dispense with technological means of exchanging information, we'd never have to worry about what location to use for the question. But I'm not willing to give up my telephone or computer, and I don't expect my clients want to give up theirs either!

Other Thoughts on Asking the Question

First, let me mention explicitly that it is perfectly legitimate to ask and answer your own questions. I doubt very many people would ever study astrology if they were excluded from studying the charts of themselves and the people closest to them, and Horary is no exception to this general rule. With experience, you may find that you lack the objectivity to read your own questions at all. Or you may find that most of the time you do fine, but occasionally you need help. Or you may find no difference between your interpretation for yourself or for others. Where you fall on this spectrum is completely personal.

There is an adage to the effect that you cannot ask the same question twice. I would go further with this and say that you cannot ask the same question twice *regardless of the divinatory technique you wish to apply*. In other words, you cannot ask the question to Tarot and then turn around and ask the question as a horary.

Let's be honest. The reason that a question gets asked a second time is because the Querent didn't like the answer the first time. This is why it's so important to encourage provisional wording in the negotiation phase, such as "Will I get married in the next two years?" instead of "Will I ever marry again?" Granted, it is possible that, following a negative answer to the "ever marry" question, that the Querent adopts such a fundamentally different outlook on life that the circumstances of the first question are no longer valid. But how can anyone truly evaluate whether circumstances have changed enough to result in the possibility of a new answer?

I have an inkling of how this could actually work in practice. A client asked a whole series of questions about relationships with different men. It was clear from the horaries that the men had no interest in her at all. It was also clear to me from our interaction that she had basic difficulty in relating to *anyone*, so it comes as no surprise that she had trouble forming a romantic relationship. Now suppose this woman went into a program of psychological counseling. She could potentially come out of it with a completely different attitude toward relationships, and I would expect any relationship horaries that she asked to change dramatically. But how can I as an outsider to the psychological process evaluate whether she has gone through enough change to warrant a new question? It is possible to get a valid new answer to the same divinatory question if there is genuine transformation in circumstance. But where does surface rearrangement end, and true change begin?

As horary astrologers, we are not in a position to answer that question. We do not pretend to know another's heart. I believe it is more prudent to avoid having to make that assessment by discouraging open-ended questions that lack ending points in time. While it may be legitimate to ask if you'll ever marry Bill B., that is much more specific and much less potentially damaging than, "Will I ever marry?"

In summary, while we are not medical doctors, it's always wise to remember the Hippocratic dictum to do no harm. Part of your acceptance of a Horary Question is your agreement to the appropriateness of the Question. While the answer that you give may be painful in that it does not reflect the Querent's desires, we should consider carefully before answering any question that may encourage the Querent to simply give up and surrender to misery concerning an area of life: that they never would have a decent relationship, job, home, income, health, or some other life theme. It's too easy for us then to become the guarantor of failure, rather than an advocate of hope.

Green Belt
Before you Run the Chart:
General Delineation Methods.
Considerations Before Judgment.
Timing and Direction.

Do not, therefore, bring to the diviner desire, or aversion, and do not approach him with trembling, but having first made up your mind that every issue is indifferent and nothing to you, but that, whatever it may be, it will be possible for you to turn it to good use, and that no one will prevent this. Go, then, with confidence to the gods as counsellors; and after that, when some counsel has been given you, remember whom you have taken as counsellors, and whom you will be disregarding if you disobey.

- Epictetus, *Encheiridon*[5]

Before you even attempt to examine a chart using classical horary, you have to know what classical astrology is. I have written an introductory book called *Classical Astrology for Modern Living* which explains the tenets of classical astrology from a natal perspective. Many of the other works in the References may be similarly helpful.

Many of the same concepts are shared between classical horary and natal. Rather than attempt to repeat these methods here, I have put a brief introduction to classical methods in Appendix A. If you do not have a background in classical methods, *please* familiarize yourself with them first. You will do yourself and the method a disservice by being unclear on fundamentals.

Okay: ready? Here we go. In this era of computers, running the chart itself is usually the least of our worries. The whole question then becomes: what do I do with it, now that I have it in front of me?

A long time ago, in what seems like a previous incarnation, or possibly a galaxy far away, I was a scientist. In one of the books I read on statistics, I came across the following formula for problem solving:

I. *Defining the problem* – what is being sought?

II. *Choosing the method* – how can the answer be found?

III. *The interpretation* – what do the results mean?[6]

In statistics, one learns to think about the method of analyzing the problem long before any data is assembled. This branch of statistics is known as the Design of Experiments. This particular method is one we would do well to incorporate into Astrology in general, and Horary (and other Interrogatory) Astrology in particular.

Here's the idea. It is far better to decide the general approach that you will take to delineating the question before you compute or even look at the chart. Why? Because it's easy to get distracted by a juicy detail in the chart that actually has nothing to do with the question. It also keeps you from being drawn to the astrological elements before you have sorted out what they mean.

The essence of good horary technique is teasing out *only* those components of a chart that apply to the question. To do this, it's easiest to begin your examination of the chart already focused on the question at hand.

To do this, we will begin with a general system for delineation. Listed below are some basic components to consider:

1. The validation of the chart

2. Describe the Querent

3. The Question/the Quesited

4. The Perfection or Emplacement (if any)

5. Timing and Direction

Let's consider each step in detail.

1. Is this a valid chart? Considerations against Judgment

Before we discuss the purpose of the considerations against judgment, we need to understand what they are. I present here two lists from the classical period in their entirety: those of William Lilly and John Gadbury. After we take a look at them, we can then decide what to do with them, and consider how others have approached these ideas.

William Lilly: *Aphorismes and Considerations for better judging any Horary Question*[7]

1. *See [that] the Question be radicall, or fit to be judged; which is, when the Lord of the ascendant and hour be of one nature or Triplicity.*

2. Be not confident of the Judgement if either the first degrees or later of any Signe be ascending: if few degrees ascend, the matter is not ripe for judgement: if the later degrees arise, the matter of the Question is elapsed, and it's probable the Querent hath been tampering with others, or despaires of any successe: however, the Heavens advise you not to meddle with it at that time.

3. The position of Saturn or Mars in the tenth, and they be peregrine or unfortunate, of the South Node in that house, the Artist hardly gets credit by that Question.

4. Judge not upon every light motion, or without premeditation of the Querent, nor upon slight and triviall Questions, or when the Querent hath not wit to know what he should demand.

9. Generally consider the state of the Moon, for if she be void of course, there's no great hopes of the Question propounded, that it shall be effected; yet if she be in Cancer, Taurus, Sagittarius or Pisces, your fear may be the lesse, for then she is not much impedited by being voyd of course.

John Gadbury: *When a Figure is Radical, and fit to be judged.*[8]

The Astrologer before he adventureth to judge a Question, ought first to consider, whether it be proper and fit to be judged: For many times, Persons propound impertinent Questions, with an intention to disgrace Art; in doing which, they do nothing but create shame to themselves. Then, the Artist shall sometimes meet with Persons that know not how to propound their desires aright, it's an Argument when such Queries are made, that (although they may be asked with good intent, yet) they are not ripe for a resolve; and the Astrologer in such cases ought to defer judgement until another time.

Now, for the discovery of the knavery of the one, and the unfitness or unpreparedness of the other, you may observe these following Rules and Aphorisms – viz.

1. When the Sign Ascending, and Planet in the Ascendant, etc. shall describe the person of the Querent exactly, you may conclude that figure Radical, and the Question propounded fit to be judged.

2. When either the very beginning of a Sign ascends, or the very later end thereof, it is not safe to give judgement; for the Querent hath been tampering with others about the business propounded, or else the Question is forged, and thereof not fit to be answered.

3. When the Moon is voyd of Course, or in Via Combusta, *the Combust way; All Matters or businesses propounded, go unluckily on: therefore the Astrologer ought to understand the Matter propounded perfectly, or else he will give but poor content to the Querent therein.*

4. *If the Moon go to a square, or opposite of the Lord of the Seventh; or the Lord of the Ascendant afflict him so the Artist may conclude his Querent a knave, for he then cometh to abuse him.*

5. *If the Seventh House be hindered, or his Lord be Retrograde, Combust, or other ways afflicted, let not the Astrologer judge any thing: for by how much more he shall adventure to judge at such a time, by so much the more shall he disgrace himself, and disparage the Art he professeth...*

6. *When Saturn is [in] the Ascendant of a Question, and infortunate, the Matter propounded is either false, and without ground, or else 'tis past all hope: And if at the same time, the Lord of the Ascendant be Combust or Retrograde, the Querent is either a knave or a fool.*

7. *When the Testimonies in your Figure are equal, the Matter propounded ought not to be judged; for the Artist knows not which way the balance may yield, wherefore he ought to defer judgement, until a more convenient time.*

8. *Some Astrologers hold the Question to be Radical, when the Lord of the Ascendant, and the Lord of the Hour, are of one nature and Triplicity; which is easily known: suppose Leo ascend the Horoscope at the Querent's Interrogation, and Mars happen to be Lord of the Hour; here the Question will be found Radical, because the Sun, who is Lord of the Horoscope, and Mars, are of one Nature, viz. Hot and Dry; Or if at the same time, Jupiter fortune to be Lord of the hour, the Question will then be admitted Radical, because Jupiter is of the same Triplicity with the Sun understand the same with the rest.*

This is actually only part of the list that Lilly gave, because this appears in a list of general ideas for how to approach reading a question. Before we proceed with discussing these lists, a word about Lilly and Gadbury. They were contemporaries, although Gadbury was the younger. Of greater significance is that they ended up on opposite sides of the English Civil War. This was not merely a personal difference, but a dangerous political disagreement. I mention this because when the two of them agree on a concept, you *know* that this is a matter of generally accepted technique, because often they tried to emphasize their differences.

What these two lists have in common is the sense that many Questions perhaps should not be read – *at least to the Querent*. Let's sort out the lists and discuss the issues they raise.

A Note on the English Civil War: In hindsight, the Stuarts were a disastrous dynasty for England. The reign of Charles I (1625-1649) was a continual struggle with the Parliament for money. 1640 marked the first session of the Long Parliament, which set up the struggle which ended, after a number of battles, with the capture, trial and execution of Charles I on 30 January 1649. Oliver Cromwell (1599-1658), who proved a brilliant general for the Parliament during the war, inaugurated the Protectorate, which abolished the office of king, and dissolved the House of Lords. The Protectorate, which Cromwell headed, did not long survive his death, as his son proved incompetent, and no other figure could step up to replace him. Charles's son was invited back to England to become king; he ruled as Charles II (1660-1685). During the War, everyone was polarized. Lilly was the somewhat unwilling captain (along with John Booker) of the astrological propagandists for the Parliament against the Crown. Almanacs and broadsides were published with predictions showing why Parliament would win. The reverse was demonstrated by the astrologers who propagandized for the Crown. The Royalists included George Wharton (who even raised a fighting company), John Gadbury, and William Ramesey. Astrologers fought astrologers in the media of the time. Later, when the Restoration of Charles II had occurred, a past history as a Roundhead or Parliamentarian was dangerous; in this period, Lilly came under suspicion for starting the Great Fire of London, since he had predicted it. Patrick Curry believes that the conservatism that accompanied the Restoration contributed to the decline of Astrology in England in the 18th Century, as people attempted to repress any of those influences which seemed so strong during the Civil War.[9]

A. Radicality

There are two ideas here to test whether a chart is radical: either the 1st House gives a good description of the Querent, or the Planetary Hour matches the Ascendant Ruler by Triplicity (i.e., their signs are in the same element). Both of these ideas touch upon one of the dangers of doing horary for others: you don't know their mind. As a result, you need methods for evaluating whether you need to apply caution to answering questions – or to whether to answer the question at all.

When these indicators appeared, was this enough to make an astrologer turn away from answering the question? Not really. In Lilly's case, out of 35 examples, 10 match the planetary hour/Ascendant criterion; 25 do not – if you count this as *sign* of the dispositors. If you figure that there are four elements, then roughly 1/4 of the time, a chart would match between Ascendant Ruler element and Planetary Hour ruler element. This works out to about 9 for 35 examples, which is approximately the actual distribution in Lilly's book. In plain English, this translates to mean that Lilly ignored these considerations as an indication that he shouldn't read the chart. In fact, the number of charts that match his desired conditions are almost exactly what you would expect by chance, meaning that Lilly did nothing to increase the number of "ideal" charts by rejecting less than ideal ones. Clearly, this proviso wasn't even important enough to encourage him to select a "better" sample for publication!

If we do the calculation as Gadbury spells out, then we have to separate out two possibilities. If we distinguish planets by their intrinsic qualities[10], we actually have three categories: of the same nature, of a different nature, or Mercury, because astrologers could never agree on a consistent set of qualities for Mercury. So in this classification, there are 5 examples which match by nature, 20 that do not, and there are 10 examples with Mercury as either Ascendant Ruler or Planetary Hour Ruler, and thus 10 with uncertain characteristics.

If we define *of the same nature* as requiring that the two planets each rule within the same Triplicity, then there are 12 that agree, and 23 that do not.

All of these systems show that, in practice, this consideration is virtually ignored, if it was ever really supposed to screen out charts. The last system using Triplicity rulerships may show a slight possibility that charts were being favored according to this system, but it could also be just a statistical anomaly. I have summarized these results in the following table.

Lilly examples showing Planetary Hour Agreement with Ascendant:

	Yes	No	Mercury Swings
Agreement by Sign of Dispositor	10	25	
Intrinsic qualities (i.e., naturally hot, cold, wet or dry)	5	20	10
Rulers in same Triplicity element	12	23	

Why did they bother with so carefully listing this rule if they then ignored it? There is absolutely no way to tell. Perhaps they thought they were paying attention to this aphorism when in fact they were not. Perhaps it was a quick test to tell them when a particular chart was going to be especially difficult to interpret. We just don't know. And curiously, there was never a discussion of this – or any other consideration against judgment – in relationship to their own personal questions. After all, if I'm asking my own question, I don't need the chart to tell me whether I'm serious about the question – or whether I'm a liar or a knave!

B. The Position of Saturn

There are three possible "bad" positions for Saturn: in the 1st, 7th, or 10th Houses. There are also two possible mitigations:

- If the Question is of the nature of that house, then Saturn there is probably just a description of the situation. For instance, when Saturn is in the 7th House in a chart for a question about buying a property, it can simply indicate that the owners are old people.

- If Saturn is highly dignified, then the consideration has little weight. By highly dignified, I mean certainly by Sign or Exaltation, possibly even by Triplicity. But, having Term or Face is not sufficient. The origin of this idea can be seen as far back as Bonatti, who cites a

> still earlier source in his 32nd Aphorism to the effect that, "An ill-planet strong in his own Home or Exaltation, not joined with any other Infortune to impede or weaken him, is better than a Fortune Retrograde afflicted." I have personally observed this and can verify its utility.

Now that we've sorted out the exceptions, what is the rule? Each of the placements of Saturn brings different dangers.

7th House: The best known is the danger of the 7th House placement. The 7th House always includes the Astrologer in a Question – the unspoken "Thou" in the "I-Thou" relationship of the Horary Question. Saturn's placement shows a potential problem, and this would represent a problem for the Astrologer. Before the days of computers, the simple interpretation was that the Astrologer would make a mistake in the calculations. Now, it's still possible to make a mistake in data entry! However, the other danger is a mistake in interpretation. Wariness is advised. But be careful. As we proceed through the different types of questions, observe that many actually involve a 7th House issue in which case Saturn becomes a Significator, part of the story. Anytime the Question has a distinct 7th House component, this doesn't apply anyway. This consideration is not applicable perhaps half the time.

10th House: The meaning of the 10th House placement is also clear. The Astrologer's reputation may be besmirched. This means that while you may be absolutely correct in a delineation, the Querent will tell 3,000 of their closest friends that you failed. Unless it is a 10th House Question, this is one consideration that I studiously observe as a ban on delineation. Frankly, I don't want to risk the possibility that this aphorism is true. It's interesting, though: since I made the decision to pay attention to this, it has only popped up in a few cases of literally hundreds of Horaries.

1st House: The meaning of Saturn in the 1st House is a bit more variable. There are two major meanings of "falsehood" in Gadbury's parlance. However, it has not been my experience as it clearly was Lilly's and Gadbury's, to have people contacting me with false questions. As a result, I have not needed to apply the measure for skepticism or deliberate deception as they clearly did.

The first meaning is simply referred to as "lying." The problem is precisely the spectrum, which runs from brazen falsehoods, to so-called white lies, to nothing more than the inability to connect the dots that would make the Horary superfluous. Let me illustrate by example.

- A woman asks whether some jewelry she posted was lost in the mail. What she doesn't admit until further questioning is that what had really happened is that she had purchased some jewelry and had it shipped to her sister in another state in order to avoid paying state sales tax, and now she was really concerned about whether someone in the Post Office stole it, or whether her sister did!

- An astrologer asks if she will marry a particular man, but omits to mention that she had already asked the question before, even though she knew that this fact made the horary invalid.

- A woman is talking to her husband, who claims that he has never engaged in sexual activity with anyone else since they were married. The chart was done for the moment that he made the statement. Here the lie is what has become known as the Clinton defense – his definition of sex included only intercourse, while hers included oral sex.

- A man asks about moving to one of several cities. When questioned as a follow-up, he mentions that his wife suffers from terrible hay fever, and in reality only one of the cities has a low pollen count, so the Question is virtually unnecessary.

In two of the cases, you may notice my wording about "upon further questioning." This reveals my approach to these questions. I simply tell the person that the chart indicates there is some additional piece of information which is crucial to the interpretation that either they didn't tell me, or that they themselves have not connected as being important to the question. This generally results in, if not a confession, at least some additional information!

There is one other variant of the "falsehood" issue that should be mentioned. The other meaning is that the Querent may have no intention of paying for the reading, or at least, that there may be a problem in payment. This is one time where I will certainly *not* expect the check to be in the mail, and there is no question that the credit card will be verified before proceeding!

C. Ascendant Too Early or Too Late

The general understanding of this consideration is that either the first three degrees, or the last three degrees of a sign, are treated differently than the intervening degrees. In most cases, however, the fact of earliness or lateness is actually part of the answer.

When reading a horary chart with late degrees rising, the essential meaning is that there is nothing else that the Querent can do to effect the situation, and that often, the Question actually has been resolved, it's just that the Querent doesn't know the answer yet.

The "too early " theme of the early degrees is a bit different. Here, the "too early" Ascendant implies that there are still unforeseen events or people that may still impinge on the outcome: the resolution to the question, the result, is not yet fixed.

Before considering the philosophical implications of "fixed" or "fated," let me mention one exception: the early or the late degrees were said not to apply if the Querent was the same age as the degree ascending, in which case the match constituted strong argument of radicality.

Now, about "fixed" and "fated." What we are implying is that each Horary Question actually begins with the phrase, "If events continue as they are unfolding, then..." Horary Astrology does not have a definite position on the question of Fate *versus* Free Will. The reason is that the functioning of Fate is next to impossible to distinguish in actual practice. The theoretical *ability* to do something different than one's first "instinct" does not imply that one *will* do something different. In Horary, we cannot tell the motivations, only the most likely sequence of subsequent events. In other words, answering a horary is like picking the favorite in a competition where the odds are maybe 90% that the favorite will win. There can always be an upset, but the horary is showing the path of least resistance at the present moment.

The usual reading that I give when an Ascendant is 1 or 2 degrees is that the delineation only represents a trend, but one that can be changed easily by subsequent events. In the case of 0 degrees Rising, while I may delineate a trend, there is simply too much Free Will in the system: the odds are not good enough to pick a winner. In fact the only thing that you can safely say is that circumstances will change – and probably quite quickly.

D. Other Considerations

The two other major considerations are the question of the Moon's placement in the ***Via Combusta*** and the question of the Moon Void of Course. The Via Combusta (Combust Way or burned path) is the region approximately from 15 degrees of Libra to 15 degrees of Scorpio. I have not found this consideration to have any particular use. I am personally uncomfortable with this idea for two reasons. The first is that I have no idea where this concept came from, even whether it is a tropical or a sidereal degree region. The second is that one of the most beneficial fixed stars, Spica, is located in it, currently at about 23 Libra![11]

There has been some recent re-envisioning of the true meaning of the Moon Void of Course, especially by English astrologer Sue Ward. At this time, I am retaining the generally accepted definition, which is that the Moon (or a planet) is Void of Course when it makes no more ***ptolemaic aspects*** (conjunction, sextile, square, trine, opposition) until it leaves the sign it is in.[12] Lilly's observation that the Moon acts differently when Void of Course in Cancer, Taurus, Sagittarius and Pisces[13] (i.e., the Moon's own sign and exaltation sign, and Jupiter's two signs) is something that I can absolutely confirm with my own experience.

What Happened to the Considerations?

In 1992, Axel Harvey presented a lecture at the United Astrology Congress concerning the notebooks of Henri Bernard, a 17th Century French physician. Bernard had a series of notebooks made when he became a physician that contained blank chart forms, plus an area in which to make notes. He used this book to record his medical cases as he received them. He calculated the ***Decumbiture*** (a chart taken for either when a patient becomes sick, or when a physician is contacted about the sickness) and then recorded the description of the illness, his observations, and even sometimes, the result. This manuscript is housed at McGill University in Montreal, and I have been privileged to examine it personally, thanks to Axel. What is so valuable about this work is that it shows someone out there in the field, so to speak, and what methods he actually employed. What is completely clear from this notebook is that Bernard never used the considerations as a reason *not* to delineate the chart. There is no evidence that Bernard ever refused to delineate a chart based on any consideration, or that he ever hesitated in prognosis based on them.

Until the 20th Century, the Considerations were called by one of two names: the considerations, or whether the chart is radical and fit to be judged. This changed with Ivy Goldstein-Jacobson and Barbara Watters. Goldstein-Jacobson referred to a similar list as "Caution."[14] Somewhat later, Watters called yet the same list "Strictures."[15] This then mutated in common usage to "cautions and strictures." Goldstein-Jacobson's "cautions" nomenclature actually captures the original meaning pretty well. However, the word "strictures" sounds much more dire than "cautions," and what resulted was various astrologers taking the usual list of suspects and dividing them up according to whether they really were cautions or strictures.

What developed out of this change in wording was the mythology that the purpose of the considerations was to ascertain whether or not to read the chart. In fact, all the classical sources that we have are full of charts with considerations. Considerations are just that: *think* about what you are doing, and *think* about whether the consideration(s) that applies actually tells you something about the nature of the Question propounded.

2. Describe the Querent

As we have already seen, the Ascendant, the Ascendant Ruler, and planets in the 1st House can all be used to describe the Querent. In addition, the Moon always co-rules the Question, whatever that means.[16] This is the stage in the delineation where the Astrologer really enters the picture: the Ascendant is the entry point to the chart, the beginning of the actual astrological delineation of the circumstances. We begin with the circumstances as they currently are.

The purpose in describing the Querent is not to impress and amaze your friends and clients with the stunning accuracy of your positioning of the marks and moles on the Querent's body – the purpose is actually twofold: to confirm that this Question was truly asked in Sacred Time, and to ascertain which Significator to use for the Querent.

The possible Significators for the Querent are:

- the Ascendant itself
- the Ascendant Ruler or Almuten
- planets in the 1st House, or occasionally
- the Moon – but this is problematic, because what the Moon *really* shows in the chart is the sequence of events

In addition, some particular types of horaries have specific means of identifying the Querent, for example as the planet that last separated from the

Moon. The Moon co-rules all questions, though it is seldom used as the Ruler of the Querent, unless Cancer is Rising.

Delineation Tip: *Notice that the object is to arrive at precisely one Significator to represent the Querent. The list of possible Significators allows you some latitude in deciding which is the appropriate one. Having chosen one Significator, all other candidates are abandoned, and only one Significator is actually delineated.*

The way to arrive at a physical description is to begin at the Ascendant, and examine both its sign ruler and its Term ruler. There is a long-standing tradition that assigns the Term ruler as being, "of the body," which is descriptive of the nature, not necessarily the talent, of the individual. A person represented by the Ascendant in the Terms of Saturn would appear serious, morose, or perhaps be in a Saturn-ruled profession. The Ascendant in the Terms of Mars – or the Ruler of the Ascendant in the Terms of Mars – might show someone with a red or ruddy complexion, a combative person, a soldier, an athlete, or someone who is angry over the content of the Question!

The ancients tell us of a method to identify the "marks and moles" – blemishes on the body which may serve as an indication of a radical chart.[17] The method is to take the sign Rising, and translate this into the portion of the body ruled by the sign (Aries = head, Taurus = neck, Gemini = shoulders, arms and hands, etc.[18]), and then further, take the decanate and assign the uppermost part of the bodily region to the 1st decanate, the middle section to the middle decanate, and the lower section to the third decanate. Of course, telling this to the Scorpio Rising Querent may become interesting!

The reason for describing the Querent *at all* is to verify that the Question was asked appropriately. After all, you cannot read the Querent's mind to see just how serious or appropriate the Question may be. But what happens when you ask your own question? Now, you yourself can verify that this is truly a horary moment, that the question is valid. And yet different rising signs will occur – and not all of them will seem to describe you. This is also a valid point if you have clients (as I do) who ask multiple horary questions in a week. In this case, the different signs often seem to correlate with either the component of the Querent's natal chart that is most engaged in the question, or with the mood or viewpoint of the Querent in asking the question. If the Ascendant of the horary chart is the natal Ascendant, Sun placement, or Moon placement, the question is viewed as being especially "hot."

3. The Question/the Quesited

The ***Quesited*** is the subject of the Horary. For example, if the question is about a job, then the job is the Quesited. If the question is about marriage, then the lucky other party is the Quesited. There is a distinction here that's worth making. Suppose you are asked the question, "Will I marry Maria?" Maria is the Quesited. But suppose you are asked the question, "Will I ever marry again?" (Presuming that you failed in convincing the Querent not to ask a lifetime question!) Now marriage *itself* is the Quesited. One way to think of this is that the Quesited is who or what the Querent is seeking in the Horary.

The Quesited is shown by:

- the House represented by the nature of the Question
- the Ruler or Almuten of that House
- planets in that house

So now, the obvious question is: what house to use? I will begin by giving a brief synopsis of the kinds of questions that occur by house, referring you to the much more complete listing in *The Book of Rulerships*. After we present this list, we will then show how to chose the proper house, because this is one of the most difficult things to do when you are learning Horary.

1st **House** Longevity, health (disease is 6th), happiness, moving vehicles (planes, trains and automobiles), best period in life, the visiting team in most sporting events.

2nd **House** Money, financial instruments directly convertible into cash (bank accounts, CD's, guaranteed bonds), salary, moveable objects (things you can pick up and carry by yourself), lawyer acting in your behalf in a lawsuit (i.e., barrister).

3rd **House** Neighbors, siblings, cousins of the same generation in age, primary education (see below), short trips (see below), religious matters (see below), whether the rumor is true, writing.

4th **House** Your father (usually), property (whether land or buildings), hidden or buried treasure, your home, inheritance of land, the home team in many sporting events, gardeners or other workers who do landscaping or other outside work.

5th **House** Entertainment, sex (see below), pleasure, gambling, ambassadors (see below), bribery, gifts, the stock market and other riskier investments, alcohol and recreational drugs, children, procreation.

6th **House** Pets, disease, accidents (as in: car accidents), employees or day laborers, small animals (i.e., smaller than a sheep, but also includes large but domesticated dogs like St. Bernards), birds, labor unions (the unions themselves, not labor actions).

7th **House** Marriage and marriage partners, partnerships of all sorts (business as well as intimate), open enemies, thieves, the other party in a buying and selling transaction, a contract labor or subcontractor situation, the default other person (see below), the other side in a lawsuit or negotiation, the other possibility for the home team in a sporting event, removals (or moving house).

8th House Death, taxes, wills, insurance, your partner's money, inheritances other than of property, lawyer representing the other side in a lawsuit.

9th House Travel, long trips (see below), philosophy, religion (see below), prophetic dreams, lawyers (see below), higher education (see below).

10th House Your mother (usually), honors and awards, promotions, high managerial jobs, judge in a lawsuit, arbiter in a negotiation, bosses higher up in the corporate ladder, perks given out at the whim of someone higher up.

11th House Friends, associations, organizations, funding bodies of government agencies, hopes and wishes.

12th House Witchcraft (see below), hidden enemies, imprisonment, all institutions of confinement, hospitals, self-undoing, large animals (horses, elephants, whales).

Notes on the Table:

Some of the concepts presented here may not seem clear without a bit of discussion. This is generally because there may be arguably more than one house you can use.

Education: Here we face a problem that Lilly and his contemporaries simply didn't have. The idea of general public education didn't exist. What they had was home tutoring for the nobility's children, boarding schools, and finally, university for the more educationally inclined. Most boys received vocational training in the form of apprenticeships, and this is why there is often an intertwining of 9th and 10th Houses for education.[19] In our modern form, I would distinguish education as follows: primary, elementary and high school (if of a general nature): 3rd House. This is considered general education: subject matter that benefits anyone, even if there are particular vocationally-oriented classes, such as car repair, there are general requirements like language and mathematics. In those countries where tracking occurs prior to university level (as Great Britain, with national O-Level and A-Level exams), the pre-university college track would still be 3rd House, but the more vocationally-oriented non-college track would be 10th House. In the USA there is some specialty training, as for talented musicians, that I would also place in the 10th House. University and beyond is unequivocally 9th House, although Medical School or Law School, even though postgraduate, would have a 10th House emphasis.

Trips and Voyages: Lilly never had to cope with travel faster than by horseback or sailing vessel, and speed has changed our concept of distance permanently. Accordingly, I believe we need to change our concept of traveling to mesh with the essence of the difference between the 3rd and the 9th House: the issue of neighborhood *vs.* foreignness. I would therefore propose some of the following ideas for how to make this determination in practice. Notice that I do not believe that there is an absolute scale based on timing or distance, but on the Querent's state of mind regarding travel.

- There are people for whom any travel is stressful and foreign. This is the kind of person who regards the next town or city down the road to be hopelessly far away. They work in their own city or neighborhood, shop locally, go to restaurants locally if at all, and never emerge from their immediate environment except under duress. For these people, the next town *is* a 9th House location, because it is foreign and unfamiliar.

- There are people for whom any airplane trip is hopelessly complex and dangerous, while travel by car is completely normal and comfortable. For this person, the distance may be less important for determining 3rd or 9th House than the means of transportation.

- Many of us have lived in multiple cities and towns. Any of these former habitation points may well remain 3rd House regardless of distance *if* we stay in touch with people still living there, and visit frequently enough to stay abreast of construction and changes to the old haunts.

- There are cities or locales we visit regularly regardless of distance whether on business or pleasure trips. If we know the language (regardless of whether it's our native language), can get around comfortably, have regular places to go to eat or for entertainment, have family or friends, and can answer simple requests for directions from other travelers, then that locale has probably become 3rd House.

Thus, I could count Geneva, Switzerland as 3rd House because I have a general idea of the city, have visited several times, I can make my way around in French (although in Geneva, anything other than English is seldom needed), and I have my favorite restaurants and bookstores. Geneva is a continent away for me, and yet Orlando, which is only an hour away by car, is absolutely a 9th House experience – I barely know how to get around without a map. Yet for another person living in my same city, the reverse would surely be more likely.

For trips, you simply have to ask the Querent to define the ease and comfort level of the proposed itinerary.

Religious Matters: In the Greek material on Astrology, the 3rd House was referred to as *Thea* (literally Goddess), while the 9th House was designated *Theos* (literally God). Rob Hand has put what I believe is the correct interpretation to this idea. He refers to the 3rd House as ruling religious matters that are not the societal orthodoxy, while the 9th refers to creeds and sects that do conform to societal expectation. This would be like saying that the 9th House represents culturally dominant religions in a particular society, whereas the 3rd

House would be minority religions, or even repressed ones. Thus, in modern Western society, Christianity and Judaism would be 9th House, while Wicca, and probably even Buddhism, Islam, Hinduism, Shintoism, and Nature cults would be 3rd House. Arguably, if you were answering a Question on religion from a Japanese person, then Shintoism and Buddhism would be the 9th House religions, while Christianity may be 3rd House.

There also seem to be some gradations within a religion. For example, we know that some of the Catholic emphasis on Mary was actually a way of supplanting indigenous goddess cults. However, when you examine charts of Mary sightings, and other marian activities, the 3rd House may be more engaged than the 9th.

Sex: There are no references to sex being associated with the 8th House, as is now common, prior to the 20th Century. The earliest known reference is Alan Leo.[20] Even though he mentioned it, he didn't actually seem to use it, as shown in his delineation of Prince Albert Victor of Wales:

> The position of Saturn in the second squared by the Sun and Moon is unsatisfactory for his finances. Great prodigality is shewn [*sic*], and as the aspect occurs from the second to the fifth houses, the expenditure will go in matters signified by the fifth house; that we need not enlarge upon.[21]

This was typical Victorian allusion to sexuality. The Prince's dalliances, especially with Lily Langtry, were commonly known. Thus, the relationship between the 2nd and 5th Houses resulted in "Increases family. Speculation. Many love affairs," while the Moon in the 8th was "Legacies. Gain or loss through deaths, as aspected." His references to the 5th house for other planets contained further comments about love affairs, while his 8th House references were restricted to legacies, partner's money, and death. Leo continued along this theme in his work, *Horary Astrology* (1907), and actually, most horary astrologers, including Robert DeLuce, Marc Edmund Jones, Ivy Goldstein-Jacobson, Barbara Watters, and Sylvia Delong, continued this pattern, assigning all love matters to the 5th House, except marriage, while not mentioning sexuality at all in the 8th House, except possibly venereal disease, which evokes occasional classical references to the "privy parts" [i.e., genitals] as being associated with the 8th House.

The change, bringing emphasis to the 8th House, occurred in natal psychological astrology sometime in the 1950s or early 1960s. Thus, we see the statement in C.E.O. Carter's 5th Edition *The Principles of Astrology,*[22] "It [the 8th House] is related to the sexual nature." (page 86). The fact that Carter is also the author of a book on psychological astrology is probably not irrelevant. However, he was not the first psychological astrologer, nor the first one to discuss sexuality. In 1928, Karl Guenter Heimsoth, M.D., published a book on homosexuality. His psychological approach was strictly Freudian, but his astrology was grounded in classical concepts, so he listed sex as a meaning of the 5th House. Several authors in the *Astrological Quarterly*, the magazine Carter edited, also used the 5th House during this period.[23]

To the pre-industrial mind, sex used to be just recreation, procreation, or sin. In any of these guises, it was 5th House in nature. I believe the shift to the 8th House resulted from the psychological tendency to view sex as a neurosis, which combined with the tendency to assign Pluto as the ruler of Scorpio. Pluto was then identified as having sexual components, mainly negative ones. There seem to be no references other than Leo's to sexuality being an 8th House matter prior to the discovery of Pluto in 1930. I believe further that we have come to glorify the 8th House in a most curious matter: we have become seduced by the taboos that we intuit as being present here. This is the living manifestation of the Eros-Thanatos (Love & Death) complex that Freud discussed. And since *real* tests of survival are, well, difficult and dangerous, what better solution than to fantasize that sex puts us on the edge in the same way that mountain climbing or hang gliding does?

The classical understanding of sex is that it's a "venereal sport" or "venereal pursuit." While Puritan Lilly may have chosen not to discuss it because of its moral implications[24], other less squeamish astrologers had no problem mentioning it, although the English text often shifts to Latin at critical points! Ramesey even included a method for electing a time for intercourse in order to select the gender of the child begotten at that time![25]

Ambassadors: There is a long-standing association of the 5th House with ambassadors, which may seem strange, at least until we reflect on the historical purpose of ambassadors. Put simply, the purpose of an ambassador was to sway a foreign leader to do your country a favor. The preferred means of obtaining your desires: bribery. Gifts and bribes (it's the same word in ancient Greek) are both matters of the 5th House.

The default "other person": Whenever there isn't an obvious house relationship to the other party in a Horary question, that person is assigned to the 7th House. Now, regarding the 7th House, we should also mention another modern tendency that seems rather strange. Consider the following two questions:

- Where is my daughter Heather?
- Where is Heather?

Both of these questions could have been asked by the same person, namely Heather's parent. Some modern astrologers would assign the Quesited differently, assigning Heather to the 5th House in the first case, and the 7th in the second case. I find this to be ludicrous. Has the parent forgotten in the second case that there is a parental relationship? I doubt it! It is more likely that the Querent has merely made the assumption that you (the astrologer) *know* what the relationship to Heather is. A daughter is a daughter is a daughter...

Lawyers: There are two types of lawyers that differ functionally, following the tradition of the English legal system. These two functions are known in that system as solicitors and barristers. The *solicitor* is the person that you employ to execute a will, write a contract, or perform any other kind of legal paperwork. A *barrister* is the lawyer that represents you in court during a lawsuit. The difference between these two types astrologically is that the solicitor is given by the 9th House, while the barrister is given by the 2nd House.

In addition, other people who are not technically lawyers can act in a solicitor capacity. Anytime that you appoint someone to act as your quasi-legal agent, it is likely that they are in a 9th House relationship to you. A Notary Public, for example, would be acting in a 9th House manner. A title company that facilitates a real estate transaction is acting in a 9th House capacity. If the agent is acting more as an ambassador, then the agent becomes 5th House. A real estate agent is acting as ambassador for your house: this is a 5th House capacity, as would be most cases when a sales person is acting for the Querent on a commission basis. However, if you as a buyer hire a real estate agent to act upon your behalf, (i.e., a buyer's agent) *that* real estate agent is now assuming a 9th House status, because he or she is negotiating for you, not selling to you. Any person who sells something for you, and then receives a commission, is 5th House.

Witchcraft: You may have been a bit surprised to see the reference to witchcraft as associated with the 12th House. Either the reference could be considered politically incorrect, or the concept itself is considered passé. Actually, it is not meant in either fashion. Witchcraft as a reference to Wicca belongs in the 3rd House – at least in our current culture. The 12th House meaning is closer to the stereotyped idea of what witches did, namely casting spells upon others. This means any system or method that attempts to coerce a person into acting in a fashion which is contrary to his or her own knowledge, benefit or desire. This could be a whole range of possibilities, from an unsavory hypnotist, to a guru who promises enlightenment for sexual favors, to a parental figure who uses guilt or intimidation to achieve dominance.

In some societies, there actually are people who function as witches. In Hispanic America, any such person is called a *brujo*. A *brujo* is the person you visit when you want a love potion, when you want to cement a business deal, or when you want to coerce someone into marrying you. In Russia, psychics are sometimes hired in the same capacity. It is rumored that Vladimir Putin hired psychics to help influence people to vote for him when he ran for President. While this may not exactly match with Northwestern European sensibilities, it seems to work in those societies that have this job description. In other societies, this function can be served by anyone skilled in psychological manipulation techniques: techniques that gain advantage over another person.

While we have listed some of the major subjects associated with each house, it does not mean that the student should already feel comfortable attacking a horary question. It is at this point of house assignment that the neophyte Horary Astrologer may encounter the most difficulty. Often, the best way through this morass is to think carefully about what the ramifications of the Question may be, as a way of assigning the Significator to each party. Let's consider a few example questions and how we would assign rulerships and Significators.

- **Will I marry José?** Here the approach is pretty straightforward. Because it's a question of marriage, José is placed as the Significator of the 7th House, and his Significator is viewed in relationship to the Querent's in order to determine the answer. This same logic would be used whether the question was marriage, or cohabitation.

- **Will I get the house in the divorce settlement?** Here you have to think a little bit about what is going on. A divorce is a lawsuit between married partners; thus, the other spouse is represented by the 7th House. (It's worth mentioning here that a bit of Horary jargon can easily creep in. It is technically correct to say that the spouse is represented by the 7th House. However, this is often abbreviated to saying that the other person *is* the 7th House. It becomes so natural to equate person with house that it becomes completely unconscious after a while.) Who gets the house? There are really four scenarios: the Querent gets it, the other spouse gets it, they can rent it out to a third party, or they sell it and then split the profit. To determine the outcome, there are really several ideas to cover, such as: does the divorce look messy? who seems to win overall? is one party associated with the house (the 4th House)? does there seem to be enough in the way of assets that the house won't have to be sold? All of these possibilities would have to be assessed to fully answer the question.

- **Will the deal go through?** Before you could answer this question you would need to know generally what kind of business deal is involved. Since most deals are really disguised versions of buying and selling, most likely it's a 1st-7th House question.

- **Will we hit the Big One?** Whether the question is this Saturday's state lottery or an oil drilling, the principal question is: what are the odds of winning? If the odds are not great, then this is definitely a 5th House question, and things better look fabulous for the gamble to pay off.

- **Will I get the commission?** Usually, this is not quite the wording of the question. But here's the idea. Suppose your Querent is working as a real estate agent or a furniture salesperson. The sale of an item results in a commission for the selling agent (sometimes the buying agent as well, as in house sales). Buying and selling is normally 1st-7th, but if the Querent doesn't actually *own* anything, they benefit by someone else buying what they are selling as a representative of the owner. A commission works as a gift, i.e., as a 5th House matter.

- **Is there an Indian burial ground on the property?** A burial ground is also known as a cemetery, which is a 4th House matter. Of course, we could also classify it as buried treasure if we are archeologically inclined.

- **Will this gardener produce a good design and implementation?** There is a trick here that Lilly uses in his discussion of towns on page 53: "The Signe of the fourth denoteth the Town, the Lord there of the Governour." When you have both a place and a person to consider, use the cusp of the house itself for the place, and the Ruler of the cusp for the person. In this case we have the place as the garden, which is then the 4th House cusp, and the gardener as the ruler of the 4th House. So we look for a relationship between cusp and ruler, and probably also a relationship to the ruler of the 1st, namely, the Querent.

- **Should I go to China this Spring?** This is where you really need to tease out the meaning of "should." The big question is: why go to China at all? Is this a vacation, is it to see relatives, or to look into doing business there? In general, when the question is worded in this fashion, you can be pretty confident of using China as a 9th House place, no matter how familiar the Querent is with it. Why? Because generally, you wouldn't be getting the question to interpret if there wasn't some issue of foreignness or bigness or distance about the concept of the trip. We don't take questions like, "Should I go to the grocery store!"

In all of these cases, we use the Question itself as a springboard for consideration of what would follow from the Question. It is in our understanding of the meaning of the question within the flow of events that we can tease out a way to examine the answer.

4. The Perfection or Emplacement (if any)

Perfection is the word applied to any condition that allows a Question to complete unimpeded.

There are two general kinds of Horaries: Perfection and Emplacement types. A perfection horary requires that some sort of action(s) or event(s) happen in order for the result to be brought about. An emplacement horary relies purely on where the planets are positioned at the time of the horary, not where they will be sometime later. Most horaries other than lost items or missing people or animal horaries are perfection horaries.

There are four typical types of perfections.

- **Approaching aspect of Querent's planet to Quesited planet.** This is by far the most common. In this case, there is an *approaching* or *partile* aspect between the Significator of the Querent and the Significator of the Quesited. Only the *Ptolemaic aspects* (conjunction, sextile, square, trine, and opposition) are allowed. Also, there is a specific proviso for perfection by opposition. The mantra for this is: "if you do, you will regret it."[26] Remember that the faster moving body *must* catch up to the slower moving one for this to work. The perfection generally has to take place without the planets changing sign, although we will discuss the exceptions to this rule later.

- **Mutual reception:** Sometimes merely having a mutual reception between Significators is enough to bring the Question forward *if* it is a strong reception (by Sign, Exaltation, Triplicity or a combination thereof) and *if the planets in reception have essential dignity apart from the reception itself.* (See Appendix A.)

- **Collection** occurs when the faster moving body is separating from the slower moving one, but both are applying to yet a slower body. The slowest one then "collects" the other two. The scenario here is that either a place or a person acts as a means to bring the two parties together, when they would likely have missed each other otherwise.

- **Translation** is also a common means of perfection. In translation, a fast moving body (generally the Moon, but occasionally Venus or Mercury) separates from one of the Significators, and applies to the other one. This is what I call the *Yenta* scenario: a third party gets involved to bring the two people together. ("So you're looking to get married? I know just the woman for you! Here, let me arrange to get you two together!")

In addition to these means of achieving perfection, there are also other ways to thwart a perfection. These include:

- ***Refranation:*** in this case, the two bodies are moving toward perfection, but before the aspect becomes exact, the faster moving body turns retrograde, and the aspect never happens until after that body goes direct again, if at all in the same sign. This is one of the most frustrating scenarios, because everything appears to be moving in the right direction until things suddenly veer off. (See Examples 28, 33 and 65.)

- ***Frustration:*** in this case, again the Significators appear to be moving to perfection, but this time the slower moving planet achieves a partile aspect with a different body before the faster moving body catches up. Again, this scenario shows hope until the person represented by the slower moving Significator goes off in a different direction.

- ***Prohibition:*** the Significators are moving to perfection, but a swifter body intervenes and completes aspects with both bodies first. Prohibition acts rather the same way as translation: the issue is really whether the *Yenta* figure ends up bringing the people together, or carrying off one of them for him or herself.

- ***Besiegement:*** if a Significator is between two malefics, it is besieged. It is not at all clear how large an orb should be allowed for this. The concept for besieged is: between a rock and a hard place. A besieged planet is not free to act, as it is hemmed in on all sides. Here's the problem though. Because there is no orb specified, it's possible to have orbs of 180 degrees! See Chart Example 82, where the orb is that large. Given that the three Outer Planets operate primarily as malefics, if we allow for their use, the number of besiegements is tremendous: more than one third of the examples in this work (See Appendix E). I have not found it necessary to interpret all, or even most besiegements. All I can say is: there's an art to the interpretation.

John Gadbury: *Of the possibility or impossibility of the Matter propounded.*[27]

Whatsoever is propounded, carryeth in the face of it, both a Negative, and an Affirmative; That is to say, it may either be brought to a wished Conclusion, or not: For all things under the Sun are Contingent. And it is as honourable, for an Artist to give a judgement in the Negative, (if he see reason so to do) as in the Affirmative; although not so pleasant to the proponent. But the possibility or impossibility of bringing to pass the Matter propounded, may be known by these following Aphorisms.

1. *Businesses are brought to pass divers ways, according to the opinion of the Ancient Astrologers, viz. When the Planets signifying the Person propounding, and the Person or thing propounded, are going to Conjunction in good places of the Figure; Or, when they are applying by sextile, or trine, unto each other. Sometimes, things are brought to pass by Translation, or Collection of Light, or by the dwelling in Houses or Dignities, etc.*[28]

2. *When the Significators of the Matter enquired, are going to conjunction in a good House of Heaven, chiefly in an Angle, the business may be brought to pass. If the Significator of the thing promised be essentially Dignified, and doth apply to the Lord of the Ascendant; the matter will be brought to perfection before 'tis expected.*

3. *If the Lords of the Matter propounded, etc., apply to each other by a sextile or trine, from Signs and Houses they delight in, the thing sought after will be brought to pass.*

4. *When the Significators are not beholding, yet, if a good Planet do Translate, or Collect, and gather their light, it prenotes good in the Matter enquired after, and shews it's possibility.*

5. When Planets dwell in Houses proper and convenient, the Matter by that means may be brought to pass; chiefly, if the Moon have a good Defluxion and Application. Now, as I have shewed the possibility of bringing things to pass, it is requisite I shew the impossibility; which is known from these following Aphorisms.

1. If the Significators of the Querent, and Quesited, etc., are nonbeholding, it is an ill sign of ever bringing the thing enquired after to perfection.

2. If the Significators shall behold each other by square, or opposition, from hateful places of the Figure; or shall be in square, or opposition the Infortunes, It is seldom known that upon such positions any things is brought to pass.

3. When the Significators are voyd of reception, or are Combust, Cadent, etc., it is a Miracle, if they perform any thing.

When the Infortunes or Cauda Draconis [☋] shall be in the House signifying the thing enquired after, or afflicting the Significators, the business propounded will come to a poor end.

Henry Coley: *By what meanes are things brought to perfection, in the business of a Horary Question.*[29]

Things are brought to pass five wayes, viz.

1. When the Planet that denotes the Querent, and the planet that signifies the thing inquired after, are applying by sextile or trine Aspect, or if they are going to a Conjunction; this argues the business shall be effected.

2. When the Significator of the matter inquired after shall apply to the Lord of the Ascendant, and be in his essential dignities, this signifies the business shall be perfected unexpectedly.

3. If the Significator apply friendly from houses they delight in, or from signs they joy in, the business, or matter sought after comes to a happy conclusion.

4. If the Significators do not behold each other, yet if a fortunate Planet collect or translate their beams of light, the matter will be brought to pass.

5. Lastly, when the promising Planets dwell in houses proper and convenient, though there be no Aspect, the matter may be brought to perfection.

Finally: is perfection enough? To read the references, one would think that it is. I began my Horary career thinking so. However, I noticed that I was getting too many horaries wrong that had perfections. When I examined these charts for commonalities, I discovered something: *peregrine planets often do not perform even if they do perfect.*

Having said this, let me be perfectly clear about which definition of peregrine I'm using, because I'm not quite using Lilly's – or Ptolemy's. A peregrine planet lacks all dignity by any of the five categories of essential dignity. Unlike Lilly, I do not allow a mutual reception to alleviate peregrine status. Also unlike Lilly, if a planet has out-of-sect Triplicity (as in Jupiter in Aries in a day chart), I would not treat it as peregrine, although I would not assign dignity points to it either.[30]

An example of this can be illustrated by an actual question I received. A woman had asked if she was going to marry a particular man. Their Significators perfected by trine, which is one of the strongest indicators of a "yes." There were no indicators against perfection, it was, in fact, a very clear chart. However, both Significators were peregrine.

What happened was: they both cared about each other. But they both lacked the will to do anything to move the relationship beyond a very casual encounter stage. Peregrine planets are either powerless, or have a tendency to wander off in a different direction. You do not get a result with peregrine planets unless the scenario allows for the peregrine person to be *absolutely passive*. Obviously, that's not how a marriage comes about!

5. Timing and Direction

If you do get a positive result, you can often (but not always) get timing or compass direction out of the chart. Timing comes from looking for a degree separation between any of the following:

- the Significators of the two parties in a simple perfection
- between the Moon and one of the Significators
- between a Significator and a nearby house cusp
- the number of degrees until the Moon changes sign, especially if the Moon is in the late degrees of a sign.

One of the big issues which we should point out is that there are actually two scales of time: symbolic, and ephemeris. All the old sources used both, but I have yet to see a discussion of the relative merits or applications of one *versus* the other. As nearly as I can determine, symbolic time (a difference of degrees between the two Significators applied to produce time units through the following table) is used most of the time, unless some significant ephemeris event itself may impact the outcome. If, for example, a significant planet is about to go retrograde or direct, it's common to refer to the actual station date as the critical timing date.

The unit of time to go with this number is given in the following table.[31]

Angles	Succedents	Cadents
Moveable Signs Give Days	Moveable Signs Give Weeks	Moveable Signs Give Months
Common Signs Give Weeks	Common Signs Give Months	Common Signs Give Years
Fixed Signs Give Months	Fixed Signs Give Years	Fixed Signs Unknown

Of course, much of the time you get mixed indicators: for example, one Significator will be Cardinal Cadent, while the other is Fixed Succedent. In these cases, you may want to adjust the units of time. The units of time also vary according to the nature of the Question itself. If you are examining a Question concerning stock trading, and your Querent is doing day trading, a short interval of time might be minutes, while a long interval of time might be days. For someone who is creating a retirement portfolio, the long interval might make more sense as years – or even possibly decades.

Direction is not always so obvious, in part because of the frequency of having mixed indicators. The general idea is this: take the major Significators in the chart. Examine their location by sign and by house. If the bulk of the planets are either in one house or one sign, then you can translate this into compass location through the following tables, as given by Lilly.[32] Be aware there are other systems of allocation, which you can find in ***The Book of Rulerships***.

Sign	Direction
Aries	East
Taurus	South
Gemini	West
Cancer	North
Leo	East
Virgo	South
Libra	West
Scorpio	North
Sagittarius	East
Capricorn	South
Aquarius	West
Pisces	North

House	Direction
1st House	East
2nd House	East-Northeast
3rd House	North-Northeast
4th House	North
5th House	North-Northwest
6th House	West-Northwest
7th House	West
8th House	West-Southwest
9th House	South-Southwest
10th House	South
11th House	South-Southeast
12th House	East-Southeast

These directions are only a guide. I have expressed them in modern language, because, evidently, the ancient sources could tell "North-Northwest" from "Northwest-North."

Significators

The most important thing to remember about this general approach to delineation is that it's important to reason your way to one Significator for each of the parties in the Question, and then to observe each Significator's strength, placement and movement in order to predict the outcome. When you delineate the chart in this fashion, you will find that you are leaving out a great number of components of the chart that you would normally utilize if this were a nativity. This is perfectly normal for horary. You can completely ignore that Mars-Saturn-Pluto combination if none of the components are sign rulers of, or posited in, the houses relevant to the Question. A Horary delineation uses only those components directly related to the question at hand. Anything else is completely ignored.

Blue Belt
Other Considerations
Orbs. Antiscia. Sect.
Pitted and other Degree Types.
Mute Signs and Other Sign Classifications.

Before we begin the fun part, namely, delineations, we need to cover a little more in the way of terminology, and to engage in a close examination of how much significance to place on the signs of the Significators.

When is Sign significant?

This may seem like a strange question, but consider an alternative starting point:

Must a forming aspect become exact within the same sign to qualify as a perfection?

The Ancients had a rather inconsistent approach to sign boundaries. Sometimes they are important. Sometimes they are not. This can be seen in a closer scrutiny of how Lilly actually utilized sign boundaries, apart from how they may have figured in his definitions.

Recall from the last chapter that the definition of Void of Course restricts the next aspect to being within sign.[33] Another definition in which Lilly restricts usage to within sign is ***combustion***, the conjunction of another planet within 8 degrees orb of the Sun. This definition was not usually restricted to within sign, but Lilly makes this exception.[34] One would therefore assume that aspects might also need to be within sign? Look again at the two definitions of perfection in the last chapter: there is no such restriction. Lilly's definition of perfection also does not stipulate that the aspect must be within sign.[35] In examining Lilly's 35 example horaries, I find out-of-sign aspects used five times in four charts.[36]

This presents a very inconsistent picture. On the one hand, sign boundaries are important enough for Lilly to restrict the definition of combustion more than other astrologers did. They are also important enough to maintain (and use) a definition of Void of Course that is at least partially based on those boundaries. But they are not important enough to present any barrier to perfection! In fact, when Lilly uses an out of sign aspect, he doesn't even bother to mention that it's out of sign, further emphasizing that to him, the out of sign perfection was absolutely normal.

The use of signs historically has had its problems. We can probably blame the Babylonians, because while their astronomy included the modern ecliptical constellations, the recording of planetary positions by sign was not nearly as important as contemporary thought would have us believe. There is a certain ambivalency about just how much of the qualities of a planet are a result of sign designation. Among the points that require sign information, we have:

- Dispositorships of other planets
- Quality of degree
- House rulership
- Essential Dignity
- House placement
- Intrinsic quality of sign; as we may designate a planet in Aries as being impetuous, while one is Taurus is more circumspect, etc.

Here we may examine some of the kinds of qualities that we can designate for the signs, as shown in the following table.

Sign	Quality	Reference
♈	Choleric	PA-004
	Ingenious	LI-538
	Ingenuous	KB-013
	Ireful	D2-005
	Luxurious (Lascivious)	D2-005
	Sanguine	D1-009
	Vicious	D2-005
	Violent	PA-004
	Witty	KB-013, LI-538
♉	Furious	PA-004
	Honest	D2-006
	Laborious	KB-015, LI-538
	Luxurious (Lascivious)	D2-006
	Religious	D2-006
♊	Fidelity Lacking	KB-016
	Judicious in Worldly Affairs	KB-016
	Lover of Arts & Sciences	KB-016, LI-538
	Lover of Curiosities	KB-016
	Lover of Learning	LI-538
	Ready Understanding	PA-005
	Sanguine	D1-009
	Sweet	D2-007
	Temperate	AB-264

Sign	Quality	Reference
♊ (cont.)	Understanding Excellent	KB-016
	Witty	D2-007, KB-016, LI-538
♋	Dumb (as in mute)	D2-007
	Given to Drinking	KB-018
	Phlegmatic	PA-005
	Unconstant	KB-018, LI-538
♌	Crafty	D2-008
	Cruel	LI-538
	Fierce	KB-019
	Honest	D2-008
	Ireful	D2-008
	Luxurious (Lascivious)	D2-008
	Proud	KB-019
	Sober & Grave	KB-020, LI-538
	Spirit Generous	KB-019
	Spirit Resolute	KB-019
	Valiant	PA-006
♍	Choleric	D1-009
	Covetous	LI-538
	Cruel	D2-009, LI-538
	Given to Learning	KB-021, LI-538, PA-006
	Judicious	KB-021
	Lover of Arts	LI-538
	Spiteful	LI-538
	Studious	KB-021, PA-006
	Wit Ingenious But Subtle	KB-021
	Wit Wholly for Its Own End	D2-009
	Witty	KB-021, PA-006
♎	Conceited	KB-023, LI-538
	Courteous	KB-023
	Crafty	LI-538
	Inconstant	LI-538
	Melancholic	D1-009
	Sanguine	PA-007
♏	Covetous	LI-538
	Cunning & Subtle	KB-025
	Impudent	KB-025, LI-538
	Indecent	KB-025
	Ireful	D2-011
	Lewdness (Priapism)	KB-026, SA-018

Sign	Quality	Reference
♏ (cont.)	Liars	KB-025
	Melancholic	D1-009
	Phlegmatic	PA-007
	Sluggish	KB-025
	Vicious	D2-011
	Violent	PA-007
♐	Apprehension Quick	KB-027
	Choleric	PA-008
	Crafty	D2-011
	Fearless	KB-027, LI-538
	Ingenious	D2-011, KB-027
	Intemperance in Sports	KB-028
	Melancholic	D1-009
	Proud	KB-027
	Quick to Anger, Soon Over It	KB-027
	Stout-Hearted	KB-027
	Valiant	KB-027, LI-538
	Witty	KB-027
♑	Cowards	KB-028
	Crooked	D2-012
	Cruel	D2-012
	Inconstant	KB-028
	Lecherous	KB-028, LI-538
	Luxurious (Lascivious)	D2-012
	Phlegmatic	D1-009
	Subtle	KB-028
	Vicious	D2-012
♒	Affable	LI-538
	Honest	D2-013
	Phlegmatic	D1-009
	Religious	D2-013
	Sanguine	PA-009
	Sweet	D2-013
♓	Dishonest	D2-014, LI-538
	Dumb (as in mute)	D2-014
	Luxurious (Lascivious)	D2-014
	Pretender of Truth	KB-031
	Vicious	D2-014

Among the qualities of planets that don't require sign placement, we have:

- Planetary speed
- Visibility
- Oriental or occidental placement
- Station points and retrogradations
- Aspects, maybe.

Historically, the designation of planetary position by sign occurred a number of centuries after planetary cycles began to be systematically studied. Apart from dignities dependent specifically upon sign placement, it is well worth the time of the horary practitioner to consider carefully how important *any* sign placement may be to the nature of the phenomenon being studied.

My own experience has been to not follow Lilly completely in his demarcations. I do not restrict combustion to within sign, because combustion is based on a question of actual astronomical visibility, and sign boundaries clearly are not visible! But I am also troubled by Lilly's opinion that out of sign aspects are normative: in other words, that they are no different than in-sign aspects.

My own position on aspects is as follows. I allow out of sign aspects only when:

- they are within orb.
- the body that changes sign either gains dignity or loses debility by doing so.

We shall have a chance to study these matters more fully in Appendix E, which enumerates the chart examples match a number of specific conditions, such as out-of-sign perfections.

Lilly would subscribe to the first restriction, but not the second. The second is really an extension of my observation that peregrine planets really don't perform well in horary. However, consider the case of the Moon in Scorpio, where she is in her Fall. When the Moon goes into Sagittarius, she is peregrine. However, the Moon generally seems so relieved to be out of Scorpio, that an out-of-sign applying aspect in Sagittarius seems to work just fine, even though peregrine!

I include as part of the story given by the delineation that there is a change in state associated with the change in sign. Conditions change. This is shown by the sign change: it must mean *something*!

Orbs

The topic of orbs receives different treatment in almost every different school of astrology. The classical method of doing orbs consists of breaking each orb into two halves, and assigning one half to each planet involved in the orb. These half orbs are called ***moieties***. The moieties for each planet as used by Lilly[37] are shown in the following table.

Planet	Moiety
Sun	7.5 – 8.5 degrees
Moon	6.0 – 6.25 degrees
Mercury	3.5 degrees
Venus	3.5 – 4.0 degrees
Mars	3.5 – 3.75 degrees
Jupiter	4.5 – 6.0 degrees
Saturn	4.5 – 5.0 degrees

We can summarize the table as follows: the Sun, the Moon, the "personal" planets, and the "social" planets each have a different moiety. Here's how to use the moieties. Suppose we're looking at a possible aspect between the Sun and Jupiter. The orb for this aspect would be 7.5 + 4.5 = 12 degrees. In other words, the orb is potentially different for each planetary pair. There is no differentiation between different types of aspects, such as between a conjunction and a square.

Having defined orb, how important is this definition in horary? Again, turning to our examples of horaries of Lilly, there were 37 instances of approaching aspects between planets that were within orb compared to only seven cases of where the aspects mentioned were out of orb. The largest degree of separation that Lilly mentioned was the case of Venus applying to Jupiter by 19 degrees.[38] Granted, this does not preclude the use of out of orb aspects because we have no referent to examine the expected frequency of one case *versus* the other.

The simplest conclusion is probably that an aspect within orb is preferred, but in the absence of a closer configuration, a more distant one will do – provided that something else doesn't happen in the meantime to frustrate the result. This latter thought may in fact be more crucial than the orb size itself. Obviously, the greater the arc difference between two planets, the greater the likelihood that something else of significance may occur before the former two planets reach an exact aspect.

Antiscia and Aversion

In Chapter 9 of ***CAML***, I discussed the various classical definitions of ***beholding***. Beholding links the idea of aspects to several other methods of planetary interaction. The principal additional interaction is through the solstice point relationship. The sign pairs that are in either antiscial or contra-antiscial relationship are shown in Appendix A. An antiscial relationship may be treated as having the same effect as a conjunction, while a contra-antiscial relationship may be treated as an opposition. Thus, we in effect have two additional aspects to consider in our evaluation of possible perfections.

There is one other concept in sign relationship that we should mention here. Specifically, what we are defining is the absence of all relationship: ***aversion***. Averse signs have no relationship either by aspect, solstice points, or mutual rulership. Mutual rulership refers to the pairs Taurus – Libra; Gemini – Virgo; Aries – Scorpio; Sagittarius – Pisces; or Capricorn – Aquarius. These pairs share the same ruler and thus are considered to have some degree of relationship, even if tenuous. The averse signs pairs would be: Aries-Taurus; Taurus-Gemini; Taurus-Sagittarius; Gemini-Scorpio; Cancer-Leo; Cancer-Aquarius; Leo-Virgo; Leo-Capricorn; Leo-Pisces; Virgo-Aquarius; Libra-Scorpio; Scorpio-Sagittarius; and Aquarius-Pisces.

The use of non-averse signs that do not behold, as Taurus – Libra, is not to produce something like an aspect, but to demonstrate affinity. For example, in questions of lost persons, having the same planet rule that person's 1st and 8th Houses would be an argument of death, just as having the same planet as ruler of the 1st and 8th Houses radically is a possible argument of death in a question concerning a disease. In these cases, there is an affinity between the person and Death – not a good thing! Similarly, having a 1st-6th relationship as demonstrated by having the same ruler of the 1st and 6th would indicate an absent party being sick.

Sect

Sect is the attribution of qualities based on day or night conditions: of the time of day, of whether the planet is in a diurnal or nocturnal placement, by sign, etc. For example, a diurnal placement in a day chart (one with the Sun in one of the houses between 12 and 7) would mean that the planet is above the horizon: in the same hemisphere as the Sun, with hemisphere defined by the Ascendant-Descendant axis. A nocturnal placement is in the hemisphere opposite the Sun.

In Horary, these considerations seem to be irrelevant except as Sect is used to determine the formulation of the Lots and Arabic Parts.[39]

Do specific degrees or degree areas have meaning in classical Horary?

One of the truly obscure tables in Lilly's *Christian Astrology* is the Table of Degree Areas on page 116, which lists masculine, feminine, light, dark, smoky, void, pitted, lame and degrees of increasing fortune. While Lilly meticulously lists them, he then proceeds to ignore them. The only common usage of them that I have found is in medical questions and medical astrology, in which there is a specific use for the lame degrees, also called *azimene*. Blagrave gives the most extensive list: if the Moon is in azimene degrees in an acute disease, or the Sun in a chronic disease, or the Ruler of the 6th House, or the Ruler of the Ascendant, then the feared result is continued sickness or even death.[40] Lilly's description for these degrees is that if the Ruler of the 6th House is square or opposite the Ruler of the 1st House in Azimene degrees, the disease is incurable, and any actions on the part of the physician are useless. Also, the disease will probably be quite painful.[41] Lilly's assessment is echoed by Coley, who adds that the pain engendered in the disease is permanent.[42]

For the rest, there doesn't seem to be any evidence that these were used consistently, so until someone decides to take on the job of studying this in depth, we shall pass on to the next topic.

Qualities of the Signs

While the qualities of degrees may be something we can skip over, the same cannot be said for the qualities of the signs. This is in addition to the common classifications which have survived into modern usage, such as Cardinal, Fixed, Mutable, Masculine, and Feminine. The following terms may have important meanings in the delineation of an answer to a Horary Question. The classification is usually obvious, based on the representative constellation for the sign.

Human Signs: Gemini, Virgo, Libra and Aquarius. These are also called the courteous signs, which gives a pretty good indication of their meaning. Whether courtesy is the primary motivator, or simply that Significators in these signs are more aware of the social context, would be difficult to determine.

Bestial or Four-footed Signs: Aries, Taurus, Leo, Sagittarius (last part), and Capricorn. Bestial signs have more voracious sex drives than other signs. They also tend to act out of desire, rather than reason. Bestial signs act instinctively, without thinking out the best strategic response. A human sign can stop and consider the outcome of a particular scenario, and what would be the best path to that desired goal. A bestial sign will charge ahead in a direct path, regardless of the odds of success from that approach.

Feral Signs: Leo and the last part of Sagittarius. The four-footed signs are animal in nature, but these feral areas are supposed to be really beastly, especially for the placement of the Ascendant. The word atavistic comes to mind in describing persons acting out of this influence.

Mute Signs: Cancer, Scorpio or Pisces. These are also called signs of slow voice.

Fruitful Signs: Cancer, Scorpio, or Pisces. The prominence of these signs in a question about pregnancy gives an affirmative answer. The old lists do not include Taurus. I do, because I have repeatedly seen it bring positive answers in pregnancy questions.

Barren Signs: Gemini, Leo and Virgo. The prominence of these signs in a question about pregnancy gives a negative answer.

Signs of Long or Short Ascension: The Babylonians noticed that different signs take different amounts of time to rise. The signs of long ascension are

Cancer through Sagittarius; the signs of short ascension are Capricorn through Gemini. Since we have no specific designation of horary as a Babylonian technique, we can only go back to the Greeks for information about how to apply these. Dorotheus discussed these signs almost immediately upon beginning his work on Interrogations.[43] His usage was simple: signs of long ascension denote matters that take longer to come to perfection or fruition. Lilly by contrast felt that an approaching square in signs of long ascension should be treated as a trine.[44] This usage directly contradicts Dorotheus, as Dorotheus' point was that, the longer it takes for something to occur, the more problems are likely to be encountered. Lilly took a square, which by its very nature implies problems, and eliminated the problem by declaring it like a trine, which certainly lessens the difficulty of the perfection. Perhaps we should consider merely the timing implication – signs that rise more slowly give events that are slower to resolve.

Of all of these types, we find the most useful are either the mute signs, or the fruitful-barren, depending on the nature of the Question. If the Significator of a party is in a mute sign, and communication is necessary to effect the result, then the mute quality means that they don't open their mouths and speak up at critical times. So a mute sign could preclude the possibility of further action if the primary action necessary is of a verbal nature.

The fruitful-barren polarity applies to more than pregnancy, but that's a good starting image. If creativity is called for, and barren signs predominate, then there is a problem! We can express the concept "fruitfulness" when it comes to an idea as well as biological fertility. Any such application would be relevant. Sometimes you get questions that involve whether it's beneficial to pursue a particular idea or plan. In this case, fruitful signs would be helpful. If you want to stop something from occurring, then barren signs would be preferred.

Now that we have covered the preliminaries, we are ready to go on to the real forms of Horary: the actual types of Questions that you will ask or be asked. We will consider these Questions according to the primary house that would be invoked to provide the answer.

Chapter One

Affairs of the 1st House:
Planes, Trains and Automobiles. Health and Happiness (Maybe not in that Order)

Questions of the 1st House as given by Lilly:[45]

- *If the Querent is likely to live long, yea or not.*
- *To what part of Heaven [i.e., global location] it's best the Querent direct his Affaires, or wherein he may live most happily.*
- *What part of his Life is like to be the best.*
- *What Accidents in future he might expect; Time when.[46]*
- *If one shall find the Party at home he would speak withall. [Note that Lilly put this in his section on the 1st House, but it is a matter of both 1st and 7th, so we will consider it later.]*
- *Of a thing suddenly happening, Whether it signifieth Good or Evill.*
- *What Marke, Mole or Scarre the Querent hath in any Member of his Body.*
- *Whether one absent be dead or alive. [Note again that Lilly put this in his section on the 1st House, but it is a matter of both 1st and the 7th or other house. We will consider it in Chapter 4.]*
- *Of a Ship, and whatever are in her, her Safety or Destruction.*

Gadbury also lists the following:[47]

- *Of the good or evil attending life.*
- *When, or in what time shall the Native undergo a change?*

We now begin our trek through the houses to illustrate the kinds of Questions that the Horary Astrologer frequently encounters. The 1st House is used in all Horaries, because it represents the Querent. However, it can also be the locus of particular questions. In the traditional lists, the three concepts most associated with the 1st House are health, longevity and happiness. Strangely, these Questions are rare. Or maybe not so strangely: astrologers today are not used to doing horary, so many of these questions would be considered as part of a natal reading. Therefore, they would never even be considered as horary questions. The bulk of 1st House horary Questions actually asked nowadays concerns something seemingly unrelated: cars.

Why are cars considered in the 1st House? For the answer, we can go back to Lilly and observe his treatment of Ships at Sea.[48] Lilly lived in the period of nautical exploration and commerce prior to the discovery of reliable means of measuring longitude. In the absence of accurate measurement, there was a level of danger in voyages that today is virtually unimaginable. As a result, there was a booming trade in Horary and Electional work at virtually any port city.[49]

The typical Horary Question was: "X (a ship at sea) is she safe or shipwrecked?" The ship itself was considered to be a matter of the 1st House. Its condition could be determined from the condition of the Ascendant Ruler, and Moon, mixed with the placement of the malefics – Mars, Saturn and the South Node. In a modern context, we could add Uranus, Neptune, and Pluto.

It is not much of an extrapolation to apply the rules for oceangoing ships to virtually any vessel of transportation, regardless of whether it moves via land, water, air – or space, for that matter. These days, we place a phone call rather than wondering where a ship (or a car) is – or even locate it through other means such as radar or global positioning satellites. While accidents and fatalities still occur, generally we hear the sad news *before* a horary even could be asked. As a result, the more common application for these transportation Questions has shifted to *buying* a car, or other vessel. Thus, the Question occurs most frequently in the form: "Should I buy this car?"

We have already discussed the pitfalls of "should" as far as its intrinsically ambiguous meaning. However, in this case the meaning of the Question is usually fairly clear with a minimum of follow-up to the Querent. The implication of this Question is generally:

- If I buy this car, is it safe? Will I be in an accident in it?
- Is the car reliable?
- If it's a used car, is there anything wrong with particular components of the car?
- If it's a used car, has it been in an accident?
- If it's a used car, is the price reasonable?

Before we go into our first example, let's review Lilly's method, so that we have a starting point for application to our newer technology:[50]

The Ancients doe put this Question to those concerning the ninth house, and I conceive for no other reason, than because it must be granted, that all Ships are made for Travell and Journeys: however in regard the most part of the Judgments concerning its safety or ruine is derived from the Ascendant and his Lord, and the Moon, I thought it fit to place this Judgment as belonging to the first House.

Generally, the Signe ascending and the Moon are Significators *of the* Ship, *and what Goods are in her, the Lord of the Ascendant of those that saile in her: if in the Question demanded you find all these unfortunate, that is, if a malevolent Planet by position be placed in the Ascendant, he having dignities in the* 8th*: or if you find the* Lord *of the Ascendant in the* 8th, *in any ill configuration with the lord of the* 8th, 12th, 4th or 6th, or the Moon combust, *or under the earth, you may judge the Ship is lost and the men drowned, (unlesse you find reception betwixt themselves) for then the Ship was casually Shipwrackt, and some of the Sea-men did escape: but if you find the preceding* Significators *all of them free from misfortune, both Men and Goods are all safe; the more safe if any reception be. But if the Ascendant and the Moon be infortunate, and the Lord of the Ascendant fortunate, the Ship is like to be drowned, but the men will be saved...*

Lilly then goes on to construct a table that shows the parts of the ship by sign, with the idea that if you see which signs are afflicted, you can translate this into a section of the ship. I have presented this with a translation into the parts of a car.

	Lilly – parts of a ship	**Lehman – parts of a car**
♈	breast of a ship	front end
♉	more towards the water	passenger compartment
♊	rudder or stern	steering mechanism, column and wheel
♋	bottom or floor	floorboards or underside; oil pan
♌	top of ship above water	moon roof, sun roof, and antennas; convertible top
♍	the belly of the ship	the trunk, or storage area
♎	section that may be above or below water	the paint job; aerodynamics
♏	crew quarters or work areas	the motor
♐	the crew	Passengers
♑	ends of the ship	bumpers and crash protectors
♒	captain	driver
♓	the oars	the wheels and axles

My list is somewhat speculative, but you should be able to see what I have done to create it is to either translate by functionality or by location, two standard ways we can use to apply rulerships to an as yet undesignated entity.

The table is used as follows: note the signs that are accidentally highlighted in the chart by being the signs of the Moon and Ascendant – then consider the Moon and Ascendant themselves. If they are fortunate, those parts of the vessel are safe and sound. If they are debilitated by conjunction or aspect to the malefics, then there is a problem with that region. If a malefic is prominent, the nature of the malefic will give a clue to the nature of potential problems.

Apart from the methodology of locating the weak points of the vessel, the system Lilly proposes is absolutely analogous to medical horary delineation, as we shall see. Essentially, he is looking for one of two conditions, which would illustrate the death of the ship: either destruction of the Ascendant, Ascendant Ruler or the Moon; or a relationship of one of those to the 8th House. This is exactly the sort of analysis that goes into determining whether a disease is potentially fatal.

Recall that Lilly had a generic method for distinguishing between inanimate objects and people that are both related to the same house – the object is the house cusp itself, the people are given by the ruler of the house. So *if there is a need to distinguish them*, the car is represented by the Ascendant itself, while the people in it are shown by the Ruler of the 1st House.

Let's return to Lilly's commentary so that we can understand the action of the malefics:[51]

> *... if you find the infortunes in Angles, or Succeeding Houses, there will chance some hindrance unto the Ship, and it shall be in that part which the Signe signifies where the unfortunate Planet is; if the same Infortune be Saturn, the Ship will be split, and the men drowned, or received hurt by some bruise, or running a ground: but if it be Mars, and he in any of his Essential Dignities, ... he shall then signifie the same as Saturn did, or very great danger and damage to the Ship: But if the Fortunes cast their benevolent rayes or aspect to the places where Mars or Saturn are, and the ... Ascendant, and the Lord of that House or Signe where the Moon is in be free, then it's an argument, the Ship shall labour hard, and suffer much damage, yet not withstanding the greater part both of Goods and Men shall be preserved. But if Mars does afflict the Lords of the Angles, and Dispositor of the Moon, the Mariners shall be in great fear of their enemies, or of Pyrates or Sea-robbers, shall even tremble for feare of them: and if also unto this evill configuration chance any other affliction of the Signes, there will happen amongst the Mariners Blood-shed, Controversies, quarreling one with another, theeving and robbing each other, purloyning the Goods of the Ship...*
>
> *If Saturn in the like nature doe afflict, as was before cited of Mars, there will be many thefts committed in the Ship, but no blood-*

shed; the Goods of the Ship consume, no body knowing which way.

If the unfortunate Signes (viz. Those which are afflicted by the presence of Saturn, Mars or South Node) be those which signifie the bottome or that part of the Ship which is under Water, it's an argument of the breaking and drowning thereof, or receiving some dangerous Leak: if the Signes so unfortunate be in the Midheaven, and Mars unfortunate them, it's like the Ship will be burnt by fire, thunder or lightening, or matter falling out of the Aire into the Ship; this shall then take place when the Signs are fiery, and neer violent fixed Stars.

If that Signe wherein Mars or the unfortunate Planet be the Signe of the 4th house, it notes firing of the Ship in the bottome of her; but if Mars be there, and the Signe humane, viz. either Gemini, Libra or Aquarius, that fire or burning of the Ship shall proceed from a fight with Enemies, or they shall cast fire into her, or shall teare the Ship in pieces in grapling with her, and the fire shall be in that part of the Ship first take hold, signified by the Signe wherein an Infortune was at the time of asking the Question.

If Saturn instead of Mars doe denunciate dammage, and be placed in the Mid-heaven, the Ship shall receive prejudice by contrary Winds, and by leaks in the Ship, by rending or using of bad Sailes...

What we can conclude from Lilly's treatment is that problems of either a Mars or Saturn (i.e., malefic) nature come from their involvement with the Ascendant or Moon – exactly as we would interpret in a matter of health. The effect of Mars trends more toward fire or violence; the effect of Saturn, mechanical breakdown or aging. Both give the possibility of theft, but it's more likely to be violent in the case of Mars. We can add in a modern context that Uranus, Neptune and Pluto each have their own style of baleful influence: Uranus through electrical problems, accidents or sudden failures, Neptune through any fluid in the car (or outside of it, as in leaks, or even danger from fog), and Pluto through corrosion and rust.

Before continuing, let me directly address one particular issue: the modern usage of the 3rd House for cars. This may have arisen from the purely functional theory that a car is used for local trips. Modern thinking hypothesizes that since local trips are a 3rd House matter, therefore, cars are a 3rd house item. Notice that Lilly addresses an analogous situation with some "ancients," who attributed sailing vessels to the 9th House for precisely the same reason: the theory being that a machine or thing that facilitates or is involved with a matter of a particular house is ruled by that same house.[52] Is that a consistent pattern in rulership attribution?

I would have to say no. Here's the issue. At first I thought, let's just look up medical instruments and see how they are assigned. But going through all of my sources, I could not find specific designations for things like scalpels, sutures, cauterizing implements, or even agricultural tools such as ploughs, or household tools such as needles. Apparently, if a tool is simply a means to an end, then the tool doesn't even rate a separate rulership citation.[53] However, a ship is not merely a tool for ocean transport, but a significant investment. It is the size, complexity and cost of the ship that makes the ship rate enough to have a specific rulership. Not to mention the presence of a human crew, and the likely presence of a valuable cargo. Actually, our closest classical analogy to cars would be horses. Horses, which would have been the principal form of land transportation in Lilly's time, are assigned to the 12th House of large animals. The use of horses does not override the fact that they are animals first, means of transportation second. One could surmise that the platonic concept of ideal forms was dominant in thinking here: an entity was first classified by relationship to other types *as far as house designations were concerned.* It's worth remembering that an item could be classified *either* by house, planet or sign – or any combination thereof. I believe it's an open question as to whether everything even *has* a house designation at all, because one is able to use a planet directly, without recourse to a specific house Significator.[54] Sometimes, trying too hard to come up with a house Significator is simply too tortured.

It is clear that planetary designation is much more likely to be a result of functionality than house assignment. For example, in ***Essential Dignities***, I showed that Culpeper's plant rulership designations were based far more closely on medical treatment usage than on plant structure, morphology, or classification.

Before we begin to study our examples, let's consider a few of the types of 1st House horaries and how we would delineate them.

What Accidents in future he might expect; Time when.

The timing of accidents, which in this context means events of a deleterious nature, is shown by an approaching aspect between the Ruler of the Ascendant and an Infortune, where Infortune is defined a little more broadly than just a malefic. Infortunes can also include the Sun by conjunction – because the conjunction to the Sun means that the Significator in question is combust. We can also include any aspect to the Ruler of the 8th House. The Ruler of the 8th House is what we might call an Accidental Malefic, and it is used in several different types of horary.[55] In any case, the number of degrees distant between the Ruler of the 1st and the Infortune is then converted to a time measurement as given in the Green Belt Chapter.

If this method does not produce a result, then the same logic may be applied using the Moon instead of the Ruler of the Ascendant.

The next option is to use any Infortune posited in the 1st House, and the degree separation of that Infortune from the cusp of the 1st as the timing mechanism.

If the Lord of the 1st is afflicted by the Ruler of the 6th, or if the Ruler of the 1st is going to combustion in the 6th, then disease is afflicting health, and the conclusion is that sickness is the outcome within the time frame given by the perfection. If the relationship is to the 8th instead of the 6th, then the outcome is a danger of death, not sickness.

If the Ruler of the 1st is afflicted by another planet, then the houses which are ruled by that afflicting planet, determine the nature of the affliction.

Of a thing suddenly happening, Whether it signifieth Good or Evil.

Here the method is to consider the dispositor of the Sun, the dispositor of the Moon, and the Ruler of the Ascendant, and decide among the three which is strongest in the 1st House, either by position or Rulership. That Planet then becomes the Significator of the event happening. That Significator is then examined for its condition: peregrinity, combustion, and approaching aspects. If it is aspecting only the Fortunes, then the outcome is good. If it is aspecting primarily Saturn, Mars or Mercury, then the outcome is problematic.

There is a related kind of horary that we will discuss in Chapter 8. It is also possible to ask if a situation is dangerous. In that case, the question becomes an 8th House question.

What Marke, Mole or Scarre the Querent hath in any member of his Body.

We have already touched upon this technique in the Green Belt Chapter. This often seems like a big theme in Lillyesque horary. The actual method is to equate the sign rising to the part of the body ruled by that sign, then to divide that organ into thirds. If the first part of the sign is rising, then the mark is in the upper part of the organ; if the middle degrees are rising, then in the middle of the organ; and if the late degrees are rising, then in the lower part of the organ. I have to admit to considerable ennui concerning this technique, although I have seen some very good results achieved.

My problem is this: the principle use of the "marks and moles" was to determine whether the chart was radical. But this implies that a non-radical chart was treated differently from a radical one – which never seems to have been the practice! This is not a question I can *ever* imagine the Querent asking, so this is merely a cute little exercise on the part of the astrologer. The only practical application that I can see for this – apart from impressing the client – is if the question were asked about another party (as in, what will my future wife look like?), then this could be one more component of the answer.

Of the good or evil attending life.

This is similar in reading to the delineation above for whether an event should have a good or evil outcome, with the added consideration that having a Fortune ruling the Ascendant bodes well for the life. Saturn as Ruler produces a melancholy and pensive person, while Mars ruling the Ascendant means the Querent is likely to be a target of knaves and thieves. If the South Node is in the 1st, then there is continual danger of scandal.

The wording is frankly archaic. A more contemporary wording might be, will the circumstances of my life work out well in this period? Since I receive a number of client referrals from Vedic astrologers, there is actually a very reasonable context for this question. If the Querent has been shown to be in an especially malefic dasa or bhukti,[56] they may be questioning their judgment about everything, or may be concerned about every possible outcome. This then becomes a way to get a second opinion on the period in question.

When, or in what time shall the Native undergo a change?

It's worth mentioning that this is a variant of the question of when accidents shall befall the Querent, which shows you the confidence the Ancients had that *any* change was usually for the worse!

Example 1: Will the car work out?

In our first example, an "experienced Querent" (an astrologer who took the time of his own question, but chose to have me do the delineation) asked the question. Hence the coordinates are for his location, not mine. He was in the market for a used car as the second family car. Having already previously discussed the problem of "should" horaries with him, he decided to ask the question in this matter, querying whether this car would be able to function as needed.

In this chart, with Capricorn Rising, we of course use Saturn to rule the car, but Jupiter has just risen, and is considered conjunct the Ascendant. Jupiter retrograde and in Fall, gives high hopes, but delivers nothing but promises. This is aggravated still more because Jupiter is at the ***bendings*** – the points square the Nodes.[57] In any buy-sell transaction, the 7th House gives the other party from the Querent: here we see the Moon in Scorpio ruling it, and the owner of the car had just recently been released from prison! The 10th House in a buy-sell situation gives the price: the debilitated Moon in the 10th House representing the seller (7th House) shows that the seller clearly needed the money: the seller lacks dignity, and his complete focus is on the 10th, namely the price.

So: do we recommend buying this car? Saturn is in Fall in Aries, and further debilitated by being retrograde. The co-Almuten of the 1st House, Mars, is at 29 Gemini, with dignity only by Term. Neither planet suggests that the car is in good condition to begin with, and Mars is about to move into Cancer, where it simultaneously is in Fall, and has Triplicity, so its condition becomes even *less* predictable.

Jupiter, the one benefic in a position to help, is so debilitated that it becomes a hindrance. The sign Capricorn highlighted brings to mind the "ends" of the car, which I take to mean the bumpers. Also, Mars at 29 degrees disposes the Moon in Scorpio, which I judge as two arguments that this car has been in at least one accident. With Mars in Gemini, I expect that the steering mechanism has sustained damage, and with Saturn in Aries, I suspect that the front end was damaged as well.

Using Lilly's idea of the house as representative of the object in question, the presence of Neptune and Uranus in the 1st House gives me pause. With Neptune in the first, I am immediately suspicious of problems with hydraulics or other fluids. With Uranus present, the electrical system is suspect. Each of these planets being retrograde surely makes the problem worse, not better.

In summary, this car does not look like a great deal. In any case, Saturn ruling the 1st and the Moon ruling the 7th are not coming into any aspect, and both are peregrine, so I don't see a deal being consummated. The Querent did not buy the car.

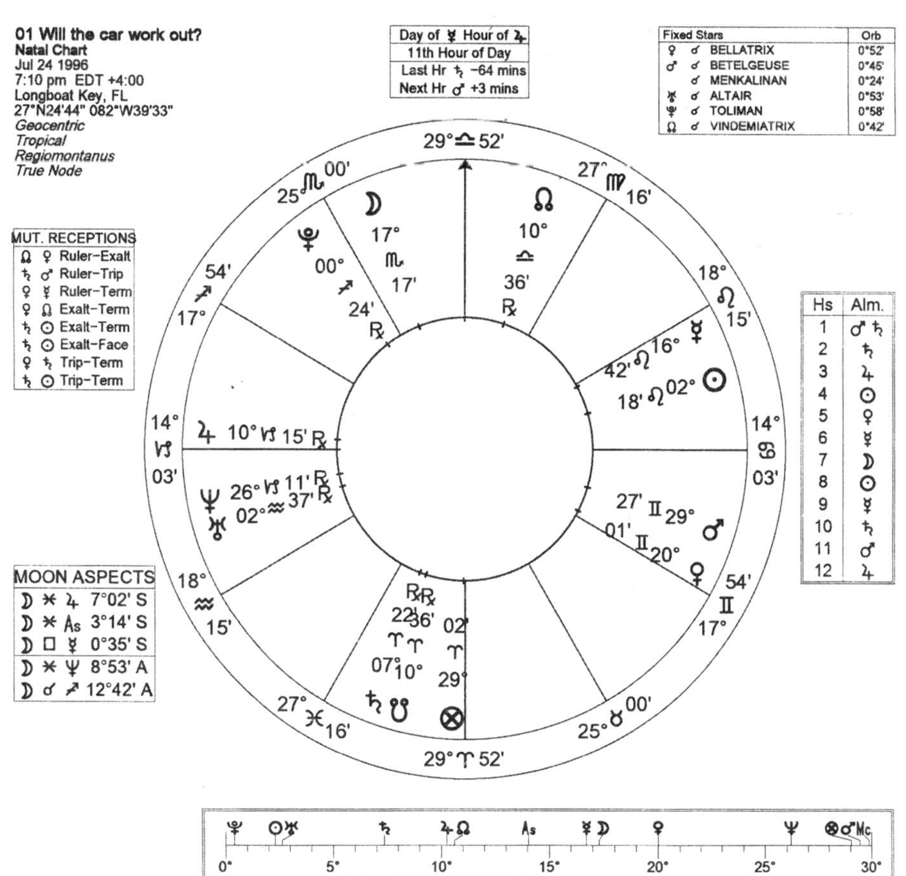

ESSENTIAL DIGNITIES (LEHMAN)								
Pt	Ruler	Exalt	Trip	Term	Face	Detri	Fall	Score
☽	♂	--	♀	♀	☉	♀	☽ -	-9 p
☉	☉ +	--	☉ +	♄	♄	♄	--	+8
☿	☉	--	☉	♀	♃	♄	--	-5 p
♀	☿	☊	♄	♀ +	☉	♃	☋	+2
♂	☿	☊	♄	♂ +	☉	♃	☋	+2
♃	♄	♂	♀	☿	♂	☽	♃ -	-9 p
♄	♂	☉	☉	♀	♂	♀	♄ -	-9 p
As	♄	♂	♀	♃	♂	☽	♃	--
Mc	♀	♄	♄	♂	♃	♂	☉	--
⊗	♂	☉	☉	♄	♀	♀	♄	--

planets.pts				
Pt	Long.	Travel	Antiscia	C.Ant.
☽	17°♏17'56"	+13°29'	12°♒42	12°♌42
☉	02°♌18'07"	+00°57'	27°♉41	27°♏41
☿	16°♌42	+01°50'	13°♉17	13°♏17
♀	20°♊01	+00°38'	09°♋58	09°♑58
♂	29°♊27	+00°40'	00°♋32	00°♑32
♃	10°♑15 ℞	-00°06'	19°♐44	19°♊44
♄	07°♈22 ℞	-00°00'	22°♍37	22°♓37
♅	02°♒37 ℞	-00°02'	27°♏22	27°♉22
♆	26°♑11 ℞	-00°01'	03°♐48	03°♊48
♇	00°♐24 ℞	-00°00'	29°♑35	29°♋35
☊	10°♎36 ℞	-00°01'	19°♓23	19°♍23
☋	10°♈36 ℞	-00°01'	19°♍23	19°♓23
As	14°♑03'02"	+00°00'	15°♐56	15°♊56
Mc	29°♎52'13"	+00°00'	00°♓07	00°♍07
⊗	29°♈02	+00°00'	00°♍57	00°♓57

Example 2. Car #4?

The Querent from Example 1 followed my advice, and even got confirmation from his mechanic, but this didn't change the fact that he needed to buy a car. What followed was a series of horary questions as he found out about still more cars. The following example is for the car he finally bought.

Here we have Virgo Rising, with the Ascendant ruled by a dignified Mercury, and the North Node in the Ascendant. Mercury rules both Ascendant and M.C., which means the Querent is in a position to affect the ultimate price. With Mercury dignified, the price will be, if not high, at least fair. Virgo rules the belly of a ship, that area I have designated as the trunk. However, neither Mercury nor the dignified Moon is afflicted by the malefics, and there are no malefics in the 1st House. The only exception is that the Moon is coming to the opposition to Neptune, which probably indicates some sort of leak related to one of the fluids in the car. Both the classical malefics are angular, but both are also in Fall.

Notice that, while neither the Moon nor Mercury perfects with Jupiter, ruler of the 7th, there is still an argument of successful sale. Often a sale is not shown through a perfection of the rulers of the 1st and 7th, but those of the 2nd and 8th, showing the movement of money from one party to the other. In 1996, Venus did complete the conjunction to Mars just before leaving the sign of Cancer.

In this case, Saturn in the 7th as well as the South Node there described elements of the circumstances – the seller was 85 years old and had cancer: the expectation was that he would die soon.

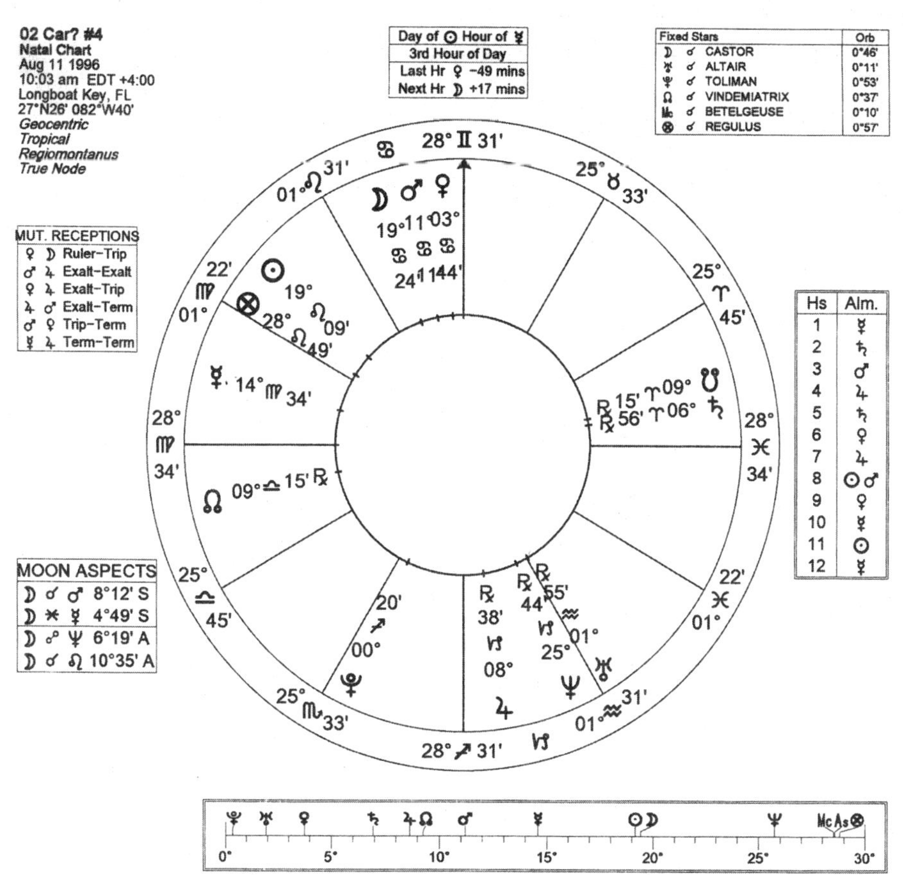

ESSENTIAL DIGNITIES (LEHMAN)								
Pt	Ruler	Exalt	Trip	Term	Face	Detri	Fall	Score
☽	☽ +	♃	♀	☿	☿	♄	♂	+5
☉	☉ +	--	☉ +	♃	♃	♄	--	+8
☿	☿ +	☿ +	♀	♃ m	♀	♃	♀	+9
♀	☽	♃	♀ +	♂	♀ +	♄	♂	+4
♂	☽	♃ m	♀	♃	☿	♄	♂ -	-9 p
♃	♄	♂ m	♀	☿ m	♃ +	☽	♃ -	-3
♄	♂	☉	☉	♀	♂	♀	♄ -	-9 p
As	☿	☿	♀	♂	☿	♃	♀	--
Mc	☿	☊	♄	♂	☉	♃	☋	--
⊗	☉	--	☉	♂	♂	♄	--	--

planets.pts				
Pt	Long.	Travel	Antiscia	C.Ant.
☽	19°♋24'42"	+11°52'	10°♊35	10°♐35
☉	19°♌09'57"	+00°57'	10°♉50	10°♏50
☿	14°♍34	+01°19'	15°♈25	15°♎25
♀	03°♋44	+00°53'	26°♊15	26°♐15
♂	11°♋11	+00°39'	18°♊48	18°♐48
♃	08°♑38 ℞	-00°04'	21°♐21	21°♊21
♄	06°♈56 ℞	-00°02'	23°♍03	23°♓03
♅	01°♒55 ℞	-00°02'	28°♏04	28°♉04
♆	25°♑44 ℞	-00°01'	04°♐15	04°♊15
♇	00°♐20	+00°00'	29°♑39	29°♋39
☊	09°♎15 ℞	-00°09'	20°♓44	20°♍44
☋	09°♈15 ℞	-00°09'	20°♍44	20°♓44
As	28°♍34'23"	+00°00'	01°♈25	01°♎25
Mc	28°♊31'43"	+00°00'	01°♋28	01°♑28
⊗	28°♌49	+00°00'	01°♉10	01°♏10

Example 3: Will I place if I compete in the national dance competition?

Our next example invokes yet another facet of the 1st House: that it always represents the condition of the Querent. A very large number of horaries are read by the relative condition of the 1st and some other house, usually the 7th. This is because many horaries are in essence the question: who is stronger, the Querent, or another party to a dispute, competition, lawsuit, quarrel, or power play. We shall see much more of this when we arrive at the 7th and the 10th Houses, but here's a simple example that emphasized the Querent's strength, apart from the strength of her competition.

The Querent has been dancing competitively for some time, but her current dance instructor has never had a pupil who has placed in a competition. Since she would be competing in the senior division, she would have less competition, and thus, a better chance. Placing means scoring in the top six.

Her ruler, the Sun, in Gemini, which seems right for a partnership, has dignity only by face. Saturn rules her competition, the 7th House (the *senior* division competition, no less!), which is peregrine. She is in better shape, although not great.

Recall that in emplacement horaries, the result is read by examining the relative strengths of the planets *where they are*, or in other words, in place. The most common emplacement question is whether to stay or to move, temporarily or permanently. Here, the question even used the word "place," a clear indication that we are looking at condition. As a variant on the contest chart, we do not get a result by seeing a perfection between the Querent and her competition!

Since we are not looking at a question of perfection in time, I considered a degree to equal a ranking. Fortuna is at 4°, and the Moon is 4° away from an opposition to peregrine Saturn. I told her that she would be able to place 4th.

Her daughter faxed three months later to say that she had placed fourth in Latin Dance.

As I have indicated, we will continue to see the use of the 1st House as we work our way through the other houses. Even here, it's obvious that sometimes the assignment of one house to represent a question is at best a simplification, more for purposes of organization than because of any abstract reality.

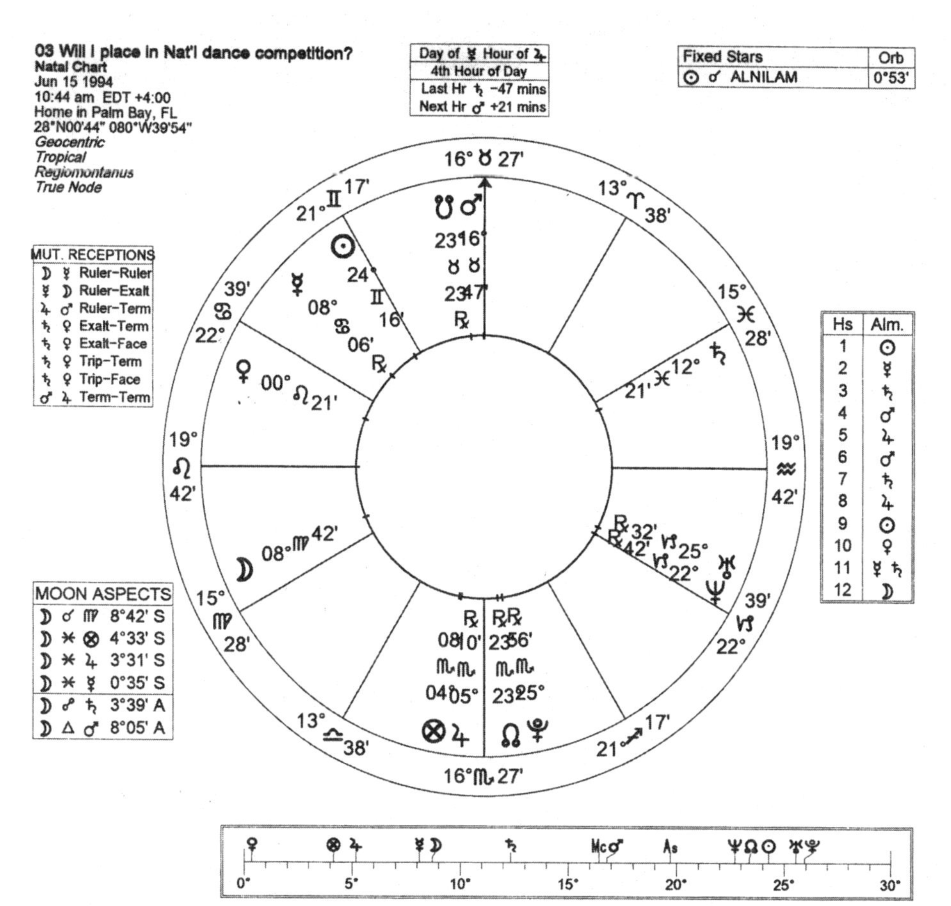

ESSENTIAL DIGNITIES (LEHMAN)								
Pt	Ruler	Exalt	Trip	Term	Face	Detri	Fall	Score
☽	☿ m	☿	♀	♀	☉	♃	♀	−5 p
☉	☿	☊	♄	♄	☉ +	♃	☋	+1
☿	☽ m	♃	♀	♃	♀	♄	♂	−5 p
♀	☉	---	☉	♄	♄	♄	---	−5 p
♂	♀	☽	♀	♃ m	☽	♂ −	---	−10 p
♃	♂	---	♀	♂ m	♂	♀	☽	−5 p
♄	♃	♀	♀	♃	♃	☿	☿	−5 p
As	☉	---	☉	♃	♃	♄	---	---
Mc	♀	☽	♀	♃	☽	♂	---	---
⊗	♂	---	♀	♂	♂	♀	☽	---

planets.pts				
Pt	Long.	Travel	Antiscia	C.Ant.
☽	08°♍42'08"	+13°35'	21°♈17	21°♎17
☉	24°♊16'14"	+00°57'	05°♋43	05°♑43
☿	08°♋06 ℞	−00°12'	21°♊53	21°♐53
♀	00°♌21	+01°10'	29°♉38	29°♏38
♂	16°♉47	+00°43'	13°♌12	13°♒12
♃	05°♏10 ℞	−00°02'	24°♒49	24°♌49
♄	12°♓21	+00°00'	17°♎38	17°♈38
♅	25°♑32 ℞	−00°01'	04°♐27	04°♊27
♆	22°♑42 ℞	−00°01'	07°♐17	07°♊17
♇	25°♏56 ℞	−00°01'	04°♒03	04°♌03
☊	23°♏23 ℞	−00°01'	06°♒36	06°♌36
☋	23°♉23 ℞	−00°01'	06°♌36	06°♒36
As	19°♌42'44"	+00°00'	10°♉17	10°♏17
Mc	16°♉27'09"	+00°00'	13°♌32	13°♒32
⊗	04°♏08	+00°00'	25°♒51	25°♌51

Chapter Two

Affairs of the 2nd House: Money

Questions of the 2nd House as given by Lilly:[58]

- *Whether the Querent shall be rich.*
- *By what means shall he attain wealth.*
- *The time when he shall obtain wealth.*
- *Whether the wealth is lasting.*
- *Whether one shall acquire that Gaine or Profit.*
- *Why the Querent shall* not *obtain Wealth.*
- *Whether the Querent shall obtain the substance which he demands, or hath lent, or the Goods he hath pawned.*
- *If the Querent be rich or in a capacity of substance without Marriage.*

More horaries utilize the 2nd House than you might expect. It's amazing how many questions have money as the background to the question asked. This does not mean that money is included in the wording of the question! The 2nd House can be examined any time that a financial subtext is stated or implied given the nature of the question. Many people hesitate to actually ask about money, even when that is the primary focus of the question. How often does a change of residence hinge on whether the family can afford to relocate? How often does the type of holiday or vacation depend on whether the people saved for it in advance? Is that trip to Tahiti simply a matter of wanting to go, or whether the Querent can afford to go? How many people decide to share the same residence partly in the hope that it will reduce their combined expenses?

The more overt examples include buying and selling. While buying and selling are generically 1st-7th House matters, the 2nd-8th shows whether the buyer can afford the transaction, and whether the seller will ever see the money. Other combinations are also possible. The two most common are: 10th-2nd, for salary ramifications of getting a job or asking for a raise, or 5th-2nd for income from the sale of a stock or bond.

How does it work? Consider Gadbury's description for whether the Querent shall be rich:[59]

1. In resolving this question, you must observe the Sign of the second and his Lord, the Planet or Planets located therein, and casting rayes either to the Cusp or the Lord thereof; the Part of Fortune also, and his position.

2. When you finde all the Significators free, and assisted by the bodies or Aspects of the Benevolent Planets, you may conclude the Querent will attain unto a very convenient degree of fortune, and shall escape Poverty.

3. When (on the contrary) you finde all the Significators afflicted, and the fortunate Stars afford them no assistance, you need not fear to say, The person interrogating will be poor, and that in a manner continually.

4. If the Lord of the Ascendant or Moon, shall be joyned to the Lord of the House of substance; or the Lord of the second, to the Lord of the Ascendant; or if the Lord of the House of substance shall be posited in the Ascendant; or if the Lord of the Ascendant or Moon, shall be in the House of substance; or if the Moon, or any other Planet, shall transfer the light of the Lord of the second, to the Lord of the Ascendant, or of the Lord of the Ascendant, to the Lord of the Second; the Querent then shall obtain Riches, and live in good esteem, according to his capacity of birth.

5. If none of these things happen, see to Jupiter the naturall Significator of substance; or Venus who is a fortune; or the North Node, which always portends good: For if they be free from the ill Beams of the infortunes, or happen to be posited in the House of substance, the Querent will most certainly be Rich, and will bear great sway in the place he lives.

6. When Saturn, Mars, or *Cauda Draconis* shall be in the second House, or afflict the Lord of the Second, Jupiter, Venus, or Fortuna, It is an Argument the Querent shall not attain Riches; or if ever he were in a good capacity, he will be reduced to beggery, or to a very mean Estate.

7. The Significators of substance swift in Motion, and in good parts of the Figure, and free from affliction, the Querent shall be rich of a sudden: but if they be slow in Motion (although they are not afflicted) the Querent will attain Riches but slowly; chiefly if the Planets signifying Riches, are ponderous and in fixed Signs."

What we have in Gadbury's considerations is a virtual catalog of all the ways that any house can be either fortified or debilitated. This is the essence of the delineation of wealth: if the Second is fortified, then wealth is possible; if the Second is debilitated, then wealth is *not* possible.[60]

The means to wealth is given by the house location of the Ruler of the 2nd, or other Significator of wealth (such as the Part of Fortune): if in the 1st, then wealth comes with little effort (one could say it comes by simply being oneself); if in the 2nd, through proper industry; if in the 3rd, through siblings, etc.

Timing is given by "the application of the Moon, or the Lord of the Ascendant, unto the Planet or Planets signifying the substance of the Querent."[61] Use the time conversions given in the Green Belt Chapter for Cardinal/Fixed/Mutable and Angular/Succedent/Cadent.

The method for determining if the Querent shall obtain the goods or monies lent is one of the most useful methods of this type of horary, because it has general application to just about any horary with a financial subtext.

Here's the idea. Remember that the 1st-7th axis represents all buying and selling. This includes borrowing and lending. Thus, we have the Querent as one party to the deal, and the 7th House as the other party. The Querent's money is ruled by the 2nd, and the other party's money by the 8th.

See if the Ruler of the Ascendant or the Moon is joined[62] to either the Ruler of the 8th, or to a planet in the 8th. If the planet representing the 8th House is not a malefic (and I would add, not peregrine), then the Querent gets the money. If the 8th House Significator is a malefic, and in reception with the Ruler of the Ascendant or the Moon, it's still okay. But without reception, and certainly if the Malefic is not in dignity, then there will be travail, hassle, and difficulty, but most likely not payment in full. It's worth remembering the operative definition of peregrine: it's the inability for things to happen by way of a direct route. When it comes to money, most people would vastly prefer a narrow straight track!

If the Ruler of either the 7th or 8th is in either the 1st or 2nd House, then it remains to be seen if that Ruler is disposed by either the Moon, Ruler of the 1st, or Ruler of the 2nd. If that is the case, then matters go forward to a good conclusion. If there is no disposition, then there is a danger of loss to the Querent if the matter is pursued.

The Fortunes[63] can also bring the matter to successful conclusion in two ways. First, if either the Lord of the Ascendant or the Moon is joined to a Fortune, which has dignity in the degree of the Ascendant, then things work out. Things will also come to a successful conclusion if the Ruler of the Ascendant or the Moon is joined to a *very* essentially dignified Malefic,[64] especially if there is reception. It is also possible that things will work out if either of the Fortunes is joined to the Ruler of the Ascendant or the Moon, and the Fortune is accidentally dignified by position, but there is no reception.

Lilly points out[65] that specific business activities may entail other house combinations than 1st-7th: the sale of birds, for example, is a 1st-6th matter. Lilly also mentions that the issue of payment is contingent on the question being propounded by parties who are truly equal before the law. In Lilly's day – and this is still occasionally true today – noblemen were often notoriously slow at repaying a debt, because they knew that they were functionally above the Law.

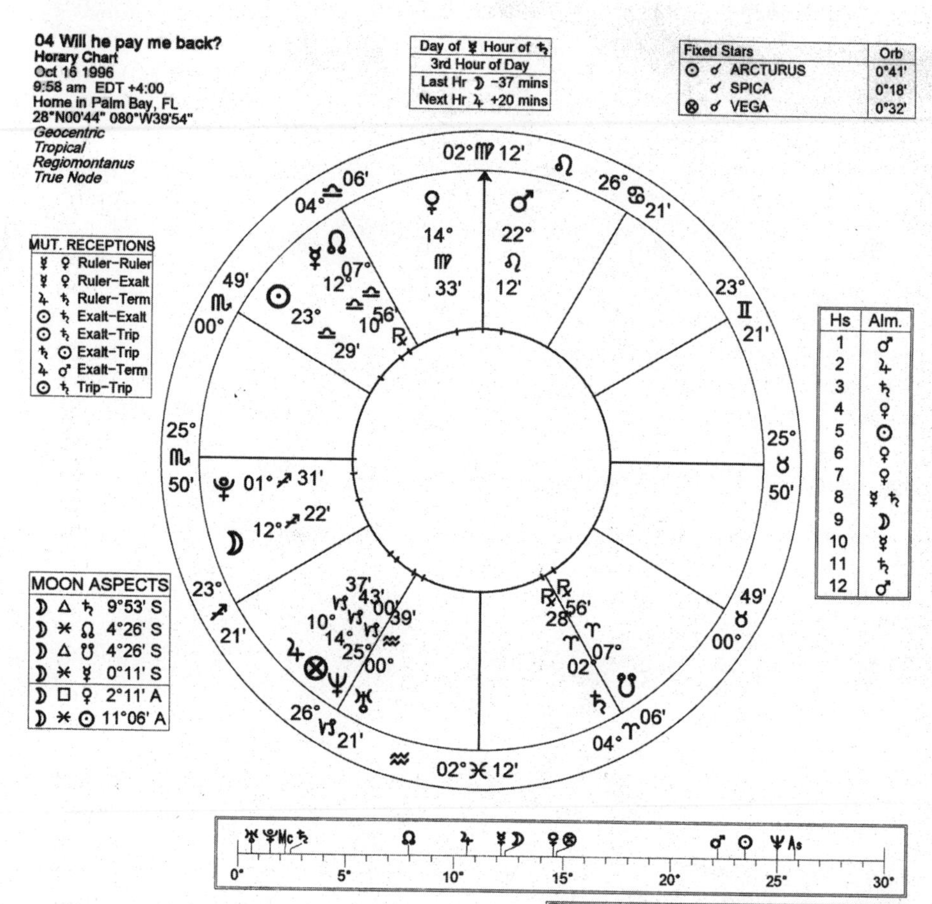

planets.pts				
Pt	Long.	Travel	Antiscia	C.Ant.
☽	12°♐22'31"	+13°41'	17°♑37	17°♋37
☉	23°♎29'00"	+00°59'	06°♓30	06°♍30
☿	12°♎10	+01°42'	17°♓49	17°♍49
♀	14°♍33	+01°11'	15°♈26	15°♎26
♂	22°♌12	+00°34'	07°♉47	07°♏47
♃	10°♑37	+00°07'	19°♐22	19°♊22
♄	02°♈28 ℞	-00°04'	27°♍31	27°♓31
♅	00°♒39	+00°00'	29°♏20	29°♉20
♆	25°♑00	+00°00'	04°♐59	04°♊59
♇	01°♐31	+00°01'	28°♑28	28°♋28
☊	07°♎56 ℞	-00°02'	22°♓03	22°♍03
☋	07°♈56 ℞	-00°02'	22°♍03	22°♓03
As	25°♏50'17"	+00°00'	04°♒09	04°♌09
Mc	02°♍12'45"	+00°00'	27°♈47	27°♎47
⊗	14°♑43	+00°00'	15°♐16	15°♊16

ESSENTIAL DIGNITIES (LEHMAN)								
Pt	Ruler	Exalt	Trip	Term	Face	Detri	Fall	Score
☽	♃	☋	☉	♀	☽ +	☿	☊	+1
☉	♀	♄ m	♄ m	☿	♃	♂	☉ −	−9 p
☿	♀ m	♄	♄	♃ m	♄	♂	☉	−5 p
♀	☿ m	☿	♀ +	♃	♀ +	♃	♀ −	+0
♂	☉	--	☉	♃	♂ +	♄	--	+1
♃	♄	♂	♀	☿ m	♂	☽	♃ −	−9 p
♄	♂	☉ m	☉ m	♃	♂	♀	♄ −	−9 p
As	♂	--	♀	☿	♀	♀	☽	--
Mc	☿	☿	♀	☿	☉	♃	♀	--
⊗	♄	♂	♀	♃	♂	☽	♃	--

Example 4. Will he pay me back?

The Querent had been in a business deal with the Quesited, and had lost over $500,000. He was the best friend of the Querent's brother, and was the Querent's friend as well, since they had all grown up together. The childhood friend was now telling the Querent that he was going to pay him back, probably completely within the year. The Querent had the possibility of suing the man, but clearly, would prefer to handle the case out of court.

After some thought, I decided to treat this question as an example of the generic type, "Is the rumor true?" The rumor, in this case, is the contention that he would be repaid.

The answer to this question lies in the Moon and the condition of the 3rd House of rumors. Uranus and Neptune are bracketing the cusp, so already we are having some doubts: and Neptune is *definitely* still close enough to be considered to be in the 3rd! Furthermore, Saturn ruling the cusp is peregrine, in Fall, and retrograde. So the 3rd House itself says the rumor is false.

The Moon is in the 1st House in Sagittarius, in dignity only by Face. Since this is Face, I judged that the issue here was fear: probably fear of what the Quesited could or would do. The Moon is coming to square Venus, ruler of the 11th House of friends. Venus herself is in Fall, although she is the daytime Triplicity ruler of the Earth Signs. The two planets in the 11th, Mercury and the Sun, are both debilitated: the Sun is in Fall and peregrine; Mercury has only out of sect triplicity. Thus, the condition of the Querent's "friend" is marginal at best. He may even *believe* that he will pay back the Querent. But there's no indication that he will be able to carry out his stated intention.

We will examine "is the rumor true" horaries in more detail in the next chapter, so let's also examine the question directly as a 2nd House matter. Here, we see the Querent's money represented by Jupiter in Capricorn: he engaged in a generous gesture, but Jupiter is in Fall! There is no relationship between the Querent (1st House) and the Quesited (the borrower, or 7th House) – and the borrower – Venus in Virgo – is not in good shape in any case. Mercury, ruling the Quesited's money (8th House) is past the square to Jupiter – the Quesited has already spent the money, and is broke, or at least not capable of honoring the debt.

I told the Querent that his friend would not repay him. I also told him that, with the Moon ruling the 9th House, that he may need to consult a lawyer. The Quesited has not repaid the money, and appears no closer to doing so than he was at the time of the question.

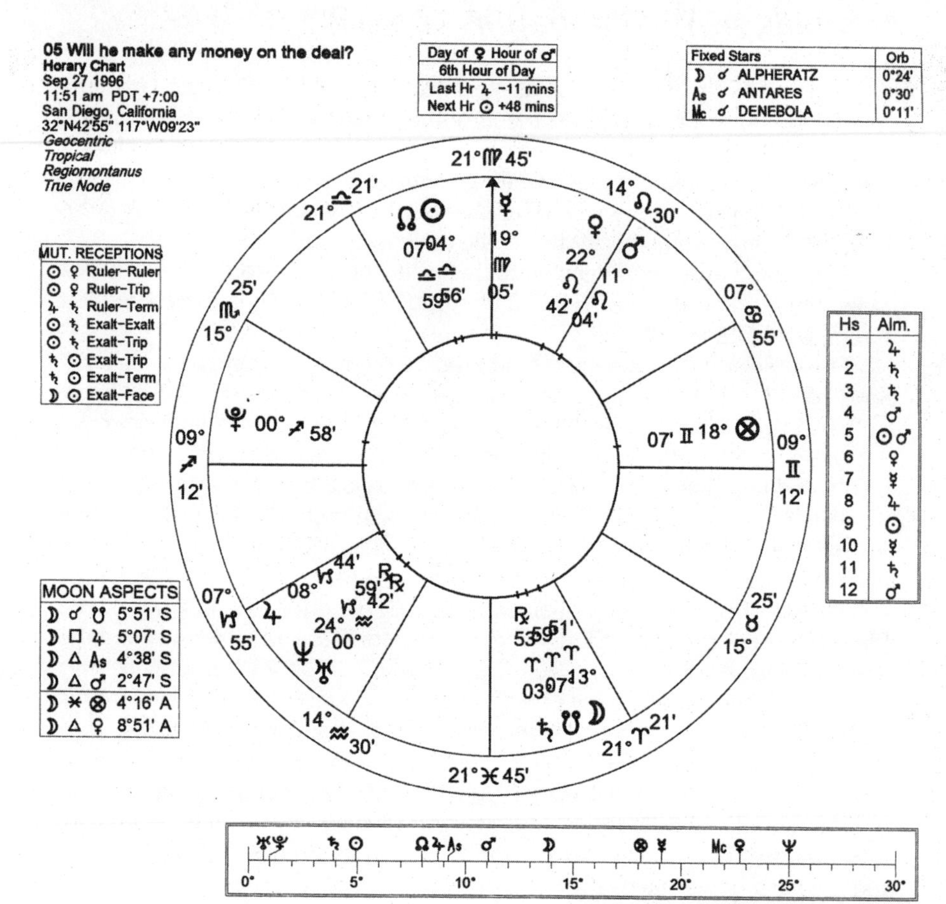

ESSENTIAL DIGNITIES (LEHMAN)								
Pt	Ruler	Exalt	Trip	Term	Face	Detri	Fall	Score
☽	♂	☉	☉	♀	☉ m	♀	♄	−5 p
☉	♀ m	♄ m	♄ m	♄	☽ m	♂	☉ −	−9 p
☿	☿ +	☿ +	♀	♄	♀	♃	♀	+9
♀	☉ m	--	☉	♃	♂	♄	--	−5 p
♂	☉	--	☉	☿	♃	♄	--	−5 p
♃	♄	♂	♀	☿	♃ +	☽	♃ −	−3
♄	♂	☉ m	☉ m	♃	♂	♀	♄ −	−9 p
As	♃	☋	☉	♀	☿	☿	☊	--
Mc	☿	☿	♀	♄	☿	♃	♀	--
⊗	☿	☊	♄	♀	♂	♃	☋	--

planets.pts				
Pt	Long.	Travel	Antiscia	C.Ant.
☽	13°♈51'20"	+14°15'	16°♍08	16°♓08
☉	04°♎56'00"	+00°58'	25°♓03	25°♍03
☿	19°♍05	+00°10'	10°♈54	10°♎54
♀	22°♌42	+01°08'	07°♉17	07°♏17
♂	11°♌04	+00°36'	18°♉55	18°♏55
♃	08°♑44	+00°04'	21°♐15	21°♊15
♄	03°♈53 ℞	−00°04'	26°♍06	26°♓06
♅	00°♒42 ℞	−00°00'	29°♏17	29°♉17
♆	24°♑59 ℞	−00°00'	05°♐00	05°♊00
♇	00°♐58	+00°01'	29°♑01	29°♋01
☊	07°♎59	+00°00'	22°♓00	22°♍00
☋	07°♈59	+00°00'	22°♍00	22°♓00
As	09°♐12'27"	+00°00'	20°♑47	20°♋47
Mc	21°♍45'26"	+00°00'	08°♈14	08°♎14
⊗	18°♊07	+00°00'	11°♋52	11°♑52

Example 5. Will he make any money on the deal?

The Querent asked this question on behalf of her friend, who had been hounding her for months to tell him about how much money he could make on a business deal. The setup was this: he was acting as intermediary to bring together two companies to do business with each other. He did not have a contract with either one to perform this service, yet he believed that he stood to make at least $100,000 for his pains.

This is a turned chart, since the Querent asked on behalf of her friend. The Querent's friend is given by Venus, ruler of the 11th House. Venus is peregrine, in a mutual reception with the Sun in Fall, not exactly much help! Given the placement in Leo, I described the man as "full of himself," completely puffed up in believing about his worth, and the worth of his services. The other party is given by the 5th House, the 7th from the 11th. Here we see Mars as the other player: the other party is likewise puffed up about *his* own worth. The Moon *does* translate the light between them, and the Moon *does* receive both parties. This indicates that he could get something. But how much? Mars rules his 2nd House, and Pluto is there. Furthermore, Jupiter is in Fall, Neptune and Uranus are in the radical 2nd House. A peregrine ruler of the 2nd certainly doesn't sound like he is going to get paid very much. Furthermore, his ruler is past applying to the Part of Fortune. His time is past for making very much.

As a matter of fact, he was offered $10,000, but he turned it down because he thought the figure was too small. He filed a lawsuit for $1,000,000; although he was prepared to settle for a mere $500,000! The lawsuit came to nothing.

Example 6. Will I get a Mac computer within six months?

The Querent had set up a freelance word processing business with a partner. She had been learning desktop publishing on a friend's Mac, and wanted to acquire the equipment to do it herself. The question was whether the business could afford the additional equipment, as they already had IBM compatibles.

There is only one consideration against judgment: the Ascendant is in the *Via combusta*. The Ascendant is ruled by Mars, which has dignity only by Face. Mars is in the 8th House of the partner's money, and the question was tied up in what the business could afford.

Jupiter rules the 2nd House of moveable objects. It is in mutual reception by Term with Mercury. This is not a very strong reception, but Mercury does rule the partner's 2nd House (the Querent's 8th) and Mercury is the strongest planet in the chart.

There are several ways we can judge this chart. First, we can use the conventional method of perfection: does Mars (Querent) go to Jupiter (the computer)? The answer is no: Mars has passed the sextile to Jupiter.

What we do have is a forming Translation of Light. In this case, the Sun, at 4 degrees Libra, has not yet reached the sextile to Jupiter, at 7 Leo. After it

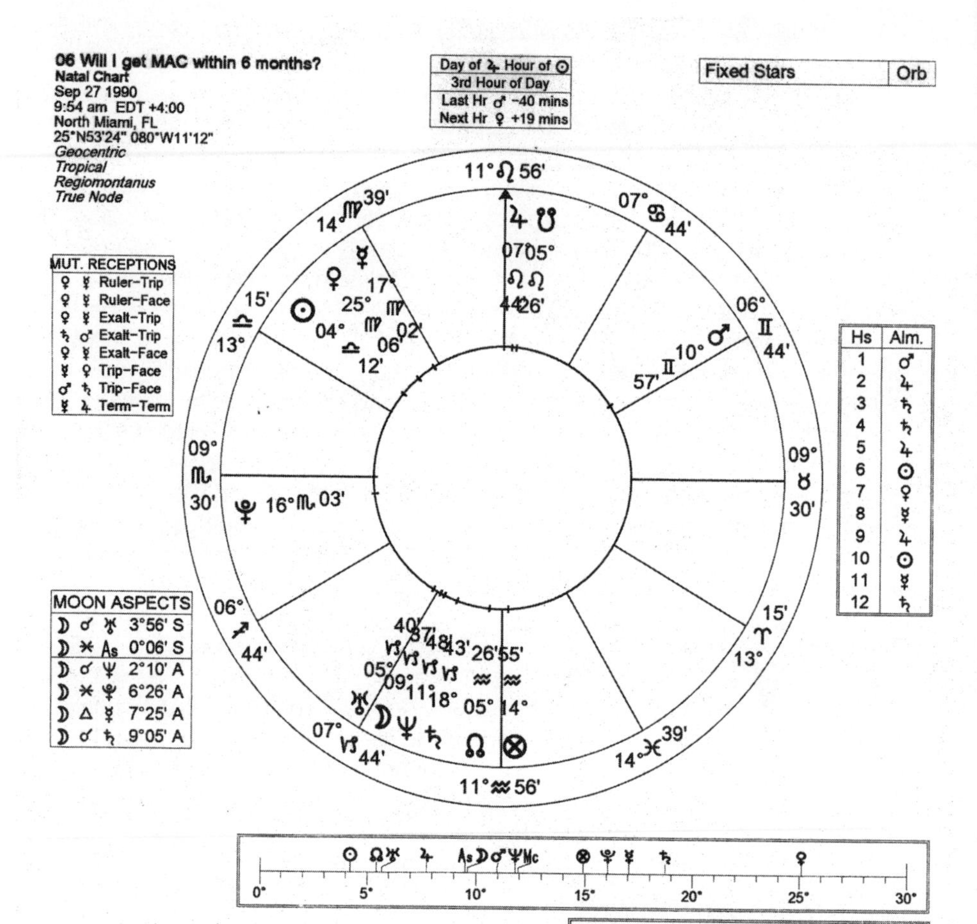

planets.pts				
Pt	Long.	Travel	Antiscia	C.Ant.
☽	09°♑37'13"	+12°01'	20°♐22	20°♊22
☉	04°♎12'17"	+00°58'	25°♓47	25°♍47
☿	17°♍02	+01°20'	12°♈57	12°♎57
♀	25°♍06	+01°14'	04°♈53	04°♎53
♂	10°♊57	+00°17'	19°♋02	19°♑02
♃	07°♌44	+00°09'	22°♉15	22°♏15
♄	18°♑43	+00°00'	11°♐16	11°♊16
♅	05°♑40	+00°00'	24°♐19	24°♊19
♆	11°♑48	+00°00'	18°♐11	18°♊11
♇	16°♏03	+00°01'	13°♒56	13°♌56
☊	05°♒26	+00°00'	24°♏33	24°♉33
☋	05°♌26	+00°00'	24°♉33	24°♏33
As	09°♏30'41"	+00°00'	20°♒29	20°♌29
Mc	11°♌56'41"	+00°00'	18°♉03	18°♏03
⊗	14°♒55	+00°00'	15°♏04	15°♉04

ESSENTIAL DIGNITIES (LEHMAN)								
Pt	Ruler	Exalt	Trip	Term	Face	Detri	Fall	Score
☽	♄	♂	♀	☿	♃	☽ −	♃	−10 p
☉	♀	♄	♄	♄	☽	♂	☉ −	−9 p
☿	☿ +	☿ +	♀	♃ m	♀ m	♃	♀	+9
♀	☿	☿	♀ +	♂	☿ m	♃	♀ −	−1
♂	☿	☊	♄	♃	♂ +	♃	☋	+1
♃	☉	—	☉	☿ m	♄	♄	—	−5 p
♄	♄ +	♂	♀	♃	♂	☽	♃	+5
As	♂	—	♀	♃	♂	♀	☽	—
Mc	☉	—	☉	☿	♃	♄	—	—
⊗	♄	—	♄	♀	☿	☉	—	—

sextiles Jupiter, the Sun will then trine Mars. ***But*** the Sun is peregrine, in the 11th of friends. Given the translation, someone else gets involved, in this case someone of an 11th House nature: perhaps a small business grant from the government, or a friend, trading up to a new Mac? Because of the weakness of the Sun, I judged that the forming translation would not be strong enough to produce the result within the time frame asked.

I interpreted the meaning this way because, while the translation can give a positive result, the weakness of the translating planet implies a weak outcome. A weak outcome could either be an undesirable Mac (too old, broken, etc.), or a delay in obtaining it, or even a substitute for a Mac.

Second, let us see if the Moon sheds any light on the Question. The Moon is in a double-quincunx pattern with Mars and Jupiter: in other words, the Moon is translating the light by quincunx. This is not exactly classically kosher, although the Moon does receive both Mars (by Exaltation) and Jupiter (by Face). This is a weak result at best, again suggesting that the desired result is not likely within the time frame given. (Non-ptolemaic aspects, if they work at all, produce weak effects.) Further, the translating body, the Moon, is weak by being in detriment and applying to Nepture, so a delay or a problem is indicated, which virtually precludes a positive result.

Third, are Mars and Jupiter in mutual reception? The answer is no, so there's no help here.

Fourth, since the decision involved the partner's funds as well as her own, would her partner spring for the Mac? Does the 8th House ruler Mercury perfect with either Mars (i.e., money goes to Querent), or Jupiter (money goes to computer)? The answer is no.

The best scenario, taking all possible interpretations into account, was that she would not get a Mac within six months. She didn't. Of course, in the interim, Windows captured considerable market share as a platform for layout and production, so she simply acquired the software for Windows, and the firm upgraded her 286's to 486's.

Example 7. Will I be successful with a 900 Line?

The Querent wanted to know if she would be successful financially if she ran a psychics 900 line: a dial-up psychic service that would automatically bill clients through their regular phone bill.

Notice that, while the Ascendant is 26 degrees and not quite "too late," it's certainly edging in that direction. I mention this because this general sensation may be significant: here this woman is proposing a new business venture, but that chart is saying, it's almost too late! This is exactly the opposite of the kind of circumstances one would expect to see for a *new* business venture, so while not an answer by itself, this observation does suggest that there may be something wrong with the idea.

Mercury rules the Ascendant. Mercury is peregrine, which means that she really has no power to create a result anyway. This again is in direct contradiction to the question as asked: she is proposing to *manage* a 900 line. Were this to be successful, she would have to set up the business, get the advertisements, develop the client base, etc. – in other words, she would be in a powerful position, not a powerless one. Mercury, her Ruler, is in a mute sign – and she is proposing a *phone* service – which clearly involves talking. Again, the circumstances of the chart testify against a good outcome.

Fortuna is in the 11th of hopes and wishes, and she certainly hoped for financial success.

Her finances are given by the 2nd House, which can be ruled by Saturn (Almuten), Venus (sign), or Jupiter (placement). None of these planets have

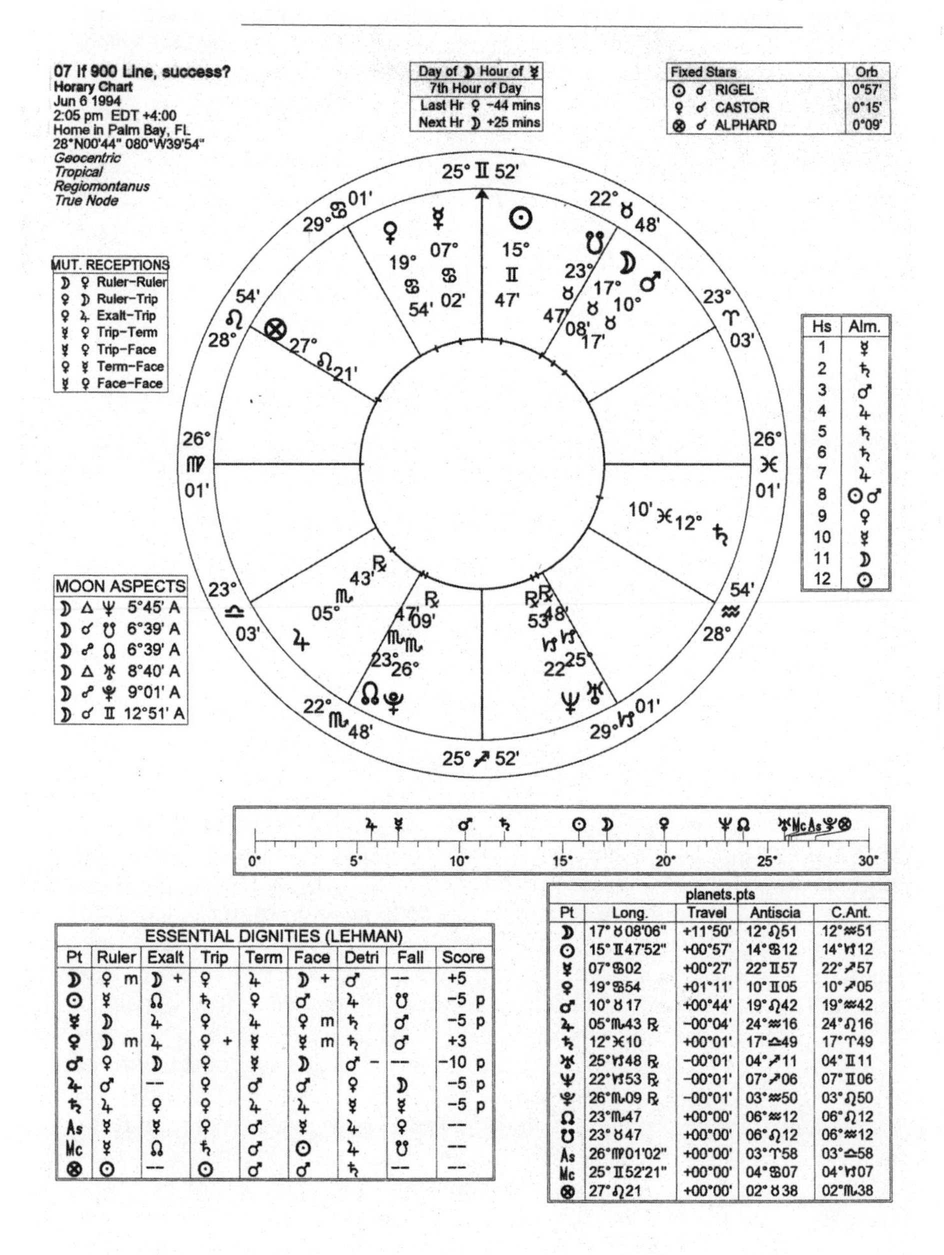

MUT. RECEPTIONS	
☽ ♀	Ruler-Ruler
♀ ☽	Ruler-Trip
♀ ♃	Exalt-Trip
☿ ♀	Trip-Term
☿ ♀	Trip-Face
♀ ☿	Term-Face
☿ ♀	Face-Face

MOON ASPECTS	
☽ △ ♆	5°45' A
☽ ☌ ☋	6°39' A
☽ ☍ ☊	6°39' A
☽ △ ♅	8°40' A
☽ ☍ ♇	9°01' A
☽ ☌ ♊	12°51' A

Hs	Alm.
1	☿
2	♄
3	♂
4	♃
5	♄
6	♄
7	♃
8	☉♂
9	♀
10	☿
11	☽
12	☉

ESSENTIAL DIGNITIES (LEHMAN)								
Pt	Ruler	Exalt	Trip	Term	Face	Detri	Fall	Score
☽	♀ m	☽ +	♀	♃	☽ +	♂	---	+5
☉	☿	☊	♄	♀	♂	♃	☋	-5 p
☿	☽	♃	♀	♃	♀ m	♄	♂	-5 p
♀	☽ m	♃	♀ +	☿	☿ m	♄	♂	+3
♂	♀	☽	♀	☿	☽	♂ -	---	-10 p
♃	♂	---	♀	♂	♂	♀	☽	-5 p
♄	♃	♀	♀	♃	♃	☿	☿	-5 p
As	☿	☿	♀	♂	☿	♃	♀	---
Mc	☿	☊	♄	♂	☉	♃	☋	---
⊗	☉	---	☉	♂	♂	♄	---	---

planets.pts				
Pt	Long.	Travel	Antiscia	C.Ant.
☽	17° ♉ 08'06"	+11°50'	12° ♌ 51	12° ♒ 51
☉	15° ♊ 47'52"	+00°57'	14° ♋ 12	14° ♑ 12
☿	07° ♋ 02	+00°27'	22° ♊ 57	22° ♐ 57
♀	19° ♋ 54	+01°11'	10° ♊ 05	10° ♐ 05
♂	10° ♉ 17	+00°44'	19° ♌ 42	19° ♒ 42
♃	05° ♏ 43 ℞	-00°04'	24° ♒ 16	24° ♌ 16
♄	12° ♓ 10	+00°01'	17° ♎ 49	17° ♈ 49
♅	25° ♑ 48 ℞	-00°01'	04° ♐ 11	04° ♊ 11
♆	22° ♑ 53 ℞	-00°01'	07° ♐ 06	07° ♊ 06
♇	26° ♏ 09 ℞	-00°01'	03° ♒ 50	03° ♌ 50
☊	23° ♏ 47	+00°00'	06° ♒ 12	06° ♌ 12
☋	23° ♉ 47	+00°00'	06° ♌ 12	06° ♒ 12
As	26° ♍ 01'02"	+00°00'	03° ♈ 58	03° ♎ 58
Mc	25° ♊ 52'21"	+00°00'	04° ♋ 07	04° ♑ 07
⊗	27° ♌ 21	+00°00'	02° ♉ 38	02° ♏ 38

any intrinsic essential dignity, except Venus by Triplicity. She might get some occasional financial lucky breaks, but this doesn't look like continuous cash flow. Mercury and Venus are doubly in reception; but each involves minor dignities, so the effect would not be strong.

The Moon is the strongest planet in the chart. She will come to sextile Venus in 2 degrees. Unfortunately, the Moon doesn't rule any of the significant houses of this chart: only her hopes and wishes. The mutual reception with Venus could possibly be helpful, since both planets are dignified to start with. But this again argues for occasional financial good news, because the principal meaning of the Moon related to the 2nd House is cash flow – money ebbing and flowing. Furthermore, her final aspect is a square to Fortuna.

I told the Querent that while I didn't see a loss, I didn't see any great windfall, and that making the money might be more trouble than it would be worth.

Example 8. Will I make money pursuing the street sign idea?

This question was asked by a Querent who is used to asking her own horary questions, and then calling me up later for delineation: the kind of person I refer to as an experienced client. In working with her, I have found that I do not have to do anything in the way of reworking either the question, or the data for the question. Accordingly, they are always set for her time and her coordinates.

This client is a small business entrepreneur who is always on the lookout for new business opportunities. She works in part from her house. One day, she was noticing how the street cleaning people would put up signs to cordon off streets while they cleaned them. She observed that the signs were cheap disposable paper that often fell off before the workmen were done. She thought that she might be able to come up with a better, reusable design, and asked whether such an idea could make money. She actually asked two questions in fairly rapid sequence, the second one concerning a variant in the design of the first idea.

Jupiter, Ruler of the Ascendant, gives the Querent. It is also worth noting that Pluto is conjunct the Ascendant, which I certainly considered. It has been noted by many modern astrologers that Pluto can denote large amounts of money – although whether by loss or gain is often unclear. That is not the only meaning of Pluto, of course, but it's relevant enough that I assumed that, once I finished the conventional classical delineation of the chart, I would probably have to take Pluto into account.

Jupiter is in Pisces but retrograde: this tells me that she is in a reasonably strong position, but that, being retrograde, there is likely to be a change of mind. Also note that Jupiter (like Mercury) is not a fighter by nature, so this tells me that she would only prevail by making an overwhelming intellectual case for her idea, not by having to fight it out. She simply wouldn't have the stomach for a prolonged conflict.

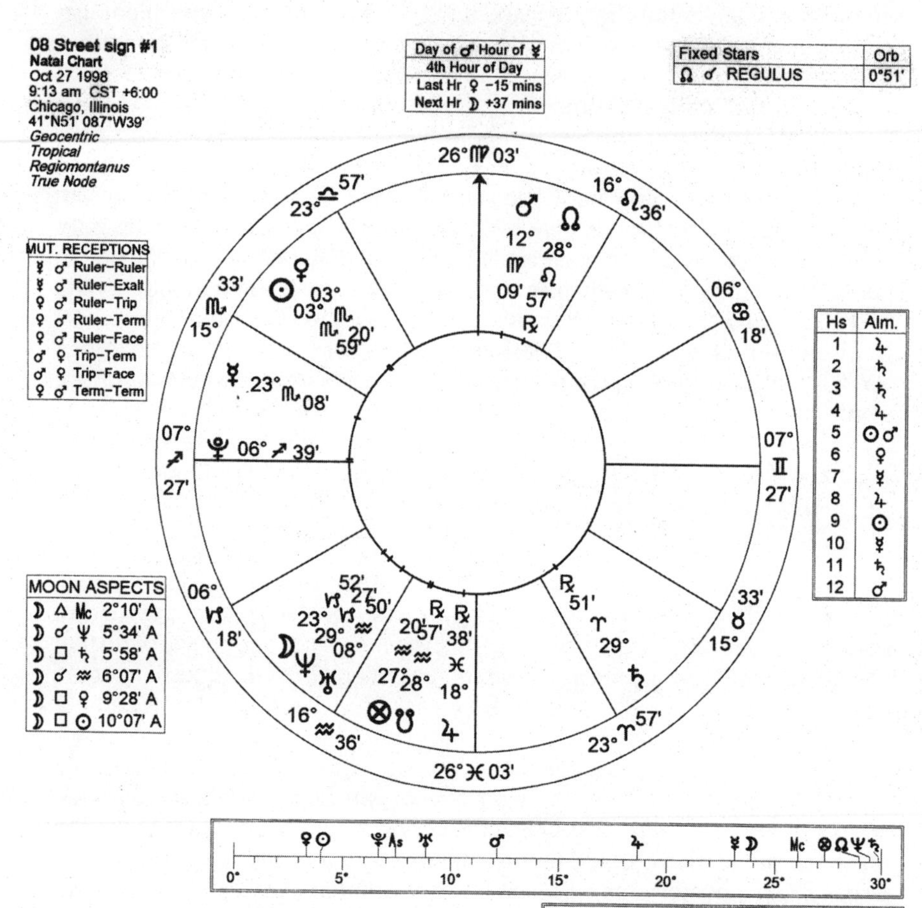

ESSENTIAL DIGNITIES (LEHMAN)								
Pt	Ruler	Exalt	Trip	Term	Face	Detri	Fall	Score
☽	♄	♂	♀	♂	☉	☽ −	♃	−10 p
☉	♂	--	♀	♂	♂	♀	☽	−5 p
☿	♂ m	--	♀	☿ +	♀	♀	☽	+2
♀	♂	--	♀ +	♂ m	♂ m	♀ −	☽	−2
♂	☿ m	☿	♀	♀ m	♀ m	♃	♀	−5 p
♃	♃ +	♀	♀	☿	♃ +	☿	☿	+6
♄	♂	☉	☉	♄ +	♀	♀	♄ −	−2
As	♃	☋	☉	♃	☿	☿	☊	--
Mc	☿	☿	♀	♂	☿	♃	♀	--
⊗	♄	--	♄	♂	☽	☉	--	--

planets.pts				
Pt	Long.	Travel	Antiscia	C.Ant.
☽	23°♑52'38"	+12°40'	06°♐07	06°♊07
☉	03°♏59'52"	+00°59'	26°♒00	26°♌00
☿	23°♏08	+01°24'	06°♒51	06°♌51
♀	03°♏20	+01°15'	26°♒39	26°♌39
♂	12°♍09	+00°35'	17°♈50	17°♎50
♃	18°♓38 ℞	−00°03'	11°♎21	11°♈21
♄	29°♈51 ℞	−00°04'	00°♍08	00°♓08
♅	08°♒50	+00°00'	21°♏09	21°♉09
♆	29°♑27	+00°00'	00°♐32	00°♊32
♇	06°♐39	+00°02'	23°♑20	23°♋20
☊	28°♌57 ℞	−00°01'	01°♉02	01°♏02
☋	28°♒57 ℞	−00°01'	01°♏02	01°♉02
As	07°♐27'30"	+00°00'	22°♑32	22°♋32
Mc	26°♍03'13"	+00°00'	03°♈56	03°♎56
⊗	27°♒20	+00°00'	02°♏39	02°♉39

While she looks to be in good shape, her money does not. Saturn rules the 2nd House, and Saturn is both in Fall and retrograde, from the 5th House. This tells me that any profit would be strictly as a result of a speculation (5th House), and that the profit would be little or negative (Saturn in Fall) and delayed as well (retrograde). This does not look good!

We can further observe that the Moon is in Detriment and approaching Neptune: deceit or deception is likely. The Moon is in a partile sextile to Mercury, which rules her open enemies – her competitors in the street sign business. Moon going from Mercury to Neptune? I'd say there's a good chance that the current sign manufacturers probably have a somewhat dubious contract that probably wouldn't withstand too much public scrutiny! Thus we get an idea about what the Pluto conjunct the Ascendant might mean: since it doesn't look like she makes money from this anyway, maybe it's better for her health and longevity if she just doesn't pursue this idea any further!

Notice that there is a translation here between the Rulers of the 1st and 2nd: but I would judge this as essentially irrelevant. The Moon isn't very strong in Capricorn, and while it separates from a sextile from Jupiter, it applies to a square to Saturn, with the conjunction to Neptune at the same degree.

If the Reader is somewhat distraught that all the examples here have negative outcomes, it's worth considering two things. First, it's unfortunate, but most ideas in business don't turn out to be successful. Unfortunately, I haven't had the clients who invented Velcro™ or masking tape. Secondly, it's also worth remembering that a valid horary has to have some emotional passion attached to it. Often that passion is actually fear or misgiving. This means that commonly we are being called upon to verify a truth that the Querent cannot bring himself or herself to face. I am continually surprised at how frequently, when I deliver a negative outcome to the Querent, the response is that they really knew already, but they needed confirmation in order to proceed.

Perhaps one of the most important generic ideas that we can derive from this discussion of the 2nd House is that we can delineate 2nd House (and other house) matters by considering the condition of the 1st and the 2nd House rulers, and whether they seem to be gaining or losing. This then gives us the information about whether financial resources are flooding – or ebbing.

Chapter Three

Affairs of the 3rd House: Is the Rumor true? Short Trips. Neighbors. Siblings.

Questions of the 3rd House as given by Gadbury:[66]

- *Shall the Querent his Brethren, &c. and Neighbours accord?*
- *Of the condition and estate of an absent Brother.*
- *Shall the Querent's Inland Journeys be prosperous?*
- *If the Reports or Rumors noys'd about, be true or false?*
- *Of the advice of a friend, &c., whether good or evil.*

Additional Questions of the 3rd House as given by Lilly:[67]

- *Whether the Querent have Brethren or Sisters.*

We will take up journeys in the 9th House, in great part because it is unusual to get a question concerning a 3rd House journey anyway. Third House trips by their very nature describe travel to familiar places, generally involving shorter time intervals: and the issue of familiarity tends to reduce the probability of concern, anxiety or fear about the trip. The method for delineating the two types of journeys is exactly the same anyway, once the primary journey house is established.

In the cultural shifts that have occurred since Lilly's time, some of the common questions of the 3rd House have almost disappeared, for no good reason other than demographics. Time was, if you were a male, chances were that you were in business with your brother, whether because the whole family was engaged in a trade, or because the whole family's trade was being part of the aristocracy. These days, we do well to grow up with our brothers and sisters, and then many of us go off to college, and from then on, we see our siblings at holidays (maybe!) and family occasions like weddings and funerals. The extended family has become an endangered breed (at least in North America), and as long as this is true, there won't be so many horaries generated concerning siblings as there were in the past. Furthermore, there are fewer questions about absent parties in the wake of the telephone and other means of instant communication.

As for neighbors, many of us are doing well to even know our neighbors' names! I have personally taken no horaries about neighbors for this reason: neither I nor my clients seem to have close enough relations with our neighbors to have enough emotional juice to ask a cogent and effective question. Occasionally, the topic of neighbors (or the neighborhood) has cropped up as a side issue in real estate horaries. In these cases, an afflicted 3rd House may reveal that a problem with the neighborhood may either reduce the property value, or reduce the enjoyment of the particular dwelling or property. But this is generally just a minor theme to the delineation; almost an afterthought. The only neighbor issue which seems to generate a lot of emotional angst is disagreements among condominium co-tenants: and there the politics seems inevitably to intrude!

Even though the mobile society of the United States in the early 21st Century has resulted in greater distance from both our relatives and our neighbors than in prior decades, that does not mean that we have less need for human emotional support. Many have transferred their emotional ties from family and environs to friends, creating what are sometimes designated "friend families." While these newer networks may not be as stable as the older systems, they can serve a valuable function. Having said this, we do have a perfectly good house to represent friends: the eleventh. I do not believe that we should redefine traditional rulerships because the contemporary fashion may be to equate friends as family – or pets as children. They are not. And future societies shall surely see things differently, anyway.

As for Lilly's example of *whether* the Querent has sisters or brothers, well – I'd rather just ask! The only value I see to this is when the Querent is attempting to trace a somewhat delicate family history, in which case, she or he may not know whether a particular party is in fact related – but this falls nicely into the one very common question of the 3rd House: Is the rumor true?

However, things have a way of showing up just when you don't expect them, so here's an example that we can use.

Example 9. Are we half sisters?

I've had several clients and students who have found out in middle age about brothers and sisters they never guessed existed. The difference between now and Lilly's time is that genetic testing can clinch the answer. This was one such case: the woman had found out about a putative half sister, and they had gone for genetic screening: but the results take about six weeks, and she was dying to know immediately!

This counts as almost a no-brainer. Lilly looks for fruitful signs on the 3rd House cusp as an indication of a positive outcome for (more) siblings.[68] Here we have Cancer, about as fruitful as you can get, and the North Node at the 3rd House cusp as well. The Moon, ruling the 3rd, and Venus, ruling the Ascendant, are in a partile square. The partile aspect also confirms the answer, but what is the tension represented by the square? I asked. It turns out that the

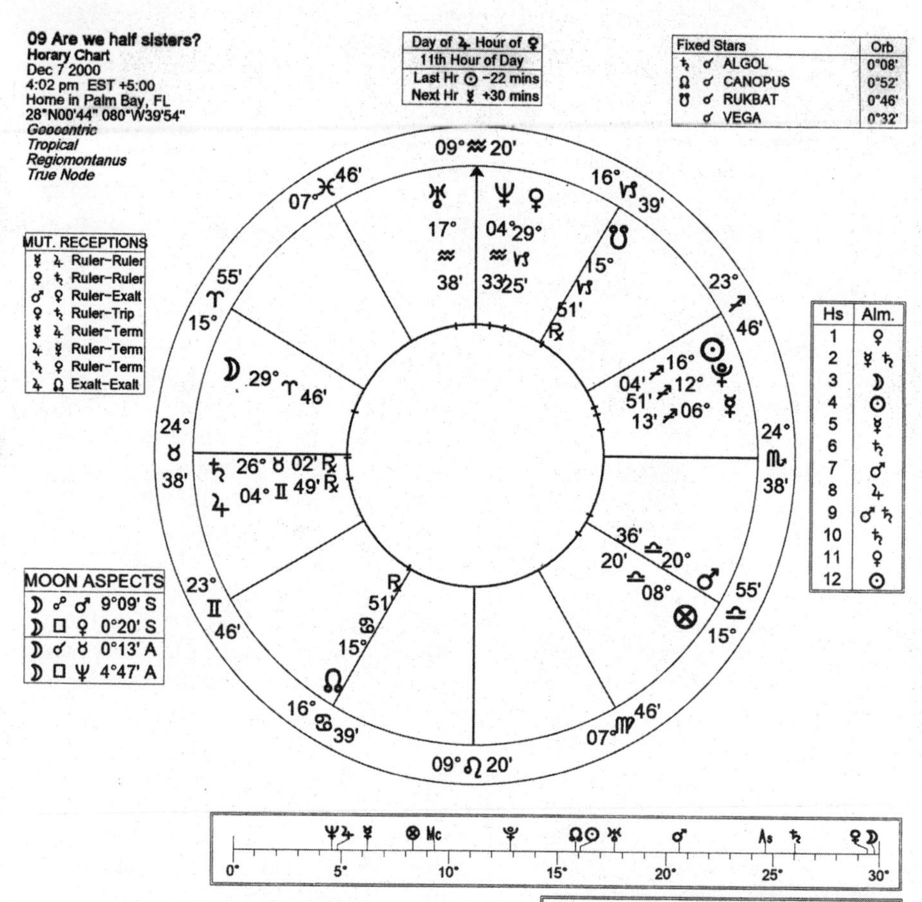

ESSENTIAL DIGNITIES (LEHMAN)								
Pt	Ruler	Exalt	Trip	Term	Face	Detri	Fall	Score
☽	♂	☉	☉	♄	♀	♀	♄	−5 p
☉	♃	☋	☉ +	☿	☽	☿	☊	+3
☿	♃ m	☋	☉	♃ m	☿ +	☿ −	☊	−4
♀	♄ m	♂	♀ +	♄	☉	☽	♃	+3
♂	♀	♄	♄	☿	♃	♂ −	☉	−10 p
♃	☿ m	☊ m	♄	☿ m	♃ +	♃ −	☋	−4
♄	♀ m	☽	♀	♂	♄ +	♂	---	+1
As	♀	☽	♀	♄	♄	♂	---	---
Mc	♄	---	♄	☿	♀	☉	---	---
⊗	♀	♄	♄	♀	☽	♂	☉	---

planets.pts				
Pt	Long.	Travel	Antiscia	C.Ant.
☽	29°♈46'09"	+13°32'	00°♍13	00°♓13
☉	16°♐04'30"	+01°00'	13°♑55	13°♋55
☿	06°♐13	+01°33'	23°♑46	23°♋46
♀	29°♑25	+01°10'	00°♐34	00°♊34
♂	20°♎36	+00°36'	09°♓23	09°♍23
♃	04°♊49 ℞	−00°07'	25°♋10	25°♑10
♄	26°♉02 ℞	−00°04'	03°♌57	03°♒57
♅	17°♒38	+00°02'	12°♏21	12°♉21
♆	04°♒33	+00°01'	25°♏26	25°♉26
♇	12°♐51	+00°02'	17°♑08	17°♋08
☊	15°♋51 ℞	−00°04'	14°♊08	14°♐08
☋	15°♑51 ℞	−00°04'	14°♐08	14°♊08
As	24°♉38'38"	+00°00'	05°♌21	05°♒21
Mc	09°♒20'06"	+00°00'	20°♏39	20°♉39
⊗	08°♎20	+00°00'	21°♓39	21°♍39

Querent's *full* sister is having a big problem adjusting to the idea, while the Querent is thrilled.

The genetic match was better than 99%. The answer is confirmed.

Is the Rumor True?

So we will concern ourselves here almost solely with the rumor type of horary. This type of construction is actually much more useful than most astrologers realize. Of all the horaries that I get from clients, this is one type that seldom is worded correctly at the first attempt. The crux of the delineation is what constitutes a rumor. We need to be clear on this before we activate this method of delineation.

In the last chapter in Example 4, we delineated whether the borrower's promise to pay back the money was true. Any promise or statement can be taken in this manner, the only warning being a reminder that this method should *not* be applied to statements heard through the various news media, unless you are absolutely sure that the broadcast is live, and that the statement was uttered for the first time.

You may recall from the Green Belt Chapter that Lilly had considerable vested interest in victory by the Parliament during the English Civil War. Thus, we can understand that in Lilly's examples, the 1st House was applied to his side, and the 7th House to the Crown, and that the delineation method often involved the stark issues of War as much as a discussion of Truth.

Here is a list of possible arguments of Truth or Falsehood, with the notations (L) for Lilly, and (G) for Gadbury, depending upon who advocated the method.

1. The rumor is true if the Lord of the Ascendant, the Moon, or the Moon's dispositor (or better, the majority of them) are fixed, not Cadent, and in good aspect to the benefics or the Sun. (L, G)

2. If those three are Cadent and afflicted by the malefics, the rumor is false whether they are in good zodiacal condition or not. (G)

3. The rumor is true if all four angles are fixed, the Moon and Mercury are fixed, and they in turn are separating from the malefics and applying to an angular benefic. (L, G)

4. If the MC/IC axis is fixed, and the Moon rules either angle, then the rumor is true. (L, G)

5. If the benefics are in the 1st, but the Moon unfortunate, the rumor is false or misleading. (G)

6. Mercury retrograde or debilitated shows a false rumor, as does the affliction of the planet to whom the Moon or Mercury next applies. (G)

7. The Ruler of the Ascendant or the Moon Under Beams brings secrecy to the matter. (L, G)

8. The Moon either Void of Course or in hard aspect to Mercury shows the rumor to be either false, or of no import. (L, G)

9. The Moon in the 1st, 3rd, 10th or 11th, separating from an easy aspect to any planet, and applying by an easy aspect to the Lord of the Ascendant argues that the rumor is true. (L)

10. The Moon square or opposite Mercury, neither in easy aspect to the Ascendant argues that the rumor is false. (L)

11. If the Lord of the 6th, 8th, or 12th House is in the 1st House, or afflicting the Ruler of the Ascendant; or Mars or Saturn retrograde and in the 1st House, or in hard aspect to either the ascending degree or the Ruler of the Ascendant; then the Querent will receive damage or prejudice from the news heard. (L)

Let's see how these ideas can be applied through our first example.

Example 10. Is the rumor true?

It's amazing how rumors start, and how easily they spread. In this case, I was at an astrological conference, when a rumor began circulating that one of the speakers was getting a special deal. As a former conference organizer, I knew how easily something like this could turn ugly, so I asked the question: is the rumor true, knowing that I could use the horary itself as an argument to confirm or squelch the rumor. Below, I have repeated the list of arguments and how they apply to this example:

1. The rumor is true if the Lord of the Ascendant, the Moon, or the Moon's dispositor (or better, the majority of them) are fixed, not Cadent, and in good aspect to the benefics or the Sun. (L, G) **The Ruler of the Ascendant is in Fall, mutable and Succedent, also retrograde. The Moon is fixed but peregrine, and applying to a conjunction to the Sun, which is considered a baleful aspect. The Sun is in Leo, fixed and dignified, but then we are just on the verge of a solar eclipse.**

2. If those three are Cadent and afflicted by the malefics, the rumor is false whether they are in good zodiacal condition or not. (G) **They are not cadent, but the Sun and Moon are definitely afflicted by malefics.**

3. The rumor is true if all four angles are fixed, the Moon and Mercury are fixed, and they in turn are separating from the malefics and applying to an angular benefic. (L, G) **Half the angles are fixed, the Moon is fixed, but Mercury is cardinal. The Moon is apply-**

ing to malefics. Mercury is slow and void of course.

4. If the MC/IC axis is fixed, and the Moon rules either angle, then the rumor is true. (L, G) **The Moon rules the 4th, but the axis isn't fixed.**

5. If the benefics are in the 1st, but the Moon unfortunate, the rumor is false or misleading. (G) **Does not apply.**

6. Mercury retrograde or debilitated shows a false rumor, as does the affliction of the planet to whom the Moon or Mercury next applies. (G) **The Moon next applies to Uranus, then to the two traditional malefics. Mercury next applies to Neptune, Jupiter and Pluto; all out of sign. What do we do with this? Uranus can be interpreted as accidentally afflicted: it is retrograde and conjunct the South Node. The Mercury applications are more problematic; because Mercury has to leave sign in order to complete them. The application to Neptune is next, but is Neptune afflicted? Yes, by retrogradation; no by angularity. Fortunately, we don't have to decide, since the application of the Moon to afflicted Uranus gives the false rumor argument.:**

7. The Ruler of the Ascendant or the Moon Under Beams brings secrecy to the matter. (L, G) **The Moon is combust (even worse than Under Beams), and the Moon is also the Almuten of the Ascendant, so used in place of Venus. Notice that this doesn't actually give an answer, but describes some circumstances surrounding the question.**

8. The Moon either Void of Course or in hard aspect to Mercury shows the rumor to be either false, or of no import. (L, G) **Does not apply.**

9. The Moon in the 1st, 3rd, 10th or 11th, separating from an easy aspect to any planet, and applying by an easy aspect to the Lord of the Ascendant argues that the rumor is true. (L) **Does not apply.**

10. The Moon square or opposite Mercury, neither in easy aspect to the Ascendant argues that the rumor is false. (L) **Does not apply.**

11. If the Lord of the 6th, 8th, or 12th House is in the 1st House, or afflicting the Ruler of the Ascendant; or Mars or Saturn retrograde and in the 1st House, or in hard aspect to either the ascending degree or the Ruler of the Ascendant; then the Querent will receive damage or prejudice from the news heard. (L) **Mercury and Jupiter are not afflicting Venus; Venus is separating by trine from Jupiter.**

Apart from running the numbers, so to speak, of the aphorisms above, this Mercury is just in terrible condition. Beyond being peregrine, it's in the 29th degree – in the Terms of Saturn. This almost compels an image of the rumor (Mercury) on its last legs.

Overall, the majority of the considerations show that the rumor is false. Even when the conditions apply, there are problems – such as the upcoming solar eclipse. I was able to confirm that the rumor was false by asking the subject of it directly – and receiving a very candid negative response.

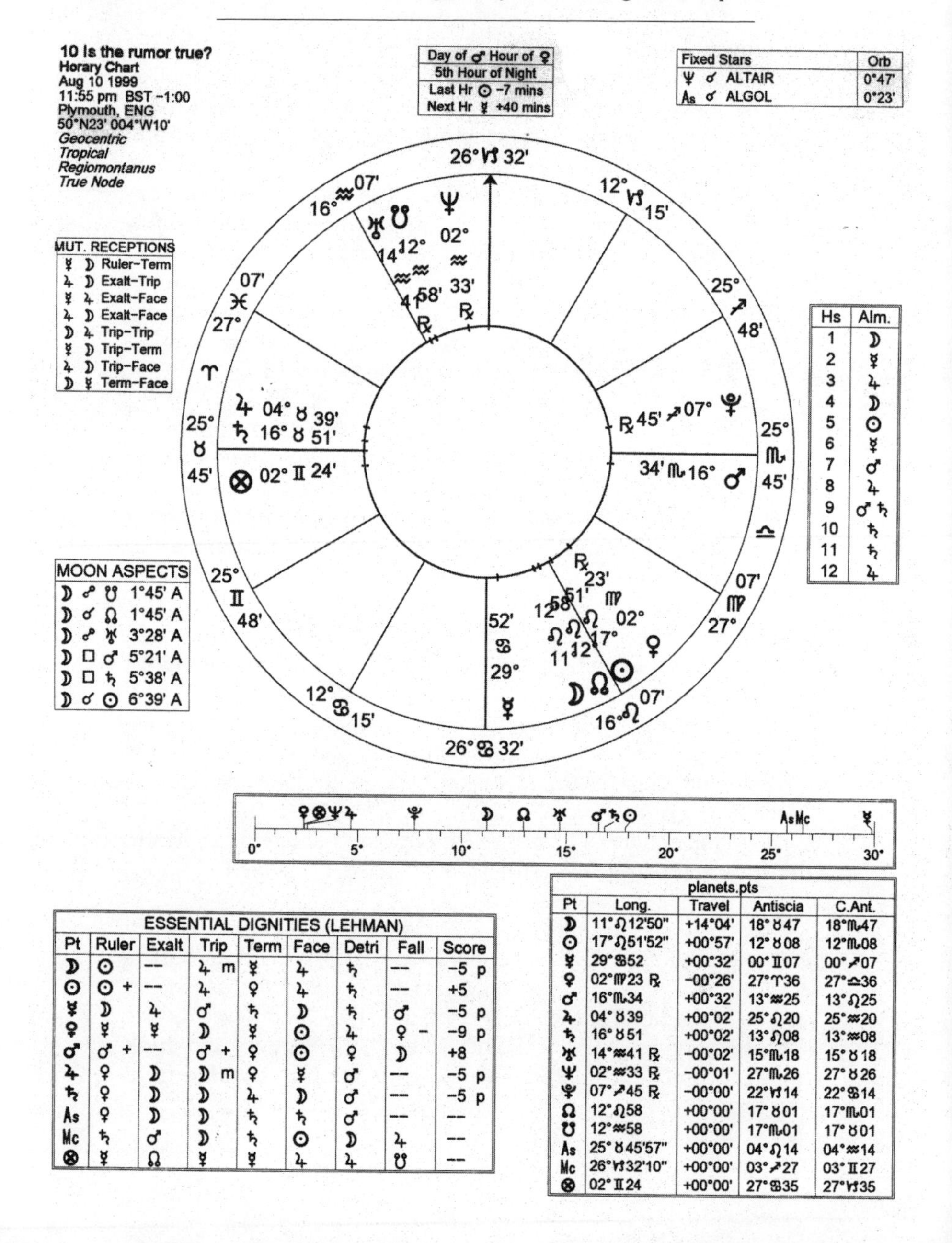

Fixed Stars	Orb
♆ ☌ ALTAIR	0°47'
As ☌ ALGOL	0°23'

MUT. RECEPTIONS
☿ ☽ Ruler-Term
♃ ☽ Exalt-Trip
☿ ♃ Exalt-Face
♃ ☽ Exalt-Face
☽ ♃ Trip-Trip
☿ ☽ Trip-Term
♃ ☽ Trip-Face
☽ ☿ Term-Face

Hs	Alm.
1	☽
2	☿
3	♃
4	☽
5	☉
6	☿
7	♂
8	♃
9	♂ ♄
10	♄
11	♄
12	♃

MOON ASPECTS
☽ ☍ ☋ 1°45' A
☽ ☌ ☊ 1°45' A
☽ ☍ ♅ 3°28' A
☽ □ ♂ 5°21' A
☽ □ ♄ 5°38' A
☽ ☌ ☉ 6°39' A

ESSENTIAL DIGNITIES (LEHMAN)								
Pt	Ruler	Exalt	Trip	Term	Face	Detri	Fall	Score
☽	☉	--	♃ m	☿	♃	♄	--	-5 p
☉	☉ +	--	♃	♀	♃	♄	--	+5
☿	☽	♃	♂	♄	☽	♄	♂	-5 p
♀	☿	☿	☽	☿	☉	♃	♀ -	-9 p
♂	♂ +	--	♂ +	♀	☉	♀	☽	+8
♃	♀	☽	☽ m	♀	☿	♂	--	-5 p
♄	♀	☽	☽	♃	☽	♂	--	-5 p
As	♀	☽	☽	♄	♄	♂	--	--
Mc	♄	♂	☽	♄	☉	☽	♃	--
⊗	☿	☊	☿	☿	♃	♃	☋	--

planets.pts				
Pt	Long.	Travel	Antiscia	C.Ant.
☽	11°♌12'50"	+14°04'	18°♉47	18°♏47
☉	17°♌51'52"	+00°57'	12°♉08	12°♏08
☿	29°♋52	+00°32'	00°♊07	00°♐07
♀	02°♍23 ℞	-00°26'	27°♈36	27°♎36
♂	16°♏34	+00°32'	13°♒25	13°♌25
♃	04°♉39	+00°02'	25°♌20	25°♒20
♄	16°♉51	+00°02'	13°♌08	13°♒08
♅	14°♒41 ℞	-00°02'	15°♏18	15°♉18
♆	02°♒33 ℞	-00°01'	27°♏26	27°♉26
♇	07°♐45 ℞	-00°00'	22°♑14	22°♋14
☊	12°♌58	+00°00'	17°♉01	17°♏01
☋	12°♒58	+00°00'	17°♏01	17°♉01
As	25°♉45'57"	+00°00'	04°♌14	04°♒14
Mc	26°♑32'10"	+00°00'	03°♐27	03°♊27
⊗	02°♊24	+00°00'	27°♋35	27°♑35

Example 11. Event: Statement about Sex

Our next example addresses the Rumor issue head on – pardon the pun! The story is this: a woman was talking to her husband on the phone while he was out of town on business. He made the statement to her that he had not had sex with anyone else since they were married. She is an astrologer, and she was at her computer during the call. Any guesses what she did?

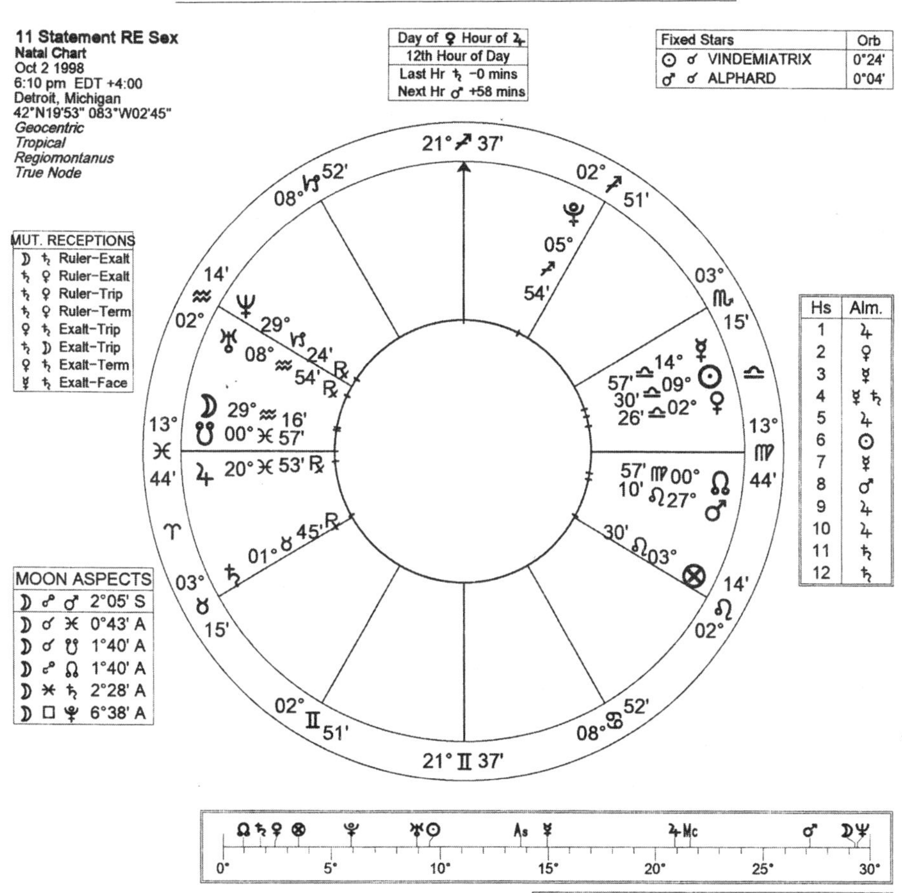

ESSENTIAL DIGNITIES (LEHMAN)								
Pt	Ruler	Exalt	Trip	Term	Face	Detri	Fall	Score
☽	♄	--	♄	♂	☽ +	☉	--	+1
☉	♀	♄	♄	♀	☽	♂	☉ −	−9 p
☿	♀	♄	♄	♃	♄ m	♂	☉	−5 p
♀	♀ +	♄	♄ m	♄ m	☽	♂	☉	+5
♂	☉	--	☉	♂ +	♂ +	♄	--	+3
♃	♃ +	♀	♀	♂	♂	☿	☿	+5
♄	♀	☽	♀ m	♀ m	☿ m	♂	--	−5 p
As	♃	♀	♀	♃	♃	☿	☿	--
Mc	♃	☋	☉	♄	♄	☿	☊	--
⊗	☉	--	☉	♄	♄	♄	--	--

planets.pts				
Pt	Long.	Travel	Antiscia	C.Ant.
☽	29°♒16'42"	+14°12'	00°♏43	00°♉43
☉	09°♎30'32"	+00°59'	20°♓29	20°♍29
☿	14°♎57	+01°41'	15°♓02	15°♍02
♀	02°♎26	+01°14'	27°♓33	27°♍33
♂	27°♌10	+00°36'	02°♉49	02°♏49
♃	20°♓53 ℞	−00°07'	09°♎06	09°♈06
♄	01°♉45 ℞	−00°04'	28°♌14	28°♒14
♅	08°♒54 ℞	−00°00'	21°♏05	21°♉05
♆	29°♑24 ℞	−00°00'	00°♐35	00°♊35
♇	05°♐54	+00°01'	24°♑05	24°♋05
☊	00°♍57	+00°00'	29°♈02	29°♎02
☋	00°♓57	+00°00'	29°♎02	29°♈02
As	13°♓44'12"	+00°00'	16°♎15	16°♈15
Mc	21°♐37'06"	+00°00'	08°♑22	08°♋22
⊗	03°♌30	+00°00'	26°♉29	26°♏29

While she couldn't resist examining the chart, she didn't know how to interpret it, so she called me. I made one adjustment to her chart: I relocated it to where her husband was. My reasoning was that we are evaluating his statement, and in the case of simultaneous transmission, I wanted to examine his situation in making the statement, not her situation in hearing it. She also asked a horary about a month later, and for that I used her for the 1st House. However, for the original statement made by her husband, we use the 1st House to represent him.

Jupiter ruling the Ascendant, close to the Ascendant, immediately struck me. Now I'm sorry folks, but mythology sometimes intrudes on my consciousness, and this was just one of those times – it seems every myth of Jupiter involves him making love with anyone other than his wife Juno! The expression, "spilling seed" just wouldn't leave my brain... And Jupiter is actually besieged between the South Node and Saturn.

Okay. This time we have all mutable angles. The Ruler of the Ascendant is in a mutable sign and retrograde. The Moon and its dispositor are fixed, but neither is in exactly happy condition, and Saturn, dispositor of the Moon is also retrograde. Mercury has only out of sect triplicity and is in a separating quincunx as well as approaching antiscion to the Ascendant, not an easy combination! If we need anything else, there's that Moon conjunct the South Node. Is he lying? Through his teeth!!

The major news story going on at the time was President Clinton's infidelities, so of course the image came to mind about Clinton choosing to believe that oral sex isn't really sex, and the Kinsey Institute came up with a survey suggesting that something like 40% of adult American men agree with that statement – or at least did before the impeachment proceedings! I therefore suggested that we might be confronting a difference of opinion concerning the definitions that at the very least seemed to be working strongly in his favor.

I also examined her horary question, although I considered the chart as secondary to the event of the phone call. This is what often happens with astrologers who aren't quite used to horary: they get a chart like the phone call in this instance, and then if for some reason, they cannot read the chart, their response is to then ask a horary *about* the event, hoping that the second chart is clearer. However, even were the second chart clearer, it's generally less valid anyway. In any case, her horary had the Moon in Capricorn and Mercury retrograde in Sagittarius, which is about enough to sink any possibility that he was telling the truth.

Delineation Tip: *The chart for an event always supercedes a question about that event. Perhaps we should visualize every event as the Universe asking a Question, and that to ask a horary about that event would be equivalent to asking the same question twice!*

Example 12. Will a letter do any good?

The very mention of a letter – a form of communication – immediately brings the 3rd House to mind, and this is an example of how we can use our method to cover yet another 3rd House matter.

The Querent committed the great occupational no-no: she became romantically involved with her employer. Now, she's dealing with issues of possible betrayal at the same time that she needs to get a raise in her salary! On a rational level, most of us would agree that this is crazy, definitely not something that one decides to do for logical reasons! So, continuing with the sequence of events that put her into this predicament in the first place, now she thinks that maybe he'll respond in a positive way if only she can just express her feelings properly. The question was whether it was a good idea to send an

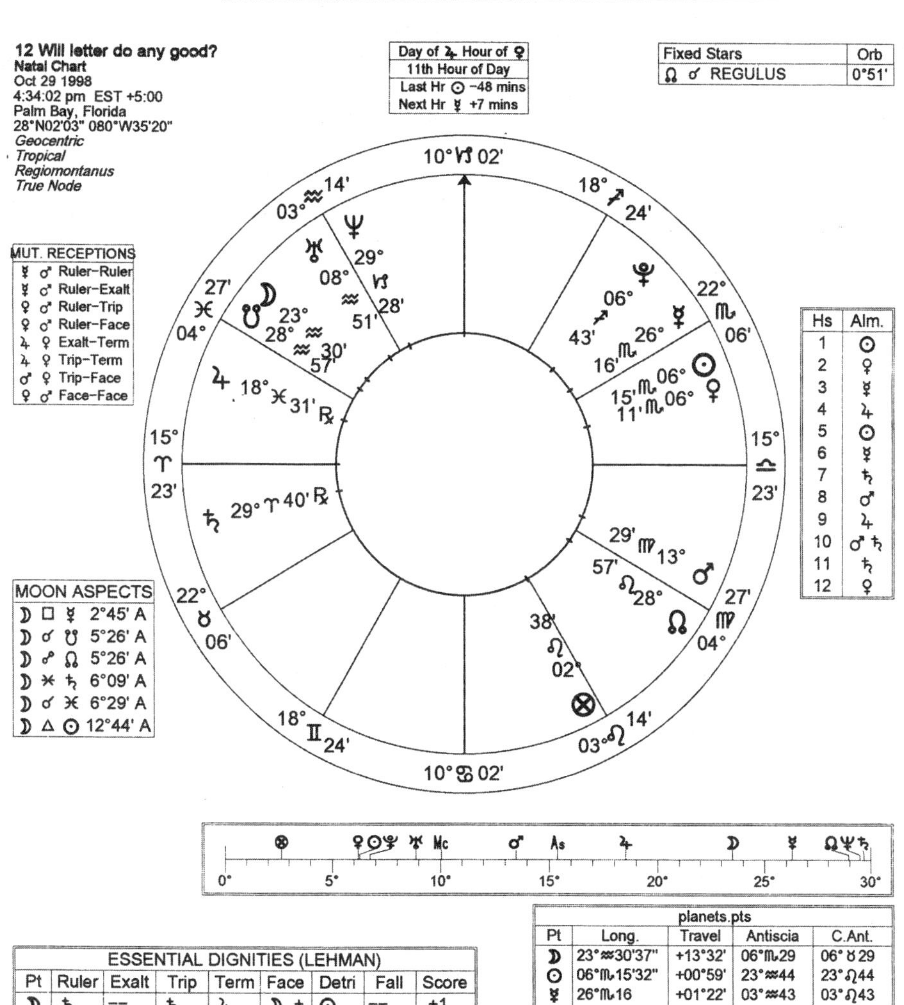

ESSENTIAL DIGNITIES (LEHMAN)								
Pt	Ruler	Exalt	Trip	Term	Face	Detri	Fall	Score
☽	♄	--	♄	♃	☽ +	☉	--	+1
☉	♂	--	♀	♃	♂	♀	☽	−5 p
☿	♂ m	--	♀	☿ +	♀	♀	☽	+2
♀	♂	--	♀ +	♃	♂ m	♀ −	☽	−2
♂	☿ m	☿	♀	♃	♀ m	♃	♀	−5 p
♃	♃ +	♀	♀	☿	♃ +	☿	☿	+6
♄	♂	☉	☉	♄ +	♀	♀	♄ −	−2
As	♂	☉	☉	☿	☉	♀	♄	--
Mc	♄	♂	♀	☿	♂	☽	♃	--
⊗	☉	--	☉	♄	♄	♄	--	--

planets.pts				
Pt	Long.	Travel	Antiscia	C.Ant.
☽	23°♒30'37"	+13°32'	06°♏29	06°♉29
☉	06°♏15'32"	+00°59'	23°♒44	23°♌44
☿	26°♏16	+01°22'	03°♒43	03°♌43
♀	06°♏11	+01°15'	23°♒48	23°♌48
♂	13°♍29	+00°35'	16°♈30	16°♎30
♃	18°♓31 ℞	−00°02'	11°♎28	11°♈28
♄	29°♈40 ℞	−00°04'	00°♍19	00°♓19
♅	08°♒51	+00°00'	21°♏08	21°♉08
♆	29°♑28	+00°00'	00°♐31	00°♊31
♇	06°♐43	+00°02'	23°♑16	23°♋16
☊	28°♌57	+00°00'	01°♉02	01°♏02
☋	28°♒57	+00°00'	01°♏02	01°♉02
As	15°♈23'09"	+00°00'	14°♍36	14°♓36
Mc	10°♑02'49"	+00°00'	19°♐57	19°♊57
⊗	02°♌38	+00°00'	27°♉21	27°♏21

e-mail that she was writing. This is completely apart from the salary issue, which was dealt with successfully as a separate horary, and via an electional chart.

Saturn is in the 1st House. You may recall that this is a consideration against judgment: either the Querent is lying (or simply omitting or not revealing something of relevance), *or* the astrologer will not get paid. So my first issue was to get the credit card approved, which actually took about three tries, because she had inadvertently given me the wrong card number!

This whole situation sure looked like Saturn in the 1st: but is she leaving something out of her narrative to me, or is she simply fooling herself? Or is there something she just doesn't know? To make things even cloudier, we have two possible Significators for her: the Sun as Almuten of Aries by day, or Mars, the sign ruler of the Aries Ascendant. Both are peregrine, but I selected the Sun, because I thought it showed her predicament precisely: peregrine, in the 7th House, conjunct the Ruler of the 7th, which is in Detriment. She works out of his house, a 7th House situation clearly describing the Sun as her ruler.

Delineation Tip: *Pick only one primary Significator for each party. The use of multiple Significators for any one person or thing adds more confusion than clarity.*

Now: is he Venus or Saturn, Saturn being the Almuten of the 7th House? I picked Venus, because he is not under her control: he's in his *own* house. Notice that they are already in a partile conjunction: they are as close now as they are ever going to be. They are cazimi – joined at the hip! Venus is in Detriment, yet not peregrine. This combination of dignity and debility often makes the person unpredictable, because generally *both* conditions apply.

Any letter that she sends is ruled by Mercury, both as natural ruler of letters generally, and as ruler of the 3rd House in this chart specifically – the fact that they are the same being a pretty good indication that this is a radical chart. Mercury is in a mute sign and has dignity only by Term, which is not strong enough to create a change in circumstances for the better. This means that if he were only wavering, it might be enough to give pause, but not to convince him to adopt a completely different point of view. Mercury is also not making an aspect to his ruler – the letter makes no impact on him directly. And Mercury is at the Bendings. But notice that the Moon is coming to square Mercury. What does this mean? Recall that we use the Moon as co-ruler of all Questions. This means some sort of unpremeditated action puts a stress into the story – remember it is a square. What happened: the e-mail that she was drafting was inadvertently sent instead of saved in the system as a draft! The missive he received in his in-box was a much starker statement than he would have gotten had she had the chance to edit more thoroughly.

Delineation Tip: *What does it mean that the Moon co-rules all Questions – or all Querents? The Moon primarily gives timing or the sequence of the events. The Moon is also a generic indicator of change, and most horary questions can only be answered in the affirmative if a change in state occurs. Beginners often try to use this idea to justify using the Moon as an alternate Significator for the Querent, and this is not generally true.*

The letter did not exactly inflame his passions, but it did shock him into acknowledging her feelings.

While we chose to use the Sun as her ruler, there is an interesting configuation between Venus and Mars in this chart. It is called a rendering.

Rendering was a concept defined by Claude Dariot, and actually used by Lilly, on page 385, although he didn't define it. Dariot gave the following definition of rendering (***rédition***):

> Rend[e]ring up or giving back is double, that is to say, of the vertue and of the light; the rend[e]ring up of the vertue is when a Planet being in his own house, or in any other of his dignities, beholdeth another which is combust or Retrograde: for that Planet because of his imbecility which cometh by his retrogradation or combustion, cannot hold or keep the vertue which the other doth communicate or give unto him by his aspect... [For example] Mercury being combust in Taurus rendereth up to the Moon her vertue, which he gives unto her by a sextile aspect. Such yielding up is good and profitable, if both the Planets be in angles, or succeeding houses, being fortunate. Likewise if the Planet that doth apply unto the other be in angle, although the other be in an house that is cadent (so that there be some reception between them) is indifferent. Finally, it will be profitable if he which yieldeth up his vertue be in an angle: otherwise it is altogether unprofitable; the yielding or rendering up of the Light is, when two Planets which do not behold one another with any aspect: yet both of them do behold some other Planet: for that the Planets do gather their lights and do cast it back again, either to themselves or to some other place of the Zodiack...[69]

The Rendering in this chart is as follows. Venus is seriously debilitated by being Combust (I don't find the Cazimi to be benefic), as well as in Fall. But Venus is disposed by Mars, and is in the approaching sextile to Mars. Mars is not strong. But the combination of aspect and disposition does bring Venus and Mars together. This does argue that the two of them will ultimately come to agreement. They did. While nothing that strong happened immediately, two years later they did marry. I wouldn't use this at the time to predict the marriage, but the result is fascinating.

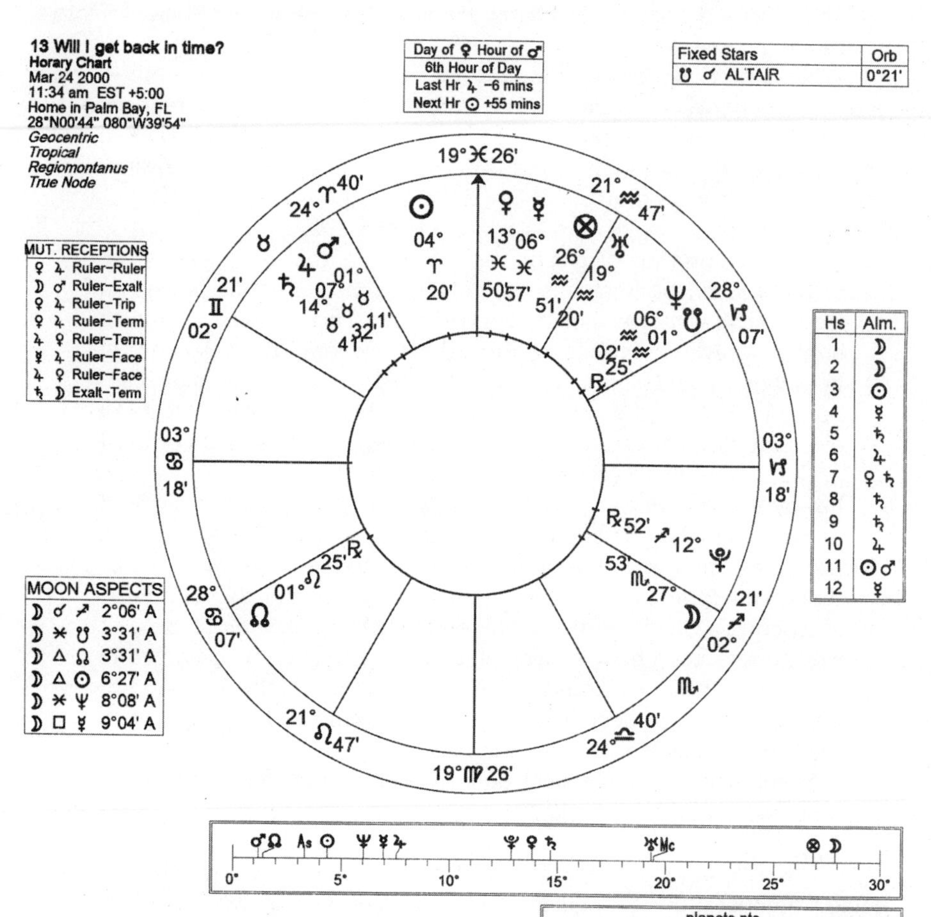

ESSENTIAL DIGNITIES (LEHMAN)								
Pt	Ruler	Exalt	Trip	Term	Face	Detri	Fall	Score
☽	♂	--	♀	♄	♀	♀	☽ -	-9 p
☉	♂	☉ +	☉ +	♃	♂	♀	♄	+7
☿	♃	♀	♀	♀	♄	☿ -	☿ -	-14 p
♀	♃ m	♀ +	♀ +	♃ m	♃	☿	☿	+7
♂	♀	☽	♀	♀	☿	♂ -	---	-10 p
♃	♀ m	☽	♀	♀ m	☿	♂	---	-5 p
♄	♀	☽	♀	☿	☽	♂	---	-5 p
As	☽	♃	♀	♂	♀	♄	♂	---
Mc	♃	♀	♀	☿	♃	☿	☿	---
⊗	♄	---	♄	♂	☽	☉	---	---

planets.pts				
Pt	Long.	Travel	Antiscia	C.Ant.
☽	27°♏53'14"	+12°14'	02°♒06	02°♌06
☉	04°♈20'19"	+00°59'	25°♍39	25°♓39
☿	06°♓57	+00°46'	23°♎02	23°♈02
♀	13°♓50	+01°14'	16°♎09	16°♈09
♂	01°♉11	+00°44'	28°♌48	28°♒48
♃	07°♉32	+00°13'	22°♌27	22°♒27
♄	14°♉41	+00°06'	15°♌18	15°♒18
♅	19°♒20	+00°02'	10°♏39	10°♉39
♆	06°♒02	+00°01'	23°♏57	23°♉57
♇	12°♐52 ℞	-00°00'	17°♑07	17°♋07
☊	01°♌25 ℞	-00°06'	28°♉34	28°♏34
☋	01°♒25 ℞	-00°06'	28°♏34	28°♉34
As	03°♋18'12"	+00°00'	26°♊41	26°♐41
Mc	19°♓26'14"	+00°00'	10°♎33	10°♈33
⊗	26°♒51	+00°00'	03°♏08	03°♉08

Example 13. Will I get back in time?

This chart is representative of the kind of question asked by flight attendants and other airline personnel, but rarely by people outside that industry. Here's the background. Airline personnel generally fly on passes, which means that they pay only a small surcharge for the flight. However, they fly standby (i.e., on a space-available basis), so there's no guarantee that they will get to their intended destination at all, let alone on schedule. So while the rest of us pay for a flight and expect to get to our destination more or less on schedule, airline employees take the chance that there will be space available for an unbeatable fare.

Having said this, the down side of this scenario is that these people have schedules to meet. This question was asked by a flight attendant who wanted to spend Easter in San Juan, Puerto Rico. Her concern was her rather tight work schedule after Easter, so she would have to count on being able to get back without delay. This can be difficult when trying to travel during a busy holiday season.

For a US-based flight attendant, a trip to Puerto Rico, or the Caribbean, for that matter, is generally a 3rd House trip, especially if that flight attendant is located on the East Coast. Anyone who travels so constantly has to go on a seriously complex or long itinerary to move the focus to the 9th House.

The 3rd House is ruled by the Sun in Aries: this looks like it could be a really fun trip! The problem is that the Moon in Scorpio represents the Querent. Right away that's a problem: the Moon naturally ebbs and flows: change is a part of the system. But the Moon slow of course and in a fixed sign simply does not look like someone who would get what she wants in a timely fashion, and the Moon fallen and Void of Course in Scorpio specifically just doesn't look happy.

Remember Lilly's aphorism: If the Lord of the 12th House is afflicting the Ruler of the Ascendant; then the Querent will receive damage or prejudice from the news heard. The Moon, Ruler of the Ascendant, is coming to an out-of-sign square to Mercury, Ruler of the 12th. So the Querent receives prejudice from this information. In other words, she isn't going to like the result.

To further confirm our suspicions, there is no perfection between Sun and Moon without changing signs – which we could possibly allow, since the Moon loses debility by moving to Sagittarius. However, since a change in sign would imply a change in plan, this trip just doesn't look like a good plan. When informed of the probability of delays, the Querent decided to defer the trip to another, less busy, time.

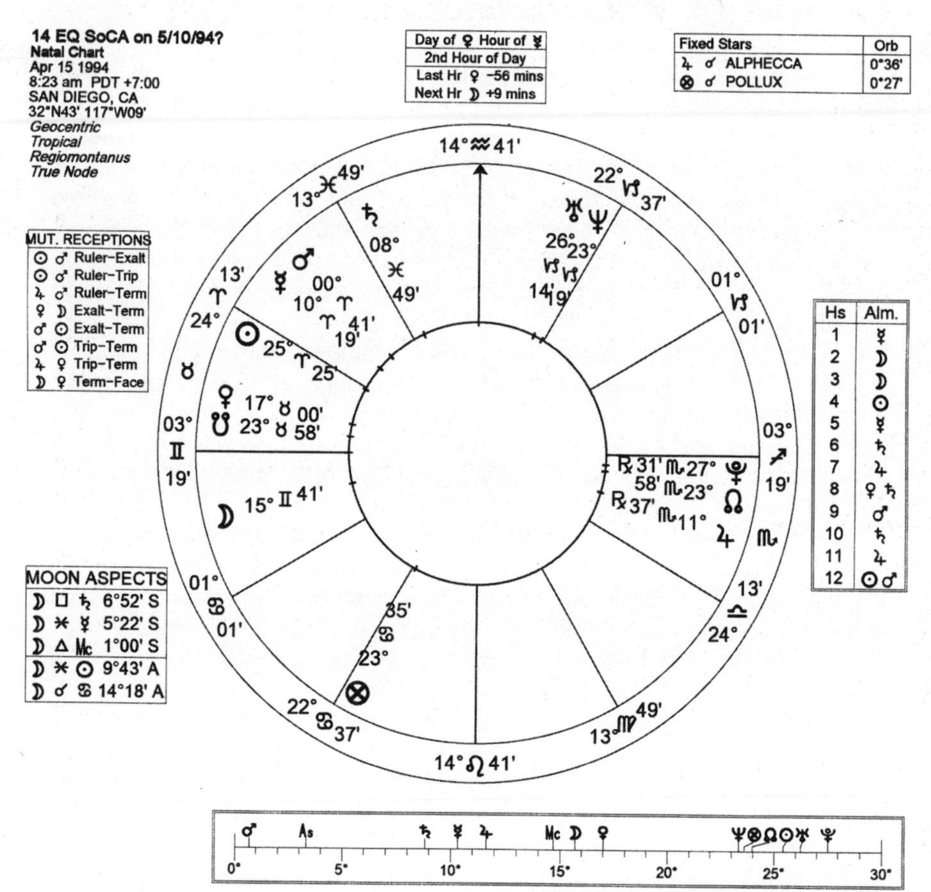

ESSENTIAL DIGNITIES (LEHMAN)								
Pt	Ruler	Exalt	Trip	Term	Face	Detri	Fall	Score
☽	☿	☊	♄	♀	♂	♃	☋	-5 p
☉	♂	☉ +	☉ +	♂	♀	♀	♄	+7
☿	♂	☉	☉	♀	☉	♀	♄	-5 p
♀	♀ +	☽	♀ +	♃	☽	♂	--	+8
♂	♂ +	☉	☉	♃	♂ +	♀	♄	+6
♃	♂	--	♀	♃ +	☉	♀	☽	+2
♄	♃	♀	♀	♃	♄ +	☿	☿	+1
As	☿	☊	♄	☿	♃	♃	☋	--
Mc	♄	--	♄	♀	☿	☉	--	--
⊗	☽	♃	♀	♀	☽	♄	♂	--

planets.pts				
Pt	Long.	Travel	Antiscia	C.Ant.
☽	15°♊41'54"	+12°00'	14°♋18	14°♑18
☉	25°♈25'43"	+00°58'	04°♍34	04°♓34
☿	10°♈19	+01°48'	19°♍40	19°♓40
♀	17°♉00	+01°13'	12°♌59	12°♒59
♂	00°♈41	+00°46'	29°♍18	29°♓18
♃	11°♏37 ℞	-00°07'	18°♒22	18°♌22
♄	08°♓49	+00°05'	21°♎10	21°♈10
♅	26°♑14	+00°00'	03°♐45	03°♊45
♆	23°♑19	+00°00'	06°♐40	06°♊40
♇	27°♏31 ℞	-00°01'	02°♒28	02°♌28
☊	23°♏58	+00°01'	06°♒01	06°♌01
☋	23°♉58	+00°01'	06°♌01	06°♒01
As	03°♊19'22"	+00°00'	26°♋40	26°♑40
Mc	14°♒41'16"	+00°00'	15°♏18	15°♉18
⊗	23°♋35	+00°00'	06°♊24	06°♐24

Example 14. Will there be a magnitude 8.5 or greater earthquake in Southern California on May 10, 1994?

This is the kind of question that my San Diego Horary Class calls the $50 "No" – charge more than your usual rate, and then just say No! Seriously, there are certain questions that you get that have such a high probability of a negative answer that they almost cannot be treated by the usual rules.

We don't often talk about probability in horary, but sometimes we need to. The average yes/no question typically has a probable ratio of yes to no of somewhere between one in ten to nine in ten. In other words, the odds may not be fifty-fifty, but they aren't astronomical either. So what do you do when the odds of success are less than a million to one?

I think the answer is that you have to apply a higher standard, so to speak. This means that *any* ambiguity or mixed result is automatically a *no*. To get a *yes*, the chart would have to *scream* yes, and even then, I'd probably want a link to something in the natal chart to confirm it!

This case, though, was a no-brainer. The Ascendant is mutable, the Moon is mutable, the Ruler of the Ascendant (and the Moon) is Cardinal; none of the rulers is fixed. Neither the Moon nor Mercury have any dignity. Mercury is weakly beholding the Ascendant by separtating sextile, but that's as close to a positive argument as this chart possesses.

Needless to say, had the outcome been true, you, the Reader, would have known about this quake!

Example 15. Is the rumor true?

This question was asked by a stockholder in a small private company, concerning a rumor that the company was about to be bought by a Fortune 500 company.

1. The rumor is true if the Lord of the Ascendant, the Moon, or the Moon's dispositor (or better, the majority of them) are fixed, not Cadent, and in good aspect to the benefics or the Sun. (L, G) **None of the three are cadent; only the Moon is fixed.**

2. If those three are Cadent and afflicted by the malefics, the rumor is false whether they are in good zodiacal condition or not. (G) **Does not apply.**

3. The rumor is true if all four angles are fixed, the Moon and Mercury are fixed, and they in turn are separating from the malefics and applying to an angular benefic. (L, G) **None of the angles are fixed. The Moon is fixed, but Mercury is mutable. Both Moon and Mercury are applying to both malefic (Mars) and benefic (Venus).**

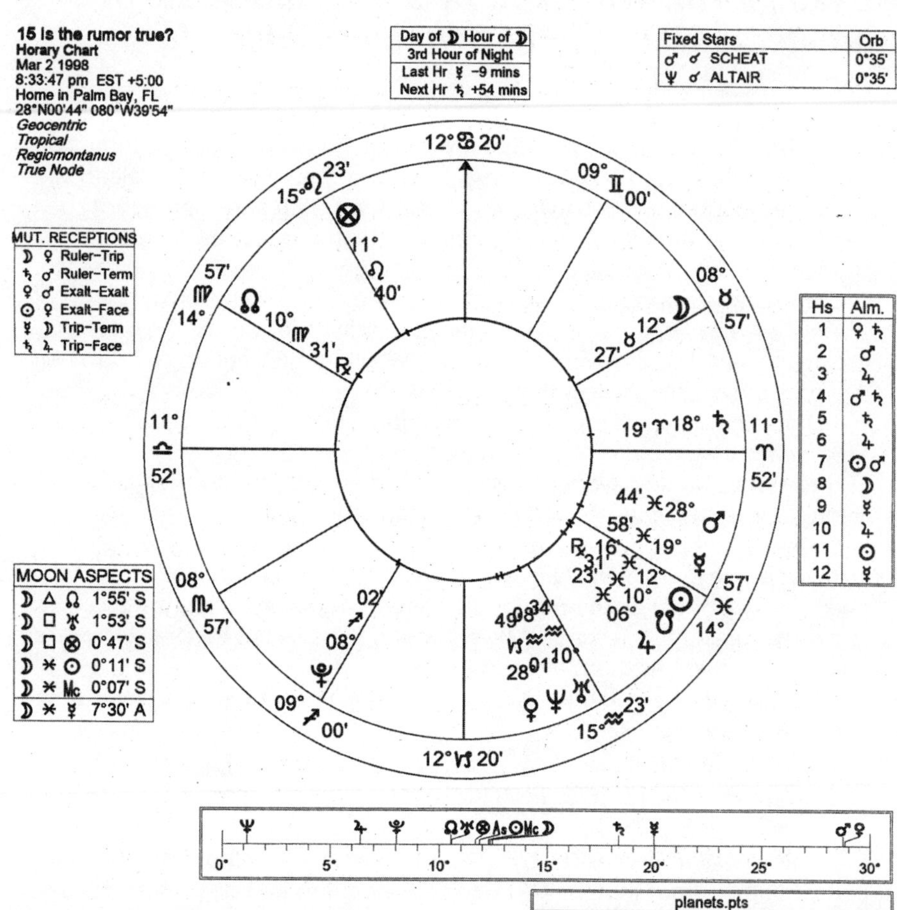

ESSENTIAL DIGNITIES (LEHMAN)								
Pt	Ruler	Exalt	Trip	Term	Face	Detri	Fall	Score
☽	♀	☽ +	☽ +	☿	☽ +	♂	--	+8
☉	♃	♀	♂	♃	♃	☿	☿	−5 p
☿	♃	♀	♂	☿ +	♃	☿ −	☿ −	−7
♀	♄	♂ m	☽	♄	☉	☽	♃	−5 p
♂	♃	♀ m	♂ +	♄	♂ +	☿	☿	+4
♃	♃ +	♀	♂	♀	♄	☿	☿	+5
♄	♂	☉	♃	☿	☉	♀	♄ −	−9 p
As	♀	♄	☿	♃	♄	♂	☉	--
Mc	☽	♃	♂	♃	☿	♄	♂	--
⊗	☉	--	♃	☿	♃	♄	--	--

planets.pts				
Pt	Long.	Travel	Antiscia	C.Ant.
☽	12° ♉ 27'44"	+14°24'	17° ♌ 32	17° ♒ 32
☉	12° ♓ 16'07"	+01°00'	17° ♎ 43	17° ♈ 43
☿	19° ♓ 58	+01°55'	10° ♎ 01	10° ♈ 01
♀	28° ♑ 49	+00°43'	01° ♐ 10	01° ♊ 10
♂	28° ♓ 44	+00°46'	01° ♎ 15	01° ♈ 15
♃	06° ♓ 23	+00°14'	23° ♎ 36	23° ♈ 36
♄	18° ♈ 19	+00°06'	11° ♍ 40	11° ♓ 40
♅	10° ♒ 34	+00°03'	19° ♏ 25	19° ♉ 25
♆	01° ♒ 08	+00°01'	28° ♏ 51	28° ♉ 51
♇	08° ♐ 02	+00°00'	21° ♑ 57	21° ♋ 57
☊	10° ♍ 31 ℞	−00°00'	19° ♈ 28	19° ♎ 28
☋	10° ♓ 31 ℞	−00°00'	19° ♎ 28	19° ♈ 28
As	11° ♎ 52'00"	+00°00'	18° ♓ 07	18° ♍ 07
Mc	12° ♋ 20'34"	+00°00'	17° ♊ 39	17° ♐ 39
⊗	11° ♌ 40	+00°00'	18° ♉ 19	18° ♏ 19

4. If the MC/IC axis is fixed, and the Moon rules either angle, then the rumor is true. (L, G) **Neither axis is fixed.**

5. If the benefics are in the 1st, but the Moon unfortunate, the rumor is false or misleading. (G) **Does not apply.**

6. Mercury retrograde or debilitated shows a false rumor, as does the affliction of the planet to whom the Moon or Mercury next applies. (G) **They both next apply to Mars, which is dignified.**

7. The Ruler of the Ascendant or the Moon Under Beams brings secrecy to the matter. (L, G) **Does not apply.**

8. The Moon either Void of Course or in hard aspect to Mercury shows the rumor to be either false, or of no import. (L, G) **Does not apply.**

9. The Moon in the 1st, 3rd, 10th or 11th, separating from an easy aspect to any planet, and applying by an easy aspect to the Lord of the Ascendant argues that the rumor is true. (L) **Does not apply.**

10. The Moon square or opposite Mercury, neither in easy aspect to the Ascendant argues that the rumor is false. (L) **Does not apply.**

11. If the Lord of the 6th, 8th, or 12th House is in the 1st House, or afflicting the Ruler of the Ascendant; or Mars or Saturn retrograde and in the 1st House, or in hard aspect to either the ascending degree or the Ruler of the Ascendant; then the Querent will receive damage or prejudice from the news heard. (L) **Here we have the problem of Venus being sign ruler of both 1st and 8th. What do we do? The simple solution is to use the Almuten Ruler of the 8th, the Moon. This makes sense anyway, because the Moon is so dignified, and in the 8th House. With this adjustment, there are no afflictions from the listed rulers. Saturn is opposite the Ascendant, but I'm reluctant to allow a seven degree orb. Mars is in a partile sextile to Venus, Ruler of the Ascendant. So this consideration doesn't apply.**

None of the conditions is completely and unequivocally met. Here a couple of other factors may apply. Generally malefic Pluto conjunct the 3rd House cusp certainly does not help the situation, nor I suspect does the Moon in the 8th – the death of the matter, so to speak. Notice that the Sun was conjunct the South Node – this fact, in tandem with the Moon being just a sextile ahead of the Sun, shows that this question was asked just a few days after a solar eclipse, which is not considered to be a good omen.

One might be tempted to look at the Part of Fortune conjunct the 11th House cusp and conclude that there is a material profit to one's hopes and wishes – one at least presumes that the Querent was hoping for a profit! Recall that the condition of the Part of Fortune is read from its dispositors. Here we have two strong ones: the Sun and Jupiter. The Sun is peregrine, but

Jupiter is strong by sign – unfortunately though, Jupiter is conjunct the South Node. We shall examine a question asked a couple weeks after this one in Example 88, Chapter 13, where Jupiter also is a prominent planet in the chart. The question is: which is more important: the dignity of Jupiter, or its conjunction to the South Node, traditionally considered a malefic? In both charts, the South Node conjunction not only precluded the benefic expression of Jupiter in Pisces, it added troubles of its own. So read in terms of its dispositors, the conjunction of Fortuna and the 11th House cusp comes closer to meaning hopes dashed than anything positive.

We can also look at the question as a buy-sell, which would represent a 1st-7th House perfection. However, the Querent is not an owner of the company, so we have to turn the chart. Her involvement is as a shareholder; thus; her relationship is a 5th House relationship. The buy-sell would therefore have to involve the 5th-11th axis. Harsh Saturn in Aries rules the 5th (already not a good sign), and the Sun the 11th – and there's no aspect between them. While the Moon translates the light via an incredibly weak pattern of sextile and semi-sextile, both Sun and Saturn are peregrine and contra antiscial, so nothing good is likely to come of it anyway. This confirms that this rather mixed but predominantly negative result really means that the rumor is false. It was.

Example 16: How long will my brother live?

The Querent's brother had AIDS. We had actually looked at a horary concerning him over a year before this one, in which his prognosis at the time looked pretty good. Unfortunately, he had taken a turn for the worse, and when this question was asked, he was hospitalized. The Querent was in a very distressed condition – not only was her brother dying, but months before she and her husband had arranged to take their young daughter on a trip to Disney World – and she was worried that her brother might die while they were on the trip.

The first issue we have to settle in delineating this chart is whether to turn the chart at all. We shall address this issue again in Chapter 6, but the question is whether she is asking this on his behalf, or for her own sake. If she is asking it on his behalf, then he is the 1st House, and her existence is essentially ignored in the chart, because she is considered merely the agent who gets the question asked. However here, given the background to asking the question, there's no doubt that she is the Querent, and so her brother is the 3rd House.

So we begin by encountering what looks at first like an anomaly: he is the Sun, ruling the 3rd House. And the Sun is in Aries! This looks too dignified to represent a man dying of AIDS – until we observe that the Sun is in his 8th House of death. Notice he is alone in this house. His next aspect is a trine to Pluto in the 6th House. In Horary, a planet alone (i.e., not sharing a house with other planets) often really is *alone* – he's not really responding to other people much, and specifically, there's nothing the Querent can do. The Moon in Capricorn rules the Querent – she is in Detriment, and that certainly describes her state at this time. She only applies to him via a dubious twelve degree sextile that is frustrated by the Moon applying to three malefics: the South Node, Mars and Neptune, all out of sign. So there really is nothing more that she can do about this.

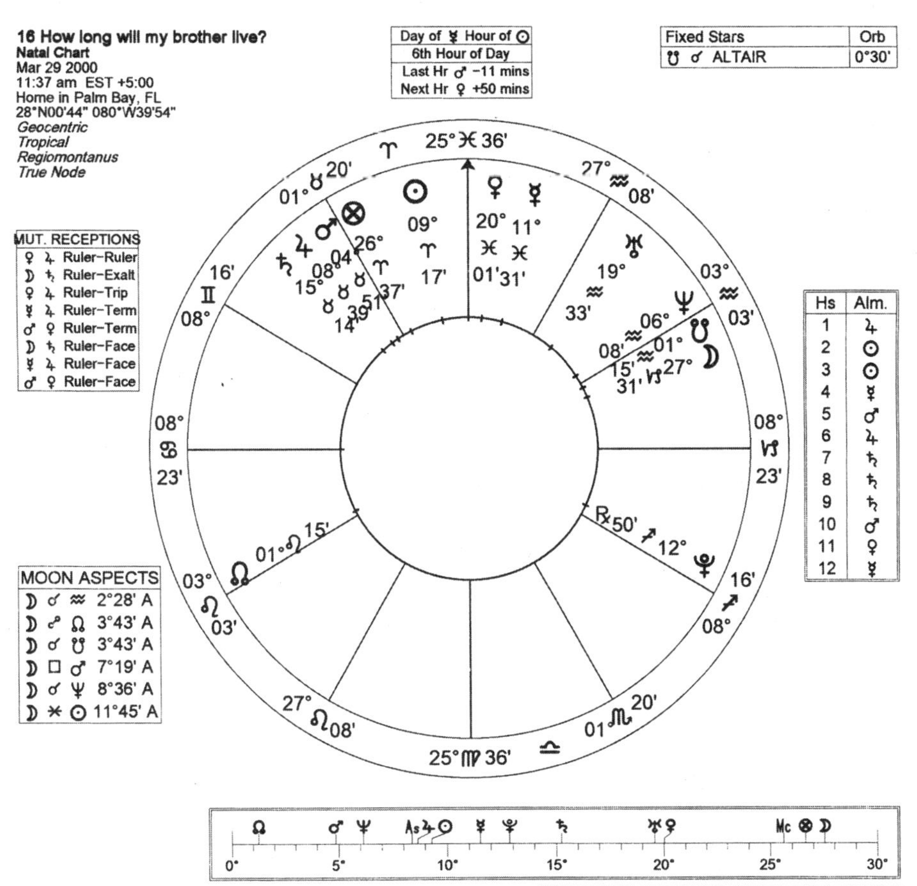

ESSENTIAL DIGNITIES (LEHMAN)								
Pt	Ruler	Exalt	Trip	Term	Face	Detri	Fall	Score
☽	♄	♂ m	♀	♄	☉	☽ −	♃	−10 p
☉	♂	☉ +	☉ +	♀	♂	♀	♄	+7
☿	♃	♀	♀	♃ m	♃ m	☿ −	☿ −	−14 p
♀	♃ m	♀ +	♀ +	♂ m	♂	☿	☿	+7
♂	♀	☽ m	♀	♀ m	☿	♂ −	---	−10 p
♃	♀ m	☽	♀	☿ m	☿ m	♂	---	−5 p
♄	♀	☽	♀	♃	☽	♂	---	−5 p
As	☽	♃	♀	♃	♀	♄	♂	---
Mc	♃	♀	♀	♂	♂	☿	☿	---
⊗	♂	☉	☉	♄	♀	♀	♄	---

planets.pts				
Pt	Long.	Travel	Antiscia	C.Ant.
☽	27°♑31'46"	+11°57'	02°♐28	02°♊28
☉	09°♈17'17"	+00°59'	20°♍42	20°♓42
☿	11°♓31	+01°01'	18°♎28	18°♈28
♀	20°♓01	+01°14'	09°♎58	09°♈58
♂	04°♉51	+00°43'	25°♌08	25°♒08
♃	08°♉39	+00°13'	21°♌20	21°♒20
♄	15°♉14	+00°06'	14°♌45	14°♒45
♅	19°♒33	+00°02'	10°♏26	10°♉26
♆	06°♒08	+00°01'	23°♏51	23°♉51
♇	12°♐50 ℞	−00°00'	17°♑09	17°♋09
☊	01°♌15	+00°00'	28°♉44	28°♏44
☋	01°♒15	+00°00'	28°♏44	28°♉44
As	08°♋23'31"	+00°00'	21°♊36	21°♐36
Mc	25°♓36'39"	+00°00'	04°♎23	04°♈23
⊗	26°♈37	+00°00'	03°♍22	03°♓22

I noted that the Moon is three degrees from changing sign. There is three degrees on his 6th House cusp – and the reciprocal 27 degrees on his Ascendant – i.e., three degrees left in that sign. And there is three degrees application of Sun (Ruler of the 3rd) to Pluto. So I said that there is a possibility of a change for the worse in a bit less than 3 (weeks) – but I didn't expect him to die until the Moon symbolically hits either the South Node (just under 4 weeks) or even possibly Neptune (nine weeks). He died April 24, 2000, just under four weeks from when the question was asked.

How "true" does a question have to be before one can say that the rumor is true? That depends. I would say that it would be necessary to get at least one condition which is unambiguously met, at least for those aphorisms that specify a true rumor. If the unambiguous match is to a condition which means that the rumor is false, then the very least that it shows is that the rumor is partially false. Once again, we have to take a measure of the preponderance of evidence; the same measure applied in Common Law civil cases.[70]

Before we conclude, let me just mention one more delineation idea: the question of good advice. I've never gotten precisely this question, but it seems like a good idea to me! Questions concerning rumors come in the flavor of true or false. Of course, what we have seen is that there is actually a gray area of partly true and partly not.

However, it might be a good idea sometimes to ask not about rumor, but about advice. People are always offering each other advice about what to do: where to go to college, whether to take that job offer, whether that salary increase is really the best one could hope for. Oftentimes such advice comes unasked – and from people whose intentions in offering it are either unknown or questionable. Is your boss saying that the on-the-job training is really good for you – or for the company? Is your mentor really addressing your needs, or reminiscing about what she or he went though at the stage you are at? Advice is not the same as a flat statement like "I have never been unfaithful." But it can be evaluated using this same style of delineation. Note that the delineation is *not* whether the advice actually *works* – but whether it is offered in good faith. The delineation method is essentially a combination of the "rumor" delineation, with one additional factor: looking for benefics or malefics associated with the 10th House, which gives you some clue to whether the advice is proposed for your benefit or detriment.

Chapter Four

Affairs of the 4th House: Housing, Buried Treasure, Removal, and Objects & Entities Lost, Stolen, Waylaid & Mislaid

Questions of the 4th House as given by Gadbury:[71]

- *Shall the Querent purchase the House or Land, &c.*
- *Of the Quality thereof, and shall the Querent do well to take it?*
- *If it be good for one to remove, or abide where he is?*
- *Of Treasure hid, if attainable?*
- *Is there Treasure in the place supposed?*
- *Shall the Querent enjoy the Estate of his Father?*
- *Of a thing mislay'd, how or where to finde it?*

Additional Questions of the 4th House as given by Lilly:[72]

- *Parents*
- *Lands*
- *Tenements*
- *Inheritance of land*
- *Cities, towns, farms, manors, and castles*
- *Of turning the course of Rivers, or bringing Waters into one's Ground or House, either by Conduit or Pipes.*

As you can see from the title of this chapter, the 4th House supports a huge number of questions. Virtually any of the points given above could constitute an entire chapter by itself. We are going to defer the discussion of buying and selling houses until the 7th House, because generically, buying and selling is a 1st – 7th House matter. Having done so, it's important to remember that questions about the *condition* of a dwelling or building belong in the 4th, even if buying and selling involves other houses as well. Simply put, the 4th House is security. Whether it's one's parents, landed possessions, or social citizenship; matters of the 4th House translate ultimately to our sense of place in the world; our foundations. The bottom line. That is the justification for considering the 4th House to be the end-of-the-matter, because matters of the 4th house are so often the ultimate concern. Having said that, I sincerely believe that the 4th House has been wildly overused as the end-of-the-matter when astrologers have not known any other way to read the chart.

For the remaining, the two most frequent questions concern lost objects, and removal.

Lost objects were mentioned by Lilly as associated with the 4th House, but he mainly discussed them in the 7th, because the 7th House relates to theft. Obviously, before the location of an object can be ascertained, we have to eliminate (or interpret!) theft. Rather than splitting the process, we shall consider all aspects of items and entities lost, stolen, waylaid, or dead in this chapter.

Before we take up this major matter, let me first say a few words about removal. Many readers have never used the word "removal" in a sentence before, because the word itself has fallen into disuse and has become archaic in areas where U.S.-style English is spoken. A "removal" is a temporary relocation from one place to another, such as going to one's summer cottage. However, it can also be used in moving from one place to another – a very important usage, as we shall see. British English has maintained the old usage.

Lost, Stolen, Mislaid & Waylaid Objects, People and Animals

Many of the logic steps for inanimate things and living entities are the same. But not all. The preliminary sequence of steps to follow is shown below.

- If a living creature, first determine whether the animal or person is dead or alive, well or injured.

- If an inanimate thing, first determine whether the item **could** have been stolen. You cannot skip this step unless you are completely convinced that theft is not a possibility. Also notice that theft is possible for living beings: then we call it kidnapping, rustling, and a host of other names!

- If an item or entity is stolen, then follow the sequence to determine where the Quesited is, in what condition, the nature of the thief, and whether the thief can be caught, and whether the Quesited will be found or returned.

- If the Quesited is a living being who is not confined, then see if a voluntary return is shown, or if further wandering will happen.

- If theft is not an issue, and the Quesited is a thing, then follow the steps to determine its location: whether in the home, property, care or possession of the Querent, or proximity to the Querent.

1. Absent Party: Dead or Alive?

Lilly is absolutely amazing at points, and this is one of those times. His section, "If the absent party be alive or dead?" beginning on page 404 can be used as is. You can, as we say, 'cookbook it!' The sequence he follows is completely dependable for both humans and animals. Here's the idea.

First, you have to determine the relationship of the absent party to the Querent.

- For pets and small animals, use the 6th House.
- For larger animals, use the 12th House.
- For friends, use the 11th House
- For one's father, the 4th House, usually, with the 10th for the mother. Sometimes, these reverse.
- For one's child, use the 5th House.
- For employees or co-workers, use the 6th House.
- For one's boss, use the 10th House.
- For all other parties where the relationship is difficult to characterize, or if it is too far along the derivative spiral (such as: Karen's friend's great granddaughter), use the 7th House. Lilly uses the 1st House in this case,[73] but I have a problem with that attribution, because it implies that the Querent is really in a position to ask on that party's behalf. This matter will be taken up in detail in Chapter 6, but the usual justification for using the 1st for a party other than the Querent is that what we might call the technical Querent is actually acting as an agent for what we might call the true Querent. But if there is no particular relationship to the absent party, how can the Querent be considered that person's agent?

The reason for paying careful attention to these assignments is that Lilly's rules apply to **both** the radical (unturned) and the turned chart – i.e., the chart that puts the house cusp defined above as the Ascendant.

Once you have determined the relationship to the Querent, you can continue to the actual considerations.

- Is the Significator of the absent party or the Moon in the absent party's 12th House? If so, is that Significator or Moon in an approaching hard aspect to a malefic? If so, this can signify death. In a separating hard aspect to the malefics, death is less likely: the party suffered or was miserable, but is probably alive.

- Is the Sun or the Moon afflicted by one or more of the malefic planets or is it in an evil placement?[74] This can also mean death.

- Is the Significator of the absent party or the Moon in the absent party's 6th House? If so, if that Significator or Moon is in hard aspect to the Ruler of the 6th – unless the two are in reception or the Significator or Moon applies to benefics - then the absent party is sick. If the absent one is separating from hard aspect to the malefics, then the absent party *was* sick. If applying to the malefics, then the absent party may yet *become* sick.

- Is the Significator of the absent party or the Moon in, or afflicted by the 8th House? This is an indicator that the party may be dead.

- The stronger the Significator of the absent party by essential dignity, and the fewer the aspects to the malefic planets, the better the condition of that party.

We can see this in action in the following example.

Example 17: Where is Patty?

Patty was the girlfriend of the Querent's part-time boss, Mr. V. Patty was living in Southeast Florida but she had previously lived on Florida's West Coast, and still had family there. She frequently drove across the state. She had left the day before, supposedly to go and visit her sons, but had never arrived.

Mr. V. called the Querent to relate that Patty was missing and request that she start calling the Highway Patrol and toll stations along Patty's presumptive route from one coast to the other. The Querent called me immediately with this question.

What ensued was a bit of a quandary about what house to use for Patty. There were actually three choices: we could view Patty as Mr. V.'s significant other (5th from the 10th), as the co-worker of the Querent (6th House - Patty also did part-time work for Mr. V., and it was actually as a result of that work that the Querent met her), or simply the 7th House as the default Other Person. There was no question of attempting to use the 11th House because Patty and the Querent were not close enough to be called friends. They were friendly acquaintances.

After some thought, I decided to work with the 7th House to signify Patty since the other connections struck me as relatively confused. In other words, there were simply too many options, and none of them were really better than the next. With eight degrees of Aries on the 7th cusp, I could have used either Mars or the Sun for her. Mars as the sign ruler; or the Sun as the Almuten. I decided to use Mars, because with the Sun in the 10th House, the implication would be that Patty was home with him– which she clearly wasn't! Patty in her own house simply meant that she was where she wanted to be: that wherever it was, she got there of her own accord.

So where is she? First we have to examine the rules for whether or not she is alive. We observe the Moon in Patty's 12th House, separating from a sextile to Neptune and applying to a square with Venus. Normally we would think:

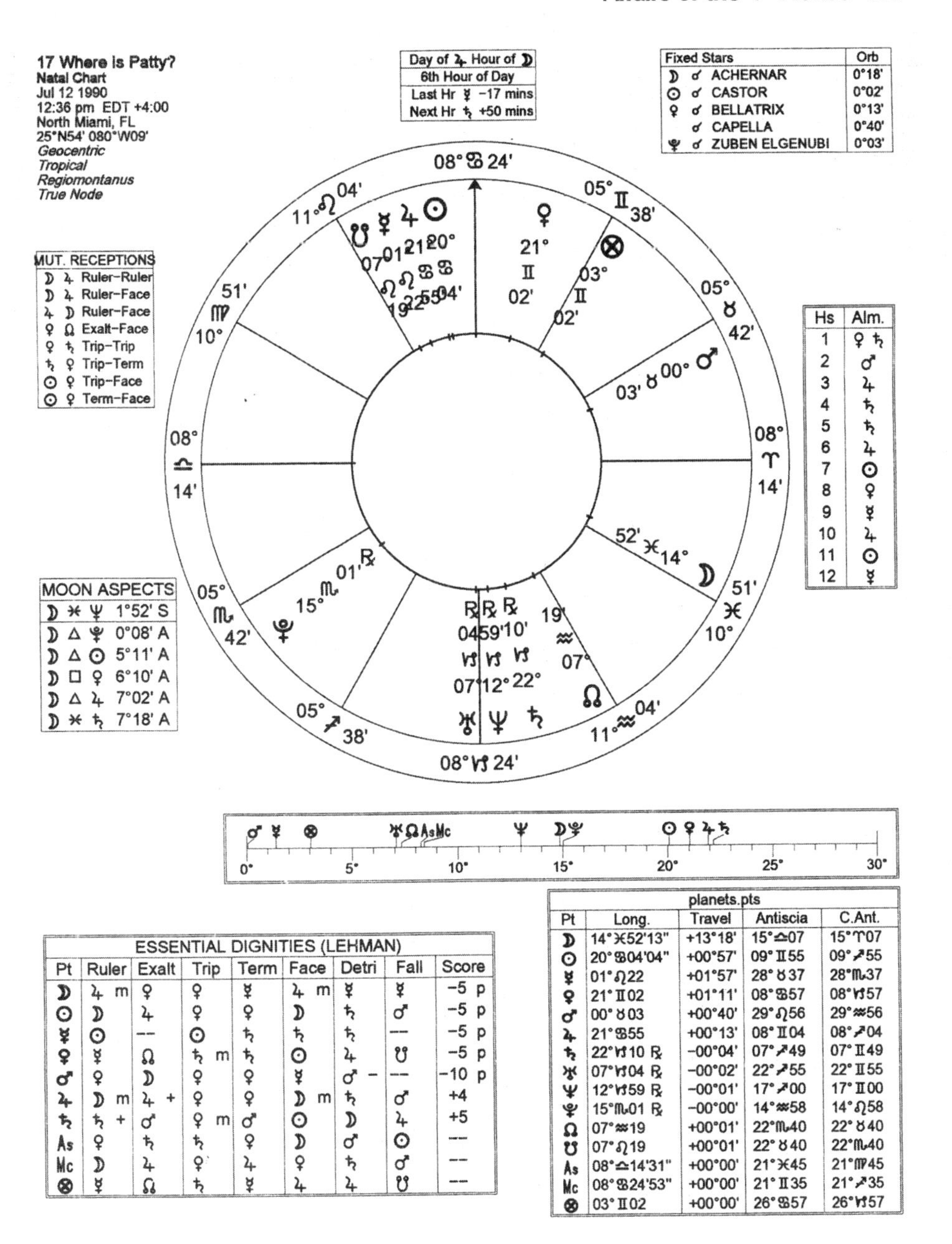

ESSENTIAL DIGNITIES (LEHMAN)								
Pt	Ruler	Exalt	Trip	Term	Face	Detri	Fall	Score
☽	♃ m	♀	♀	☿	♃ m	☿	☿	−5 p
☉	☽	♃	♀	♀	☽	♄	♂	−5 p
☿	☉	--	☉	♄	♄	♄	--	−5 p
♀	☿	☊	♄ m	♄	☉	♃	☋	−5 p
♂	♀	☽	♀	♀	☿	♂ −	--	−10 p
♃	☽ m	♃ +	♀	♀	☽ m	♄	♂	+4
♄	♄ +	♂	♀ m	♂	☉	☽	♃	+5
As	♀	♄	♄	♀	☽	♂	☉	--
Mc	☽	♃	♀	♃	♀	♄	♂	--
⊗	☿	☊	♄	☿	♃	♃	☋	--

planets.pts				
Pt	Long.	Travel	Antiscia	C.Ant.
☽	14°♓52'13"	+13°18'	15°♎07	15°♈07
☉	20°♋04'04"	+00°57'	09°♊55	09°♐55
☿	01°♌22	+01°57'	28°♉37	28°♏37
♀	21°♊02	+01°11'	08°♋57	08°♑57
♂	00°♉03	+00°40'	29°♌56	29°♒56
♃	21°♋55	+00°13'	08°♊04	08°♐04
♄	22°♑10 ℞	−00°04'	07°♐49	07°♊49
♅	07°♑04 ℞	−00°02'	22°♐55	22°♊55
♆	12°♑59 ℞	−00°01'	17°♐00	17°♊00
♇	15°♏01 ℞	−00°00'	14°♒58	14°♌58
☊	07°♒19	+00°01'	22°♏40	22°♉40
☋	07°♌19	+00°01'	22°♉40	22°♏40
As	08°♎14'31"	+00°00'	21°♓45	21°♍45
Mc	08°♋24'53"	+00°00'	21°♊35	21°♐35
⊗	03°♊02	+00°00'	26°♋57	26°♑57

great, Venus is a benefic, but Venus is the ruler of the radical 8th House! This makes Venus an accidental malefic. Mars, ruling Patty, is ruler of both her 1st *and* her 8th, and the Moon's next aspect is a trine to Pluto. Furthermore, Mars is debilitated – both peregrine and in Detriment, so her condition is not good. This is further confirmed because Mars is at the Bendings.

This in fact turned out to be the case. There are simply too many arguments that Patty is - or is about to be – dead. Actually, I was not at all convinced that she already was – but that it was impending. Mars being ruler of both her 1st and 8th is symbolic that she is the cause of her own death. With the Moon departing from Neptune and applying to Pluto, we can hypothesize a method: drugs. One further note: with Mars in her own house, I thought it likely that Patty actually hadn't gone far – she was very close to where she "should" be. Relative to the Querent, the 7th House represents West, so I thought she might be a little bit West of the Querent.

This turned out to be the case. Patty had not gone across the state to see her sons as she had announced. She checked into a local motor inn where she used a bottle of vodka to wash down a bottle of prescription sedatives in a successful effort to kill herself.

A number of years ago I presented this horary as an example at a particular astrological conference where we were comparing horaries to nativities. It so happened that one of the astrologers there had a client who was an astro-twin of Patty's, and this astrologer was most upset with my characterization of the inevitability of this scenario. Her client had gone through some deeply disturbing psychological problems during this same period, but had survived.

The important point to remember here is that it isn't necessarily the *natal* chart that shows the inevitability of the death, but the *horary*. Obviously, the same question was not asked about the astro-twin!

2. Stolen or kidnapped?

In addition to the usual good advice from Lilly, there is an entire 17th Century work by Anthony Griffin devoted to theft. Combining the two sources together, let's create a sequence of steps to examine.

Arguments for No Theft from Griffin. [75]

- First examine the Dispositor of the Moon and the ruler of the 2nd House. If they do not separate from each other, or from any other planets, then the item is not stolen.

- If the Dispositor of the Moon and the Ruler of the Ascendant are conjunct, the item is in the Querent's home.

- If the Ruler of the Ascendant separates from either Jupiter or the Lord of the 2nd, then the Querent put it down and forgot about it.

- If the Planetary Hour Ruler is in the 1st House, then the item is in the Querent's home.

- If the chart has Cancer Rising and the Moon is in the 4th, and the Ruler of the 2nd House is in the 7th, or in the sign of the 8th, and the Moon is sextile or trine the Ruler of the 2nd, then the item may have been temporarily moved or removed as a joke.

- If the Moon is in the 7th, in the same sign as the Planetary Hour Ruler, provided the Planetary Hour Ruler is also Ruler of the 7th, then there is no theft, the item being overlooked or mistaken for something else.

- If the Ruler of the Ascendant is conjunct the Planetary Hour Ruler, the item is not stolen.

- If several of the following are conjunct, then the item is not stolen, but near the Querent: the Planetary Hour Ruler, the Ruler of the 4th, a planet in the 4th, the Moon, or the Dispositor of the Moon.

Arguments for Theft, mainly from Griffin:

- If the Dispositor of the Moon or the Ruler of the 2nd separates from *any* planet, then the item is stolen.

- If a peregrine planet disposes the Moon, or vice versa, the item is stolen. (I find this to be too pervasive, since much of the time, the number of peregrine planets exceeds the number in dignity!)

- A putative thief is symbolized by a peregrine planet either angular or in the 2nd House that beholds the Descendant; lacking this, the thief can be given by the Ruler of the Descendant. In Lilly's restrictive definition which he cited as that of Master Allen,[76] the Ruler of the 7th has to behold the Descendant to qualify as thief, in which case the planet to whom the Moon applies may be counted as thief provided that planet beholds the Descendant. Lilly went on to say that he never encountered a planet in the 1st House as thief, and also found the 2nd House option unlikely. No thief, no theft, according to Lilly's definition. Griffin uses the short version: either an angular peregrine planet, or, lacking that, the Ruler of the 7th House.

- If the Ruler of the Ascendant disposes the Significator of the thief, it is stolen.

- If the Significator of the Thief is peregrine, it is stolen.

- If the Significator of the Thief is conjunct or in hard aspect to the Ruler of the Ascendant, it is stolen.

- If the Significator of the Thief disposes any planet in the 1st House, it is stolen.

- If a peregrine planet is in the 1st or the 2nd, the item is stolen. (Here Griffin rather seems to be adopting Lilly's citation of Master Allen above.)

- If both the Part of Fortune and its Dispositor are unfortunate, then the item is stolen.

Griffin suggests comparing the arguments for "stolen" and "not stolen" and interpreting according to the preponderance of the evidence. One more point: for the Disposition arguments, I suspect that disposition needs to be by the major dignities: sign, exaltation or Triplicity; not the minor ones: term or face.

3. Lost or Mislaid?

Let's briefly consider the rules for finding lost objects as given by Gadbury,[77] this is essentially the same as Lilly's, except for being a bit better organized.

> Having erected your Figure, and rightly considered your Ascendant, &c. You may proceed to judgment after this manner, viz.
>
> 1. If the Lord of the Second be in an Angle, the thing missing is within the House of the Querent; but if the Lord of the Second, or the Moon be in the Ascendant, or in the Sign of the Lord of the Ascendant is in, or disposed of by him, the thing missing is in that part of the House, which the Querent himself most frequents.
>
> 2. The Lord of the Second or Moon, in the 10th House, declares the thing hid or mislaid to be in the Hall or Dining room, if a Gentleman ask the Question; If a Tradesman, 'tis in his Shop, or Counting House.
>
> 3. But, if the Lord of the Second, or Moon, be in the 7th, the Thing is in that part of the House where the Querent's wife or Maidservants use most to be. If in the sixth, where his servants alone have most to do, &c.
>
> 4. To judge of the Nature or Quality of the place, you must observe the Nature and Quality of the signs the Significators are in; which, if they be Aiery, the thing wanting is in the upper part of the House; if fiery, 'tis neer a Chimney, or where Iron is layd; If earthy, it is neer some Pavement or Floor, or in some low place: If watry, then it is neer to some Sink or Wash-house, or in some Moorish moyst place, &c.
>
> 5. You must also observe the Quarters the Signs govern, for that directs you to the right Angle or part of the House where the thing is hid or mislaid.

A handy way to apply Lilly or Gadbury's system is to turn it into a table.[78] We score the *element* of the sign of the component listed. We shall then use this table in our examples.

Table 1. Table for assessing location according to Lilly's method, page 204.

	Element
Ascendant	
Ruler of Ascendant	
4th House Cusp	
Ruler of 4th House	
Moon	
2nd House Cusp	
Ruler of 2nd House	
Part of Fortune	

After we list the elements and add them up, we look for a preponderance of an element to help pinpoint a location. We shall have occasion to return to this table as we go through our examples. I have found this system useful, although almost never sufficient to actually walk to the item and pick it up. Perhaps its greatest use is in *eliminating* places to look: for example, if water is prevalent, then the kitchen, bathroom and laundry room are the obvious first places to look, if water is lacking, those rooms can be eliminated.

4. Arguments of Recovery – or Not!

Perhaps even more important than what happened is whether the Querent can hope to recover the lost object! These are the arguments for recovery as given by Griffin[79] and Lilly[80]

1. A soft aspect between the Moon and the Ruler of the 2nd House, or natural Significator of the object.

2. If the Planetary Hour Ruler, the Term Ruler and the Sign Ruler of the Moon are direct, and increasing in light and motion, and free from the affliction of the malefics, the item will be recovered whole and intact.

3. If the Ruler of the Ascendant is in its own sign, the item will be recovered.

4. If the Term Ruler or the Sign Ruler of the 2nd applies by a soft aspect to the Ruler of the Ascendant, the item will be recovered.

5. If the Ruler of the Ascendant is in the 2nd or 10th, it means recovery, but with a great amount of effort by the Querent.

6. If the Ruler of the 2nd is in the 2nd or in soft aspect to the 2nd House cusp, then at least part of the goods are recovered; the amount being given by the essential dignities of the 2nd House ruler.

7. Cross positions between the 1st and 4th Houses and their respective rulers denote recovery.

8. If the Moon is opposite the Sun, the thief is caught, but without the goods.

9. The Moon or the ruler of the 2nd in the 1st gives recovery.

10. If the Sun and Moon both behold the Ascendant, then the goods will be recovered.

11. The Moon in the 1st with a benefic denotes recovery.

12. If both the Sun and Moon are angular and behold each other by a soft aspect, it gives recovery.

13. The Ruler of the 2nd in the 8th denies recovery.

Example 18. Where is my jewelry?

The Querent had taken out three bracelets, a gold necklace and a large gold lapis ring from her jewelry case. She was in a hurry, and she thought that she had left them out on her dresser. However, she had a lot on her mind, and she has a tendency to hide jewelry in various strange places. One of those places is her wastebasket. Unfortunately, the trash was picked up the next day, and she forgot about the whole thing until after the trash people had come! I ran charts for three scenarios: the approximate time she remembered the jewelry, the time she called me and left a message on my message service, and the time I listened to the message.

Using her natal chart as a referent, I could justify either of the later two, but chose the time of her call because I felt the Neptune Rising chart was more descriptive of the scenario, since the real issue was forgetfulness. At the time, I asked her about the possibility of theft and while she indicated it was possible, she felt it was more likely that she had misplaced them, and was especially concerned about having put them in the garbage.

First, we have to determine if the items are stolen. There are two peregrine angular planets: Venus and Mars. The Moon and Mars are in a partile trine. The Moon is separating from Saturn, ruler of the Second. The latter is an argument that the item is *not* "in its own place".[81] The Lord of the Ascendant, Saturn does separate from Jupiter, an indicator that the Querent laid it down and forgot it, but we already know this. None of Griffin's other arguments for the "item not stolen" (i.e., being in the house) apply.

As for arguments that the "items are stolen," both the Lord of the House of the Moon[82] (Jupiter) and the Lord of the 2nd, separate from various planets, including mutually from each other. Saturn, the Lord of the Ascendant gives virtue to Mars, the Significator of the thief (they are in mutual reception by Face, and Saturn is the Term Ruler of Mars).[83] Saturn is peregrine, and is in the 2nd House.[84] Therefore, we have strong indicators that the item is stolen.

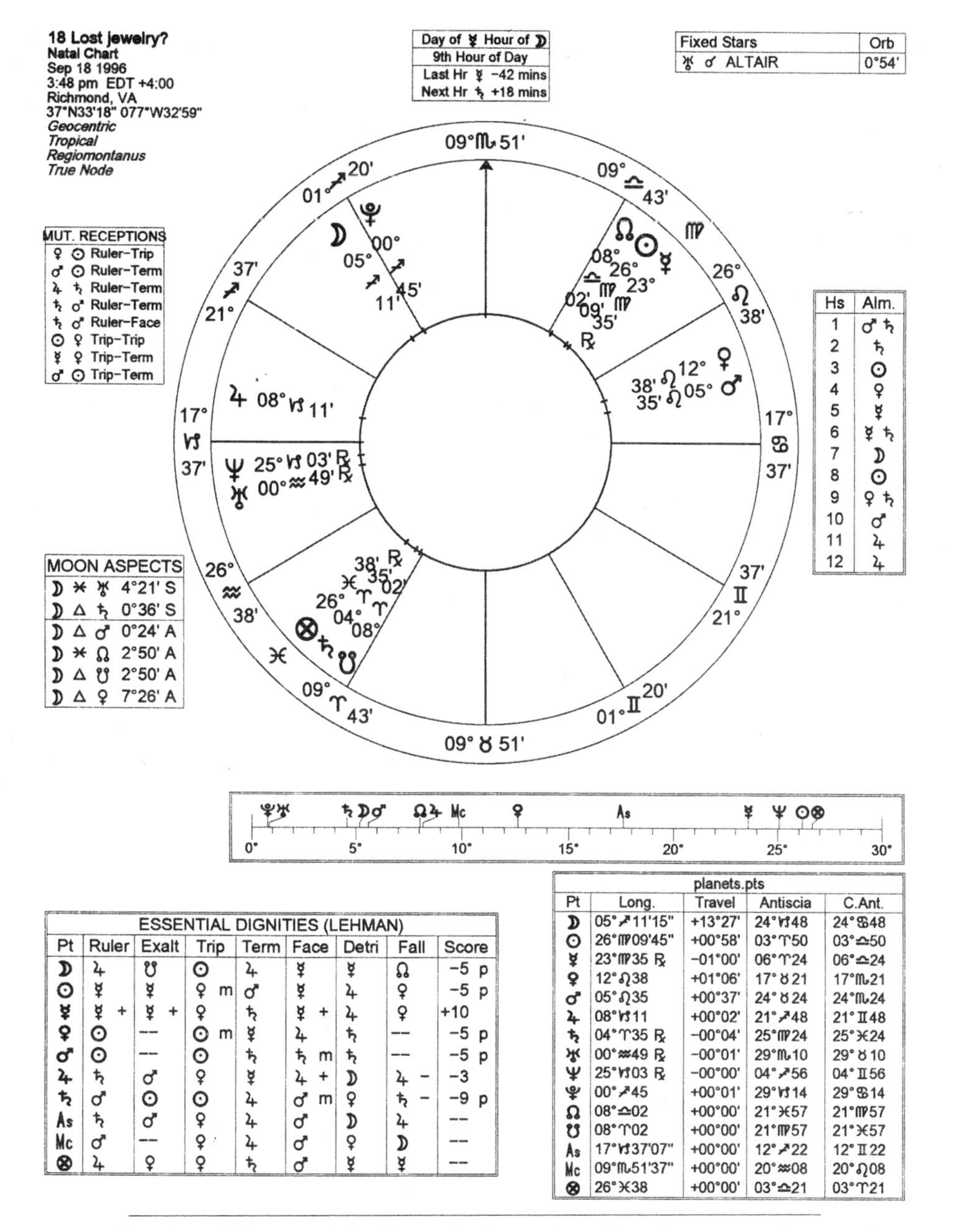

MUT. RECEPTIONS
♀ ☉ Ruler–Trip
♂ ☉ Ruler–Term
♃ ♄ Ruler–Term
♄ ♂ Ruler–Term
♄ ♂ Ruler–Face
☉ ♀ Trip–Trip
☿ ♀ Trip–Term
♂ ☉ Trip–Term

MOON ASPECTS
☽ ⚹ ♅ 4°21' S
☽ △ ♄ 0°36' S
☽ △ ♂ 0°24' A
☽ ⚹ ☊ 2°50' A
☽ △ ☋ 2°50' A
☽ △ ♀ 7°26' A

Hs	Alm.
1	♂ ♄
2	♄
3	☉
4	♀
5	☿
6	☿ ♄
7	☽
8	☉
9	♀ ♄
10	♂
11	♃
12	♃

ESSENTIAL DIGNITIES (LEHMAN)								
Pt	Ruler	Exalt	Trip	Term	Face	Detri	Fall	Score
☽	♃	☋	☉	♃	☿	☿	☊	−5 p
☉	☿	☿	♀ m	♂	☿	♃	♀	−5 p
☿	☿ +	☿ +	♀	♄	☿ +	♃	♀	+10
♀	☉	--	☉ m	☿	♃	♄	--	−5 p
♂	☉	--	☉	♄	♄ m	♄	--	−5 p
♃	♄	♂	♀	☿	♃ +	☽	♃ −	−3
♄	♂	☉	☉	♃	♂ m	♀	♄ −	−9 p
As	♄	♂	♀	♃	♂	☽	♃	--
Mc	♂	--	♀	♃	♂	♀	☽	--
⊗	♃	♀	♀	♄	♂	☿	☿	--

planets.pts				
Pt	Long.	Travel	Antiscia	C.Ant.
☽	05°♐11'15"	+13°27'	24°♑48	24°♋48
☉	26°♍09'45"	+00°58'	03°♈50	03°♎50
☿	23°♍35 ℞	−01°00'	06°♈24	06°♎24
♀	12°♌38	+01°06'	17°♉21	17°♏21
♂	05°♌35	+00°37'	24°♉24	24°♏24
♃	08°♑11	+00°02'	21°♐48	21°♊48
♄	04°♈35 ℞	−00°04'	25°♍24	25°♓24
♅	00°♒49 ℞	−00°01'	29°♏10	29°♉10
♆	25°♑03 ℞	−00°00'	04°♐56	04°♊56
♇	00°♐45	+00°01'	29°♑14	29°♋14
☊	08°♎02	+00°00'	21°♓57	21°♍57
☋	08°♈02	+00°00'	21°♍57	21°♓57
As	17°♑37'07"	+00°00'	12°♐22	12°♊22
Mc	09°♏51'37"	+00°00'	20°♒08	20°♌08
⊗	26°♓38	+00°00'	03°♎21	03°♈21

By whom? Mars and the Moon both in masculine signs argue for a male thief. There may be two, but probably one thief.[85] Mars being located in the Quadrant from the 10th to the 7th House denotes a youthful thief, while Mars denotes middle age. I would therefore conclude the thief's age is probably thirty-something, but probably somewhat more youthful in appearance. The thief is not a member of the family, but with the Lord of the Ascendant in the 2nd, it would argue for a household servant.[86] I would extend this argument to any non-relative or friend who has a key to the house, thereby possibly adding a landlord or other person who has access to the place for reason of his job. The description doesn't fit the neighbor who does have a key, and none of her friends or relatives has keys.

Since Mars is early in Leo, the thief has not left town. Given that Mars is in the 7th House, I would judge him to be West of the Querent. The Ascendant ruler, the Planetary Hour Ruler and the Moon are not angular. This suggests that the jewelry is not too near the house.[87]

As for a description of the thief's house, the doors (Moon in a common sign) have been broken, but repaired. (Moon trine Saturn), but since the Moon is also peregrine, the door or gate still has problems. The door opens to the Southeast.[88]

Given that the Moon and Mars, the Significator of the thief, are in a partile trine, the thief does not live very far away. This also argues for the goods still being in the thief's hands.[89]

There are not strong indicators that the thief will be caught.[90] There is poor indication that the goods will be recovered in full.[91] A hope of partial recovery is given by the fact that the Lord of the 2nd is in the 2nd, but Saturn is debilitated, which reduces the possibility for the recovery of anything meaningful.

Unfortunately, when this is true, we seldom find out what actually happened, except that the item is never found, as in this case.

As you can see from the full description above, Griffin gives a lot of detail about exactly what the nature of the thief's relationship to the Querent is, where the thief lives, what the door of the thief's residence looks like and about the nature of the circumstances of the theft. I highly recommend this reference for further detail.

Example 19. Where is my diamond ring?

After her mother died, the Querent could not locate the diamond wedding band her mother had worn for most of her life. It was not in the safety deposit box that they shared. She was concerned because, in the last days of her fatal illness, her mother had given away some things indiscriminately, and she was afraid that her mother had given the ring either to a neighbor, or that a relative had taken it around the time of the funeral.

The Querent would normally be described by the planet ruling the Ascendant, Venus. The Almuten of the 1st House is Saturn, which is far more descriptive of the Querent who was in a fog of grief following her mother's death (Significator conjunct Neptune). Her Ruler in the 3rd House shows her concerns about neighbors and relatives (both 3rd House.) If that is not enough, Saturn is in Jupiter's Face; Jupiter being Ruler of the 3rd House. Remember, Dignity by Face often shows fear and anxiety, rather than what we would normally consider a more positive dignity.

In classical astrology, the mother is given by the Midheaven and its ruler – in this case the Moon. The Moon was peregrine, and in the degree of the Nodes,[92] and her Mother was dead! The Part of Fortune was in the tenth House, indicating that there was hope that something concerning her Mother could still turn out well.

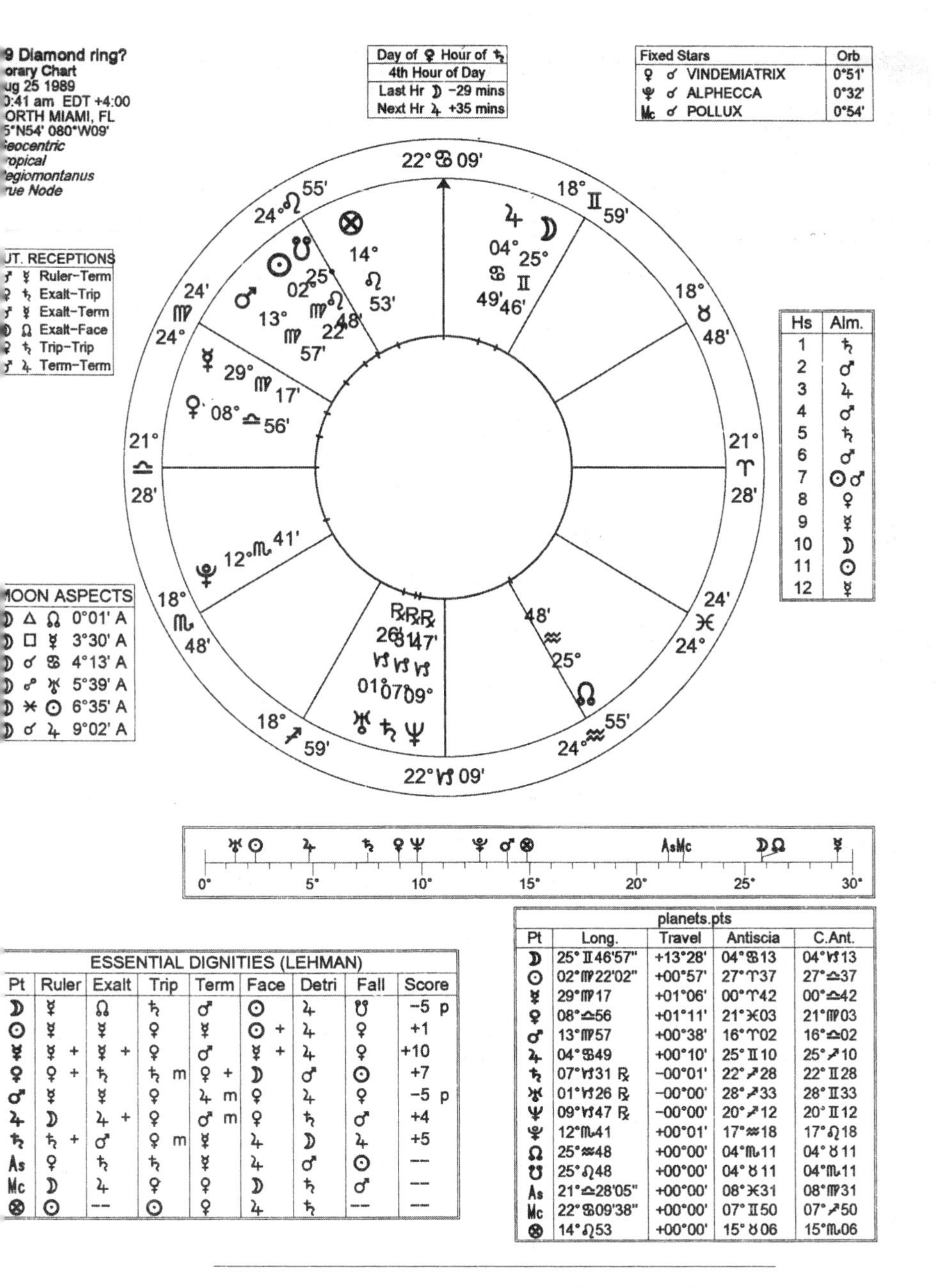

Pt	Ruler	Exalt	Trip	Term	Face	Detri	Fall	Score
☽	☿	☊	♄	♂	☉	♃	☋	−5 p
☉	☿	☿	♀	☿	☉ +	♃	♀	+1
☿	☿ +	☿ +	♀	♂	☿ +	♃	♀	+10
♀	♀ +	♄	♄ m	♀ +	☽	♂	☉	+7
♂	☿	☿	♀	♃ m	♀	♃	♀	−5 p
♃	☽	♃ +	♀	♂ m	♀	♄	♂	+4
♄	♄ +	♂	♀ m	☿	♃	☽	♃	+5
As	♀	♄	♄	☿	♃	♂	☉	---
Mc	☽	♃	♀	♀	☽	♄	♂	---
⊗	☉	--	☉	♀	♃	♄	---	---

ESSENTIAL DIGNITIES (LEHMAN)

planets.pts

Pt	Long.	Travel	Antiscia	C.Ant.
☽	25°♊46'57"	+13°28'	04°♋13	04°♑13
☉	02°♍22'02"	+00°57'	27°♈37	27°♎37
☿	29°♍17	+01°06'	00°♈42	00°♎42
♀	08°♎56	+01°11'	21°♓03	21°♍03
♂	13°♍57	+00°38'	16°♈02	16°♎02
♃	04°♋49	+00°10'	25°♊10	25°♐10
♄	07°♑31 ℞	-00°01'	22°♐28	22°♊28
♅	01°♑26 ℞	-00°00'	28°♐33	28°♊33
♆	09°♑47 ℞	-00°00'	20°♐12	20°♊12
♇	12°♏41	+00°01'	17°♒18	17°♌18
☊	25°♒48	+00°00'	04°♏11	04°♉11
☋	25°♌48	+00°00'	04°♉11	04°♏11
As	21°♎28'05"	+00°00'	08°♓31	08°♍31
Mc	22°♋09'38"	+00°00'	07°♊50	07°♐50
⊗	14°♌53	+00°00'	15°♉06	15°♏06

Venus is the natural ruler of jewelry, and Venus in Libra, her own sign, is strong. The ring contained twenty-one cut diamonds in a platinum setting. Venus is in the 12th House, hidden from view. If the Almuten of the Ascendant were not used, there would be confusion between whether Venus represented the ring or the Querent: a strong Venus is not a good description of a daughter devastated by grief. A strong Saturn, maybe – but not a strong Venus! Also notice that Venus rules the 8th House of death and inheritance, and that's a meaning we may wish to reserve for Venus. Also Mars, the Ruler of the 2nd, would be inappropriate for the jewelry: peregrine Mars in Virgo simply would not describe the finest piece of jewelry that her mother had owned. Further, the ring had symbolized a marriage that had ended forty years previously: the Querent's mother had remained a widow, but continued to wear the ring. Venus is conjunct Vindemiatrix, the widow's star.

Which is a good thing – because Mars is the obvious putative thief candidate in the chart: peregrine and ruling the 7th House. Saturn, Almuten of the 1st, does not dispose Mars. (Note here how we must stick to one Significator, or we shall confuse the issue completely.) Mars is *not* in hard aspect to Saturn, the Almuten of the Ascendant and thus Significator of our Querent. The only 1st House planet is Pluto, which cannot become involved in an issue of disposition with Mars in any case. Mars only disposes the Moon by term (which as I mentioned, is a weak argument) and the Moon does not dispose Mars. There is thus very little argument here for theft.

It is interesting that one of the two peregrine planets, the Moon, represents the Querent's Mother: could she have been the "thief" i.e., given the ring away? The Part of Fortune in the 10th House argues against this. There is also an argument of recovery through the double strong mutual reception of Venus and Saturn.

So where is the ring? It is hidden away, with papers (Venus with Mercury in the Twelfth). The 4th House cusp and the ruler of the 4th House can also give a description: Saturn in Capricorn is on or near the earth, in a dark place.

Having eliminated theft as the likely situation, we can fill out the table we derived from Lilly for the description of the location.

	Element
Ruler of Ascendant	Air (Venus – sign ruler) Earth (Saturn–Almuten)
4th House Cusp	Earth (Capricorn)
Ruler of 4th House	Earth (Saturn)
Moon	Air (Gemini)
2nd House Cusp	Water (Scorpio)
Ruler of 2nd House	Earth (Mars)
Part of Fortune	Fire (Leo)

We then total the numbers:

Fire = 1
Earth = 4
Air = 2
Water = 1

It is tempting to add Venus into the list as the natural ruler of jewelry. I simply don't know whether this is a good idea yet, as no mention in the aphorisms concerning recovery ever mention natural rulers.

How can a place be both Earth and Air? One answer is that the item will not actually be located on the floor, but up a certain distance (air), hidden from view in an obscure place (earth). The solidity of a bank vault strikes me as very earthy, but the presence of so much air reminds us again that it isn't actually on the ground.

The ring was found 17 months later hidden away from view in the safety deposit box at the bank - where it was all along and where it belonged. It was inside another box (gray) jammed into the back of the safety deposit box (also gray) under the unhinged part of the lid. The position of the safety deposit box in the larger bank vault was just a few centimeters off the floor.

Actually, this chart is a very good argument for the importance of taking great care in assigning Significators. This chart required more than the usual number of players:

- The Querent.
- The Ring (Quesited).
- The Querent's deceased mother.
- The possible thief.

It is often tempting to just go on autopilot and assign Significators by rote. However, the more possible parties to a transaction, the more you will find yourself having to think about how to assign their Significators. While there is a certain art to the process, the most important thing is to remember to keep everything as clear and simple as possible.

Example 20. Where are the videos?

I was asked the following question by e-mail.

"I have a question which is very important to me. I am producing television programs. Some time ago a friend of mine borrowed from me four videotapes, with 16 programs on them. I have spent about two months full working time to produce these tapes. And they are the originals and cannot be substituted by some copy. So they are very valuable for me.

"When my friend did not need them any longer he was supposed to mail them to me in a packet. It took a long time and after some time I contacted him to ask what had happened. He then said that his wife had mailed them to me a couple of weeks earlier, i.e., she must have mailed them sometime between the 5th and 15th of April. I have checked with our post offices and my friend's wife has tried to check with the post where they live. A problem is that she did not keep the paper with the number on which one gets from the post when mailing packets. Such number can help to track a lost packet. So our investigations have not given any results.

"So therefore I wonder if you can see where these four tapes are and whether I will eventually get them back and, if so, when will I receive them?

The Querent was the husband of one of my horary students, so that the answer I gave was also designed to help her learn how to interpret a lost item chart. It's important when examining a question to first consider what the possible scenarios may be.

In this case, the likelihood of theft was very low, while the likelihood of a problem with the post office was very high. The videos would simply not have been of use to someone else, and it's a pretty desperate thief that would be looking to fence videotapes with no value other than to re-record something

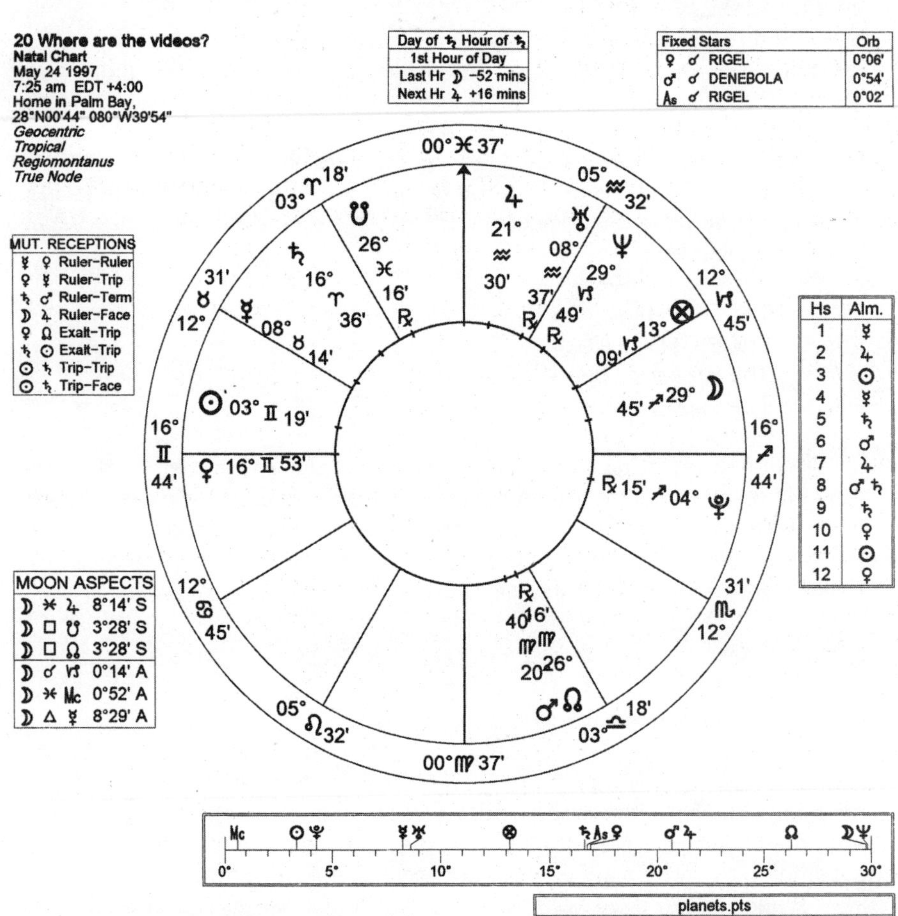

ESSENTIAL DIGNITIES (LEHMAN)								
Pt	Ruler	Exalt	Trip	Term	Face	Detri	Fall	Score
☽	♃	☋	☉	♂	♄	☿	☊	−5 p
☉	☿	☊	♄ m	☿	♃	♃	☋	−5 p
☿	♀ m	☽	♀	☿ +	☿ +	♂	--	+3
♀	☿ m	☊	♄	♀ +	♂	♃	☋	+2
♂	☿	☿	♀	♄	☿	♃	♀	−5 p
♃	♄	--	♄	♃ +	☽	☉	--	+2
♄	♂	☉	☉ m	☿	☉	♀	♄ −	−9 p
As	☿	☊	♄	♀	♂	♃	☋	--
Mc	♃	♀	♀	♀	♄	☿	☿	--
⊗	♄	♂	♀	♃	♂	☽	♃	--

planets.pts				
Pt	Long.	Travel	Antiscia	C.Ant.
☽	29°♐45'00"	+13°49'	00°♑14	00°♋14
☉	03°♊19'41"	+00°57'	26°♋40	26°♑40
☿	08°♉14	+01°02'	21°♌45	21°♒45
♀	16°♊53	+01°13'	13°♋06	13°♑06
♂	20°♍40	+00°16'	09°♈19	09°♎19
♃	21°♒30	+00°03'	08°♏29	08°♉29
♄	16°♈36	+00°05'	13°♍23	13°♓23
♅	08°♒37 ℞	−00°00'	21°♏22	21°♉22
♆	29°♑49 ℞	−00°00'	00°♐10	00°♊10
♇	04°♐15 ℞	−00°01'	25°♑44	25°♋44
☊	26°♍16 ℞	−00°09'	03°♈43	03°♎43
☋	26°♓16 ℞	−00°09'	03°♎43	03°♈43
As	16°♊44'18"	+00°00'	13°♋15	13°♑15
Mc	00°♓37'26"	+00°00'	29°♎22	29°♈22
⊗	13°♑09	+00°00'	16°♐50	16°♊50

on them! The only other possibility that I could envision was that either the videos had never been mailed in the first place, or that somehow they had been received, but in a way in which they were not recognized for what they were.

Thus, I did not feel the need to go through the considerations for theft. I began with an examination of the ruler of the second House. The ruler of the 2nd is in the 7th, and this indicates the spouse's area of the house or office as the location for the tapes. But which spouse? The late Sagittarius Moon, Void, but in one of the semi-void signs, suggests they will be found, and soon. As for their condition, with the Moon peregrine, there may be some problem with one or more of them. On the other hand, considering that Lilly considered this sign highly enough to exclude a true Void state for the Moon there, I would question how much the equation of peregrine and damaged actually applies, although with the Moon at the Bendings, it may.

I would surmise that the Querent's wife might have received the package, but not realized what it was, possibly because the labeling was unclear. Or else, the friend's wife really forgot to mail them at all, and will find a way to hand deliver them to save face. It turned out that the friend's wife did have the tapes and had never mailed them. The Querent received them back a few weeks later. This is certainly consistent with the out-of-sign application of the Moon to the trine of Mercury, although the Moon loses dignity by going into Capricorn later.

Here we can examine the arguments for location:

	Element
Ascendant	Air (Gemini)
Ruler of Ascendant	Earth (Mercury – sign ruler)
4th House Cusp	Earth (Virgo)
Ruler of 4th House	Earth (Mercury)
Moon	Fire (Sagittarius)
2nd House cusp	Water (Cancer)
Ruler of 2nd House	Fire (Moon) + Air (Jupiter Almuten)
Part of Fortune	Earth (Capricorn)

We then total the numbers:

Fire = 2
Earth = 4
Air = 2
Water = 1

This is a pretty strong argument for Earth. This would indicate that the items were in a ground floor room, on the floor, or low down in height in the room, or possibly in a place dominated by earthy colors. Unfortunately, we don't have that information in this case, although I'm tempted to think of all the people who stack things up near the front door in anticipation of mailing them!

Example 21. Where are the Textbooks?

The Querent had just attended a seminar concerning the healing technique, *Jin Shin Jyutsu* ™. She had laid her textbook manuals down somewhere in her house, or possibly at either her daughter's apartment, or her ex-husband's house.

Mars rules the 2nd house and notice also the 7th house. Mars is in a slightly wide conjunction with the fixed star Spica, although in debility and slow of course. However, Spica is one of the most benefic placements in the zodiac, and hence the conjunction does much to offset the effect of the debility. Mars in the 1st House shows it is in the room the Querent uses the most. Saturn rules the 4th, indicating low down, and dark colors. The color given by Lilly for the 1st House is white. The Querent's partner (7th House ruler is the same as the 2nd) found the books in the Querent's office in a black and white folder that was placed on top of a box on the floor approximately 15 minutes after this horary was asked.

Here's our table.

	Element
Ascendant	Air (Libra)
Ruler of Ascendant	Fire (Venus - sign ruler) + Earth (Saturn - Almuten)
4th House Cusp	Earth (Capricorn)
Ruler of 4th House	Earth (Saturn)
Moon	Earth (Virgo)
2nd House Cusp	Water (Scorpio)
Ruler of 2nd House	Air (Mars)
Part of Fortune	Fire (Sagittarius)

We then total the numbers:

Fire = 2
Earth = 4
Air = 2
Water = 1

This is an argument for Earth: low down, ground floor room, earthy tones. In Florida, there are no basements or cellars, so ground floor is as extreme as it is likely to get. In this case, the box in which the manuals were found was sitting right on the floor of the room.

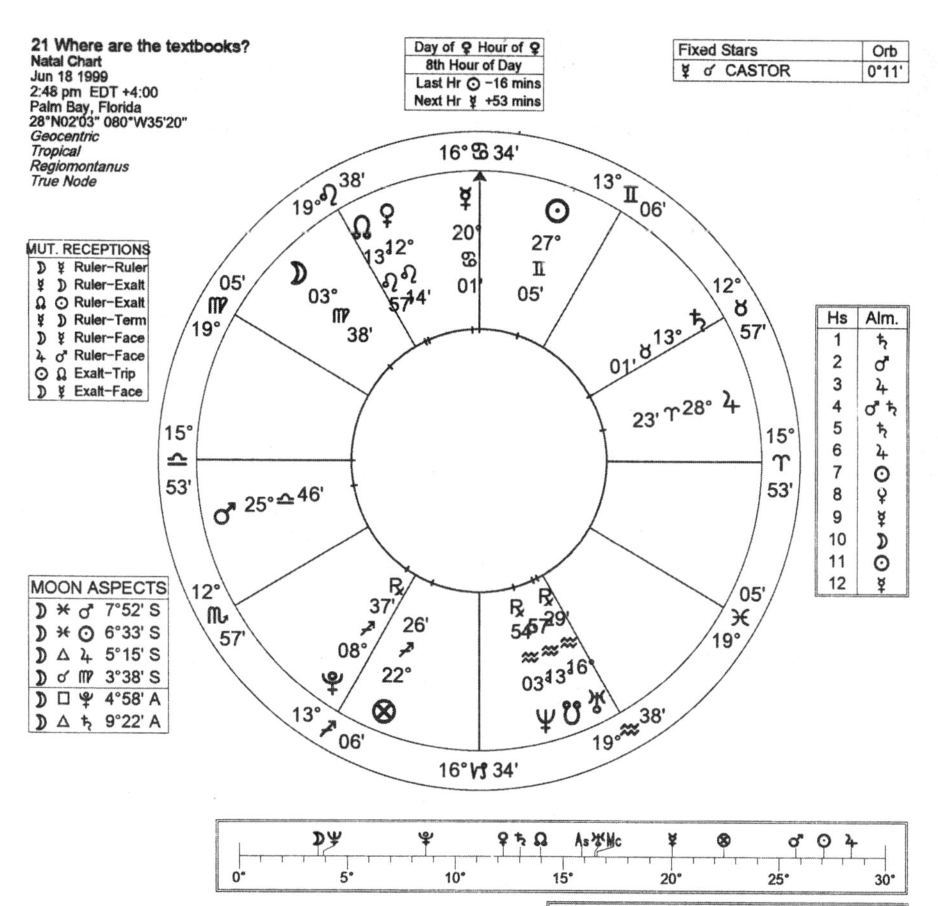

ESSENTIAL DIGNITIES (LEHMAN)								
Pt	Ruler	Exalt	Trip	Term	Face	Detri	Fall	Score
☽	☿ m	☿	♀	☿	☉	♃	♀	−5 p
☉	☿	☊	♄	♂	☉ +	♃	☋	+1
☿	☽ m	♃	♀	♀ m	☽	♄	♂	−5 p
♀	☉	--	☉	☿ m	♃ m	♄	--	−5 p
♂	♀	♄	♄	♂ +	♃	♂ −	☉	−3
♃	♂	☉	☉	♄	♀ m	♀	♄	−5 p
♄	♀	☽	♀	☿	☽	♂	--	−5 p
As	♀	♄	♄	♃	♄	♂	☉	--
Mc	☽	♃	♀	☿	☿	♄	♂	--
⊗	♃	☋	☉	♄	♄	☿	☊	--

planets.pts				
Pt	Long.	Travel	Antiscia	C.Ant.
☽	03°♍38'59"	+13°12'	26°♈21	26°♎21
☉	27°♊05'46"	+00°57'	02°♋54	02°♑54
☿	20°♋01	+01°26'	09°♊58	09°♐58
♀	12°♌14	+00°53'	17°♉45	17°♏45
♂	25°♎46	+00°10'	04°♓13	04°♍13
♃	28°♈23	+00°10'	01°♍36	01°♓36
♄	13°♉01	+00°06'	16°♌58	16°♒58
♅	16°♒29 ℞	−00°01'	13°♏30	13°♉30
♆	03°♒54 ℞	−00°01'	26°♏05	26°♉05
♇	08°♐37 ℞	−00°01'	21°♑22	21°♋22
☊	13°♌57	+00°01'	16°♉02	16°♏02
☋	13°♒57	+00°01'	16°♏02	16°♉02
As	15°♎53'12"	+00°00'	14°♓06	14°♍06
Mc	16°♋34'45"	+00°00'	13°♊25	13°♐25
⊗	22°♐26	+00°00'	07°♑33	07°♋33

Example 22. Where is my gold bracelet?

The woman who asked the question had just lost a gold bracelet valued at $2,000. As she is not a wealthy woman herself, this loss disturbed her greatly. She was a college student who shared an apartment with a friend, and typical of this circumstance, a lot of people come in and out of their apartment. Accordingly, I had to eliminate the possibility of theft before going on to examine the location of the bracelet.

Jupiter gives the Querent: retrograde in Aquarius, where it enjoys the very dubious mixed or participating Triplicity - a dignity that is useless in horary, although not in natal delineation. Again, we have the challenge of deciding upon which Significator to use for each of the possible components of this horary. We could use Venus, as natural ruler of jewelry. We could use Saturn, as Ruler of the 2nd House. Saturn is retrograde, in Fall, and Peregrine. Or we could use Mars in Detriment as Almuten. But Mars and Saturn do not sound like an expensive bracelet. Venus is in Virgo, her Fall, but she has dignity by Triplicity. This makes Venus a better candidate for representing the jewelry than Saturn. Accordingly, we need to adjust our rules to take into account the fact that we are not using the second House ruler.

The Moon and Venus are both in Virgo, with the Moon applying to Venus. This is a very good sign, one that bodes well for recovery. Mercury, the Dispositor of both the Moon and Venus, separates from only one planet, Pluto, and that some distance past. There are only two possible candidates for thief: Mars and Saturn. They are both angular, and they both behold the Descendant. However, Jupiter, ruler of the Ascendant, does not dispose Saturn, and Mars only by face. Mars separates from Jupiter, and Jupiter separates from Saturn because Jupiter is retrograde. Therefore, we have weak indication of theft, and strong indications of no theft. So we can conclude that the bracelet is not stolen.

So, if it's not stolen, where is it? The ruler of the second is in the 4th House, which is an argument that the bracelet is in the home. Venus, the natural ruler of the bracelet, is in the 9th House; and thus cadent. Given the fact that the Querent had not been on any trips lately, I tended to take the argument more strongly from the ruler of the 2nd House. A fire sign on the cusp of the 4th House is argument that the item is near fire or metal. The Querent lives in Florida, and does not have a fireplace in her apartment.

The important point for the Querent is that she would get the item back and that it was not stolen. She had contacted me at a time when I was really not in a position to study the horary closely, so I got back to her and told her that the bracelet was not stolen and that it was probably in her apartment. I told her that she would find it, but if she had any real difficulty in doing so, I would be happy to examine the chart further. As it turned out, I didn't need to, because armed with the conviction that she would find it, she searched the living room and found the bracelet down among the cushions of the couch. The couch has a metal frame. Also the Part of Fortune is near the cusp of the second house indicating that it would be found "between," behind or at the boundary of something; in this case, the cushions.

As you will see below, our table for assessing the elemental balance could have given me additional information had I taken the time to fill it out.

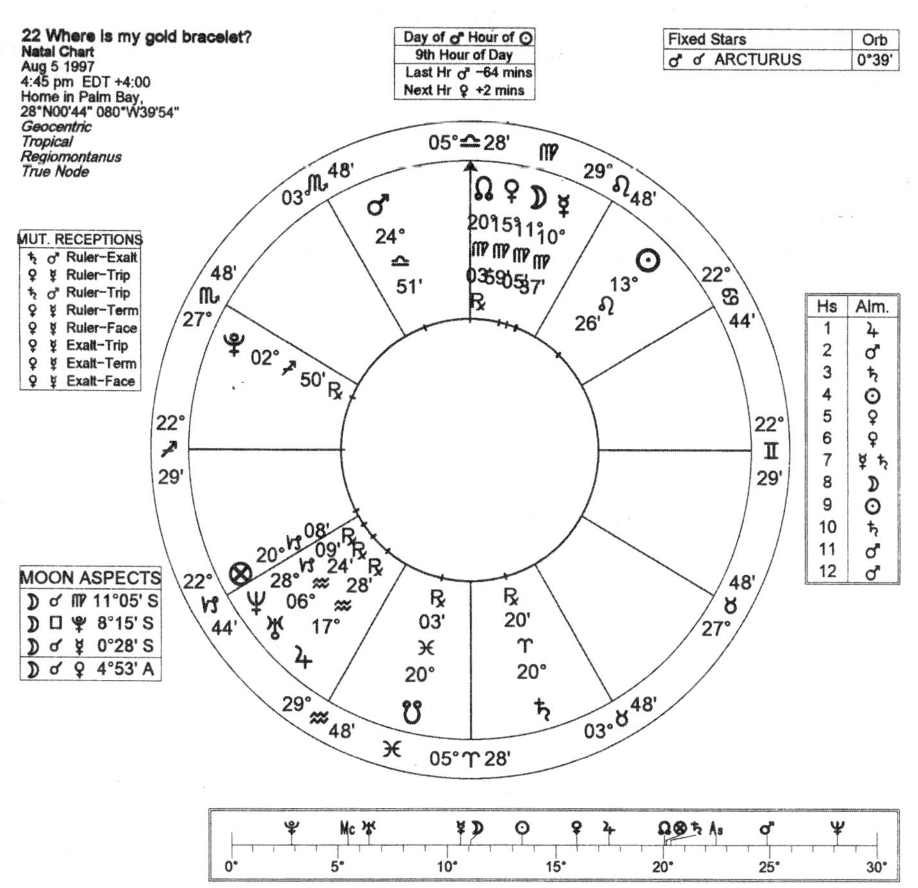

ESSENTIAL DIGNITIES (LEHMAN)								
Pt	Ruler	Exalt	Trip	Term	Face	Detri	Fall	Score
☽	☿	☿	♀	♀	♀	♃	♀	−5 p
☉	☉ +	--	☉ +	♀	♃	♄	--	+8
☿	☿ +	☿ +	♀	♀	♀	♃	♀	+9
♀	☿	☿	♀ +	♃ m	♀ +	♃	♀ −	+0
♂	♀	♄	♄	♂ +	♃	♂ −	☉	−3
♃	♄	--	♄	♀ m	☿	☉	--	−5 p
♄	♂	☉	☉	☿	♀	♀	♄ −	−9 p
As	♃	☋	☉	♄	♄	☿	☊	--
Mc	♀	♄	♄	♄	☽	♂	☉	--
⊗	♄	♂	♀	♂	☉	☽	♃	--

planets.pts				
Pt	Long.	Travel	Antiscia	C.Ant.
☽	11°♍05'45"	+11°48'	18°♈54	18°♎54
☉	13°♌26'54"	+00°57'	16°♉33	16°♏33
☿	10°♍37	+00°51'	19°♈22	19°♎22
♀	15°♍59	+01°11'	14°♈00	14°♎00
♂	24°♎51	+00°35'	05°♓08	05°♍08
♃	17°♒28 ℞	−00°07'	12°♏31	12°♉31
♄	20°♈20 ℞	−00°00'	09°♍39	09°♓39
♅	06°♒24 ℞	−00°02'	23°♏35	23°♉35
♆	28°♑09 ℞	−00°01'	01°♐50	01°♊50
♇	02°♐50 ℞	−00°00'	27°♑09	27°♋09
☊	20°♍03 ℞	−00°01'	09°♈56	09°♎56
☋	20°♓03 ℞	−00°01'	09°♎56	09°♈56
As	22°♐29'24"	+00°00'	07°♑30	07°♋30
Mc	05°♎28'10"	+00°00'	24°♓31	24°♍31
⊗	20°♑08	+00°00'	09°♐51	09°♊51

	Element
Ascendant	Fire (Sagittarius)
Ruler of Ascendant	Air (Jupiter)
4th House Cusp	Fire (Aries)
Ruler of 4th House	Air (Mars - by sign) + Fire (Sun - Almuten)
Moon	Earth (Virgo)
2nd House Cusp	Earth (Capricorn)
Ruler of 2nd House	Fire (Saturn - by sign) + Air (Saturn - Almuten)
Part of Fortune	Earth (Capricorn)

We then total the numbers:

Fire = 4
Earth = 3
Air = 3
Water = 0

This doesn't give a definitive answer *except* for eliminating the issue of being near water. This in turn eliminates the kitchen and bathroom as possible places.

Delineation Tip: *Note that while the Moon is intercepted, we didn't interpret that fact as part of the delineation. It's hard to find any classical references at all to the concept of interception.*

Example 23. Where is my cat?

The cat in question (I never got the name or sex) is an inside cat. The cat became lost when the workman who was working in the Querent's attic left the door open while changing the air conditioning filters. When the Querent returned home, she could not find her cat, and was concerned that the cat had gotten out, and then didn't know how to get back.

She had searched the immediate neighborhood to no avail, and then called me with the question The cat is given by Jupiter, ruler of the 6th House, technically peregrine, but in out-of-sect Triplicity and swift of course. The cat is in the 10th House, which means that the cat is still at home. The sign on the 4th House cusp is Libra, which suggests an upper room, thus I thought the cat was still up in the attic. Since the Querent lives in Georgia, and temperatures there can get pretty hot in the Spring, and given the number of fire indicators (since this is a cat horary, we take out the references to the 2nd and substitute the 6th) – 6th House cusp, the Ruler of the 6th, and the sign of the Moon, I suggested that she put water up in the attic because I was concerned about desiccation, but I emphasized that the cat was still in the attic.

The cat jumped down of its own accord three days later.

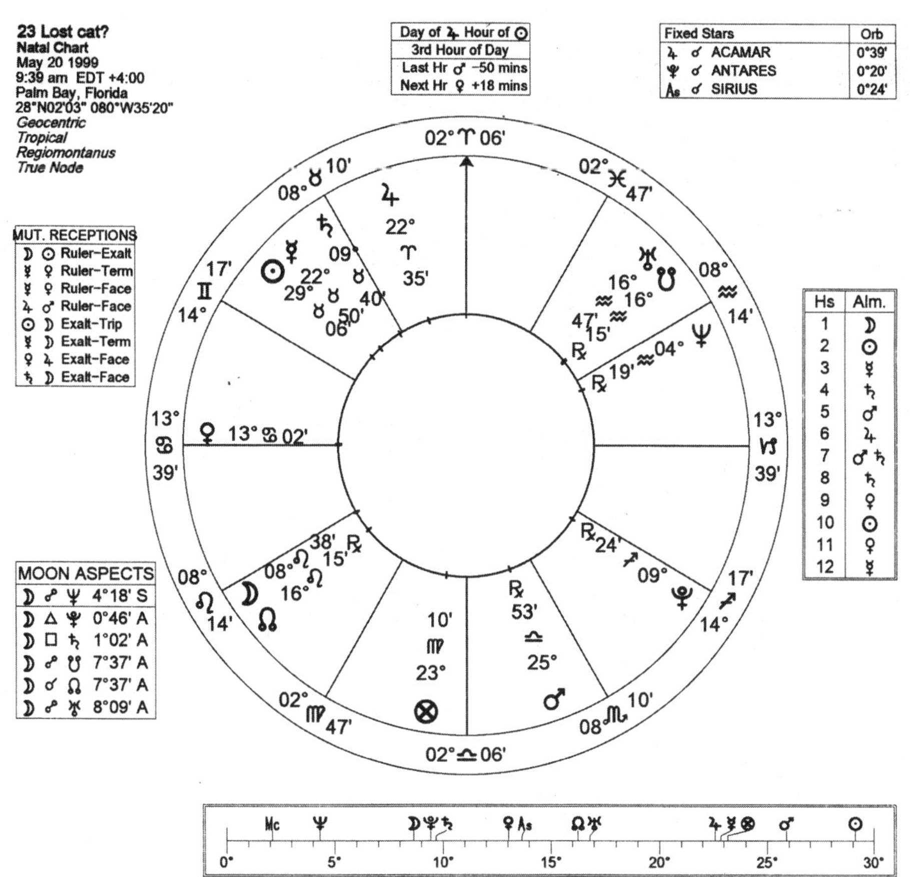

ESSENTIAL DIGNITIES (LEHMAN)								
Pt	Ruler	Exalt	Trip	Term	Face	Detri	Fall	Score
☽	☉	--	☉	☿	♄	♄	--	-5 p
☉	♀	☽	♀	♂	♄	♂	--	-5 p
☿	♀	☽	♀	♄ m	♄ m	♂	--	-5 p
♀	☽	♃	♀ +	☿	☿	♄	♂	+3
♂	♀	♄	♄	♂ +	♃	♂ -	☉	-3
♃	♂	☉	☉	♂	♀	♀	♄	-5 p
♄	♀	☽	♀	☿ m	☿ m	♂	--	-5 p
As	☽	♃	♀	☿	☿	♄	♂	--
Mc	♂	☉	☉	♃	♂	♀	♄	--
⊗	☿	☿	♀	♄	☿	♃	♀	--

planets.pts				
Pt	Long.	Travel	Antiscia	C.Ant.
☽	08°♌38'02"	+13°38'	21°♉21	21°♏21
☉	29°♉06'31"	+00°57'	00°♌53	00°♒53
☿	22°♉50	+02°07'	07°♌09	07°♒09
♀	13°♋02	+01°04'	16°♊57	16°♐57
♂	25°♎53 ℞	-00°11'	04°♓06	04°♍06
♃	22°♈35	+00°12'	07°♍24	07°♓24
♄	09°♉40	+00°07'	20°♌19	20°♒19
♅	16°♒47	+00°00'	13°♏12	13°♉12
♆	04°♒19 ℞	-00°00'	25°♏40	25°♉40
♇	09°♐24 ℞	-00°01'	20°♑35	20°♋35
☊	16°♌15 ℞	-00°00'	13°♉44	13°♏44
☋	16°♒15 ℞	-00°00'	13°♏44	13°♉44
As	13°♋39'07"	+00°00'	16°♊20	16°♐20
Mc	02°♈06'23"	+00°00'	27°♍53	27°♓53
⊗	23°♍10	+00°00'	06°♈49	06°♎49

Housing and Renovation

Among the other kinds of questions that are grouped under the 4th House are questions concerning land, houses, renovation, addition, and other changes to both structures and the property itself. Lilly also includes putting in conduits or changing the course of a river. Other applications include such matters as adding a new room, putting in a garden, constructing a deck, treating for termites, buying new appliances, or changing the electrical wiring.

It is also possible to use the 4th House to assess the condition of a house you wish to purchase. This is apart from issues concerning the sale itself, such as whether you'll get the house, or what price you might pay. The purpose here is to determine the actual quality of the house and any maintenance issues that you might have to address. This in turn can be valuable information that you may use to decide whether to purchase the house at all.

Example 24: What is the condition of Giroux?

We were considering the purchase of this house. When we viewed the house, the layout was great. There was space for two large offices, a huge eat-in kitchen, and plenty of storage space.

The two biggest misgivings we had were the location (it was not far from a small shopping center with a fire house nearby) and the absence of a swimming pool. While the latter may seem like a somewhat frivolous requirement, this was Florida, and homes with pools give owners here a much better return on their investment than those without.

We offered what we considered a fair price for the house. Later, as the witching hour approached (offers are technically only good for 24 hours, although this limitation is typically ignored), the question was asked: What is the condition of the house and property?

Notice that the question was not, *Will we get the house?* Accordingly, there is no need to consider whether there is perfection between Significators representing the buyer and the seller. As such, this is strictly a fourth House question, because the fourth House rules the house itself, and the land on which it sits.

Notice also early degrees of Sagittarius rising: it is early in the game. We made a mental note to observe later just what this "too soon" message signified.

There are four possible rulers for the house and land:

Jupiter	Sign ruler and Almuten of the 4th House	(Triplicity)
Sun	located in the 4th House	(peregrine)
Mercury	located in the 4th House	(peregrine)
Moon	located in the 4th House	(peregrine)

None of these planets, except Jupiter, had dignity.

The Sign on the 4th House cusp, as well as the sign of two of the 4th House planets, was Pisces, a water sign. The other two rulers are in Aries and Leo (i.e., the other 4th House planet, plus the Ascendant ruler), both fire signs. This strong dichotomy suggests that we may have two conditions to the house and land: hot and dry, and cold and wet.

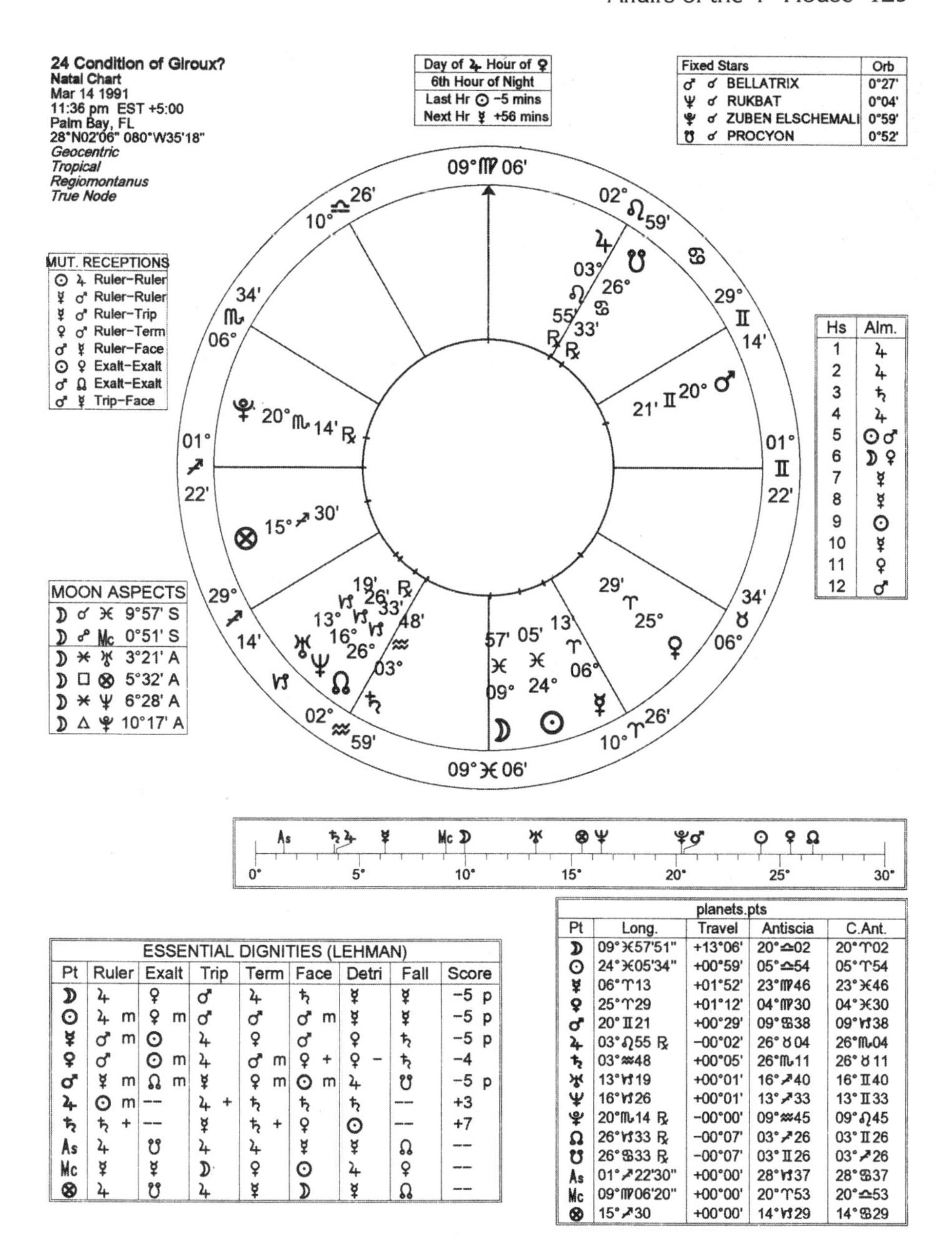

Fixed Stars	Orb
♂ ☌ BELLATRIX	0°27'
♆ ☌ RUKBAT	0°04'
♇ ☌ ZUBEN ELSCHEMALI	0°59'
☋ ☌ PROCYON	0°52'

MUT. RECEPTIONS
☉ ♃ Ruler-Ruler
☿ ♂ Ruler-Ruler
☿ ♂ Ruler-Trip
♀ ♂ Ruler-Term
♂ ☿ Ruler-Face
☉ ♀ Exalt-Exalt
♂ ☊ Exalt-Exalt
♂ ☿ Trip-Face

Hs	Alm.
1	♃
2	♃
3	♄
4	♃
5	☉♂
6	☽♀
7	☿
8	☿
9	☉
10	☿
11	♀
12	♂

MOON ASPECTS
☽ ☌ ♓ 9°57' S
☽ ☍ Mc 0°51' S
☽ ⚹ ♅ 3°21' A
☽ □ ⊗ 5°32' A
☽ ⚹ ♆ 6°28' A
☽ △ ♇ 10°17' A

ESSENTIAL DIGNITIES (LEHMAN)							
Pt	Ruler	Exalt	Trip	Term	Face	Detri	Fall	Score
☽	♃	♀	♂	♃	♄	☿	☿	-5 p
☉	♃ m	♀ m	♂	♂	♂ m	☿	☿	-5 p
☿	♂ m	☉	♃	♀	♂	♀	♄	-5 p
♀	♂	☉ m	♃	♂ m	♀ +	♀ –	♄	-4
♂	☿ m	☊ m	☿	♀ m	☉ m	♃	☋	-5 p
♃	☉ m	--	♃ +	♄	♄	♄	--	+3
♄	♄ +	--	☿	♄ +	♀	☉	--	+7
As	♃	☋	♃	♃	☿	☿	☊	--
Mc	☿	☿	☽	♀	☉	♃	♀	--
⊗	♃	☋	♃	☿	☽	☿	☊	--

planets.pts				
Pt	Long.	Travel	Antiscia	C.Ant.
☽	09°♓57'51"	+13°06'	20°♎02	20°♈02
☉	24°♓05'34"	+00°59'	05°♎54	05°♈54
☿	06°♈13	+01°52'	23°♍46	23°♓46
♀	25°♈29	+01°12'	04°♍30	04°♓30
♂	20°♊21	+00°29'	09°♋38	09°♑38
♃	03°♌55 ℞	-00°02'	26°♉04	26°♏04
♄	03°♒48	+00°05'	26°♏11	26°♉11
♅	13°♑19	+00°01'	16°♐40	16°♊40
♆	16°♑26	+00°01'	13°♐33	13°♊33
♇	20°♏14 ℞	-00°00'	09°♒45	09°♌45
☊	26°♑33 ℞	-00°07'	03°♐26	03°♊26
☋	26°♋33 ℞	-00°07'	03°♊26	03°♐26
As	01°♐22'30"	+00°00'	28°♑37	28°♋37
Mc	09°♍06'20"	+00°00'	20°♈53	20°♎53
⊗	15°♐30	+00°00'	14°♑29	14°♋29

The only cold and wet portions of the house are generally the kitchen, laundry area and the bathrooms. With the Sun in Pisces peregrine, we judged that the condition of these rooms was not so good. This didn't look much like our cursory inspection, which turned up no obvious anomalies. However, it turns out that the land is prone to flooding and heavy rain. But what was hot and dry? And what of the peregrine Moon?

The cardinal point associated with fire is East[93]. The Eastern side of the house was where the presumptive offices were located, the rooms in which we would spend the most time. Enclosing the outside porch had created one of the two "offices". Because of this, most likely the air conditioning would prove inadequate, because it had not originally been designed to be under air.

Our other concern had been the neighborhood. The 3rd House shows the neighborhood. Saturn rules the 3rd, and is located in the 3rd, dignified, but opposite Jupiter. Jupiter will oppose Saturn before turning direct. There is an opposition between the house and the neighborhood. In other words, our surmise about the neighborhood being a bit problematic was correct. The house was located midway in the block of a dead-end street. The very large house at the endpoint of the cul-de-sac was in very poor condition. The residents had let the house go into disrepair.

The horary basically confirmed most of our assumptions about the house, as well as pointing out one potential problem in the air conditioning. We decided not to proceed with the purchase.

Buried Treasure

I have only had two instances of this type of question in my practice, and I don't know what happened in either case, so I can only relate the teachings in this matter. Lilly distinguished a couple of different scenarios.

- If the Querent hid or buried his or her own treasure, so to speak, then the chart is read using a variation on the rules for lost objects, i.e., with the treasure represented as the 2nd House. Before the reader declares this a bit farfetched, one of the two horaries that I have done was precisely this scenario: a family burying their valuables in the wake of the Russian Revolution, and an ancestor wondering whether any of the treasure was still recoverable.

- The other case was for treasure of what we might call an anonymous nature: who buried it is unknown; the question is whether there is anything of value to recover. There is if there are planets in the 4th unimpeded. If there are no planets in the 4th, then the Ruler of the 4th is judged along with the Ruler of the 7th House for the quality of the treasure, which is taken from the nature of the Significator as well as its sign and dignity.

- Recovery is gauged from an applying aspect between the Significator of the treasure and the Ruler of the Querent.

The rules for buried treasure can also be applied to questions concerning ore deposits or other underground assets that may be present on a piece of property.

Removal

It is really difficult to decide where to take up this topic, because not one, but three houses are involved: the 1st, 4th, and 7th.[94] Here's the way the houses share in the decision:

- The 1st House relates to staying in the place that one currently occupies.
- The 4th House represents one's current abode.
- The 7th house represents either moving or the place one wishes to go to.

Actually the logic applies in the same fashion whether the question is a temporary move or permanent one. There are three major methods of comparison to evaluate the two options of staying or going. The first possibility is to compare the relative dignity of the different rulers. The second possibility is to examine house placements, for example the ruler of the Ascendant in the 7th House is an argument that the Querent will in fact go. The third factor that should always be mentioned is to see whether the angles are in fixed signs. If the angles are fixed, then it is unlikely that any movement will take place. If the Significators for staying and going are of roughly equal strength, then the real answer is that it doesn't matter.

Example 25: Better to move for sake of daughter's education?

The Querent is understandably concerned about her daughter's education. Her daughter is in primary school, and Mom wants her to have the best possible opportunity. The interpretation of this chart depends on being very clear about when to use derived houses for clarification of the interpretation.

The Ascendant is ruled by the Sun, exalted in Aries. A dignified, if retrograde Mars rules the fourth house. A fast but peregrine Saturn rules the 7th House. Furthermore, there are fixed signs on the angles. The alternative of moving as represented by the 7th house certainly does not look appealing! It also does not look likely in any case because of the fixed angles. Let's examine this situation a little more closely to see exactly why this might be. The fifth house ruler, Jupiter in Aries, gives the Querent's daughter. Jupiter has out-of-sect dignity - it is weakened by combustion, although the Sun renders its virtue, reducing the debility of the combustion. The daughter's education is given by the third from the fifth house: the 7th House. The only reason that they would consider moving is for the daughter's education, therefore the poor condition of Saturn argues strongly that the private school in the new location would not provide her with the education her parents desire.

Can we draw conclusions based on the fact that Mars, the Significator of their home, is retrograde? Because the horary question was couched as a move between cities, it's possible that the retrograde may indicate either moving within the existing city, to another place a short distance away, or even ultimately to someplace completely different. The mutual reception between the Sun and Mars is technically weak, since Mars is in the Sun's Face. But perhaps this shows some fear that they won't be able to get a house or property as good as the one they have, if they are forced to move: a weak, but a possibly contributing argument in the equation! However, the fixed angles suggest that any move is not likely in the near future. They did not move.

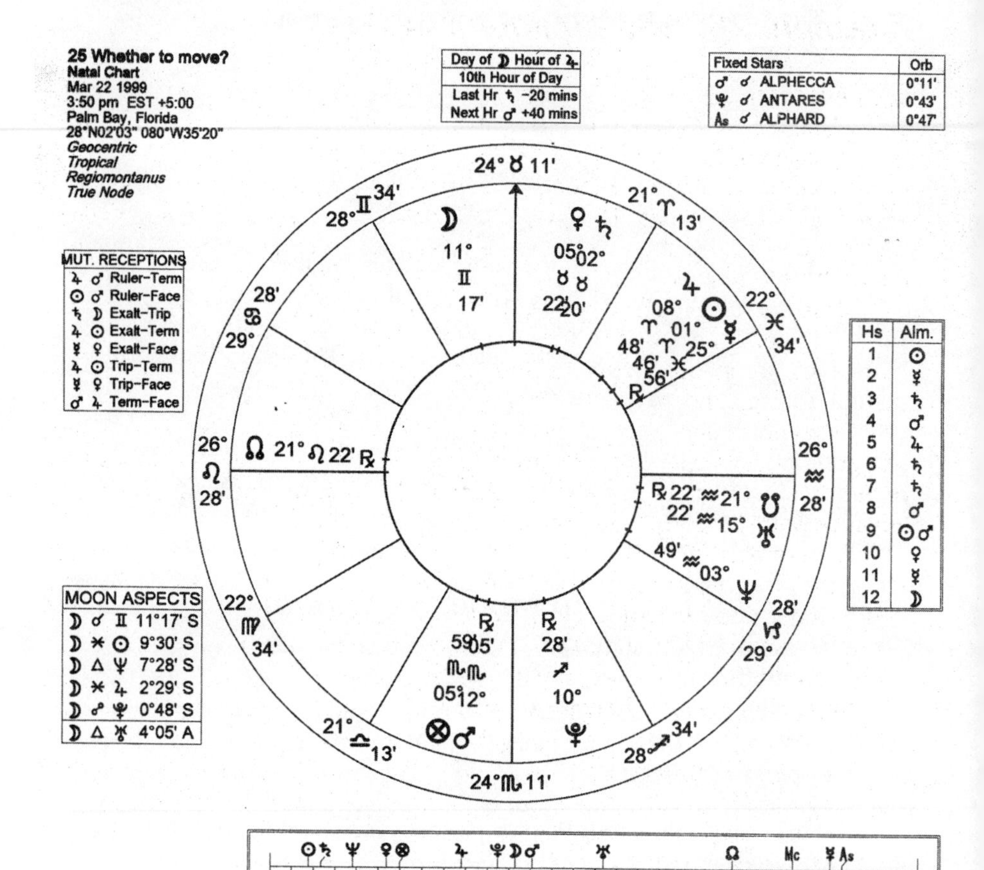

ESSENTIAL DIGNITIES (LEHMAN)								
Pt	Ruler	Exalt	Trip	Term	Face	Detri	Fall	Score
☽	☿	☊	♄	♃	♂	♃	☋	−5 p
☉	♂	☉ +	☉ +	♃	♂ m	♀	♄	+7
☿	♃	♀	♀	♂	♂	☿ −	☿ −	−14 p
♀	♀ +	☽	♀ +	♀ +	☿	♂	---	+10
♂	♂ +	---	♀	♃	☉ m	♀	☽	+5
♃	♂	☉	☉	♀	♂	♀	♄	−5 p
♄	♀	☽	♀	♀	☿	♂	---	−5 p
As	☉	---	☉	♂	♂	♄	---	---
Mc	♀	☽	♀	♄	♄	♂	---	---
⊗	♂	---	♀	♂	♂	♀	☽	---

planets.pts				
Pt	Long.	Travel	Antiscia	C.Ant.
☽	11°♊17'18"	+14°20'	18°♋42	18°♑42
☉	01°♈46'56"	+00°59'	28°♍13	28°♓13
☿	25°♓56 ℞	−00°52'	04°♎03	04°♈03
♀	05°♉22	+01°12'	24°♌37	24°♒37
♂	12°♏05 ℞	−00°03'	17°♒54	17°♌54
♃	08°♈48	+00°14'	21°♍11	21°♓11
♄	02°♉20	+00°06'	27°♌39	27°♒39
♅	15°♒22	+00°02'	14°♏37	14°♉37
♆	03°♒49	+00°01'	26°♏10	26°♉10
♇	10°♐28 ℞	−00°00'	19°♑31	19°♋31
☊	21°♌22 ℞	−00°02'	08°♉37	08°♏37
☋	21°♒22 ℞	−00°02'	08°♏37	08°♉37
As	26°♌28'44"	+00°00'	03°♉31	03°♏31
Mc	24°♉11'43"	+00°00'	05°♌48	05°♒48
⊗	05°♏59	+00°00'	24°♒00	24°♌00

Example 26: Shall we Remove?

One of the advantages of being a horary astrologer is knowing that one can ask certain kinds of questions. In Lilly's time, one of the issues that he had to consider was that bubonic plague still stalked England. In those frightening days, it was generally recognized that it was safer to go to the country than to stay in one's town house. Thus, when Lilly delineated questions having to do with removal to the countryside, there was often an edge of life and death about the interpretation.

Disasters still occur today, even though most of us live our lives as if this were not true. Considering how many people live in areas that are affected by hurricanes, tornadoes, floods, earthquakes, mudslides, and a host of other natural disasters, not to mention human-induced catastrophes such as environmental poisoning, it becomes obvious that this sort of question has really not gone out of style. In my household, we have asked this question with regard to such matters as California earthquakes and whether evacuation in advance of major hurricanes and fires was a wise move.

The example given here was asked because my partner was concerned about the news reports concerning the launch of the satellite Cassini. Cassini had a larger nuclear payload then anything that had been launched previously. We live only 40 minutes from Cape Canaveral, so had there been any problem with the launch, we would have been right in the zone for possible nuclear contamination. Granted, the possibility was remote but the question becomes: how much risk do you want to add to your life when you are receiving no potential benefit for the added risk? It was in that spirit that the question was asked.

The first thing that is obvious upon gazing at the chart is that the angles are in fixed signs. Already, we've barely spent 10 seconds on the chart and we almost have the answer. But let's try to confirm our initial impression. Venus rules the first, and Venus is peregrine. The Sun rules the 4th House and it is both peregrine and in its Fall. Mars rules the 7th, and it is fast but peregrine. Clearly, none of the Significators has any dignity, and as a result, there's no strong argument to do anything at all.

In examining the chart a little more closely, we begin to see an indicator for why this might be true. What house would we use to designate the launch? I would pick the 9th House, since this is about as distant a journey as we are capable of as a species. The ninth house is ruled by a very debilitated Saturn: retrograde, in the 12th House and in Fall. Among other things, Saturn rules delays, and being retrograde, I strongly suspected that the launch would not get off on the first attempt anyway. As a result, this horary was being asked for the wrong time period! This turned out to be the case. The first launch window did not produce a launch.

About Saturn in this chart. Its condition looks dreadful. Does this mean that the mission is doomed? Not necessarily. One sees fire signs as kind of a natural ruler for launches – after all, they are explosions. Since Saturn is not angular, I suspected that what this really meant was that this would be an average or mediocre mission. So far, this seems to be the case.

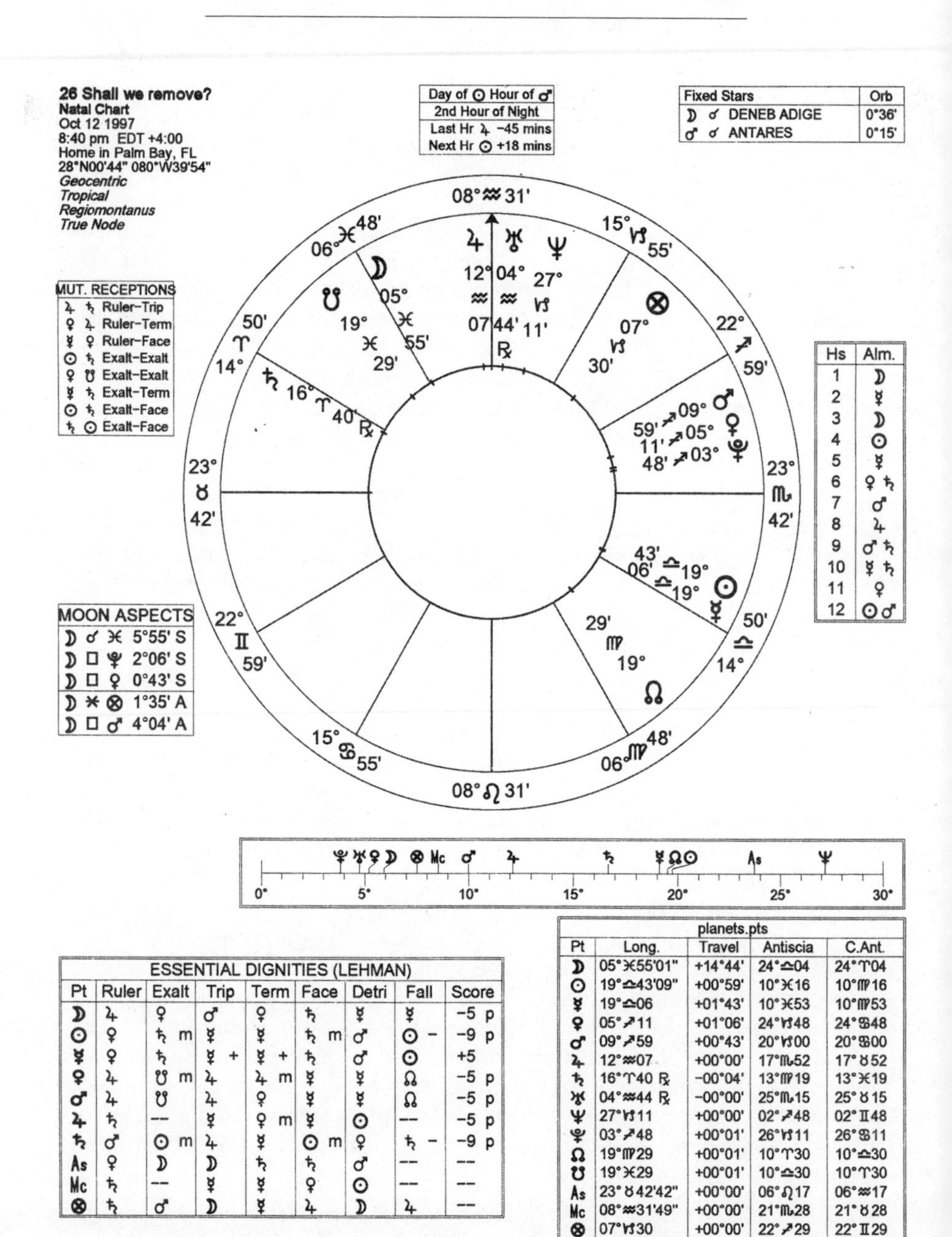

Pt	Ruler	Exalt	Trip	Term	Face	Detri	Fall	Score
ESSENTIAL DIGNITIES (LEHMAN)								
☽	♃	♀	♂	♀	♄	☿	☿	-5 p
☉	♀	♄ m	☿	☿	♄ m	♂	☉ -	-9 p
☿	♀	♄	☿ +	☿ +	♄	♂	☉	+5
♀	♃	☋ m	♃	♃ m	☿	☿	☊	-5 p
♂	♃	☋	♃	♀	☿	☿	☊	-5 p
♃	♄	—	☿	♀ m	☿	☉	—	-5 p
♄	♂	☉ m	♃	☿	☉ m	♀	♄ -	-9 p
As	♀	☽	☽	♄	♄	♂	—	—
Mc	♄	—	☿	☿	♀	☉	—	—
⊗	♄	♂	☽	☿	♃	☽	♃	—

Pt	Long.	Travel	Antiscia	C.Ant.
planets.pts				
☽	05°♓55'01"	+14°44'	24°♎04	24°♈04
☉	19°♎43'09"	+00°59'	10°♓16	10°♍16
☿	19°♎06	+01°43'	10°♓53	10°♍53
♀	05°♐11	+01°06'	24°♑48	24°♋48
♂	09°♐59	+00°43'	20°♑00	20°♋00
♃	12°♒07	+00°00'	17°♏52	17°♉52
♄	16°♈40 ℞	-00°04'	13°♍19	13°♓19
♅	04°♒44 ℞	-00°00'	25°♏15	25°♉15
♆	27°♑11	+00°00'	02°♐48	02°♊48
♇	03°♐48	+00°01'	26°♑11	26°♋11
☊	19°♍29	+00°01'	10°♈30	10°♎30
☋	19°♓29	+00°01'	10°♎30	10°♈30
As	23°♉42'42"	+00°00'	06°♌17	06°♒17
Mc	08°♒31'49"	+00°00'	21°♏28	21°♉28
⊗	07°♑30	+00°00'	22°♐29	22°♊29

Chapter Five

Affairs of the 5th House:

Sex, Children, Agents, the Stock Market, and other Gambling.

Questions of the 5th House as given by Gadbury:[95]

- *Whether a Woman shall have children?*
- *In what time may she conceive?*
- *If a Woman enquiring be with child?*
- *If she be impregnated of a Boy or Girle?*
- *Shall she have Twins?*
- *When will the birth be?*

Additional Questions of the 5th House as given by Lilly:[96]

- *Whether the Querent shall have Children, be he Man or Woman that asketh?*
- *If a Man shall have Children by his Wife yea or not, or of any other Woman whom he nominates.*
- *Whether Unity is like to be betwixt the Infant and the Parent, or betwixt the Parent and any of his Children of elder Yeers.*
- *Ambassadors and Messengers*
- *Sending for someone to collect payment*

The 5th House has several rather disparate uses – pregnancy and children, pleasure, and representation to another party. I have found that this is one house where the old rules are not an entirely happy fit, and where there has been a substantial shift in emphasis and importance of the questions. The reason for this shift is fairly obvious: people are simply not having children in the quantity that was typical in the absence of birth control. It is now almost impossible to even imagine how the fear of pregnancy could actually control behavior – sometimes. Now, we are more likely to fear disease. As longevity has increased, the assumption in the more developed areas of the world is that any child born will live to old age. This is not completely the case, but it is much truer than in Lilly's day.

As a result of the change in infant mortality, it is generally not necessary to worry about having multiple sons – and in societies where girls inherit as readily as boys, the gender mix has become less critical – at least among those people who do not belong to religious or ethnic groups that have maintained traditional sexist views.

Thus, I find myself receiving comparatively few questions concerning pregnancy. Modern questions about pregnancy have a different slant, as will be obvious in the following section.

Matters of Pregnancy

Because infertility seems to have increased in rather mysterious ways, questions of conception often extend beyond "Will we be able to have a child?" to "Which of us needs fertility treatment?" For this question to work, it's necessary to careful about the wording of the question in such a way that *one* of the couple asks the question – otherwise the "we" of the plural Querents makes it impossible to separate the woman's and the man's biological contributions to the total process. This may not be as simple as it sounds – the person who calls with the Question cannot automatically be assumed to be the Querent if the couple is already experiencing doubts or suspicions about the possible nature of the infertility. The astrologer needs to be very clear about this before taking the question.

What makes for a successful conception, from a horary perspective?

- Predominance of fruitful signs (see below) associated with the 1st and 5th Houses.

- An association by aspect, translation, antiscion , rendering, collection or possibly reception between the Ruler of the Ascendant or the Moon and the Ruler of the 5th House. The more direct and the closer the association, the sooner the pregnancy comes to pass. As for reception, it is seldom sufficient unless it's by sign, exaltation or Triplicity; where the two planets in the reception have dignity apart from the reception.

- The Moon or the Ruler of the 5th in the 1st, or the Ruler of the 1st in the 5th.

- An approaching aspect between the planet from whom the Moon separates with the planet to whom the Moon applies, provided that they are both in good dignity and free from affliction.

- Lilly allowed for the Ruler of the 1st in the 7th as an affirmative if a woman asked the question; I can only take this as signifying that the woman would please her husband. These days, I'm not always certain that an announcement of pregnancy is necessarily pleasing, so I would be reluctant to use this argument on its own.

- Finally, the barren signs should not assume prominence in the chart. The barren signs are Gemini, Leo and Virgo in Lilly's list.

I have not found Lilly's list to work as well as Partridge's.[97] Partridge classifies the signs in the following table.

Aries	Barren
Taurus	More fruitful than barren
Gemini	Barren
Cancer	Very fruitful
Leo	Barren
Virgo	Barren except in matters intellectual
Libra	Rather fruitful
Scorpio	Fruitful but less so
Sagittarius	Rather fruitful
Capricorn	Barren
Aquarius	Barren
Pisces	Most fruitful

Example 27: Will my wife get pregnant? Where is the problem?

This Question was asked because the couple had been trying for some time to have a child, and they were uncertain about whether there was a fertility issue blocking their effort.

Mercury, ruler of the 1st, and hence, the Querent, is in a fertile sign, swift, but dignified only by Face. The Querent is definitely anxious about the question, the typical state for a planet with only Face. The fear given by Face alone is akin to the belief that this is the last chance: if it doesn't work this time, it's never going to work. His wife is Jupiter, ruler of 7th House, posited in the 10th, also in a fertile sign. This fact already suggests that neither of them is infertile, so the problem is most likely transient in nature.

The Moon is swift and in fertile Taurus, and Venus, ruler of the 5th, likewise in fertile Taurus, is coming to sextile Jupiter in 2 degrees. So I told him that they could expect a pregnancy within two months.

Mercury, the husband's actual Significator, is in fertile Cancer. But Mars is rising in Gemini, so I see pregnancy ultimately, but the temporary problem is on the husband's side. Mars in Gemini is in a barren sign. Also, Mercury is to be sextiled by the Moon. The Moon is fast, and Mercury is in an angular house, which argues for a faster conclusion. Note also that Pluto is in 6th, with Mars separating – perhaps the problem may have passed its peak. Again, Descen-

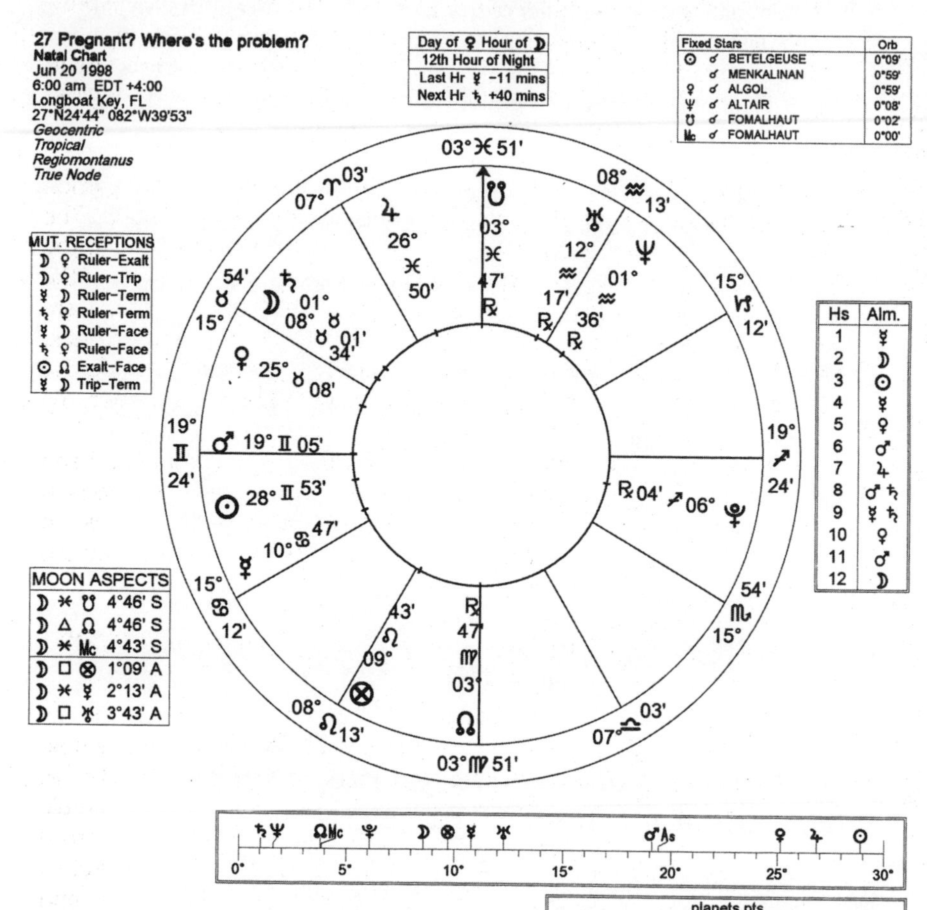

ESSENTIAL DIGNITIES (LEHMAN)								
Pt	Ruler	Exalt	Trip	Term	Face	Detri	Fall	Score
☽	♀	☽ +	☽ +	☿	☿	♂	--	+7
☉	☿	☊	☿	♂	☉ +	♃	☋	+1
☿	☽	♃	♂ m	♃	☿ +	♄	♂	+1
♀	♀ +	☽	☽	♄ m	♄	♂	--	+5
♂	☿	☊	☿ m	♀	♂ +	♃	☋	+1
♃	♃ +	♀	♂	♄	♂	☿	☿	+5
♄	♀	☽	☽	♀ m	☿	♂	--	-5 p
As	☿	☊	☿	♀	♂	♃	☋	--
Mc	♃	♀	♂	♀	♄	☿	☿	--
⊗	☉	--	♃	☿	♄	♄	--	--

planets.pts				
Pt	Long.	Travel	Antiscia	C.Ant.
☽	08°♉34'06"	+14°29'	21°♌25	21°♒25
☉	28°♊53'04"	+00°57'	01°♋06	01°♑06
☿	10°♋47	+02°00'	19°♊12	19°♐12
♀	25°♉08	+01°10'	04°♌51	04°♒51
♂	19°♊05	+00°41'	10°♋54	10°♑54
♃	26°♓50	+00°05'	03°♎09	03°♈09
♄	01°♉01	+00°05'	28°♌58	28°♒58
♅	12°♒17 ℞	-00°01'	17°♏42	17°♉42
♆	01°♒36 ℞	-00°01'	28°♏23	28°♉23
♇	06°♐04 ℞	-00°01'	23°♑55	23°♋55
☊	03°♍47 ℞	-00°06'	26°♈12	26°♎12
☋	03°♓47 ℞	-00°06'	26°♎12	26°♈12
As	19°♊24'25"	+00°00'	10°♋35	10°♑35
Mc	03°♓51'02"	+00°00'	26°♎08	26°♈08
⊗	09°♌43	+00°00'	20°♉16	20°♏16

dant ruler Jupiter was squared by the Sun in the 1st House 2 degrees before – again, the angularity argues for two weeks – or even days – ago.

I was wrong: it wasn't two months, it was two weeks! The Moon actually gave the hint, by coming to sextile Jupiter in a unit of 18: 18 days is pretty close to two weeks. And she delivered a very healthy Aries son the next year.

While we are on the subject of pregnancy, let me mention that a common question in Lilly's day was concerning the gender of an unborn child. The assessment was done by counting up the signs and planets assigned to the Ascendant cusp, Ruler of the Ascendant, 5th house cusp, and the Ruler of the 5th house, and then classifying them by gender (the earth and water signs are female; the fire and air signs are male; the Moon and Venus are female; Mars, Sun, Jupiter and Saturn are male; Mercury vacillates) and counting up the indicators. I have not been entirely pleased with this method. As a result, my typical answer is to suggest ultrasound.

In a similar vein, it was common to ask how long the woman had been pregnant, or when she would deliver. I would prefer to defer these questions to the health care personnel working with the woman. Thus, the only question apart from fertility that I commonly receive is concerning whether or not the pregnancy will be completed with a live birth.

Example 28: Will we be able to have another child?

The husband also asked this question. His wife is a physician, and they were both living lives of perpetual stress. Notice that the most fertile axis possible is on the Ascendant-Descendant: Scorpio and Taurus. Furthermore, his ruler, Mars, is swift and in fertile Cancer; her ruler, Venus, is also in fertile Cancer. The two bodies even conjoin; in less than two degrees, which is probably two months, since the conjunction occurs in a cadent house. The actual date of the conjunction was September 3rd. The signs on the Ascendant and Descendant were actually the Sun signs of the husband and wife.

The 5th House cusp was also a fertile sign. Fertility at the time of the question and in the immediate aftermath should not be a problem. But there were a few things about this chart not to like. The first is that nasty retrograde Saturn in Fall in the 5th House itself. Normally, I think of Saturn associated with the 5th as being a severe case of contraception. Its placement here as well as its debility at the very least suggests that this would be the last child – if not the last chance at conception! The alternate reading is one that the Astrologer simply doesn't want to have to delineate – a problem with any child conceived.

The 5th House ruler is Jupiter. Jupiter is also in Fall, and retrograde, like Saturn, and disposed by Saturn. While Jupiter applies to the square of Saturn, it refrains from actually squaring by turning direct a week later. Furthermore, Jupiter is at the Bendings. But the poor condition of both the ruler of the 5th and a planet in the 5th definitely shows a problem relating to conception or childbearing – as would the poor condition of the Ascendant ruler as well. I did not know it at the time, but his wife had miscarried three times! They were engaged in a rigorous schedule of temperature-taking and sex on command, which was stressful, and anything but fun.

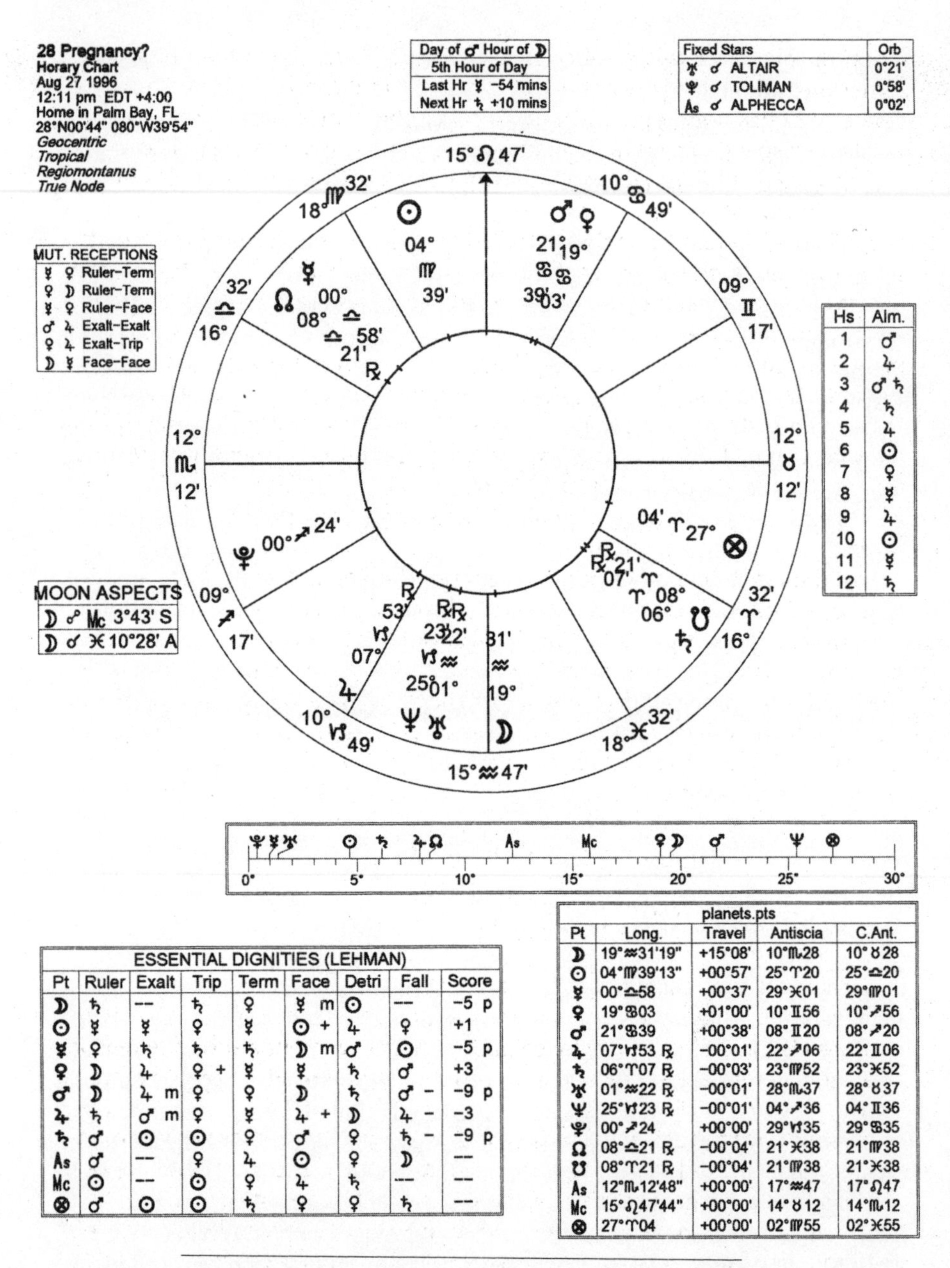

Fixed Stars	Orb
♅ ☌ ALTAIR	0°21'
♇ ☌ TOLIMAN	0°58'
As ☌ ALPHECCA	0°02'

MUT. RECEPTIONS
☿ ♀ Ruler-Term
♀ ☽ Ruler-Term
☿ ♀ Ruler-Face
♂ ♃ Exalt-Exalt
♀ ♃ Exalt-Trip
☽ ☿ Face-Face

Hs	Alm.
1	♂
2	♃
3	♂ ♄
4	♄
5	♃
6	☉
7	♀
8	☿
9	♃
10	☉
11	☿
12	♄

MOON ASPECTS
☽ ☍ Mc 3°43' S
☽ ☌ ♓ 10°28' A

ESSENTIAL DIGNITIES (LEHMAN)								
Pt	Ruler	Exalt	Trip	Term	Face	Detri	Fall	Score
☽	♄	---	♄	♀	☿ m	☉	---	−5 p
☉	☿	☿	♀	☿	☉ +	♃	♀	+1
☿	♀	♄	♄	♄	☽ m	♂	☉	−5 p
♀	☽	♃	♀ +	☿	☿	♄	♂	+3
♂	☽	♃ m	♀	♀	☽	♄	♂ −	−9 p
♃	♄	♂ m	♀	☿	♃ +	☽	♃ −	−3
♄	♂	☉	☉	♀	♂	♀	♄ −	−9 p
As	♂	---	♀	♃	☉	♀	☽	---
Mc	☉	---	☉	♀	♃	♄	---	---
⊗	♂	☉	☉	♄	♀	♀	♄	---

planets.pts				
Pt	Long.	Travel	Antiscia	C.Ant.
☽	19°♒31'19"	+15°08'	10°♏28	10°♉28
☉	04°♍39'13"	+00°57'	25°♈20	25°♎20
☿	00°♎58	+00°37'	29°♓01	29°♍01
♀	19°♋03	+01°00'	10°♊56	10°♐56
♂	21°♋39	+00°38'	08°♊20	08°♐20
♃	07°♑53 ℞	−00°01'	22°♐06	22°♊06
♄	06°♈07 ℞	−00°03'	23°♍52	23°♓52
♅	01°♒22 ℞	−00°01'	28°♏37	28°♉37
♆	25°♑23 ℞	−00°01'	04°♐36	04°♊36
♇	00°♐24	+00°00'	29°♑35	29°♋35
☊	08°♎21 ℞	−00°04'	21°♓38	21°♍38
☋	08°♈21 ℞	−00°04'	21°♍38	21°♓38
As	12°♏12'48"	+00°00'	17°♒47	17°♌47
Mc	15°♌47'44"	+00°00'	14°♉12	14°♏12
⊗	27°♈04	+00°00'	02°♍55	02°♓55

I further considered that the swift Moon would change signs to fertile Pisces in a bit more than 10 (weeks)? This should be a good sign for fertility, but almost just as soon as the Moon changes sign, she squares Pluto. Not good!

Combining all these factors together, I told him the window was from the time of the question through October, into the 1st week of November, but that after that time, it might not be possible to have another child.

Unfortunately, I was all too right! They had a son the following June. But the Querent died unexpectedly in November 1996, almost exactly when the

Moon of this chart was symbolically squaring Pluto! The Querent's sister remembers him telling her about this chart, and that I had said to him: you can conceive a child between August and October, but then nothing - no more!

In retrospect, can we find the Querent's death in this chart? I will be showing a horary that he asked me a week before he died in our 8th House chapter. But obviously, who thinks to look for this when someone asks you about having a child – I certainly don't! Yes, we can find some hints: Jupiter, Ruler of the 5th, at the Bendings and square Saturn conjunct the South Node. But this can just as easily be a warning about no more children. Further, this chart contains a very good argument for using the Dorothean Triplicity Rulers (for day and night) compared to the Lilly ones. They only differ for the water signs. In Lilly's system, Mars is both the day and night Ruler of the water signs, while in the Dorothean system, Venus is the daytime Ruler. The Dorothean system gives the wife as the stronger of the two: Venus in Cancer in Triplicity, with Mars in Cancer for the husband – no points of dignity, and also being in Fall. This shows him in a much weaker condition, while Lilly's Triplicities would show the reverse.

And there is one other oddity: the mutual *de*ception of Mars and Jupiter (the Querent and the presumptive child). While each of the two Significators is in each other's Exaltation, making this a strong reception indeed, each planet is in its own Fall. The two come together – the man contributes to producing the child – but what is the cost? The symbolic square of the Moon to Pluto does show the timing, but I wouldn't want to use that as an indicator in another horary. I have to conclude that while the chart laid down three tantalizing hints, it was the kind that could only be fully understood in retrospect. I often suspect that there are simply some things we aren't supposed to know in advance, and when this is the case, the chart simply won't tell us about it.

Example 29: Will Karen carry to term?

The potential child's grandmother asked this question, so we have to establish which house to use for Karen. She is the Querent's daughter-in-law, so Karen is the 11th ; the 7th House partner of the Querent's son. The reason that the Querent asked the question was because Karen has a thyroid problem.

Venus rules the eleventh House. Venus rules the throat, which is where the thyroids are located. Venus is in detriment in Aries, and peregrine as well. Karen's health (remember that health is the first House, while disease is the sixth; since this is Karen's health, the house in question is the eleventh) is therefore damaged, so this confirms the scenario we were given.

Karen's child would be her fifth House, which in the radical chart is the 3rd House. The House cusp is Virgo, a barren sign, the ruler, Mercury is also in a barren sign, swift, as well as being Under the Sun's Beams, and separating from a conjunction to Saturn. The child is not in good condition. Karen's Ascendant was in the fertile sign of Taurus (she was pregnant, after all), but its dispositor the Aries Venus is barren.

Since we know that Karen has health problems, we need to examine her 6th. Her 6th House is the radical 4th. The Almuten of the 4th House is Saturn, which is dignified in Aquarius. This is effectively saying that her disease is

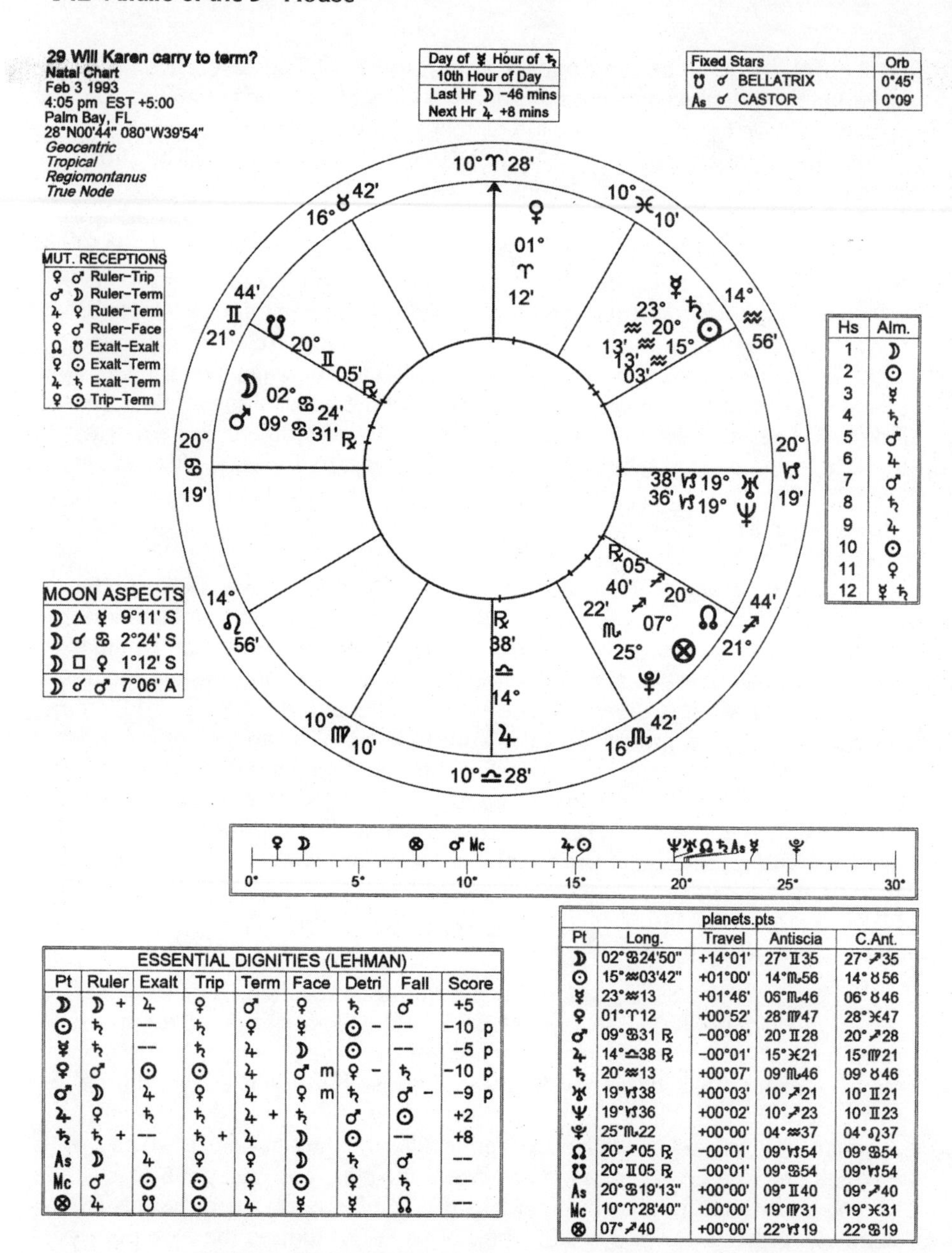

ESSENTIAL DIGNITIES (LEHMAN)								
Pt	Ruler	Exalt	Trip	Term	Face	Detri	Fall	Score
☽	☽ +	♃	♀	♂	♀	♄	♂	+5
☉	♄	---	♄	♀	☿	☉ -	---	-10 p
☿	♄	---	♄	♃	☽	☉	---	-5 p
♀	♂	☉	☉	♃	♂ m	♀ -	♄	-10 p
♂	☽	♃	♀	♃	♀ m	♄	♂ -	-9 p
♃	♀	♄	♄	♃ +	♄	♂	☉	+2
♄	♄ +	---	♄ +	♃	☽	☉	---	+8
As	☽	♃	♀	♀	☽	♄	♂	---
Mc	♂	☉	☉	♀	☉	♀	♄	---
⊗	♃	☋	☉	♃	☿	☿	☊	---

planets.pts				
Pt	Long.	Travel	Antiscia	C.Ant.
☽	02°♋24'50"	+14°01'	27°♊35	27°♐35
☉	15°♒03'42"	+01°00'	14°♏56	14°♉56
☿	23°♒13	+01°46'	06°♏46	06°♉46
♀	01°♈12	+00°52'	28°♍47	28°♓47
♂	09°♋31 ℞	-00°08'	20°♊28	20°♐28
♃	14°♎38 ℞	-00°01'	15°♓21	15°♍21
♄	20°♒13	+00°07'	09°♏46	09°♉46
♅	19°♑38	+00°03'	10°♐21	10°♊21
♆	19°♑36	+00°02'	10°♐23	10°♊23
♇	25°♏22	+00°00'	04°♒37	04°♌37
☊	20°♐05 ℞	-00°01'	09°♑54	09°♋54
☋	20°♊05 ℞	-00°01'	09°♋54	09°♑54
As	20°♋19'13"	+00°00'	09°♊40	09°♐40
Mc	10°♈28'40"	+00°00'	19°♍31	19°♓31
⊗	07°♐40	+00°00'	22°♑19	22°♋19

stronger than she is (6th is stronger than 1st). Mercury, ruler of the child (the turned 5th, or the radical 3rd), had separated from Saturn, but was approaching a square to Pluto.

All these factors indicated that there was no sign of improvement in the near future, and that the child was in danger. I told the Querent that Karen would not carry to term. Later that month, her health problems worsened, and they elected to abort the pregnancy.

Example 30: Will I carry this pregnancy to term?

The circumstances surrounding this question were considerably different than the last example. Karen had an identifiable health problem which could – and did – endanger the pregnancy. In this case, the Querent already has two children, and believes in what we could call high intensity parenting – she will do anything for her kids, and spends a considerable amount of time on them.

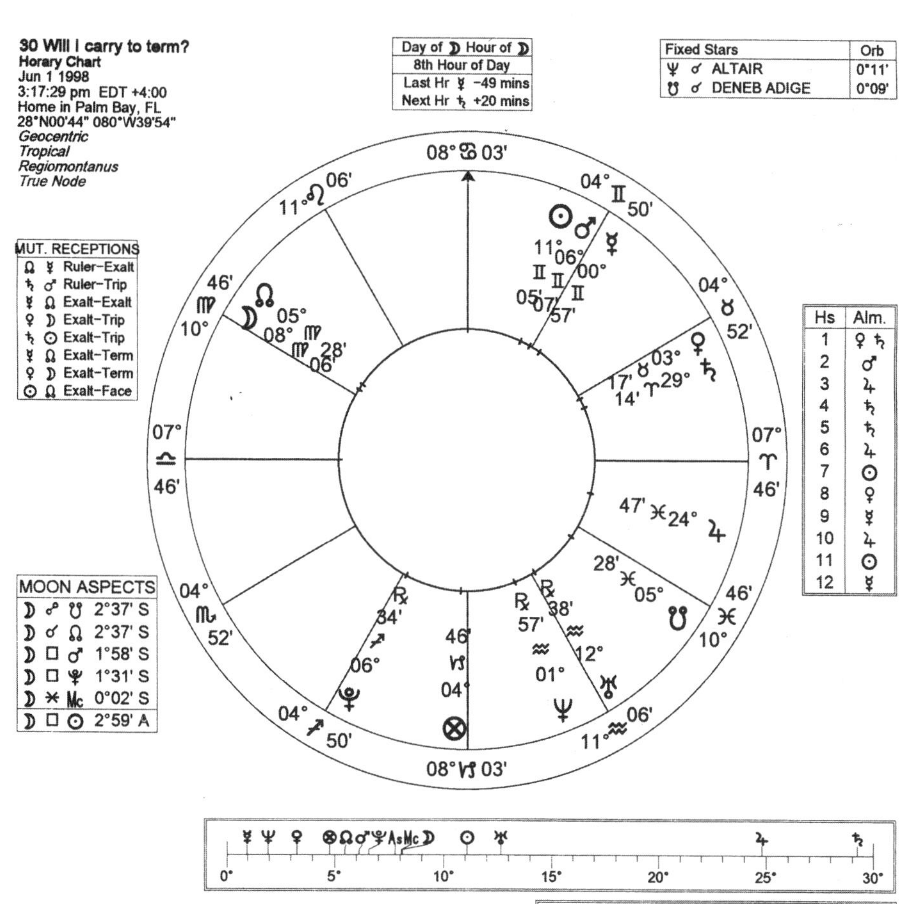

ESSENTIAL DIGNITIES (LEHMAN)								
Pt	Ruler	Exalt	Trip	Term	Face	Detri	Fall	Score
☽	☿	☿	♀	♀	☉	♃	♀	−5 p
☉	☿	☊	♄ m	♃	♂	♃	☋	−5 p
☿	☿ +	☊ m	♄	☿ +	♃	♃	☋	+7
♀	♀ +	☽	♀ +	♀ +	☿	♂	--	+10
♂	☿	☊	♄	☿	♃ m	♃	☋	−5 p
♃	♃ +	♀	♀	♂	♂ m	☿	☿	+5
♄	♂	☉	☉ m	♄ +	♀	♀	♄ −	−2
As	♀	♄	♄	♀	☽	♂	☉	--
Mc	☽	♃	♀	♃	♀	♄	♂	--
⊗	♄	♂	♀	♀	♃	☽	♃	--

planets.pts				
Pt	Long.	Travel	Antiscia	C.Ant.
☽	08°♍06'00"	+12°06'	21°♈53	21°♎53
☉	11°♊05'33"	+00°57'	18°♋54	18°♑54
☿	00°♊57	+02°03'	29°♋02	29°♑02
♀	03°♉17	+01°09'	26°♌42	26°♒42
♂	06°♊07	+00°42'	23°♋52	23°♑52
♃	24°♓47	+00°07'	05°♎12	05°♈12
♄	29°♈14	+00°06'	00°♍45	00°♓45
♅	12°♒38 ℞	−00°00'	17°♏21	17°♉21
♆	01°♒57 ℞	−00°00'	28°♏02	28°♉02
♇	06°♐34 ℞	−00°01'	23°♑25	23°♋25
☊	05°♍28	+00°00'	24°♈31	24°♎31
☋	05°♓28	+00°00'	24°♎31	24°♈31
As	07°♎46'06"	+00°00'	22°♓13	22°♍13
Mc	08°♋03'41"	+00°00'	21°♊56	21°♐56
⊗	04°♑46	+00°00'	25°♐13	25°♊13

She was worried that she wouldn't be able to devote that kind of energy to a third child, and so was contemplating having an abortion.

I judged that she would not carry to term, for the following reasons:

- South Node in the 5th bodes destruction of the fetus.

- The Moon is slow and in a barren sign.

- Uranus at the cusp of the 5th suggests a sudden turn or event.

- Saturn is ruling the 5th, at 29 degrees (a critical degree), in its Detriment, and hardly in a fertile sign.

- With her ruler Venus in Taurus, *becoming* pregnant is not her problem! Her ruler conjunct the 8th House cusp does suggest that Death is the subject of this pregnancy – whether hers, or the child's.

- The Moon conjunct the 12th House cusp of confinement is yet one more indicator of misfortune associated with this pregnancy,

Notice that this is a case where we are using the sign ruler of the Ascendant instead of the co-Almuten. There are two reasons to do this. First, it's essential to have different Significators for the Querent and her fetus, so that we can tease out the different priorities. Second, Venus is so much stronger than Saturn that the choice is fairly obvious. Venus in Taurus sounds far more like a pregnant woman than Saturn in Aries!

However, the co-Almuten of the 1st being also the ruler of the 5th, and said ruler having dignity only by Term while being in Fall does indicate that her health could be somewhat endangered by the continuation of the pregnancy.

She suffered a miscarriage several weeks after this horary was asked.

Example 31: Will my boyfriend call [again]?

We will revisit the use of the 5th House for love and sex in Chapter 13, when we examine the choice between multiple alternatives. However, when it comes to affairs of the heart or gonads, the choice of 5th vs. 7th is not as simple as it might seem. Part of the reason is that many Querents are in denial about 5th House relationships: they may always prefer to think of the relationship as 7th, even when no one else would define it that way! When receiving a question such as the one stated above, the differentiation for house rulership purposes is simple: ask her if they are living together. If they are, then the boyfriend is 7th; otherwise, he's 5th. Now obviously, this particular question precluded them living together: if she's asking about whether he will call her again, it's precisely because they are *not* living together.

Mercury, ruling the 1st House, signifies the Querent in this chart. Notice that Mercury is slow and peregrine. Right away, this tells you that there is nothing that the Querent can do to change the situation: she's powerless to affect the result. She is concerned that she hasn't heard from her boyfriend because he believes that the relationship is over; this tells you that she cannot

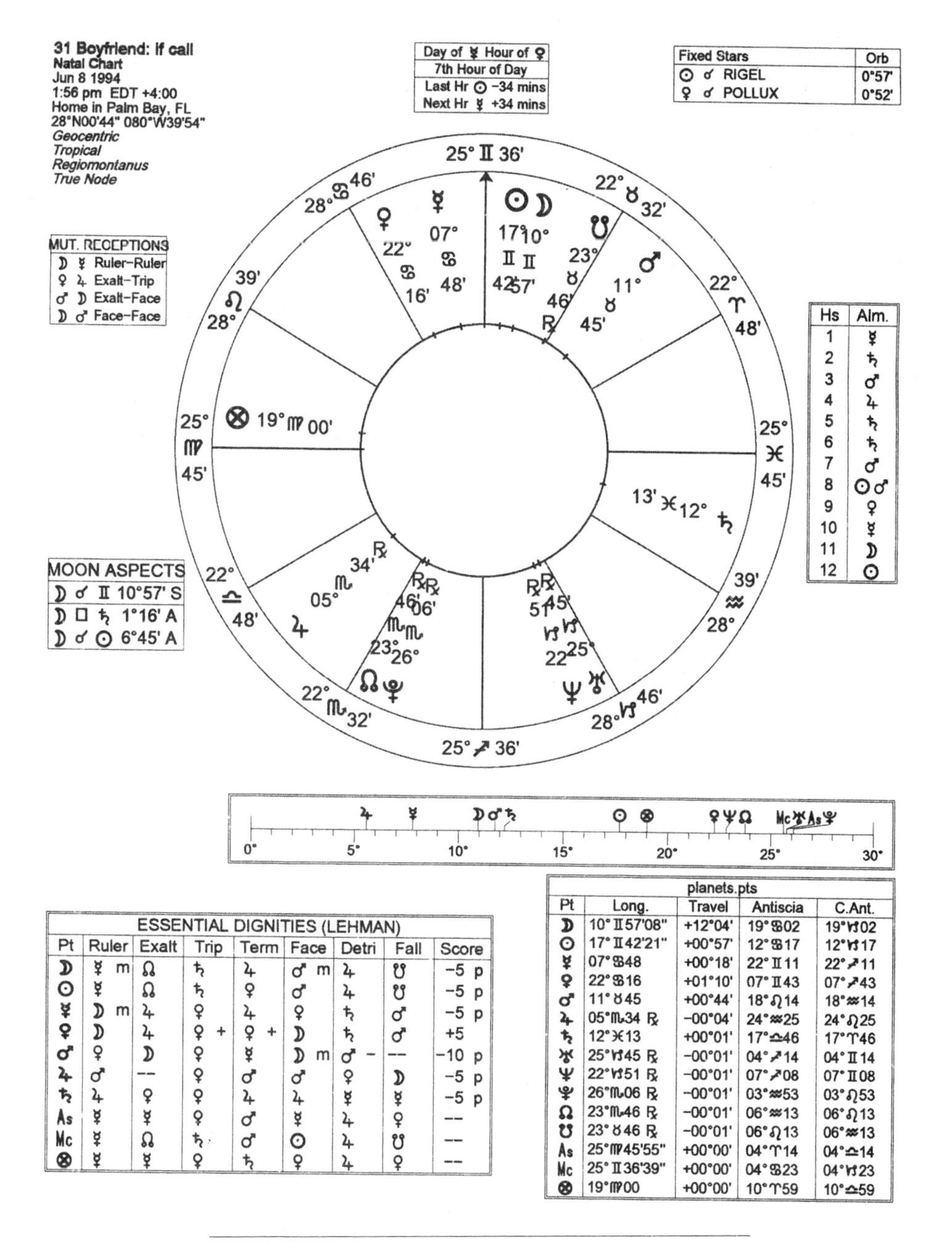

ESSENTIAL DIGNITIES (LEHMAN)								
Pt	Ruler	Exalt	Trip	Term	Face	Detri	Fall	Score
☽	☿ m	☊	♄	♃	♂ m	♃	☋	−5 p
☉	☿	☊	♄	♀	♂	♃	☋	−5 p
☿	☽ m	♃	♀	♃	♀	♄	♂	−5 p
♀	☽	♃	♀ +	♀ +	☽	♄	♂	+5
♂	♀	☽	♀	☿	☽ m	♂ −	--	−10 p
♃	♂	--	♀	♂	♂	♀	☽	−5 p
♄	♃	♀	♀	♃	♃	☿	☿	−5 p
As	☿	☿	♀	♂	☿	♃	♀	--
Mc	☿	☊	♄	♂	☉	♃	☋	--
⊗	☿	☿	♀	♄	♀	♃	♀	--

planets.pts				
Pt	Long.	Travel	Antiscia	C.Ant.
☽	10°♊57'08"	+12°04'	19°♋02	19°♑02
☉	17°♊42'21"	+00°57'	12°♋17	12°♑17
☿	07°♋48	+00°18'	22°♊11	22°♐11
♀	22°♋16	+01°10'	07°♊43	07°♐43
♂	11°♉45	+00°44'	18°♌14	18°♒14
♃	05°♏34 ℞	−00°04'	24°♒25	24°♌25
♄	12°♓13	+00°01'	17°♎46	17°♈46
♅	25°♑45 ℞	−00°01'	04°♐14	04°♊14
♆	22°♑51 ℞	−00°01'	07°♐08	07°♊08
♇	26°♏06 ℞	−00°01'	03°♒53	03°♌53
☊	23°♏46 ℞	−00°01'	06°♒13	06°♌13
☋	23°♉46 ℞	−00°01'	06°♌13	06°♒13
As	25°♍45'55"	+00°00'	04°♈14	04°♎14
Mc	25°♊36'39"	+00°00'	04°♋23	04°♑23
⊗	19°♍00	+00°00'	10°♈59	10°♎59

jump start the relationship by any effort on her part. So everything is in the hands of the boyfriend.

He is Saturn, Ruler of the 5th House. He's also slow and peregrine. So he's not going to do anything that he isn't already doing. So while the two Significators do perfect, nothing will come of the matter, because neither will put out the effort to become closer. The Moon is also not in a position to bring about the result by translation: in the first place, translation by semi-sextile and square isn't exactly a strong one to begin with; secondly, the Moon is also peregrine. With a configuration like this, the two people simply drift apart, with no precipitating event to mark the end of the relationship.

When I told her this, she confirmed that this was precisely how it felt; she had simply wanted to get confirmation from an outside source.

Example 32: Will my client win a big pile of money from the publisher's sweepstakes?

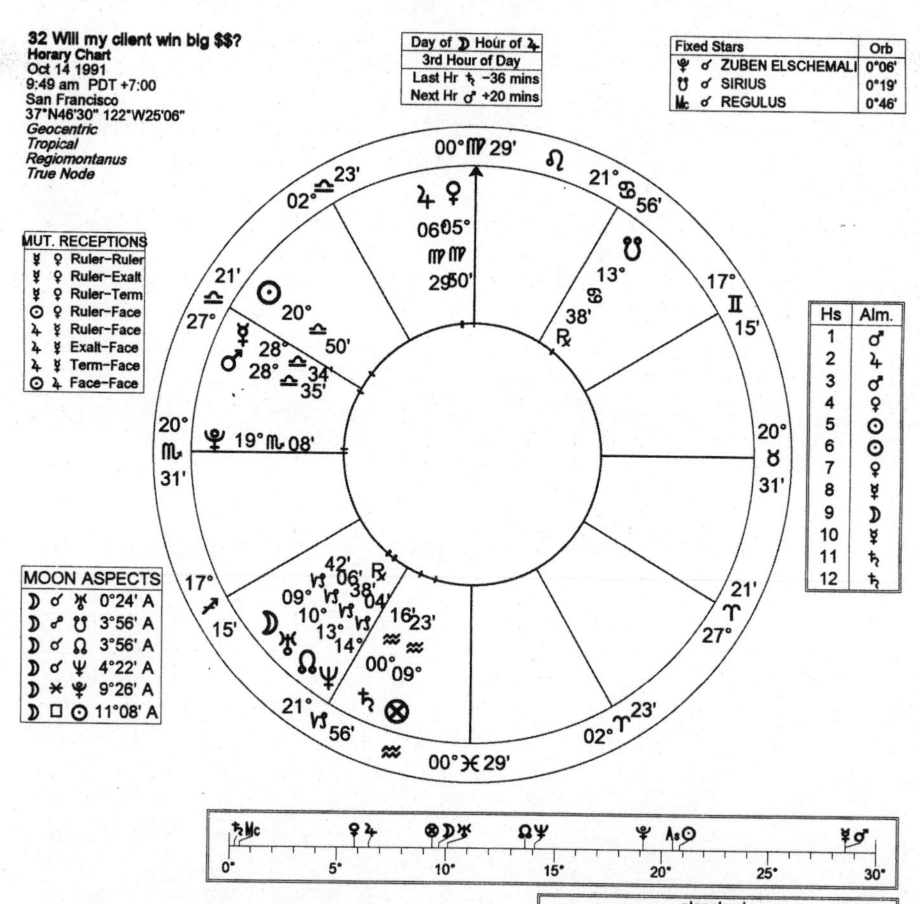

ESSENTIAL DIGNITIES (LEHMAN)								
Pt	Ruler	Exalt	Trip	Term	Face	Detri	Fall	Score
☽	♄	♂	♀	☿	♃	☽ −	♃	−10 p
☉	♀	♄	♄	☿	♃ m	♂	☉ −	−9 p
☿	♀ m	♄	♄	♂	♃	♂	☉	−5 p
♀	☿ m	☿	♀ +	☿	☉	♃	♀ −	−1
♂	♀	♄	♄	♂ +	♃	♂ −	☉	−3
♃	☿	☿	♀	☿	☉ m	♃ −	♀	−10 p
♄	♄ +	---	♄ +	♄ +	♀	☉	---	+10
As	♂	---	♀	♀	♀	♀	☽	---
Mc	☿	☿	♀	☿	☉	♃	♀	---
⊗	♄	---	♄	☿	♀	☉	---	---

planets.pts				
Pt	Long.	Travel	Antiscia	C.Ant.
☽	09°♑42'24"	+11°49'	20°♐17	20°♊17
☉	20°♎50'41"	+00°59'	09°♓09	09°♍09
☿	28°♎34	+01°37'	01°♓25	01°♍25
♀	05°♍50	+00°48'	24°♈09	24°♎09
♂	28°♎35	+00°40'	01°♓24	01°♍24
♃	06°♍29	+00°11'	23°♈30	23°♎30
♄	00°♒16	+00°00'	29°♏43	29°♉43
♅	10°♑06	+00°01'	19°♐53	19°♊53
♆	14°♑04	+00°00'	15°♐55	15°♊55
♇	19°♏08	+00°02'	10°♒51	10°♌51
☊	13°♑38 ℞	−00°00'	16°♐21	16°♊21
☋	13°♋38 ℞	−00°00'	16°♊21	16°♐21
As	20°♏31'18"	+00°00'	09°♒28	09°♌28
Mc	00°♍29'41"	+00°00'	29°♈30	29°♎30
⊗	09°♒23	+00°00'	20°♏36	20°♉36

You just know that those ads you get in the mail must be deceptive somehow when you are told that you are one of ten "finalists" for the grand prize. I have always assumed that they have actually picked the winner, and that by publishing that person's name with nine others selected at random, that the letter could be sent to thousands of people at once!

Anyway, this question was asked by one of my students on behalf of her client, who was completely convinced that the letter was real. This is the kind of question that I frankly have difficulty taking seriously, because the odds of it happening are so low. But what this means is that you have to be *very* convinced by the chart in order to say yes.

Since the question is asked by the astrologer, the client in question is the 7th House. He is given by Venus, which is in mixed condition, being in Fall in Virgo, yet having Triplicity there. Because Triplicity signifies luck, he might win something; being in Fall, you wouldn't expect this to be The Big One. Also, Venus is a bit slow.

The sweepstakes is given by his 5th House, which is the 11th. That same Venus is the sign ruler, but the Almuten is Saturn, the only planet in the chart decently dignified. The bad news, however, is that Venus is not aspecting Saturn, the Moon is not aspecting Saturn, and Mercury, ruler of his 2nd House only aspects Saturn by square after leaving the sign of Libra, where Mercury has nighttime Triplicity. Thus, Mercury is losing dignity by changing sign. Because Mercury is losing dignity by changing sign, and the aspect is a square anyway, we can hardly expect good things to be produced for him.

Also, the Moon was slow of course. Would you be surprised to learn that he didn't win?

On Representation by Another

I really wish I got these questions more often, because I think it's a very important type. We often don't think about it, but many of our affairs are actually conducted by someone else. We don't always act on our own behalf. Even when buying and selling, we often don't buy directly from the owner, but through an agent. Any time that a transaction occurs through a proxy, the 5th House is involved. Hence, this type of question is to assay whether a strategy for obtaining something through another will be successful.

Let us remember that gifts are traditionally associated with the 5th House. The Greek word for "gift" is also the word for "bribe." We can therefore understand the connection of the 5th House with ambassadors: the traditional purpose of an ambassador was to bribe a foreign monarch into a policy friendly to the ambassador's monarch!

Bearing this in mind, Lilly's rules for ambassadors or messengers become clear. An ambassador is simply someone who represents your interests to a third party. One of the most common places that we encounter such ambassadors today is when we buy and sell houses: the real estate agent is usually legally an agent for the seller, so the agent can be represented by the 5th house from the seller.

Example 33: When will I sell my house?

The Querent, an Astrologer, had elected a time to put her house up for sale. She asked this question with the assumption that the house would in fact sell.

Normally in a real estate question, or any buy-sell transaction, we look for perfection between the 1st House ruler and the 7th House ruler. In this particular case, the sale is already assumed, so the 1st –7th perfection is not necessary. In fact, there is no perfection between Sun, Almuten of the 1st, and Saturn, Almuten of the 7th. Mars and Venus, the sign rulers of these two houses, don't perfect either, although they are in mutual reception.[98] However, the two Almutens do receive each other by Face, an almost pitifully weak linkage.

Dignified Saturn rules the 10th; the 10th House rules the price in all buy-sell questions. Hence the price should be respectable, but leaning toward favoring the 7th House party. Mars, the Ruler of the 1st appears to be retrograding back to trine Saturn, but Mars actually turns direct before the trine is partile. Thus, it will appear that the Querent is going to get her price, but something will thwart this before it comes to conclusion.

How do we interpret these facts? Since the result is not forthcoming from the 1st-7th axis, then we need to consider the impact of the question. If the Querent sells her house, she gets the money from the sale. Therefore, we can see the sale through money coming to the 2nd House. The choices for 2nd House ruler are Venus, the ruler of the cusp, and Mars, present in the 2nd House. The money is coming from the sellers, whose money is the 8th House. This can be represented either by Mars again, or Pluto, posited in the 8th. We can also use the Moon to show the action.

The Moon comes to Mars by opposition in three degrees, or 3 months. Because Mars is retrograde, we may expect the timing to be different from the timing given.[99] The Moon is slow of course, which suggests delay. The Moon is in Fall: something about the action will be wrong, or not what the Querent wants or anticipates. It's a perfection by opposition, which means there will be something to regret about the matter. Mars is conjunct the Pleiades, the Seven Sisters. There will be something to cry about.

Remember that the seller asked the question; thus the agent is the 5th House, because he is hired to act on her behalf. How good an ambassador for her is he? He is the Sun in Sagittarius, in mutual reception with retrograde Jupiter in the 5th House. The Sun has Triplicity; so he's lucky. But he's square the Part of Fortune. This suggests that he will actually cost the Querent money. How is this possible?

The couple that bought the house put down a contract in February for a July 1st closing. Thus, the chart worked fine for timing as far as the contract signing was concerned. However, the actual close date was 27 June 1991. The price received was less than 5% lower than the asking price. However, the settlement was not entirely satisfactory to the seller, since her realtor had neglected to inform her that since the buyers had acquired an F.H.A. mortgage, this meant that she (the seller) had to pay closing costs. This was only revealed by the agent at the closing. The agent, who legally was working on her behalf, had apparently withheld this information from her in order to prevent the deal from being cancelled. With the influence of the Pleiades, she literally

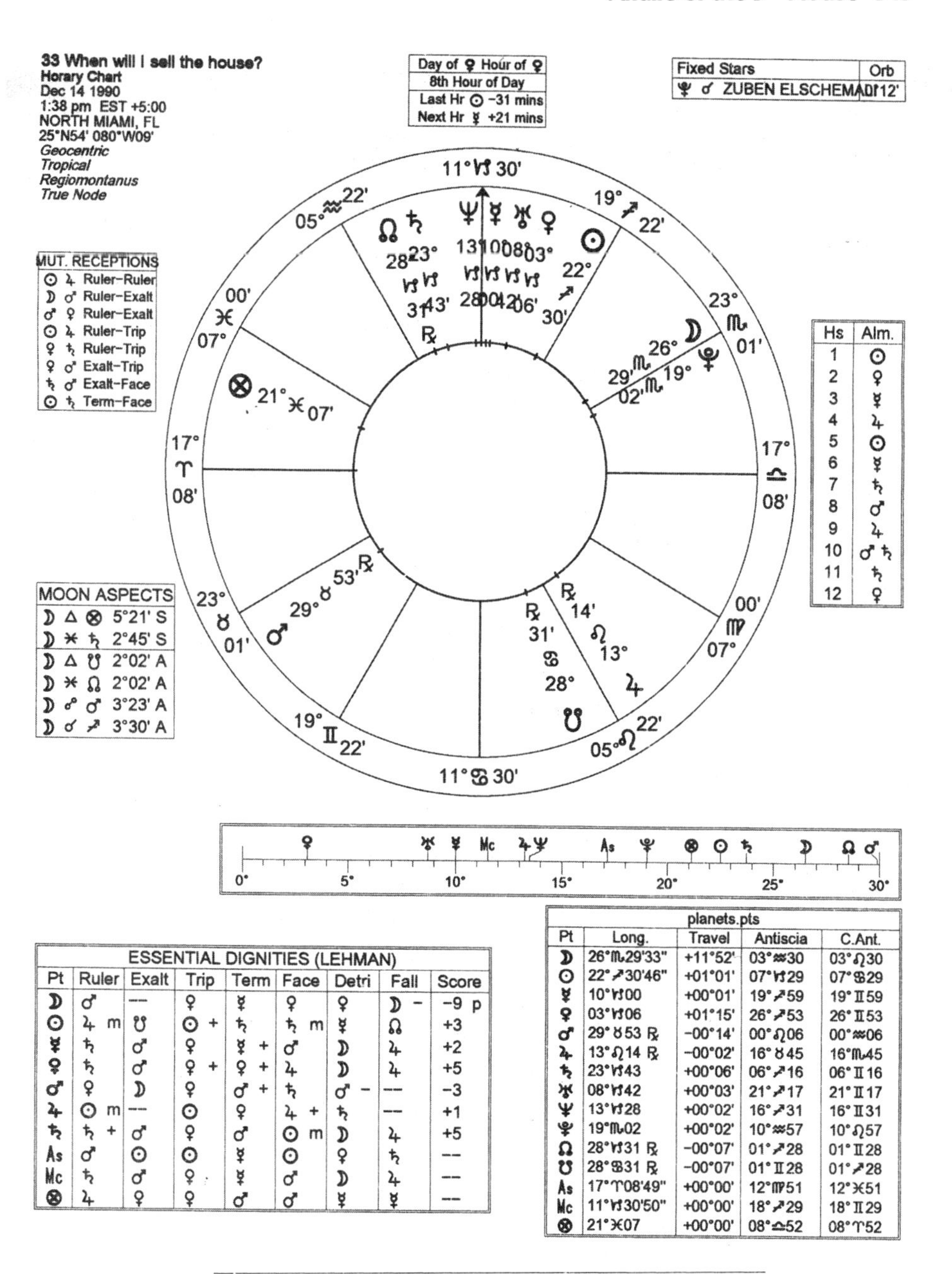

Fixed Stars	Orb
♆ ☌ ZUBEN ELSCHEMALI	1°12'

MUT. RECEPTIONS
☉ ♃ Ruler-Ruler
☽ ♂ Ruler-Exalt
♂ ♀ Ruler-Exalt
☉ ♃ Ruler-Trip
♀ ♄ Ruler-Trip
♀ ♂ Exalt-Trip
♄ ♂ Exalt-Face
☉ ♄ Term-Face

Hs	Alm.
1	☉
2	♀
3	☿
4	♃
5	☉
6	☿
7	♄
8	♂
9	♃
10	♂ ♄
11	♄
12	♀

MOON ASPECTS
☽ △ ⊗ 5°21' S
☽ ⚹ ♄ 2°45' S
☽ △ ☋ 2°02' A
☽ ⚹ ☊ 2°02' A
☽ ☍ ♂ 3°23' A
☽ ☌ ♐ 3°30' A

ESSENTIAL DIGNITIES (LEHMAN)								
Pt	Ruler	Exalt	Trip	Term	Face	Detri	Fall	Score
☽	♂	---	♀	☿	♀	♀	☽ −	−9 p
☉	♃ m	☋	☉ +	♄	♄ m	☿	☊	+3
☿	♄	♂	♀	☿ +	♂	☽	♃	+2
♀	♄	♂	♀ +	♀ +	♃	☽	♃	+5
♂	♀	☽	♀	♂ +	♄	♂ −	---	−3
♃	☉ m	---	☉	♀	♃ +	♄	---	+1
♄	♄ +	♂	♀	♂	☉ m	☽	♃	+5
As	♂	☉	☉	☿	☉	♀	♄	---
Mc	♄	♂	♀	☿	♂	☽	♃	---
⊗	♃	♀	♀	♂	♂	☿	☿	---

planets.pts				
Pt	Long.	Travel	Antiscia	C.Ant.
☽	26°♏29'33"	+11°52'	03°♒30	03°♌30
☉	22°♐30'46"	+01°01'	07°♑29	07°♋29
☿	10°♑00	+00°01'	19°♐59	19°♊59
♀	03°♑06	+01°15'	26°♐53	26°♊53
♂	29°♉53 ℞	−00°14'	00°♌06	00°♒06
♃	13°♌14 ℞	−00°02'	16°♉45	16°♏45
♄	23°♑43	+00°06'	06°♐16	06°♊16
♅	08°♑42	+00°03'	21°♐17	21°♊17
♆	13°♑28	+00°02'	16°♐31	16°♊31
♇	19°♏02	+00°02'	10°♒57	10°♌57
☊	28°♑31 ℞	−00°07'	01°♐28	01°♊28
☋	28°♋31 ℞	−00°07'	01°♊28	01°♐28
As	17°♈08'49"	+00°00'	12°♍51	12°♓51
Mc	11°♑30'50"	+00°00'	18°♐29	18°♊29
⊗	21°♓07	+00°00'	08°♎52	08°♈52

---

cried at the closing. And the agent certainly did not represent her interests very well.

Lilly's rules for representation by another primarily involved whether there was a relation between the 5th and the 10th Houses: the 10th House being used to represent the king. We can apply this for our purposes by deciding which house is the most appropriate to represent the party being courted. In our example here, the ambassador or agent was attempting to put a deal together between the 1st House Querent and the 7th House buyers. Here we see Venus departing from the conjunction to the Sun, and the Sun is actually void of course: the agent wasn't really serving the buyers' interests either, but his own.

Lilly mentions that a sextile or trine between the Ruler of the 1st and the Ruler of the 5th means that the ambassador "performe his trust with much sincerity."[100] Here, we have Jupiter in a departing trine from the Ascendant cusp itself. I'm sure the agent *thought* he was doing a good job for the Querent, but of course, he wasn't.

Collecting Money

When it was a matter of collecting money, Lilly assigned the rulerships as follows: the 1st to the Querent, the 5th to the party attempting to collect the money, and the 7th to the party owing the money. Then, Lilly looked for a fortunate aspect or relationships between the Rulers of 5th and 7th.

Buying and Selling Stock – and other Gambling

Lilly did not address the issue of "play," the word that Gadbury chose for gambling. So let's review Gadbury's rules:[101]

1. *The Lord of the Ascendant and Sign Ascending, shall signifie the Querent; the Lord of the Fifth, and fifth House, the Play or Game; the seventh House and his Lord, the Persons you are to play or Game withal.*

2. *If the Lord of the Fifth be in reception with the Lord of the Ascendant, and in good Aspect, viz. a sextile, or trine, the Person enquiring may advantage himself by his Play.*

3. *If the Lord of the Fifth, or Moon, shall translate the light and vertue of the Lord of the Eighth to the Lord of the Second, or the Ascendant, the Querent will gain much of his Adversaries moneys by Play; or if Venus, being a natural Significator of Play, shall be in a sextile or trine to the Lord of the Ascendant, or Second, or unto the Cuspes of the Ascendant or Second, it signifies the same.*

4. *Venus in the Ascendant, or second House, in sextile or trine to a Planet in the 5th, or to the Lord of the Fifth, declares the Querent to be a gainer by his play; Jupiter so posited, the same.*

5. *The Lord of the Fifth, in the Dignities of Jupiter or Mercury, thence casting a good Aspect to the Part of Fortune, or transferring the Light of the Dispositor of the Part of Play*[102] *to the Lord of the Ascendant or second House, shews gain by play.*

6. *But if none of these happen, but both the Lord of the Ascendant and second House be afflicted by the position of the Infortunes, or the square or opposition of Venus, or the Lord of the Fifth, the Querent*

will then lose by his Gaming. If the South Node afflict the second House at the same time, and Mercury happen to be Lord of the Seventh, although he be in sextile or trine to the Ascendant or Lord thereof, yet the Querent will be cheated and abused in his Play.

Example 34: Sell stock and take the profit?

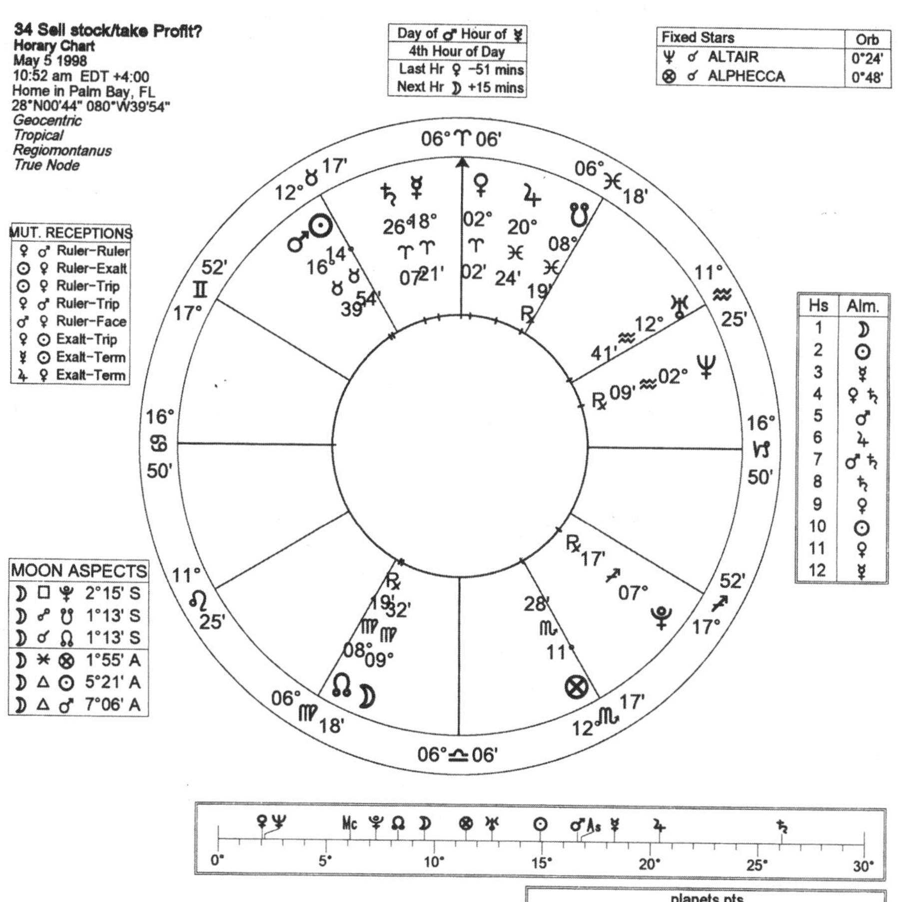

planets.pts				
Pt	Long.	Travel	Antiscia	C.Ant.
☽	09°♍32'43"	+11°56'	20°♈27	20°♎27
☉	14°♉54'42"	+00°58'	15°♌05	15°♒05
☿	18°♈21	+01°01'	11°♍38	11°♓38
♀	02°♈02	+01°07'	27°♍57	27°♓57
♂	16°♉39	+00°43'	13°♌20	13°♒20
♃	20°♓24	+00°11'	09°♎35	09°♈35
♄	26°♈07	+00°07'	03°♍52	03°♓52
♅	12°♒41	+00°00'	17°♏18	17°♉18
♆	02°♒09 ℞	−00°00'	27°♏50	27°♉50
♇	07°♐17 ℞	−00°01'	22°♑42	22°♋42
☊	08°♍19 ℞	−00°00'	21°♈40	21°♎40
☋	08°♓19 ℞	−00°00'	21°♎40	21°♈40
As	16°♋50'40"	+00°00'	13°♊09	13°♐09
Mc	06°♈06'42"	+00°00'	23°♍53	23°♓53
⊗	11°♏28	+00°00'	18°♒31	18°♌31

ESSENTIAL DIGNITIES (LEHMAN)								
Pt	Ruler	Exalt	Trip	Term	Face	Detri	Fall	Score
☽	☿	☿	♀	♀	☉ m	♃	♀	−5 p
☉	♀	☽	♀ m	☿	☽ m	♂	--	−5 p
☿	♂	☉	☉	☿ +	☉	♀	♄	+2
♀	♂ m	☉	☉ m	♃	♂	♀ −	♄	−10 p
♂	♀ m	☽	♀	♃ m	☽	♂ −	--	−10 p
♃	♃ +	♀	♀	♂ m	♂	☿	☿	+5
♄	♂	☉	☉	♄ +	♀	♀	♄ −	−2
As	☽	♃	♀	☿	☿	♄	♂	--
Mc	♂	☉	☉	♀	♂	♀	♄	--
⊗	♂	---	♀	♃	☉	♀	☽	--

The Querent who asked this question had already had a pretty good run with this stock: it was up considerably over the price she had paid for it. So the question was whether it was time to let go and sell it.

When we examine questions with respect to the stock market, we use the gambling rules, except that we mostly ignore the 7th. Buying and selling stocks is, of course, a buy-sell situation, which is intrinsically 1st-7th, but the other party is anonymous from the Querent's perspective, and so this anonymous party is mainly ignored.

Here we see the Moon in Virgo representing the Querent – it's in the 3rd House, just separating from the North Node. The Querent is thinking about profit, and she has just seen her stock go up. Fortuna is conjunct the 5th House cusp: gambling profits ripe for the picking? The Moon is slow and will symbolically come to the sextile to Fortuna shortly. Mars, the Ruler of the 5th House, is in Taurus, its Detriment and Combust.

I therefore judged that she should take her profits and sell, because that debilitated Mars would show that the company was about to take a sharp downturn, at least from the market's standpoint. She took my advice and sold; shortly thereafter, the stock plummeted on news of a possible merger.

Example 35: Buy more, or sell?

The stock was riding high. The Querent had already made a good profit on it. So now she wanted to know whether she should buy more of the stock, or cash in on what she already had. Jupiter rules the Querent, a sign the chart is radical, since she is a Sagittarius Sun.

Jupiter, the Ruler of the Ascendant, is in Pisces but retrograde; Saturn, ruling the 2nd and in Fall is also retrograde. Venus ruling the 5th is in Detriment, at the Bendings, and combust – but fast. Two of the three major Significators retrograde argues for a change in position; the Ruler of the 5th combust looks suspiciously like something nefarious going on behind closed doors. Remember that a prime interpretation of a combust ruler is secrecy – something going on out of sight.

Neptune in the 2nd House I took to represent the Querent gleefully eyeing a financial coup – Neptune and stocks don't mix where clarity and objectivity are useful values. Ironically, my Atlanta study group has found that when it comes to the stock market, Neptune acts primarily as a benefic: glamour tends to raise the value of a stock. However, in a horary about investing, Neptune if configured with the Querent's Significator is far more likely to bring wishful thinking to the mix.

Given the overall condition of the Significators, I told her to sell. She decided to wait to sell until just before the Moon squared Venus – and she watched her shares climb $16 per share right up to the square and her sale – and then crash on a negative report about the company.

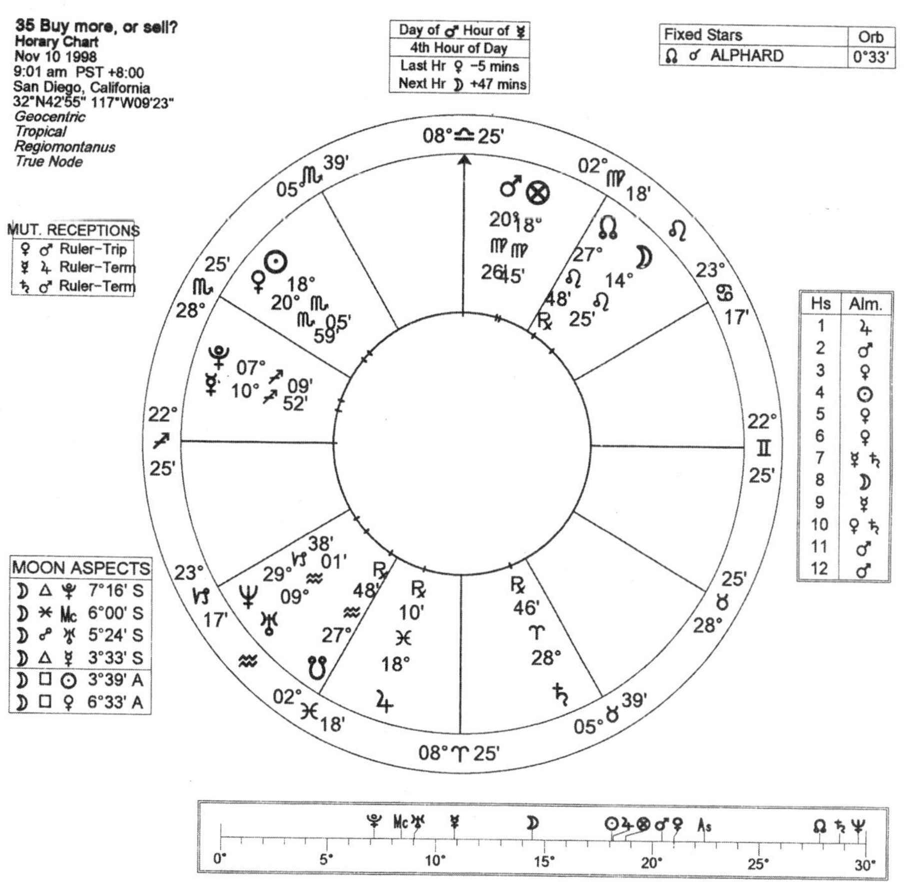

ESSENTIAL DIGNITIES (LEHMAN)								
Pt	Ruler	Exalt	Trip	Term	Face	Detri	Fall	Score
☽	☉	--	☉	♀	♃	♄	--	-5 p
☉	♂	--	♀	♀	☉ +	♀	☽	+1
☿	♃	☋	☉	♀	☽	☿ -	☊	-10 p
♀	♂	--	♀ +	♀ +	♀ +	♀ -	☽	+1
♂	☿	☿	♀	♄	☿	♃	♀	-5 p
♃	♃ +	♀	♀	☿	♃ +	☿	☿	+6
♄	♂	☉	☉	♄ +	♀	♀	♄ -	-2
As	♃	☋	☉	♄	♄	☿	☊	--
Mc	♀	♄	♄	♀	☽	♂	☉	--
⊗	☿	☿	♀	♄	♀	♃	♀	--

planets.pts				
Pt	Long.	Travel	Antiscia	C.Ant.
☽	14°♌25'58"	+12°51'	15°♉34	15°♏34
☉	18°♏05'27"	+01°00'	11°♒54	11°♌54
☿	10°♐52	+01°02'	19°♑07	19°♋07
♀	20°♏59	+01°15'	09°♒00	09°♌00
♂	20°♍26	+00°34'	09°♈33	09°♎33
♃	18°♓10 ℞	-00°00'	11°♎49	11°♈49
♄	28°♈46 ℞	-00°04'	01°♍13	01°♓13
♅	09°♒01	+00°01'	20°♏58	20°♉58
♆	29°♑38	+00°00'	00°♐21	00°♊21
♇	07°♐09	+00°02'	22°♑50	22°♋50
☊	27°♌48 ℞	-00°00'	02°♉11	02°♏11
☋	27°♒48 ℞	-00°00'	02°♏11	02°♉11
As	22°♐25'08"	+00°00'	07°♑34	07°♋34
Mc	08°♎25'55"	+00°00'	21°♓34	21°♍34
⊗	18°♍45	+00°00'	11°♈14	11°♎14

Chapter Six

Affairs of the 6th House: Health, Pets, Working Conditions and Hiring.

"Avoid the treatment, cutting with a knife or scalpel from the limb whose government belongs to the sign in which the Moon or Ascendant is at that hour."

Dorotheus of Sidon[103]

Questions of the 6th House as given by Gadbury:[104]

- *What part of the body is afflicted?*
- *Is the disease in the body, or minde, or both?*
- *Shall the distemper be Chronique, or acute?*
- *Shall the sick party recover, or die of the disease?*
- *Of servants, shall they prove just or knavish?*
- *Of small Cattel, shall the Querent thrive by them, or not?*

Additional Questions of the 6th House as given by Lilly:[105]

- *Arguments that the Querent shall live and not dye of the infirmity now afflicting.*
- *Whether the Disease be in the right or left side or part of the Body of him that demands the Question or is sick.*
- *Of the Crysis, or days Criticall.*
- *From what Cause the Sickness was.*

Like the 5th House, the 6th House has several themes that don't connect together very well. As a result, the rules for each have to be given separately.

Questions concerning Health, Dis-ease and Illness.

Because Astrology was so well integrated into medicine for centuries, the literature on this subject is vast, and frequently contradictory. Unfortunately, to really master the Art of Horary, we must also learn something of the traditional Art of Medicine, and this can be very daunting. The modern concept of disease as understood by experimental science and allopathic medicine is completely unrelated to traditional ideas about disease. However, the traditional ideas of Western medicine are closely related to those practiced in India as Ayurvedic medicine, and quite analogous to those of Traditional Chinese Medicine (TCM) as well.

In the modern "scientific" understanding, there are three forms of disease, what we might call accidents, internal, and external. Accidents include bodily injury or trauma, such as a broken leg or sunburn. Internal disease is caused by the breakdown of various components of the body, such as the mutation of genes that can happen as part of the aging process. Neither requires an outside causative agent, apart from circumstance. External disease requires an agent or pathogen: thus, flu or the common cold is externally "caused" by a virus, the agent or pathogen. Following upon the 19th Century work of Koch and Pasteur, by definition, a person cannot manifest the flu in the absence of the flu virus.

The earliest theories that stand in the direct lineage of traditional Western medicine are those of Hippocrates, dating to the 4th Century BC. In this paradigm, what we now call symptoms *are* the disease. To Hippocrates, a fever was a disease. It remained for the practitioner to characterize the nature of this disease by describing the details of the fever: how high is it, is it accompanied by sweating, what time(s) of day does it occur, what parts of the body show the most obvious heat, etc. The job of the physician would then be to treat the fever, and any other accompanying symptoms/diseases, until the patient's body returned to normal functioning.

Today, that same fever would be considered part of a complex of symptoms that serve to allow the doctor to diagnose or classify the "real" disease, and through that, the "real" pathogen. It would then be preferable, but not always possible, to treat the "disease" through a regimen that directly attacks the pathogen, under the theory that, once the pathogen is destroyed or expelled, the symptoms will disappear and the body will return to normal.

Both ideas have their merits. If allopathy were truly successful at targeting specific pathogens and removing them, there would probably be much less objection to it. However, two objections to this approach have become increasingly apparent. The first is that there are very few truly specific treatment protocols apart from vaccines.[106] Otherwise, the drugs developed tend to have broad specificity, and because they react with multiple pathogens, they get widespread usage, which then provokes the second objection. Organisms, whether viral, bacterial or fungal, adapt to their environment, so they eventually find ways to subvert the anti-pathogenic agents anyway. The result is a stronger pathogen, pre-selected for the most robust individuals. This in turn can provoke much more extreme symptoms in the hosts: namely, us.

The traditional approach is to treat the "symptoms," and then let the body heal itself. This also has limitations, many of which were based on an incomplete understanding of the constellation of symptoms which comprise a disease complex, or the inability to match the severity of the symptoms with the speed of functioning of the curative agent.

The two systems differ in their philosophical approach to a cure. Take, for example, a condition such as congestive heart failure: the diagnosis when the heart muscle loses the ability to pump enough blood for the body to function properly. Often, there is so much fluid in the body's tissues that the heart has to overwork to pump the blood, and ultimately, the heart cannot maintain a high enough blood pressure differential through the kidneys to maintain kidney function. Thus, the kidneys cease to function, not as a result of any organic "failure," but simply because they require a gradient in fluid pressure that is no longer present.

The conventional allopathic "solution" involves salt intake restriction, and various pharmaceutical solutions such as antibiotics, anti-hypertensives, vasodilators; and chemical diuretics. Progressing to kidney dialysis or heart transplant surgery when other methods fail. Curiously, there are only a few chemical diuretics commonly tried.

In traditional medicine, the water retention (traditionally called edema or dropsy) would be treated as the disease. Most traditional societies have literally dozens, if not hundreds of herbal diuretics; it is one of the most common classifications of plant functions in many cultures. As a result, if one particular plant drug doesn't work, another would be tried until something effective could be found.

If an effective diuretic is found, then is the disease still present? Technically, perhaps, but functionally no, unless the systemic damage prior to the successful treatment with diuretics was simply too great, or unless the edema is a secondary effect, rather than a contributing factor to the disease. In modern allopathic medicine, this route is ignored, because the edema is viewed as a compensatory mechanism for an already damaged heart, rather than a symptom that could be putting additional strain on the heart, thereby causing the heart damage. What we have here is the potential for a chicken *vs.* egg argument: which comes first, and which is the primary symptom. And like most chicken and egg scenarios, the controversy comes more from diverging world views than from so-called objective reality.

Curiously, some people have complained that the modern physician isn't usually even sensitive to the possible severity of "symptoms" such as edema, in great part because of modern dependence on chemical testing, and a lack of emphasis on the physical appearance of the patient. A Chinese or Ayurvedic practitioner would be much more likely to see the problem before it gets serious. My own mother died of complications of this nature. Photographs of her last months show greatly increasing edema, and yet during multiple visits to a physician who had been seeing her for years, no treatment of the edema was proffered. It wasn't until she manifested a health "crisis" that the edema was even considered – too late, as it turned out. The physician's practices and procedures were absolutely normal for the profession.

When we attempt to study medical conditions astrologically, there are several overarching classifications that can be applied. The first system is whether the disease is physical, mental, or spiritual.

Before we can examine this classification, we need to define the astrological houses that are used in beginning a medical horary analysis.

- The 1st House represents the health and vitality of the patient/ Querent.
- The 6th House shows the disease.
- The 7th House shows the health care practitioner
- The 8th House shows the possibility of the death of the patient
- The 10th House shows either the method of cure, or the diagnostic method or technique, depending on the nature of the question.

Body, mind and spirit are an uneasy triad in this material, because spirit and mind are not always distinguished, and in some sources, spirit and mind may be considered synonymous. We can begin by considering that only diseases of the body may be treated conventionally, by which we mean through herbs, drugs, and physical, biological or chemical means. Disease of the mind or spirit may be treated by bio-energetic means[107] (which can also be used for physical disease), psychotherapy, or spiritual healing. Note that some diseases are transitioning between the categories as the biochemistry of the brain becomes more fully understood. As certain so-called mental illnesses are found to respond to chemicals or drugs, they cease to be classified as mental, but can then be classified as nervous system dysfunctions, which we would understand astrologically as being "of the body."

Table One compares some of the astrological indicators of physical vs. mental or spiritual disease.

Table 1. Typical configurations for physical and mental diseases, as described by Lilly and others.

Physical	Mental/Spiritual
Ascendant and Moon afflicted; their rulers not afflicted.	The Ascendant and the Moon not afflicted; but their rulers afflicted.
Mars or Saturn afflicting the Moon, but not the Ascendant.	Mars or Saturn afflicting the Ascendant, but not the Moon.
Jupiter in the 1st or 6th	Ruler of the 9th or 12th in the 6th (witchcraft)
Ruler of the 1st in the 6th	Ruler of the 6th is Mercury (witchcraft)
Moon or Ruler of the Ascendant in the 12th.	Ruler of the Moon or Ascendant in the 12th.

The debate in classical medical astrology was about whether the Moon and the Ascendant, or their rulers, represented the body or the mind. However, the presence of a 12th House influence was an argument for witchcraft. Witchcraft in those days was believed to be a spiritual affliction. In modern parlance, we would translate the use of "witchcraft" as involuntary coercion, a psychological affliction.

This classification is useful for determining the best pathway to follow to alleviate the symptoms. If the disease is purely mental/spiritual, then following the sequence of physical states may be beside the point. Attempting to treat the condition physically may also expose the body to unwarranted chemicals. And it is the over-prescribing of drugs such as antibiotics that has resulted in massive evolution of antibiotic-resistant bacteria.

Having said this, can physical disease be treated only physically? My own experience tells me no, having personally experienced healing crises brought on by acupressure, or even by homeopathy, where no detectable chemical agent is present.

The normal diagnosis assumes a condition of physical disease. While there are literally thousands of aphorisms that apply to medical astrology[108], the basic rules are fairly simple. Among the most important rules are:

- The Moon represents acute conditions (ones that are less than ninety days in duration); the Sun chronic ones. All the rules that are given as applying to the Moon are subsequently interpreted according to the placement of the Sun after 90 days.

- It is better to have as little relationship as possible between the 1st and 8th Houses, and the Moon and the 8th House. When there are ties between these, it is an indication of death. We define death as meaning that the person would have died in the 17th Century, prior to the advent of modern medical crisis procedures. Nowadays, we would call this a life-threatening illness.

- A relationship between the 1st and 6th Houses means that the patient is the "cause" of his or her own disease. This usually translates to a lifestyle choice or decision, like eating the wrong foods or ignoring a serious food allergy, taking a drug that provokes a reaction, or having to cope with too much stress.

- A relationship between the 6th and 8th Houses means that there is a danger of the patient having the disease *unto* death, meaning that the patient is likely to still have the condition at death. This does not mean the patient dies as a result of this condition.

As for a description of the disease, the process is similar to what we use for lost objects: we tally the planets that can be considered Significators (planets associated with the 1st or 6th Houses - either by rulership, Almuten, or placement) - and see if we have a pattern or predominance by planet and sign. The planetary rulers are mainly expressed through the descriptions of that planet as the Ruler of the 6th House. Then, there are two principal choices: either (1) the disease in the part of the body ruled by the sign of the 6th House ruler, of the nature of the planet ruling the 6th House, or (2) in an organ ruled by the Ruler of the 6th, of the nature of the sign element of that ruler.

For example, if Saturn in Leo rules the 6th House, then the disease could be (1) heart disease (Leo) of a chronic type (Saturn), or (2) an acute flare-up (Leo as hot and dry) in one or more of the bones (Saturn).

Taking this to mean general predominance, we can describe the conditions by planet as follows.

Saturn as Ruler of the Disease[109]

The patient is subject to the following general health issues: rheumatism, leprosy, obstructions, trembling, right ear problems, palsies, toothache, deafness, vain fears, gout, rashes with itching, knee problems, hemorrhoids, fractures, dislocations, ruptures, sciatica, bladder infections, madness, chronic disease, or forgetfulness. Saturn produces a disease of long duration[110], with the danger that it will become chronic[111]. Saturn tends to affect the right side of the body more than the left[112].

> "... the sick party labours with some affliction of the Minde, or with some vexatious care whereof his minde is much troubled." [113]

> " [Saturn] produceth continued and tedious Sicknesses, quartan Agues [malaria, or periodic fever], Coughs, consumptions, &c." [114]

> "[Saturn] causeth the falling-sickness [epilepsy], black Choler and Leprosie, Morphew [leprous or scurvy eruptions], Fistulas, and Podagra. [foot gout]" [115]

Table 2. Some parts of the body ruled by Saturn.

Item	Reference
Bladder	D2-017, E1-195, PA-127, PT-319, SA-014
Bones	AB-247, E1-195, KB-037, LI-579, PA-011, PT-319, SA-014
Hair	AB-247
Knees	AB-248
Marrow	AB-247
Skin	AB-247
Spleen	AB-247, D2-017, E1-195, KB-037, LI-059, PA-011, PT-319, RA-050, SA-014
Teeth	D2-017, KB-037, LI-059, PA-011, SA-014

Jupiter as Ruler of the Disease

The patient is subject to the following general health issues: liver disease, venous problems, lung inflammation, convulsions, pleurisy, swelling, pain or abscesses about the breast, quinsy (tonsillitis), inflammations, windiness, blood corruption, gluttony, scurvy, liver obstructions, or stomach obstructions.

Jupiter produces conditions of shorter duration[116], primarily affecting the right side of body. [117]

Table 3. Some parts of the body ruled by Jupiter.

Item	Reference
Arteries	AB-247, D2-019, LI-246, PA-128, PT-319, SA-014
Blood	AB-247, CU-051, E1-197, KB-042, PA-012
Bone Marrow	AB-247
Cartilage (Gristle)	D2-019, LI-246, PA-128, SA-014
Liver	CU-051, D2-019, E1-196, KB-042, LI-063, PA-012, RA-052, SA-014
Lungs (Lights)	CU-051, D2-019, LI-246, PA-012, PT-319, SA-014
Ribs	CU-051, D2-019, E1-196, KB-042, LI-063, PA-012, SA-014
Seed, Reproductive	AB-247, D2-019, LI-246, PT-319, SA-014
Semen	D2-019, PT-319, SA-014
Sides	CU-051, D2-019, KB-042, PA-012, SA-014
Thighs	AB-248
Veins	CU-051, KB-042, LI-063, PA-012, SA-014

Mars as the Ruler of the Disease

The patient is subject to the following general health issues: anger, pestilence, fevers, malaria, migraines, carbuncles, sores, burning, scalding, ringworm, blisters, frenzy, hepatitis, dysentery, fistula, shingles, St. Anthony's fire [erysipelas, gangrene, or ergotism], genital disease, kidney stones, bladder stones, small pox, measles, injury through sharp instruments, diabetes, and dog-like hunger.

Mars produces a condition of short duration[118] which will tend to afflict the right side of body. [119]

Table 4. Some parts of the body ruled by Mars.

Item	Reference
Back, Small of the	LI-246, RA-054
Bile	AB-247, E1-198, SA-020
Face	KB-047
Gall	D2-020, KB-047, LI-067, PA-013, RA-054, SA-014
Gall Bladder	AB-248, CU-051
Genitals	CU-051, LI-246, PA-128, PT-319
Head	PA-128
Kidneys	AB-248, CU-051, D2-020, E1-198, PT-319, SA-014

Reproductive Organs	CU-051, E1-198, SA-014
Veins	AB-247, D2-020, PA-128, PT-319, RA-054, SA-014

Sun as the Ruler of the Disease

The patient is subject to the following general health issues: heart disease, pimples in the face, break-outs, eye weakness, swooning, malaria or burning fevers.

About the male-female differentiation given in the table: sometimes it works, sometimes it doesn't - always check this one out for yourself.

Solar conditions are short in duration[120], primarily affecting the right side of body.[121]

Table 5. Some parts of the body ruled by the Sun.

Item	Reference
Arteries	CU-052, KB-052, PA-014
Back	KB-052
Brain	AB-247, LI-247, PT-319, RA-057
Eye, Left (Women)	CU-052, D2-022, KB-052, LI-071, PA-014, RA-057
Eye, Right	AB-248, PA-129, SA-014
Eye, Right (Men)	CU-052, D2-022, KB-052, LI-071, PA-014, RA-057
Head	AB-248, SA-014
Heart	CU-052, D2-022, KB-052, LI-247, PA-014, PT-319, RA-057, SA-014
Right Side of Body	D2-022, PT-319, SA-014
Sinews	D2-022, LI-579, PA-129, PT-319, SA-014

Venus as the Ruler of the Disease

The patient is subject to the following general health issues: suffocation, sudden and brief illnesses, kidney disease, problems related to carbohydrate metabolism, dislocation, venereal disease, menstrual or uterine problems.

> "Venus is Temperate in Heat and Cold, in Moist and Dry, but yet more Cold than Hot, and more Moist than Dry, Decreasing, and Descending, Passive, Flegmatick, causing thin Flegm and Water." [122]

Table 6. Some parts of the body ruled by Venus.

Item	Reference
Back, Small of the	D2-023, PA-015, SA-014
Breasts	CU-051, KB-057
Buttocks (Hamms)	D2-023, SA-014
Dimples	D2-024

Item	Reference
Flesh	E1-200, PT-321, SA-014
Kidneys	CU-051, KB-057, PA-129, SA-014
Loins	D2-023, PA-015, SA-014
Nipples	D2-023, LI-247, SA-014
Reproductive Organs	AB-248, CU-051, D2-023, KB-057, LI-247, PA-015, SA-014, S2-056
Seed, Reproductive	CU-051, D2-023, E1-200, KB-057, LI-247, PA-015, SA-014
Throat	CU-051, D2-023, KB-057, LI-247, PA-015, SA-014

Mercury as the Ruler of the Disease

The patient is subject to the following general health issues: inflammations, especially of mucous membranes, sciatica, stammering, lisping, hoarseness, coughs, snuffling in the nose, hepatitis, imperfection in the tongue, and all diseases of the brain: vertigo, apoplexy, and madness, also diseases of the lungs, such as asthma, tuberculosis, and other diseases that belong to the brain, tongue and memory.

> "Mercury is naturally more Cold and Dry than Hot and Moist, but of a superfluous Humidity, and is Moveable, Quick in Melancholick causes, Thin, Melancholick and Subtil." [123]
>
> "… the sick party hath his Brain disaffected, is disturbed with an unquiet Fancy or Minde, with a Frenzie, Falling-sicknessse, Cough, Ptisick [tuberculosis], or the like." [124]

The condition is more likely on the right side of the body[125]

Table 7. Some parts of the body ruled by Mercury.

Item	Reference
Brain	CU-051, D2-025, KB-063, LI-247, RA-061, SA-015
Fingers	D2-025, LI-247, PA-130
Gall Bladder	AB-247, D2-025, SA-015
Hands	CU-051, D2-025, KB-063, LI-247, PA-017, SA-015
Larynx	AB-248, E1-201, SA-015
Nerves	E1-201
Tongue	AB-248, CU-051, D2-025, E1-201, KB-063, LI-247, PA-017, PT-321, RA-061, SA-015

Moon as the Ruler of the Disease

The patient is subject to the following general health issues: all obstructions, colic, stomach aches, edema, excessive flows, cerebral hemorrhage, embolisms, rheumatism, menstrual flow and other conditions of the genitals, gluttony, eye rheums, worms, rotten coughs, convulsions, epilepsy, scrofula (associated with moral corruption), abscesses, smallpox, measles, lethargy, and excess phlegm.

In the table, just as with the solar attribution for the eyes, sometimes the gender differentiation works, sometimes it doesn't - always check this one out for yourself.

The left side of body is the more afflicted.[126]

Table 8. Some parts of the body ruled by the Moon.

Item	Reference
Belly	D2-026, PT-321, SA-015
Bladder	CU-051, KB-068, LI-082, PA-018, SA-015
Bowels	CU-052, KB-068, PA-018, SA-015
Brain	CU-052, D2-026, KB-068, LI-247, PA-018, SA-015
Breasts	AB-248, D2-026
Eye, Left	AB-248
Eye, Left (Diurnal)	E1-202
Eye, Left (Men)	CU-052,D2-026, KB-068, LI-082, PA-018, SA-015
Eye, Right (Nocturnal)	E1-202
Eye, Right (Women)	CU-052, D2-026, KB-068, LI-082, PA-018, SA-015
Left Side Of Body	D2-026, E1-015, PT-321, SA-015
Nerves	CU-052, KB-068
Stomach	AB-248, CU-052, D2-026, KB-068, PA-018, PT-321, SA-015
Vulva	SA-198
Womb	D2-026, LI-082, PT-321, RA-064

Dis-ease Rulership by Sign

Once we have a description of the planet, we then modify our delineation by considering the sign of the planet. There are two ways that this can be done. The signs themselves rule parts of the body, and there is also a specific assignment by planet and sign. These are the sign attributions as given by multiple sources.

Aries	Item	Reference
	Atlas Joint	CU-053
	Brain	CU-053
	Ear	D2-015, SA-015
	Eyebrows	SA-015
	Eyes	CU-053, D2-005, SA-015
	Face	BL-029, CU-053, D2-005, SA-015

Aries (cont) Item	Reference
Hair	CU-053
Head	AR-045, BL-029, CU-053, D2-005, LI-245, SA-015
Nose	CU-053, SA-015
Teeth	CU-053
Tongue	CU-053

Taurus Item	Reference
Buttocks (Hamms)	D2-007
Cervical Vertebrae	CU-053
Chin, Area Under	SA-015
Clavicle	CU-053
Neck	AR-045, BL-029, CU-053, D2-006, LI-245, SA-015
Shoulder Blade	CU-053
Throat	BL-029, CU-053, D2-006, LI-245, SA-015

Gemini Item	Reference
Arms	AR-046, BL-029, CU-053, D2-007, LI-245, SA-015
Fingers	CU-053, SA-015
Hands	CU-053, D2-007, LI-245, SA-015
Shoulders	BL-029, CU-053, D2-007, LI-245, SA-015
Wrists	SA-015

Cancer Item	Reference
Breasts	AR-046, BL-029, CU-053, D2-007, LI-095, SA-015
Lungs	AR-046, CU-053, LI-245, SA-015
Nipples	D2-007, LI-095, SA-015
Ribs	BL-029, CU-053, D2-007, SA-015
Sides	SA-015
Spleen	AR-046, D2-007, LI-245, SA-015
Stomach	AR-046, BL-029, CU-053, LI-095

Leo Item	Reference
Back, thoracic	AR-046. BL-029, CU-049, D2-008, SA-015
Backbone	LI-246
Chest; pericardium	AR-046, CU-053
Diaphragm	AR-046
Gall	SA-015
Heart	AR-046, BL-029, CU-053, D2-008, LI-095, SA-015
Ribs & Sides	D2-008, LI-095

Virgo Item	Reference
Belly	AR-046, BL-029, CU-053, D2-009, SA-015
Bowels	BL-029, CU-053, D2-009, LI-096, SA-015
Diaphragm	KB-022
Navel	CU-053, SA-015
Omentum (Bowel membrane)	CU-049, KB-022
Spleen	CU-053, KB-022

Libra Item	Reference
Back, small of the	AR-046, D2-010, KB-024, SA-015
Bladder	D2-010, SA-015
Buttocks (Hamms)	D2-010, SA-015
Genitals	AR-046
Hinder Parts	AR-046
Kidneys (reins)	AR-046, BL-029, CU-053, ED-048, KB-024, LI-096, SA-015
Loins	BL-029, CU-053, D2-010, LI-096, SA-015
Navel	D2-010, SA-015
Uterus	ED-048

Scorpio Item	Reference
Anus	CU-054, D2-010, LI-245
Bladder	BL-029, CU-054, D2-010, LI-097, SA-015
Genitals	AR-046, BL-029, CU-054, D2-010, LI-097, SA-015
Groin	LI-246
Ovum	S2-056
Reproductive Organs	AR-046, CU-054, D2-010, LI-246, SA-015
Sperm	S2-056

Sagittarius Item	Reference
Back, Lower	SA-015
Buttocks (Hamms)	SA-015, LI-097
Hips	D2-011, LI-246, SA-015
Os Sacrum	CU-054, SA-015
Thighs	AR-046, BL-029, CU-054, D2-011, LI-097, SA-015

Capricorn Item	Reference
Bladder	CU-050
Bones	CU-050
Buttocks (Hamms)	CU-054, LI-246, SA-015

Capricorn Item	Reference
Knees	AR-046, BL-029, CU-054, D2-012, LI-098, SA-015
Legs, Upper Part	SA-015
Spleen	CU-050
Teeth	CU-050

Aquarius Item	Reference
Ankles	D2-013, LI-098
Calves Of Legs	LI-246
Legs	BL-029, CU-054, D2-013, LI-098
Legs, Lower	AR-046
Shanks	AR-046, SA-015
Tibia (shin)	AR-046, LI-246, SA-015

Pisces Item	Reference
Ankles	CU-054, LI-246, SA-015
Feet	AR-046, BL-029, CU-054, D2-014, LI-099, SA-015
Heels	D2-014
Instep	SA-015
Skin & Flesh of Foot	CU-054

Dis-ease Rulership by Sign & Planet[127]

Tables were given for the combination of planet and sign. What is less clear was the priority that was assigned to this information compared to using the list by planet, and then by sign of the planet, as shown in the table. Unfortunately, anything resembling a statistical study is simply unknown from this period.

I do not consistently use this table, which makes me somewhat suspicious of it. To test it, I extracted 256 people from the AstroDataBank®[128] who have had heart conditions. In counting up the number of cases where the heart showed up as one of the organs affected by the combination of planet and sign (like Moon in Leo), I tabulated 22 out of the total of 84 positions listing the heart as a possible organ; this gave an expected value of 22/84 = 26.2% of a population should have one of these placements ruling either 1st or 6th House – by chance. If these attributions were really kicking, I reasoned, we should see an elevation in the frequency of these placements.

There isn't much of an effect. The 1st House ruler matched one of these combinations 74 times; the 6th House 67. The expected amount was 26.2 x 256 = 67. The slight elevation in the 1st House probably isn't significant.

Therefore, I include this table for completeness; not out of conviction.

Table 8. Dis-ease Rulership by Sign and Planet

	Saturn	Jupiter	Mars	Sun	Venus	Mercury	Moon
Aries	Breast Arms	Neck Throat Heart Belly	Belly Head	Thighs	Kidneys Feet	Genitals Legs	Knees Head
Taurus	Heart Breast Belly	Shoulders Arms Belly Neck	Kidneys Throat	Knees	Genitals Head	Thighs Feet	Legs Throat
Gemini	Belly Heart	Breast Kidneys Genitals	Genitals Arms Breast	Legs Ankles	Thighs Throat	Knees Head	Feet Shoulders Thighs Arms
Cancer	Kidneys Belly Genitals	Heart Genitals Thighs	Breast Thighs	Feet	Knees Shoulders Arms	Legs Throat Eyes	Head Breast Stomach
Leo	Genitals Kidneys	Belly Thighs Knees	Knees Heart Belly	Head	Legs Breast Heart	Feet Arms Shoulder Throat	Throat Stomach Heart
Virgo	Thighs Genitals Feet	Kidneys Knees	Legs Belly	Throat	Feet Stomach Heart Belly	Head Breast Heart	Arms Shoulders Bowels
Libra	Knees Thighs	Genitals Legs Head Eyes	Feet Kidneys Genitals	Shoulders Arms	Head Small Intestine	Throat Heart Stomach Belly	Breast Kidneys Heart Belly
Scorpio	Knees Legs	Thighs Feet	Head Genitals ArmsThighs	Breast Heart	Throat Kidneys Genitals	Shoulders Arms Bowels Back	Stomach Heart Genitals Belly
Sagittarius	Legs Feet	Knees Head Thighs	Throat Thighs Hands Feet	Heart Belly	Shoulders Arms Genitals Thighs	Breast Kidneys Heart Genitals	Bowels Thigh Back
Capricorn	Head Feet	Legs Neck Eyes Knees	Arms Shoulders Knees Legs	Belly Back	Breast Heart Thighs	Stomach Heart Genitals	Kidneys Knees Thighs
Aquarius	Neck Head	Feet Arm Shoulders Breast	Breast Legs Heart	Kidneys Genitals	Heart Knees	Bowels Thighs Heart	Secrets Legs Ankles
Pisces	Arms Shoulders Neck	Head Breast Heart	Heart Feet Belly Ankles	Genitals Thighs	Belly Legs Neck Throat	Kidneys Knees Genitals Thighs	Thighs Feet

Dis-ease Rulership by House

There are only two subject groupings in classical astrology where house and sign meanings almost coincide – one is medical astrology where you find, for instance, that both Pisces and the 12th House rule the feet. The other case is geographical places. Today we no longer delineate the houses as a method of describing the disease: we use the 6th House to show the disease.

As more astrologers have begun to study the Greek horoscopic period, we have learned that the original house system was what we now classify as Whole Sign. In a whole sign house system, your 1st House is Aries if you have Aries Rising, regardless of whether the Ascendant is one degree, or twenty-nine degrees. The actual Ascendant would simply be a point located somewhere in the 1st House. In other words, house cusps were not expressed as beginning at a degree within a sign, but the house encompassed precisely one whole sign. It is from this system that we have residual references to "house" and "sign" as being occasionally synonymous, as in the expression: "Mars is in Mercury's house" as equivalent for Mars in Virgo.

The use of the different houses to describe diseases is essentially a vestigial holdover from this period. Thus, what references we have to diseases by house derive from this primordial association of the two. Since house is almost never used for the description of a disease, we have not presented what would be a redundant and possibly misleading table.

Example 36: Is this a good doctor? Is my condition treatable?

The Querent simply does not like allopaths. She was showing symptoms of a systemic infection, periodic outbreaks that just appeared and disappeared seemingly at random. She talked to a couple of health care practitioners about it; they suggested that systemic infection was the most likely condition. She checked around for references on doctors, and had selected one. However, she was unwilling to go through the treatment protocol (massive doses of antibiotics) if the procedure was not going to alleviate the condition permanently.

The Querent is given by either Venus in Scorpio or Saturn in Aries, depending on whether we decide to use the sign ruler, Venus, or the Almuten of the 1st House, Saturn. What a choice! I opted for Venus in Scorpio because its Direct nature is in slightly better condition than fallen and retrograde Saturn - the usual method of choosing between sign ruler and Almuten ruler.

Venus in Scorpio shows the Querent's condition, which is not great. The cardinal sign on the 1st House shows the possibility of change, although the Ascendant ruler in a fixed sign shows that change is not easy: nor is it guaranteed.

The doctor looks excellent: once again we have a choice of a sign ruler or an Almuten ruler, and the sign ruler, Mars in Scorpio, looks very good. Venus and Mars are in mutual reception, so the two would probably get along.

The Moon rules the physic, or treatment. It is strong in Taurus, but coming to an opposition to her Significator, Venus. The Moon is translating the light between Venus and Mars. Even though they are coming to conjunction, the actual conjunction did not occur until 20 Sagittarius, after both had left sign. Therefore, she and the doctor were unlikely to meet without the help or intercession of another, namely the Moon.

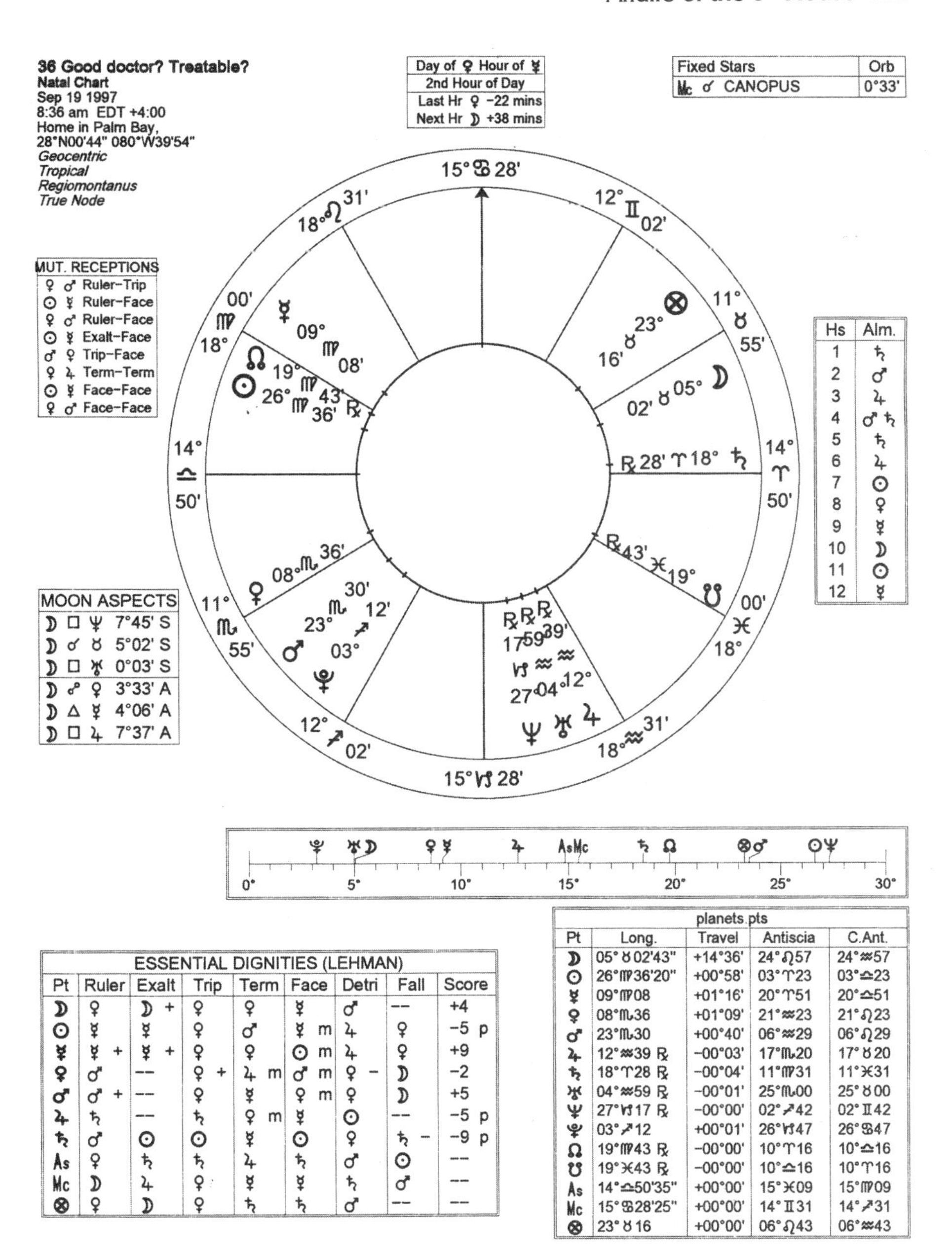

Fixed Stars	Orb
Mc ☌ CANOPUS	0°33'

MUT. RECEPTIONS
♀ ♂ Ruler–Trip
☉ ☿ Ruler–Face
♀ ♂ Ruler–Face
☉ ☿ Exalt–Face
♂ ♀ Trip–Face
♀ ♃ Term–Term
☉ ☿ Face–Face
♀ ♂ Face–Face

Hs	Alm.
1	♄
2	♂
3	♃
4	♂ ♄
5	♄
6	♃
7	☉
8	♀
9	☿
10	☽
11	☉
12	☿

MOON ASPECTS
☽ □ ♆ 7°45' S
☽ ☌ ☋ 5°02' S
☽ □ ♅ 0°03' S
☽ ☍ ♀ 3°33' A
☽ △ ☿ 4°06' A
☽ □ ♃ 7°37' A

ESSENTIAL DIGNITIES (LEHMAN)								
Pt	Ruler	Exalt	Trip	Term	Face	Detri	Fall	Score
☽	♀	☽ +	♀	♀	☿	♂	--	+4
☉	☿	☿	♀	♂	☿ m	♃	♀	−5 p
☿	☿ +	☿ +	♀	♀	☉ m	♃	♀	+9
♀	♂	--	♀ +	♃ m	♂ m	♀ −	☽	−2
♂	♂ +	--	♀	☿	♀ m	♀	☽	+5
♃	♄	--	♄	♀ m	☿	☉	--	−5 p
♄	♂	☉	☉	☿	☉	♀	♄ −	−9 p
As	♀	♄	♄	♃	♄	♂	☉	--
Mc	☽	♃	♀	☿	☿	♄	♂	--
⊗	♀	☽	♀	♄	♄	♂	--	--

planets.pts				
Pt	Long.	Travel	Antiscia	C.Ant.
☽	05° ♉ 02'43"	+14°36'	24° ♌ 57	24° ♒ 57
☉	26° ♍ 36'20"	+00°58'	03° ♈ 23	03° ♎ 23
☿	09° ♍ 08	+01°16'	20° ♈ 51	20° ♎ 51
♀	08° ♏ 36	+01°09'	21° ♒ 23	21° ♌ 23
♂	23° ♏ 30	+00°40'	06° ♒ 29	06° ♌ 29
♃	12° ♒ 39 ℞	−00°03'	17° ♏ 20	17° ♉ 20
♄	18° ♈ 28 ℞	−00°04'	11° ♍ 31	11° ♓ 31
♅	04° ♒ 59 ℞	−00°01'	25° ♏ 00	25° ♉ 00
♆	27° ♑ 17 ℞	−00°00'	02° ♐ 42	02° ♊ 42
♇	03° ♐ 12	+00°01'	26° ♑ 47	26° ♋ 47
☊	19° ♍ 43 ℞	−00°00'	10° ♈ 16	10° ♎ 16
☋	19° ♓ 43 ℞	−00°00'	10° ♎ 16	10° ♈ 16
As	14° ♎ 50'35"	+00°00'	15° ♓ 09	15° ♍ 09
Mc	15° ♋ 28'25"	+00°00'	14° ♊ 31	14° ♐ 31
⊗	23° ♉ 16	+00°00'	06° ♌ 43	06° ♒ 43

Because the Moon rules the 10th House, the nature of the intercession is not through a person, but the treatment itself. The scenario collapses to the almost trivial story: without the intermediary of the consultation, the two would never meet. The problem is that the Moon completes the translation by opposition, so we are confronted with the "if you do, you will regret it" mantra. So even though the issue does not appear to be the doctor's innate competency, he just doesn't look like the doctor for her.

Venus rules both 1st and 8th, raising the possibility of death. However, this is not exactly the most expected outcome in modern times. And it's worth considering the nature of the wording of the question. The Querent did not say, what disease do I have, and is it treatable? She asked, will this doctor be able to treat it? Because her primary question was about *this* doctor and *this* treatment, I have to address the possibility that the death being shown could be from the treatment administered by this doctor, and not from the disease itself.

Jupiter in Aquarius, the Ruler of the 6th House, shows the condition itself. Jupiter is peregrine[129] and retrograde. While in a fixed sign, the peregrine and retrograde qualities argue against the condition having a constant nature. A peregrine disease is not necessarily weak. Instead, it may be unpredictable because its nature or location keeps shifting, or its susceptibility to a particular treatment protocol may vary. We also see the South Node at the 6th House cusp. Notice that both Jupiter and Aquarius have some relationship to the concept of "bad blood" when we attempt to describe the disease – and in this case, a systemic infection is a pretty good match. However, notice again as we saw for the possibility of death that the South Node at the 6th, combined with the fixed nature of Jupiter in Aquarius could argue for the disease remaining, and the retrograde direction of Jupiter could show the condition becoming worse should the Querent pursue this treatment.

Because the Moon is in Taurus, I judged she could successfully treat the infection; because it's coming to opposition in fixed signs, I said the process would be long. She decided to forego the treatment at that time. She has reduced the severity of the condition by Qi Jong[130] practice to such an extent that, most of the time, she barely remembers that she has the condition.

Example 37: Should we give our cat Epogen®?

A student of mine asked this question during a course session. One of her cats had kidney failure, and she and her husband were trying desperately to give the cat the chance to recover from her condition, or at least to stabilize. She asked about the drug Epogen®, because her concern was that perhaps a third of the animals given this drug have an allergic reaction, and she didn't want her cat to go through the distress.

Despite the concern that we often have about "should" questions, the wording of this one is absolutely clear: there's no point giving the drug either if it provokes a reaction, or if the drug will be ineffective.

Do we turn the chart because the Querent is asking about a drug for her cat? The cat is given by the 6th House, the cat's illness by the 6th from the 6th (the 11th), the possible drug treatment by the 10th from the 6th (the 3rd), and the possibility of the death of the cat from the 8th from the 6th (the 1st). Stop! Mars in Aries gives the cat? Either the cat has just gotten radically better, or something is *very* wrong with this chart! The traditional rules for using the 1st House as the patient if the patient grants permission seemingly excludes animals, which to date are not considered capable of giving permission as generally understood. But which would we rather use to describe a cat with kidney failure: Mars in Aries ruling the 6th, or Mercury in Pisces ruling the 1st? I have to

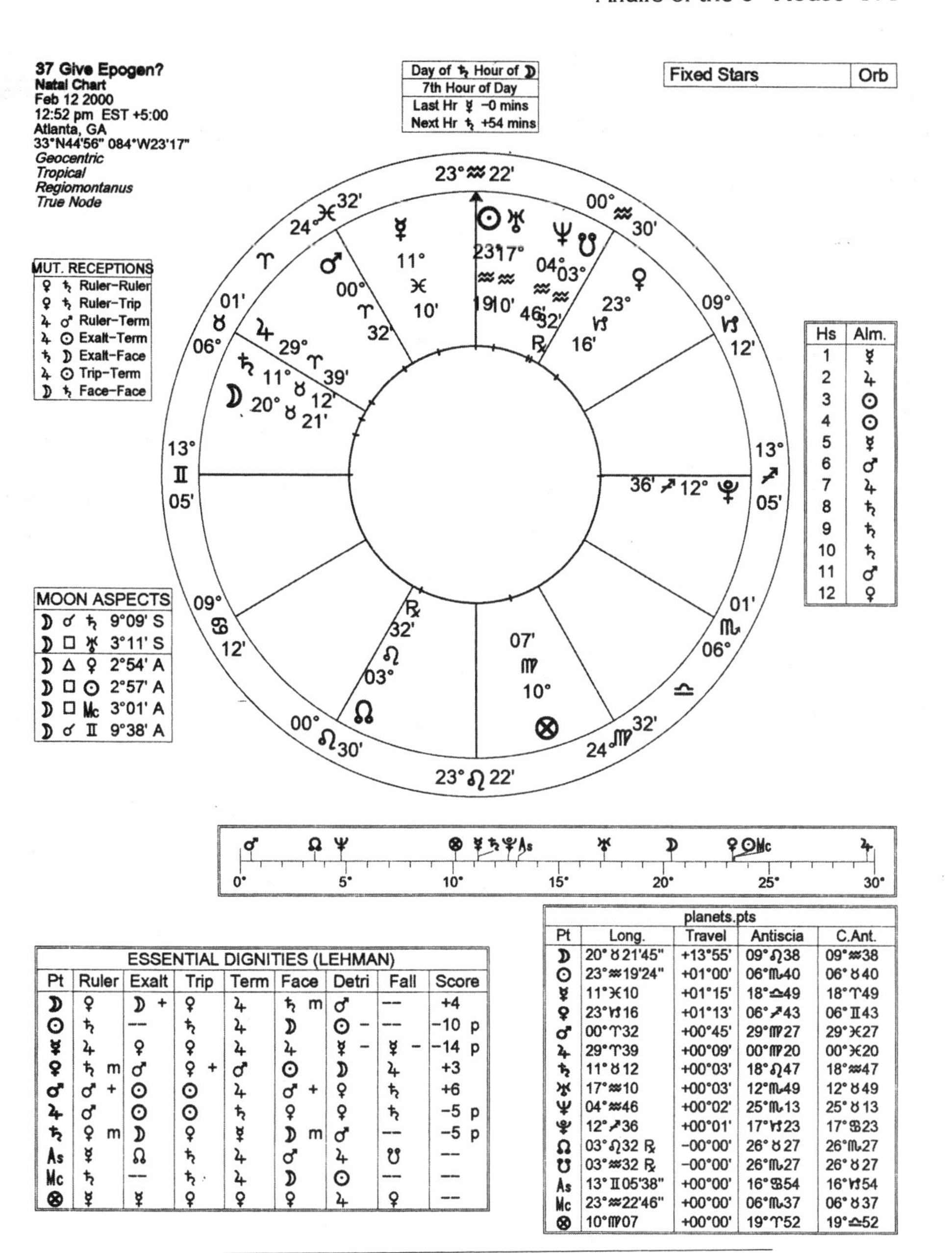

MUT. RECEPTIONS
♀ ♄ Ruler-Ruler
♀ ♄ Ruler-Trip
♃ ♂ Ruler-Term
♃ ☉ Exalt-Term
♄ ☽ Exalt-Face
♃ ☉ Trip-Term
☽ ♄ Face-Face

MOON ASPECTS			
☽ ☌ ♄	9°09'	S
☽ □ ♅	3°11'	S
☽ △ ♀	2°54'	A
☽ □ ☉	2°57'	A
☽ □ Mc	3°01'	A
☽ ☌ ♊	9°38'	A

Hs	Alm.
1	☿
2	♃
3	☉
4	☉
5	☿
6	♂
7	♃
8	♄
9	♄
10	♄
11	♂
12	♀

ESSENTIAL DIGNITIES (LEHMAN)								
Pt	Ruler	Exalt	Trip	Term	Face	Detri	Fall	Score
☽	♀	☽ +	♀	♃	♄ m	♂	--	+4
☉	♄	--	♄	♃	☽	☉ -	--	-10 p
☿	♃	♀	♀	♃	♃	☿ -	☿ -	-14 p
♀	♄ m	♂	♀ +	♂	☉	☽	♃	+3
♂	♂ +	☉	☉	♃	♂ +	♀	♄	+6
♃	♂	☉	☉	♄	♀	♀	♄	-5 p
♄	♀ m	☽	♀	☿	☽ m	♂	--	-5 p
As	☿	☊	♄	♃	♂	♃	☋	--
Mc	♄	--	♄	♃	☽	☉	--	--
⊗	☿	☿	♀	♀	♀	♃	♀	--

planets.pts				
Pt	Long.	Travel	Antiscia	C.Ant.
☽	20°♉21'45"	+13°55'	09°♌38	09°♒38
☉	23°♒19'24"	+01°00'	06°♏40	06°♉40
☿	11°♓10	+01°15'	18°♎49	18°♈49
♀	23°♑16	+01°13'	06°♐43	06°♊43
♂	00°♈32	+00°45'	29°♍27	29°♓27
♃	29°♈39	+00°09'	00°♍20	00°♓20
♄	11°♉12	+00°03'	18°♌47	18°♒47
♅	17°♒10	+00°03'	12°♏49	12°♉49
♆	04°♒46	+00°02'	25°♏13	25°♉13
♇	12°♐36	+00°01'	17°♑23	17°♋23
☊	03°♌32 ℞	-00°00'	26°♉27	26°♏27
☋	03°♒32 ℞	-00°00'	26°♏27	26°♉27
As	13°♊05'38"	+00°00'	16°♋54	16°♑54
Mc	23°♒22'46"	+00°00'	06°♏37	06°♉37
⊗	10°♍07	+00°00'	19°♈52	19°♎52

say this looks a lot more like Mercury in Pisces. As a result, the chart tells me that we *have* to use the radical 1st House for the cat, given what we know about the circumstances.

Our valiant cat, being Mercury in Pisces, is damaged. No surprise, and Pisces shows the nature of the problem. Notice that Mercury is in a partile sextile to Saturn, Ruler of the 10th. Saturn is peregrine and just barely still at the Bendings, so it looks doubtful that the treatment will do any good, but the partile sextile suggests that the cat would not suffer from the treatment by reacting badly to it. Even so, with the same planet ruling both 10th and 8th, one would still worry about the treatment hastening death.

Because of the shift to using the radical 6th as the illness instead of the cat, here we see the illness very strong, and just having entered a new phase.

Unfortunately, it had. The Querent decided against the Epogen® treatment, but shortly thereafter the cat was seized by convulsions and died a few days later. Which is quite well shown here by Pluto conjunct the 7th House cusp, the Portal of Death in a chart.

The death of the cat is shown several other ways, including through the translation by the Moon from Saturn, Ruler of the 8th, to Venus, located in the 8th. The Moon reached Venus symbolically in three days.

Example 38: Event – Chest Pains

When an event is available, it should be interpreted in preference to a horary about the event. Questions about illness have myriad events: appointments with health care practitioners, times of diagnosis, treatment times, hospital admission times, not to mention health crisis times. When available, these are the better option. They are interpreted just as if there were an implicit horary: What is the nature of my condition, and how and when will I recover from it?

In an event, the event itself is the First House. Practically speaking, this makes the patient the 1st, because the patient is the subject of the event. This chart is presented in proportional houses to show the effect of the high latitude on the delineation. The event was chest pains. The subject assumed he was having a heart attack, so he checked himself into the hospital.

The condition of the patient is shown through the Ruler of the Ascendant, Saturn in Aries. He is having an acute condition, so Aries certainly seems descriptive enough. The Ruler of the 6th House (trust me, there *is* a 6th House!) is Mercury in Capricorn in the 1st. This doesn't look like heart disease. It looks like a chronic problem (Capricorn) of the nerves (Mercury) or an intermittent or variable problem (Mercury) with the bones (Capricorn).

The heart is most usually associated with the Sun and Leo. There is no relationship of any of these components to the 6th House. The Sun is in the 1st – but so are most of the possible placements, given the size of the 1st! So we see absolutely no indication of heart problems.

The obvious question is: what was it? The two other likely culprits are indigestion, or possibly thoracic (mid spinal) vertebrae out of alignment, as both these conditions can cause chest pains. Stomach conditions are associated with the Moon and Cancer; again, we seem to be lacking any indicators of this nature. Mercury in Capricorn does rule the 6th, so I would surmise that he needed a chiropractic or spinal adjustment.

The patient is not of an alternative health frame of mind. The doctors he consulted are allopaths. They examined him, performed a battery of tests and found nothing, except the opportunity to bill his insurance company. He has not had a recurrence of the symptoms, although the hint that does suggest the chiropractic hypothesis was that he was in a car accident a few weeks before this incident occurred.

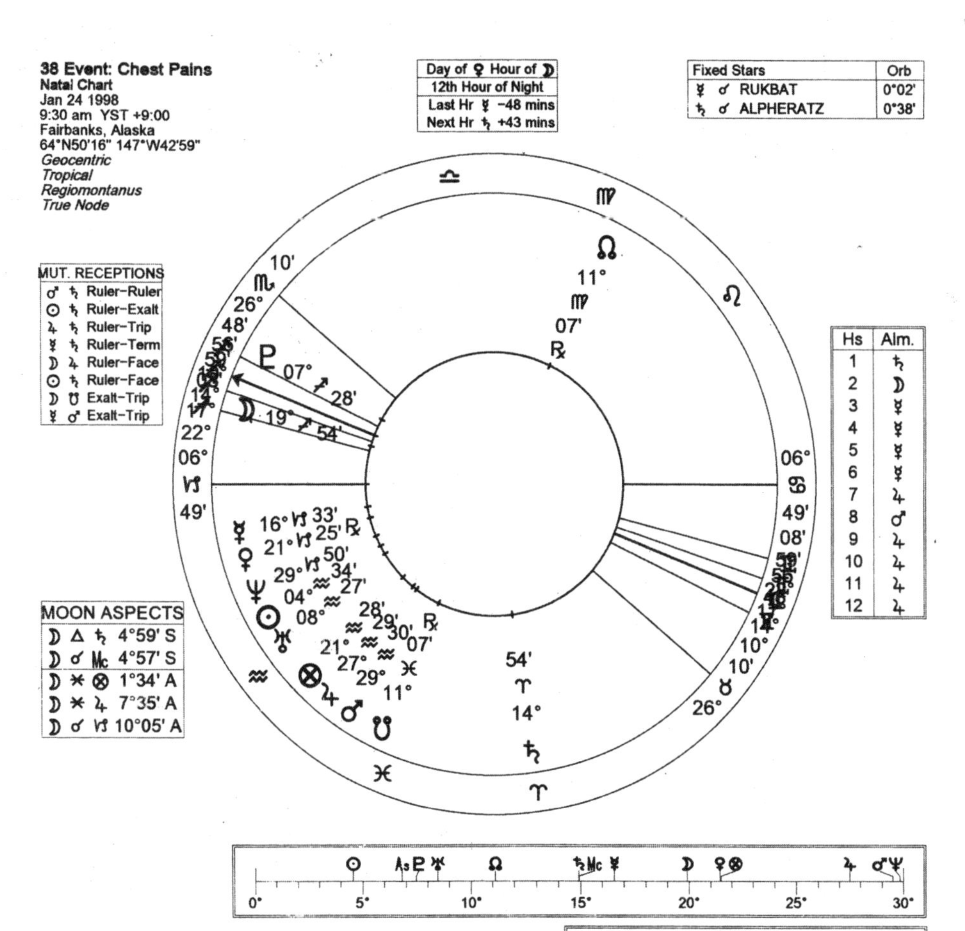

planets.pts				
Pt	Long.	Travel	Antiscia	C.Ant.
☽	19°♐54'29"	+13°11'	10°♑05	10°♋05
☉	04°♒34'03"	+01°01'	25°♏25	25°♉25
☿	16°♑33	+01°27'	13°♐26	13°♊26
♀	21°♑25 ℞	−00°28'	08°♐34	08°♊34
♂	29°♒30	+00°47'	00°♏29	00°♉29
♃	27°♒29	+00°13'	02°♏30	02°♉30
♄	14°♈54	+00°04'	15°♍05	15°♓05
♅	08°♒27	+00°03'	21°♏32	21°♉32
♆	29°♑50	+00°02'	00°♐09	00°♊09
♇	07°♐28	+00°01'	22°♑31	22°♋31
☊	11°♍07 ℞	−00°05'	18°♈52	18°♎52
☋	11°♓07 ℞	−00°05'	18°♎52	18°♈52
As	06°♑49'02"	+00°00'	23°♐10	23°♊10
Mc	14°♐56'34"	+00°00'	15°♑03	15°♋03
⊗	21°♒28	+00°00'	08°♏31	08°♉31

ESSENTIAL DIGNITIES (LEHMAN)								
Pt	Ruler	Exalt	Trip	Term	Face	Detri	Fall	Score
☽	♃	☋	♃	♄	☽ +	☿	☊	+1
☉	♄	--	☿	♄	♀ m	☉ −	---	−10 p
☿	♄	♂	☽	♃	♂	☽	♃	−5 p
♀	♄	♂	☽	♂	☉ m	☽	♃	−5 p
♂	♄ m	--	☿	♂ +	☽	☉	--	+2
♃	♄	--	☿	♂	☽	☉	--	−5 p
♄	♂ m	☉	♃	☿	☉	♀	♄ −	−9 p
As	♄	♂	☽	☿	♃	☽	♃	--
Mc	♃	☋	♃	☿	☽	☿	☊	--
⊗	♄	--	☿	♃	☽	☉	---	--

Questions concerning Pets and Small Animals.

Pets, birds and small animals are considered matters of the 6th House, although it has become common for some astrologers to try to use the 5th House, under the argument that many people treat pets as their children. While this may be true, I have not shifted my mode of delineation, because there are certain differences which go beyond merely the species boundary, although the species barrier may be the cause of the difference. Obviously the type of scenarios we face in keeping our pets safe are often very different than those we encounter with minor children, the easiest analogy to the circumstances of pethood.

In theory, we can ask any questions about animals that we can ask about humans, given the lifestyle differences. In my practice, almost no questions about animals are asked except either missing animals, animal health problems, or concerning adopting a new pet. For these, we can look to the Ruler of the 6th House, and see its dignity, and also we would look for an interaction between the Rulers of the 1st and 6th to see the effect of a successful transition on both sides.

In these horaries, the animals were generally read just as they would have been for a turned chart for a sister, a father, or some other non-first House person: in other words, using the 6th House as the cat or dog, just as we would use the 3rd for a sibling, or the 7th for a spouse. Although it is still necessary to check for the possibility that you need to read the chart in its radical positions, as in Example 37.

Questions concerning Jobs and Working Conditions.

There is a tendency among horary astrologers to adopt a convention much in use by natal astrologers when it comes to job questions. That tendency is to attribute so-called blue collar jobs to the 6th, and management jobs to the 10th. I accepted this uncritically for quite a while, but I became increasingly unhappy about the results for many so-called management jobs.

The more I thought about this, the more I realized that the real culprit was the tendency of our society to inflate job titles. When you have corporations with hundreds of vice presidents, just how valuable is that title? In a feudal society, the 10th House applied to the higher nobility: the king, princes, dukes, and earls – and just how many were there in a typical country? In a business, the only unequivocal 10th House parties are the owner(s) and the chief executive officers. Even the other "chief" officers – the chief financial officer, chief operating officer, chief information officer – may or may not be 10th, depending on the individual corporate structure.

In reality, there are two primary ways that most of us experience the 10th House: as our boss, i.e., the person further up the hierarchy; or as honors and rewards. Thus, a question about promotion may be legitimately 10th House because it represents a change in status, or an honor, both 10th House matters.

In any case, the 6th House is valuable in virtually all job questions, because it highlights working conditions. One of the biggest issues in working conditions is fellow employees. This is where we see them.

Example 39: Is it worth trying to make it?

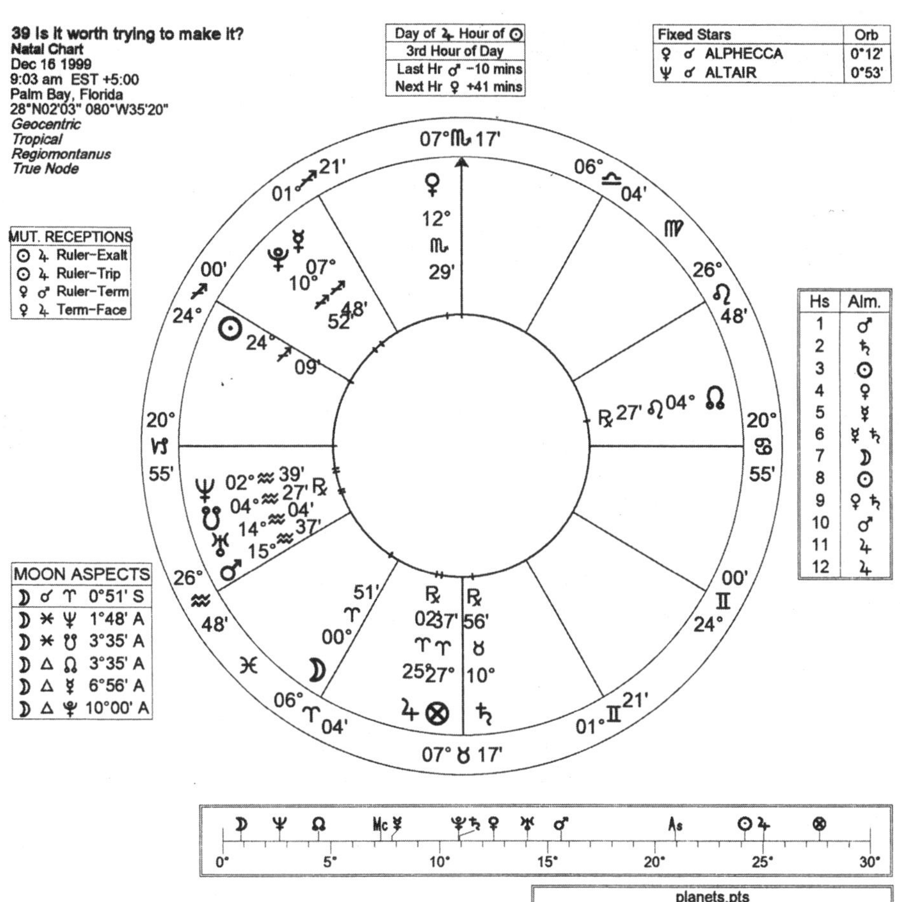

ESSENTIAL DIGNITIES (LEHMAN)								
Pt	Ruler	Exalt	Trip	Term	Face	Detri	Fall	Score
☽	♂	☉	☉	♃	♂	♀	♄	−5 p
☉	♃	☋	☉ +	♄	♄	☿	☊	+3
☿	♃	☋	☉	♃	☿ +	☿ −	☊	−4
♀	♂	---	♀ +	♃	☉	♀ −	☽	−2
♂	♄	---	♄	♀	☿	☉	---	−5 p
♃	♂	☉	☉	♂	♀	♀	♄	−5 p
♄	♀	☽	♀	☿	☽	♂	---	−5 p
As	♄	♂	♀	♂	☉	☽	♃	---
Mc	♂	---	♀	♃	♂	♀	☽	---
⊗	♂	☉	☉	♄	♀	♀	♄	---

planets.pts				
Pt	Long.	Travel	Antiscia	C.Ant.
☽	00°♈51'25"	+13°17'	29°♍08	29°♓08
☉	24°♐09'41"	+01°01'	05°♑50	05°♋50
☿	07°♐48	+01°27'	22°♑11	22°♋11
♀	12°♏29	+01°11'	17°♒30	17°♌30
♂	15°♒37	+00°46'	14°♏22	14°♉22
♃	25°♈02 ℞	−00°00'	04°♍57	04°♓57
♄	10°♉56 ℞	−00°02'	19°♌03	19°♒03
♅	14°♒04	+00°02'	15°♏55	15°♉55
♆	02°♒39	+00°01'	27°♏20	27°♉20
♇	10°♐52	+00°02'	19°♑07	19°♋07
☊	04°♌27 ℞	−00°00'	25°♉32	25°♏32
☋	04°♒27 ℞	−00°00'	25°♏32	25°♉32
As	20°♑55'58"	+00°00'	09°♐04	09°♊04
Mc	07°♏17'01"	+00°00'	22°♒42	22°♌42
⊗	27°♈37	+00°00'	02°♍22	02°♓22

The Querent works as a financial analyst. His firm, which is big enough for the name to be recognizable by virtually everyone, had not succeeded in getting a contract from a government agency; a project that had been his major focus for over a year. In the aftermath, he was reduced to playing computer game and working out in the office gym. What he wanted was guidance about whether he should try to take control and get back on track in his company, or start sending his resume out to potential employers.

We have a choice of using Mars (Almuten) or Saturn (sign) ruler of the 1st for the Querent. Mars is not in any better shape than Saturn. I rather thought Saturn at the Bendings sounded sufficiently morose and depressed to signify the Querent. Also, I needed to be free and clear to use Mars for his bosses, because this whole question hinges on the client's ability to reconnect to his bosses, to get them to assign him new responsibilities, and to turn the work experience around. Notice that they are doubly separating from each other by square, no less. His boss(es) are peregrine – they don't actually have any idea what to do, but being Mars, they will try to do something! It's just not likely to involve the Querent.

Notice that the job or working conditions are given by Mercury – in Detriment in Sagittarius. The sign of Saturn and the sign of Mercury don't even behold – there is absolutely no tie here between the Querent and his work environment.

Consider that this job we are talking about has annual compensation of over $100,000 – a pretty good sum! Many of us would be very loath to assign such a job to the 6th, but consider – the Querent has no autonomy to set up his own agenda. He may have quite a bit once he is assigned a project, but without the initial assignment, he is reduced to complete inertia. This illustrates how we cannot let our assumptions about a job or profession based upon the magnitude of compensation blind us to the fact that a 10th House position involves considerable power and independence – not merely a commanding salary.

So I didn't see how he would turn this situation around. By January 8th, he was let go with a month's notice; he agreed after negotiating better severance pay, and left February 1st.

Example 40: Will this potential employee be a problem?

The Querent had posted a job listing for a clerk to process mail orders. Because this was a mail-order situation, the applicant's location was much less important than his or her computer skills. Furthermore, the Querent was somewhat apprehensive, because this position would be completely telecomputing, meaning that on-site supervision would not be possible.

The specific reason that alarm bells were raised in her mind was that the woman who applied indicated that she was not a morning person, and intended to do most of the work late at night. Although this is hardly unknown in the computer world, the Querent was uneasy about whether the late night schedule in fact masked a more important problem.

Let us first examine the Querent, who has dignity by Triplicity. Her Significator is in the 10th house: very good, since she is the boss with respect

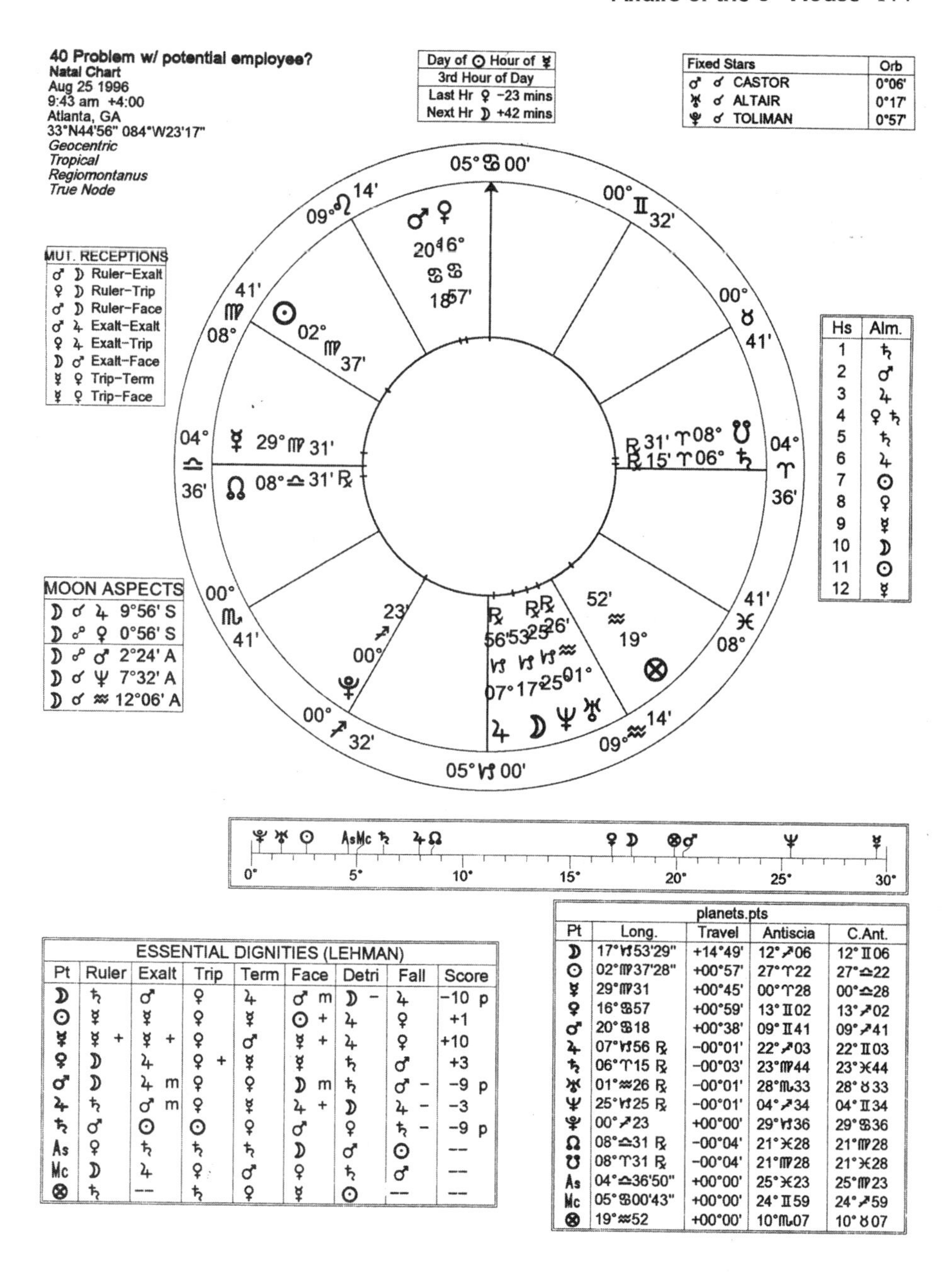

Pt	Ruler	Exalt	Trip	Term	Face	Detri	Fall	Score
ESSENTIAL DIGNITIES (LEHMAN)								
☽	♄	♂	♀	♃	♂ m	☽ −	♃	−10 p
☉	☿	☿	♀	☿	☉ +	♃	♀	+1
☿	☿ +	☿ +	♀	♂	☿ +	♃	♀	+10
♀	☽	♃	♀ +	☿	☿	♄	♂	+3
♂	☽	♃ m	♀	♀	☽ m	♄	♂ −	−9 p
♃	♄	♂ m	♀	☿	♃ +	☽	♃ −	−3
♄	♂	☉	☉	♀	♂	♀	♄ −	−9 p
As	♀	♄	♄	♄	☽	♂	☉	---
Mc	☽	♃	♀	♂	♀	♄	♂	---
⊗	♄	---	♄	♀	☿	☉	---	---

planets.pts

Pt	Long.	Travel	Antiscia	C.Ant.
☽	17°♑53'29"	+14°49'	12°♐06	12°♊06
☉	02°♍37'28"	+00°57'	27°♈22	27°♎22
☿	29°♍31	+00°45'	00°♈28	00°♎28
♀	16°♋57	+00°59'	13°♊02	13°♐02
♂	20°♋18	+00°38'	09°♊41	09°♐41
♃	07°♑56 ℞	−00°01'	22°♐03	22°♊03
♄	06°♈15 ℞	−00°03'	23°♍44	23°♓44
♅	01°♒26 ℞	−00°01'	28°♏33	28°♉33
♆	25°♑25 ℞	−00°01'	04°♐34	04°♊34
♇	00°♐23	+00°00'	29°♑36	29°♋36
☊	08°♎31 ℞	−00°04'	21°♓28	21°♍28
☋	08°♈31 ℞	−00°04'	21°♍28	21°♓28
As	04°♎36'50"	+00°00'	25°♓23	25°♍23
Mc	05°♋00'43"	+00°00'	24°♊59	24°♐59
⊗	19°♒52	+00°00'	10°♏07	10°♉07

to this question.

There are two ways to consider the Quesited: either as a 7th House person, or a 6th House one. Normally, a subcontractor (7th House) is treated as a specialist: an "equal" as it were, while an employee (6th) is subservient. This had the feel of a 6th House position, with the legal status of a 7th House position. Which to use? I examined both, figuring that if one house proved sufficiently better than the other, then perhaps the Querent could structure the job to work with the better house.

Using the 7th House as the Quesited, we see a retrograde Saturn sitting near the cusp, and near the South Node. This *definitely* does not look like a good idea! If we use the 6th, we have Jupiter in Fall, again retrograde, at the Bendings, in the 4th House. The latter is at least descriptive: she would be working at home. But retrograde, at the Bendings and in Fall? I don't think so!

Either method pointed to this potential employee not being a good choice. However, in examining further, the Querent's Significator, Venus, is coming to conjoin Mars. While Mars was a possible candidate for being the Quesited, I rejected Mars for three reasons: (1) the Sun is Almuten of the 7th, not Mars; (2) the Sun has small Dignity, while Mars has mixed Dignity and Debility,[131] so the Almuten would override the sign ruler; and (3) Saturn in the 7th described the Quesited better anyway: an older woman. So, if Mars were not the Quesited, then Mars would have to be somebody else!

So I advised the Querent that there was someone else out there who would be a better choice. And so it proved.

Example 41: Leave my job today?

The Querent had been working for a software company for about seven months when she asked this question. Her Significator, the Moon, was in the 9th House: leaving this job would also result in her moving, as her husband had taken a job in another city, and she would prefer to join him. The Ascendant degree is the natal Sun of the owner of the business.

The importance of this chart is in thinking about exactly how we delineate the houses in questions about jobs. The reason I got the call from the Querent was because she had gotten especially aggravated with her boss. But we don't even see a direct conflict here. The Moon signifying her is not making an aspect with Mars, Ruler of the 10th House. The boss's Mars retrograde is right on her 2nd House cusp, so we can surmise that she probably was looking for better financial compensation, but still, the two are not shown as in conflict – *which most likely means that he is unaware that she is experiencing this problem with him*. A conflict requires that both parties conflict – in the absence of an aspect such as a square to show the conflict, then all the pressure and frustration is on one side. A contributing argument in this case is that both boss and employee are Cancers – so there's a good chance that whatever the real conflict, it was not taking place in the open.

The Moon was approaching Scheat, one of the principal shipwreck fixed stars. This does not bode well for her and her position! The South Node in the 10th House clearly shows that, from her perspective anyway, the boss was a baleful influence. The peregrine Sun rules the 2nd House - her money. The only two planets with any dignity greater than Face are Jupiter and Venus, who rule the 4th, 6th, 9th and 11th Houses, not terribly relevant in this question, with the exception of the 6th. Notice that dignified Jupiter rules the work environment and the job – the 6th House. Her problem is not with her fellow employees, or the employees under her, but with her boss. Also note that this Jupiter is in a weak mutual reception with the Querent's Significator, the Moon. Could the Querent be nervous about finding another job if she walks away from this one?

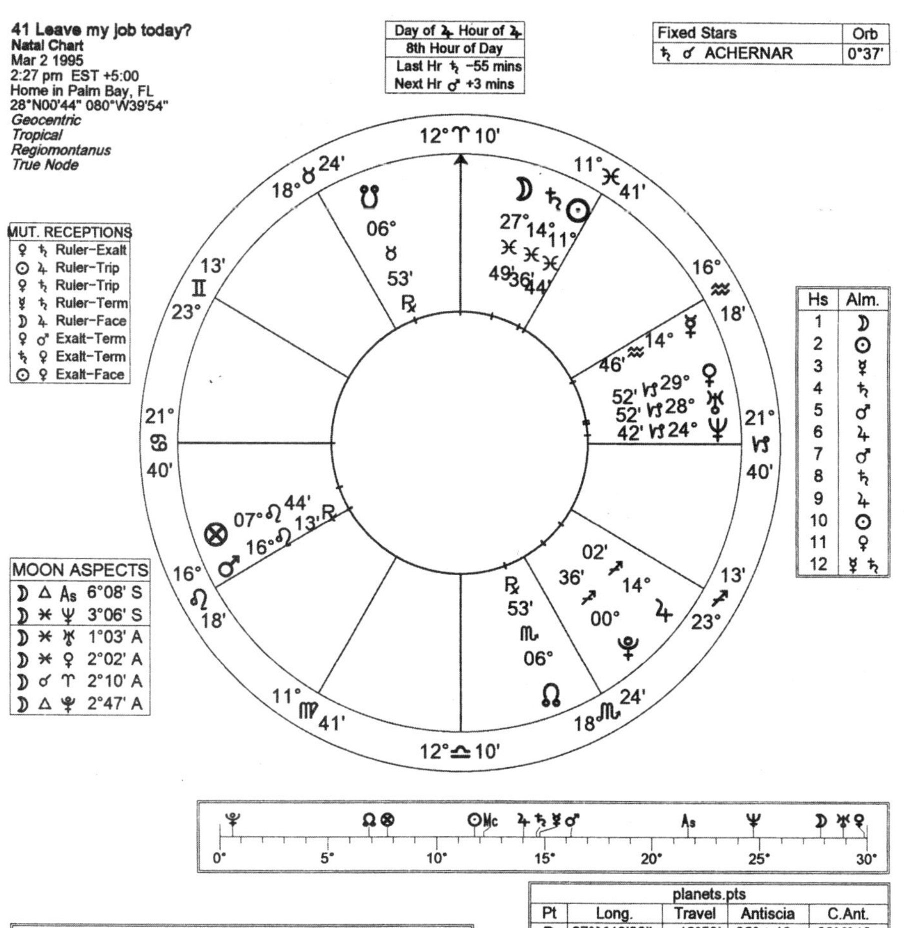

Pt	Long.	Travel	Antiscia	C.Ant.
☽	27°♓49'00"	+12°58'	02°♎10	02°♈10
☉	11°♓44'56"	+01°00'	18°♎15	18°♈15
☿	14°♒46	+01°03'	15°♏13	15°♉13
♀	29°♑52	+01°10'	00°♐07	00°♊07
♂	16°♌13 ℞	-00°16'	13°♉46	13°♏46
♃	14°♐02	+00°05'	15°♑57	15°♋57
♄	14°♓36	+00°07'	15°♎23	15°♈23
♅	28°♑52	+00°02'	01°♐07	01°♊07
♆	24°♑42	+00°01'	05°♐17	05°♊17
♇	00°♐36	+00°00'	29°♑23	29°♋23
☊	06°♏53 ℞	-00°06'	23°♒06	23°♌06
☋	06°♉53 ℞	-00°06'	23°♌06	23°♒06
As	21°♋40'14"	+00°00'	08°♊19	08°♐19
Mc	12°♈10'34"	+00°00'	17°♍49	17°♓49
⊗	07°♌44	+00°00'	22°♉15	22°♏15

ESSENTIAL DIGNITIES (LEHMAN)

Pt	Ruler	Exalt	Trip	Term	Face	Detri	Fall	Score
☽	♃	♀	♀	♄	♂	☿	☿	-5 p
☉	♃	♀	♀	♃	♃	☿	☿	-5 p
☿	♄	--	♄	♀	☿ +	☉	--	+1
♀	♄	♂	♀ +	♄	☉	☽	♃	+3
♂	☉	--	☉	♀	♃	♄	--	-5 p
♃	♃ +	☋	☉	☿	☽	☿	☊	+5
♄	♃	♀	♀	☿	♃	☿	☿	-5 p
As	☽	♃	♀	♀	☽	♄	♂	--
Mc	♂	☉	☉	♀	☉	♀	♄	--
⊗	☉	--	☉	☿	♄	♄	--	--

The Moon with Scheat represents her job situation floundering on the rocks, but is her job floundering *today*? The Moon is in a mutable sign in a cadent House: this does not suggest the same immediacy as today. Remember – cadent placements slow down the flow of events. With the Sun ruling the 2nd House and peregrine, leaving the company *today* (i.e., the time frame of her question) would *not* bode well for her financially. Mars is sitting, retrograde, right on the 2nd House cusp. A planet retrograde brings delays or sudden results – we might simply call this instability.

The Moon, in addition to coming to Scheat, is also about to change signs, but in a little over 2 degrees. The one planet that is immediately about to change signs is Venus, with Triplicity, in the 7th House.

I judged the following to the client. With Venus angular and in a cardinal sign, someone, probably female, is about to leave the company: this is definitely immediate. The Querent's job is precarious, but it does not require leaving today: in fact, leaving today would be financially disadvantageous to the Querent. I suggested that, since the aspects and dignity patterns were generally wretched until the Sun got into Aries, that she at least try to hold on for the two weeks or two months that it will take to get there (interestingly, the same timing that it takes for the Moon to symbolically change signs if we pick weeks as the unit of measure). With so many Significators peregrine, the people are too weak to do anything effective anyway.

The Part of Fortune is at the Bendings: this puts her financial compensation at risk. I counseled her to be ready to leave at any time, to take each day as if it were her last, and to get her resume out, preferably with some good electional work backing the time to send it out, and the time to contact prospective employers.

Within the week, a long-standing female employee did leave. The Querent left her job several months later.

We will revisit the subject of jobs in Chapter Ten. The differentiation between the houses can be somewhat tricky. Perhaps the simplest way to determine this is to ask whether the Querent has a boss figure over her or him that needs to be considered. If the Querent has considerable autonomy and there is no supervising figure, then the job itself is 10th House. If there is a day-to-day supervisor, then the job is probably not 10th House.

Chapter 7

Affairs of the 7th House:

Marriage and Partnerships. Theft. Fugitives. Buying, Selling, Competitions, Lawsuits and Wars. Open Enemies

Questions of the 7th House as given by Lilly:[132]

- *Of marriage*
  - *The time of marriage*
  - *The number of spouses*
  - *The nature of the spouse*
  - *Whether the partners agree after marriage*
  - *Whether the marriage shall be broken*
  - *Who dies first*
  - *Whether the intended is a virgin*
  - *Whether the spouse has a lover*
  - *Whether the child conceived is the child of the husband*
  - *Whether the spouses, living apart, shall be reconciled*
- *Of items, people and animals lost, mislaid, or stolen*
  - *Of servants fled*
  - *Of animals strayed*
  - *Of items lost*
  - *Theft*

- *Battles, Wars and other Contentions*
  - *Whether the Querent shall return home from the war*
  - *What will ensue of the war*
  - *On the competency of commanders*
  - *Of whether a town besieged shall be taken*
  - *Who shall do the best in a suit of law*
- *Of [business] partnership*
- *Of removal from place to place*
- *Of hunting*
- *Of buying and selling commodities*
- *If the Querent have Open Enemies, or any Adversaries*

That's quite a list! Gadbury's list of categories of questions is subsumed under Lilly's.[133] We have already taken up lost objects, theft and removal under Chapter 4. Two additional thoughts, however. First, the rules for theft can be applied – within reason – for questions concerning the commission of any felony. In other words, the word "criminal" can be substituted for the word "thief." Second, while it's not listed officially as a category in Lilly, the 7th House is used as the "default other person"- that particular Quesited who doesn't fit the classification of any other house in the chart.

When we examine 1st-7th House questions, we should be aware that there are only a relatively small number of planetary pairs that we use, as shown in Table One. This idea of a small number of pairs does *not* necessarily hold for other house combinations, because any house combination which is not in a polar relationship can have variations imposed by house interceptions: e.g., what sign is on the 5th House cusp is not entirely predictable if the chart has, for example, Scorpio Rising. Pisces would merely be the most common answer, but not the only answer.

Table 1. Planetary Pairs that are encountered in 1st-7th questions.

1st House	7th House	Ruler - 1st	Ruler - 7th	Almuten 1st	Almuten 7th
♈	♎	♂	♀	☉ (day)	♄ (day)
♉	♏	♀	♂	☽ (night)	
♊	♐	☿	♃		
♋	♑	☽	♄	♃	♂
♌	♒	☉	♄		
♍	♓	☿	♃		♀ ♂

This table makes it clear that only certain pairs are involved in 1st-7th questions: by far the most common being Venus-Mars, Mercury-Jupiter, and (Sunand Moon)-Saturn. Some variants are also given because they are commonly the Almutens of certain signs.

Each of these common pair types gives a different flavor or undertone to the Question, especially considering the exact type of Question or circumstance. The Venus-Mars combination gives passion, but not just sexual passion. This pair highlights the emotional agenda that each person brings to the matter at hand. Emotions are very hard for the average human to imagine controlling – so these circumstances are difficult for the parties to think through, or approach with any degree of objectivity. The Mercury-Jupiter combination gives a more intellectual focus, which makes for more objectivity, but also less emotional glue to hold the pairing together whenever difficulty ensues. The Sun/Moon-Saturn combinations give an emotionally-charged power differential, as the two parties approach the relationship with completely different agendas. These different perspectives can then become a part of the story surrounding the Question. They become especially important if the Question puts the two parties into a conflict situation as exemplified by the use of the 7th House for enemies, competitors, and even business clients.

Questions of Marriage

We will begin by succinctly stating Lilly's rules with regard to these matters, and then we will examine these questions further by going through specific examples.

However, before considering the specifics, let's be sure to mention the general. In a question of whether a marriage (or other 7th House relationship) will occur, the affirmative is obtained from an approaching aspect of Significators representing the 1st and 7th House parties, or via the other means of perfection that we outlined in the Green Belt Chapter.[134] As already discussed, dignity is crucial in the judgment of whether positive indications will actually occur.

Now, touching Lilly's subcategories of relationship questions,

- **The time of marriage:** This can be given either by the application between the Significators of the 1st and 7th Houses, or by the application of the Moon to the Sun or Venus.[135]

- **The number of spouses:** Lilly gives several possibilities. The ones he considers best are:
  (1) many planets in the 7th denote multiple spouses (especially if the Sun is sextile or trine these planets); or
  (2) to consider the relationship of the Lord of the 7th to the Sun: the number of planets between represents the number of spouses, provided Mars is in a mutable sign.

  Lilly doesn't actually give an example using this rule, and this is somewhat obscured because he refers only to the number of husbands. By common usage, one might then hypothesize that in the case of a question about wives, Venus might be substituted for

Mars, and the Moon for the Sun. Since I have never been asked this specific question, I haven't had the opportunity to clarify this method.[136]

- **The nature of the spouse:** Generally, this is obtained from examining the sign and house placement of the Ruler of the 7th. For example, the Ruler of the 7th in the 9th could indicate a foreign partner, but also the possibility of a partner of a 9th House type, such as a teacher, book publisher, cleric or philosopher. The relative angular placements of 1st and 7th rulers give the relative class backgrounds of the two parties. For example, both Rulers Succedent would be both parties essentially from the Middle Class; one Significator Angular and the other Succedent would mean that the Angular ruler is from a higher class than the Succedent one. One can also judge physical appearance by the planets beholding the Sun (if the Quesited is a male) or the Moon (if the Quesited is a female).[137] For questions concerning the wealth of the Quesited, examine the condition of the Ruler of the 8th House.[138]

- **Whether the partners agree after marriage:** If the Ascendant and 7th House Ruler behold each other by trine or sextile, this means agreement; the Moon unfortunate means discord. The house Rulership of the afflicting planet gives a hint of who (if anyone on the outside) is contributing to the strife between the partners. The Moon beholding either her dispositor or the exaltation Ruler of the house where she is located is also an indication of agreement between the two. As with disagreement, the house rulership of planets that the Moon beholds favorably can denote which people are particular allies of the couple. The placement of 1st and 7th House rulers in angular houses gives autonomy within the marriage; cadent placement puts that party at a power disadvantage.[139]

- **Whether the marriage shall be broken:** In Lilly's usage, this applied primarily to whether a marriage agreed to would actually take place. A contract could be agreed upon, but then broken off, or one party could die before the marriage occurred. We can also extend this to questions of divorce. In this question, look to the planet that each of the two Significators (of the 1st and 7th) applies. If the planet applied to (in each case) is a superior planet, and that superior planet is in a hard aspect to a malefic, or in cadent placement, then the marriage can be broken off. The house rulership(s) of the offending malefic gives the reason. For example, suppose that Mercury rules the Ascendant, Mercury applies to Saturn (here acting as a superior planet, not a malefic), and Saturn is squared by Mars.[140] The marriage can be broken off. Assuming that Mars is Ruler of the 8th House (as could easily be the case with Virgo Rising), then the reason that the marriage breaks off is money relating to the Quesited: a dowry, or simply financial arrangements, such as a problem with a prenuptial contract.[141]

- **Who dies first:** This is shown by which of the two Significators (1st or 7th) becomes combust first. Lilly also gives the possibility of using the Sun generically for the man, and Venus generically for the woman: one significantly more debilitated argues that this is the party who dies first.[142] This is a question that I have received only a couple of times, possibly because with the greater accessibility of divorce, this question arises only upon the arrival of a life-threatening illness of one of the partners. The option of two different methods makes me nervous, because clearly they can produce different results. The cases I have taken are still open, as fortunately, both partners are still alive.

- **Whether the intended is a virgin:** This is also a kind of horary that's gotten a bit archaic, but then, styles change! However, for whatever it's worth, look to the Ruler of the Ascendant (yes, I think that's odd too, since it's not the Querent asking if he or she is chaste!), the Moon and Venus. If they are in fixed signs, and applying to benefics (which in this case includes the Sun), then the Quesited is judged a virgin. The Moon and Sun in aspect to each other and to Mars is an argument that she or he is not chaste. Also, the angles fixed, but the Ruler of the Ascendant or the Moon in mutable signs likewise gives virginity. The Ruler of the Ascendant combust and in a cardinal sign, or the Moon in the 1st with Saturn means that she (most likely) was the victim of sexual violence.[143]

- **Whether the spouse (or fiancé) has a lover:** When this question has come before me, I have used the rules for whether the rumor is true, rather than Lilly's rules for uncovering a lover. When I have gotten this question, the partner (usually the wife) was asking in response to a particular conversation in which the spouse had declared faithfulness, and where the Querent was doubtful. For Lilly's method, there are three possibilities:

  - The Ascendant, its Ruler, the Moon and the planet that the Moon separates from are used for the Querent. Look to the planets joined to the Moon and the Ruler of the 7th. If both are in reception with the Ruler of the 1st, or conjunct the Ruler of the 1st, then there is no lover. If the Moon separates from the Ruler of the 1st, and the Moon or the Ruler of the 7th is joined (again, one assumes by conjunction or reception) to the Triplicity Ruler of the 1st, then the Quesited has moved on from the Querent to a new love. The Ruler of the 7th void of course argues that there is no third person.

    Use the following table to assess the meaning of any planet in the 7th House.

Saturn	Loves another, but they're not sleeping together
Jupiter	It's tough to resist

Mars	Yes, there's a lover
Venus	There is the appearance of a lover, but not the fact
Mercury	The lover is in past tense
Moon	Not yet, but probable in the future
Sun or North Node	No lover

- Any planet in the 7th, except the Ruler of the 7th (and one must presume, the Ruler of the 1st) denotes a lover. The Ruler of the 7th void of course or conjunct the North Node means no lover. The Ruler of the 7th or the Moon conjunct Mars means a friend, but not necessarily a lover.[144]

  If we go back and examine Example 11 from Chapter 3, page 91 ("Statement about Sex ") using this method, we get the following result: Method One, the Moon is with the South Node, which looks bad in the lover department. Method two gives a negative, but the appearance of a lover, because of Venus' presence. Mercury, as Ruler of the 7th, is not read as having anything to do with the question. Using the third method, there is a lover, or possibly two, because there are planets in the 7th House, and the Ruler of the 7th isn't Void of Course, if Neptune is used.

  In my opinion, Lilly has presented way too many possibilities here, both because of the multiple Significators, and the multiple methods of assessing the question.

- **Whether the child conceived is the child of the husband:** This is another case where I have treated this question as a variation of an "is the rumor true" type. Lilly's method is an interesting throwback to Hellenistic astrology, which used the 11th House for children as much as the 5th House. Although here we could hypothesize that the real derivation is that the 11th House for a man as Querent would be the wife's child. Here Lilly uses the Ruler of the Ascendant and the Moon for the Querent (male), and the 11th House cusp and the Ruler of the 11th for the child. If there is perfection between the two, then the child is legitimate. This is also true if the Ruler of the 1st or the Moon is in the 5th, or if the Ruler of the 5th is in the 1st, both cases being in the absence of hard aspects from the Malefics. If the Fortunes aspect the Ruler of the 5th, then the child is legitimate. Lacking these arguments, the child is not.

- **Whether the spouses, living apart, shall be reconciled:** This is one case where Lilly violates the fundamental principle that the 1st House always gives the Querent. His reasoning is that the 7th House must give the banished spouse (or I would hypothesize, the spouse who left), as the 7th House gives strays. If the Ruler of the 7th beholds the Ascendant; then the two shall be reconciled. Another planet beholding the Ascendant can represent a third party who reconciles the two. If the Sun is above the horizon and Venus beholds the Ascendant by a soft aspect, it also denotes reconciliation, but of course this symbolism implies that the male of a heterosexual relationship is the Querent. If the Sun is below the horizon and Venus beholds the Ascendant by a soft aspect, then the reconciliation is more difficult, and the difficulties are more public. If the Moon is either increasing in light, or in the last Quarter, but not Under Beams, and the Moon is in soft aspect to the Ascendant, then there is reconciliation. Again, from the standpoint of a male Querent, if Venus is occidental, retrograde and hastening to combustion, then she returns of her own accord.[145]

Example 42. Will my husband come back to me?

At the time that I first judged this Question, I took a very simplistic approach: the Ruler of the 1st and the Ruler of the 7th are approaching an opposition. Therefore, using my interpretation of Lilly's rule for perfection by opposition,[146] if they were to get back together, they would regret it. Furthermore, using my normal expectation of the story surrounding a perfection by opposition, the parties are drawn to the matter like a moth to a flame; it's a fatal attraction. However, further examination of the chart gives more detail.

First, the Querent in this case is the wife. She is given by the Moon peregrine in the 8th House. The husband is Saturn, in Detriment and peregrine in the 2nd House. Both rulers are in their spouse's money house: the issue here is money! However, given the condition of both rulers, scarcity of money is the watchword. The Querent's husband had a reasonably successful business, but one that shortly saw costs go up, while revenue dropped. His business ultimately was superceded by newer technology, and he never retooled.

However, consider the situation further. The husband is the one who left home, not the wife. And he did so after establishing a fairly long-term relationship with his secretary. Thus, part of the answer to this question involves not whether he was dallying, but whether the lover relationship would end, and he would be reconciled with his wife.

Using Lilly's rules for lovers, the Sun is applying to Saturn, Ruler of the 7th. Further, Saturn is in the Sun's sign, while the Sun is in Saturn's exaltation: they are in mutual reception. Even better, the Sun is the exaltation ruler of the husband's 5th House, the radical 11th. So the lover is shown in Lilly's rules, although Mars rates as the Significator of the lover generally, since Mars is both Ruler and Almuten of the 11th House. (Notice that the Querent didn't ask if there was a lover; she already knew. So while it's nice to find confirmation through Lilly's rules for lovers, this usage won't supercede the normal use of the husband's 5th House in the question at hand.)

What about the rules for reconciliation? In this case, we have to decide what to do about Lilly's assumption that the fled party is female. The normal approach would be to substitute either the Sun or Mars for Venus; the rules don't make any sense with the Sun, which can be neither retrograde nor combust, and Mars is already reserved for the girlfriend. So the only other possible choice for a male would be Saturn, which makes sense anyway as Ruler of the 7th. So we see that Saturn does not behold the Ascendant, and the Sun is below the horizon, an argument against reconciliation. This is further argued

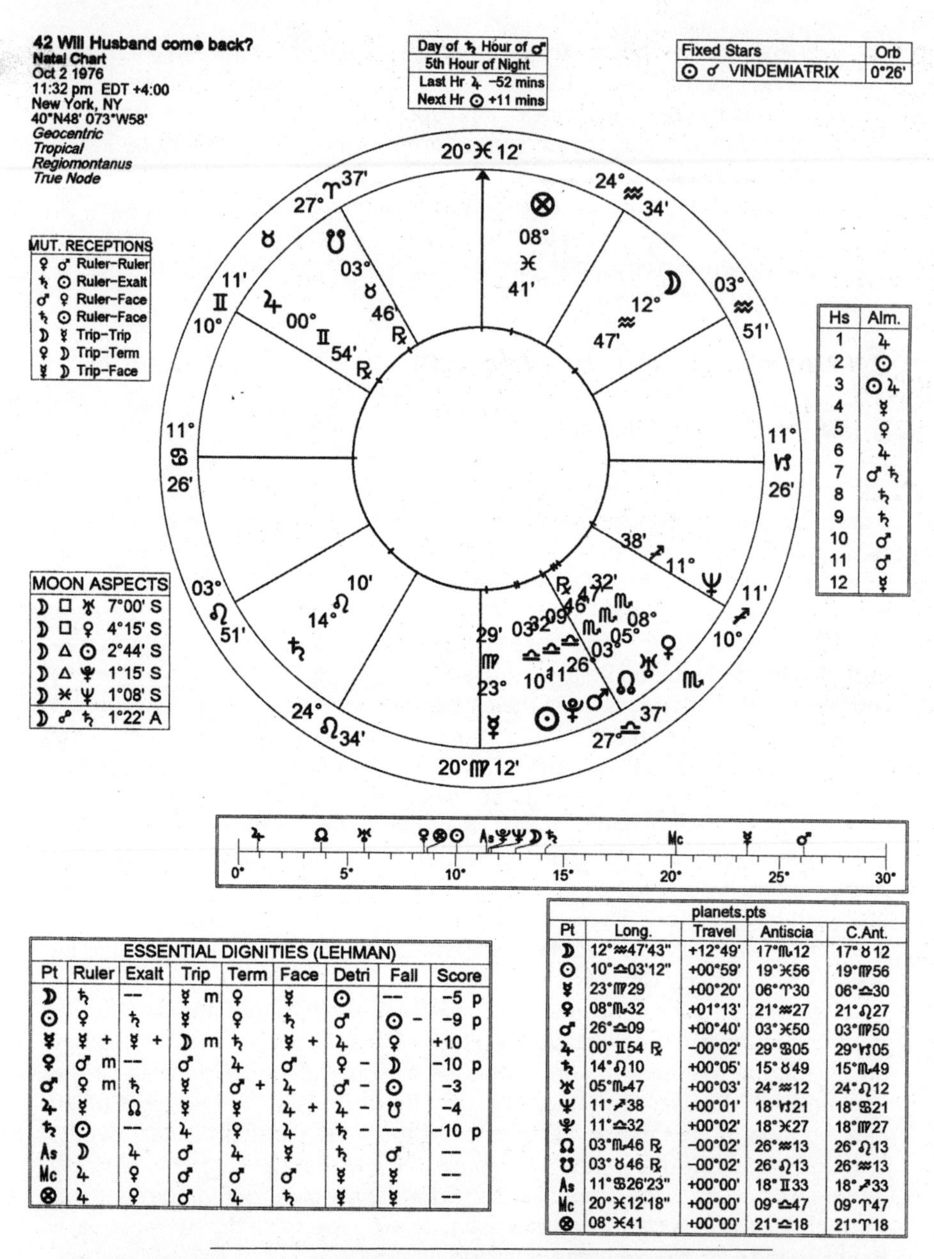

ESSENTIAL DIGNITIES (LEHMAN)

Pt	Ruler	Exalt	Trip	Term	Face	Detri	Fall	Score
☽	♄	—	☿ m	♀	☿	☉	—	-5 p
☉	♀	♄	☿	♀	♄	♂	☉ -	-9 p
☿	☿ +	☿ +	☽ m	♄	☿ +	♃	♀	+10
♀	♂ m	—	♂	♃	♂	♀ -	☽	-10 p
♂	♀ m	♄	☿	♂ +	♃	♂ -	☉	-3
♃	☿	☊	☿	☿	♃ +	♃ -	☋	-4
♄	☉	—	♃	♀	♃	♄ -	—	-10 p
As	☽	♃	♂	♃	☿	♄	♂	—
Mc	♃	♀	♂	♂	♂	☿	☿	—
⊗	♃	♀	♂	♃	♄	☿	☿	—

planets.pts

Pt	Long.	Travel	Antiscia	C.Ant.
☽	12°♒47'43"	+12°49'	17°♏12	17°♉12
☉	10°♎03'12"	+00°59'	19°♓56	19°♍56
☿	23°♍29	+00°20'	06°♈30	06°♎30
♀	08°♏32	+01°13'	21°♒27	21°♌27
♂	26°♎09	+00°40'	03°♓50	03°♍50
♃	00°♊54 ℞	-00°02'	29°♋05	29°♑05
♄	14°♌10	+00°05'	15°♉49	15°♏49
♅	05°♏47	+00°03'	24°♒12	24°♌12
♆	11°♐38	+00°01'	18°♑21	18°♋21
♇	11°♎32	+00°02'	18°♓27	18°♍27
☊	03°♏46 ℞	-00°02'	26°♒13	26°♌13
☋	03°♉46 ℞	-00°02'	26°♌13	26°♒13
As	11°♋26'23"	+00°00'	18°♊33	18°♐33
Mc	20°♓12'18"	+00°00'	09°♎47	09°♈47
⊗	08°♓41	+00°00'	21°♎18	21°♈18

through the Moon, which, while increasing in light, also does not behold the Ascendant, although she does rule it. The only planets beholding the Ascendant are the Sun and Pluto, both by square, and Venus and Uranus by trine, so reconciliation through a 3rd party is too contentious to be useful. The two do not reconcile.

They didn't, a statement that we can absolutely make, since the husband has since died. But interestingly, with the emphasis on the 2nd-8th House, he never divorced her, and so he supported her financially for the rest of his life, and through his will and last testament after death.

Example 43. Will J & R split up?

Beware the Double Negative, my son!
The jaws that bite, the claws that catch!
With apology to Lewis Carroll

Be careful how you word your Question because you just might have to answer it the way you asked it! I asked this question about a business associ-

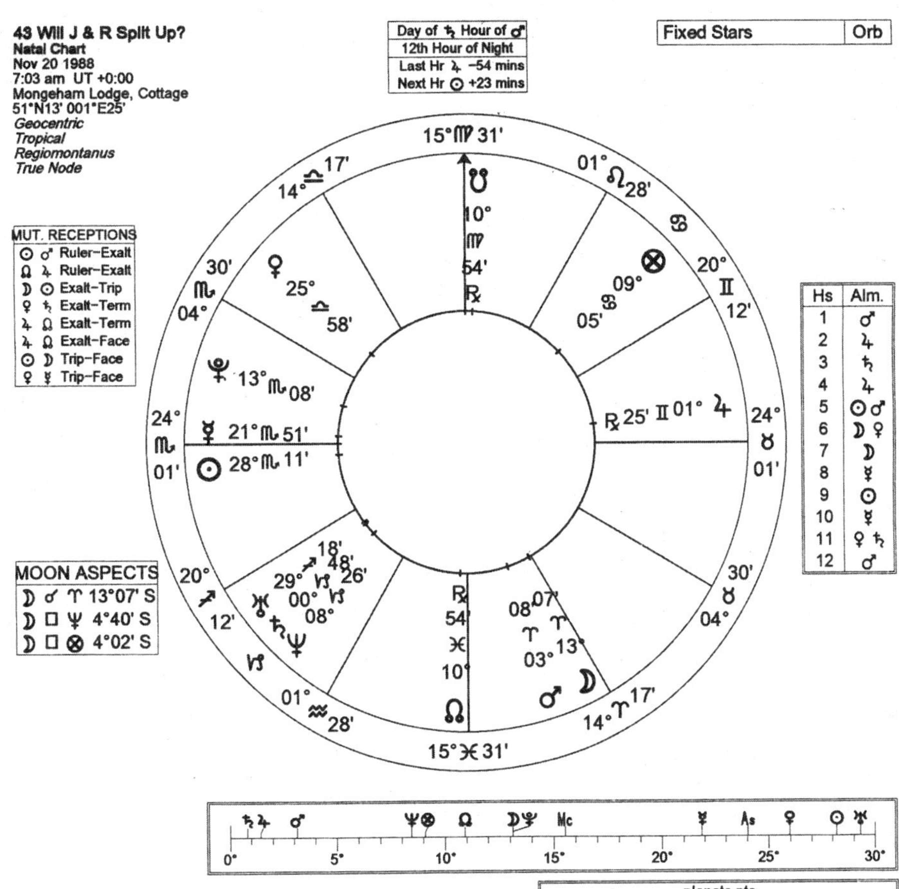

ESSENTIAL DIGNITIES (LEHMAN)								
Pt	Ruler	Exalt	Trip	Term	Face	Detri	Fall	Score
☽	♂	☉	♃	♀	☉	♀	♄	−5 p
☉	♂	---	♂	♄	♀	♀	☽	−5 p
☿	♂	---	♂	☿ +	♀	♀	☽	+2
♀	♀ +	♄	☿	♂	♃	♂	☉	+5
♂	♂ +	☉	♃	♃	♂ +	♀	♄	+6
♃	☿	☊	☿	☿	♃ +	♃ −	☋	−4
♄	♄ +	♂	☽	♀	♃	☽	♃	+5
As	♂	---	♂	☿	♀	♀	☽	---
Mc	☿	☿	☽	♃	♀	♃	♀	---
⊗	☽	♃	♂	♃	♀	♄	♂	---

planets.pts				
Pt	Long.	Travel	Antiscia	C.Ant.
☽	13°♈07'24"	+14°27'	16°♍52	16°♓52
☉	28°♏11'04"	+01°00'	01°♒48	01°♌48
☿	21°♏51	+01°35'	08°♒08	08°♌08
♀	25°♎58	+01°13'	04°♓01	04°♍01
♂	03°♈08	+00°16'	26°♍51	26°♓51
♃	01°♊25 ℞	−00°08'	28°♋34	28°♑34
♄	00°♑48	+00°06'	29°♐11	29°♊11
♅	29°♐18	+00°03'	00°♑41	00°♋41
♆	08°♑26	+00°01'	21°♐33	21°♊33
♇	13°♏08	+00°02'	16°♒51	16°♌51
☊	10°♓54 ℞	−00°04'	19°♎05	19°♈05
☋	10°♍54 ℞	−00°04'	19°♈05	19°♎05
As	24°♏01'20"	+00°00'	05°♒58	05°♌58
Mc	15°♍31'52"	+00°00'	14°♈28	14°♎28
⊗	09°♋05	+00°00'	20°♊54	20°♐54

ate. Her marriage was new, and I felt her husband was interfering with the business dealings that I had with her. So I basically wanted to know if the marriage was going to last.

In my own case, I have observed that when Scorpio ascends, it generally means that I have an ulterior motive for asking the question. This question was one of my early arguments for this observation, since I certainly had a strong financial motive in knowing the outcome. My involvement in this question is further confirmed by the Moon placement. The antiscion of the Moon is my Sun position, both located on the M.C. of this horary question.

But where are J and R? J was a friend. So she's the 11th House. R, her new husband, would therefore be the 5th House, the 7th from the 11th.

Venus and Mars are both strong in their own signs. J's Significator is even in her own house. They are in opposite signs, but past the actual opposition between the Significators, although the Moon translates the light (by opposition) between them. The Moon is fast but weak, so it is possible that someone else (i.e., the Moon) may make an attempt to split them up, or may say something to put a strain on the relationship, but the weak Moon will be unable to carry off a separation between two planets that are so strong to begin with.

Now it remains to translate this information into a judgment. We interpret a perfection as a "yes," but this is a "yes" to a negative question. In other words, the question was whether they would split up. The answer is "no," they won't split up. Notice that the intrinsic wording of the question produces results from the planets that are the opposite of how one might expect. Normally in a relationship horary, you would expect John and Nancy to come together if their Significators produce a trine. The planets come together, the people come together. If you ask whether John and Nancy will divorce, if their Significators produce a trine, does this mean they divorce, but amicably? The planets come together, the people may split apart.

The primary combination given above shows no perfection, so J and R do not split up. The only perfection is by opposition through a Translation. This would indicate that, if they split up, they will regret it.

J and R do not split up.

Example 44. Will J & S divorce?

J's mother asked this question. J and S were having a lot of friction in their relationship, and the mother wanted to know if it would go as far as divorce.

J is given by Mars or the Sun, sign ruler or Almuten of the 5th. The Sun clearly has better dignity. Using the Sun further has the advantage of leaving Mars for the Querent, who, we may assume, does have somewhat of a vested interest in the outcome of this question. S is therefore Saturn, Almuten of the 11th, which also has more dignity than sign-ruler Venus.

The two Significators, both dignified, are doubly separating from each other by opposition. This certainly shows their current impasse. But Saturn is aspecting the turned Ascendant, an argument for reconciliation in Lilly's list. Notice also that neither planet is with another planet. The Sun ultimately will apply to Jupiter, although it has to get through the square to Pluto first. But

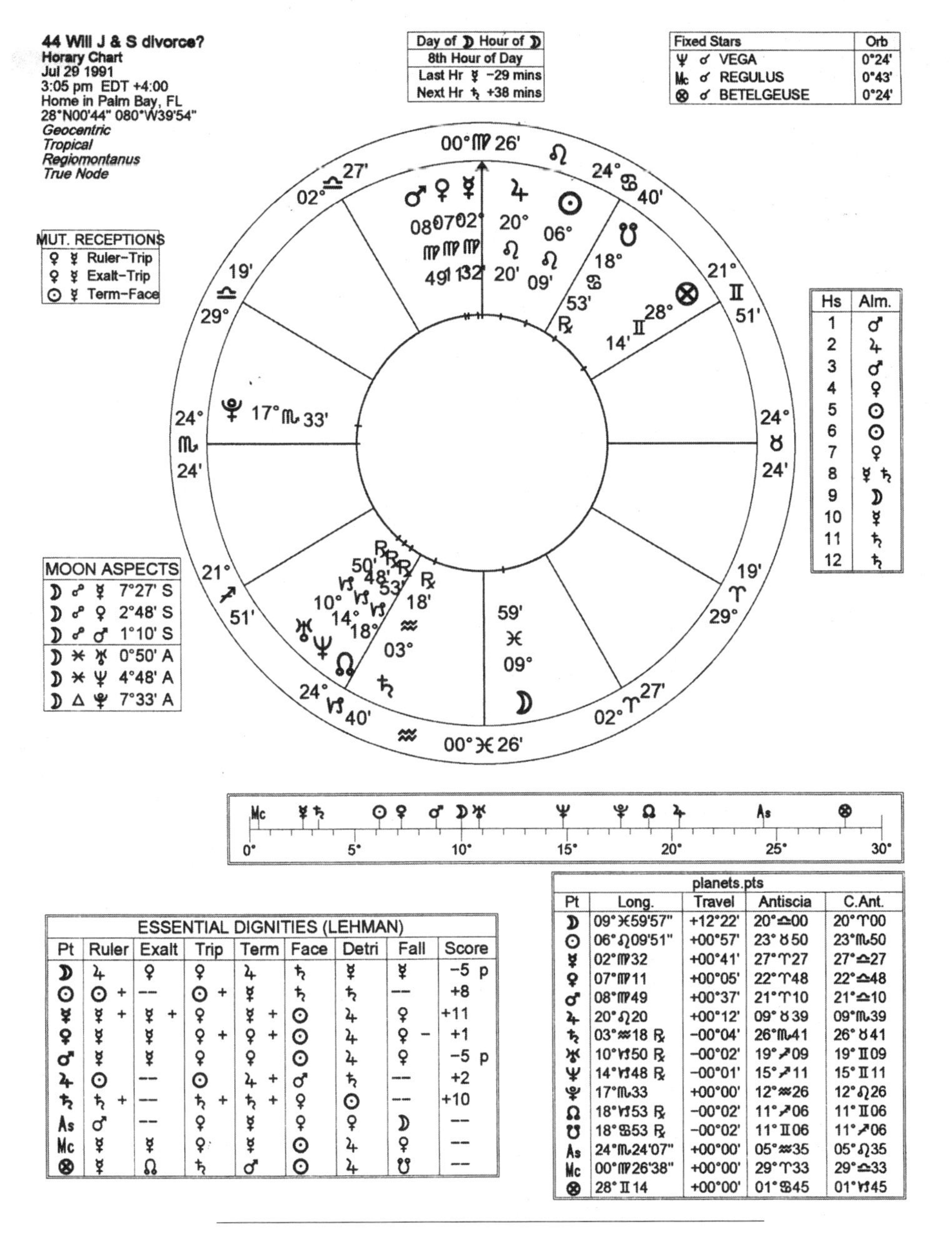

Pt	Long.	Travel	Antiscia	C.Ant.
☽	09°♓59'57"	+12°22'	20°♎00	20°♈00
☉	06°♌09'51"	+00°57'	23°♉50	23°♏50
☿	02°♍32	+00°41'	27°♈27	27°♎27
♀	07°♍11	+00°05'	22°♈48	22°♎48
♂	08°♍49	+00°37'	21°♈10	21°♎10
♃	20°♌20	+00°12'	09°♉39	09°♏39
♄	03°♒18 ℞	−00°04'	26°♏41	26°♉41
♅	10°♑50 ℞	−00°02'	19°♐09	19°♊09
♆	14°♑48 ℞	−00°01'	15°♐11	15°♊11
♇	17°♏33	+00°00'	12°♒26	12°♌26
☊	18°♑53 ℞	−00°02'	11°♐06	11°♊06
☋	18°♋53 ℞	−00°02'	11°♊06	11°♐06
As	24°♏24'07"	+00°00'	05°♒35	05°♌35
Mc	00°♍26'38"	+00°00'	29°♈33	29°♎33
⊗	28°♊14	+00°00'	01°♋45	01°♑45

ESSENTIAL DIGNITIES (LEHMAN)

Pt	Ruler	Exalt	Trip	Term	Face	Detri	Fall	Score
☽	♃	♀	♀	♃	♄	☿	☿	−5 p
☉	☉ +	—	☉ +	☿	♄	♄	—	+8
☿	☿ +	☿ +	♀	☿ +	☉	♃	♀	+11
♀	☿	☿	♀ +	♀ +	☉	♃	♀ −	+1
♂	☿	☿	♀	♀	☉	♃	♀	−5 p
♃	☉	—	☉	♃ +	♂	♄	—	+2
♄	♄ +	—	♄ +	♄ +	♀	☉	—	+10
As	♂	—	♀	☿	♀	♀	☽	—
Mc	☿	☿	♀	☿	☉	♃	♀	—
⊗	☿	☊	♄	♂	☉	♃	☋	—

this is an argument that neither party is currently with another, although there is the possibility that J will end up with a lover eventually. But there are no planets in either the turned 1st or 7th, and no planets apart from S's Significator applying to the turned Ascendant. So the problem is just between them, and there is an argument that their differences can be transcended, through the offices of dignified Saturn.

They did resolve their differences, and they are still together.

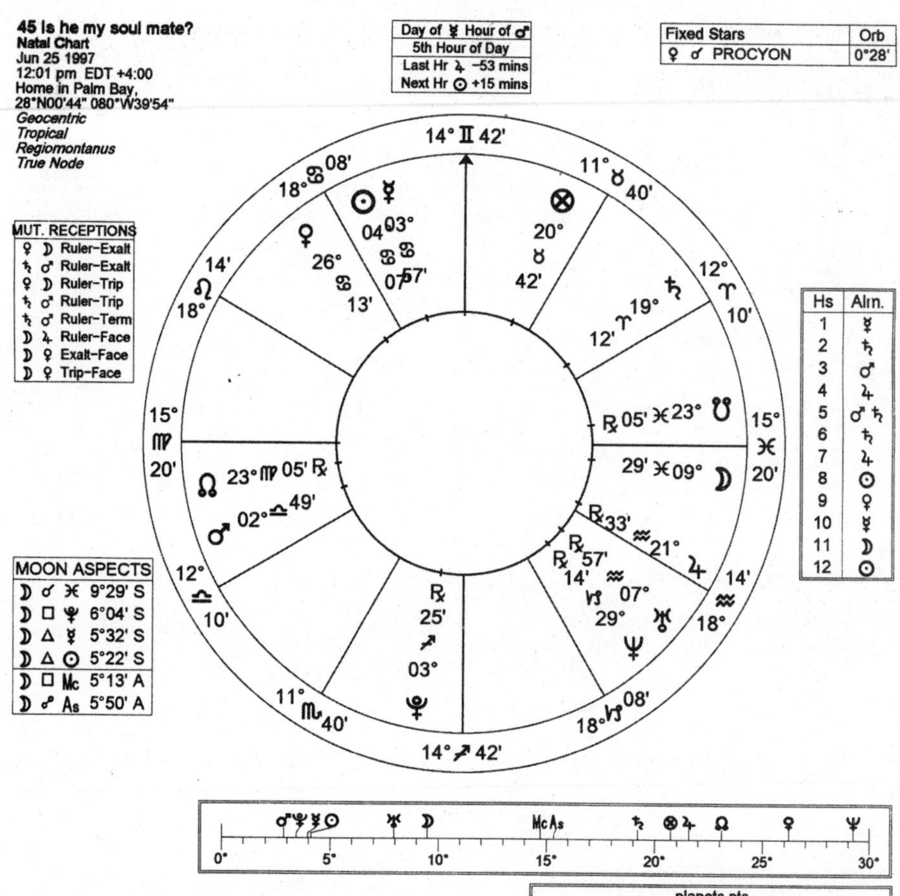

ESSENTIAL DIGNITIES (LEHMAN)								
Pt	Ruler	Exalt	Trip	Term	Face	Detri	Fall	Score
☽	♃	♀	♀	♃	♄	☿	☿	−5 p
☉	☽	♃	♀	♂	♀	♄	♂	−5 p
☿	☽	♃	♀	♂	♀	♄	♂	−5 p
♀	☽	♃	♀ +	♀ +	☽	♄	♂	+5
♂	♀	♄	♄	♄	☽	♂ −	☉	−10 p
♃	♄	---	♄	♃ +	☽	☉	---	+2
♄	♂	☉	☉	☿	☉	♀	♄ −	−9 p
As	☿	☿	♀	♃	♀	♃	♀	---
Mc	☿	☊	♄	♀	♂	♃	☋	---
⊗	♀	☽	♀	♃	♄	♂	---	---

planets.pts				
Pt	Long.	Travel	Antiscia	C.Ant.
☽	09°♓29'46"	+14°19'	20°♎30	20°♈30
☉	04°♋07'11"	+00°57'	25°♊52	25°♐52
☿	03°♋57	+02°11'	26°♊02	26°♐02
♀	26°♋13	+01°12'	03°♊46	03°♐46
♂	02°♎49	+00°27'	27°♓10	27°♍10
♃	21°♒33 ℞	−00°02'	08°♏26	08°♉26
♄	19°♈12	+00°03'	10°♍47	10°♓47
♅	07°♒57 ℞	−00°01'	22°♏02	22°♉02
♆	29°♑14 ℞	−00°01'	00°♐45	00°♊45
♇	03°♐25 ℞	−00°01'	26°♑34	26°♋34
☊	23°♍05 ℞	−00°01'	06°♈54	06°♎54
☋	23°♓05 ℞	−00°01'	06°♎54	06°♈54
As	15°♍20'13"	+00°00'	14°♈39	14°♎39
Mc	14°♊42'59"	+00°00'	15°♋17	15°♑17
⊗	20°♉42	+00°00'	09°♌17	09°♒17

Example 45. Is he my soul mate?

Yes, yes, I know we shouldn't take the question quite this way, but every so often, I just have to try!

With South Node in the 7th, I said, "The good news is that you knew him in a former life." With no perfection between Mercury and Jupiter I continued, "the bad news is that there is no relationship with him in this life." Based on Saturn's dispositorship of Jupiter, I described him as a man with very clear boundaries. Two years previously, when Saturn went into Aries, he became extremely impatient. I said, "were I reading this planet for a woman of 40 instead of a man, I would say that the biological clock issue had just struck." I added further, with Mercury in Cancer *versus* Jupiter in Aquarius, that she loved him more than he loved her. This is simply comparing the Rulers of 1st and 7th. The difference in the natures is pretty obvious once one stops to consider it. She was a bit surprised, although on reflection, she realized that she could be mistaking zeal for passion. With Mercury Cazimi, she was probably dazzled by him. He's a lawyer, who she'd known just two months. He had been hounding her to get married. This would entail selling her house, moving out of state, and dropping her educational plans. She was worried that, having done all that, he would turn into a different person. Considering the Saturn dispositorship, and Saturn moving into Taurus, I said that most likely he would eventually revert to his usual tendencies, which would make him a different person than the one she knew.

Now obviously, with the background that she gave me, the question about being soul mates was a substitute for some variation of, "Would marriage be a good idea?" The soul mate issue was a screen for her reaction to how quickly he was moving, since she was uncomfortable with two months of knowing someone being sufficient for completely changing her life. What is interesting here is that Mercury is very fast in speed, over two degrees per day. This confirms that events were moving much too quickly for her. But in any case, the rulers of the 1st and 7th do not perfect, Mercury is peregrine, and Jupiter has dignity only by Term, and accidental debility by retrogradation. Nothing permanent is going to happen anyway.

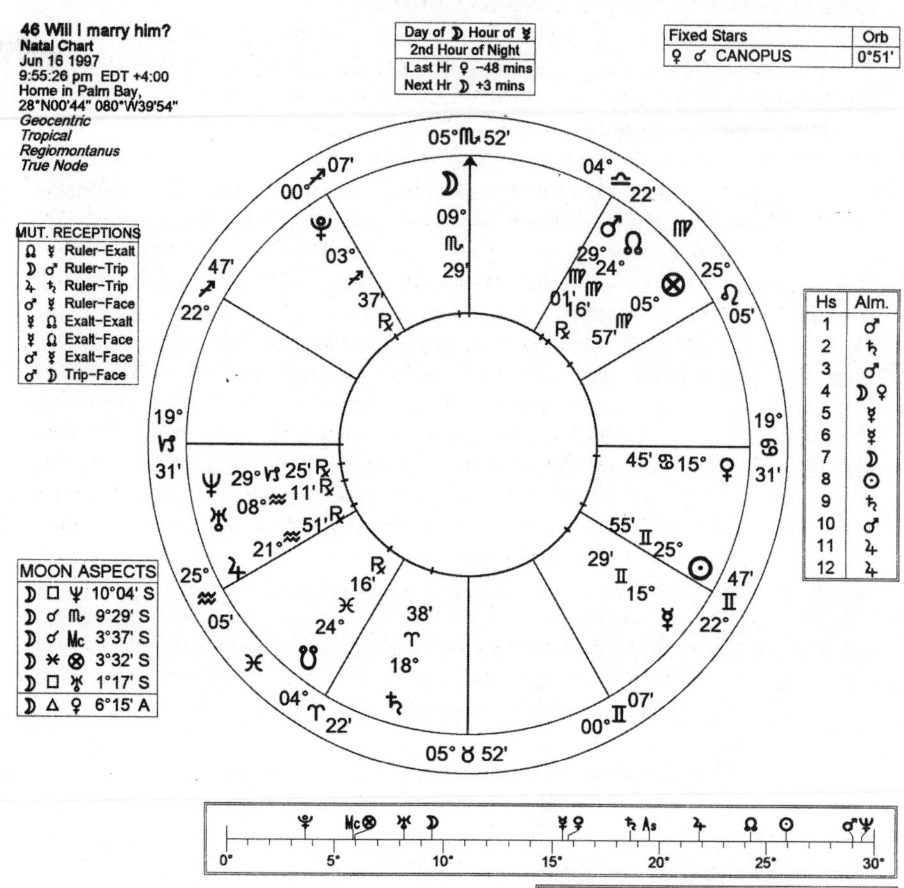

ESSENTIAL DIGNITIES (LEHMAN)								
Pt	Ruler	Exalt	Trip	Term	Face	Detri	Fall	Score
☽	♂	--	♂ m	♃	♂	♀	☽ −	−9 p
☉	☿	☊	☿	♂	☉ +	♃	☋	+1
☿	☿ +	☊ m	☿ +	♀ m	♂ m	♃	☋	+8
♀	☽	♃	♂	☿ m	☿	♄	♂	−5 p
♂	☿	☿	☽ m	♂ +	☿ m	♃	♀	+2
♃	♄	--	☿	♃ +	☽	☉	--	+2
♄	♂	☉	♃	☿	☉	♀	♄ −	−9 p
As	♄	♂	☽	♂	♂	☽	♃	--
Mc	♂	--	♂	♂	♂	♀	☽	--
⊗	☿	☿	☽	☿	☉	♃	♀	--

planets.pts				
Pt	Long.	Travel	Antiscia	C.Ant.
☽	09°♏29'54"	+12°44'	20°♒30	20°♌30
☉	25°♊55'43"	+00°57'	04°♋04	04°♑04
☿	15°♊29	+02°03'	14°♋30	14°♑30
♀	15°♋45	+01°13'	14°♊14	14°♐14
♂	29°♍01	+00°25'	00°♈58	00°♎58
♃	21°♒51 ℞	−00°01'	08°♏08	08°♉08
♄	18°♈38	+00°04'	11°♍21	11°♓21
♅	08°♒11 ℞	−00°01'	21°♏48	21°♉48
♆	29°♑25 ℞	−00°01'	00°♐34	00°♊34
♇	03°♐37 ℞	−00°01'	26°♑22	26°♋22
☊	24°♍16 ℞	−00°06'	05°♈43	05°♎43
☋	24°♓16 ℞	−00°06'	05°♎43	05°♈43
As	19°♑31'44"	+00°00'	10°♐28	10°♊28
Mc	05°♏52'05"	+00°00'	24°♒07	24°♌07
⊗	05°♍57	+00°00'	24°♈02	24°♎02

Example 46. Will I marry him?

Her sign ruler is Saturn, peregrine and in Fall. The Almuten ruler of the 1st is Mars, which marginally improves her condition, giving her dignity by Term, but being posited in the 29th degree and about to enter the Sign of its Fall!

With Moon in Scorpio in no aspect to Saturn, and out of orb to the sextile to Mars, the answer is no. I told her that he is a user: someone who willfully takes advantage of others. The reason I said this is that the Moon in Scorpio does not look like a benign influence. Another strong possibility, with the Significator in a fixed sign, is that he wouldn't take no for an answer, but keep trying and trying and trying ... With Neptune and Uranus in the 1st, she was open to major changes, possibly of a spiritual nature. Along he came into this time when she knew herself to be transitional and perhaps he personified the process for her. At any rate, with her sign ruler square the Ascendant, it wouldn't be long before she rejected the whole idea of the relationship. Still, the double reception between her Significator and his Significator does show a tie between them. However, Neptune in the 1st is as easily someone in complete denial about the circumstances of the Question, as someone desiring to make spiritual changes. In that case, possibly the Uranus shows the possibility for a sudden change in either the nature of the denial, or in whether the overly optimistic viewpoint can continue.

She had already pretty much nixed the possibility of marriage between the time she asked the question, and the time she called for the reading. So my delineation did not come as much of a surprise.

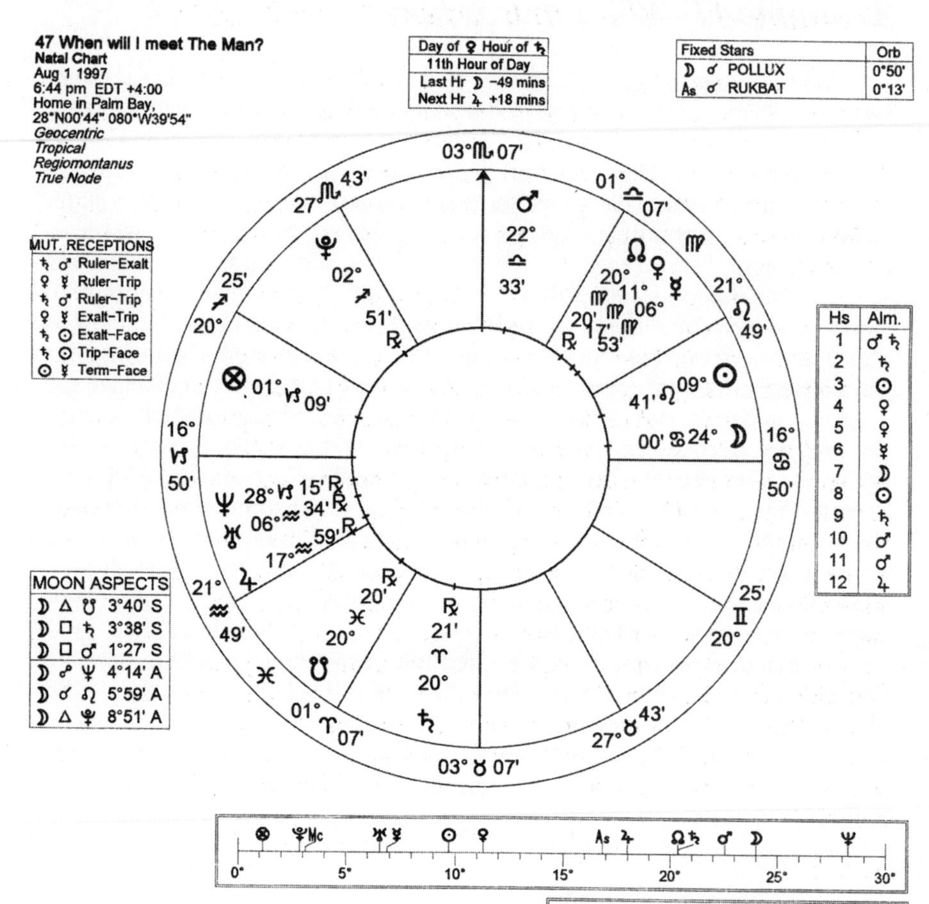

ESSENTIAL DIGNITIES (LEHMAN)								
Pt	Ruler	Exalt	Trip	Term	Face	Detri	Fall	Score
☽	☽ +	♃	♀	♀	☽ +	♄	♂	+6
☉	☉ +	--	☉ +	☿	♄	♄	--	+8
☿	☿ +	☿ +	♀	☿ +	☉	♃	♀	+11
♀	☿	☿	♀ +	♀ +	♀ +	♃	♀ -	+2
♂	♀	♄	♄	☿	♃	♂ -	☉	-10 p
♃	♄	--	♄	♀	☿	☉	--	-5 p
♄	♂	☉	☉	☿	♀	♀	♄ -	-9 p
As	♄	♂	♀	♃	♂	☽	♃	--
Mc	♂	--	♀	♂	♂	♀	☽	--
⊗	♄	♂	♀	♀	♃	☽	♃	--

planets.pts				
Pt	Long.	Travel	Antiscia	C.Ant.
☽	24°♋00'37"	+12°18'	05°♊59	05°♐59
☉	09°♌41'48"	+00°57'	20°♉18	20°♏18
☿	06°♍53	+01°02'	23°♈06	23°♎06
♀	11°♍17	+01°11'	18°♈42	18°♎42
♂	22°♎33	+00°35'	07°♓26	07°♍26
♃	17°♒59 ℞	-00°07'	12°♏00	12°♉00
♄	20°♈21 ℞	-00°00'	09°♍38	09°♓38
♅	06°♒34 ℞	-00°02'	23°♏25	23°♉25
♆	28°♑15 ℞	-00°01'	01°♐44	01°♊44
♇	02°♐51 ℞	-00°00'	27°♑08	27°♋08
☊	20°♍20 ℞	-00°07'	09°♈39	09°♎39
☋	20°♓20 ℞	-00°07'	09°♎39	09°♈39
As	16°♑50'21"	+00°00'	13°♐09	13°♊09
Mc	03°♏07'36"	+00°00'	26°♒52	26°♌52
⊗	01°♑09	+00°00'	28°♐50	28°♊50

Example 47. When will I meet "The Man"?

The full question was, "When will I meet the man of my dreams?" The setup of this chart is very similar to the last example, but what a difference a couple of months made! I also found it amusing, with Neptune again in the 1st, that she should be asking about an ideal lover. Again, we have the choice of Mars or Saturn for the Ruler of the Querent; with both planets in such shoddy cosmic condition, it's anybody's guess about which Significator you would want to have!

However, the important difference from the last example is that now the Moon, ruling the 7th House, is dignified in Cancer! The man is in his own house and very dignified. But now how do we interpret the fact that he is separating from Significators that we could use for the Querent?

Here, we have to fall back on the importance of how the question is worded. She did not ask, "*Will* I meet the man of my dreams?" She asked *when*. Within the context of the question, the answer becomes obvious: she already *has* met the man of her dreams. So what's the problem? The problem is that she knows him, but not what he's going to be for her! It's one of those cases where it is *not* love at first sight, (maybe even conflict or disdain, with Moon square Mars and Saturn) but only after their interactions change, so that she can see him in another light. Notice that Mars (slightly less debilitated than Saturn, being direct, not retrograde), becomes highly dignified by entering Scorpio: (symbolically, in 7.5 months?) when her condition improves considerably. The same indicators we saw in the previous chart show the need for this improvement. The presence of Uranus and Neptune in the 1st House shows that her current condition is in flux, so it will take her that long to probably even notice him.

And so it proved. They were married in 2000. And by the way, he's a Cancer.

Example 48. Is it my dharma to "help" this man?

The Querent had previously asked me about a yoga instructor that she worked with. He had made a series of passes at her, and she was concerned about whether she could even work in the same location with him, and worried that he might be dangerous. The answer was no. He already had his eye on someone else. I told her that he did not have control of his *kundalini*, and that as long as that was true, he was going to continue to hit on women in inappropriate circumstances. (Sometimes it is necessary to translate the obvious: that he had difficulty controlling his sexual urges, and that he had no incentive to do otherwise when surrounded by women who have difficulty saying no.)

It was in response to my answer that she asked this second question. It's very difficult for an independent observer not to scream, "He's using you!" Her response absolutely struck me as that of a woman who simply is in denial that a man with a zipper problem is not likely to be thinking of enlightenment when sex is an alternative! However, I kept my cool and calculated the chart ...

Her Significator, Mars, is in Detriment and conjunct Algol by ecliptic degree. Beyond the traditional association of Algol with hanging, the psycho-

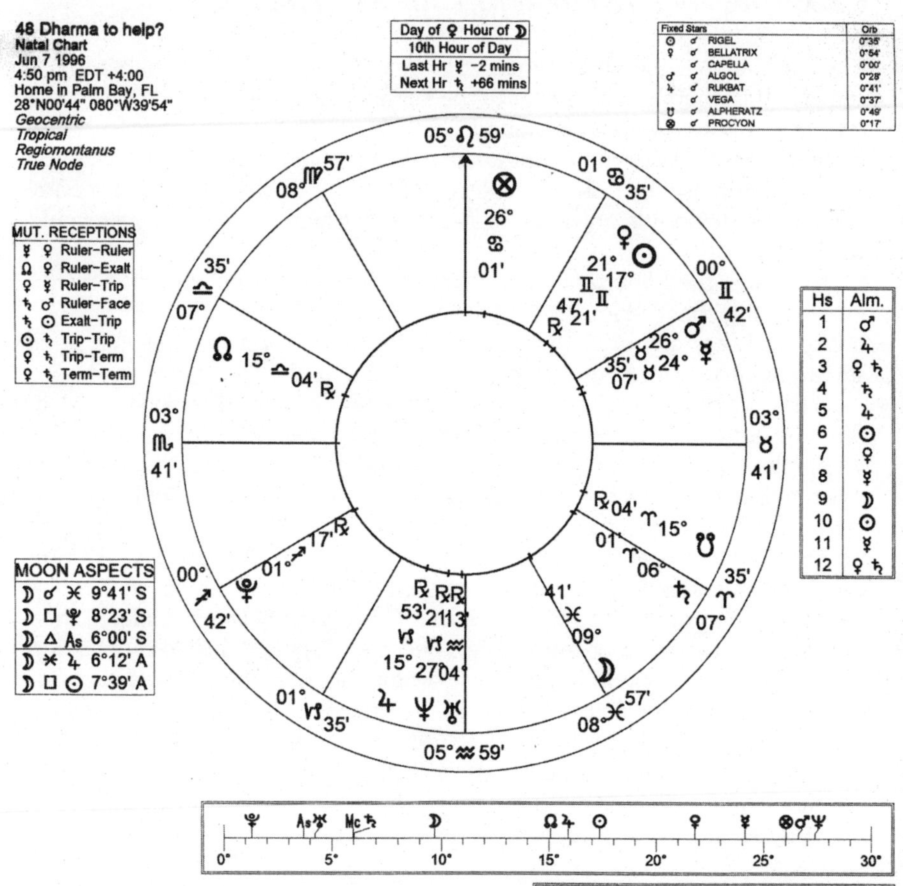

planets.pts				
Pt	Long.	Travel	Antiscia	C.Ant.
☽	09°♓41'30"	+13°57'	20°♎18	20°♈18
☉	17°♊21'28"	+00°57'	12°♋38	12°♑38
☿	24°♉07	+00°47'	05°♌52	05°♒52
♀	21°♊47 ℞	−00°36'	08°♋12	08°♑12
♂	26°♉35	+00°43'	03°♌24	03°♒24
♃	15°♑53 ℞	−00°05'	14°♐06	14°♊06
♄	06°♈01	+00°03'	23°♍58	23°♓58
♅	04°♒13 ℞	−00°01'	25°♏46	25°♉46
♆	27°♑21 ℞	−00°01'	02°♐38	02°♊38
♇	01°♐17 ℞	−00°01'	28°♑42	28°♋42
☊	15°♎04 ℞	−00°00'	14°♓55	14°♍55
☋	15°♈04 ℞	−00°00'	14°♍55	14°♓55
As	03°♏41'09"	+00°00'	26°♒18	26°♌18
Mc	05°♌59'04"	+00°00'	24°♉00	24°♏00
⊗	26°♋01	+00°00'	03°♊58	03°♐58

ESSENTIAL DIGNITIES (LEHMAN)								
Pt	Ruler	Exalt	Trip	Term	Face	Detri	Fall	Score
☽	♃	♀	♀	♃	♄	☿	☿	−5 p
☉	☿	☊	♄ m	♀	♂	♃	☋	−5 p
☿	♀ m	☽	♀	♄	♄	♂	---	−5 p
♀	☿ m	☊	♄	♄ m	☉	♃	☋	−5 p
♂	♀	☽	♀	♂ +	♄ m	♂ −	---	−3
♃	♄	♂	♀	♃ +	♂	☽	♃ −	−2
♄	♂	☉	☉ m	♀ m	♂ m	♀	♄ −	−9 p
As	♂	---	♀	♂	♂	♀	☽	---
Mc	☉	---	☉	♄	♄	♄	---	---
⊗	☽	♃	♀	♀	☽	♄	♂	---

logical association I have observed is that the person gets a bee in his/her proverbial bonnet, gets completely fixated on someone or something and ends up "hanging" purely because of stubborn obsession. This told me she was fixated on the man. (I should have known this because when she first called me about the passes he made at her, she neglected to mention to me that she had a live-in relationship. A man in a spiritual community propositioning a "married" woman? This *should* have been a tip-off!) Furthermore, her Significator was immediately applying to Neptune. While this could indicate a spiritual contact, it more likely meant that she was deluding herself. Her Significator is in the 7th House. Since we are dealing with a generic "other," the man is given by the 7th House, hence, she is in his sway. His Significator is in the 8th house, peregrine but for mutual reception, and with the Sun, therefore with another person.

In short, the Moon at the 5th House cusp in a fertile sign actually encapsulates the whole question! The Moon is spotlighting the issue of sexuality (shall we call it second chakra?) in an environment which, as a spiritual program, is supposed to involve the 9th House!

Is there any future interaction between the parties shown? The Moon *will* come to a square of his Significator before sextiling hers. This means that, were she to pursue this idea, it would be fraught with hassle. And the sextile is *not* that strong a conclusion. However, there are other aspects of the Moon before this happens. I judged that she should just let it be, there being no strong indication that they needed to have any more interaction.

Questions about Battles, Wars and other Contentions

Lilly lived during one of the most difficult kinds of war: civil war (see "Green Belt"). Lilly not only had plenty of opportunities to ask these questions for himself, but also to answer them for others. Here is a summary of his method.

- **Whether the Querent shall return home from the war (or dangerous voyage):** If the Rulers of the 1st and 7th, and the Moon, are dignified and beholding benefics, then there is no need to fear. The more of these factors that are debilitated, the greater the fear. A benefic in the 1st bodes well. The Ruler of the 1st combust is unfortunate. The Ruler of the 1st with a malefic planet and the Ruler of the 7th with a benefic, produces danger, but not death. Malefics in the 8th are dangerous, and possibly fatal. The Ruler of the 1st conjunct a malefic, but a benefic planet in the 1st denotes wounding, but not death. Do not go if Saturn is in the 1st or with the Ruler of the 1st. The combination of a malefic in the 1st and a malefic with the Ruler of the 1st denotes wounding or death. The same is true if the Ruler of the 7th is combust, and the Sun is in the 7th, 8th or 10th.[147]

- **What will ensue of the war?:** The outcome is given by evaluating the relative strength and condition of the 1st and 7th Houses and their rulers. Give the 1st to the side favored by the Querent. The Ruler of the 1st in the 8th, or the Ruler of the 8th in the 1st, or the Ruler of the 8th with the Ruler of the 1st can denote the death of the Querent as a result of war. The Ruler of the 7th in the 2nd, or the Ruler of the 7th with the Ruler of the 2nd can denote the death of the adversary. If both the Rulers of the 1st and 7th are in the 1st, and the 2nd House cusp is favorably aspected, then the Querent can make a profit through the war.[148]

- **On the competency of commanders:** This is a variant of the last type, but here's the twist – this question is addressed from the standpoint that the commander *is* the Querent. The former question is asked from the viewpoint of a common soldier, or someone who is called upon to provision a war. This question addresses whether the war is just, how it will be fought and the specifics of what will and won't work in the war. As a result, this is the kind of Question that is easiest to translate to a modern question concerning a lawsuit, as the "commander" is most analogous to a litigant. Begin by assigning the 1st and the 7th Houses as before, according to the allegiance of the Querent. Then look for the presence of the Fortunes, or if they are beholding a House cusp (especially by trine or sextile); or the Infortunes, and if they are beholding a House cusp (especially by square or opposition), as relating to the following issues by House:

    - The 1st House denotes the general conduct of affairs by the Querent's side, and whether the cause is just. In Medieval warfare, the question of whether a cause was just was paramount, because only a just cause could allow for expenditure of public funds, and give the right of spoils to the victor.[149] The "right" of spoils was an absolutely necessary ingredient in warfare, because without pillage and ransoming of the leaders of the other side, it was almost impossible to fund a campaign. Thus, this was not a trivial matter.

    - The 2nd House is the friends or seconds of the 1st House partisan. If this is too badly afflicted, it's virtually impossible to have a war at all.

    - The 3rd House shows the provisioning of the army – which means the quality of soldiers provisioned. This means the enlisted soldiers, in modern parlance.

    - The 4th House shows the quality of ground where the war is to be fought.

    - The 5th House shows the ability of the soldiers to take orders and to be trained.

- The 6th House shows the quality of carriage horse. Now we would say tanks and troop carriers.

- The 7th House shows both the quality of fortifications, guns *and* the Enemy. I'd love to see these distinguished, unless, of course, the implication is that this Question would only be asked by a potential invader, in which case the fortifications and the Enemy may well be considered as one.

- The 8th House shows the amount of death resulting from the war. Fortunes here reduce the carnage. Saturn retrograde produces many prisoners, as well as ruin and destruction.

- The 9th House shows an Enemy that will operate by misinformation, using false reports as a strategy. Hmm - the house of lawyers ...

- The 10th House shows the ability of the commander-in-chief and principal officers.

- The 11th House shows the lesser officers: the ones who get the army to where it needs to go, and handle the mundane affairs of the army.

- The 12th House shows the enemy of the army.

  After reading this way for the Querent, read the twelve houses in like fashion, beginning with the 7th House, for the enemy. Also, consider whether there is any relationship between the Ruler of the 1st and the 7th either by aspect or reception, because without a relationship, there is no fight.

  Mars has a special place in these interpretations, because Mars is of the nature of war itself. The presence of Mars denotes courage and warlike qualities, but the danger of whether that quantity ruled by Mars is governable. Saturn, on the other hand, means feeble, old, rotten, etc. – a true malefic.[150]

- **Of whether a town besieged shall be taken:** Here Lilly uses methods derived from Medieval warfare, as delineated in Electional by Guido Bonatti.[151] In this method, the 1st House is given to the besieging party, the town or fortress is given the 4th House and the army belonging to the 4th is given to the 7th House.[152] Again, like the more conventional open-field warfare, it's a question of which side is stronger.

The rules of warfare apply to sporting events as well, at least those games that are regarded by the participants as true competition. (I am not at all sure that much of professional sport in the USA is competition anymore.) In these cases, rather than use horary questions to determine the results, the scheduled time of the game is used. This is a method that I worked on with Bernadette Brady, and we distinguished between those events where the castle besiegement model applied, versus the 1st-7th open-field contest as follows:

> "Castle besiegement may be suspected for any sport where one team holds a trophy or a title and must be beaten in order to lose that title, and where a draw means the title or trophy stays with the holder. When besiegement applies, the holder has an intrinsic advantage over the challenger. The challenger must clearly defeat the holder in order to win the title. The winner is then the champion and holds that title until retirement or loss to a new challenger.
>
> "These are quite different from 'battle chart' sporting conflicts which is where a group of teams compete over a season and the top teams play off for the trophy. In that type of contest, the winner of the trophy in any one year does not have any special claim or privileges to the trophy in the next year."[153]

What's essential to mention about our model is that it hearkens back to an historical truism: to win at a besiegement, the castle or town must be forced. To "win" *as* the castle or fort, the inhabitants merely have to survive. Winning, in other words, is strongly stacked in favor of the 4th House side, although there have been many pyrrhic victories of this nature.

- **Who shall do the best in a suit of law?** This is the most obvious for modern application. Not surprisingly, the method is to use the Rulers of the 1st and 7th Houses, with the 1st House going to the Querent and the 7th to her or his adversary. If both Rulers are angular, it is doubtful that either will be overcome. If one of the two is cadent and joined to malefics, that party loses. If both are joined to malefics, then both are undone by the lawsuit. If one of the Rulers is stronger, and neither cadent nor joined to a malefic, then that party prevails. **In lawsuits and wars, dignity by exaltation is stronger than by sign.**[154] In general, victory goes to the side whose Significator is most powerful. Lilly also considers the circumstance where one of the two Significators is an inferior planet (or faster), and the other a superior (hence slower). In this case, the faster planet "commits his disposition to the other,"[155] and so then the slower planet responds, rather than initiates any agreement. Both retrogradation and cadent placements are arguments of considerable weakness.

Agreement between the parties (without the need for the case proper) is given by a conjunction, sextile, or trine between Rulers of the 1st and 7th. This may also occur by Reception. If the aspect is by square or opposition, but there is mutual reception, then agreement is still possible, but after some strife.[156]

The condition of the 10th House Ruler is carefully considered, as that planet represents the judge. The condition of the Ruler shows the quality of the judgment, and conjunction of one of the Rulers of the 1st or 7th to the Ruler of the 10th can show the judge favoring that side. Reception between them can have the same effect. A retrograde judge may produce a ruling which is not strictly speaking according to law. A less ponderous planet representing the judge in aspect to either the 1st or 7th House Ruler will result in the judge doing that side's bidding, and not even necessarily from being told to do so by that side. If the 10th House Ruler receives both the 1st and 7th House Rulers, the judge will attempt to bring about a settlement without the benefit of trial. The Ruler of the 10th dignified, and in the 10th, brings justice.[157]

I would add one factor that Lilly does not. Not all lawsuits are 1st -7th. This is illustrated by the speed trap: speeding tickets given out by small towns in the U.S. Here there is a preference for ticketing out-of-state vehicles, and the odds of ever beating such a traffic ticket in court are near zero. Clearly the assumption that "Justice is blind" does not always apply. Accordingly, whenever one is confronted with a legal situation where, for whatever reason, the odds are considerably better for one side of the conflict, that lawsuit should be regarded as a castle besiegement, and the favored side should be assigned to the 4th.

It's worth emphasizing that, when questions concerning lawsuits arise, if the lawsuit has already been engaged, use the chart for the event of the filing of the papers, or the opening of the case, in preference to a horary about such a case.

Example 49. Event: The Microsoft Antitrust Trial

This chart is a particularly good example of how important it is to understand the ramifications of a particular situation. Earlier in the 20th Century, the Government won a very large percentage of the antitrust cases that it brought. However, this all changed in 1975, when the number of cases filed by the government dropped from about 100 cases per year to a handful. What happened? Interested readers can examine the contentions made by the Antitrust Law and Economics Review,[158] but their argument is that a group of major corporations took it upon themselves to "educate" the US judiciary in a series of seminars held in Florida in the Winter, and that since this education process occurred, the decisions handed down have completely reinterpreted the antitrust statutes to encourage consolidation, curiously as a spur to economic activity. Whether the reader chooses to accept in whole the contentions of this group, the fact remains that the number of cases has dwindled, and the number of decisions declaring monopolistic practices has diminished to such an extent that we clearly *must* declare such suits to be castle besiegements, with the curious situation of the Government as challenger, and the corporation as the 4th House.

This chart was drawn for the time that the Microsoft antitrust court case began. As soon as we view the chart from this standpoint, we see the problem from the Government's side. The Government is Mars, Ruler of the 1st House. Mars has only out-of-sect Triplicity: something, but not much. Microsoft is given by Jupiter, Ruler of the 4th House, in its own house, dignified by Sign and Face, albeit retrograde.

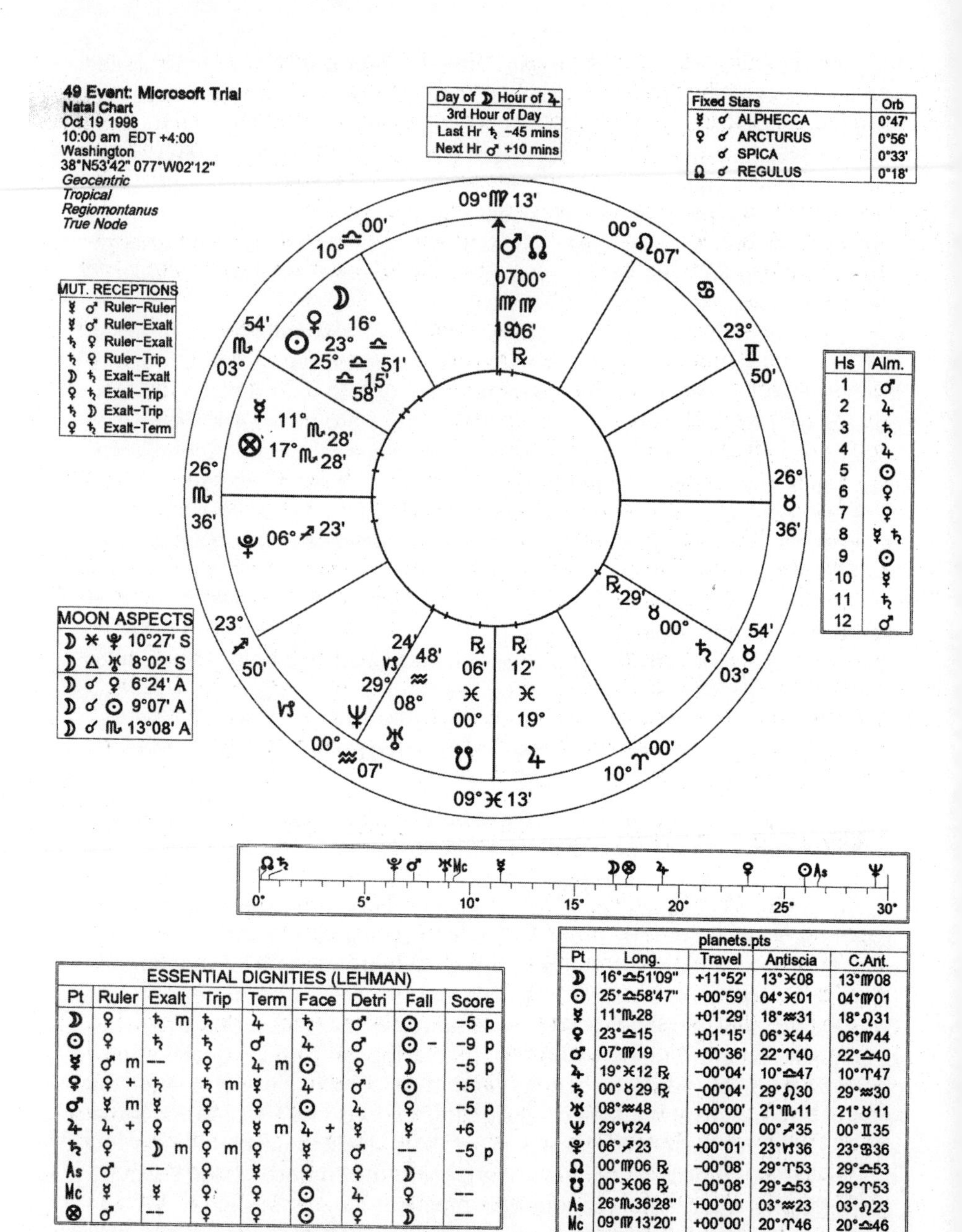

Fixed Stars		Orb
☿ ☌	ALPHECCA	0°47'
♀ ☌	ARCTURUS	0°56'
☌	SPICA	0°33'
☊ ☌	REGULUS	0°18'

MUT. RECEPTIONS	
☿ ♂	Ruler-Ruler
☿ ♂	Ruler-Exalt
♄ ♀	Ruler-Exalt
♄ ♀	Ruler-Trip
☽ ♄	Exalt-Exalt
♀ ♄	Exalt-Trip
♄ ☽	Exalt-Trip
♀ ♄	Exalt-Term

Hs	Alm.
1	♂
2	♃
3	♄
4	♃
5	☉
6	♀
7	♀
8	☿ ♄
9	☉
10	☿
11	♄
12	♂

MOON ASPECTS	
☽ ⚹ ♇	10°27' S
☽ △ ♅	8°02' S
☽ ☌ ♀	6°24' A
☽ ☌ ☉	9°07' A
☽ ☌ ♏	13°08' A

ESSENTIAL DIGNITIES (LEHMAN)								
Pt	Ruler	Exalt	Trip	Term	Face	Detri	Fall	Score
☽	♀	♄ m	♄	♃	♄	♂	☉	−5 p
☉	♀	♄	♄	♂	♃	♂	☉ −	−9 p
☿	♂ m	---	♀	♃ m	☉	♀	☽	−5 p
♀	♀ +	♄	♄ m	☿	♃	♂	☉	+5
♂	☿ m	☿	♀	♀	☉	♃	♀	−5 p
♃	♃ +	♀	♀	☿ m	♃ +	☿	☿	+6
♄	♀	☽ m	♀ m	♀	☿	♂	---	−5 p
As	♂	---	♀	☿	♀	♀	☽	---
Mc	☿	☿	♀	♀	☉	♃	♀	---
⊗	♂	---	♀	♀	☉	♀	☽	---

planets.pts				
Pt	Long.	Travel	Antiscia	C.Ant.
☽	16°♎51'09"	+11°52'	13°♓08	13°♍08
☉	25°♎58'47"	+00°59'	04°♓01	04°♍01
☿	11°♏28	+01°29'	18°♒31	18°♌31
♀	23°♎15	+01°15'	06°♓44	06°♍44
♂	07°♍19	+00°36'	22°♈40	22°♎40
♃	19°♓12 ℞	−00°04'	10°♎47	10°♈47
♄	00°♉29 ℞	−00°04'	29°♌30	29°♒30
♅	08°♒48	+00°00'	21°♏11	21°♉11
♆	29°♑24	+00°00'	00°♐35	00°♊35
♇	06°♐23	+00°01'	23°♑36	23°♋36
☊	00°♍06 ℞	−00°08'	29°♈53	29°♎53
☋	00°♓06 ℞	−00°08'	29°♎53	29°♈53
As	26°♏36'28"	+00°00'	03°♒23	03°♌23
Mc	09°♍13'20"	+00°00'	20°♈46	20°♎46
⊗	17°♏28	+00°00'	12°♒31	12°♌31

In a lawsuit, the judge is given by the 10th House.[159] Here we see Judge Jackson, personified by Mercury in Scorpio, peregrine in the 12th House. Mars and Mercury are in mutual reception by sign. Mars is conjunct the 10th House cusp. These two factors show a considerable affinity between Judge Jackson and the Government. In fact, Judge Jackson ended up accepting most of the Government's case against Microsoft. He declared Microsoft a monopoly, however, his opinion was immediately appealed, and in the change of presidential administrations between Clinton and Bush, it's pretty obvious that Microsoft is likely to emerge with a wrist slap, at most.

We almost don't have to go any further. I would hypothesize that Pluto in the 1st at the Bendings shows the Government's determination in this case to take Microsoft apart, but Mars is just separating from the square, which may show either tactical errors on the Government's part, or the inability to keep righteous indignation in check.

Curiously, Judge Jackson translates the light between the Government and Microsoft. He may yet broker some sort of agreement, although I cannot believe that it would be seriously to Microsoft's disadvantage.

We also haven't mentioned Microsoft's army: Venus, Ruler of the 7th House. We haven't really had to. Venus is as dignified as Jupiter here, even more so by being direct. The Moon is coming to Venus. But who is Microsoft's army? I would suggest that their army includes the news media, specifically Microsoft's partially owned affiliate, MSNBC, which has conducted a very effective propaganda campaign to reduce the likelihood of any serious corporate damage.

The Moon is also slow in this chart, which could certainly illustrate the glacial speed of events surrounding this trial.

Example 50. Will we win the debate?

In 1986, Mary Ellen Glass, an astrologer, then living in Baltimore, was teaching Astrology as a community education course at Towson State University. This was somehow brought to the attention of certain members of the Physics Department, who evidently had connections to CSICOP (Committee for the Scientific Investigation of Claims of the Paranormal, a skeptics organization with a fairly high media profile), who objected that such "pseudo-science" was being taught at Towson State. Mary Ellen's class was cancelled. Oops! She had a contract! Mary Ellen agreed to forgo teaching the class provided that Towson State set up and run a public, formal, debate between the two sides, which they agreed to do. Mary Ellen assembled a debating team of three people: Mary Shea, Holly Law, and myself. Many kind astrologers, who sent us preparatory materials, citations, and quotes, in turn aided us.

This question was asked by one of the participating astrologers. The answer was almost a no-brainer. As Ruler of the 1st House we are represented by the Moon in its *exaltation* (remember Lilly's comment about the superiority of the exaltation in matters of warfare?). The opposition is given by Saturn, cadent, retrograde and peregrine. If that isn't enough, Mars, the warrior, is conjunct our 1st House, and Neptune, confusion, conjunct their 7th House. I therefore judged that we almost couldn't lose – and that the opposition would show up unprepared, believing that they were so much in the right that they wouldn't

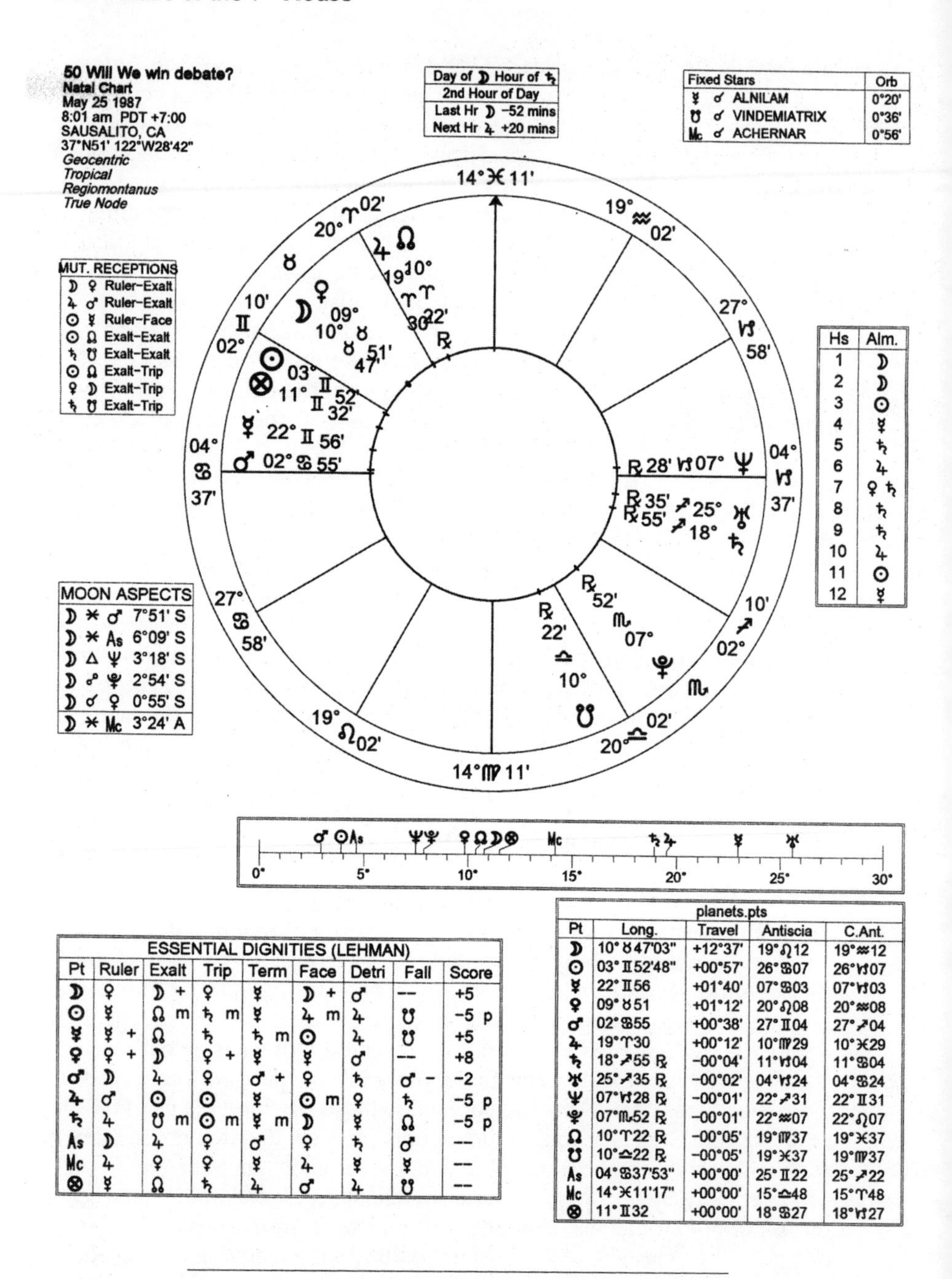

Fixed Stars	Orb
☿ ☌ ALNILAM	0°20'
☋ ☌ VINDEMIATRIX	0°36'
Mc ☌ ACHERNAR	0°56'

MUT. RECEPTIONS
☽ ♀ Ruler-Exalt
♃ ♂ Ruler-Exalt
☉ ☿ Ruler-Face
☉ ☊ Exalt-Exalt
♄ ☋ Exalt-Exalt
☉ ☊ Exalt-Trip
♀ ☽ Exalt-Trip
♄ ☋ Exalt-Trip

Hs	Alm.
1	☽
2	☽
3	☉
4	☿
5	♄
6	♃
7	♀ ♄
8	♄
9	♄
10	♃
11	☉
12	☿

MOON ASPECTS
☽ ⚹ ♂ 7°51' S
☽ ⚹ As 6°09' S
☽ △ ♆ 3°18' S
☽ ☍ ♇ 2°54' S
☽ ☌ ♀ 0°55' S
☽ ⚹ Mc 3°24' A

ESSENTIAL DIGNITIES (LEHMAN)

Pt	Ruler	Exalt	Trip	Term	Face	Detri	Fall	Score
☽	♀	☽ +	♀	☿	☽ +	♂	--	+5
☉	☿	☊ m	♄ m	☿	♃ m	♃	☋	-5 p
☿	☿ +	☊	♄	♄ m	☉	♃	☋	+5
♀	♀ +	☽	♀ +	☿	☿	♂	--	+8
♂	☽	♃	♀	♂ +	♀	♄	♂ -	-2
♃	♂	☉	☉	☿	☉ m	♀	♄	-5 p
♄	♃	☋ m	☉ m	☿ m	☽	☿	☊	-5 p
As	☽	♃	♀	♂	♀	♄	♂	--
Mc	♃	♀	♀	☿	♃	☿	☿	--
⊗	☿	☊	♄	♃	♂	♃	☋	--

planets.pts

Pt	Long.	Travel	Antiscia	C.Ant.
☽	10°♉47'03"	+12°37'	19°♌12	19°♒12
☉	03°♊52'48"	+00°57'	26°♋07	26°♑07
☿	22°♊56	+01°40'	07°♋03	07°♑03
♀	09°♉51	+01°12'	20°♌08	20°♒08
♂	02°♋55	+00°38'	27°♊04	27°♐04
♃	19°♈30	+00°12'	10°♍29	10°♓29
♄	18°♐55 ℞	-00°04'	11°♑04	11°♋04
♅	25°♐35 ℞	-00°02'	04°♑24	04°♋24
♆	07°♑28 ℞	-00°01'	22°♐31	22°♊31
♇	07°♏52 ℞	-00°01'	22°♒07	22°♌07
☊	10°♈22 ℞	-00°05'	19°♍37	19°♓37
☋	10°♎22 ℞	-00°05'	19°♓37	19°♍37
As	04°♋37'53"	+00°00'	25°♊22	25°♐22
Mc	14°♓11'17"	+00°00'	15°♎48	15°♈48
⊗	11°♊32	+00°00'	18°♋27	18°♑27

think that they would have to do any work in advance (the Neptune clouding the situation, combined with Saturn in a fire sign, hence hasty).

This proved to be the case. We came prepared to the teeth; they almost didn't have a note with them. When the neutral moderator called for a show of hands of who presented the better case, even the skeptics' partisans admitted by about a ratio of 2:1 that we had presented the stronger case. We won!

Example 51. If I run for Democratic chair?

A lawyer who was contemplating running for Democratic Chair in her county asked this question. She had several options at the time for things to do, and she had been assured that she had the support of key people.

I was reluctant to answer the question at all, because of Saturn in the 10th. I was eventually prevailed upon to say something, since Saturn is the Ruler of

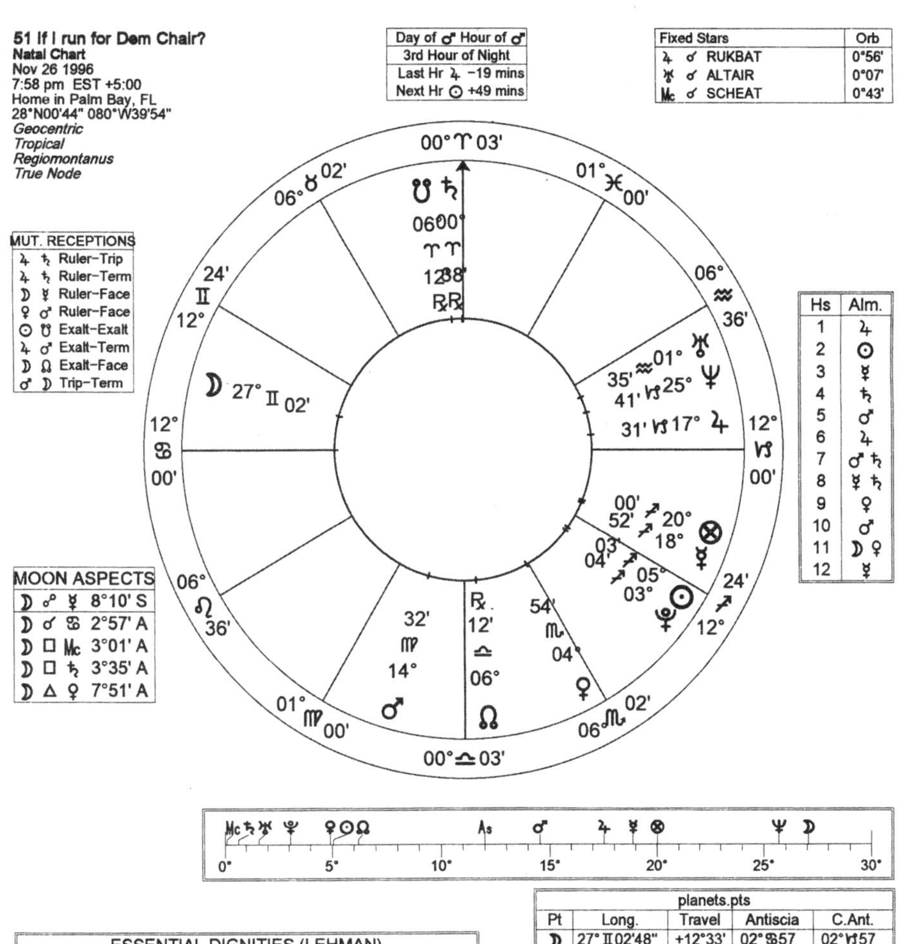

ESSENTIAL DIGNITIES (LEHMAN)								
Pt	Ruler	Exalt	Trip	Term	Face	Detri	Fall	Score
☽	☿	☊	☿	♂	☉	♃	☋	-5 p
☉	♃	☋ m	♃	♃	☿	☿	☊	-5 p
☿	♃	☋	♃	☿ +	☽	☿ -	☊	-3
♀	♂	--	♂	♂	♂ m	♀ -	☽	-10 p
♂	☿	☿	☽	♃	♀ m	♃	♀	-5 p
♃	♄	♂	☽	♃ +	♂	☽	♃ -	-2
♄	♂	☉	♃	♃	♂	♀	♄ -	-9 p
As	☽	♃	♂	♃	☿	♄	♂	--
Mc	♂	☉	♃	♃	♂	♀	♄	--
⊗	♃	☋	♃	♄	♄	☿	☊	--

planets.pts				
Pt	Long.	Travel	Antiscia	C.Ant.
☽	27°♊02'48"	+12°33'	02°♋57	02°♑57
☉	05°♐03'40"	+01°00'	24°♑56	24°♋56
☿	18°♐52	+01°30'	11°♑07	11°♋07
♀	04°♏54	+01°14'	25°♒05	25°♌05
♂	14°♍32	+00°29'	15°♈27	15°♎27
♃	17°♑31	+00°12'	12°♐28	12°♊28
♄	00°♈38 ℞	-00°00'	29°♍21	29°♓21
♅	01°♒35	+00°02'	28°♏24	28°♉24
♆	25°♑41	+00°01'	04°♐18	04°♊18
♇	03°♐04	+00°02'	26°♑55	26°♋55
☊	06°♎12 ℞	-00°11'	23°♓47	23°♍47
☋	06°♈12 ℞	-00°11'	23°♍47	23°♓47
As	12°♋00'05"	+00°00'	17°♊59	17°♐59
Mc	00°♈03'58"	+00°00'	29°♍56	29°♓56
⊗	20°♐00	+00°00'	09°♑59	09°♋59

the 7th, and hence involved in the question.

The chart is a good illustration of Lilly's weighting system for factors.

The Querent can be given by two possible Rulers: the Moon, as sign Ruler of the 1st or Jupiter, as Almuten. What a choice! The Moon is peregrine in the 12th, a cadent house. Jupiter is in Fall, although not peregrine, in the 7th – the House of the enemy!

The enemy, meanwhile, is Saturn, Ruler of the 7th. Saturn is retrograde, in Fall and peregrine but angular – partile conjunct the M.C. to be exact!

Both Rulers are debilitated! So who wins? Well, in this case, angular Saturn did. Observe the Uranus and Neptune in the 7th House. Everything seemed to be going in the Querent's favor until the day before the election when she became the victim of a smear campaign! She chose not to fight the lies and lost by a narrow margin.

It was during this period that Bernadette Brady and I were knee deep in our separate researches concerning sporting events. We had both noticed independently how vicious Saturn was acting in Aries, just as Mars is much nastier in Libra. These planetary placements would stop at nothing to achieve victory. Thus, while we might turn our noses up at the means, this Saturn does have a way of being effective!

Example 52. Chance to file an appeal?

The Querent was going through the Divorce from Hell, and so far, the Judge had basically agreed with her ex-husband on everything. She had even been ordered to pay to support him, even though he had a higher paying job!

Her question was whether to file an appeal to the judge's rulings. While I would have loved to give her an affirmative answer, this chart just didn't support it. The Querent is given by retrograde cadent peregrine Jupiter. Her ex, given by the Ruler of the 7th House, is Mercury in Virgo – cadent, but otherwise wildly dignified.

Furthermore, Mercury ruled the 10th as well. Her ex and the judge were absolutely on the same wavelength – they are the very same planet! The speedy Moon did not produce a result either, applying only to a square of Neptune in the Querent's 2nd House – more financial bad news, probably. It was. She continued to have problems with this settlement for years afterward, and her appeal was denied.

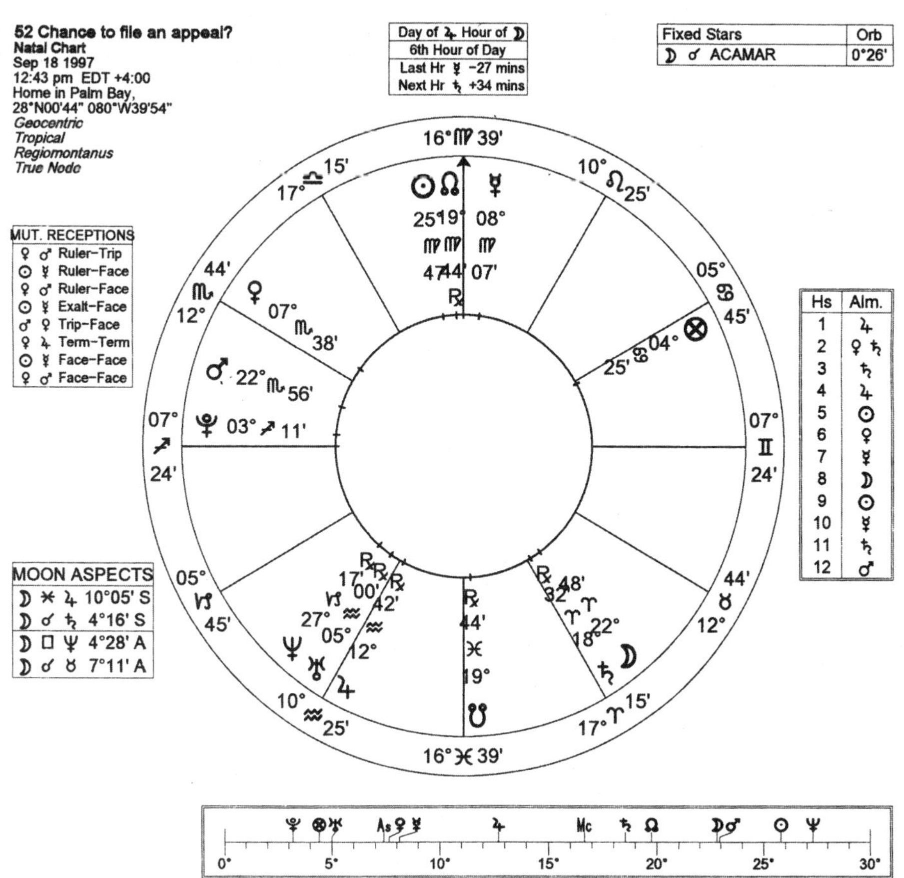

ESSENTIAL DIGNITIES (LEHMAN)								
Pt	Ruler	Exalt	Trip	Term	Face	Detri	Fall	Score
☽	♂	☉	☉	♂	♀	♀	♄	-5 p
☉	☿	☿	♀	♂	☿ m	♃	♀	-5 p
☿	☿ +	☿ +	♀	♀	☉ m	♃	♀	+9
♀	♂	---	♀ +	♃ m	♂ m	♀ -	☽	-2
♂	♂ +	---	♀	☿	♀ m	♀	☽	+5
♃	♄	---	♄	♀ m	☿	☉	---	-5 p
♄	♂	☉	☉	☿	☉	♀	♄ -	-9 p
As	♃	☋	☉	♃	☿	☿	☊	---
Mc	☿	☿	♀	♃	♀	♃	♀	---
⊗	☽	♃	♀	♂	♀	♄	♂	---

planets.pts				
Pt	Long.	Travel	Antiscia	C.Ant.
☽	22°♈48'47"	+14°54'	07°♍11	07°♓11
☉	25°♍47'49"	+00°58'	04°♈12	04°♎12
☿	08°♍07	+01°11'	21°♈52	21°♎52
♀	07°♏38	+01°09'	22°♒21	22°♌21
♂	22°♏56	+00°40'	07°♒03	07°♌03
♃	12°♒42 ℞	-00°03'	17°♏17	17°♉17
♄	18°♈32 ℞	-00°04'	11°♍27	11°♓27
♅	05°♒00 ℞	-00°01'	24°♏59	24°♉59
♆	27°♑17 ℞	-00°00'	02°♐42	02°♊42
♇	03°♐11	+00°01'	26°♑48	26°♋48
☊	19°♍44 ℞	-00°00'	10°♈15	10°♎15
☋	19°♓44 ℞	-00°00'	10°♎15	10°♈15
As	07°♐24'07"	+00°00'	22°♑35	22°♋35
Mc	16°♍39'26"	+00°00'	13°♈20	13°♎20
⊗	04°♋25	+00°00'	25°♊34	25°♐34

Questions concerning Business Partnership

Lilly treats these questions in a somewhat analogous way, although less adversarial, to questions of war. Business partnerships are 1st-7th, and to the extent that the interests of the partners differ, they may be examined using the rules of war to see who is the stronger. Again, Lilly emphasizes cadent placements and exaltation as especially important considerations.

Here, however, harmonious aspects between 1st and 7th denote agreement and harmony between the partners. Even planets of the same nature can produce this agreement.[160]

Business partnership also includes the category of business relationship encompassed by consulting. A 1st-7th business relationship that qualifies for the consulting title is any in which one party does not become an employee of the other party. Each maintains an independent existence. Doctors, psychologists, housing subcontractors, astrologers, and free-lancers of all types share this business category with persons who officially wear the title of consultant. We can think of consultancy as a kind of task-based temporary business partnership. After a period of time, the two parties to the agreement go their separate ways. In other cases, although the period of services may be long, the consultant generally has multiple clients.

Example 53. Should I end the contract with her?

The Querent, an artist, had entered a contract with a woman who agreed to represent her by getting the Querent's work placed in art galleries and museums. She had agreed to work for both a commission on works placed, and a monthly guaranteed fee of several thousand dollars. There had been no placements for several months, and so the Querent asked the question, as the consultant claimed that there were a whole series of deals in process that just needed some time to complete.

So would you trust this consultant? We can look at this chart in two ways: either about the desirability of the partnership, or in terms of whether the consultant is telling the truth.

The Querent is shown either by Venus in Sagittarius, located in the consultant's 2nd House, or the Moon in Capricorn. That certainly describes the situation! Either the Querent is peregrine, or mixed dignity, since the Moon had Triplicity, but Debility. The consultant is Mars in Virgo, not a bad description of a technical consultant, but with dignity only by Term and cadent placement. The cadent placement alone argues that the consultant is ineffectual.

The purpose of the consultant's work is to enhance the Querent's 10th House position (her visibility) and so the partile trine between Mars and Saturn, Ruler of the 10th, does argue that the consultant is genuinely working to achieve this. The problem is that Saturn has dignity only by Face, and is retrograde, so I would doubt that she (the consultant) would be successful in this endeavor. With the partile trine things may be promised, but with dignity only by Face, they simply won't come to pass. In any case, with Saturn in the Querent's 1st House (apart from my own concern about what the Querent was

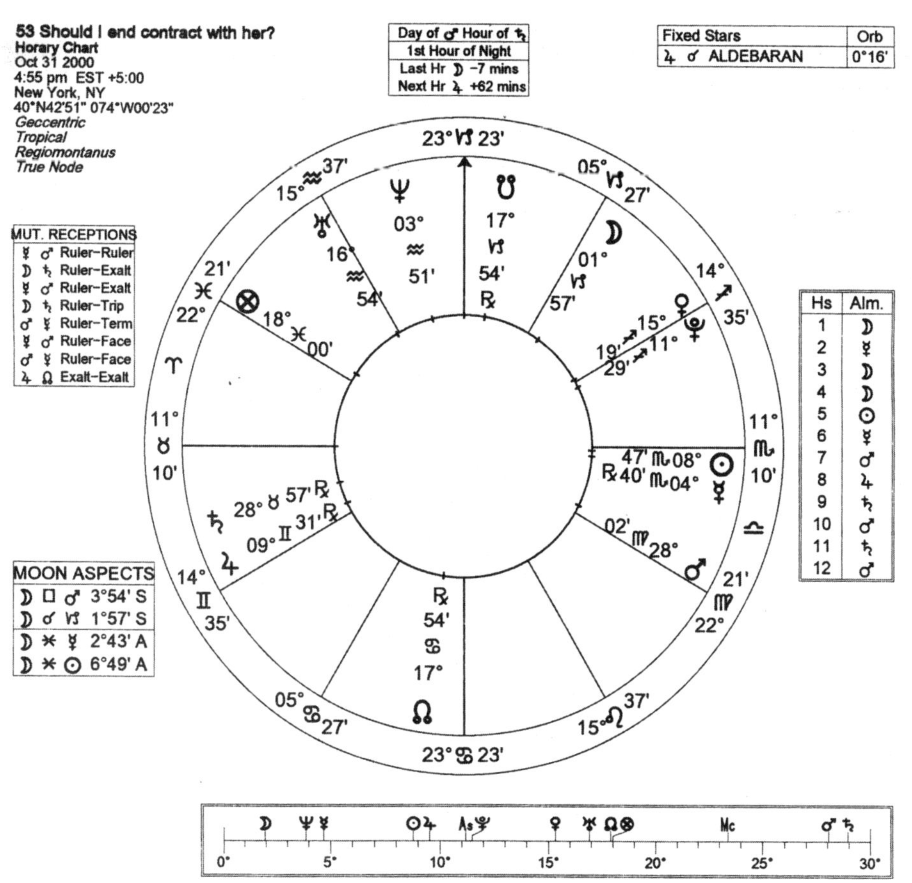

ESSENTIAL DIGNITIES (LEHMAN)								
Pt	Ruler	Exalt	Trip	Term	Face	Detri	Fall	Score
☽	♄	♂	☽ +	♀	♃	☽ −	♃	−2
☉	♂	--	♂	♃	♂	♀	☽	−5 p
☿	♂ m	--	♂	♂	♂ m	♀	☽	−5 p
♀	♃	☋	♃	☿	☽	☿	☊	−5 p
♂	☿ m	☿	☽	♂ +	☿ m	♃	♀	+2
♃	☿	☊ m	☿	♃ +	♃ +	♃ −	☋	−2
♄	♀	☽	☽	♂	♄ +	♂	--	+1
As	♀	☽	☽	☿	☽	♂	--	--
Mc	♄	♂	☽	♂	☉	☽	♃	--
⊗	♃	♀	♂	☿	♃	☿	☿	--

planets.pts				
Pt	Long.	Travel	Antiscia	C.Ant.
☽	01°♑57'02"	+12°00'	28°♐02	28°♊02
☉	08°♏47'00"	+01°00'	21°♒12	21°♌12
☿	04°♏40 ℞	−01°11'	25°♒19	25°♌19
♀	15°♐19	+01°12'	14°♑40	14°♋40
♂	28°♍02	+00°37'	01°♈57	01°♎57
♃	09°♊31 ℞	−00°06'	20°♋28	20°♑28
♄	28°♉57 ℞	−00°04'	01°♌02	01°♒02
♅	16°♒54	+00°00'	13°♏05	13°♉05
♆	03°♒51	+00°00'	26°♏08	26°♉08
♇	11°♐29	+00°02'	18°♑30	18°♋30
☊	17°♋54 ℞	−00°02'	12°♊05	12°♐05
☋	17°♑54 ℞	−00°02'	12°♐05	12°♊05
As	11°♉10'58"	+00°00'	18°♌49	18°♒49
Mc	23°♑23'48"	+00°00'	06°♐36	06°♊36
⊗	18°♓00	+00°00'	11°♎59	11°♈59

not telling) it looks rather like the Querent already knows many of the people with whom the consultant is negotiating. Those people are, after all, in the Querent's own house!

Once finishing with the trine to Saturn, Mars goes Void of Course – only to move into a sign of debility. So I judged that the consultant was not doing the Querent any good.

Now – is the consultant telling the truth when she claimed to be working on various deals? That contention is, after all, the justification for continuing to pay the monthly fee. The chart, as we have read it so far, suggests that she is in fact working on arrangements – but ones that the Querent could achieve herself. We reproduce here the rules from Chapter 3 for assessing whether the rumor is true – in this case, whether the consultant is acting in good faith.

1. The rumor is true if the Lord of the Ascendant, the Moon, or the Moon's dispositor (or better, the majority of them) are fixed, not Cadent, and in good aspect to the benefics or the Sun. (L, G) **Here, two out of three are not fixed (only Saturn, Dispositor of the Moon, is fixed), so the rumor is not confirmed as true.**

2. If those three are Cadent and afflicted by the malefics, the rumor is false whether they are in good zodiacal condition or not. (G) **None are cadent, and Saturn *is* a malefic, the Moon is weak, but unafflicted, and Venus is weak, but separating from Pluto. I would judge this item as not applying.**

3. The rumor is true if all four angles are fixed, the Moon and Mercury are fixed and they in turn are separating from the malefics and applying to an angular benefic. (L, G) **Two angles are fixed. No call.**

4. If the MC/IC axis is fixed, and the Moon rules either angle, then the rumor is true. (L, G) **Does not apply.**

5. If the benefics are in the 1st, but the Moon unfortunate, the rumor is false or misleading. (G) **Jupiter is barely in the first, and debilitated anyway, and the Moon is debilitated. The rumor is false or misleading.**

6. Mercury retrograde or debilitated shows a false rumor, as does the affliction of the planet to whom the Moon or Mercury next applies. (G) **False again.**

7. The Ruler of the Ascendant or the Moon Under Beams brings secrecy to the matter. (L, G) **Does not apply.**

8. The Moon either Void of Course or in hard aspect to Mercury shows the rumor to be either false, or of no import. (L, G) **Moon is sextile Mercury, both are debilitated. Maybe not an argument of falsehood, but hardly an argument of truth.**

9. The Moon in the 1st, 3rd, 10th or 11th, separating from an easy aspect to any planet, and applying by an easy aspect to the Lord of the Ascendant argues that the rumor is true. (L) **Does not apply.**

10. The Moon, square or opposite Mercury, neither in easy aspect to the Ascendant argues that the rumor is false. (L) **Does not apply.**

11. If the Lord of the 6th, 8th, or 12th House is in the 1st House, or afflicting the Ruler of the Ascendant,; or Mars or Saturn retrograde and in the 1st House, or in hard aspect to either the ascending degree or the Ruler of the Ascendant; then the Querent will receive damage or prejudice from the news heard. (L) **Saturn is retrograde in the 1st House, so there is damage from the consultant.**

Thus, what criteria do apply in this particular chart point to a false rumor. Combining the two methods of delineation, we conclude that the consultant is working on "leads" that she either knows are futile, or knows that the Querent could pursue on her own. Thus, the consultant is effectively lying to preserve her fees. The Moon, Slow of Course, doesn't help the situation either, because it certainly does not portend a swift breakthrough in anything related to the Question.

Questions about hunting

In Spanish, the word for marriage is *casar*. The word for hunting is *cazar*. In most Spanish-speaking countries, these would almost be homonyms. Perhaps this is significant! This is another Question I have never taken, but basically, the delineation calls for looking for bestial signs prominent with respect to the 1st, 7th, or planetary hour ruler. Without them, a hunt is not successful.[161] I would assume that if the question were concerning fishing, then the water signs would be the appropriate indicators. Perhaps we should also speculate on the use of bestial signs as an indicator for behavior in singles bars!

Buying and selling commodities (or any items owned)

It's very easy to default into language of our own time and misconstrue exactly what Lilly was conveying. Today, the word "commodity" is a word that is applied mainly to a type of financial instrument, a somewhat riskier variant of the stock market. Lilly's use was much more general. He referred to buying or selling anything *tangible*, hence, the older meaning of commodity.

A sales transaction is like a marriage. It works when there is an approaching soft aspect between the Rulers of the 1st and 7th, or when another party translates the light.

However, it's worth considering Lilly's specific warnings with respect to the Moon:

> "If the Moon be voyd of course, unless the *Significators* apply

strongly, there's seldome any Bargaine concluded, or Commodity at the time bought, and yet both parties wrangle, and have some meetings to no purpose: If the Planet from whom the Moon separates enters Combustion, he that sells his Land or House at that time, shall never recover them againe: but if the Planet from whom the Moon did last separate, be free from misfortune, and beholds the Lord of that Signe from whence the Judgment, or thing in question is required: it's then possible the *Seller* may in time re-purchase the Lands or Commodities againe, or others of as good value."[162]

At this point, it's worth mentioning that Lilly puts high stock in the use of the last aspect and the next aspect of the Moon in many of his horaries. This is a technique I mostly ignore. I have come to this primarily because of being struck by the frequency of conflicting advice when multiple techniques apply in a single delineation. However, in this section, Lilly actually gives a purpose to what we could classify as a secondary factor, namely the condition of the last planet the Moon aspected. Lilly spells out how the condition of this planet can show whether the sale is permanent, which is an interesting sub-question by itself. Thus, we can see three considerations in this delineation of buy-sell, as follows:

Primary consideration	The Rulers of the 1st and 7th	Shows whether the intention for the sale is present
Primary consideration	The condition of the Moon	Shows if the sale will die for lack of energy
Secondary consideration	The condition of the planet that last was aspected by the Moon	Shows whether the sale is permanent

By assigning a different function to each of the factors we clarify the reading rather than introduce a source of confusion.

Example 54. Event: News of Sale of Store

This is the event of a phone conversation when the "Querent" first heard the news from her ex-husband that he had succeeded in selling his store. Her ears were especially perked up for this news for two reasons: first, because this meant that he could retire, and second, because he had had a previous buyer default on the loan. This chart is done in exactly the style that Lilly used for hearing news of the war, except that obviously, this topic is a bit more benign. This is a chart for the time of hearing a piece of news, then reading it as if the question were: "Is the rumor true?"

Here we have all fixed angles, although the Ruler of the Ascendant (the Sun), the Moon and the Moon's dispositor are not fixed. Mercury is very swift and dignified and in a sextile to the Ascendant. We have two good indications of truth, the fixed angles and the condition of Mercury. Is this enough? Probably, but the situation is clinched by the fact that the Moon is translating the

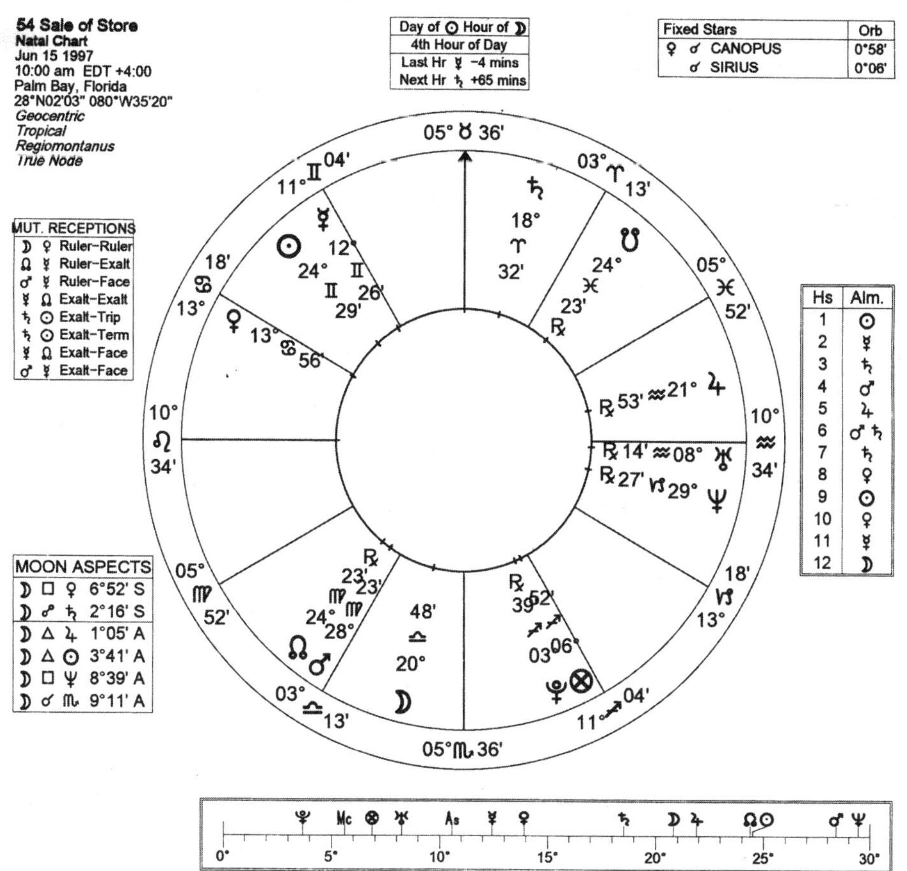

ESSENTIAL DIGNITIES (LEHMAN)								
Pt	Ruler	Exalt	Trip	Term	Face	Detri	Fall	Score
☽	♀ m	♄	♄	☿	♃ m	♂	☉	−5 p
☉	☿	☊	♄ m	♄	☉ +	♃	☋	+1
☿	☿ +	☊ m	♄	♃	♂ m	♃	☋	+5
♀	☽ m	♃	♀ +	☿	☿	♄	♂	+3
♂	☿	☿	♀	♂ +	☿ m	♃	♀	+2
♃	♄	--	♄	♃ +	☽ m	☉	--	+2
♄	♂	☉	☉ m	☿	☉	♀	♄ −	−9 p
As	☉	--	☉	☿	♃	♄	--	--
Mc	♀	☽	♀	♀	☿	♂	--	--
⊗	♃	☋	☉	♃	☿	☿	☊	--

planets.pts				
Pt	Long.	Travel	Antiscia	C.Ant.
☽	20°♎48'13"	+12°15'	09°♓11	09°♍11
☉	24°♊29'59"	+00°57'	05°♋30	05°♑30
☿	12°♊26	+02°00'	17°♋33	17°♑33
♀	13°♋56	+01°13'	16°♊03	16°♐03
♂	28°♍23	+00°24'	01°♈36	01°♎36
♃	21°♒53 ℞	−00°01'	08°♏06	08°♉06
♄	18°♈32	+00°04'	11°♍27	11°♓27
♅	08°♒14 ℞	−00°01'	21°♏45	21°♉45
♆	29°♑27 ℞	−00°01'	00°♐32	00°♊32
♇	03°♐39 ℞	−00°01'	26°♑20	26°♋20
☊	24°♍23 ℞	−00°02'	05°♈36	05°♎36
☋	24°♓23 ℞	−00°02'	05°♎36	05°♈36
As	10°♌34'04"	+00°00'	19°♉25	19°♏25
Mc	05°♉36'09"	+00°00'	24°♌23	24°♒23
⊗	06°♐52	+00°00'	23°♑07	23°♋07

light between Saturn and the Sun, the rulers of 1st and 7th. (Remember, this is a buy-sell situation.) However, given that the Moon is peregrine, this probably would not have worked, except that the Sun and Saturn are in mutual reception by Triplicity. Notice, the sale has already occurred. In this case nothing happens if things continue as they are, which is that the sale continues to be in effect. The peregrine Moon and Saturn may in fact show the difficulty that would ensue were the seller to try to go to the trouble of backing out.

Notice that the issue here is not primarily whether her ex was telling the truth – she didn't doubt that he believed what he was saying. The question was really about whether it was true that the sale would go through. Here we see the affirmative both through the "is the rumor true" construct, and through the buy-sell method. The sale went through six weeks later, and unlike the last time, he has not had to take the store back.

While Saturn, the planet that the Moon last aspected, is in Fall, it is not retrograde, nor is it afflicted by other malefics. And while the Moon in Libra is peregrine, it happens to be conjunct the seller's natal Moon.

Example 55. Restaurant: Would it be profitable?

The Querent wanted to buy a restaurant that he had seen, so he asked whether it would be a profitable investment.

First: can he succeed in buying the restaurant? Probably. Mercury, Ruler of the seller, is coming to a trine to Jupiter, Ruler of the buyer/Querent. Mercury has out-of-sect Triplicity, and Jupiter is mixed: being in Detriment, and in Term. What does this mean? One interpretation that came to my mind pretty quickly was that he was definitely capable of acting to his own detriment. I checked his past horary record, and discovered that his last horary had been concerning a romance that would have seemed futile to anyone but him, and so then I knew that he *definitely* could be his own worst enemy!

If we need confirmation of the sale, the Moon is also translating the light between buyer and seller. But notice that both the perfection and the translation involve the Moon or Mercury first passing through Neptune. Not a good omen in a property sale!

Mercury not only rules the seller (7th House), it rules the price (10th House). This tells me that the seller sets the price. Since Mercury is barely not peregrine (remember the out-of-sect Triplicity?), it doesn't look like the seller is being unreasonable about the price. And with Mercury swift of course, the seller is probably eager for a quick sale.

But what about the profitability? That, of course, was the question. Here, I was very concerned to see the Moon, South Node and Neptune all in the 2nd House, although Neptune could be judged to be cadent in the 3rd. Moon in the 2nd sends me immediately thinking of cash flow issues; the Moon in the 2nd peregrine makes me think of negative cash flow issues. Money comes in, but more money goes out. The Moon Slow of Course emphasizes the odds that this situation will take a long time to change. This got me thinking. So I asked him if this was a cash business? Yes, it is. Do the books look a little odd? Well, yes, they do. So is this place being used for money laundering? Maybe! Which means that there's no way that the buyer is actually going to have any idea

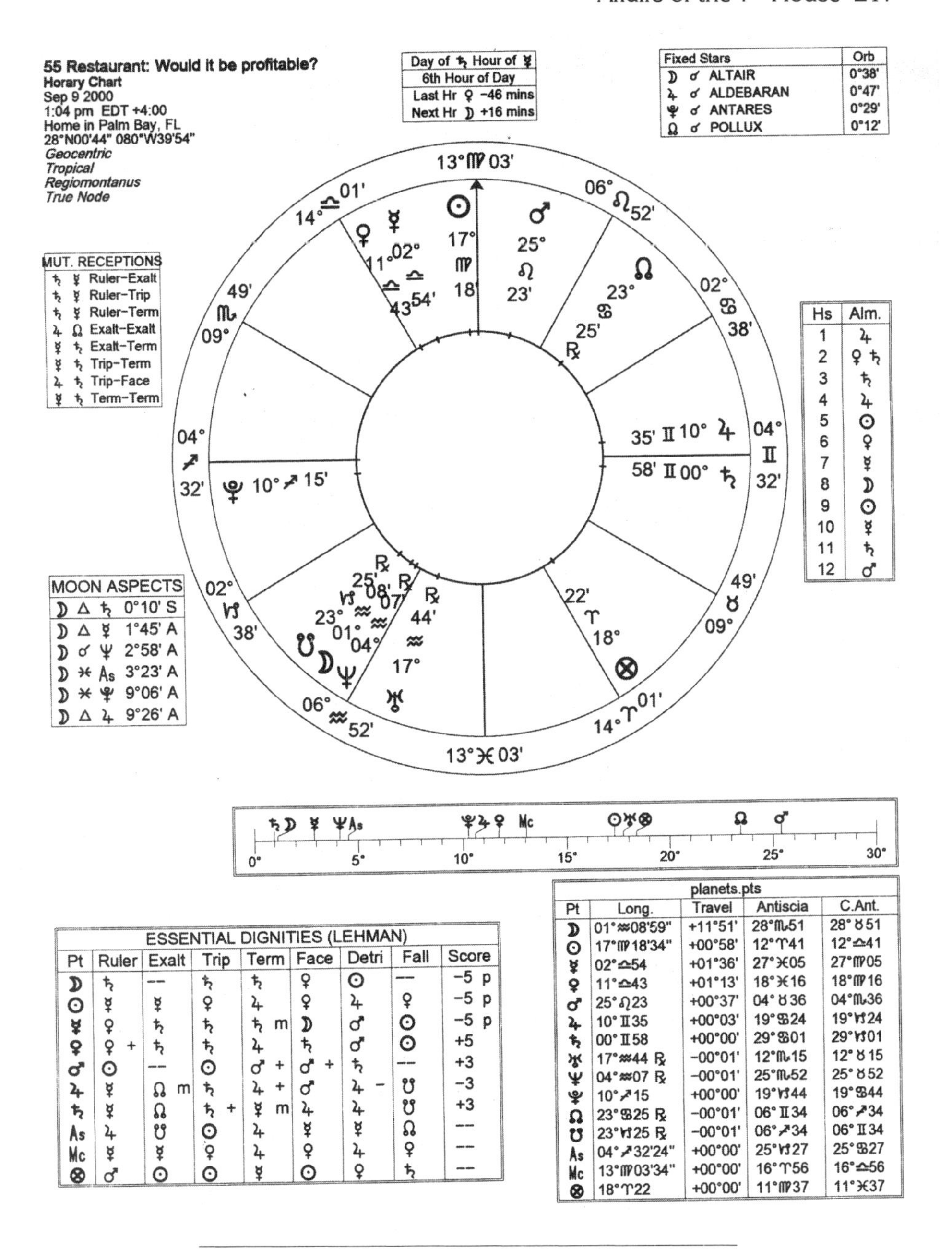

ESSENTIAL DIGNITIES (LEHMAN)								
Pt	Ruler	Exalt	Trip	Term	Face	Detri	Fall	Score
☽	♄	--	♄	♄	♀	☉	--	-5 p
☉	☿	☿	♀	♃	♀	♃	♀	-5 p
☿	♀	♄	♄	♄ m	☽	♂	☉	-5 p
♀	♀ +	♄	♄	♃	♄	♂	☉	+5
♂	☉	--	☉	♂ +	♂ +	♄	--	+3
♃	☿	☊ m	♄	♃ +	♂	♃ -	☋	-3
♄	☿	☊	♄ +	☿ m	♃	♃	☋	+3
As	♃	☋	☉	♃	☿	☿	☊	--
Mc	☿	☿	♀	♃	♀	♃	♀	--
⊗	♂	☉	☉	☿	☉	♀	♄	--

planets.pts				
Pt	Long.	Travel	Antiscia	C.Ant.
☽	01°♒08'59"	+11°51'	28°♏51	28°♉51
☉	17°♍18'34"	+00°58'	12°♈41	12°♎41
☿	02°♎54	+01°36'	27°♓05	27°♍05
♀	11°♎43	+01°13'	18°♓16	18°♍16
♂	25°♌23	+00°37'	04°♉36	04°♏36
♃	10°♊35	+00°03'	19°♋24	19°♑24
♄	00°♊58	+00°00'	29°♋01	29°♑01
♅	17°♒44 ℞	-00°01'	12°♏15	12°♉15
♆	04°♒07 ℞	-00°01'	25°♏52	25°♉52
♇	10°♐15	+00°00'	19°♑44	19°♋44
☊	23°♋25 ℞	-00°01'	06°♊34	06°♐34
☋	23°♑25 ℞	-00°01'	06°♐34	06°♊34
As	04°♐32'24"	+00°00'	25°♑27	25°♋27
Mc	13°♍03'34"	+00°00'	16°♈56	16°♎56
⊗	18°♈22	+00°00'	11°♍37	11°♓37

---

what either the true cash flow is, or what the profitability is. I therefore suggested that I didn't think this was a good idea. With a dignified Saturn in Gemini ruling the 2nd, I said that *eventually* the restaurant *might* turn a profit, but it would take a long time, and it probably wouldn't be a major profit.

He bought it anyway. And six weeks later, he asked about what he could do to turn it around, because he discovered that it was losing money like crazy. But that is another horary …

Example 56. Sell to soon-to-be ex?

This question was asked during the course of a natal reading for this client. We were discussing her upcoming divorce, which she described as "friendly." They had no children, but they did have some debts, some retirement money, and two houses. All of these would need to be split. As we were discussing this, she said that since she was living in one of the houses, and he was living in the other, maybe the simplest thing would be for each to sell "half" of each house to the other, so each would end up with a single house as a primary residence. She asked me if this would be a good idea, and I took the question as a horary.

I'm glad I did! This chart has a number of red flags which proved to be very accurate. The first oddity is the presence of all fixed angles. This is rather like fixed angles with respect to moving: selling means that a commodity *changes* ownership. Change and fixed don't work together. I'm wondering just how likely this sale is – or at least, how quickly it will occur.

The next thing is Neptune so close to the Ascendant. I have found that sometimes Neptune conjunct the Ascendant means that the person is having a psychic hit, and they want confirmation. More generally, it indicates that the Querent is confused or in denial or deluded about what the real circumstances are. So I gently asked whether she'd just had the notion to sell and she said no, she'd been mulling it over for a while. So much for Neptune's insight – more likely Neptune's miasma is showing here. Then I observed the South Node so close to the Ascendant – this also doesn't look like a good deal for the Querent.

Will the sales go through? Remember, this is a double swap, so each person is both buyer and seller. There is no perfection between the Rulers of 1st and 7th *and* the Moon is Void of Course. So by Lilly's estimation, there can be to'ing and fro'ing, but no sale. So I told her that it didn't look like the double sale would be possible. This surprised her considerably, because it just seemed so logical.

The condition of the Moon is actually even worse than Lilly's description encapsulates: because it is also at the Bendings, out of sign. Curiously, the Moon is fast. Fast but void: perhaps the illusion of speed, rather than speed itself?

A year later the answer emerged. The so-called "friendly" divorce was still dragging on with no settlement in sight – and by then, it was a lot less friendly!

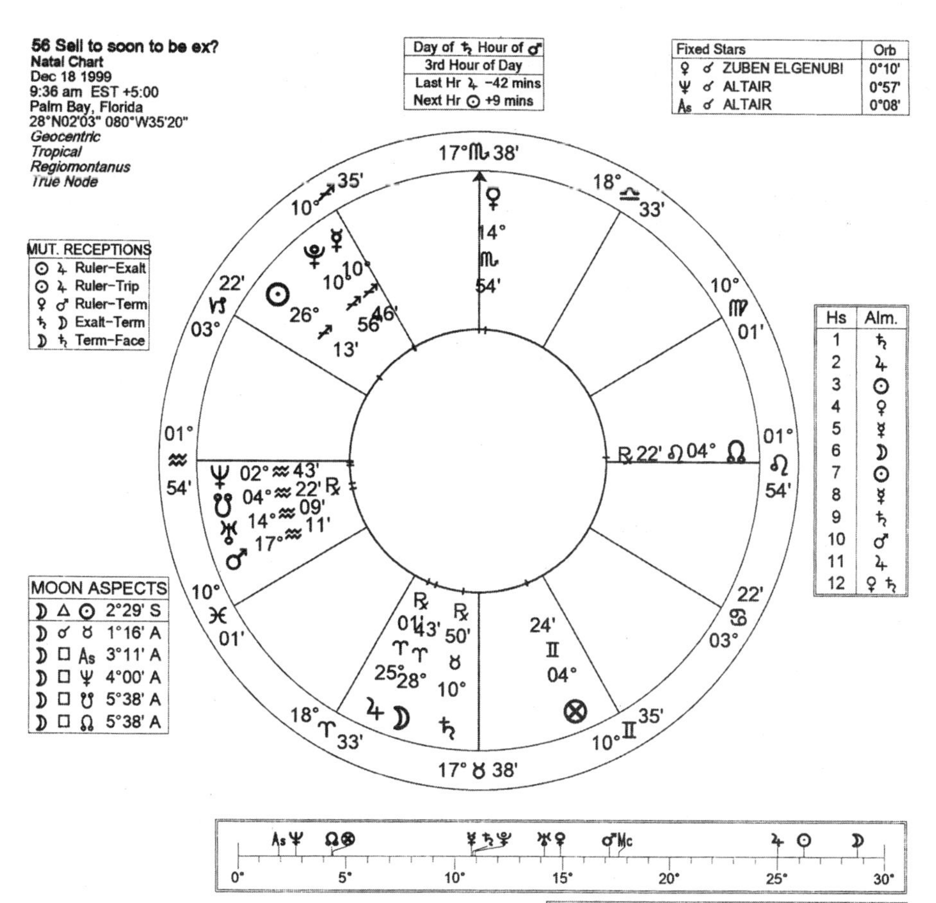

ESSENTIAL DIGNITIES (LEHMAN)								
Pt	Ruler	Exalt	Trip	Term	Face	Detri	Fall	Score
☽	♂	☉	☉	♄	♀	♀	♄	−5 p
☉	♃	☋	☉ +	♂	♄	☿	☊	+3
☿	♃	☋	☉	♀	☽	☿ −	☊	−10 p
♀	♂	--	♀ +	♀ +	☉	♀ −	☽	+0
♂	♄	--	♄	♀	☿	☉	--	−5 p
♃	♂	☉	☉	♂	♀	♀	♄	−5 p
♄	♀	☽	♀	☿	☽	♂	--	−5 p
As	♄	--	♄	♄	♀	☉	--	--
Mc	♂	--	♀	♀	☉	♀	☽	--
⊗	☿	☊	♄	☿	♃	♃	☋	--

planets.pts				
Pt	Long.	Travel	Antiscia	C.Ant.
☽	28°♈43'07"	+14°15'	01°♍16	01°♓16
☉	26°♐13'12"	+01°01'	03°♑46	03°♋46
☿	10°♐46	+01°28'	19°♑13	19°♋13
♀	14°♏54	+01°11'	15°♒05	15°♌05
♂	17°♒11	+00°46'	12°♏48	12°♉48
♃	25°♈01 ℞	−00°00'	04°♍58	04°♓58
♄	10°♉50 ℞	−00°02'	19°♌09	19°♒09
♅	14°♒09	+00°02'	15°♏50	15°♉50
♆	02°♒43	+00°01'	27°♏16	27°♉16
♇	10°♐56	+00°02'	19°♑03	19°♋03
☊	04°♌22 ℞	−00°04'	25°♉37	25°♏37
☋	04°♒22 ℞	−00°04'	25°♏37	25°♉37
As	01°♒54'46"	+00°00'	28°♏05	28°♉05
Mc	17°♏38'33"	+00°00'	12°♒21	12°♌21
⊗	04°♊24	+00°00'	25°♋35	25°♑35

If the Querent have Open Enemies, or any Adversaries

For a long time I thought: what good is this type of question? People who have open enemies know it, don't they? Silly me! That was before one of my clients was threatened with bodily harm!

So back to Lilly. Open enemies are, of course, the 7th House. Open enemies are indicated when:

- There is a hard aspect between the Ruler of the 7th with either the Ruler of the 1st or the Moon.
- The Ruler of the 7th is in the 12th House, or in the 12th House from the place of the Moon, or in the 12th House from the House where the Ruler of the Ascendant is.
- If the Ruler of the 7th is conjunct or aspecting a planet which is in a hard aspect to either the Ruler of the 1st or the Moon, without reception.[163]

Whether there are any enemies also involves the 12th House as well as the 7th House.

Example 57. How bad is it?

The Querent and her husband had been threatened with bodily harm. The husband had been a charismatic preacher, whose marriage to my client had upset some of the members of his flock. The threat had arisen from the turmoil of severed dreams, and they felt it to be seriously considered.

This is a direct threat, so we see the threatening enemy as Mars, Ruler of the 7th House. Mars is in the 1st House – so while dignified, he is in some way at their disposal. Venus, ruling the 1st, is dignified, and moving away from the trine to Mars. The Moon is moving away from the conjunction to Mars, but at the Bendings. The Moon is also fixed and slow, which doesn't suggest quick development.

I judged that the man who threatened them was powerfully affected by the perceived change in circumstance, but that his pain was mainly in the past, as the aspects were departing. Mars is slow-of-course, which makes the man more a thinker than a doer. They were not in any danger, and, probably, he could be brought around because, while posited in stubborn Scorpio, the Mars is dignified, and so should listen to reason – eventually.

They were not harmed.

The Default Other Person

Sometimes, it's hard to decide what house to use for the Quesited, either because the person is fulfilling too many roles, or because there is simply no

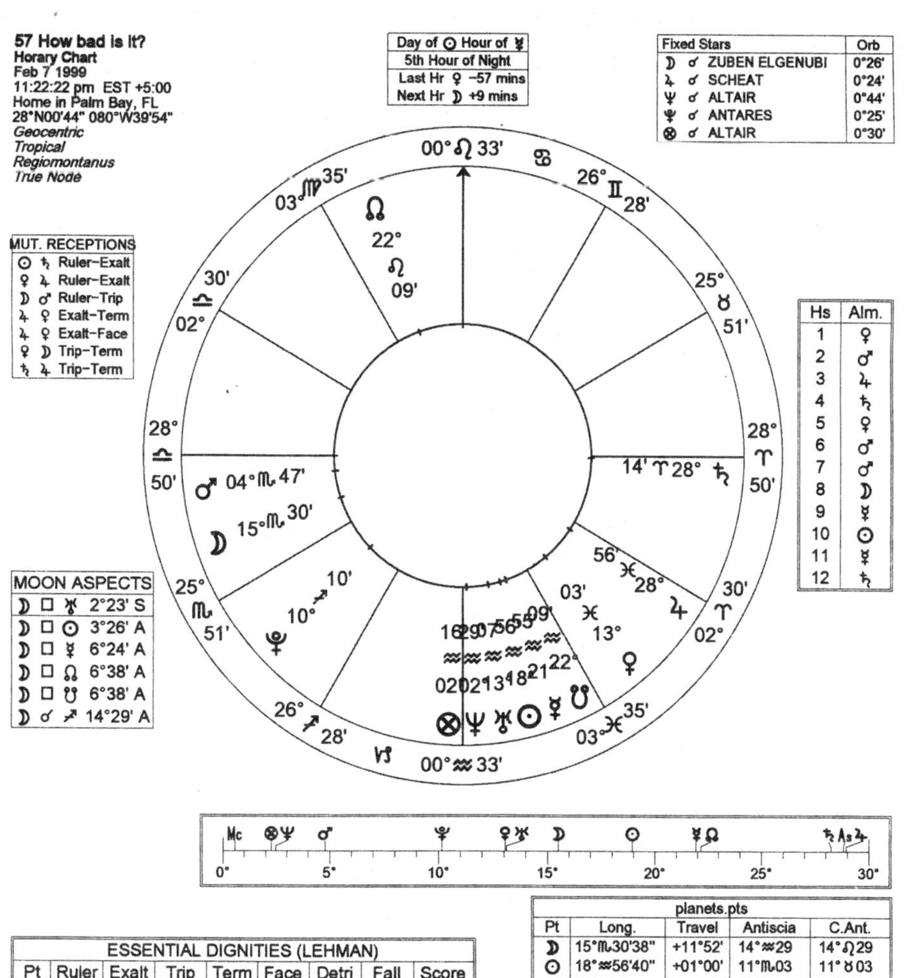

Pt	Ruler	Exalt	Trip	Term	Face	Detri	Fall	Score
ESSENTIAL DIGNITIES (LEHMAN)								
☽	♂	--	♂	♀	☉	♀	☽ -	-9 p
☉	♄	--	☿	♀	☿	☉ -	--	-10 p
☿	♄	--	☿ +	♃	☽	☉	--	+3
♀	♃	♀ +	♂	♃	♃	☿	☿	+4
♂	♂ +	--	♂ +	♂ +	♂ +	♀	☽	+11
♃	♃ +	♀	♂	♄	♂	☿	☿	+5
♄	♂	☉	♃	♄ +	♀	♀	♄ -	-2
As	♀	♄	☿	♂	♃	♂	☉	--
Mc	☉	--	♃	♄	♄	♄	--	--
⊗	♄	--	☿	♄	♀	☉	--	--

planets.pts

Pt	Long.	Travel	Antiscia	C.Ant.
☽	15°♏30'38"	+11°52'	14°♒29	14°♌29
☉	18°♒56'40"	+01°00'	11°♏03	11°♉03
☿	21°♒55	+01°47'	08°♏04	08°♉04
♀	13°♓03	+01°14'	16°♎56	16°♈56
♂	04°♏47	+00°20'	25°♒12	25°♌12
♃	28°♓56	+00°12'	01°♎03	01°♈03
♄	28°♈14	+00°04'	01°♍45	01°♓45
♅	13°♒07	+00°03'	16°♏52	16°♉52
♆	02°♒29	+00°02'	27°♏30	27°♉30
♇	10°♐10	+00°01'	19°♑49	19°♋49
☊	22°♌09	+00°00'	07°♉50	07°♏50
☋	22°♒09	+00°00'	07°♏50	07°♉50
As	28°♎50'02"	+00°00'	01°♓09	01°♍09
Mc	00°♌33'47"	+00°00'	29°♉26	29°♏26
⊗	02°♒16	+00°00'	27°♏43	27°♉43

real relationship to the person yet. The 7th House then becomes the house to use for the Quesited.

Example 58. Is it in our interest to rent a floor to this guy?

The director of a spiritual center contacted me concerning a possible business circumstance. They had heard about someone who allegedly has considerable psychic powers, and there was some discussion going on about renting him a floor of their center, and then ultimately collaborating with him on a healing center. The question was really, whether it would be a good idea to not only rent the floor, but to go into business with this person.

I made five statements concerning this prospect to the director, and then explained myself astrologically as follows.

1. *He thinks his powers are spiritual, but they are more occult than spiritual.*

   He is Mercury, Ruler of the 7th House, so Mercury rules both his 1st and 9th Houses. He wants to be spiritual, but his ruler is in his 5th House; i.e., hooked up with his sexuality. Mercury is peregrine, so he hasn't achieved real stability here in any case, and it's late in the sign.

2. *While he will be able to achieve some (sudden) cures, he will likely harm more people than he helps.*

   Note Uranus at his 6th House cusp. That's the sudden cures; but Saturn rules his 6th, and it's pretty close to Algol, Retrograde and in his 8th (the Center's 2nd House of money). Saturn's dignified only by the minor dignities Term and Face. So this doesn't look like he helps most people, and it looks like this fact could have an impact on the Center's finances.

3. *In general, your Center would do okay financially as far as the rent is concerned but he will have a tendency to delay paying rent when he wants to get something out of you.*

   Venus in Pisces rules the 2nd, which is good, except that it's in the 12th House.

4. *It is premature to expect that there would be any real partnership here: more like two separate groups doing their own thing.*

   Mercury and Jupiter simply don't connect in this chart until *after* Mercury changes sign, and when a sign change is involved, some major changes will happen and there's no guarantee that the result will occur anyway.

5. *It is distinctly possible that he may actually move to a higher spiritual level in either three months or three years. If that occurs, you really would have much more in common with him than you do now, and then there would be the possibility for a positive*

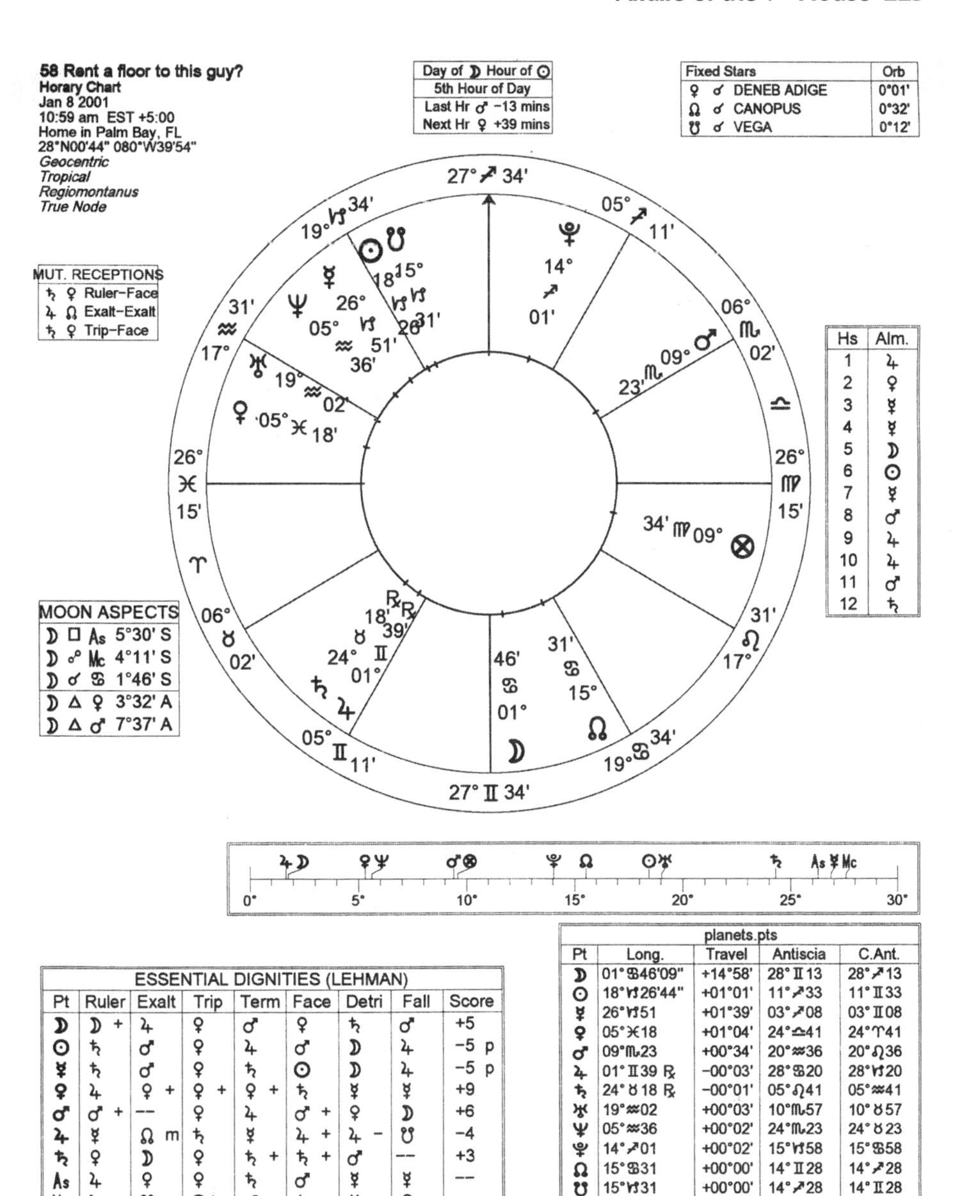

ESSENTIAL DIGNITIES (LEHMAN)								
Pt	Ruler	Exalt	Trip	Term	Face	Detri	Fall	Score
☽	☽ +	♃	♀	♂	♀	♄	♂	+5
☉	♄	♂	♀	♃	♂	☽	♃	−5 p
☿	♄	♂	♀	♄	☉	☽	♃	−5 p
♀	♃	♀ +	♀ +	♀ +	♄	☿	☿	+9
♂	♂ +	--	♀	♃	♂ +	♀	☽	+6
♃	☿	☊ m	♄	☿	♃ +	♃ −	☋	−4
♄	♀	☽	♀	♄ +	♄ +	♂	--	+3
As	♃	♀	♀	♄	♂	☿	☿	--
Mc	♃	☋	☉	♂	♄	☿	☊	--
⊗	☿	☿	♀	♀	☉	♃	♀	--

planets.pts				
Pt	Long.	Travel	Antiscia	C.Ant.
☽	01°♋46'09"	+14°58'	28°♊13	28°♐13
☉	18°♑26'44"	+01°01'	11°♐33	11°♊33
☿	26°♑51	+01°39'	03°♐08	03°♊08
♀	05°♓18	+01°04'	24°♎41	24°♈41
♂	09°♏23	+00°34'	20°♒36	20°♌36
♃	01°♊39 ℞	−00°03'	28°♋20	28°♑20
♄	24°♉18 ℞	−00°01'	05°♌41	05°♒41
♅	19°♒02	+00°03'	10°♏57	10°♉57
♆	05°♒36	+00°02'	24°♏23	24°♉23
♇	14°♐01	+00°02'	15°♑58	15°♋58
☊	15°♋31	+00°00'	14°♊28	14°♐28
☋	15°♑31	+00°00'	14°♐28	14°♊28
As	26°♓15'17"	+00°00'	03°♎44	03°♈44
Mc	27°♐34'23"	+00°00'	02°♑25	02°♋25
⊗	09°♍34	+00°00'	20°♈25	20°♎25

---

relationship. But of course, there's no guarantee he will reach this level, although he could, Mercury does rule his 9th too.

Again, Mercury improves by changing signs. But no guarantee, especially as Mercury is slowing down!

And on that note, we will move to a higher occult number, and examine the 8th House!

Chapter 8

Affairs of the 8th House:
Death, Inheritance, Debts, Taxes & Insurance

There's no avoiding it. The 8th House is depressing! The least onerous meaning of the 8th House is the financial resources of the Querent's partner, but even this seldom occurs as part of a question unless divorce or separation is in the works.

Questions of the 8th House as given by Lilly:[164]

- *If the absent party be dead or alive*
- *When, or about what time the Querent may die*
- *Whether the husband or wife shall die first*
- *The manner of death of the Querent*
- *Whether the spouse's portion (i.e. dowry) shall be great or small, and whether it shall be obtained*
- *Inheritance of money or goods (not land)*
- *Whether a fear is justifiable; whether danger is real or imaginary*

Gadbury's list of categories of questions differs only slightly from Lilly's.

I would add some additional categories:

- paying off a long-term debt, or concerning a long-term loan or mortgage
- insurance, whether a good or necessary investment
- questions concerning taxes, such as whether the Querent will undergo an audit

Death

We have already considered death in two houses: the 4th, for our discussion of absent persons; and the 6th, for considerations surrounding illness and disease. Briefly, it is not good to see the Ruler of the Querent either posited in or in aspect to the Ruler of the 6th, 8th or 12th Houses. The greater the relation between the Significator of the Querent, and the 8th House, the greater the danger to the Querent.

In this house, we consider Death generically. And it becomes obvious immediately that society has changed since Lilly's day. I have never received some of the questions that Lilly got routinely. For example, the question of who in a marriage will die first has ceased to be common. The only way that this question has occurred – and this is somewhat tangential – is in questions concerning the death (or more likely, the danger of death) of a spouse. Here, the question becomes, when will my husband/wife die? This may imply that the Querent expects to outlive the spouse, because this question is only asked when the spouse has a reason to be fearful of death – such as a medical diagnosis of a life-threatening disease.

Were the question about the relative length of life between two partners to be asked, Lilly advises to determine the outcome not through horary, but through examination of the nativities of the two parties.[165] In the absence of natal delineation to obtain the answer, examine the relative strength of the Rulers of the 1st and 7th. Whoever has the stronger Significator lives longer. Gadbury adds the following:

"In this Question, behold the Lord of the Ascendant and Lord of the Seventh, and see which of them goeth to conjunction, square or opposition of the Lord of the eighth House, or to Combustion of the Sun, or to the evil Aspects of the unfortunate Planets, and so judge."[166]

Obviously, we begin to see that questions of death can involve much more than the absent party! There are only two limitations:

1. whether the Querent has enough emotional involvement to ask the question at all

2. whether the Astrologer chooses to delineate the answer to the Querent

While I do not refrain entirely from taking questions concerning death, I at least want to ascertain the motivations of the Querent for asking the question, as well whether the Querent is sufficiently involved to ask a good horary question about death.

Example 59. Is it the transmission?

Cars die too. The car in this case had passed around among various family members, most recently, the Querent's brother, and now his niece. At first, I was reluctant to commit to just what house to use, and whether to turn the chart, but as he talked on about the car, I realized he might have been

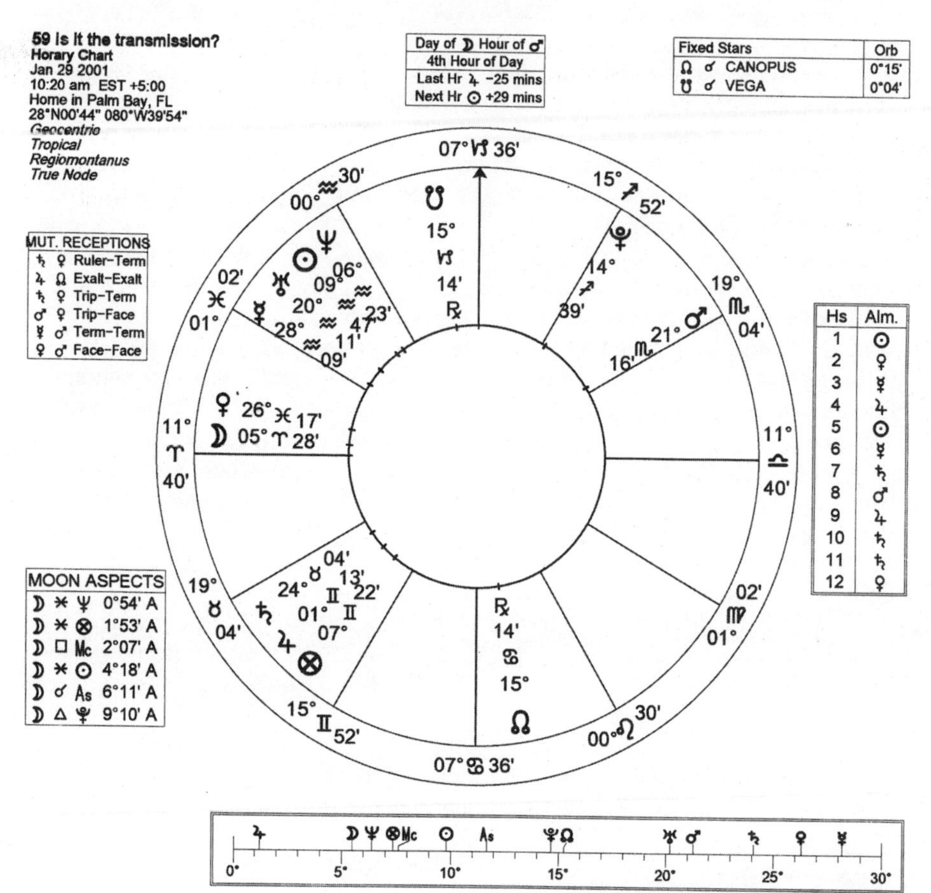

ESSENTIAL DIGNITIES (LEHMAN)								
Pt	Ruler	Exalt	Trip	Term	Face	Detri	Fall	Score
☽	♂	☉	☉	♃	♂	♀	♄	-5 p
☉	♄	--	♄	☿	♀	☉ -	--	-10 p
☿	♄	--	♄	♂ m	☽	☉	--	-5 p
♀	♃	♀ +	♀ +	♄	♂ m	☿	☿	+7
♂	♂ +	--	♀	☿ m	♀ m	♀	☽	+5
♃	☿	☊ m	♄	☿	♃ +	♃ -	☋	-4
♄	♀	☽	♀	♄ +	♄ +	♂	--	+3
As	♂	☉	☉	♀	☉	♀	♄	--
Mc	♄	♂	♀	☿	♃	☽	♃	--
⊗	☿	☊	♄	♃	♃	♃	☋	--

planets.pts				
Pt	Long.	Travel	Antiscia	C.Ant.
☽	05°♈28'54"	+12°16'	24°♍31	24°♓31
☉	09°♒47'32"	+01°00'	20°♏12	20°♉12
☿	28°♒09	+00°52'	01°♏50	01°♉50
♀	26°♓17	+00°54'	03°♎42	03°♈42
♂	21°♏16	+00°33'	08°♒43	08°♌43
♃	01°♊13	+00°00'	28°♋46	28°♑46
♄	24°♉04	+00°00'	05°♌55	05°♒55
♅	20°♒11	+00°03'	09°♏48	09°♉48
♆	06°♒23	+00°02'	23°♏36	23°♉36
♇	14°♐39	+00°01'	15°♑20	15°♋20
☊	15°♋14 ℞	-00°03'	14°♊45	14°♐45
☋	15°♑14 ℞	-00°03'	14°♐45	14°♊45
As	11°♈40'52"	+00°00'	18°♍19	18°♓19
Mc	07°♑36'09"	+00°00'	22°♐23	22°♊23
⊗	07°♊22	+00°00'	22°♋37	22°♑37

talking about a beloved family member! This was a "good car" that had recently been diagnosed with transmission problems, which would cost $600 to repair. If that was the only problem, they were willing to do it, but there was the fear that there was something lurking underneath the obvious, and that $600 was just going to go down the drain, so to speak.

All doubts lifted when I looked at the chart. Here is Mars, Ruler of the 1st House (and hence the car; see Examples 1 and 2), right at the 8th House cusp of death! Yes, it's a strong car, since Mars is dignified, but its placement just doesn't add up to prolonged life.

We can clarify these circumstances further by noting a few other things about the chart. Mars has just separated from a square to Uranus, and is approaching the opposition to Saturn, which in turn is located in the 2nd House of money, further debilitating Mars. So I judged that the car had either been in an accident recently, or some particular odd occurence or event had damaged the car, and that repairing it would simply result in further financial drain, as more damage would be found after the initial repair round.

Time for a new car!

Example 60. Will Noriega die soon?

This question was asked by a Panamanian citizen who was a student in Switzerland. A member of the political Left, she urgently wanted Noriega to be out of power. Since I understood her question to be when would General Noriega no longer be in power, I asked her repeatedly if she didn't see any alternative way to ask the question. She explained that, in her opinion, the only way that General Noriega would cease to be leader of Panama was to die. Her determination in asking the question in this particular fashion convinced me that she had sufficient standing to ask.

As the head of state of the country of origin of the Querent, Noriega is shown by Mars, both Sign Ruler and Almuten of the 10th House. Mars is in the 9th, Noriega's 12th. The General is in involved in something undercover: but we knew that! He is in a strong position, since Mars is in Aries. Just on immediate impression, this does not look like a man about to die.

Death of the Head of State is the 8th House from the 10th House, or the radix 5th House. Noriega's death is ruled by Jupiter. Jupiter is in Detriment and retrograde: neither is a strong indicator of death any time soon. Death is incompetent, as it were! Furthermore, Mars is past the sextile to Jupiter, and the Moon is past Mars (Noriega), so there is no perfection and no translation between either Noriega's Ruler or the Moon with the Ruler of the 8th House. Death simply does not look like the outcome in this chart. If anything, the chart looks like his life was more in danger three years (months/days?) earlier when Mars was square the 5th House Saturn.

So what does the chart tell about the outcome? At four degrees, the Moon is at the Bendings. With Mars, Noriega's ruler, in his own 12th House, he contributes to his self-undoing, but that doesn't imply death. In this chart he is simply too strong to die, although we might surmise that, with the Ruler of his 8th in his 1st, that he had a certain level of paranoia or fear of death. Probably quite a reasonable position!

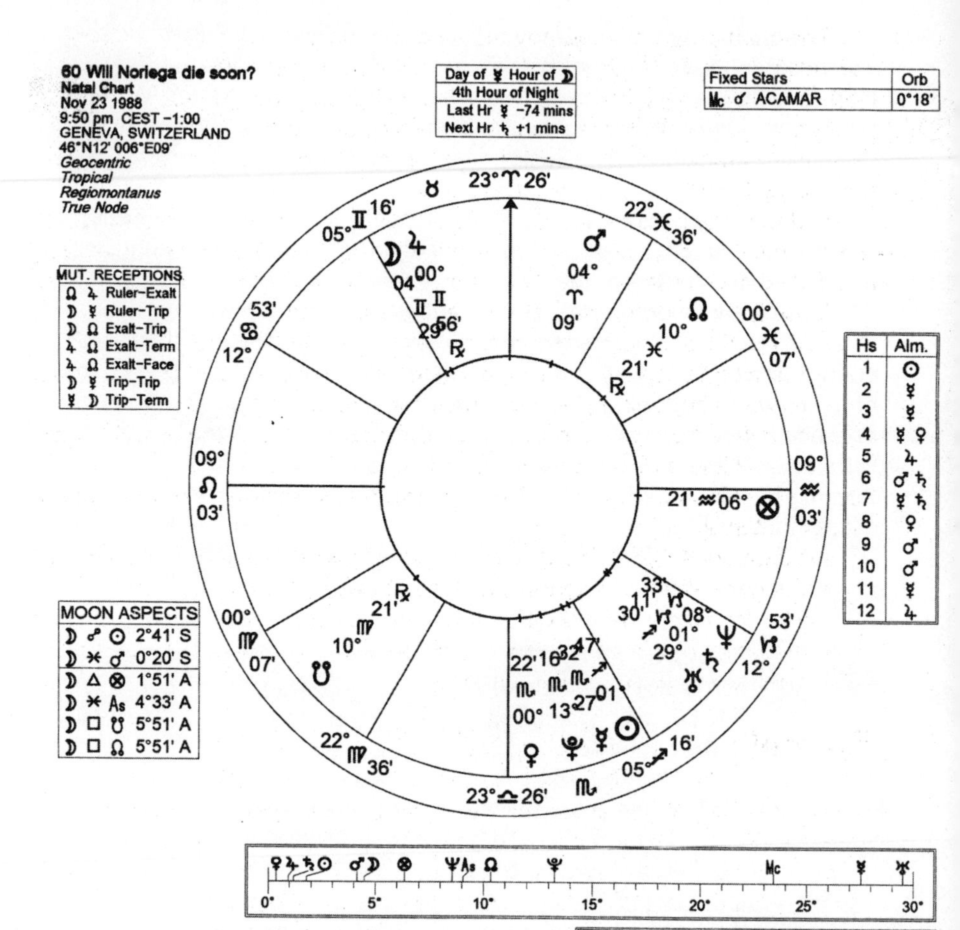

ESSENTIAL DIGNITIES (LEHMAN)								
Pt	Ruler	Exalt	Trip	Term	Face	Detri	Fall	Score
☽	☿	☊	☿	☿	♃	♃	☋	−5 p
☉	♃	☋	♃	♃	☿	☿	☊	−5 p
☿	♂	--	♂	♄	♀	♀	☽	−5 p
♀	♂	--	♂	♂	♂	♀ −	☽	−10 p
♂	♂ +	☉	♃	♃	♂ +	♀	♄	+6
♃	☿	☊	☿	☿	♃ +	♃ −	☋	−4
♄	♄ +	♂	☽	♀	♃	☽	♃	+5
As	☉	--	♃	☿	♄	♄	--	--
Mc	♂	☉	♃	♂	♀	♀	♄	--
⊗	♄	--	☿	☿	♀	☉	--	--

planets.pts				
Pt	Long.	Travel	Antiscia	C.Ant.
☽	04°♊29'36"	+14°04'	25°♋30	25°♑30
☉	01°♐47'41"	+01°00'	28°♑12	28°♋12
☿	27°♏32	+01°35'	02°♒27	02°♌27
♀	00°♏22	+01°13'	29°♒37	29°♌37
♂	04°♈09	+00°17'	25°♍50	25°♓50
♃	00°♊56 ℞	−00°08'	29°♋03	29°♑03
♄	01°♑11	+00°06'	28°♐48	28°♊48
♅	29°♐30	+00°03'	00°♑29	00°♋29
♆	08°♑33	+00°01'	21°♐26	21°♊26
♇	13°♏16	+00°02'	16°♒43	16°♌43
☊	10°♓21 ℞	−00°12'	19°♎38	19°♈38
☋	10°♍21 ℞	−00°12'	19°♈38	19°♎38
As	09°♌03'08"	+00°00'	20°♉56	20°♏56
Mc	23°♈26'06"	+00°00'	06°♍33	06°♓33
⊗	06°♒21	+00°00'	23°♏38	23°♉38

The chart does not show any more detail than this, but then the Querent was adamant in her belief that the only possible scenario to create a post-Noriega Panama was the death of this leader. Clearly, the Querent's supposition is not supported by this chart. As for timing of whatever change this chart portended, I took the approaching trine of the Moon to the Part of Fortune. Clearly, the Querent considered the removal of Noriega to be a benefit, so this seemed the only possible indicator. Both 4th House rulers disposed Fortuna, which indicates that an "end-of-the-matter" other than death may be an appropriate outcome. In viewing a question concerning the fate of a country, the 4th House is the country itself. Both the sign ruler and the co-almuten of the 4th are in the 4th, and both are peregrine, with Venus in Detriment as well. The country is in bad shape, and this affects the fortune of the Querent. If the trine of the Moon to Fortuna represents an increase in her fortune, and if this can only occur with Noriega's removal, then this may be appropriate symbolism. In that case, Noriega is out of the picture in less than two years. (I picked years because the Moon was in a Mutable sign, and Fortuna in fixed, both indicating a longer interval.)

On January 4, 1990, Noriega surrendered to the invading Americans after entering the Vatican Embassy on December 24, 1989.

The chart did not show the U.S. invasion. However, given the way that the Querent chose to ask the Question, this is hardly surprising. The Question was too narrow to show the full outcome.

Example 61. Is she dead?

I received a phone call from an astrologer who was extremely concerned because she had heard that a client of hers was kidnapped the day before in Miami. She had been abducted as she got out of her car in a parking garage, and the kidnappers grabbed her two children as well. The victim's family had gotten a phone message from her where she appeared to be drugged. The family had contacted the astrologer/Querent, in hopes that she could give them some information, or at least reassure them that their loved ones had a chance to survive this ordeal.

Kidnapping is a terrible circumstance for anyone. Just how bad is a chart likely to look because the circumstances are already so grim, *versus* how bad the chart would look if the result were death? The Querent's client is a 7th House person. Also, in this case, the actual Querent could hardly have been asked by the kidnapped woman to do a horary on it! Here we see Venus, Ruler of the 7th, in Detriment and at the Bendings, but in her 1st House, just over the edge from her 2nd House, indicating that she is being held in the neighborhood, but a strong argument that she has some control of the situation. I decided to unequivocally use Venus for the woman, because Saturn, the co-Almuten, also rules her 5th House, and her children were also abducted. Thus, the relationship of Saturn to the house signifying the woman shows her concern and fears for her children as well as herself. Remember that in Example 17, "Where is Patty," Patty's Significator was also in the 1st House, which in Patty's case meant that she got there under her own power, and that she was where she wanted to be, even if that place was a place to commit suicide.

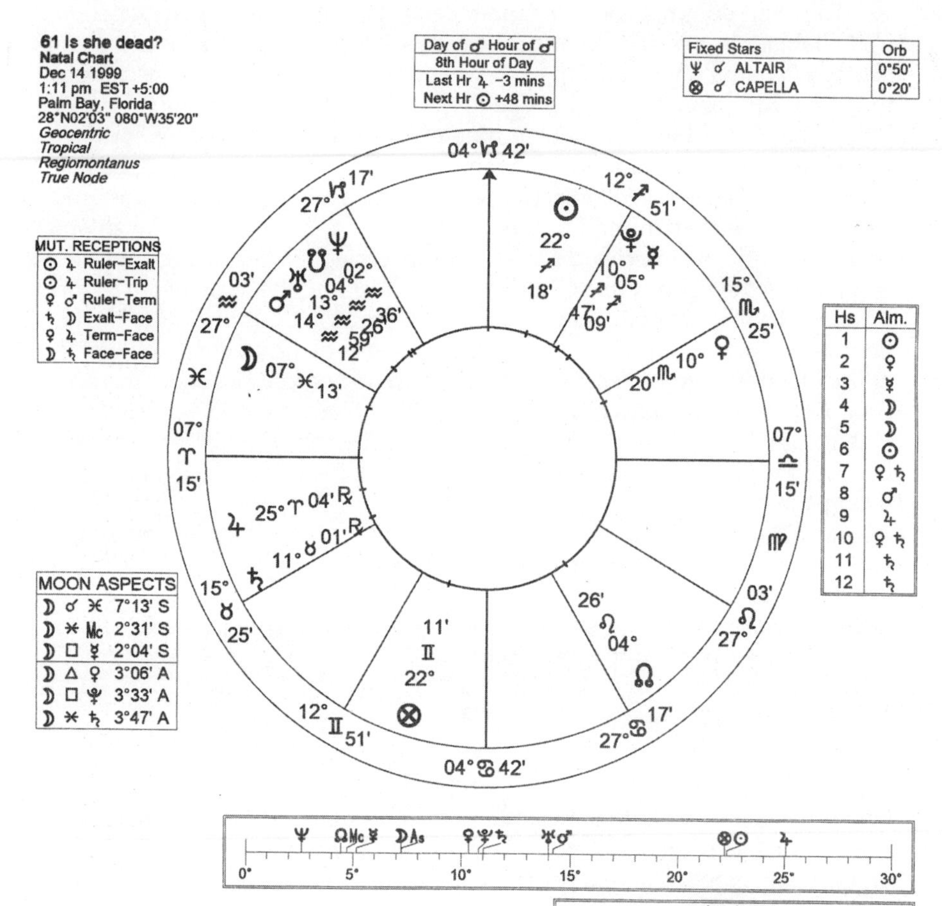

ESSENTIAL DIGNITIES (LEHMAN)								
Pt	Ruler	Exalt	Trip	Term	Face	Detri	Fall	Score
☽	♃	♀	♀	♀	♄ m	☿	☿	-5 p
☉	♃	☋	☉ +	♄	♄	☿	☊	+3
☿	♃	☋	☉	♃	☿ +	☿ -	☊	-4
♀	♂	--	♀ +	♃	☉	♀ -	☽	-2
♂	♄	--	♄	♀	☿	☉	--	-5 p
♃	♂	☉	☉	♂	♀	♀	♄	-5 p
♄	♀	☽	♀	☿	☽ m	♂	--	-5 p
As	♂	☉	☉	♀	♂	♀	♄	--
Mc	♄	♂	♀	♀	♃	☽	♃	--
⊗	☿	☊	♄	♄	☉	♃	☋	--

planets.pts				
Pt	Long.	Travel	Antiscia	C.Ant.
☽	07°♓13'58"	+12°35'	22°♎46	22°♈46
☉	22°♐18'08"	+01°01'	07°♑41	07°♋41
☿	05°♐09	+01°26'	24°♑50	24°♋50
♀	10°♏20	+01°10'	19°♒39	19°♌39
♂	14°♒12	+00°46'	15°♏47	15°♉47
♃	25°♈04 ℞	-00°01'	04°♍55	04°♓55
♄	11°♉01 ℞	-00°02'	18°♌58	18°♒58
♅	13°♒59	+00°02'	16°♏00	16°♉00
♆	02°♒36	+00°01'	27°♏23	27°♉23
♇	10°♐47	+00°02'	19°♑12	19°♋12
☊	04°♌26	+00°01'	25°♉33	25°♏33
☋	04°♒26	+00°01'	25°♏33	25°♉33
As	07°♈15'50"	+00°00'	22°♍44	22°♓44
Mc	04°♑42'43"	+00°00'	25°♐17	25°♊17
⊗	22°♊11	+00°00'	07°♋48	07°♑48

Here we know that the woman is not under her own power, unless she colluded with her kidnappers over the whole scenario. We can examine that possibility when we look at the Significator for the kidnappers. The 1st House placement means that she has some sort of control, which speaks to the fact that she must be alive at the moment the horary was asked, but I can believe that Venus in Detriment is totally descriptive of the situation.

The most significant thing about this chart, I felt, was that Venus is angular. Venus also rules the Quesited's 8th House, but clearly there is already a danger of death by the very circumstances of the chart. Had Venus been posited in the turned 8th, or even the 12th, I would have had much greater fear for her safety.

I told the Querent that her client was alive, but would be in the most danger within a day (her Significator coming to oppose Saturn, although this could also indicate danger for the children the next day), but that she definitely had a good chance to get through this. I felt especially that she had a good chance to get out within three days – the Moon coming to trine Venus and square Pluto in the same degree, then sextile Saturn – remember that her children are ruled by Saturn. Notice that her survival is shown by house placement – the lack of dignity of the rulers shows her kidnapped state.

What of the kidnapper(s)? There is no angular peregrine planet, unless we consider Jupiter, which might be construed as peregrine, although it has out-of-sect dignity. I decided to use Mars, the ruler of the turned 7th (the radix 1st), as the "thief" (abductor in this case), and observe Mars just past the conjunction to Uranus – a sudden event. I felt that it would be especially good if she were out before Venus squared Mars. The square of Venus to Mars clinches the conclusion that she was not in collusion with her kidnappers. There is a weak reception between the two Significators, but this could simply mean that she was trying to appeal to her captor personally, or trying to reach out to him to treat her as a human being – but probably not entirely successfully. I would look to an easy aspect and mutual reception if the kidnapping was actually a setup. In this case, Mars being the principal dispositor of Venus is yet one more argument that she is truly under their control.

The Querent e-mailed to tell me that her client came back safely with her kids.

Example 62. Is she pregnant? Will she be pregnant?

This may seem like an odd question to list in this section on death, but this is the follow-up chart to Example 28 concerning his wife's pregnancy. In this case, he had asked an earlier question about whether they would have an additional child. I had given him a "window of opportunity," after which, I said, there was no chance of having more children. This question was asked at the end of that window. And what I didn't know at the time is that the Querent would be dead less than one week later!

Of all the things we don't expect in this chart in hindsight, observe the zero degrees rising! This is a *very* mixed reading, and with zero rising, I couldn't express any certainty to him.

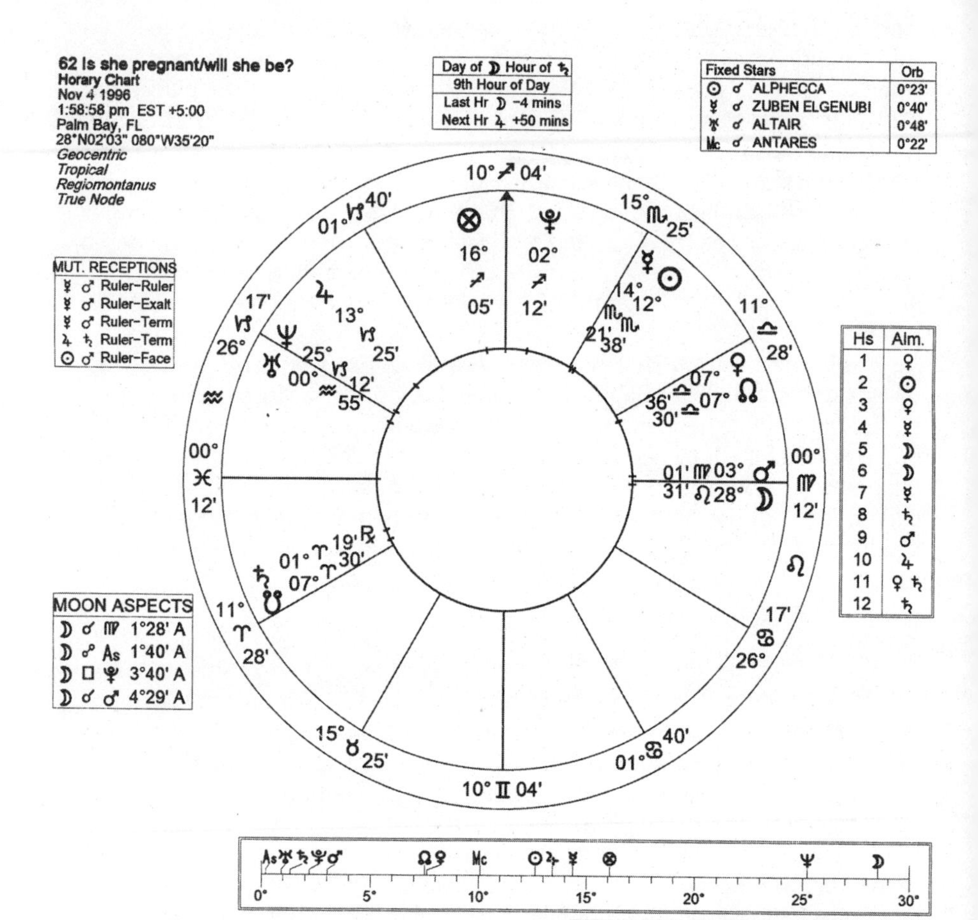

ESSENTIAL DIGNITIES (LEHMAN)								
Pt	Ruler	Exalt	Trip	Term	Face	Detri	Fall	Score
☽	☉	--	☉	♂	♂	♄	--	-5 p
☉	♂	--	♀	♃	☉ +	♀	☽	+1
☿	♂ m	--	♀	♀	☉	♀	☽	-5 p
♀	♀ +	♄	♄	♀ +	☽	♂	☉	+7
♂	☿ m	☿	♀	☿	☉	♃	♀	-5 p
♃	♄	♂	♀	♃ +	♂	☽	♃ -	-2
♄	♂	☉	☉	♃	♂	♀	♄ -	-9 p
As	♃	♀	♀	♀	♄	☿	☿	--
Mc	♃	☋	☉	♀	☽	☿	☊	--
⊗	♃	☋	☉	☿	☽	☿	☊	--

planets.pts				
Pt	Long.	Travel	Antiscia	C.Ant.
☽	28°♌31'42"	+11°53'	01°♉28	01°♏28
☉	12°♏38'23"	+01°00'	17°♒21	17°♌21
☿	14°♏21	+01°36'	15°♒38	15°♌38
♀	07°♎36	+01°12'	22°♓23	22°♍23
♂	03°♍01	+00°32'	26°♈58	26°♎58
♃	13°♑25	+00°09'	16°♐34	16°♊34
♄	01°♈19 ℞	-00°02'	28°♍40	28°♓40
♅	00°♒55	+00°01'	29°♏04	29°♉04
♆	25°♑12	+00°00'	04°♐47	04°♊47
♇	02°♐12	+00°02'	27°♑47	27°♋47
☊	07°♎30	+00°01'	22°♓29	22°♍29
☋	07°♈30	+00°01'	22°♍29	22°♓29
As	00°♓12'16"	+00°00'	29°♎47	29°♈47
Mc	10°♐04'53"	+00°00'	19°♑55	19°♋55
⊗	16°♐05	+00°00'	13°♑54	13°♋54

Arguments for pregnancy:

- Ascendant in a fertile sign.
- 5th House cusp in a fertile sign.
- Ruler of the 7th (the wife) in a fertile sign but combust, so that would argue that if she were, she doesn't know yet.
- Ruler of the 5th at the 7th House cusp. Not listed as a criterion, but symbolically, the possible child is literally "with" the mother.

Arguments against pregnancy:

- Moon in a barren sign.
- 7th House cusp in a barren sign.

This is leaning toward pregnancy, although the arguments against are troubling. However, I felt that since Mercury, the 7th House ruler, had just departed from a sextile to Fallen Jupiter, the 1st House ruler, she probably had just recently gotten pregnant. And the Moon is Void of Course, so whatever is going to happen concerning this Question probably already has. I told him that, provisionally, it looked like she already was, but circumstances were about to change. Did they ever! In retrospect, perhaps the most telling thing about the chart is that the *only* planet with any major dignity is Venus, Ruler of the 8th House and Almuten of the 1st. And further, Venus is within the five degrees of the 8th House cusp, making Venus placement 8th House as well! So Death is the only thing dignified.

Did that occur to me at the time? No! I was simply struck by how mixed the indicators were. Notice also that the arguments against pregnancy are actually descriptive: she's pregnant now, but barren henceforth! Now I can wonder if the mixed indicators were there because, although they achieved their intention, the circumstances were tragic.

Debt, Taxes and Insurance

Financial instruments have changed since William Lilly's day, and sometimes it seems that the major effect has been to produce more methods to get into debt. As has been noted elsewhere, ancient Greek astrology used all the succedent houses for financial matters. Al-Biruni came right out and listed "expenditures" as well as "buried treasure" as matters of the 8th House.[167] However, for the most part, this usage was ignored. I can only surmise that as we have multiplied the methods of obtaining credit, we have multiplied the problems associated with paying for credit.

Mostly, debt arrived at the 8th House through secondary means. Thus, Dorotheus treats debt as a matter of the 7th House, because he considers borrowing to be effectively a partnership agreement.[168] He then treats the payment or nonpayment of debt as a variant of an "is the rumor true" scenario, with added emphasis on the condition of the partner. It's worth mentioning that there was a historical religious ban on charging interest (even though Lilly gives usurers to Mercury) which worked to retard the growth of capital in the late Middle Ages and into the Renaissance. Jews were permitted to charge interest, but Christians were not supposed to charge interest to each other. Until this technicality was solved, the modern banking system could not evolve, and of course, this meant that the ease of getting a loan was so much less that questions of this nature simply could not arise with the frequency with which they do now.

Thus, we work by analogy. If, as most sources agree, the 8th House is the spouse's portion – also known as a dowry – then the 8th is also the (business) partner's money. And then there is one special case: in matters related to taxes, the government that collects them may be seen as a 7th House entity – the open enemy of the Querent, in which case, the taxes owed are 8th House – the open enemy's money.

Insurance is a somewhat new concept in all of its ramifications, but the oldest form of insurance is no doubt either property or life. In the case of property insurance, you are essentially betting with the insurance company that you will be able to maintain your goods. If you "win," then you have given them the premium – it's then their money. If you lose, they pay you more than you paid them – they experience a decline in their money. Life insurance relates to the 8th for the obvious reason that it's about wagers concerning death, clearly an 8th House matter.

Now that we've justified our house attributions, let's examine some examples that show how we might utilize this house.

Example 63. Can we handle the loan?

The question was asked concerning a real estate loan. The Querent and her husband had put down an offer on the house. They had been financially pre-approved the previous month, but she did not like the terms and conditions of the loan offered, so she decided to shop for a different loan. This question concerned the second choice: a loan package offered by "the friend of a friend." In this case, however, the loan was for more money than the original plan, so she was concerned about whether they could afford it.

With 0 degrees rising, I told her that there was *definitely* something which hadn't come to light about the loan yet. Given that the Moon in Taurus was ruling both the 1st and 2nd Houses, I told her that it didn't appear that the problem was whether they could afford it. I observed that with Neptune conjunct the 8th House cusp, there was something fishy about the loan offer itself. With the Moon about to square Uranus, also in the 8th House, I suggested that something might suddenly be revealed about it, but that, in general, I would be leery about the whole deal.

After we had finished the delineation, the Querent, a student of horary, told me that she had asked a horary question several weeks before about whether the "friend-of-a-friend" was the appropriate person as a mortgage broker. The chart (in retrospect, of course) had clearly indicated that he wasn't the appropriate broker.

One more thing. We can apply Dorotheus' idea about examining the chart from the standpoint of whether the other party to the loan has good intentions.[169] Dorotheus advocates examining the Moon and Mercury. The Moon in this chart specifically defaults to the Querent, as the chart has Cancer Rising.

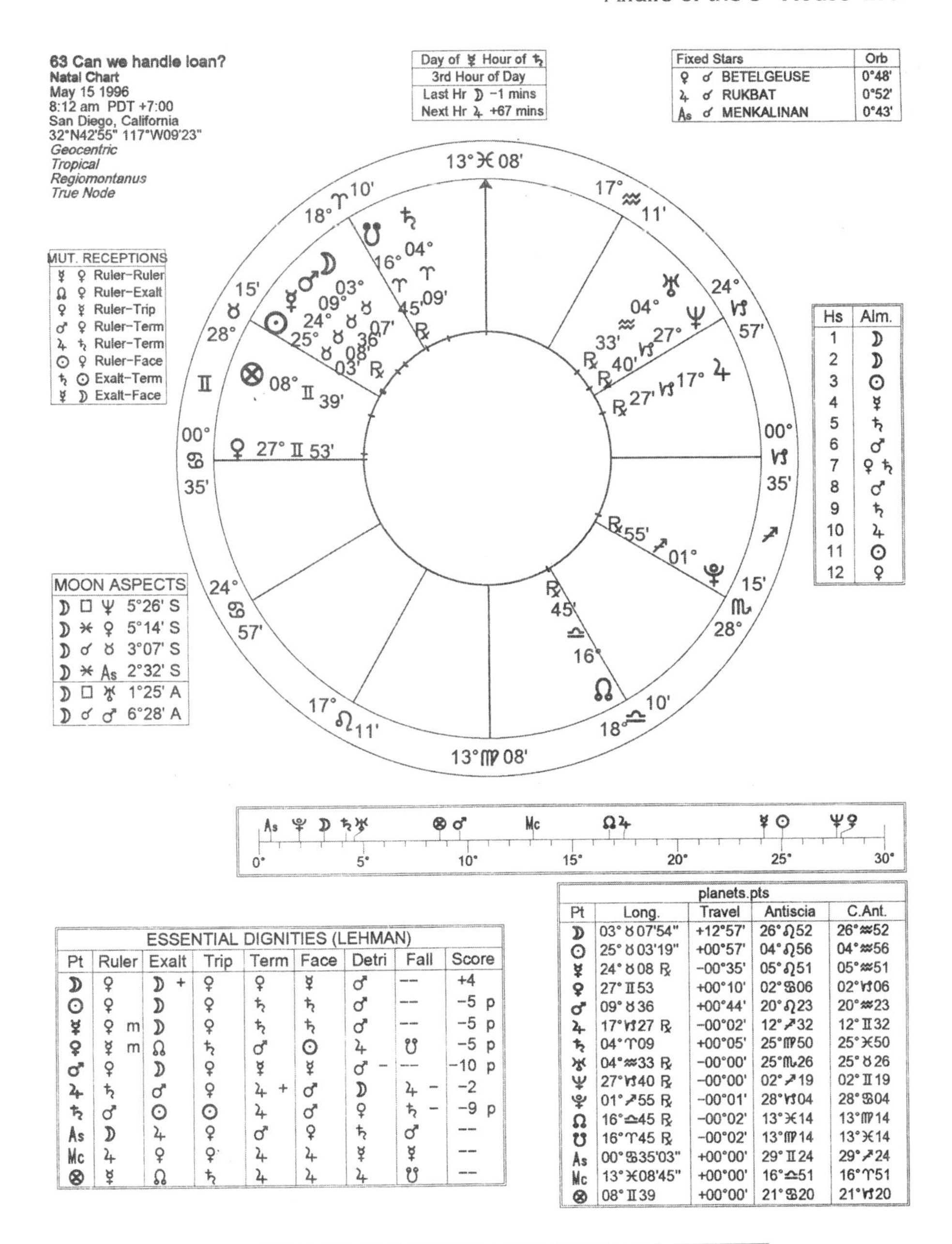

Fixed Stars	Orb
♀ ☌ BETELGEUSE	0°48'
♃ ☌ RUKBAT	0°52'
As ☌ MENKALINAN	0°43'

MUT. RECEPTIONS
☿ ♀ Ruler-Ruler
☊ ♀ Ruler-Exalt
♀ ☿ Ruler-Trip
♂ ♀ Ruler-Term
♃ ♄ Ruler-Term
☉ ♀ Ruler-Face
♄ ☉ Exalt-Term
☿ ☽ Exalt-Face

Hs	Alm.
1	☽
2	☽
3	☉
4	☿
5	♄
6	♂
7	♀ ♄
8	♂
9	♄
10	♃
11	☉
12	♀

MOON ASPECTS		
☽ □ ♆	5°26'	S
☽ ⚹ ♀	5°14'	S
☽ ☌ ♉	3°07'	S
☽ ⚹ As	2°32'	S
☽ □ ♅	1°25'	A
☽ ☌ ♂	6°28'	A

ESSENTIAL DIGNITIES (LEHMAN)								
Pt	Ruler	Exalt	Trip	Term	Face	Detri	Fall	Score
☽	♀	☽ +	♀	♀	☿	♂	--	+4
☉	♀	☽	♀	♄	♄	♂	--	-5 p
☿	♀ m	☽	♀	♄	♄	♂	--	-5 p
♀	☿ m	☊	♄	♂	☉	♃	☋	-5 p
♂	♀	☽	♀	☿	☿	♂ -	--	-10 p
♃	♄	♂	♀	♃ +	♂	☽	♃ -	-2
♄	♂	☉	☉	♃	♂	♀	♄ -	-9 p
As	☽	♃	♀	♂	♀	♄	♂	--
Mc	♃	♀	♀	♃	♃	☿	☿	--
⊗	☿	☊	♄	♃	♃	♃	☋	--

planets.pts				
Pt	Long.	Travel	Antiscia	C.Ant.
☽	03°♉07'54"	+12°57'	26°♌52	26°♒52
☉	25°♉03'19"	+00°57'	04°♌56	04°♒56
☿	24°♉08 ℞	-00°35'	05°♌51	05°♒51
♀	27°♊53	+00°10'	02°♋06	02°♑06
♂	09°♉36	+00°44'	20°♌23	20°♒23
♃	17°♑27 ℞	-00°02'	12°♐32	12°♊32
♄	04°♈09	+00°05'	25°♍50	25°♓50
♅	04°♒33 ℞	-00°00'	25°♏26	25°♉26
♆	27°♑40 ℞	-00°00'	02°♐19	02°♊19
♇	01°♐55 ℞	-00°01'	28°♑04	28°♋04
☊	16°♎45 ℞	-00°02'	13°♓14	13°♍14
☋	16°♈45 ℞	-00°02'	13°♍14	13°♓14
As	00°♋35'03"	+00°00'	29°♊24	29°♐24
Mc	13°♓08'45"	+00°00'	16°♎51	16°♈51
⊗	08°♊39	+00°00'	21°♋20	21°♑20

With the Moon in Taurus, the buyer has good intentions. However, Mercury is peregrine, combust, retrograde and not far from Algol, so this confirms the suspicions raised about this loan by Neptune's proximity to the 8th House cusp.

Here, the zero rising actually showed that they didn't have all the information they needed to make their decision. They had not exhausted all possible loan sources. As it turned out, they decided to accept a different loan offer.

One absolutely safe reading when the chart has zero degrees rising is that you don't know or have all your options yet. "Too much free will in the system" is the default meaning I give to zero rising.

The "friend of a friend" turned out to be a really disreputable character. The Querent is glad that they never took this loan.

Example 64. Should I buy health insurance?

I think this is actually one of the really useful applications of horary; a type of question I have used myself on occasion, although this particular example is for a client. All insurance is really a gamble: the person buying it is willing to pay a certain amount to prevent having to pay a larger amount if unfortunate circumstances ensue. Thus, the purchase of insurance is really a form of risk assessment: how much are you willing to pay to avoid the risk of catastrophic conditions?

As the price of health insurance has increased, to anyone who actually has to write the check for the coverage, this is a question worth pondering. The scenario is simple: if you don't get sick, the premiums are a total waste. But if you need it, the coverage can be vital.

So this was the question asked by the Querent. Because of the ramifications, there are several ways to approach the chart:

- Will the Querent get sick? If not, then the answer to the question is "no."
- Will the coverage be worthwhile?
- Does the other party have good intentions?

Here, the Querent is given by Mercury in Capricorn, peregrine and retrograde. The Querent is not in good shape, but that is not the same as saying the Querent is sick. As a matter of fact, she has some chronic health problems, but they are not ones that would require the health insurance unless there were flare-ups. Mars rules the 6th, and hence Mars ruling the illness is quite strong in Capricorn, but there is no aspect between Mercury and Mars: the Querent is not "approaching" sickness. The Moon will ultimately square Mars and translate the light of Mercury, but not before it conjoins Saturn. So the answer is: no, in the immediate future the Querent is not going to get sick enough to need coverage. But this is the kind of question that begs for the definition of a time frame, or time limit.

The quality of the coverage itself is Saturn, ruler of the 8th House, in Fall and retrograde. The coverage isn't very good anyway, and with the translation of the Moon by square, any treatment that the Querent might receive under this policy would have to be fought for all the way.

Does the other party have good intentions? We have to use Mercury for the Querent, but that leaves the seller as Jupiter, Ruler of the 7th. The insurance itself is 8th House, but any buy and sell transaction still involves the 1st-7th axis. Jupiter is peregrine. The insurance company does not have especially

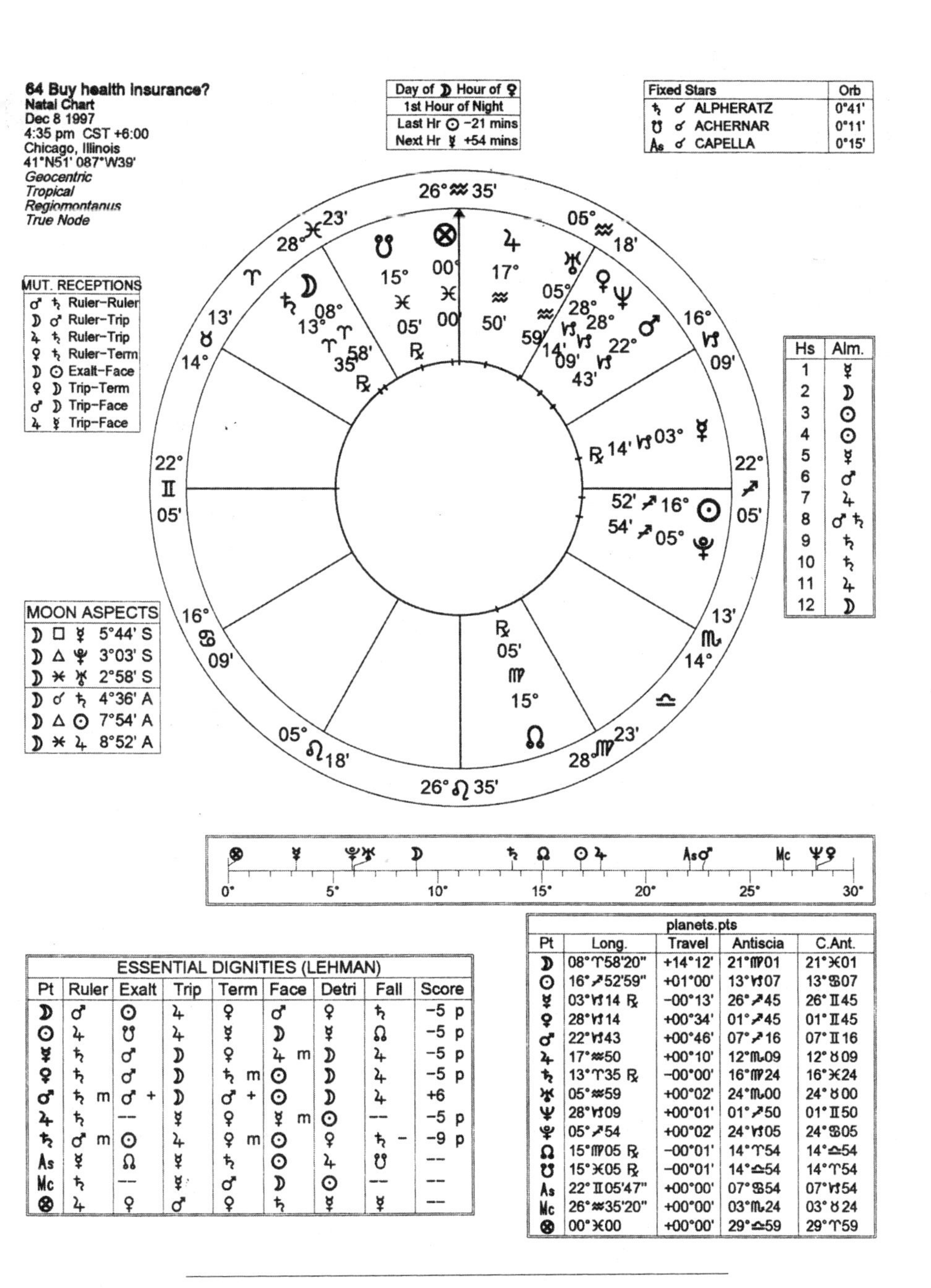

Fixed Stars	Orb
♄ ☌ ALPHERATZ	0°41'
☋ ☌ ACHERNAR	0°11'
As ☌ CAPELLA	0°15'

MUT. RECEPTIONS
♂ ♄ Ruler–Ruler
☽ ♂ Ruler–Trip
♃ ♄ Ruler–Trip
♀ ♄ Ruler–Term
☽ ☉ Exalt–Face
♀ ☽ Trip–Term
♂ ☽ Trip–Face
♃ ☿ Trip–Face

Hs	Alm.
1	☿
2	☽
3	☉
4	☉
5	☿
6	♂
7	♃
8	♂ ♄
9	♄
10	♄
11	♃
12	☽

MOON ASPECTS
☽ □ ☿ 5°44' S
☽ △ ♇ 3°03' S
☽ ⚹ ♅ 2°58' S
☽ ☌ ♄ 4°36' A
☽ △ ☉ 7°54' A
☽ ⚹ ♃ 8°52' A

ESSENTIAL DIGNITIES (LEHMAN)								
Pt	Ruler	Exalt	Trip	Term	Face	Detri	Fall	Score
☽	♂	☉	♃	♀	♂	♀	♄	−5 p
☉	♃	☋	♃	☿	☽	☿	☊	−5 p
☿	♄	♂	☽	♀	♃ m	☽	♃	−5 p
♀	♄	♂	☽	♄ m	☉	☽	♃	−5 p
♂	♄ m	♂ +	☽	♂ +	☉	☽	♃	+6
♃	♄	--	☿	♀	☿ m	☉	--	−5 p
♄	♂ m	☉	♃	♀ m	☉	♀	♄ −	−9 p
As	☿	☊	☿	♄	☉	♃	☋	--
Mc	♄	--	☿	♂	☽	☉	--	--
⊗	♃	♀	♂	♀	♄	☿	☿	--

planets.pts				
Pt	Long.	Travel	Antiscia	C.Ant.
☽	08°♈58'20"	+14°12'	21°♍01	21°♓01
☉	16°♐52'59"	+01°00'	13°♑07	13°♋07
☿	03°♑14 ℞	−00°13'	26°♐45	26°♊45
♀	28°♑14	+00°34'	01°♐45	01°♊45
♂	22°♑43	+00°46'	07°♐16	07°♊16
♃	17°♒50	+00°10'	12°♏09	12°♉09
♄	13°♈35 ℞	−00°00'	16°♍24	16°♓24
♅	05°♒59	+00°02'	24°♏00	24°♉00
♆	28°♑09	+00°01'	01°♐50	01°♊50
♇	05°♐54	+00°02'	24°♑05	24°♋05
☊	15°♍05 ℞	−00°01'	14°♈54	14°♎54
☋	15°♓05 ℞	−00°01'	14°♎54	14°♈54
As	22°♊05'47"	+00°00'	07°♋54	07°♑54
Mc	26°♒35'20"	+00°00'	03°♏24	03°♉24
⊗	00°♓00	+00°00'	29°♎59	29°♈59

good intentions, or perhaps I should say that, whatever their true intentions may be, they are ineffectual. The Moon translates the light between the two, but the Moon is also peregrine. This does not show a company ready to extend itself for their policy holders.

She didn't buy health insurance for that year, and she didn't get sick.

Example 65. Will they refinance the loan?

An astrologer, who was looking to change his mortgage from a balloon payment to more conventional financing, asked this question. This is the chart for when he asked the question, in his location. I also studied a chart for when he asked me for a second opinion, but I believe this is the primary chart.

I had the choice of rulers for the Querent: Venus as the sign ruler of Libra, or Saturn as the Almuten. Both are dignified, so the only way to choose is to evaluate which shows the circumstances better. I would prefer to choose Venus, because the late degree described a Querent who was running out of time before the balloon payment was due, and a little desperate to get the new financing in place. However, Venus also rules the 8th, and so it would work better to use Saturn for him, and Venus for the loan itself.

The fact that Venus ruled both 1st and 8th actually shows the circumstance: he already has a loan with the same company that he's approaching for refinancing.

If we follow Dorotheus' logic, Mars (or Sun) as the ruler/Almuten of the 7th House shows the lending institution; here, we pick Mars, as the stronger of the two. Mars has Triplicity rulership in Pisces by day and night if we use Lilly, by night alone if we use Dorotheus. Thus, the lender is a good company, and in fact, the company he named was familiar to me by name, if not reputation. Unfortunately, while Mars did eventually make the sextile with Saturn (the Querent), the aspect is out of orb, and Saturn went retrograde before the perfection occurred, showing a change in conditions. In fact, Saturn was stationing retrograde at the time of this Question!

What about the Moon and Mercury, Dorotheus' harbingers of good intentions? In this case, we can use both of them, as neither is a specific ruler of one of the parties. Mercury has dignity only by Term, and is retrograde. The Moon has out-of-sect Triplicity. Neither is very strong, and the retrograde status of Mercury will more than compensate for the minor dignity of Term. As a result, while the parties have the best of intentions, this doesn't look as if an agreement will be worked out.

Furthermore, the Moon comes to oppose Mars by one degree. It translates the Light to Saturn but this takes place out of orb. Any perfection by opposition is not usually a good outcome, and here the out of orb translation makes it even more dubious.

The refinancing did not come through.

Inheritance of Money

Inheritance is not covered as explicitly by the ancient sources as one might be led to believe. The 8th House is given as referring to the estates of dead persons, and to legacies, but there is a dearth of examples that show us how to proceed with these questions.

Having said this, it occurs to me that there are two basic approaches. They depend on whether the question involves future legacies from a specific person who hasn't died, or whether they involve the eventual result of probate, or other such means of inheritance.

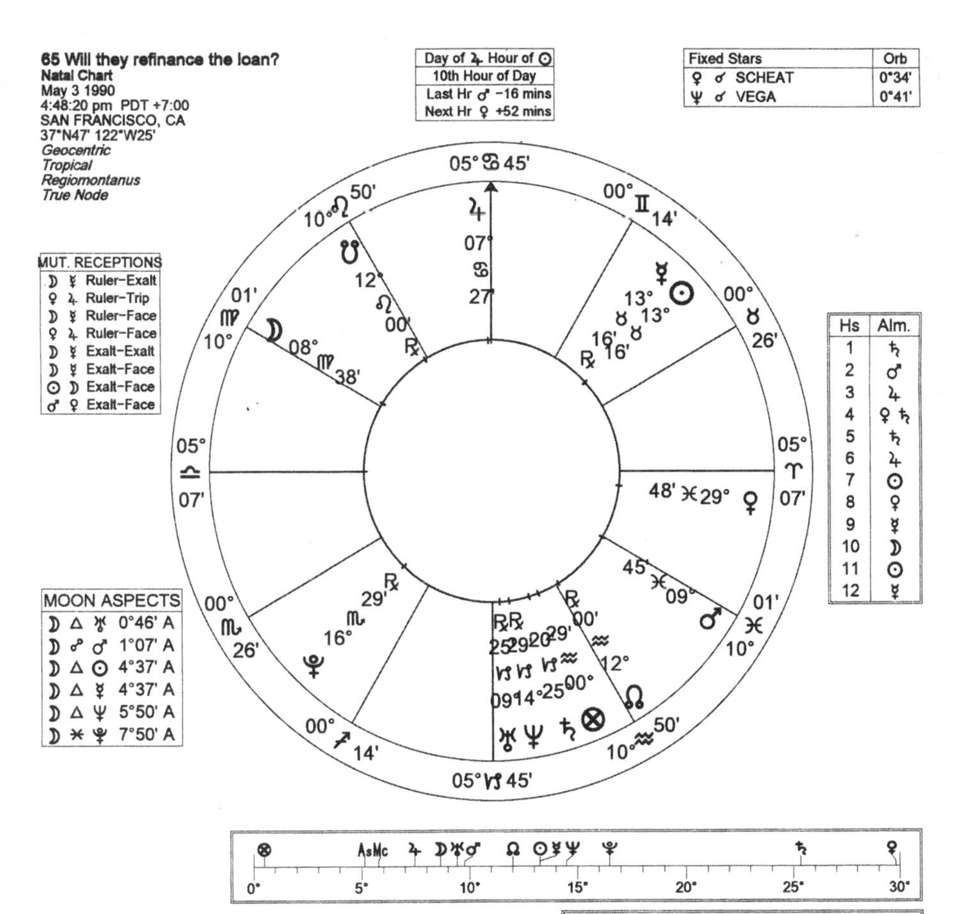

ESSENTIAL DIGNITIES (LEHMAN)								
Pt	Ruler	Exalt	Trip	Term	Face	Detri	Fall	Score
☽	☿	☿ m	♀	♀	☉ m	♃	♀	−5 p
☉	♀	☽	♀	☿	☽ m	♂	--	−5 p
☿	♀	☽ m	♀	☿ +	☽	♂	--	+2
♀	♃	♀ +	♀ +	♄	♂	☿	☿	+7
♂	♃	♀	♀	♃	♄	☿	☿	−5 p
♃	☽	♃ +	♀	♃ +	♀	♄	♂	+6
♄	♄ +	♂	♀	♄ +	☉	☽	♃	+7
As	♀	♄	♄	♄	☽	♂	☉	--
Mc	☽	♃	♀	♂	♀	♄	♂	--
⊗	♄	--	♄	♄	♀	☉	--	--

planets.pts				
Pt	Long.	Travel	Antiscia	C.Ant.
☽	08°♍38'39"	+12°28'	21°♈21	21°♎21
☉	13°♉16'22"	+00°58'	16°♌43	16°♒43
☿	13°♉16 ℞	−00°38'	16°♌43	16°♒43
♀	29°♓48	+01°07'	00°♎11	00°♈11
♂	09°♓45	+00°44'	20°♎14	20°♈14
♃	07°♋27	+00°10'	22°♊32	22°♐32
♄	25°♑20	+00°00'	04°♐39	04°♊39
♅	09°♑25 ℞	−00°00'	20°♐34	20°♊34
♆	14°♑29 ℞	−00°00'	15°♐30	15°♊30
♇	16°♏29 ℞	−00°01'	13°♒30	13°♌30
☊	12°♒00 ℞	−00°02'	17°♏59	17°♉59
☋	12°♌00 ℞	−00°02'	17°♉59	17°♏59
As	05°♎07'09"	+00°00'	24°♓52	24°♍52
Mc	05°♋45'44"	+00°00'	24°♊14	24°♐14
⊗	00°♒29	+00°00'	29°♏30	29°♉30

If the question is concerning inheritance from a still living relative, the obvious point is that said relative has to die in order for the Querent to inherit. In this case, the question is twofold:

- When is the person in question going to die? This is interpreted using the 1st and the 8th House pertaining to the person, such as the 10th House for the mother, and the 8th from the 10th (the 5th) for the death of the mother.

- How good is the inheritance for the Querent? In this case, the Querent's inheritance is the radical 8th house, and one would look for some relationship between the presumptive dead relative (or the 2nd House from that person's 1st House) and the radical 8th.

Only the latter condition is relevant if the person in question has already died. In the case of a question such as, "Will I ever inherit a substantial sum of money?" one would look for perfection between 8th and 2nd, showing the transfer of wealth from one house to the other.

Example 66. Will I have my share?

The Querent was effectively asking whether her mother-in-law would die soon, specifically within three months, which would automatically free up a certain proportion of a family trust for the Querent's use, and preclude the necessity for her to go back to work.

The Querent is Venus in Pisces, a strong position. Her mother-in-law is her husband's mother, the 10th from the 7th, or the 4th. The mother-in-law's death is the 8th from the 4th, or the 11th. Death is the Sun in Detriment, while the Quesited is Saturn – how appropriate for an elderly lady.

The Sun, Ruler of the turned 8th, does come to sextile Saturn, Ruler of the turned Ascendant. However, the unit is a factor of seven, and with the Sun in a fixed sign, this could be seven months at the earliest. The cadent Moon trines the Sun by one degree translates the light to Saturn, but this most likely gives a year since the combination involves cadent/mutable with fixed/succedent. Because the time frame suggested by these two methods falls outside the time range specified by the Querent, I had less certainty about the accuracy of the timing apart from the obvious negative answer concerning the next three months. The mother-in-law didn't die in that time.

Danger

The odd thing about these questions concerning danger is that, while Lilly assigned them to the 8th House, the actual delineation protocol has very little to do with the 8th. Among the rules that Lilly specifies for determining if a danger is real, are the following[170]:

- If the Moon or the Lord of the Ascendant is unfortunate, the danger is real.

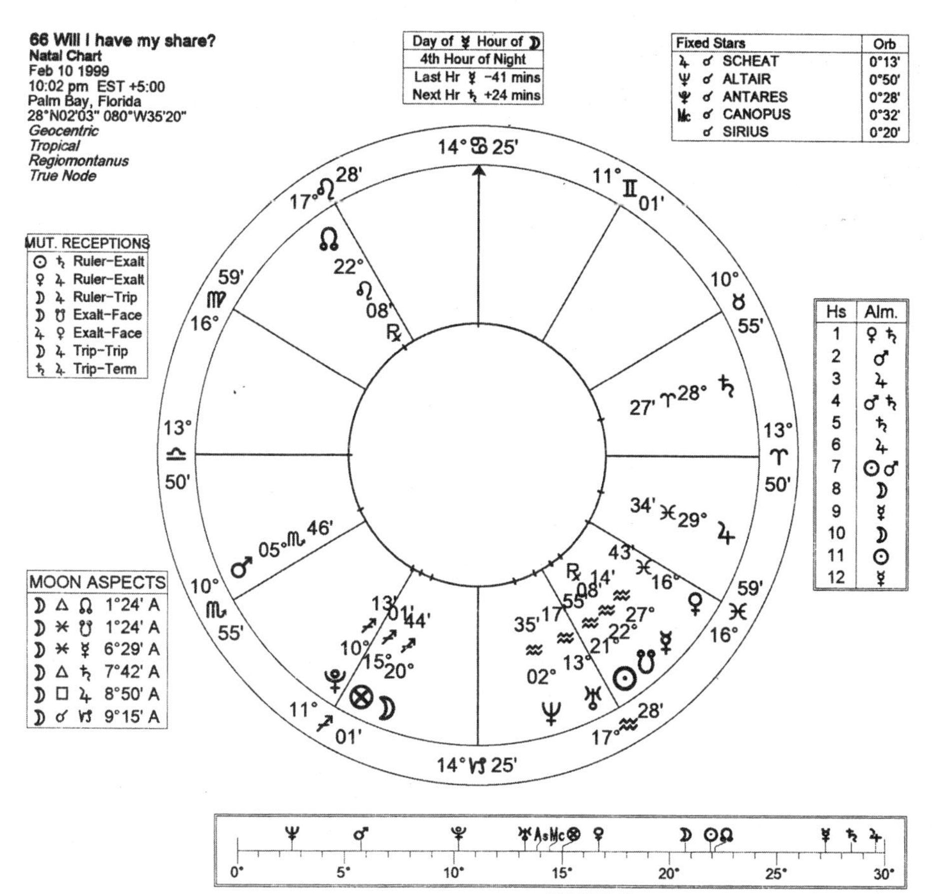

ESSENTIAL DIGNITIES (LEHMAN)								
Pt	Ruler	Exalt	Trip	Term	Face	Detri	Fall	Score
☽	♃	☋	♃	♄	♄	☿	☊	−5 p
☉	♄	--	☿	♃	☽	☉ −	--	−10 p
☿	♄	--	☿ +	♂	☽	☉	--	+3
♀	♃	♀ +	♂	☿	♃	☿	☿	+4
♂	♂ +	--	♂ +	♂ +	♂ +	♀	☽	+11
♃	♃ +	♀	♂	♄	♂	☿	☿	+5
♄	♂	☉	♃	♄ +	♀	♀	♄ −	−2
As	♀	♄	☿	♃	♄	♂	☉	--
Mc	☽	♃	♂	☿	☿	♄	♂	--
⊗	♃	☋	♃	☿	☽	☿	☊	--

planets.pts				
Pt	Long.	Travel	Antiscia	C.Ant.
☽	20°♐44'34"	+12°10'	09°♑15	09°♋15
☉	21°♒55'32"	+01°00'	08°♏04	08°♉04
☿	27°♒14	+01°48'	02°♏45	02°♉45
♀	16°♓43	+01°14'	13°♎16	13°♈16
♂	05°♏46	+00°19'	24°♒13	24°♌13
♃	29°♓34	+00°12'	00°♎25	00°♈25
♄	28°♈27	+00°04'	01°♍32	01°♓32
♅	13°♒17	+00°03'	16°♏42	16°♉42
♆	02°♒35	+00°02'	27°♏24	27°♉24
♇	10°♐13	+00°01'	19°♑46	19°♋46
☊	22°♌08 ℞	−00°00'	07°♉51	07°♏51
☋	22°♒08 ℞	−00°00'	07°♏51	07°♉51
As	13°♎50'21"	+00°00'	16°♓09	16°♍09
Mc	14°♋25'04"	+00°00'	15°♊34	15°♐34
⊗	15°♐01	+00°00'	14°♑58	14°♋58

- If the Moon or the Ruler of the Ascendant is in the 12th House (unless leaving the 12th House to arrive at the 11th), the danger is real.

- If the Ascendant Ruler applies to Fortunes, then the danger is only apparent, unless received by an Infortune, in which case the danger is real.

- If the Ascendant Ruler applies to an Infortune, the danger is real.

Example 67. Is he dangerous?

This question was asked concerning her former boyfriend. She was concerned about whether he would do something violent. While I would normally have used the 5th House for the boyfriend, because of the concern about danger, I placed him as the 7th House. Let's follow our rules above.

- If the Moon or the Lord of the Ascendant is unfortunate, the danger is real. **Both the Moon and the Ruler of the 1st are unfortunate: the Moon is in Fall in Scorpio; Jupiter is both in Fall, and retrograde. The Moon also applies to a square to Uranus, which would make me very nervous about a sudden, unprovoked attack.**

- If the Moon or the Ruler of the Ascendant is in the 12th House (unless leaving the 12th House to arrive at the 11th), the danger is real. **Not true in this case.**

- If the Ascendant Ruler applies to Fortunes, then the danger is only apparent, unless received by an Infortune, in which case the danger is real. **Nothing applies in orb to Jupiter, the Ascendant Ruler, although the debilitated Moon applies ultimately by sextile. Jupiter is at the Bendings, a critical placement.**

- If the Ascendant Ruler applies to an Infortune, the danger is real. **Not true in this case.**

With two of the four conditions true, I told her to change the locks on her apartment, and to vary her usual routes of travel, as the biggest danger appears to be from a chance, not a planned encounter. She did, and she was fine.

And with this last type of question, we can now escape to the 9th House.

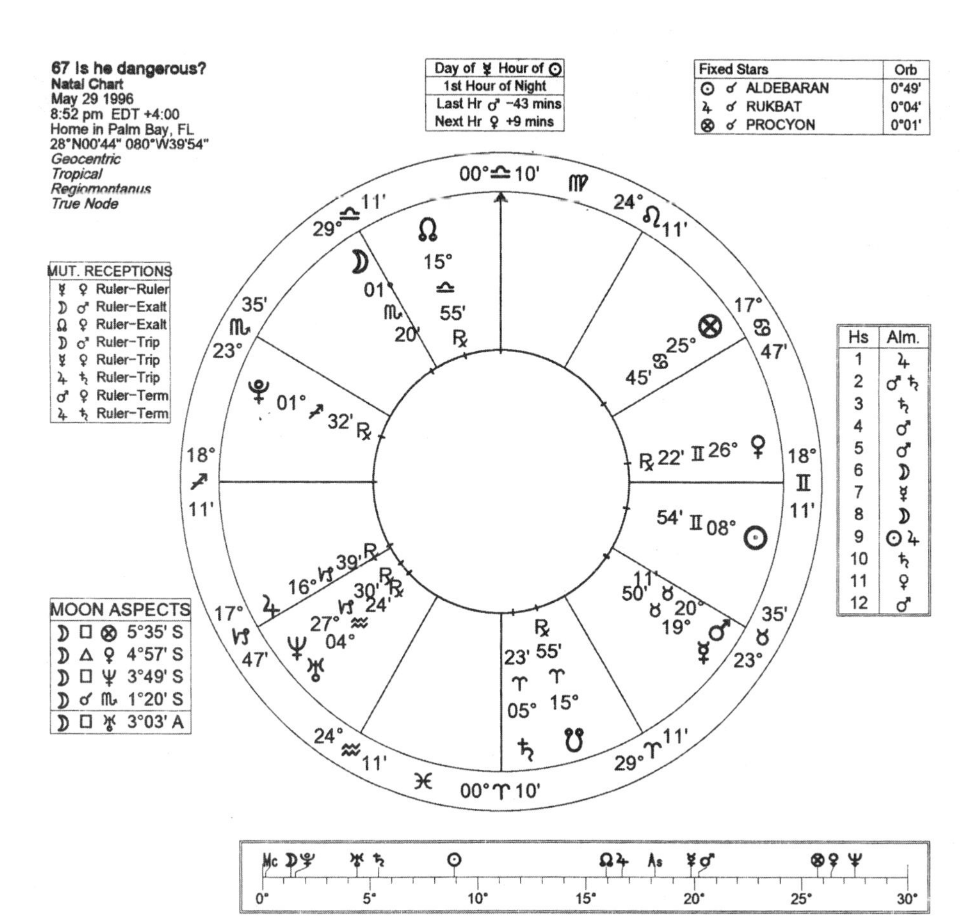

ESSENTIAL DIGNITIES (LEHMAN)								
Pt	Ruler	Exalt	Trip	Term	Face	Detri	Fall	Score
☽	♂	--	♂ m	♂	♂	♀	☽ −	−9 p
☉	☿	☊	☿	♃	♃	♃	☋	−5 p
☿	♀ m	☽	☽	♃	☽	♂	--	−5 p
♀	☿ m	☊	☿	♂	☉	♃	☋	−5 p
♂	♀	☽	☽ m	♃	♄ m	♂ −	--	−10 p
♃	♄	♂	☽	♃ +	♂	☽	♃ −	−2
♄	♂	☉	♃	♃	♂ m	♀	♄ −	−9 p
As	♃	☋	♃	☿	☽	☿	☊	--
Mc	♀	♄	☿	♄	☽	♂	☉	--
⊗	☽	♃	♂	♀	☽	♄	♂	--

planets.pts				
Pt	Long.	Travel	Antiscia	C.Ant.
☽	01°♏20'20"	+13°38'	28°♒39	28°♌39
☉	08°♊54'09"	+00°57'	21°♋05	21°♑05
☿	19°♉50	+00°10'	10°♌09	10°♒09
♀	26°♊22 ℞	−00°23'	03°♋37	03°♑37
♂	20°♉11	+00°43'	09°♌48	09°♒48
♃	16°♑39 ℞	−00°04'	13°♐20	13°♊20
♄	05°♈23	+00°04'	24°♍36	24°♓36
♅	04°♒24 ℞	−00°01'	25°♏35	25°♉35
♆	27°♑30 ℞	−00°00'	02°♐29	02°♊29
♇	01°♐32 ℞	−00°01'	28°♑27	28°♋27
☊	15°♎55 ℞	−00°02'	14°♓04	14°♍04
☋	15°♈55 ℞	−00°02'	14°♍04	14°♓04
As	18°♐11'14"	+00°00'	11°♑48	11°♋48
Mc	00°♎10'05"	+00°00'	29°♓49	29°♍49
⊗	25°♋45	+00°00'	04°♊14	04°♐14

Chapter 9

Affairs of the 9th House:
Travel, Religion & Education

Questions of the 9th House as given by Lilly:[171]

- *Of a voyage by sea, and success thereof*
- *Of journeying, and success thereof*
- *Of learning or wisdom, whether it be true or not*
- *Whether a minister/priest shall obtain a parsonage*
- *Of dreams, whether they signify something important or not*

Gadbury's list of categories of questions differs only slightly from Lilly's.

I would add some additional categories:

- Whether a particular course of education is beneficial
- All questions concerning institutionalized religion
- Questions concerning publishing
- Questions concerning lawyers – apart from their status as trial attorneys

Journeys

We deferred the discussion of journeys from the 3rd House to the 9th House. So now we can consider both 3rd and 9th House trips, because the method of delineation is identical, once the Significator can be found. Let's split out the difference between the 3rd and 9th. While I touched upon this previously, let us look now at the differences in a table format.

Table 1. Differences between 3rd and 9th House trips

3rd House	9th House
Has visited city before; may have lived there.	May not have visited before; if lived there, it was a long time ago and the city has changed a lot.
Can navigate, probably without a map	Need a map to navigate
Has favorite restaurants, shops and entertainment places Can speak the language	Uses city guide for restaurants, shops and entertainment places May not know the language
Knows city customs, like how late you can call someone on the phone; what places are open all night	Does not know city customs
Traveling there is routine	Traveling there is long, difficult, or via an uncomfortable means of transportation
Familiar with neighborhoods Has friends	Doesn't know neighborhoods May not have friends
Can give directions to strangers	Cannot give directions to strangers in city center

The differences between 3rd and 9th are mental, not physical. All cities are 3rd House to some people and 9th House to others, just as all cities are home to residents and places to visit for everyone else.

Having said this, it is the very routine and familiar nature of 3rd House places that results in fewer horary questions about them. Stop and think about this. Why would you ask a question about going to a familiar place? The only likely reason would be because you need to see someone where the meeting is likely to be awkward; but in this case, the question would be about that meeting, not about the trip itself. The only way that the question might be restricted to the trip is if there were some safety issues involved. Granted, all the statistics show that most automobile accidents occur relatively close to home, so safety is of course as legitimate for one trip as the next, but casualness about the location usually mitigates against worry over getting there.

So once we've decided on the House (3rd or 9th), what do we do? The simple answer is that having the benefics associated with the 9th (or 3rd) is good for a trip; malefics in the House are bad. Malefics associated with the 9th House show that the logistics of the trip are difficult.

- For business trips, examine the 10th and 8th Houses. The 8th represents the possibility for gain (i.e., the other party's money), while the 10th shows the actual gain from that trip. Malefics associated with these houses show the trip is not profitable.[172]

- Fortunate planets associated with the Angles show which phase of a trip produces the most satisfaction: a benefic in the 1st shows success before the trip ever begins; in the 10th, on the first part of the trip, or on the way there; in the 7th, once the Querent arrives; in the 4th, either on the trip home, or upon arriving home.[173]

- Angular Significators give a fast trip, as does the trip Significator (Ruler of the 9th or 3rd) swift of motion, as does an application or translation between the Ruler of the 1st and the trip Significator. Speed also happens when the Ruler of the 1st is in the 7th, or *vice versa*. Non-angular placements, especially in fixed signs, give delays. Mutable placements indicate changes in plans.

- The last planet to which the Querent's Significator applied is used to judge the Querent's immediate past condition. The next planet to which this Significator applies gives the immediate or present circumstances; the next aspect following shows future circumstances.[174]

- Combustion in a Question of an absent person (as in, a traveling person) can mean incarceration – the person is out of sight, so to speak.

Example 68. Should I go on the trip?

While the question was worded, "should," the Querent certainly gave me enough clarity so that the semantics were not a problem. The trip in question was a business trip back to her old hometown. She still has a number of clients there, so the purpose of this trip was to see them.

Since this was her hometown, and since she was not entirely comfortable in her new location, this has to be judged as a 3rd House trip. While the purpose of the trip was business, there was no question that she would be seeing her friends.

Will the trip work? The first thing we observe is that her Ruler, Venus, is in Detriment in Scorpio. She is not in a good position. Why? Using Lilly's system of using the last aspect of the 1st House Ruler as an indicator of the immediate past as it relates to the trip, we see that Venus has just separated from the square to Jupiter. Jupiter rules the 3rd, which may describe her separation from a city that she prefers over the one that she lives in now. But Jupiter also rules the 6th – and the 6th House cusp is in the degree of Scheat, one of the nastiest fixed stars. So the other possible interpretation is that she is sick – and that turned out to be the case. She asked the question in part because she was feeling so poorly, and was really wondering whether it would be worth it to try to get her body functional enough to get on a plane and fly to her destination.

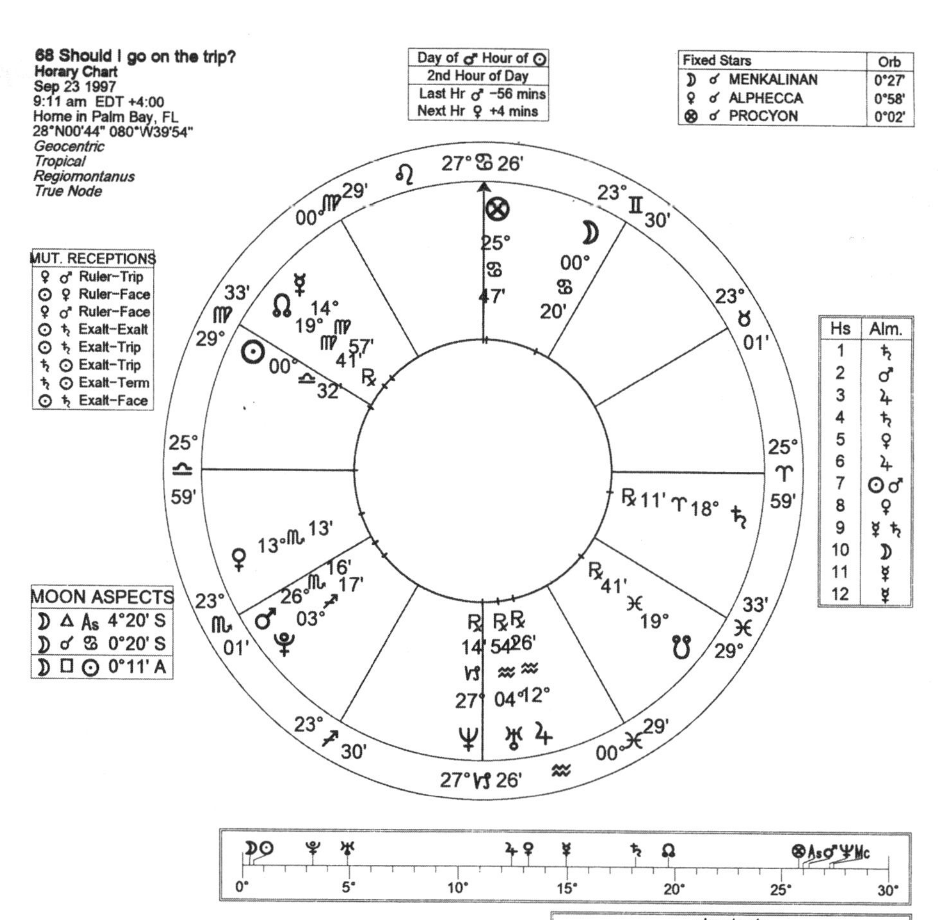

ESSENTIAL DIGNITIES (LEHMAN)								
Pt	Ruler	Exalt	Trip	Term	Face	Detri	Fall	Score
☽	☽ +	♃	♀	♂	♀	♄	♂	+5
☉	♀	♄ m	♄ m	♄	☽	♂	☉ −	−9 p
☿	☿ +	☿ +	♀	♃	♀	♃	♀	+9
♀	♂	--	♀ +	♃ m	☉	♀ −	☽	−2
♂	♂ +	--	♀	☿	♀	♀	☽	+5
♃	♄	--	♄	♀ m	☿	☉	--	−5 p
♄	♂	☉ m	☉ m	☿	☉	♀	♄ −	−9 p
As	♀	♄	♄	♂	♃	♂	☉	--
Mc	☽	♃	♀	♄	☽	♄	♂	--
⊗	☽	♃	♀	♀	☽	♄	♂	--

planets.pts				
Pt	Long.	Travel	Antiscia	C.Ant.
☽	00°♋20'27"	+12°52'	29°♊39	29°♐39
☉	00°♎32'26"	+00°58'	29°♓27	29°♍27
☿	14°♍57	+01°35'	15°♈02	15°♎02
♀	13°♏13	+01°08'	16°♒46	16°♌46
♂	26°♏16	+00°41'	03°♒43	03°♌43
♃	12°♒26 ℞	−00°02'	17°♏33	17°♉33
♄	18°♈11 ℞	−00°04'	11°♍48	11°♓48
♅	04°♒54 ℞	−00°01'	25°♏05	25°♉05
♆	27°♑14 ℞	−00°00'	02°♐45	02°♊45
♇	03°♐17	+00°01'	26°♑42	26°♋42
☊	19°♍41 ℞	−00°00'	10°♈18	10°♎18
☋	19°♓41 ℞	−00°00'	10°♎18	10°♈18
As	25°♎59'38"	+00°00'	04°♓00	04°♍00
Mc	27°♋26'22"	+00°00'	02°♊33	02°♐33
⊗	25°♋47	+00°00'	04°♊12	04°♐12

Recall that the 2nd House from the trip house shows the profit from the trip. In this case that would be the 4th House – the 2nd from the 3rd. Neptune partile conjunct the cusp just doesn't look good. Neither does Saturn in Fall, the Ruler of the 4th, retrograde in Aries! Uranus in the 4th surely doesn't look very good either, but what about Jupiter, the Ruler of the 3rd?

The Ruler of the 3rd in the 4th should be good for the profit of the trip *if* the Ruler of the 3rd is in good condition. As we noted in 1997 Jupiter was in Aquarius where it has participating Triplicity[175]. It definitely acts peregrine. So this too is an argument that the trip is not a good idea.

The Querent used her illness to cancel her flights without penalty, and so she did not go.

Example 69. Event – Romantic interlude in the Caribbean

What could be better than a little romantic interlude in the Caribbean? How about: a romantic interlude at the right *time*?! The female protagonist was not an astrology client, but an acquaintance that was casually aware of our interest in Astrology, but not sophisticated enough to really understand how it could work in her favor. She had given us the time of the airline departure, but she wasn't really that interested in any kind of delineation, except on the topic of whether there was any danger from the flight itself, because she had a mild fear of flying.

As far as danger of death is concerned, the delineation is similar to all our other death scenarios: we look for a relationship between 1st and 8th. We don't find one from the Rulers. The Sun, ruling the 1st, is past the opposition to Jupiter, Ruler of the 8th. However, the Sun is in a partile square to Saturn, a planet in the 8th. What is going on here?

Mars is the trip ruler: this is an overseas trip for two people who seldom go out of the county, let alone out of the country! Mars is in the 1st, which is certainly an appropriate signature. Mars is past the square to Jupiter, Ruler of the 8th. The number of past aspects suggests that there was danger in the past; that there is some sort of immediate danger with the partile square of Sun and Saturn, yet the sense is that the immediate risk is a continuation of the past (saturnian) danger, rather than something new.

How's the trip itself? Mars, the 9th House Ruler is peregrine. The Sun, the 1st House Ruler, has dignity only by Face. The Moon is fast and at the Bendings (out of sign) and partile conjunct Uranus, which indicates the possibility of some kind of break or disruption. This does not look like the kind of dream vacation that people anticipate when they vacation in the islands. And it wasn't. It turned out that their relationship had become rather tense before they left, and the time together brought up all their disagreements (note *Mars* ruling the trip!), and so they broke up before they returned to the mainland. And of course, Jupiter ruled not only the 8th, but the 5th: their relationship!

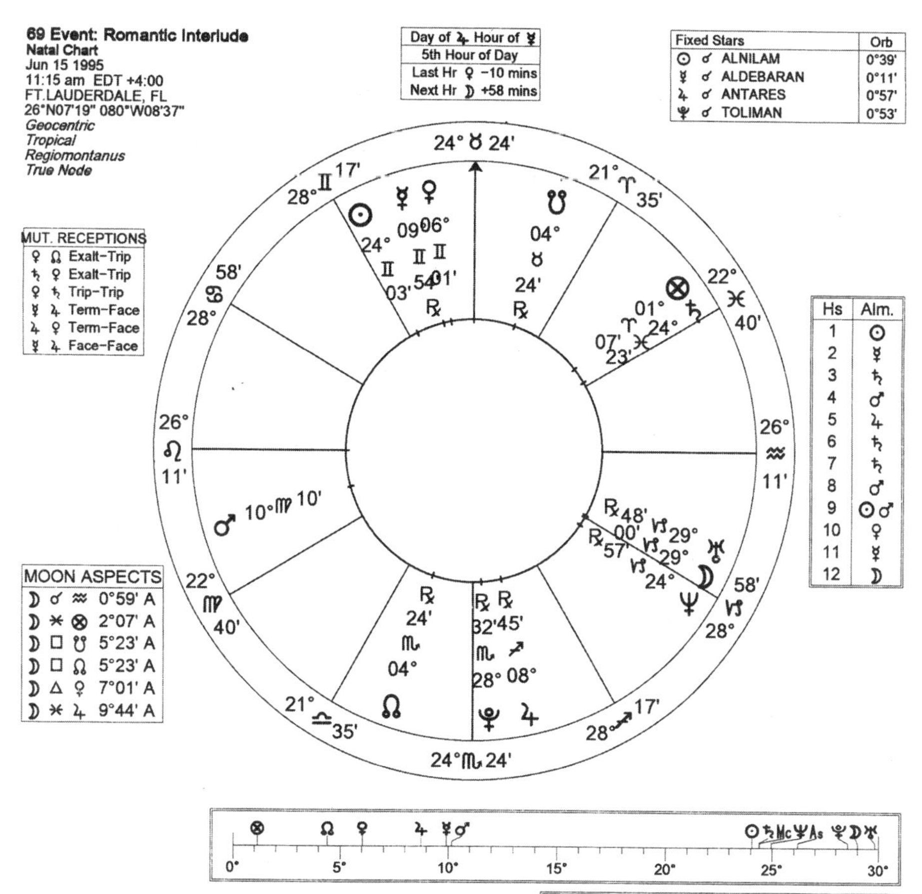

ESSENTIAL DIGNITIES (LEHMAN)								
Pt	Ruler	Exalt	Trip	Term	Face	Detri	Fall	Score
☽	♄	♂	♀	♄	☉	☽ −	♃	−10 p
☉	☿	☊	♄	♄	☉ +	♃	☋	+1
☿	☿ +	☊	♄	♃	♃ m	♃	☋	+5
♀	☿	☊	♄ m	☿	♃	♃	☋	−5 p
♂	☿	☿	♀	♀	♀	♃	♀	−5 p
♃	♃ +	☋	☉	♀	☿ m	☿	☊	+5
♄	♃	♀	♀ m	♂	♂	☿	☿	−5 p
As	☉	--	☉	♂	♂	♄	--	--
Mc	♀	☽	♀	♄	♄	♂	--	--
⊗	♂	☉	☉	♃	♂	♀	♄	--

planets.pts				
Pt	Long.	Travel	Antiscia	C.Ant.
☽	29°♑00'21"	+14°47'	00°♐59	00°♊59
☉	24°♊03'41"	+00°57'	05°♋56	05°♑56
☿	09°♊54 ℞	-00°07'	20°♋05	20°♑05
♀	06°♊01	+01°13'	23°♋58	23°♑58
♂	10°♍10	+00°30'	19°♈49	19°♎49
♃	08°♐45 ℞	-00°07'	21°♑14	21°♋14
♄	24°♓23	+00°02'	05°♎36	05°♈36
♅	29°♑48 ℞	-00°01'	00°♐11	00°♊11
♆	24°♑57 ℞	-00°01'	05°♐02	05°♊02
♇	28°♏32 ℞	-00°01'	01°♒27	01°♌27
☊	04°♏24 ℞	-00°06'	25°♒35	25°♌35
☋	04°♉24 ℞	-00°06'	25°♌35	25°♒35
As	26°♌11'17"	+00°00'	03°♉48	03°♏48
Mc	24°♉24'19"	+00°00'	05°♌35	05°♒35
⊗	01°♈07	+00°00'	28°♍52	28°♓52

Education

While no modern astrologer would be surprised at this heading, the emphasis that we place on education nowadays was simply missing from the cultural context of our 17th Century colleagues. I think we can attribute several reasons for this.

First, education was not a commodity: the university-educated population was a small minority indeed. Vocational training was the order of the day, and much of that occurred at home. The noble son would have tutors; the commoner would be an apprentice. In either case, the die was cast about his career because the kinds of choices that we assume today simply did not exist. Thus, many of the questions that we would ask concerning education could not be asked. The only kind of question I can imagine Lilly taking would be, Is this a good tutor for my son?

Second, the demographics of living were very truncated by our standards. Both boys and girls reached the age of maturity by their mid teens, an age where, in our society, they are still in high school. That meant that education was mostly finished by the age of fourteen or so.

Third, universal primary education and universal literacy didn't exist. Not even the entire nobility believed in literacy, and they could certainly afford it.

Yet wisdom was accorded to the 9th House, and we have seen how 9th and 3rd were combined for long and short trips. We shall see again shortly that the 9th and the 3rd were combined in an analogous fashion for matters of religion. So it makes sense to apply the same distinctions here for education: "shorter" education in the 3rd, and "longer" education in the 9th. And in understanding the analogical nature of what we are doing, we need to keep in mind that the definition of "shorter" and "longer" lies with the Querent. For a family of multiple doctorates, the undergraduate years may seem virtually 3rd House. For a family where no one has gone to college, high school may be 9th House.

Before we get to the examples, which concern the more formal aspects of education, we should reflect on the nature of the wisdom questions as received by Lilly. Lilly gave an example called, "If attaine the Philosopher's Stone?"[176] in which he was asked by an alchemist whether he would attain the level of purity required to create its physical manifestation, the philosopher's stone. In Lilly's day, alchemists were understood to be engaged in what we might now classify as a religious practice: individual purification through which manifested physical signs: the ability to create elixirs of increasing purity. Ultimately a pure Art could produce gold from lead, a "refined" metal from a "base" metal. The chemical processes, in other words, recapitulated the spiritual ones. Like Buddhism, Alchemy has its Greater and Lesser Vehicles; in the case of Alchemy, the Greater Vehicle is this quest for individual purity, while the Lesser Vehicle was spagyrics, the process of preparing medicines and herbal tinctures of maximum potency based on alchemical theory.[177] Spagyric horaries would be addressed as medical questions concerning a physic or medicine, and thus would be delineated primarily through the 10th House. But people who engage in years of learning and purification ask the greater alchemical questions. This is a spiritual quest which illustrates learning at its best. There is no difference between this and the decades-long study of martial arts, or the years of studying for a doctorate, or years of study in a monastery, nunnery, or ashram.

Example 70. Will my daughter graduate from college?

Questions concerning education seem to come most frequently from the parents or grandparents. This one is typical. Dawn's Mother asked this question. Dawn had just graduated from High School, and had been accepted to college for the following autumn semester.

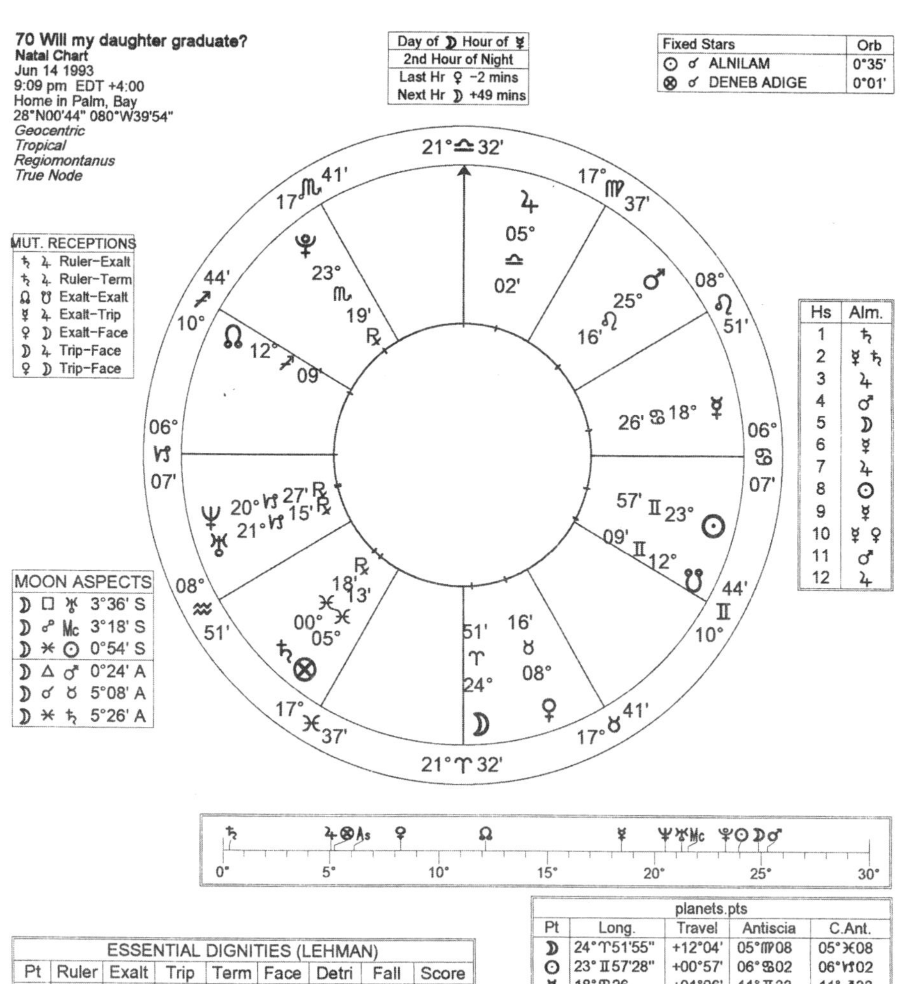

				ESSENTIAL DIGNITIES (LEHMAN)				
Pt	Ruler	Exalt	Trip	Term	Face	Detri	Fall	Score
☽	♂	☉	♃	♂	♀	♀	♄	−5 p
☉	☿	☊	☿	♄	☉ +	♃	☋	+1
☿	☽	♃	♂	☿ +	☿ +	♄	♂	+3
♀	♀ +	☽	☽	☿	☿	♂	--	+5
♂	☉	--	♃	♂ +	♂ +	♄	--	+3
♃	♀	♄	☿	♄	☽	♂	☉	−5 p
♄	♃	♀	♂	♀	♄ +	☿	☿	+1
As	♄	♂	☽	☿	♃	☽	♃	--
Mc	♀	♄	☿	☿	♃	♂	☉	--
⊗	♃	♀	♂	♀	♄	☿	☿	--

		planets.pts		
Pt	Long.	Travel	Antiscia	C.Ant.
☽	24°♈51'55"	+12°04'	05°♍08	05°♓08
☉	23°♊57'28"	+00°57'	06°♋02	06°♑02
☿	18°♋26	+01°06'	11°♊33	11°♐33
♀	08°♉16	+00°59'	21°♌43	21°♒43
♂	25°♌16	+00°33'	04°♉43	04°♏43
♃	05°♎02	+00°02'	24°♓57	24°♍57
♄	00°♓18 ℞	-00°00'	29°♎41	29°♈41
♅	21°♑15 ℞	-00°02'	08°♐44	08°♊44
♆	20°♑27 ℞	-00°01'	09°♐32	09°♊32
♇	23°♏19 ℞	-00°01'	06°♒40	06°♌40
☊	12°♐09	+00°01'	17°♑50	17°♋50
☋	12°♊09	+00°01'	17°♋50	17°♑50
As	06°♑07'37"	+00°00'	23°♐52	23°♊52
Mc	21°♎32'59"	+00°00'	08°♓27	08°♍27
⊗	05°♓13	+00°00'	24°♎46	24°♈46

The fifth House represents the Querent's daughter. The Almuten is the Moon. The Moon is peregrine in Aries. Dawn had just been diagnosed with Epstein-Barr syndrome, so she literally was weak - and listless as well. While fairly late in Aries, the Moon would still trine Mars in Leo before leaving the sign. We shall see the import of that trine shortly.

The Daughter's ninth House (higher education) was the radical first House. The Almuten and sign ruler of the 1st is Saturn, which had just gone retrograde. The Moon will sextile Saturn from out-of-sign. The Moon is within orb of the sextile and its condition will improve by moving from Aries to Taurus, its exaltation sign.

Thus, I judged that Dawn would graduate. Because the Moon is just over five degrees from the sextile to Saturn, I judged that it might take five years to do so, although the fact that Saturn is retrograde may bode for a sudden resolution of the matter. Because the Moon must change signs in order to complete the sextile, I further judged that there would be a change of circumstance (for the better) in that last year.

Both turned out to be the case. She graduated in five years, she did change majors, and she had a further change in circumstance – she became engaged – and then got married right after graduation! Remember the Moon coming to trine Mars? Mars rules her 7th House!

Example 71. Will I finish the course?

The Querent had signed up for a correspondence course, and wanted to know if she would finish. The Querent is Venus in Aries in her 12th House – and this is the problem. She is impatient, and eager to get through this material. She is also combust, which makes her invisible – we presume from the standpoint of the teacher, because I cannot imagine whom else the interpretation could apply to.

The teacher is given by 9th House Ruler Saturn in Capricorn – which fits, because not only is the teacher elderly, but clearly, she has all the power. With Saturn conjunct Neptune, she was off in a world of her own. These two Significators are separating from each other by square. So they have already quarreled. The Moon in Gemini at the Bendings is neither in a sign to bring the two back together, nor in zodiacal condition by dignity to be able to effect a result.

With the Moon approaching Mars, I judged that within nine weeks or months, they would have yet one more argument that would completely end the matter, and that she would not finish the course. Within nine months, that proved to be the case.

Religious Affairs

Lilly got religious questions; we seem to get education and lawyer questions. The questions that I have received about religion have involved questions concerning religious teachers and hierarchies; the questions that Lilly answered concerned the more practical matter of whether the Querent would receive a parsonage; i.e., whether he would be able to make money through religion.

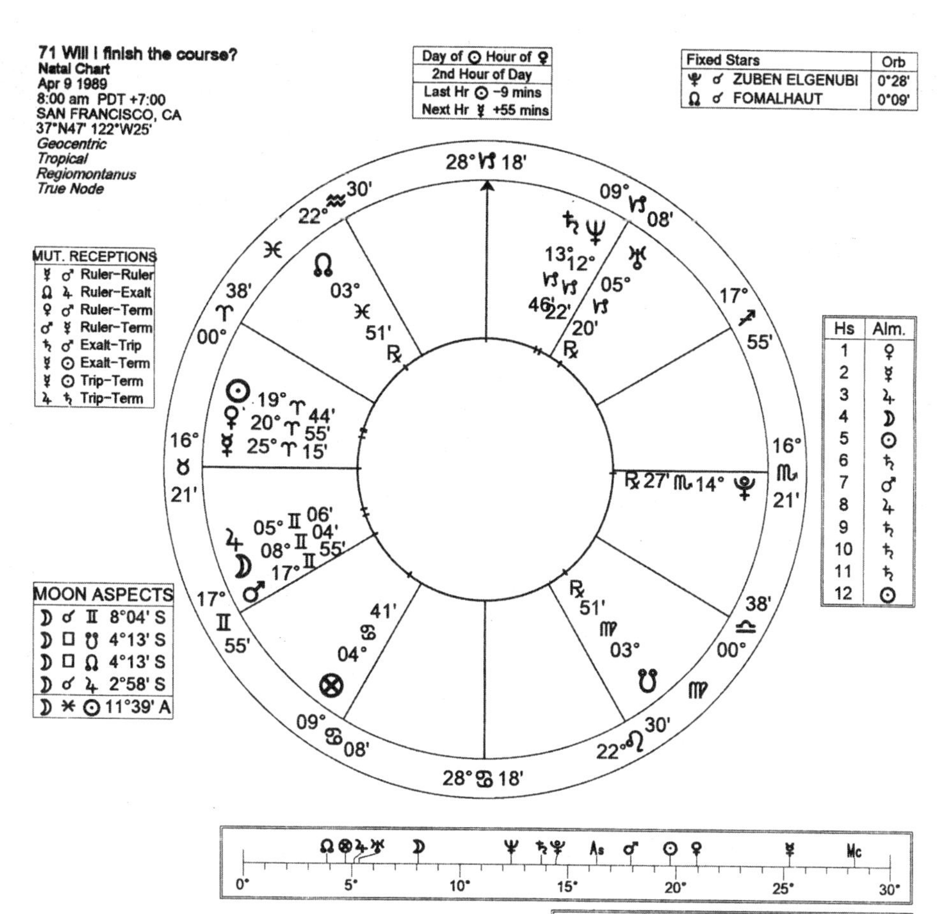

ESSENTIAL DIGNITIES (LEHMAN)								
Pt	Ruler	Exalt	Trip	Term	Face	Detri	Fall	Score
☽	☿	☊	♄	♃	♃	♃	☋	-5 p
☉	♂	☉ +	☉ +	☿	☉ +	♀	♄	+8
☿	♂ m	☉	☉	♂	♀	♀	♄	-5 p
♀	♂	☉	☉	☿	♀ +	♀ -	♄	-4
♂	☿ m	☊	♄	♀	♂ +	♃	☋	+1
♃	☿	☊	♄	☿	♃ +	♃ -	☋	-4
♄	♄ +	♂	♀	♃	♂	☽	♃	+5
As	♀	☽	♀	♃	☽	♂	--	--
Mc	♄	♂	♀	♄	☉	☽	♃	--
⊗	☽	♃	♀	♂	♀	♄	♂	--

planets.pts				
Pt	Long.	Travel	Antiscia	C.Ant.
☽	08° ♊ 04'38"	+14°14'	21° ♋ 55	21° ♑ 55
☉	19° ♈ 44'03"	+00°58'	10° ♍ 15	10° ♓ 15
☿	25° ♈ 15	+02°05'	04° ♍ 44	04° ♓ 44
♀	20° ♈ 55	+01°14'	09° ♍ 04	09° ♓ 04
♂	17° ♊ 55	+00°36'	12° ♋ 04	12° ♑ 04
♃	05° ♊ 06	+00°11'	24° ♋ 53	24° ♑ 53
♄	13° ♑ 46	+00°01'	16° ♐ 13	16° ♊ 13
♅	05° ♑ 20 ℞	-00°00'	24° ♐ 39	24° ♊ 39
♆	12° ♑ 22	+00°00'	17° ♐ 37	17° ♊ 37
♇	14° ♏ 27 ℞	-00°01'	15° ♒ 32	15° ♌ 32
☊	03° ♓ 51 ℞	-00°05'	26° ♎ 08	26° ♈ 08
☋	03° ♍ 51 ℞	-00°05'	26° ♈ 08	26° ♎ 08
As	16° ♉ 21'24"	+00°00'	13° ♌ 38	13° ♒ 38
Mc	28° ♑ 18'24"	+00°00'	01° ♐ 41	01° ♊ 41
⊗	04° ♋ 41	+00°00'	25° ♊ 18	25° ♐ 18

Granted, Lilly was more than a little cynical about these matters, as can be told from his section heading, "If an idle covetous Priest upon his Question propounded shall Obtaine a good Parsonage, yea or no?"[178] Lilly recognized that to the churchmen of his era, a parsonage was a job: it was more often a source of income, than an opportunity to provide spiritual inspiration or guidance.

Lilly looked for a relationship between Significators of the 1st and 9th to indicate a positive response, possibly substituting the Moon for the Ruler of the Ascendant, or Jupiter for the Ruler of the 9th. The nature of the aspect matters: Lilly coyly tells us that a square aspect between the Ruler of the Ascendant and the 9th, with reception, can bring a benefice provided there is a bribe attached. A translation implies success through the intervention of a third party. And the imposition of malefics can impede or destroy the process.

Example 72. Share my predicament with my students?

What if a teacher asks the Question? The circumstances were these. The Querent has been participating in an Eastern tradition for decades – long enough that he has his own students, although he is by no means at the top of the hierarchy. He has an American supervisor, then that supervisor in turn has supervisors in Asia. The Querent had reached an impasse with his supervisor about matters of practice. He had already asked a horary about whether it would be worthwhile to travel to Asia to meet with the people higher up – the answer was no.

When he had a chance to think about matters – and his prior horary also suggested that things were not going to improve with his immediate supervisor any time soon – he became concerned that he was going to be putting his students in an awkward position the longer that the disagreements dragged out. An upcoming national meeting that his senior students would be attending precipitated his question. So how do we get him an answer?

The slow, peregrine Moon in Aquarius rules the Querent. Who are his students? If his teachers (i.e., his superiors) are the 9th, then his students must in turn be the 3rd, unless we wish to use Jupiter as the natural ruler of students.[179] My choice would be to use Mercury, Ruler of the 3rd, because we would want to keep Jupiter in reserve as the Ruler of the Querent's superiors.

Notice, by the way, the slightly awkward situation that we have concerning superiors. Normally, a superior would be a 10th House person: a person further up the food chain. However, in spiritual or educational organizations, one's superior is recognized as part of a hierarchy of that nature, which is 9th, rather than a secular hierarchy, which is 10th. In an educational institution, one approaches this difference with caution. The head of a department, as a fellow teacher, is probably the 9th, while the Chancellor of the university, being primarily an administrator, would be 10th.

And we need different Significators for the three players! The Querent's Significator - the Moon - comes to trine his students in eight degrees (eight months?) and then squares Jupiter, his immediate superior, in Taurus. Because the Moon is slow, things may drag even longer. Jupiter has dignity only

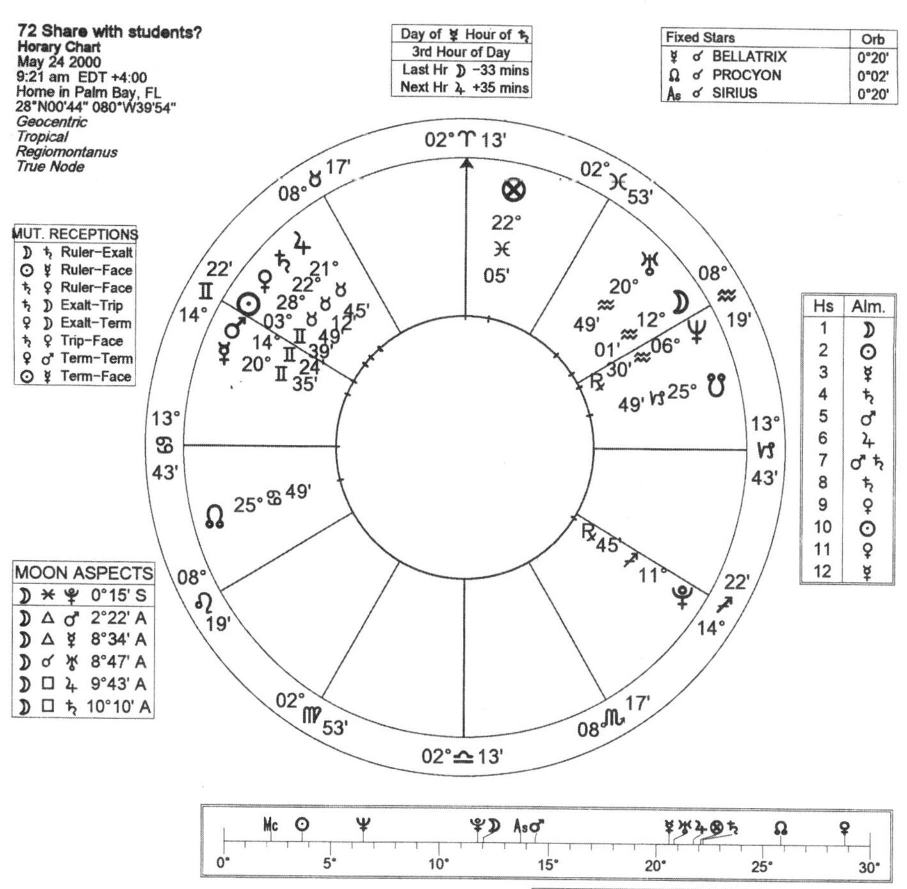

ESSENTIAL DIGNITIES (LEHMAN)								
Pt	Ruler	Exalt	Trip	Term	Face	Detri	Fall	Score
☽	♄	--	♄	♀	☿	☉	--	-5 p
☉	☿	☊	♄	☿	♃	♃	☋	-5 p
☿	☿ +	☊	♄	♀	☉	♃	☋	+5
♀	♀ +	☽	♀ +	♂ m	♄	♂	--	+8
♂	☿	☊	♄	♀ m	♂ +	♃	☋	+1
♃	♀	☽	♀	♃ +	♄	♂	--	+2
♄	♀	☽	♀	♄ +	♄ +	♂	--	+3
As	☽	♃	♀	☿	☿	♄	♂	--
Mc	♂	☉	☉	♃	♂	♀	♄	--
⊗	♃	♀	♀	♂	♂	☿	☿	--

planets.pts				
Pt	Long.	Travel	Antiscia	C.Ant.
☽	12°♒01'41"	+11°55'	17°♏58	17°♉58
☉	03°♊39'56"	+00°57'	26°♋20	26°♑20
☿	20°♊35	+01°48'	09°♋24	09°♑24
♀	28°♉49	+01°13'	01°♌10	01°♒10
♂	14°♊24	+00°41'	15°♋35	15°♑35
♃	21°♉45	+00°14'	08°♌14	08°♒14
♄	22°♉12	+00°07'	07°♌47	07°♒47
♅	20°♒49	+00°00'	09°♏10	09°♉10
♆	06°♒30 ℞	-00°00'	23°♏29	23°♉29
♇	11°♐45 ℞	-00°01'	18°♑14	18°♋14
☊	25°♋49	+00°01'	04°♊10	04°♐10
☋	25°♑49	+00°01'	04°♐10	04°♊10
As	13°♋43'47"	+00°00'	16°♊16	16°♐16
Mc	02°♈13'00"	+00°00'	27°♍46	27°♓46
⊗	22°♓05	+00°00'	07°♎54	07°♈54

by Term. The trine to the students takes place at the same time as the conjunction of the Moon to Uranus. So the best scenario we can hypothesize is that eight months (or years!) from now (succedent and fixed) he tells his students, and then one to two months later, possibly because he told his students, he will have yet one more disagreement with his superior, possibly resulting in a permanent break. However, his Significator is applying to a trine to Mars, representing the authorities higher in the structure. He then translates the Light between his students and the higher authorities. The trine means that his students will mostly support him: they do not behold his immediate superior. So it looks like the immediate superior could ultimately be the one shut out.

Almost ten months later, the Powers that Be in Asia proposed a change in the organizational structure that left the Querent with greater autonomy, and took away the restrictions that his superior had placed upon him.

Legal Matters

Fortunately for him, Lilly didn't have to worry about lawyers as much as we do! Our culture supports a level of complexity in human interactions that often makes technical advice a necessity, not merely a luxury. As a result, questions concerning the actual or potential quality of advice or service are often highly relevant.

What's the difference between 9th and 3rd House advice? The 3rd House issues are mainly associated with truth itself – if the advice is *true*. In the 9th, the advice is a matter of technical expertise.

To judge the quality of legal counsel, examine the 9th House and the condition of its ruler. These can then be examined with relation to the 1st, because without connection, the best legal guidance in the world may not be understood or implemented.

Example 73. Use this lawyer?

This Querent was interested in hiring a lawyer to help her uncover some assets that she believed were her due. So she asked whether he would be able to do the job for her.

The eye is immediately drawn to the 29 degrees Ascendant – this situation is too late. This suggests that the money the Querent thought was hers was probably already allocated to someone else, even if it hasn't technically been paid yet. Beyond that, would you trust a lawyer represented by Saturn at one degree Taurus coming to *square* Neptune in Aquarius *in the* 9th *House*? I wouldn't! I told her to find a different lawyer if she wanted to pursue it, but that recovery of her assets was unlikely no matter the quality of the lawyer.

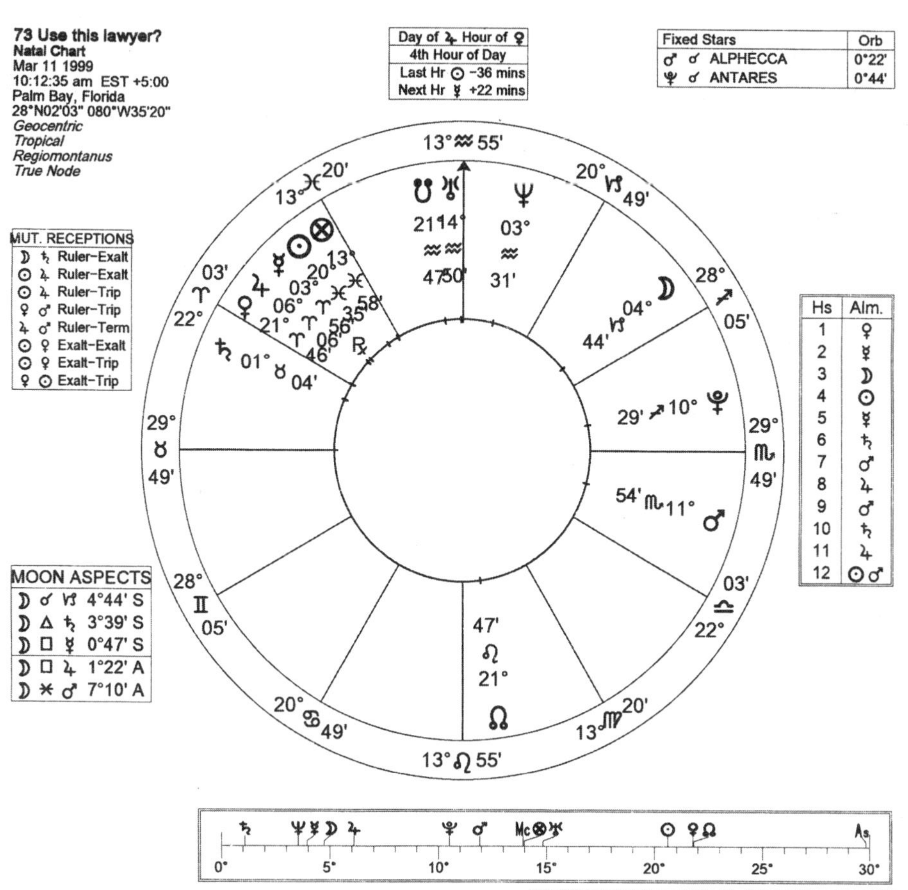

ESSENTIAL DIGNITIES (LEHMAN)								
Pt	Ruler	Exalt	Trip	Term	Face	Detri	Fall	Score
☽	♄	♂	♀	♀	♃	☽ −	♃	−10 p
☉	♃	♀ m	♀ m	♂	♂ m	☿	☿	−5 p
☿	♂	☉	☉	♃	♂	♀	♄	−5 p
♀	♂	☉ m	☉ m	♂	♀ +	♀ −	♄	−4
♂	♂ +	--	♀	♃	☉ m	♀	☽	+5
♃	♂	☉	☉	♀	♂	♀	♄	−5 p
♄	♀	☽	♀	♀	☿	♂	--	−5 p
As	♀	☽	♀	♂	♄	♂	--	--
Mc	♄	--	♄	♀	☿	☉	--	--
⊗	♃	♀	♀	♃	♃	☿	☿	--

planets.pts				
Pt	Long.	Travel	Antiscia	C.Ant.
☽	04°♑44'17"	+12°14'	25°♐15	25°♊15
☉	20°♓35'38"	+00°59'	09°♎24	09°♈24
☿	03°♈56 ℞	−00°10'	26°♍03	26°♓03
♀	21°♈46	+01°13'	08°♍13	08°♓13
♂	11°♏54	+00°04'	18°♒05	18°♌05
♃	06°♈06	+00°14'	23°♍53	23°♓53
♄	01°♉04	+00°06'	28°♌55	28°♒55
♅	14°♒50	+00°02'	15°♏09	15°♉09
♆	03°♒31	+00°01'	26°♏28	26°♉28
♇	10°♐29	+00°00'	19°♑30	19°♋30
☊	21°♌47	+00°01'	08°♉12	08°♏12
☋	21°♒47	+00°01'	08°♏12	08°♉12
As	29°♉49'51"	+00°00'	00°♌10	00°♒10
Mc	13°♒55'51"	+00°00'	16°♏04	16°♉04
⊗	13°♓58	+00°00'	16°♎01	16°♈01

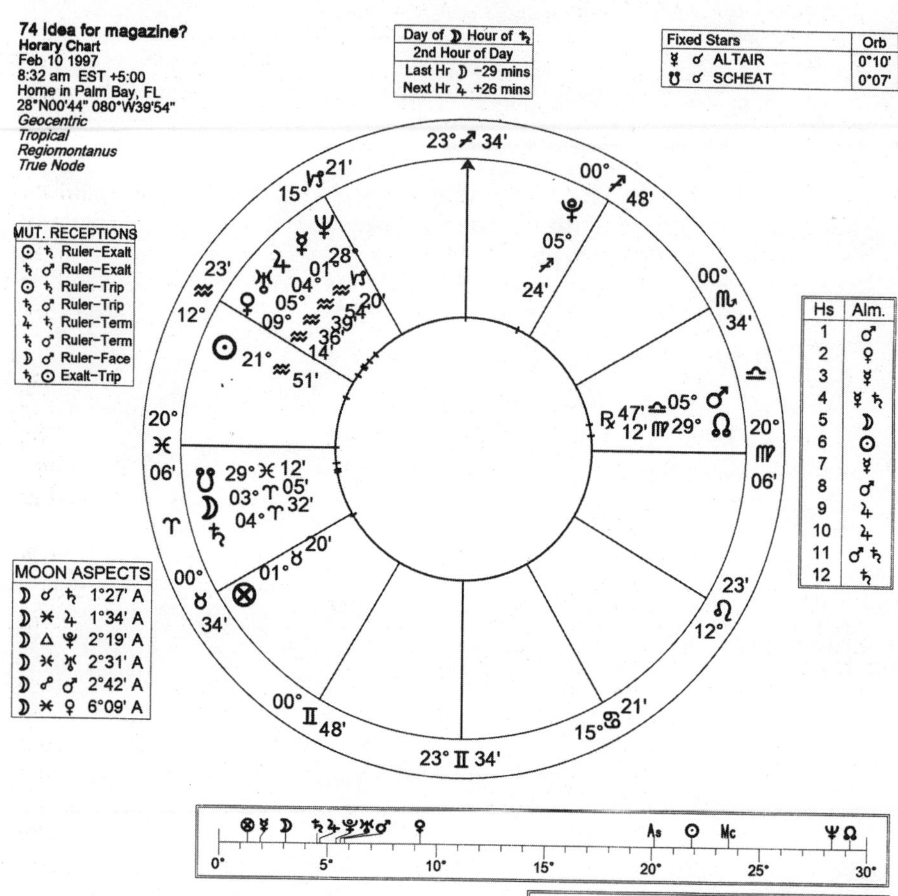

ESSENTIAL DIGNITIES (LEHMAN)								
Pt	Ruler	Exalt	Trip	Term	Face	Detri	Fall	Score
☽	♂	☉	☉	♃	♂ m	♀	♄	−5 p
☉	♄	---	♄ m	♃	☽	☉ −	---	−10 p
☿	♄	---	♄	♄	♀	☉	---	−5 p
♀	♄	---	♄	☿	♀ +	☉	---	+1
♂	♀	♄	♄	♄	☽ m	♂ −	☉	−10 p
♃	♄	---	♄	♄ m	♀	☉	---	−5 p
♄	♂	☉	☉ m	♃ m	♂	♀	♄ −	−9 p
As	♃	♀	♀	♂	♂	☿	☿	---
Mc	♃	☋	☉	♄	♄	☿	☊	---
⊗	♀	☽	♀	♀	☿	♂	---	---

planets.pts				
Pt	Long.	Travel	Antiscia	C.Ant.
☽	03°♈05'06"	+14°37'	26°♍54	26°♓54
☉	21°♒51'42"	+01°00'	08°♏08	08°♉08
☿	01°♒54	+01°27'	28°♏05	28°♉05
♀	09°♒14	+01°15'	20°♏45	20°♉45
♂	05°♎47 ℞	−00°03'	24°♓12	24°♍12
♃	04°♒39	+00°13'	25°♏20	25°♉20
♄	04°♈32	+00°06'	25°♍27	25°♓27
♅	05°♒36	+00°03'	24°♏23	24°♉23
♆	28°♑20	+00°02'	01°♐39	01°♊39
♇	05°♐24	+00°00'	24°♑35	24°♋35
☊	29°♍12	+00°00'	00°♈47	00°♎47
☋	29°♓12	+00°00'	00°♎47	00°♈47
As	20°♓06'38"	+00°00'	09°♎53	09°♈53
Mc	23°♐34'22"	+00°00'	06°♑25	06°♋25
⊗	01°♉20	+00°00'	28°♌39	28°♒39

Example 74. Idea for magazine?

The Querent called me up one morning. She had been talking to some business people about starting a slick mass media astrology/New Age magazine that would attract women readers through gossip concerning [movie!] stars. Did I think that this would be a successful venture?

This allows us to transition to yet another 9th House possibility: publishing. Again, we don't have a good classical lineage here, most likely because of cultural changes regarding publishing. Writers and writing are generally given to Mercury[180], but books are given to the 9th if a house attribution is given.[181] If books are the 9th, we can feel fairly safe generalizing to publications, and publishers as well.

In this chart, we have Jupiter ruling both 1st and 9th. There was no question that the Querent completely identified with this project, although she would not be an investor, but a writer and editor. Given the nature of the previous horary questions that we had been working with – a dwindling inheritance – I knew that the question very strongly included the issue of whether she could make money through this venture.

Jupiter is fast. In Aquarius it has mixed Triplicity; which in Horary, is too weak to be helpful. Right away, I'm questioning whether this project will ever make it to the first issue. The speed of Jupiter may just mean that the sprint at the beginning precludes a finish at the end.

The 1st House tells the rest of the tale. The South Node is in the 1st conjunct the shipwreck star Scheat, which certainly would make it next to impossible for her to benefit from this project, no matter how successful it would become. And we see the peregrine Moon applying to both of the traditional malefics, in rapid succession, and with both malefics debilitated. The Moon is besieged. And furthermore, Venus rules her 2nd, and Venus has dignity only by Face. The Part of Fortune at the 2nd House cusp is disposed by that same weak Venus, as well as by debilitated Mars.

This just isn't going to work. And it didn't. The project never left the idea stage.

Dreams

Lilly cited Haly as the source for the interpretation of dreams as follows: interpret the nature of the dream as being according to the nature of any planet in the 9th House. If nothing is in the 9th, then use the 10th; if nothing is there, the 1st; then on to the 7th or 4th, 3rd, 2nd, 5th, 6th, 8th, 11th, or 12th, going as far as you need to find a planet! The condition of that dream Ruler can then be studied through its relationship to the Ruler of the Ascendant and the Moon.[182] Notice that the 11th, the house most modern astrologers would actually take first for dreams, is pretty far down the list. Lilly reiterates the use of the 9th House for dreams in his section on nativities,[183] in which it is very clear that he was referring to the quality of dreams as shown by the Ruler of the 9th House. Gadbury doesn't mention dreams at all in his horary section, but in his section on nativities, he discusses the issue, "Shall the Natives Dreams prove true or false" under the 9th House.[184] Partridge give dreams to the 9th House as well.[185]

While I have not traced the exact lineage of the shift of dreams from the 9th to the 11th, I would suspect that the change is associated with the English usage of "dreams" as a synonym for "hopes," which is a legitimate 11th House matter.

I have never taken one of these questions, but it's good to be prepared! But I suppose these days, Querents ask their analysts about dreams, not their astrologers!

And now we can transition from dreams to the hard nature of reality as we next consider the 10th House.

Chapter 10

Affairs of the 10th House: Governments in the Broader Sense. Promotions, Honors & Higher-ups.

Questions of the 10th House as given by Lilly:[186]

- Of government, office, dignity, preferment, or any place of Command or Trust, whether obtainable or not?
- If one shall continue in the Office or Command he is in.
- Whether a King expulsed his Kingdom, or an Officer removed from his government shall return to his Kingdom or Office.
- Of the Profession, Magistery or Trade any one is capable of.
- If attain the Preferment desired?

Gadbury's list of categories of questions differs only slightly from Lilly's, except that Gadbury, having been on the losing side of the Civil War, did not present the politically charged horaries that Lilly did.[187]

I would add one additional category:

- Questions concerning a major corporation.

What is a government? This may seem like an odd question, but it's not. This issue is the real key to understanding the 10th House. A generation ago, this question would not have been asked, because the answer would have seemed obvious: a government is the administration of a nation-state. The entire world is divided into nation-states, with the exception of Antarctica, so what's the problem?

The problem is that, following the collapse of Communism, it has become apparent that the kind of tribal warfare that was easy to dismiss as transitory to the formation of the modern state has assumed massively greater significance. It is seemingly far more likely that the nation-state was a convenient myth of the so-called developed countries: a concept that described *them* well enough, but which represented a square peg in a round hole for other portions of the globe.[188] In much of Africa, South America, Eastern

Europe and the Middle East, national governments are completely ineffective at providing even the illusion of domestic tranquility, as "countries" implode into a patchwork of special interest groups that fight civil wars spanning generations.

Bringing this rather depressing political situation back to the realm of Astrology, what does this say for our conceptualization of both the 10th and 11th Houses? Traditionally, the 10th House was the King and Magistrates, the latter category being, by definition, the nobility. As Western Europe and its cultural offshoots like the USA, Canada, New Zealand and Australia developed into democracies, or some facsimile of democracies, the tendency among modern astrologers has been to assign the legislative branch (Congress, Parliament) to the 11th House, and the head of government (President, Prime Minister) to the 10th House. Government as a general entity is placed in the 10th.[189] Foreign countries can be classified by proximity. Thus, neighboring countries may be placed in the 3rd House, while distant countries are 9th. In this sense, a country is related to travel, which certainly in earlier times showed a direct relationship between duration of trip and geographical distance.

Consider one more factor. What does it mean astrologically when 51 of the world's 100 largest economies are corporations, not countries?[190] Clearly, we cannot just approach these facts without rethinking how our definitions work.

Interestingly, Lilly forbore from giving a rulership to Parliament, except in horaries related to the outcome of battles of the English Civil War, in which the Parliament, as one of the two opposing sides, was assigned to the 1st House when the Querent was a partisan for the Parliament. His use of the 11th House is for those giving counsel to the government.[191] What he does specify is that the nobility is given by the 10th House.[192]

I would contend that astrologers have only really asked the question, who is the nobility in a given society? A question far more interesting and useful is to ask, what function makes a person (or institution) *like* the aristocracy?

In a classless society, the equivalent people to the aristocracy are the rich and powerful; possibly the glamorous and famous. The equivalent *function* to the aristocracy is the ability to do what you want, with different rules applying to you compared to other people. This gives a somewhat different slant, and has some results that may even be surprising.

If being able to pay for the best legal representation will change the outcome of a lawsuit, then the side that can afford it is the aristocracy. But it goes further. Ultimately, the issue is whether a typical citizen has any effective power when pitted against another individual, or an institution. Consider a family-run restaurant. You become a regular patron. You get to know the owner by name. Maybe you don't formally get a discount, but your serving portions are a little larger, or they don't charge you for the dessert. In other words, your tacit agreement to patronize the restaurant regularly results in better service or product. And if you have a problem, you know that the owner will listen to it. Now consider McDonalds. You can go to the same McDonalds five days a week, and your hamburger and fries will be exactly the same size – because McDonalds, like most large chains, has strict portion control. And the prices are completely determined by the computer programs they are using.

If you have a problem, and you are buying from a multinational corporation, how much leverage do you have as a consumer? Almost none. The only recourse that you really have is to sue, but that means that whatever they did to annoy you better be pretty clear and illegal! Can you do anything about prices? Not a chance! Individual buyers are not in a position to engage in commerce in the old style, which included the ability to negotiate the price, terms and conditions of a sale. Our greater population density has resulted in the appearance of institutions that sell to individuals on a commodity basis. Sometimes, the effect is somewhat softened by deliberate catering to repeat business, such as an airline's frequent flyers. But how much real power does any consumer have in negotiating with United Airlines or the phone company? While there may be multiple rate plans, they are not *really* going to tailor one specifically for you.

And this is the essence of the 10th House. We have gone from the gulf created by birth status to the gulf created by shear mass of numbers. When one-on-one buying and selling goes out of the realm of possibility, then the transaction becomes 1st-10th. When you are a customer of Citicorp, and Citicorp has millions of customers, how much can you say about your clout? In essence, a 10th House figure is anyone or anything that can treat you arbitrarily – whether they in fact consciously choose to do so or not. The only fair fight – or fair chance – in horary is 1st-7th. When you are dealing with any other combination of houses, the stronger party doesn't necessarily win, because power differentials are built into the system.

It's worth mentioning that, as we begin studying questions about the government, that the traditional view of government office has metamorphosed over time. By definition, the nobility in many countries was *already* in government simply as a result of holding particular titles: whether through a parliament, a king's council, or other such body. Thus, there were questions about particular positions, such as the governor of a colony, or the general-ship of an army, or the chancellorship. However, the circle of eligible candidates was likely to be much smaller than current job seekers experience!

Governmental Questions

There were essentially two functions that were taken as governmental questions: either a boon granted by the government; or retention, removal or return to government office. And it is always worth remembering that government was not a faceless monolith. It was the king, or duke, or earl, who granted the boon, after all.

The setup for both kinds of questions was essentially the same. Is there a relationship between 1st and 10th House? If there is, the desired 10th house result will be effected. If not, it won't. The Moon may either mitigate or deny the result. Also, if the Ruler of the 1st or the Moon is in the 10th, this alone can indicate a positive result, especially if the Ruler of the 10th beholds the 10th House cusp.[193] Of course, translations, collections, and renderings also can produce the desired result, although they indicate the involvement of a third party.

Lilly also mentions the importance of aspects of Significators to angular planets.[194] He mentions that danger of placements of, and aspects to planets below the horizon, as this fact alone can mitigate against return to office once an office is lost. Further, being angular in the 4th House – or applying to 4th House planets - may not be a placement strong enough to achieve a positive result. An angular planet going retrograde or into combustion may wreck its ability to act in a positive fashion.

Example 75: Is it worth pursuing the Department of Insurance?

This story is everybody's nightmare. The Querent was a victim of bank fraud, and bogus insurance policies were taken out in her name that she was charged for. The question is whether the Department of Insurance in her state will prosecute this without her having to find some consumer advocacy group to make the affair public. The problem, of course, is that in many US states the agency that oversees the insurance companies is often far more sympathetic to those same insurance companies than to a mere citizen.

There are in fact several houses that are relevant to this question. Here is a list of the players:

- The Querent, shown through Venus, Ruler of the 1st.
- The insurance company, given by the 8th House, shown by Jupiter, Ruler of the 8th conjunct the Ascendant.
- The perpetrators of the fraud, either the 7th House ruler, or an angular peregrine planet not otherwise designated as a Significator. Here we pick Mars, Ruler of the 7th in the 12th of secret enemies.
- The state government itself, given by either Mars as Almuten of the 10th, or Saturn, the Ruler of the 10th.
- The 11th House, the usual house designated for the administrative agencies of the government, and ruled by Saturn, gives the Department of Insurance.

Just by the lineup of the potential Significators, we can reach certain conclusions:

1. Either the criminal(s) are part of the state government, or they are in league with some person(s) in the government, given Mars' dual position as Ruler of the perpetrators and Almuten of the 10th. It cannot be stated often enough that when two houses are ruled by the same planet, the affairs of those houses are linked. Notice that the only angular peregrine planet in this chart is Saturn, which we are using for the Insurance Department. Were Saturn the perpetrator, then we could conclude that:
   a. She knows the perpetrator(s), since Saturn is in the 1st House, and her Significator is in two mutual receptions with Saturn.

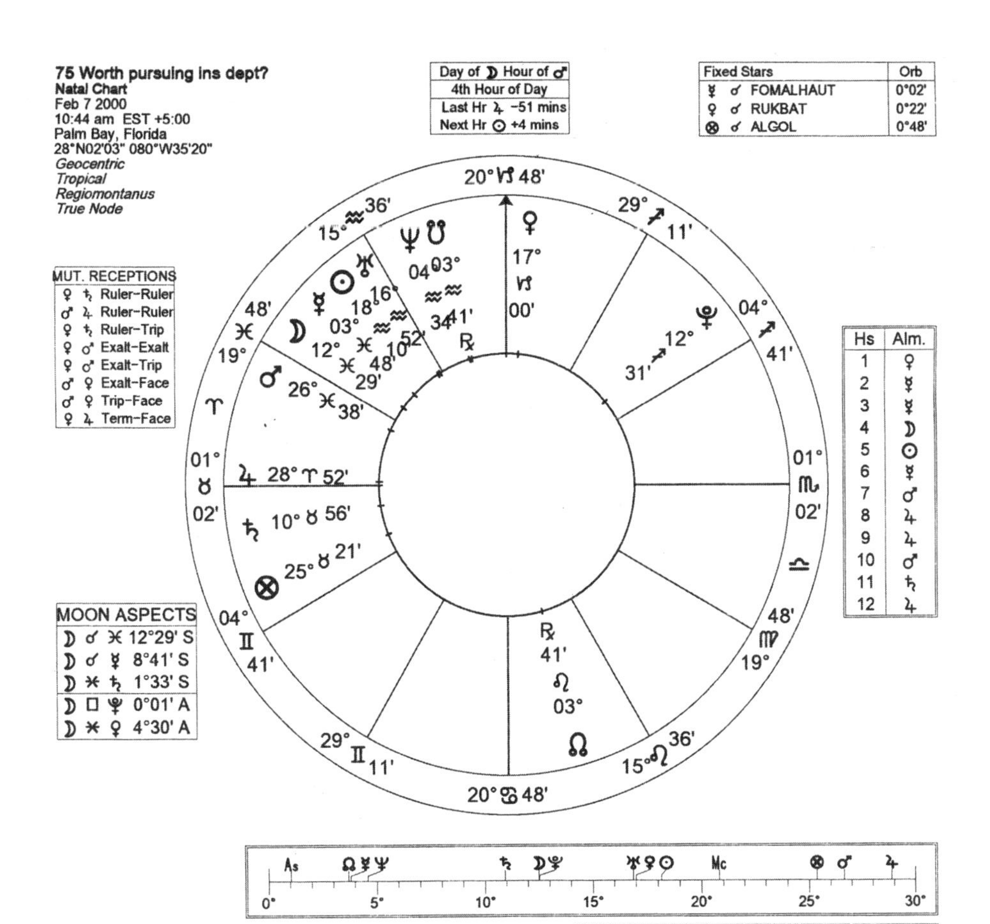

ESSENTIAL DIGNITIES (LEHMAN)								
Pt	Ruler	Exalt	Trip	Term	Face	Detri	Fall	Score
☽	♃	♀	♀	♃	♃	☿	☿	-5 p
☉	♄	---	♄	♀	☿	☉ -	---	-10 p
☿	♃	♀	♀	♀	♄	☿ -	☿ -	-14 p
♀	♄ m	♂ m	♀ +	♃	♂	☽	♃	+3
♂	♃ m	♀ m	♀	♄	♂ +	☿	☿	+1
♃	♂ m	☉	☉	♄	♀	♀	♄	-5 p
♄	♀ m	☽	♀	☿	☽	♂	---	-5 p
As	♀	☽	♀	♀	☿	♂	---	---
Mc	♄	♂	♀	♂	☉	☽	♃	---
⊗	♀	☽	♀	♄	♄	♂	---	---

planets.pts				
Pt	Long.	Travel	Antiscia	C.Ant.
☽	12°♓29'37"	+12°45'	17°♎30	17°♈30
☉	18°♒10'17"	+01°00'	11°♏49	11°♉49
☿	03°♓48	+01°35'	26°♎11	26°♈11
♀	17°♑00	+01°13'	12°♐59	12°♊59
♂	26°♓38	+00°45'	03°♎21	03°♈21
♃	28°♈52	+00°08'	01°♍07	01°♓07
♄	10°♉56	+00°02'	19°♌03	19°♒03
♅	16°♒52	+00°03'	13°♏07	13°♉07
♆	04°♒34	+00°02'	25°♏25	25°♉25
♇	12°♐31	+00°01'	17°♑28	17°♋28
☊	03°♌41 ℞	-00°02'	26°♉18	26°♏18
☋	03°♒41 ℞	-00°02'	26°♏18	26°♉18
As	01°♉02'01"	+00°00'	28°♌57	28°♒57
Mc	20°♑48'09"	+00°00'	09°♐11	09°♊11
⊗	25°♉21	+00°00'	04°♌38	04°♒38

b. The perpetrator(s) are in league with the Department of Insurance.
2. The insurance company where the bogus policies were written is in substantial danger from her, given that their ruler is conjunct the Ascendant: they are in her hands, so to speak. Perhaps the company feels that they would stand to lose in terms of reputation were this fraud revealed.

Let's take this delineation even further. The import of this question is really: will the Department of Insurance do anything about her case, or is she either going to have to pursue legal channels, or get involved with media exposé of this kind of practice, thereby shaming the Department into action? Notice that Venus (the Querent) is past the trine to the Agency (Saturn). However, the Moon translates the light between them. Just this fact is enough to tell us that a Third Party is necessary to affect a result. The Querent's planet Venus has dignity by Triplicity, so she should be able to get out of this having achieved a good portion of her goals.

Since she was not aware of knowing the perpetrators of the crime, then Saturn gets used exclusively as the Department, and not the perpetrators. In this case, the major problem with the department appears to be inertia (the peregrine and fixed Saturn), not culpability. This chart does suggest the possibility of culpability elsewhere in the state government system. Given the translation of light, I suggested that a bit of publicity might do everyone some good.

Example 76: Will I win my lawsuit against the city?

The Querent had been harassed and falsely imprisoned for fortune-telling. As is often the case in these circumstances, someone in power – whether the police, or some other municipal body – decides to "clean up" – and civil rights are not considered a priority. When their legal case against her fell apart, she decided to sue for damages.

Normally, we would place a lawsuit as a 1st-7th matter. However, there is a very good reason not to do so here. There is an old adage about not fighting City Hall. The message behind the adage is clear: to beat a government in court, you have to have a case that is airtight. The government is *always* stronger than an ordinary individual. The very nature of a 1st-7th conflict is that it takes place between equals – or perhaps we should say peers. It's not so much that the two sides are necessarily equal, but that they are *comparable*. How does an individual compare with a government? Not very well!

Because of disparity between the two sides, I opt to interpret this as a castle besiegement, like the Microsoft case in Example 49. Recall that the castle besiegement is viewed not as a 1st-7th matter, but as a 1st-4th. Cases against the government are almost inevitably castle besiegements. This may seem strange, given the association of the government with the 10th, but remember: the 4th House is the land, and governments are intimately associated with sovereignty over, if not outright ownership, of land. In a castle

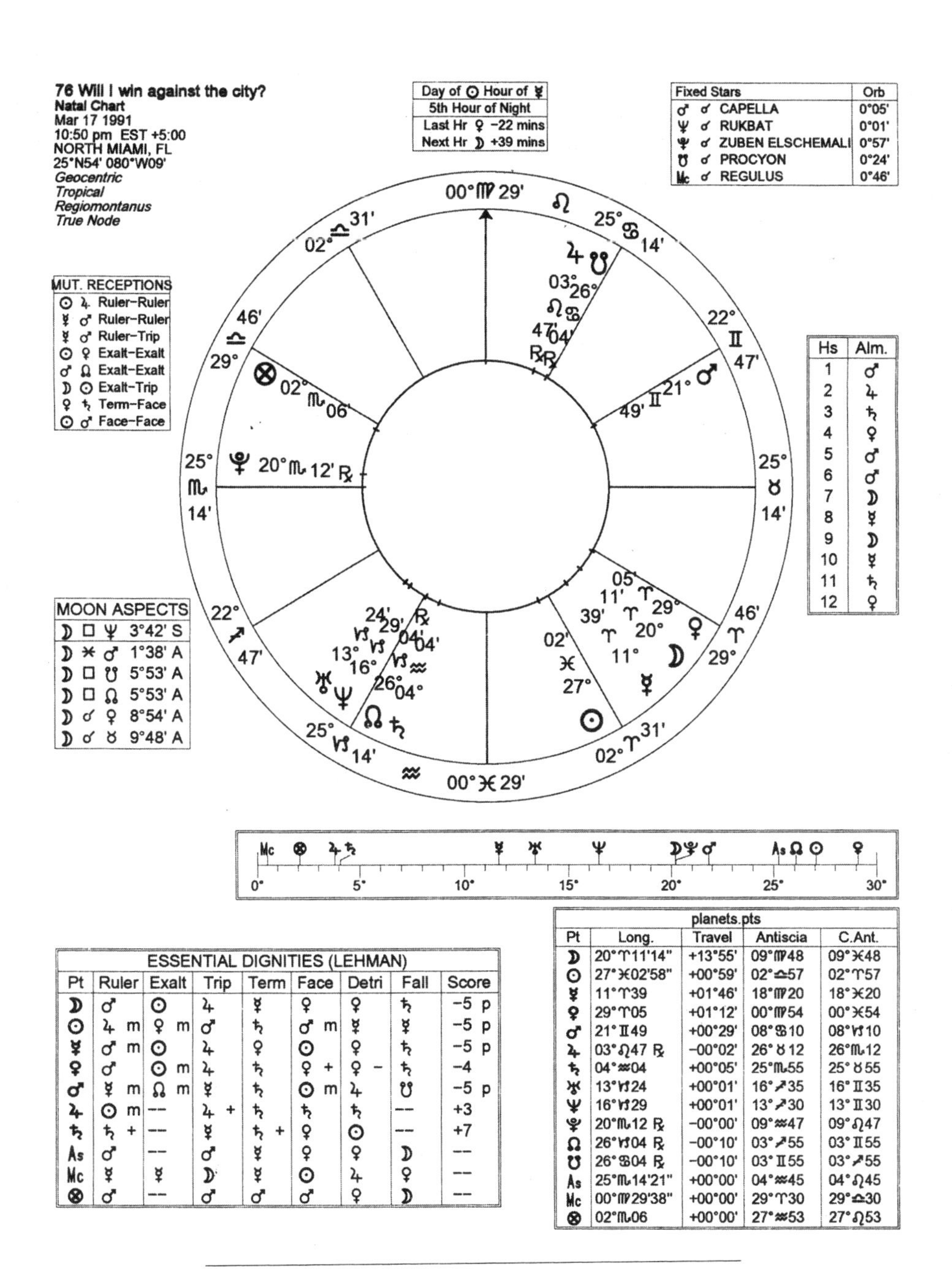

Fixed Stars	Orb
♂ ☌ CAPELLA	0°05'
♆ ☌ RUKBAT	0°01'
♇ ☌ ZUBEN ELSCHEMALI	0°57'
☋ ☌ PROCYON	0°24'
Mc ☌ REGULUS	0°46'

MUT. RECEPTIONS
☉ ♃ Ruler-Ruler
☿ ♂ Ruler-Ruler
☿ ♂ Ruler-Trip
☉ ♀ Exalt-Exalt
♂ ☊ Exalt-Exalt
☽ ☉ Exalt-Trip
♀ ♄ Term-Face
☉ ♂ Face-Face

Hs	Alm.
1	♂
2	♃
3	♄
4	♀
5	♂
6	♂
7	☽
8	☿
9	☽
10	☿
11	♄
12	♀

MOON ASPECTS
☽ □ ♆ 3°42' S
☽ ⚹ ♂ 1°38' A
☽ □ ☋ 5°53' A
☽ □ ☊ 5°53' A
☽ ☌ ♀ 8°54' A
☽ ☌ ♉ 9°48' A

ESSENTIAL DIGNITIES (LEHMAN)								
Pt	Ruler	Exalt	Trip	Term	Face	Detri	Fall	Score
☽	♂	☉	♃	☿	♀	♀	♄	−5 p
☉	♃ m	♀ m	♂	♄	♂ m	☿	☿	−5 p
☿	♂ m	☉	♃	♀	☉	♀	♄	−5 p
♀	♂	☉ m	♃	♄	♀ +	♀ −	♄	−4
♂	☿ m	☊ m	☿	♄	☉ m	♃	☋	−5 p
♃	☉ m	--	♃ +	♄	♄	♄	--	+3
♄	♄ +	--	☿	♄ +	♀	☉	--	+7
As	♂	--	♂	☿	♀	♀	☽	--
Mc	☿	☿	☽	☿	☉	♃	♀	--
⊗	♂	--	♂	♂	♂	♀	☽	--

planets.pts				
Pt	Long.	Travel	Antiscia	C.Ant.
☽	20°♈11'14"	+13°55'	09°♍48	09°♓48
☉	27°♓02'58"	+00°59'	02°♎57	02°♈57
☿	11°♈39	+01°46'	18°♍20	18°♓20
♀	29°♈05	+01°12'	00°♍54	00°♓54
♂	21°♊49	+00°29'	08°♋10	08°♑10
♃	03°♌47 ℞	−00°02'	26°♉12	26°♏12
♄	04°♒04	+00°05'	25°♏55	25°♉55
♅	13°♑24	+00°01'	16°♐35	16°♊35
♆	16°♑29	+00°01'	13°♐30	13°♊30
♇	20°♏12 ℞	−00°00'	09°♒47	09°♌47
☊	26°♑04 ℞	−00°10'	03°♐55	03°♊55
☋	26°♋04 ℞	−00°10'	03°♊55	03°♐55
As	25°♏14'21"	+00°00'	04°♒45	04°♌45
Mc	00°♍29'38"	+00°00'	29°♈30	29°♎30
⊗	02°♏06	+00°00'	27°♒53	27°♌53

---

besiegement delineation, the party considered in the advantageous position going into the trial is the 4th. This is for an event. In Horary, generally the challenging side asks the question, because the besieged party is usually not as worried! Remember that the challenger has to be significantly stronger than the besieged party in order to win. If there is anything approaching parity, then the 4th House party prevails.

In this case, our Querent is given by a peregrine Mars in Gemini. This is not a good start, although Mars as her ruler correctly reflects her rage at how she was treated. The city is shown through Jupiter, Ruler of the 4th House. Jupiter, while retrograde, still has Triplicity. The effect of the retrogradation is effectively eliminated because Saturn renders his virtue to Jupiter. Already we can see that this chart is not favoring the Querent.

But there's more. In a lawsuit or other legal action, the 2nd House represents the 1st House party's lawyers. So here the 2nd House gives the Querent's lawyers. Due to a specific component of besiegement delineation, the castle's lawyer(s) are not the 5th as you might think, but the 7th – the army of the 4th. Here we see Venus as the city's lawyers – in bad shape, but about to become very dignified. Contrast this with Jupiter, the Querent's lawyer. We already saw that Jupiter rules the city, so what does this little twist mean? It means that there is a danger that her lawyer is "bought off" by the City! They are closely linked; they are one. It may not be something so obvious as a bribe, but the same ruler does suggest some level of collusion.

One more practical consideration. One of the things that Bernadette and I noticed in looking at multiple sports is how useless Mercury and Jupiter truly are as Significators of combatants. Jupiter and Mercury simply are not fighters. They can get very involved in technique (Mercury) or strategy (Jupiter), but neither maintains its focus on the object of the game, namely to *win*. Put this into any conflict, and the side(s) represented by these planets will not be willing to do everything necessary to win.

The Moon doesn't help the situation either: it's peregrine and at the Bendings.

In this question, it looks like her lawyer lacked the stamina to pursue the case. As it turned out, the lawsuit fizzled, and she never got a satisfactory settlement for her discomfiture, even though it was obvious to all that the police had overstepped its authority.

Profession or Trade

The conundrum presented by the attribution – in both horary and natal – of profession or trade to the 10th House is this: very few professions or trades are actually 10th House in nature. They are not positions of leadership and command. What is command? For a start, it's setting your own personal working hours and making decisions without being second-guessed by a committee. While one accrues honor and dignity most directly through whatever one does for a living, unless there is true autonomy, the job itself isn't a 10th House matter.

Lilly's principal method is to examine the following points:

- The Ascendant and the Ruler of the Ascendant
- The 10th House cusp and the Ruler of the 10th House
- The sign of Mars
- The sign of Venus

From these components, look for a preponderance in one sign, or if there isn't a strong trend, pick whichever of the components is the strongest by dignity and angularity. Here's a table of typical careers by sign.[195] Obviously, we need to add a few newer professions to this list!

Sign	Lilly's Trades
Aries	Cart- or coach-maker, shepherd, cattle driver, groom, farrier (shoer of horses), butcher, brick maker, smith
Taurus	Husbandry, tree-planting, all things agricultural or with large animals, soap-maker, cloth manufacturer, and other manufacture for women
Gemini	Clerk, arithmetician (astrologer), rent collector, surveyor, astronomer, astrologer
Cancer	Fishermen, water fowl, or seamen
Leo	Servant, use of fire or hot things, huntsman, rider, coachman, smith, watchmaker, glassmaker
Virgo	Secretary (administrative assistant), schoolmaster, accountant, stationer, printer, politician, astrologer, diviner
Libra	Poet, orator, singer, musician, silk manufacturer, linen draper, go between
Scorpio	Surgeon, druggist, physician, brass worker, brewer, vintner, waterman, maltster
Sagittarius	Buying and selling cattle, chemist, churchman, cook, or baker
Capricorn	Shopkeeper, farrier, jeweler, farmer, woolen dealer, commodity trader, husbandry
Aquarius	Ship carpenter, other ship construction and repair, sailor, merchant
Pisces	Jester, singer, gambler, brewer, fishmonger

Example 77: The business deal: Good or bad?

The Querent asked about a business deal that he was setting up with a partner: the partner has the money, while the Querent was doing the work. Notice that he didn't ask about the quality of the partnership itself, which would have been a 7th House question.

I was struck by the 19 degrees Scorpio rising: the so-called "cursed degree of the cursed sign."[196] I felt that he was already starting in a hole as a result. He was given by peregrine Mars in the 8th: he was completely dependent on his partner's money. His partner is given by Venus, ruler of the 7th. With the slow Venus having dignity only by Term, the partner isn't shown as being in the best shape either.

Both the men are described by double-bodied signs, so I described the situation as being in flux.

Ultimately, however, the 2nd House gives the quality of the deal from the standpoint of the Querent's bottom line. Jupiter rules the 2nd, which is generally fortunate, but Jupiter is in Exile in Capricorn. Furthermore, Jupiter is retrograde, and at the Bendings. And the Moon, while past the opposition to Jupiter, is also at the Bendings. This position square the Nodes is a critical

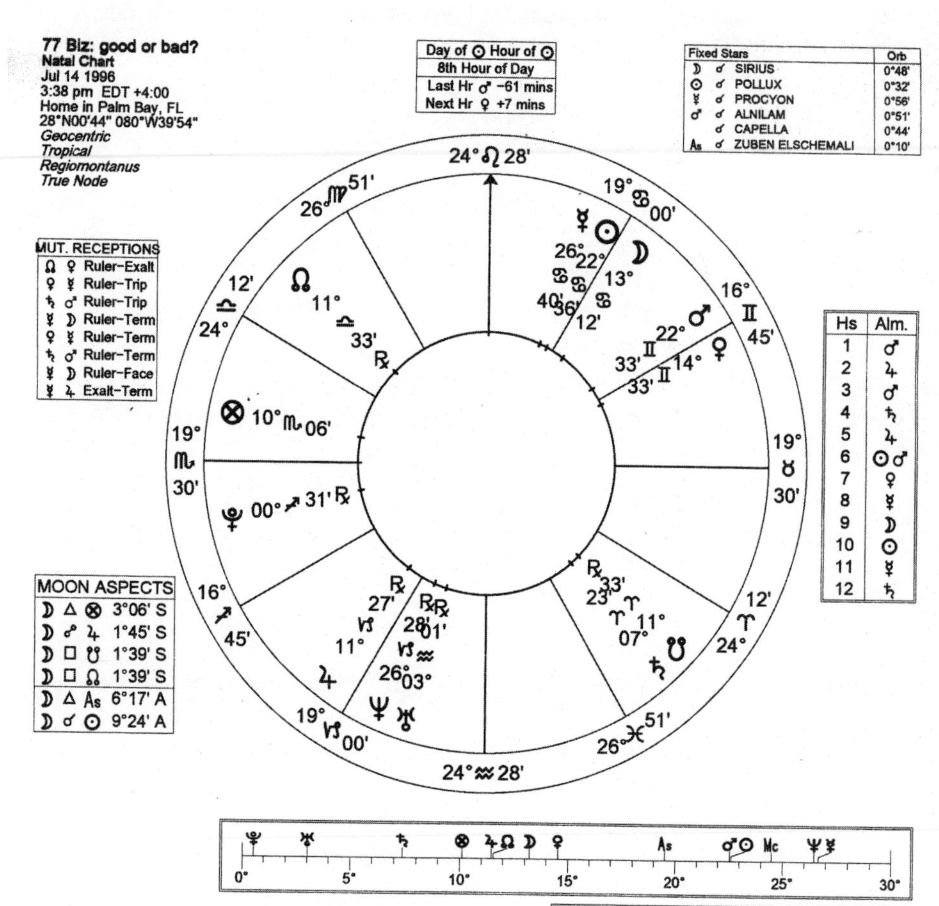

ESSENTIAL DIGNITIES (LEHMAN)								
Pt	Ruler	Exalt	Trip	Term	Face	Detri	Fall	Score
☽	☽ +	♃	♀	☿	☿ m	♄	♂	+5
☉	☽	♃	♀	♀	☽	♄	♂	-5 p
☿	☽	♃	♀	♀	☽ m	♄	♂	-5 p
♀	☿	☊	♄	♀ +	♂	♃	☋	+2
♂	☿	☊	♄	♄	☉	♃	☋	-5 p
♃	♄	♂	♀	☿	♂	☽	♃ -	-9 p
♄	♂	☉	☉	♀	♂	♀	♄ -	-9 p
As	♂	--	♀	♀	☉	♀	☽	--
Mc	☉	--	☉	♃	♂	♄	---	--
⊗	♂	--	♀	♃	☉	♀	☽	--

planets.pts				
Pt	Long.	Travel	Antiscia	C.Ant.
☽	13°♋12'47"	+11°55'	16°♊47	16°♐47
☉	22°♋36'54"	+00°57'	07°♊23	07°♐23
☿	26°♋40	+02°06'	03°♊19	03°♐19
♀	14°♊33	+00°25'	15°♋26	15°♑26
♂	22°♊33	+00°41'	07°♋26	07°♑26
♃	11°♑27 ℞	-00°07'	18°♐32	18°♊32
♄	07°♈23	+00°00'	22°♍36	22°♓36
♅	03°♒01 ℞	-00°02'	26°♏58	26°♉58
♆	26°♑28 ℞	-00°01'	03°♐31	03°♊31
♇	00°♐31 ℞	-00°00'	29°♑28	29°♋28
☊	11°♎33 ℞	-00°13'	18°♓26	18°♍26
☋	11°♈33 ℞	-00°13'	18°♍26	18°♓26
As	19°♏30'31"	+00°00'	10°♒29	10°♌29
Mc	24°♌28'50"	+00°00'	05°♉31	05°♏31
⊗	10°♏06	+00°00'	19°♒53	19°♌53

placement: any Significator located here is not likely to be fortunate.

The appropriateness of the business deal may be shown from an analysis using Lilly's method for determining the career. Here is the break-out

10th House cusp	Leo
Ruler of the 10th	Cancer
Mars	Gemini
Venus	Gemini
1st House cusp	Scorpio
Ruler of 1st House cusp	Gemini

Gemini clearly wins. So is this deal a Gemini business? I didn't know at first what the business was: it turned out that it was selling pornographic videotapes! This is not usually the image that the Gemini predominance brings to mind! But it does sound like Scorpio ruling the privy parts on the Ascendant, not to mention Fortuna also in Scorpio! This therefore becomes an argument that this business was not really a very good idea. Neither is the fact that the antiscion of the Part of Fortune is square the Ascendant.

As a result, I told him that, while he would make some money at the deal, it wouldn't be as much as he had hoped for. Furthermore, with a fixed sign rising, I warned him that it might be difficult to back out of the business once it did get started. I encouraged him to consider other options, stating that this question did not support the idea of putting all his eggs in this particular basket.

This turned out to be the case. He went ahead with the deal and discovered that it was a lot of work for minimal profit.

Example 78: Will I go to X Airlines?

The Querent is a pilot, and he is ruled by the Moon, which is peregrine and in Fall in Scorpio. While not Void-of-Course, her only remaining aspects are to Uranus and Neptune. Granted, these are both relevant in the context of flight and aviation in general. However, the 10th House rules the job itself. The interesting thing about being a pilot is that, while you are in the air, you are a 10th House Captain; while you are on the ground, you are a 6th House employee. Pilots definitely think of themselves in their 10th House capacity! The Almuten of the 10th is the Sun, in a mutual reception with Mars, the sign ruler of the 10th, by Sign-Triplicity. I would not consider this enough to mitigate the peregrine condition of either planet. Since Mars is retrograde, we would use the Sun as 10th House Ruler.

The job is weak. There is no perfection anyway, except an out-of-sign aspect of the Moon to square the Sun. Given the fact that the only dignity the Moon gains by going into Sagittarius is that she ceases to be in Fall, that's not very much. Also the presumptive perfection is by square: success with difficulty.

One might think that the Part of Fortune in a partile conjunction to the MC would be a strong argument in favor of him getting the job. Remember, however, that the condition of Fortuna is given by the strength of its dispositors.

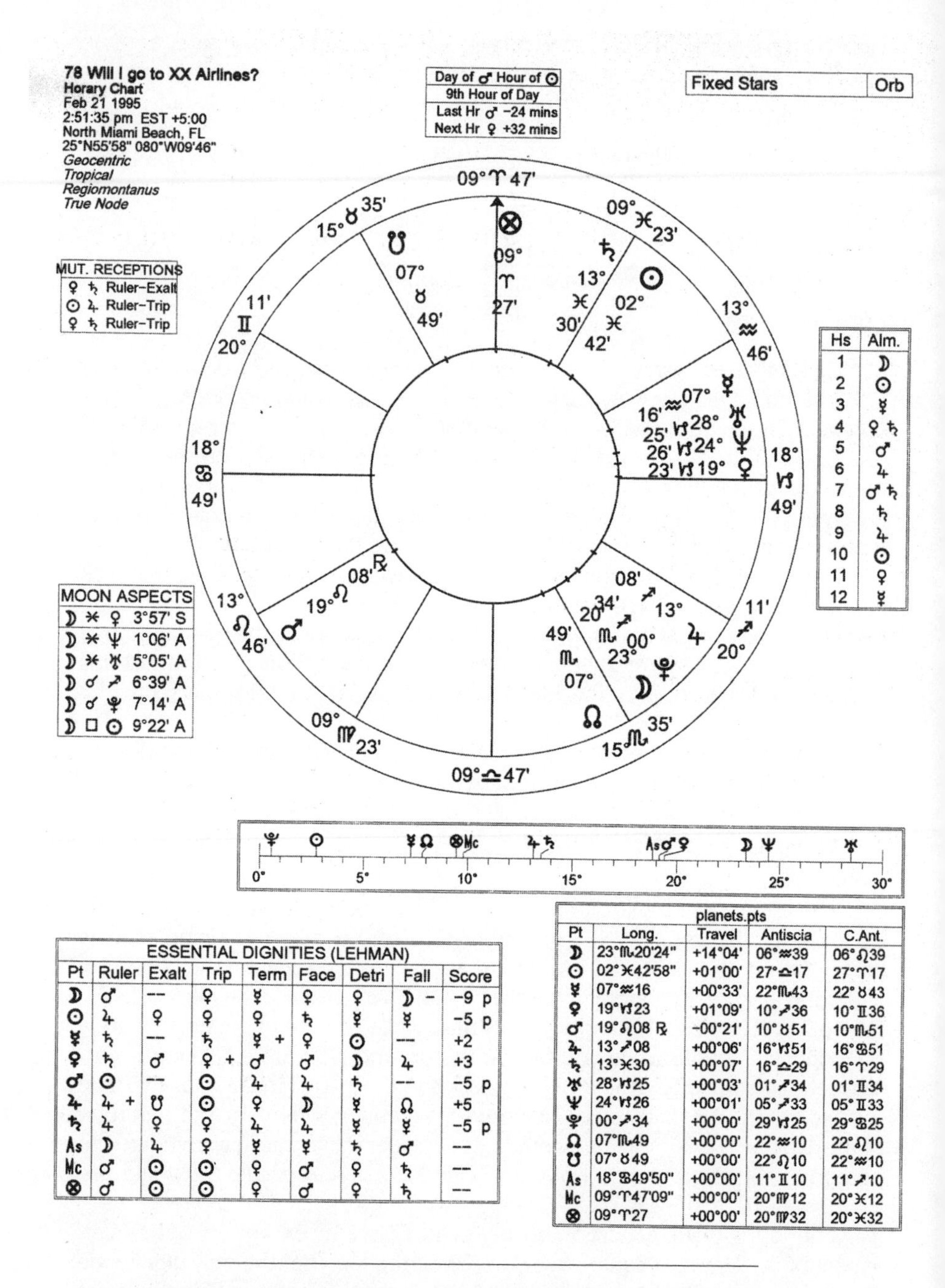

ESSENTIAL DIGNITIES (LEHMAN)								
Pt	Ruler	Exalt	Trip	Term	Face	Detri	Fall	Score
☽	♂	---	♀	☿	♀	♀	☽ −	−9 p
☉	♃	♀	♀	♀	♄	☿	☿	−5 p
☿	♄	---	♄	☿ +	♀	☉	---	+2
♀	♄	♂	♀ +	♂	♂	☽	♃	+3
♂	☉	---	☉	♃	♃	♄	---	−5 p
♃	♃ +	☋	☉	♀	☽	☿	☊	+5
♄	♃	♀	♀	♃	♃	☿	☿	−5 p
As	☽	♃	♀	☿	☿	♄	♂	---
Mc	♂	☉	☉	♀	♂	♀	♄	---
⊗	♂	☉	☉	♀	♂	♀	♄	---

planets.pts				
Pt	Long.	Travel	Antiscia	C.Ant.
☽	23°♏20'24"	+14°04'	06°♒39	06°♌39
☉	02°♓42'58"	+01°00'	27°♎17	27°♈17
☿	07°♒16	+00°33'	22°♏43	22°♉43
♀	19°♑23	+01°09'	10°♐36	10°♊36
♂	19°♌08 ℞	−00°21'	10°♉51	10°♏51
♃	13°♐08	+00°06'	16°♑51	16°♋51
♄	13°♓30	+00°07'	16°♎29	16°♈29
♅	28°♑25	+00°03'	01°♐34	01°♊34
♆	24°♑26	+00°01'	05°♐33	05°♊33
♇	00°♐34	+00°00'	29°♑25	29°♋25
☊	07°♏49	+00°00'	22°♒10	22°♌10
☋	07°♉49	+00°00'	22°♌10	22°♒10
As	18°♋49'50"	+00°00'	11°♊10	11°♐10
Mc	09°♈47'09"	+00°00'	20°♍12	20°♓12
⊗	09°♈27	+00°00'	20°♍32	20°♓32

Here, the principal dispositors are Mars and the Sun, both peregrine. So this is more the Part of *Mis*fortune than the Part of Fortune.

Given the general weakness of the Significators, I judged that the job would not be forthcoming, and if it were, that it would be too difficult a situation for the Querent to successfully pursue.

The Querent didn't get the job.

Example 79: Will my boss stay off drugs? What is my relationship with him?

This question on its surface seems like a fairly simple question. It wasn't. The reason it wasn't so simple is that the answer hinges on selecting the correct houses. Here's the problem. Our immediate tendency would be to assume that the boss is a 10th House figure. Fortunately, however, I had asked

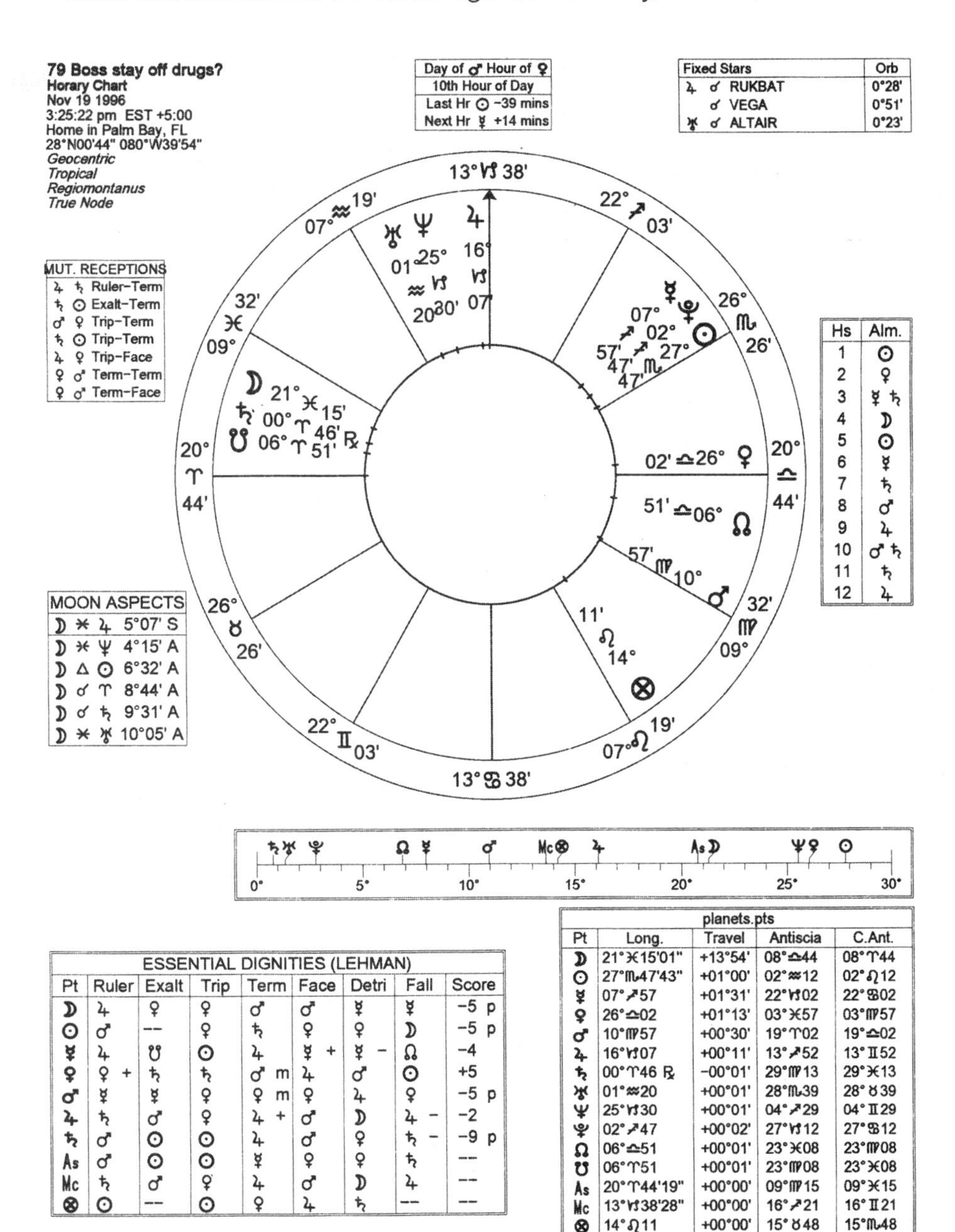

Fixed Stars		Orb
♃ ☌	RUKBAT	0°28'
☌	VEGA	0°51'
♅ ☌	ALTAIR	0°23'

MUT. RECEPTIONS
♃ ♄ Ruler−Term
♄ ☉ Exalt−Term
♂ ♀ Trip−Term
♄ ☉ Trip−Term
♃ ♀ Trip−Face
♀ ♂ Term−Term
♀ ♂ Term−Face

Hs	Alm.
1	☉
2	♀
3	☿ ♄
4	☽
5	☉
6	☿
7	♄
8	♂
9	♃
10	♂ ♄
11	♄
12	♃

MOON ASPECTS
☽ ⚹ ♃ 5°07' S
☽ ⚹ ♆ 4°15' A
☽ △ ☉ 6°32' A
☽ ☌ ♈ 8°44' A
☽ ☌ ♄ 9°31' A
☽ ⚹ ♅ 10°05' A

ESSENTIAL DIGNITIES (LEHMAN)								
Pt	Ruler	Exalt	Trip	Term	Face	Detri	Fall	Score
☽	♃	♀	♀	♂	♂	☿	☿	−5 p
☉	♂	--	♀	♄	♀	♀	☽	−5 p
☿	♃	☋	☉	♃	☿ +	☿ −	☊	−4
♀	♀ +	♄	♄	♂ m	♃	♂	☉	+5
♂	☿	☿	♀	♀ m	♀	♃	♀	−5 p
♃	♄	♂	♀	♃ +	♂	☽	♃ −	−2
♄	♂	☉	☉	♃	♂	♀	♄ −	−9 p
As	♂	☉	☉	☿	♀	♀	♄	--
Mc	♄	♂	♀	♃	♂	☽	♃	--
⊗	☉	--	☉	♀	♃	♄	--	--

planets.pts				
Pt	Long.	Travel	Antiscia	C.Ant.
☽	21°♓15'01"	+13°54'	08°♎44	08°♈44
☉	27°♏47'43"	+01°00'	02°♒12	02°♌12
☿	07°♐57	+01°31'	22°♑02	22°♋02
♀	26°♎02	+01°13'	03°♓57	03°♍57
♂	10°♍57	+00°30'	19°♈02	19°♎02
♃	16°♑07	+00°11'	13°♐52	13°♊52
♄	00°♈46 ℞	−00°01'	29°♍13	29°♓13
♅	01°♒20	+00°01'	28°♏39	28°♉39
♆	25°♑30	+00°01'	04°♐29	04°♊29
♇	02°♐47	+00°02'	27°♑12	27°♋12
☊	06°♎51	+00°01'	23°♓08	23°♍08
☋	06°♈51	+00°01'	23°♍08	23°♓08
As	20°♈44'19"	+00°00'	09°♍15	09°♓15
Mc	13°♑38'28"	+00°00'	16°♐21	16°♊21
⊗	14°♌11	+00°00'	15°♉48	15°♏48

about the nature of the business and discovered that this was a small business, and that while his "boss" was titular head, they each had a substantial investment, something like 60%-40%. As a result, they were more partners than superior-subordinate, and hence, the boss should be understood correctly as the 7th House, and so the 10th House is freed up to show their joint business venture, and the status and honor derived from it.

This chart shows the challenge of choosing between Almuten and sign Ruler. Technically, we should choose Venus to represent the boss, because Venus is dignified, while Saturn is seriously debilitated – *if* we apply our rule of using the one that has greater dignity. However, remember that there is the exception that if the Querent or Quesited is better described by a more debilitated planet, than the less dignified of the two may be selected. Does this reasoning apply, given the boss's past history of drug use? I asked the Querent how well the boss had been doing off drugs, and the answer was: pretty well. So I decided to start with Venus and see where it led me.

The boss looks very strong as Venus in Libra. He's in his own sign, in his own house. The problem is that Venus is close to the end of sign, and when she changes signs, she not only loses dignity, she gains debility. Further confirmation is given by the Moon sextiling Neptune in four degrees. Given the question about drugs, I was immediately afraid that this represented failure in his drug rehabilitation program. So I told him that the boss was likely to return to taking drugs in 4-5 weeks or months. It turned out to be months. Since Venus also rules the 2nd House, I told him that when his boss slips back into drugs, it would represent a downturn in the financial return from the company – and this also turned out to be the case.

As for his relationship with his boss, we can use either the Sun in Scorpio as Almuten of the 1st, or Mars in Virgo, as the sign Ruler of the 1st, to represent the Querent. I picked the Sun in Scorpio, because he had told me that he was feeling very depressed about his circumstances, and the Sun in Scorpio seemed to fit the description better. But the reading is no different: there is no relationship between Querent and partner. Even the Moon does not translate the light. However, with the Moon coming up to trine the Querent's ruler just two degrees later than the ingress of Venus into Scorpio, I judged that he would cut his ties to the partner about a week/month after his partner lapsed back to drugs.

The company is problematic as shown by many indicators. Saturn, Ruler of the 10th, is in the 12th House, retrograde and in Fall. Jupiter, conjunct the 10th House cusp is in Fall. Neptune and Uranus both are in the 10th House. None of this bodes well for the firm's reputation. Needless to say, the company did not survive much after the boss went back to his old ways.

As the reader can see from these examples, 10th House questions are seldom strictly 10th House. Other houses almost inevitably come into play. We will next consider one of the most common 10th House partners: the 11th. A king would rule through his councilors; a verdict may be given to a judge by a jury. Both councilors and juries are 11th House parties. But they don't even begin to exhaust the functions of the 11th House.

Chapter 11

Affairs of the 11th House: Friends, Organizations & Administrative Bodies.

Questions of the 11th House as given by Lilly:[197]

- *Of good or ill in questions concerning this House*
- *If a man shall have the thing hoped for?*
- *Of the agreeing of friends.*
- *Of the love between two [friends].*
- *Substance or riches of kings*[198]

Gadbury's list of categories of questions differs only slightly from Lilly's, emphasizing instead whether the friends of the Querent shall prove faithful.[199]

I would add two additional categories:

- Questions concerning administrative agencies of the government.
- Questions concerning legislative bodies.

One gets the impression upon arriving at the 11th House in most horary books that the author is straining to write anything at all. Lilly devotes scarcely more than two pages to the subject (compare this to 107 pages for the 7th House), with not one example. It is true: by comparison, the number of horaries relating to this house is few. However, it is not zero either, so we still need to know how to delineate this house.

It is so sad that the frequency of horaries is so low for the house the Greeks called the Good Spirit, or Daemon. But perhaps, that says it all!

Friends

I have never gotten an unequivocally 11th House question concerning friends. The reason that I refer to the issue of the 11th House type of question is that the question that I *do* get concerning friends is of the "is the rumor true" variety, where the Querent wants to know if the friend is telling the truth. Lilly's and Gadbury's methods for delineating 11th House questions are similar: if there is a benevolent aspect between the Rulers of the 1st and 11th Houses they will agree; if the Moon aspects the Ruler of the 11th, or better, translates the light between the Rulers of 1st and 11th, agreement is also favored. Hard aspects between the two Significators, or the presence of malefics in the 11th House can destroy amity. Gadbury also mentions that having the two benefics in the 1st, or in a soft aspect to the Ascendant can produce a good result, as Venus and Jupiter are the natural rulers of friendship.

Hopes and Wishes

Lilly gives two methods of delineating whether hopes and wishes will be fulfilled: and the first method is the same for whether friends shall agree: harmonious aspects between the Rulers of the 1st and 11th, or second, a harmonious disposition between the two. Reception with mutable placement gives only partial attainment. Reception with cardinal signs, cadent houses, combustion, peregrine, or retrogradation, denies the matter according to Gadbury.[200]

Organizations and Administrative Bodies

The ideas for the rest of the 11th House matters, as well as what should now be horary common sense, can combine to tell us how to interpret charts of this type, even if explicit methods were not given in the classical texts. However, we should spend a moment thinking about why we might want to assign organizations in general to the 11th House, since that is a bit of a stretch over classical definition, which was silent on the topic.

Organizations are administrative bodies. They may also be understood through the old concept of fellowship: a space in which like-minded people may meet. Like-minded about *something*, at any rate! The fellowship idea is what brings us to the 11th House. In fact, many organizational members forge strong friendships through these organizations. And unfortunately, all too often, organizational boards of directors begin acting far more like friendship circles than business people gathered together to make the right decisions!

Example 80: Will there be another UAC?

UAC is the acronym for the United Astrology Congress, a corporation formed to hold the first tri-annual conference in 1986. UAC was formed as an independent body to run a conference cosponsored by three astrological organizations in the USA. As such, it was always a nexus for political maneuvering between the co-sponsors, as this was the only venue in which the three organizations worked together.

The question was asked by one of the UAC committee members prior to the very successful conference in Monterey, California, in April 1995. By this time – this was to be the fourth UAC – there was talk about whether UAC could continue to innovate, and whether its purpose had not already been fulfilled. It

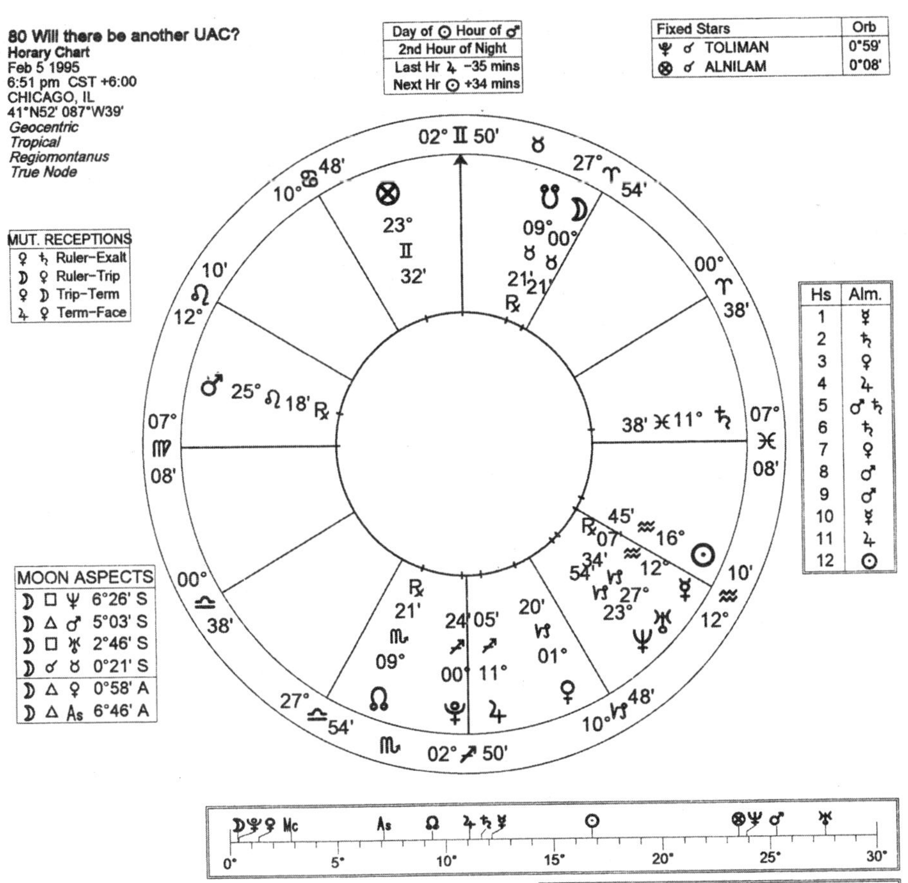

ESSENTIAL DIGNITIES (LEHMAN)								
Pt	Ruler	Exalt	Trip	Term	Face	Detri	Fall	Score
☽	♀	☽ +	☽ +	♀	☿	♂	---	+7
☉	♄	---	☿	♀	☿	☉ –	---	−10 p
☿	♄	---	☿ +	♀	☿ +	☉	---	+4
♀	♄	♂	☽	♀ +	♃	☽	♃	+2
♂	☉	---	♃	♂ +	♂ +	♄	---	+3
♃	♃ +	☋	♃ +	♀	☽	☿	☊	+8
♄	♃	♀	♂	♃	♃	☿	☿	−5 p
As	☿	☿	☽	♀	☉	♃	♀	---
Mc	☿	☊	☿	☿	♃	♃	☋	---
⊗	☿	☊	☿	♄	☉	♃	☋	---

planets.pts				
Pt	Long.	Travel	Antiscia	C.Ant.
☽	00°♉21'23"	+12°04'	29°♌38	29°♒38
☉	16°♒45'33"	+01°00'	13°♏14	13°♉14
☿	12°♒07 ℞	−01°11'	17°♏52	17°♉52
♀	01°♑20	+01°07'	28°♐39	28°♊39
♂	25°♌18 ℞	−00°23'	04°♉41	04°♏41
♃	11°♐05	+00°08'	18°♑54	18°♋54
♄	11°♓38	+00°06'	18°♎21	18°♈21
♅	27°♑34	+00°03'	02°♐25	02°♊25
♆	23°♑54	+00°02'	06°♐05	06°♊05
♇	00°♐24	+00°00'	29°♑35	29°♋35
☊	09°♏21 ℞	−00°00'	20°♒38	20°♌38
☋	09°♉21 ℞	−00°00'	20°♌38	20°♒38
As	07°♍08'19"	+00°00'	22°♈51	22°♎51
Mc	02°♊50'48"	+00°00'	27°♋09	27°♑09
⊗	23°♊32	+00°00'	06°♋27	06°♑27

was in the spirit of these questions that this horary was asked. Conferences seem like an especially 11th House outlet for organizations: a social and learning event, and a time for catching up with your friends.

It's worthwhile to stop for a moment and consider how we might want to delineate this chart. The Querent who is asking the question has a vested interest in the result but whether or not there is another UAC is not directly in her control. Furthermore, there is no guarantee that she would be involved in the next one. As a result, there is no necessity for perfection between 1st and 11th. In effect, this chart reads almost exclusively through the 11th House itself.

The Virgo Rising is rather amusing in this chart, because historically, UAC always had a large cadre of Virgos working for it. In this case we see Mercury at the Bendings, and retrograde in Aquarius, dignified by Triplicity and Face, although the latter is probably not very important. The organization is given by the Moon in Taurus, Ruler of the 11th House.

The Moon in Taurus says it all. This is a Moon that is going to barrel through any obstacle to get what it wants. It's also too stubborn to quit! However, look at its aspects. After an initial trine to Venus, the Moon encounters a whole series of squares before ending up with trines to Uranus and Neptune, planets you maybe wouldn't want involved at all. And the Moon is at Zero degrees! How do we read this?

There's no way the next UAC wouldn't happen. That Moon is too persistent! But the early Moon shows a change in leadership, an initial honeymoon period, and then severe roadblocks and obstacles, but ultimately a successful conference because despite it all, the Moon is exalted.

And that is what happened. The internal politics were more severe for this conference than any previous one, eventually resulting in UAC, Inc. dissolving itself as a corporation – *after* a very large and successful conference in 1998.

Example 81: Will I get the grant?

The grant that the Querent inquired about is an Artists' grant, given by the Commonwealth of Pennsylvania. He had received it in a prior year. He had not yet sent in the application when he asked the question.

The Querent is represented by the Scorpio Ascendant and potentially the Moon, since it's in the 1st House. For the grant, we could use:

- Eighth House, other people's money, or

- Eleventh House, the treasury of the government, or counselors (agents of the government).

This dual nature is important, because the government agency must approve the Querent in order for him to receive the grant, and there are probably several rounds before money even comes into the question. Venus, the eleventh House ruler, is in fall, though dignified by Triplicity and reception by Face. The granting agents are downcast, feeling themselves to be in exile, probably with diminished funds, downhearted. However, the Almuten of the eleventh House is Saturn. Saturn in Capricorn has dignity, but probably represents a

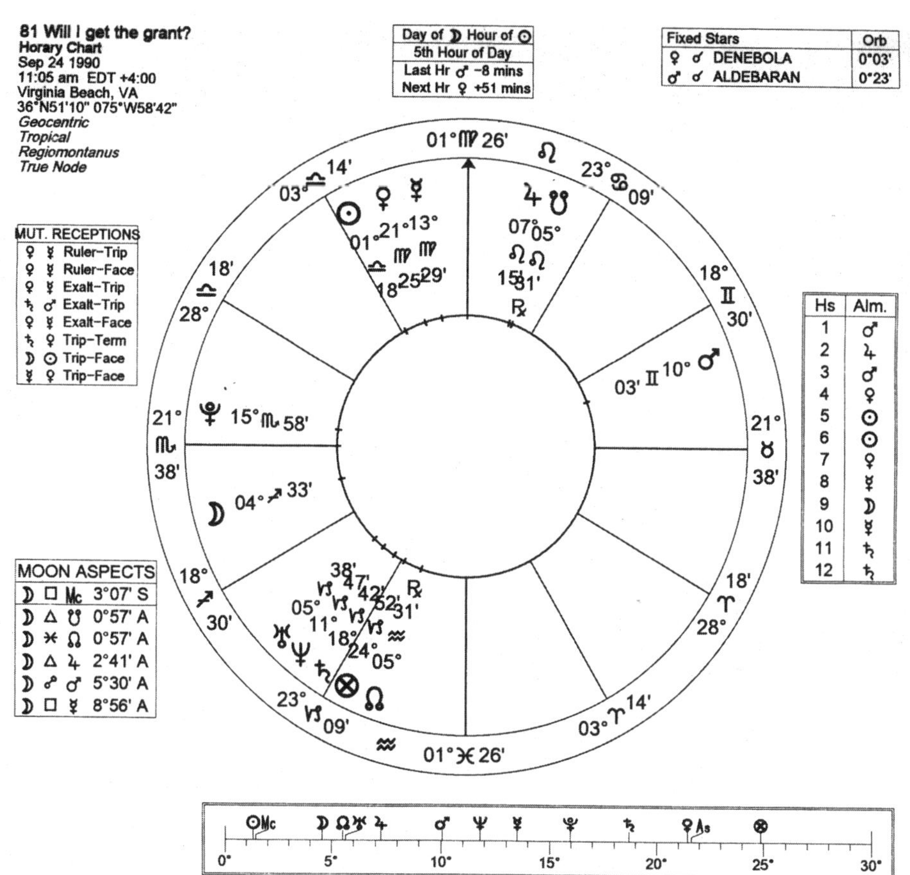

Pt	Ruler	Exalt	Trip	Term	Face	Detri	Fall	Score
ESSENTIAL DIGNITIES (LEHMAN)								
☽	♃	☋	☉	♃	☿	☿	☊	−5 p
☉	♀	♄	♄	♄	☽	♂	☉ −	−9 p
☿	☿ +	☿ +	♀	♃ m	♀ m	♃	♀	+9
♀	☿	☿	♀ +	♄	☿ m	♃	♀ −	−1
♂	☿	☊	♄	♃	♂ +	♃	☋	+1
♃	☉	--	☉	☿ m	♄	♄	--	−5 p
♄	♄ +	♂	♀	♃	♂	☽	♃	+5
As	♂	--	♀	☿	♀	♀	☽	--
Mc	☿	☿	♀	☿	☉	♃	♀	--
⊗	♄	♂	♀	♂	☉	☽	♃	--

Pt	Long.	Travel	Antiscia	C.Ant.
planets.pts				
☽	04°♐33'25"	+11°51'	25°♑26	25°♋26
☉	01°♎18'43"	+00°58'	28°♓41	28°♍41
☿	13°♍29	+01°02'	16°♈30	16°♎30
♀	21°♍25	+01°14'	08°♈34	08°♎34
♂	10°♊03	+00°19'	19°♋56	19°♑56
♃	07°♌15	+00°10'	22°♉44	22°♏44
♄	18°♑42	+00°00'	11°♐17	11°♊17
♅	05°♑38	+00°00'	24°♐21	24°♊21
♆	11°♑47	+00°00'	18°♐12	18°♊12
♇	15°♏58	+00°01'	14°♒01	14°♌01
☊	05°♒31 ℞	−00°04'	24°♏28	24°♉28
☋	05°♌31 ℞	−00°04'	24°♉28	24°♏28
As	21°♏38'06"	+00°00'	08°♒21	08°♌21
Mc	01°♍26'00"	+00°00'	28°♈33	28°♎33
⊗	24°♑52	+00°00'	05°♐07	05°♊07

more conservative approach to art than had been present previously. Saturn has just gone direct, so there's a different outlook concerning the grants than that which was in place previously. The government itself, Mercury-ruled, is sitting pretty, with Mercury in Virgo, in its own sign and exaltation and mutual reception by Face. Unfortunately we have no way to distinguish which of these two planets, Saturn or Venus, more correctly describes the agency. The government feels good, but the money's not there, at least as much as before, and the government staff feels disheartened. Both Venus (the grant) and Mercury (the government) are past the square to Mars (the Querent): they are moving away from him.

There are two translations here. The Moon translates the light between Mars (the Querent) and Venus (grant?)/Mercury (government), but the aspects are by opposition and square respectively, and the Moon is peregrine. Mercury translates the light between Mars and Venus. No perfection is given by Mars to Saturn, except through reception. But even there, Saturn has all the power. The grant, if obtained at all, will require increased effort on the Querent's part. Notice that whether we choose Venus or Saturn for the grant, the result is the same.

When I discussed this judgment with the Querent, he added some information. The grants are given following peer judgment of quality. He did confirm that, pursuant to the Venus in Fall situation vis-à-vis the state's finances, that few grants were being given that year, although they were supposed to be for more money than he received the previous year, but less than they were advertising.

Since it is a contest, I looked at the seventh House of open enemies. Venus rules the seventh House. Though Venus is in Fall, note the trine of both Venus and the seventh House cusp to Fortuna. I had not considered this in the original reading because I did not see how good fortune for the government's money had anything to do with the Querent. But with Mars, his ruler, located in the seventh House, his open enemies would have the upper hand. He told me that in light of Senator Jesse Helms's hearings on art and pornography, a friend had suggested that he submit poems having to do either with the Earth or with women in a nonsexual way. I observed that the ruler of the seventh House was Venus in Virgo bringing together those two themes. With the addition of the trines to Fortuna, I believed that his enemies, the other contestants, would be triumphant. The 7th and 11th share a Ruler; thus, the 7th House party has considerable advantage.

The Querent wrote me several months later to tell me that he had been turned down for the grant.

Example 82: Will they have to cancel the conference?

I asked this horary a few weeks prior to an astrological conference. The advance registration was terrible, and what I really wanted to know was whether I should go ahead and pay for the airfare, which would be superfluous if the conference didn't happen.

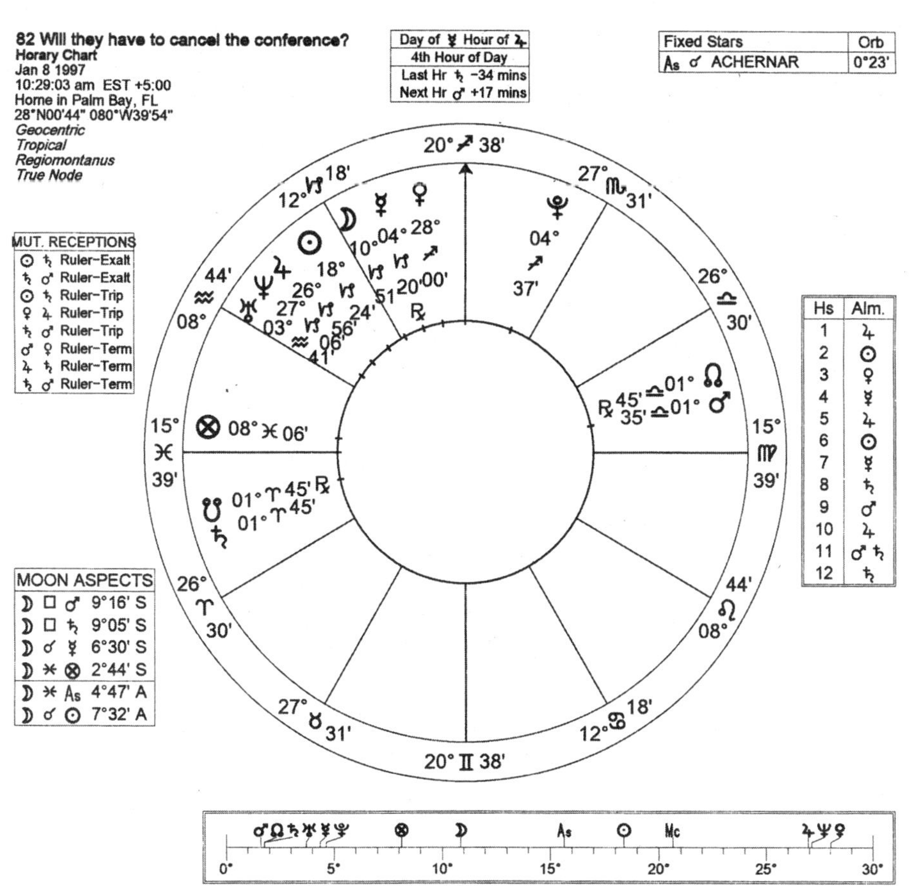

ESSENTIAL DIGNITIES (LEHMAN)								
Pt	Ruler	Exalt	Trip	Term	Face	Detri	Fall	Score
☽	♄	♂	♀	☿	♂ m	☽ −	♃	−10 p
☉	♄	♂	♀ m	♃	♂	☽	♃	−5 p
☿	♄	♂	♀	♀	♃	☽	♃	−5 p
♀	♃	☋	☉ m	♂	♄	☿	☊	−5 p
♂	♀	♄	♄	♄	☽ m	♂ −	☉	−10 p
♃	♄	♂	♀	♄ m	☉	☽	♃ −	−9 p
♄	♂	☉	☉	♃ m	♂	♀	♄ −	−9 p
As	♃	♀	♀	☿	♃	☿	☿	--
Mc	♃	☋	☉	♄	♄	☿	☊	--
⊗	♃	♀	♀	♃	♄	☿	☿	--

planets.pts				
Pt	Long.	Travel	Antiscia	C.Ant.
☽	10°♑51'44"	+14°56'	19°♐08	19°♊08
☉	18°♑24'07"	+01°01'	11°♐35	11°♊35
☿	04°♑20 ℞	−00°40'	25°♐39	25°♊39
♀	28°♐00	+01°15'	01°♑59	01°♋59
♂	01°♎35	+00°16'	28°♓24	28°♍24
♃	26°♑56	+00°14'	03°♐03	03°♊03
♄	01°♈45	+00°03'	28°♍14	28°♓14
♅	03°♒41	+00°03'	26°♏18	26°♉18
♆	27°♑06	+00°02'	02°♐53	02°♊53
♇	04°♐37	+00°01'	25°♑22	25°♋22
☊	01°♎45 ℞	−00°11'	28°♓14	28°♍14
☋	01°♈45 ℞	−00°11'	28°♍14	28°♓14
As	15°♓39'22"	+00°00'	14°♎20	14°♈20
Mc	20°♐38'29"	+00°00'	09°♑21	09°♋21
⊗	08°♓06	+00°00'	21°♎53	21°♈53

My Significator Jupiter is in the 11th House conjunct Neptune. Furthermore, Saturn is partile, exactly conjunct the South Node in the 1st House. If I were reading this for a client, I would probably refuse! Either of the above could indicate that the Querent was lying, but I am lying to myself? In a way, I was, because I assumed that if the conference was going to be too small, that it would make better fiscal sense to cancel it than to go ahead with it!

Here, we can clearly see that the conference is a failure: Saturn, the 11th House ruler is conjunct the South Node, so the conference is destroyed. And this is precisely what happened: attendance was way beneath the break-even point. However, the aggressive Saturn in Aries, in a partile opposition to the other malefic, Mars, shows the complete unwillingness to do the right thing, which would be to cancel the conference. This belligerency was reflected in the Board of Directors of the organization, which at the time was in a severe state of political factions. The hit to the organization's finances is clearly shown by Saturn ruling the 12th House: the organization's finances.

I concluded from this chart that while the organization probably *should* cancel the conference, this was not a time when cooler heads would prevail, and so they would go ahead with it. The weak reception between me and the conference probably shows that I do actually end up going to it, even with considerable ambivalence. They did go ahead and hold the conference, but attendance was as bad as projected.

Perhaps these examples of organization charts should remind us of why so few conventional horaries are asked involving the 11th House. We don't ask about our friends unless something goes wrong. We don't ask about our hopes and wishes unless we are anxious about them. The very angst which is so necessary to guarantee getting a good horary mitigates against situations in which the Querent doesn't in some way sense that something is wrong.

Bearing this rather depressing thought in mind, it's time to move on to the House that has the worse reputation of all: the 12th House!

Chapter 12

Affairs of the 12th House:

Enemies, Imprisonment & Obsessions

Questions of the 12th House as given by Lilly:[201]

- *Of secret enemies, not named*
- *Any man committed to prison, whether he shall be soon delivered*
- *Of a captive or slave*
- *If one be bewitched or not*
- *Horses, or other large cattle*

Gadbury's list of categories of questions differs only slightly from Lilly's.

Secret Enemies

Lilly's way of wording the distinction between secret and open enemies is slightly arbitrary; or perhaps we should say that he splits hairs where he doesn't need to do so. The issue of naming the enemies in the wording of the horary question is not important. While this is never explicit in the classical material, I would define a secret enemy as being the kind that one doesn't know about or anticipate, either because the enemy is not personally known to the Querent, or the enemy is masquerading as neutral or positive toward the Querent.

Lilly gives the rules for this question as being analogous to the rules for public enemies, except that the 12th House is used for the enemies instead of the 7th. Thus, look at whether the Ruler of the 12th aspects the Ruler of the Ascendant by hard aspect, or the Ruler of the 12th is in the 2nd, 4th, 6th, 8th, 10th or 12th Houses. The additional houses besides those used for open enemies include those houses that are in mundo square or non-aspect to the Ascendant.

The nature of the secret enemies is given by reading the qualities of the 12th House Ruler: its dignities, house placements, and aspects to other planets.

Strangely, I have never gotten this type of question, although it seems like a perfectly applicable type in our time!

Imprisonment

This seems to be the most popular 12th House question, in one variation or another. However, I find that the far more common question is *whether* a person will go to jail, rather than whether a prisoner shall be released. Lilly didn't give rules for whether a person would go to jail, quite possibly because, in his day, a suspected criminal already *was* in jail, and hence, many of his questions about release would involve release by judicial process.

Thus, for whether someone will go to jail or be released, I mainly look at the condition of the 12th House Ruler with respect to the 1st House Ruler, and also the condition of the Moon. Among the rules concerning release are:

- A fast Moon brings the imprisonment to conclusion faster.

- Examine the angles of the chart. Significators in feminine signs denote quicker release; masculine slower. Mutable signs may give re-imprisonment. The Rulers of the angles angular does not bode well for release. Other angular planets speak ill, but the effect is somewhat mitigated if those planets are swift of course.

Example 83. When will my son be released?

The mother asked this question. Her son was serving a long sentence for drug possession and sales. I immediately noticed the Uranus-South Node partile conjunction at the son's 1st House (the radical 5th). Uranus by itself might give a sudden release, but not with the South Node there! I was also struck that the Widow's Star, Vindemiatrix, was Rising (in zodiacal coordinates, not in actual azimuth). While this is her son and not her husband, the same image of a woman alone, and in mourning, seems appropriate to her situation.

The son's 12th House is the radical 4th, and here is Neptune. He's imprisoned for drug violations, and most modern astrologers would feel totally comfortable assigning Neptune to this duty!

This question falls into Lilly's category, "If a Question be asked for a captive or prisoner;" i.e., on the prisoner's behalf. Lilly certainly recognized that the prisoner was seldom in a position to pop the horary question. The rules are:

- See if the Ruler of the Ascendant and the Ruler of the 4th are separating from each other; if so, then the release is quick. **Here Venus and Saturn are approaching a sextile, which does not bode well for quick release. Here we have to stop and think about what to do when one planet, in this case, Saturn, is a possible Co-Almuten for each cusp. We can sort this out two ways. For the Ascendant, given the choice of Venus or Saturn,**

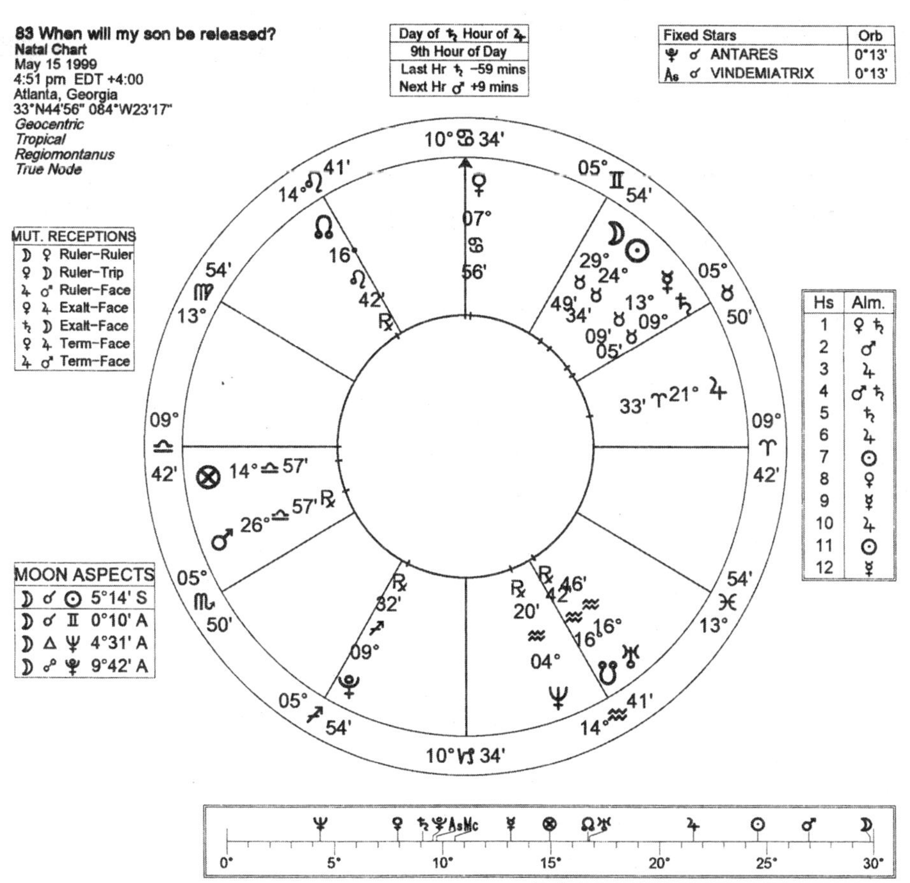

ESSENTIAL DIGNITIES (LEHMAN)								
Pt	Ruler	Exalt	Trip	Term	Face	Detri	Fall	Score
☽	♀ m	☽ +	♀	♂	♄	♂	--	+4
☉	♀	☽	♀	♄	♄	♂	--	-5 p
☿	♀	☽	♀	☿ +	☽	♂	--	+2
♀	☽ m	♃	♀ +	♃	♀ +	♄	♂	+4
♂	♀	♄	♄	♂ +	♃	♂ -	☉	-3
♃	♂	☉	☉	♂	♀	♀	♄	-5 p
♄	♀	☽	♀	☿	☿	♂	--	-5 p
As	♀	♄	♄	♀	☽	♂	☉	--
Mc	☽	♃	♀	♃	☿	♄	♂	--
⊗	♀	♄	♄	♃	♄	♂	☉	--

planets.pts				
Pt	Long.	Travel	Antiscia	C.Ant.
☽	29°♉49'39"	+15°19'	00°♌10	00°♒10
☉	24°♉34'45"	+00°57'	05°♌25	05°♒25
☿	13°♉09	+01°59'	16°♌50	16°♒50
♀	07°♋56	+01°05'	22°♊03	22°♐03
♂	26°♎57 ℞	-00°15'	03°♓02	03°♍02
♃	21°♈33	+00°13'	08°♍26	08°♓26
♄	09°♉05	+00°07'	20°♌54	20°♒54
♅	16°♒46	+00°00'	13°♏13	13°♉13
♆	04°♒20 ℞	-00°00'	25°♏39	25°♉39
♇	09°♐32 ℞	-00°01'	20°♑27	20°♋27
☊	16°♌42 ℞	-00°10'	13°♉17	13°♏17
☋	16°♒42 ℞	-00°10'	13°♏17	13°♉17
As	09°♎42'48"	+00°00'	20°♓17	20°♍17
Mc	10°♋34'27"	+00°00'	19°♊25	19°♐25
⊗	14°♎57	+00°00'	15°♓02	15°♍02

Venus is more dignified. For the 4th, in deciding between Mars and Saturn, Saturn is less debilitated. But when confronted with dual possibilities, it may just be simpler to default to the sign rulers!

- See if the Ruler of the Ascendant separates from the Sun, or if the Moon is Under Beams. Either represents escape. **The Moon is Under Beams, actually Combust, but the Ruler of the Ascendant is not separating from the Sun.**

- It is better for the Moon to be waning, descending, and applying to a Fortune, with the Ascendant and the Ruler of the Ascendant fortunate.[202] **Here the Moon is just New, descending, but applying to Saturn, but only by an out-of-sign semi-sextile, which isn't enough (Does the word desperate come to mind). The Moon is fast, however.**

I unfortunately had to tell his mother that the odds of his early release were rather slim.

Example 84. Will I go to jail?

People find themselves in strange circumstances. The Querent had been taking care of her mother-in-law, who was ill and bedridden. The older woman needed virtually around-the-clock care. After the woman died, the Querent found herself answering some very pointed questions from the police; questions that perhaps implied that they believed she could have murdered her mother-in-law. It was under these circumstances that she asked whether she would go to jail.

Here we have a choice of the Sun (as Almuten) or Mars (the sign ruler) to represent the Querent. Using our usual rule, I picked Mars. We see Mars in the 9th but conjunct the 10th House cusp, and exalted, which certainly does not indicate going to jail. Maybe to a religious retreat, but not to jail! So why am I sure that she's Mars, and not the Sun? Remember that our rule is to use the more dignified planet *unless* the circumstances warrant the reverse logic. Here, the Querent has not been arrested, but she feels that she is under some suspicion. One could argue that that sounds rather like the Sun in Scorpio – and if we followed that line of reasoning, she looks a lot guiltier. Were the Querent under arrest, then I would be more tempted to think about the Sun as descriptive.

However, two things in this chart struck me. First, Saturn was in the 1st House. Saturn in the 1st is telling me that the Querent is lying (I'd already eliminated the other interpretation of not getting paid). Oops, I thought – better check to see whether she's really guilty! The 4th House, the 10th from the 7th, gives the mother-in-law. The Moon rules the 4th, and the Moon and Mars are completely unrelated by aspect. The Moon is in a partile trine to Neptune, I assumed the mother-in-law had died of "drowning," which generally these days means a condition with fluid in the lungs, such as pneumonia.

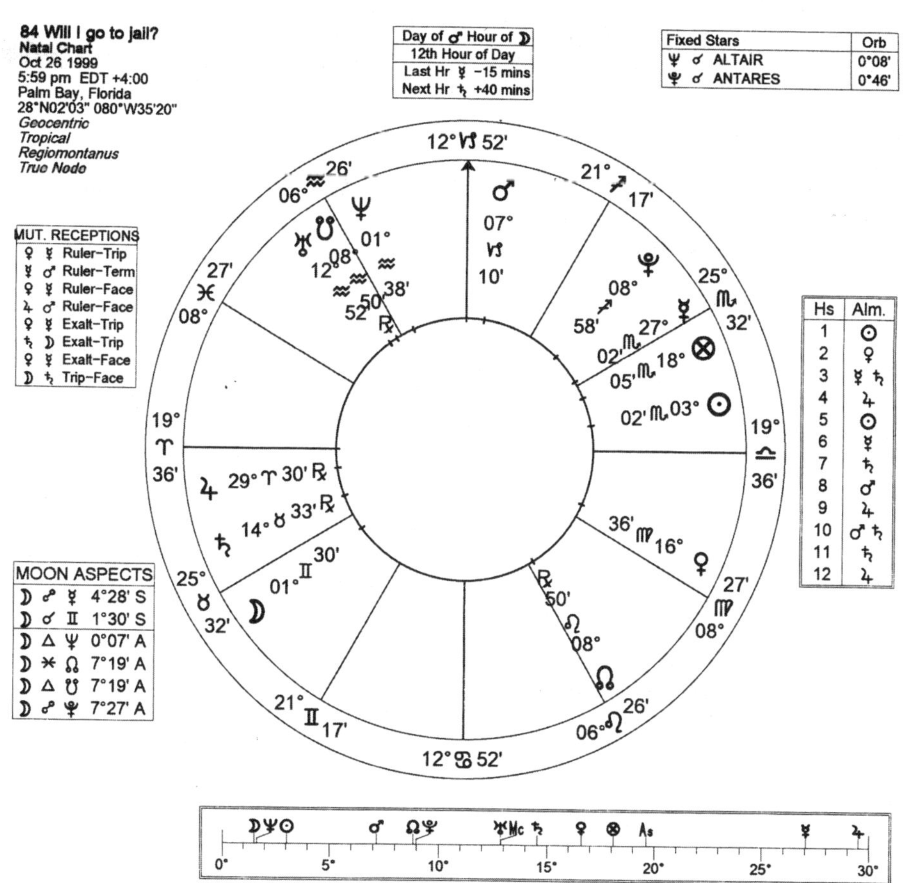

ESSENTIAL DIGNITIES (LEHMAN)								
Pt	Ruler	Exalt	Trip	Term	Face	Detri	Fall	Score
☽	☿	☊	♄	☿	♃	♃	☋	-5 p
☉	♂	--	♀	♂	♂	♀	☽	-5 p
☿	♂	--	♀	♄ m	♀	♀	☽	-5 p
♀	☿	☿	♀ +	♃	♀ +	♃	♀ –	+0
♂	♄	♂ +	♀	☿	♃	☽	♃	+4
♃	♂	☉	☉	♄	♀	♀	♄	-5 p
♄	♀	☽	♀	☿ m	☽	♂	---	-5 p
As	♂	☉	☉	☿	☉	♀	♄	--
Mc	♄	♂	♀	♃	♂	☽	♃	--
⊗	♂	--	♀	♀	☉	♀	☽	--

planets.pts				
Pt	Long.	Travel	Antiscia	C.Ant.
☽	01°♊30'58"	+14°58'	28°♋29	28°♑29
☉	03°♏02'05"	+00°59'	26°♒57	26°♌57
☿	27°♏02	+00°53'	02°♒57	02°♌57
♀	16°♍36	+00°58'	13°♈23	13°♎23
♂	07°♑10	+00°44'	22°♐49	22°♊49
♃	29°♈30 ℞	-00°08'	00°♍29	00°♓29
♄	14°♉33 ℞	-00°04'	15°♌26	15°♒26
♅	12°♒52	+00°00'	17°♏07	17°♉07
♆	01°♒38	+00°00'	28°♏21	28°♉21
♇	08°♐58	+00°01'	21°♑01	21°♋01
☊	08°♌50 ℞	-00°09'	21°♉09	21°♏09
☋	08°♒50 ℞	-00°09'	21°♏09	21°♉09
As	19°♈36'59"	+00°00'	10°♍23	10°♓23
Mc	12°♑52'42"	+00°00'	17°♐07	17°♊07
⊗	18°♏05	+00°00'	11°♒54	11°♌54

So the Querent didn't do it. So what's the missing piece of information? With Saturn as Almuten of the 7th, I speculated that maybe there was something to do with the husband – perhaps there was something that was making the police suspicious about her in the first place.

The second thing I wasn't wild about was the Ruler of the 12th in the 1st. However, Jupiter was disposed by Mars, retrograde, and only blocked from being peregrine by having out-of-sect Triplicity. Jupiter and Mars share a very weak reception by Ruler and Face. The involvement by Face tells me that what this is showing is *fear* of jail, not jail itself. As a result, I judged that this 12th House connection was more likely expressing her anxiety about imprisonment rather than the real thing.

I told her that she would not go to jail, and that there was something possibly regarding her husband that could help her situation if she could only remember it or connect to it. While I never found out about that piece of information, she didn't go to jail.

Captives and Slaves

These rules aren't commonly used anymore, but we can go back and examine them for Example 61, "Is she dead?" After all, a victim of kidnapping is surely a captive.

1. Look for a planet in the 6th or the 12th. This planet becomes the Significator of the captive. Lacking such a planet, use a planet Under Beams. **The Moon is in the 12th House, so this is our captive.**

2. Examine the planetary hour of the time of capture. A benefic as planetary hour gives a short imprisonment; a malefic a long one. **We don't have the time of capture. In the Horary, the planetary hour ruler is Mars, which should give trouble in prison and beatings, but we don't know whether this rule applies to a horary.**[203]

So Lilly's system doesn't seem terribly applicable. But if instead we examine some of his rules for release, we find that the cardinal signs on the angles bode well. The Moon is slow in speed, so that should prolong the imprisonment. But the four angle rulers are mostly not angular (only Venus, Ruler of the 7th, which is judged as angular by only 5 minutes), so that bodes well, as does the fact that three of the four are in feminine signs, which give quicker release than masculine ones.

Bewitchment

We now arrive at the most politically uncomfortable issue of the 12th House. It's very easy to dismiss this section of Lilly by rationalizing it as an historical anomaly. Lilly lived in a time when witches and warlocks were believed to exist, and that they were capable of having a baleful (or occasionally good) influence on the behavior of others.[204] Recently, of course, the Feminist Movement has rehabilitated witchcraft, and introduced an offspring, Wicca, as a serious religion.

However, I don't make a living at dismissing Lilly lightly. And while Northern European-derived culture in the United States chooses to believe that psychic control of others was just a laughable superstition of primitive peoples, the fact remains that plenty of other cultures today have practitioners of exactly what Lilly would have recognized as witches. In Latin America, these are the *brujos*, and they do a thriving business.

Beyond the absence of a mechanism from science as we know it, the very concept of witchcraft is uncomfortable to many people, because we don't like to think that our actions – let alone our thoughts! – could be controlled by others against our will, and even without our knowledge. But that is exactly the function of the Unconscious as described by Freud and others. And this is also exactly what an obsession accomplishes. So what, in reality is the difference between an irrational urge that comes from within – or one that comes from without?

Lilly's rules for ascertaining bewitchment are:[205]

- The Ruler of the 12th in the 6th, or vice versa; or the Ruler of the 12th in the 1st, or vice versa, or the Ruler of the 8th in the 1st or vice versa; give strong suspicion of witchcraft.

- The same Ruler of 1st and 12th denotes witchcraft.

- The Ruler of the Ascendant combust, or unfortunate in the 12th denotes witchcraft.

Example 85. Will I marry P?

One of my students asked me for help in delineating this question. The Querent, a Latin American woman, was one of her regular clients.

We can dispense with the conventional reading of her question quite quickly. Jupiter, ruling the Querent, is peregrine and retrograde. Mercury, Ruler of the 7th and her "intended," is strong in Virgo. However, there is no aspect between Mercury and Jupiter. The Moon, while strong, is past the trine to Mercury, in orb of the square to Jupiter, so the Moon is translating the Light, but via a square aspect to the second planet. And the two principals involved are not even making a *separating* aspect to each other! So we have the possible intercession of another (i.e., the Moon; what I sometimes call the "Yenta effect" in marriage questions) but the aspect pattern is both weak and difficult – and the aspects are only with the Moon, not with each other. Furthermore, it's a late Ascendant, implying that everything is done, except that the Querent doesn't know the result. So there's no question that, left to their own devices, these two people would not get together – even with the help of a third party yenta.

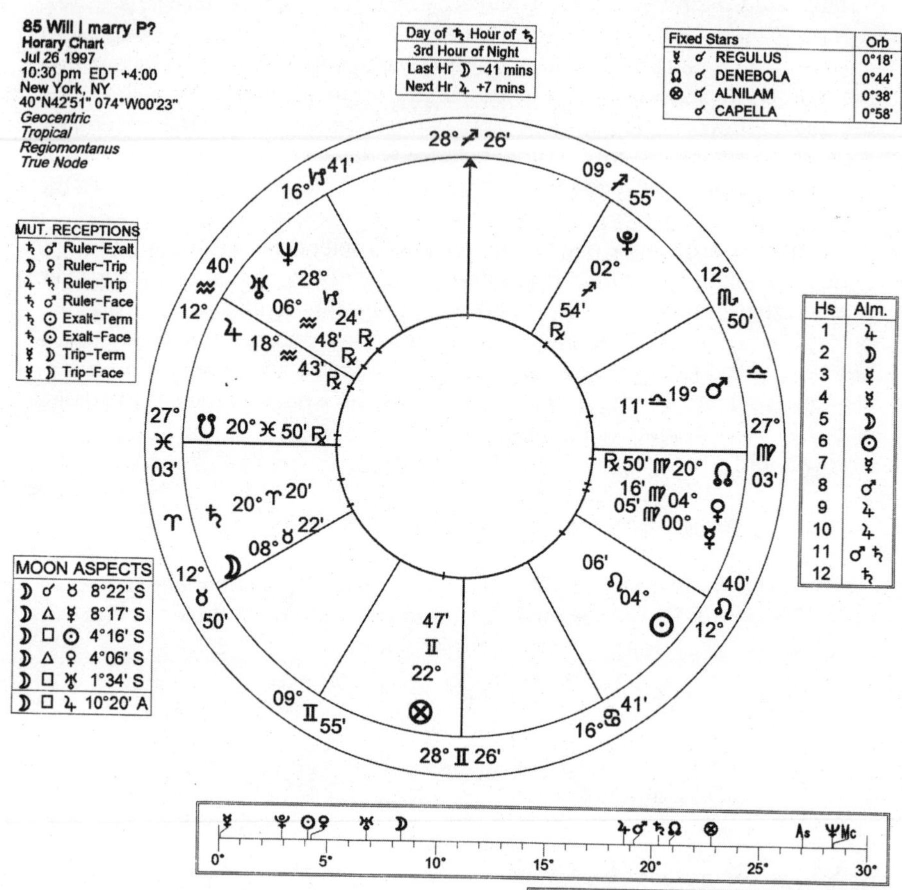

ESSENTIAL DIGNITIES (LEHMAN)								
Pt	Ruler	Exalt	Trip	Term	Face	Detri	Fall	Score
☽	♀	☽ +	☽ +	☿	☿	♂	---	+7
☉	☉ +	---	♃	♄	♄	♄	---	+5
☿	☿ +	☿ +	☽	☿ +	☉	♃	♀	+11
♀	☿	☿	☽	☿	☉	♃	♀ −	−9 p
♂	♀	♄	☿	☿	♄	♂ −	☉	−10 p
♃	♄	---	☿	♀	☿	☉	---	−5 p
♄	♂	☉	♃	☿	♀	♀	♄ −	−9 p
As	♃	♀	♂	♄	♂	☿	☿	---
Mc	♃	☋	♃	♂	♄	☿	☊	---
⊗	☿	☊	☿	♄	☉	♃	☋	---

planets.pts				
Pt	Long.	Travel	Antiscia	C.Ant.
☽	08°♉22'53"	+13°40'	21°♌37	21°♒37
☉	04°♌06'29"	+00°57'	25°♉53	25°♏53
☿	00°♍05	+01°16'	29°♈54	29°♎54
♀	04°♍16	+01°12'	25°♈43	25°♎43
♂	19°♎11	+00°34'	10°♓48	10°♍48
♃	18°♒43 ℞	−00°07'	11°♏16	11°♉16
♄	20°♈20	+00°00'	09°♍39	09°♓39
♅	06°♒48 ℞	−00°02'	23°♏11	23°♉11
♆	28°♑24 ℞	−00°01'	01°♐35	01°♊35
♇	02°♐54 ℞	−00°00'	27°♑05	27°♋05
☊	20°♍50 ℞	−00°00'	09°♈09	09°♎09
☋	20°♓50 ℞	−00°00'	09°♎09	09°♈09
As	27°♓03'38"	+00°00'	02°♎56	02°♈56
Mc	28°♐26'54"	+00°00'	01°♑33	01°♋33
⊗	22°♊47	+00°00'	07°♋12	07°♑12

However, the Ruler of the 1st in the 12th House, and the Ruler of the 12th in the 1st House struck me. Knowing that my answer would be appropriate for the Querent's cultural background, I told my student to tell her that, under normal circumstances, they probably wouldn't marry, but she'd probably hire a *brujo* to fix it up, and then it would happen. She did. Suddenly, he changed from completely indifferent to her, to passionately in love with her, and they were married two years later!

I use the rules for witchcraft to examine any kind of psychological coercion. This can include the effect of charismatic spiritual leaders, or counselors, for that matter. It also may occur among family members.

Compulsion or obsession is a difficult matter. It's easy to see why some religions have classified it as evil. The problem lies in the absence of boundaries between conscious thought and decision making. We are often ignorant of our own compulsions, let alone any imposed by others. But is it evil, our shadow side, or simply an alternate reality? That is for each of us to discover.

Chapter 13

Red Belt: Alternate Methods

Distinguishing between multiple members of a class.

Revisiting the 5th & 7th Houses.

The Consultation Chart

This chapter addresses techniques that cut across the boundaries of houses. First, we shall study multiple-choice horaries. Then, we will proceed to reconsider some philosophical questions about which horaries belong to the 5th or to the 7th House. Finally, we shall examine the consultation chart, a chart often used by natal astrologers, but interpreted in a horary way.

Most horary questions implicitly revolve around a two-state universe of exclusive either/or:

- Will I get the job?
- Will I marry Paula?
- Will we buy this house?
- Will I have children with this man?
- Should I get long-term medical insurance?

Many answers are worded as yes/no, or could be easily reworded as such. Yes/no is a two-state universe. Two-state universes are marvelous from the standpoint of simplicity, but of course Life is not always that simple! So now we need to consider what to do when the choices are not so easy. Unfortunately, the multiple-case scenario was never discussed by classical horary authors, so we have no idea what they actually did, if they did, or even if they had a theory to address this possibility! As a result, any horary astrologer faced with multiple existing possibilities has to invent a method, or adopt the one common method proposed in natal astrology in modern times.

Modern astrologers use a system of successive alternate houses for multiple entities of the same type: the 1st marriage is 7th House, the second is 9th House, the third is 11th House, etc. Marriage as a concept would still be 7th, and presumably *any* marriage would be 7th House, unless for some reason both spouses needed to be delineated in the same horary. But what would the Ancients have done?

There is no evidence in classical astrology for any use of alternate houses to represent multiple cases. The closest analogy to this type of situation occurs in nativities, when one is interested in multiple periods of the life. Here, the classical procedure was to use the three Triplicity rulers of the cusp in question for the three periods of life: the in-sect Triplicity ruler for the first period, the out-of-sect Triplicity ruler for the second, and the participating or mixed Triplicity ruler for the third.[206] This is one of the techniques that I have used in horary: when there is a chronological sequence of entities, the first one in the sequence is the in-sect Triplicity ruler, etc. Generally speaking, three is probably as many alternatives as a Horary can comfortably handle anyway. Any more and you have to break the question down into several separate questions.

Feel a little confused by the three Triplicity rulers? Here's a table to show how they work in sequence.

	1st one of the series	2nd one of the series	3rd one of the series
Daytime Chart[207]	Daytime Triplicity Ruler	Nighttime Triplicity Ruler	Mixed Triplicity Ruler
Nighttime Chart[208]	Nighttime Triplicity Ruler	Daytime Triplicity Ruler	Mixed Triplicity Ruler

I have employed this method quite successfully in those cases where there is a temporal sequence to the multiple cases. You will see this below in Example 88.

That is not the only method I have used. The other method has been to go back to the very fundamental idea that the horary chart should look like the question. In this method of delineation, I decide upon the rulers of the parties involved *without first looking at the chart*, based on planetary characteristics alone. Then I use the chart to examine how each of these parties actually fares with the Querent.

This is the reverse of most horary analysis. Instead of deciding upon the house to use, planets are assigned – houses at this point are absent, because the chart has not been calculated yet. Once the players have been assigned to planets,[209] *then* the chart is computed, and the relevant house to the question is examined to see which of the planets selected have any relation to the house in question.

In assigning planets using this method, more attention than usual is paid to the age of the Querent, and to the gender of the Quesited.

For example, if the Querent is middle aged, then the only two planets that really can indicate an older person are either Jupiter or Saturn, while a younger person could be the Moon, Mercury, Venus, or Mars. The Sun – and possibly Mars as well – would represent an age contemporary.

If the Querent has not yet had the first Saturn Return, then Saturn, Jupiter and the Sun would all tend to represent older people, while Mars would either denote someone older or the same age. Venus, Mercury and the Moon would all tend to show someone the same age or younger.

For a Querent under eighteen, only the Moon or Mercury would generally be used for a younger Quesited, while Mercury and Venus would be the usual choices for someone the same age. The rest of the planets would represent –

just like real life – everybody older.

For a senior citizen, only Saturn could represent either an older person or a person of the same age, while any other planet would represent a younger person.

Age is a strong consideration, but not the only one. The profession of a person can override the normal choice if the profession is sufficiently stereotypic for the planet. For example, an accountant would be Mercury, but how about a sixty-year-old computer programmer? In this case, Saturn in Gemini, or Mercury in Capricorn might be perfect choices!

Generally speaking, assigning Venus to a male in our society is much more problematic than assigning Mars to a female; this is more a cultural taboo than anything else. But if the male is an interior decorator, it might make some sense to use Venus; or to use the Moon for a chef.

Here's the rule I use to decide which of these two methods to employ in a specific case. In those instances where the multiple choice quesiteds are distinct enough in the Querent's mind that they can truly describe each possibility clearly enough to result in a distinctive planetary picture for each, I assign the planets as natural rulers of the alternatives. However, if there isn't such strong differentiation, as in the case below where the Querent was interviewing for two job positions that were essentially the same in two different companies, I assign the multiple options temporally to the Triplicity rulers of the House in question, as in the in-sect Triplicity Ruler of the first job prospect, the out-of-sect Triplicity Ruler for the second job prospect, and the participating Triplicity Ruler for the third job prospect.

Let's see how these ideas apply in some actual examples.

Example 86: What is this person?

This question usually arises either after the Querent has "gone to the 5th House" with the Quesited, or is strongly considering it! While the issue may not be entirely spelled out, the Question is whether the Quesited will end up 5th, 7th, or 11th – or none of the above! In the case of this particular question, the Querent was married to someone else.

Before I examined the chart, I asked the Querent to describe the Quesited. Her answer was that he is older than she is, but not extremely so. She is middle aged. He has salt-and-pepper hair. And he's a New Age minister at a church located in her neighborhood.

At this stage in the delineation, it's well to know what signs the planets are in, even if you don't want to envision the full chart yet. If she's middle aged, and he's older than her, then the only two possible planets which could represent him would be Saturn or Jupiter. Saturn would generally be significantly older than she is, but Jupiter is a mature person, generally male. So my choice is between Jupiter in Sagittarius or Saturn in Pisces. If he were a minister at a more typical denomination, I would pick Jupiter. But New Age? I pick Saturn in Pisces!

Now I can examine the chart. Saturn is Retrograde in Pisces, in the 3rd House. So far, that's actually a pretty good description, since his church is in her neighborhood! Since Saturn isn't located in one of the three houses of interest, then the next question is: does Saturn rule any of them?

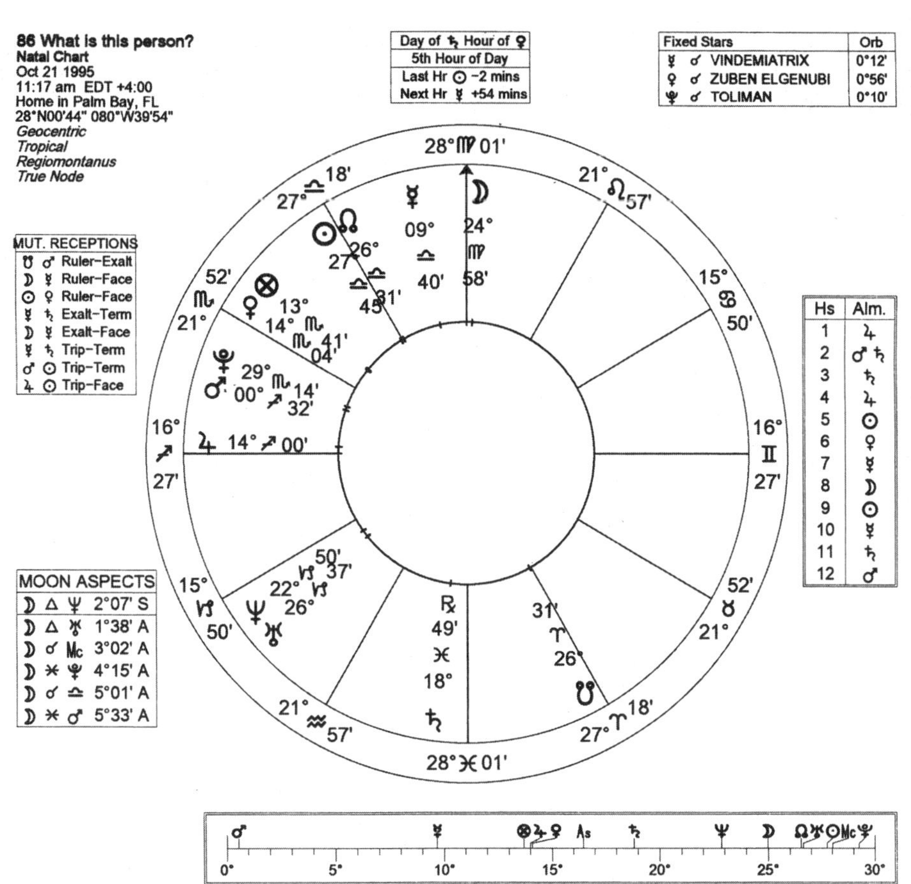

ESSENTIAL DIGNITIES (LEHMAN)								
Pt	Ruler	Exalt	Trip	Term	Face	Detri	Fall	Score
☽	☿	☿	♀	♂	☿ m	♃	♀	-5 p
☉	♀	♄	♄	♂	♃	♂	☉ -	-9 p
☿	♀	♄	♄	♀	☽ m	♂	☉	-5 p
♀	♂	--	♀ +	♀ +	☉	♀ -	☽	+0
♂	♃	☋	☉	♃	☿	☿	☊	-5 p
♃	♃ +	☋	☉	☿	☽	☿	☊	+5
♄	♃	♀	♀	☿	♃	☿	☿	-5 p
As	♃	☋	☉	☿	☽	☿	☊	--
Mc	☿	☿	♀	♂	☿	♃	♀	--
⊗	♂	--	♀	♃	☉	♀	☽	--

planets.pts				
Pt	Long.	Travel	Antiscia	C.Ant.
☽	24°♍58'51"	+13°21'	05°♈01	05°♎01
☉	27°♎45'00"	+00°59'	02°♓14	02°♍14
☿	09°♎40	+01°06'	20°♓19	20°♍19
♀	14°♏04	+01°14'	15°♒55	15°♌55
♂	00°♐32	+00°42'	29°♑27	29°♋27
♃	14°♐00	+00°11'	15°♑59	15°♋59
♄	18°♓49 ℞	-00°03'	11°♎10	11°♈10
♅	26°♑37	+00°00'	03°♐22	03°♊22
♆	22°♑50	+00°00'	07°♐09	07°♊09
♇	29°♏14	+00°02'	00°♒45	00°♌45
☊	26°♎31	+00°00'	03°♓28	03°♍28
☋	26°♈31	+00°00'	03°♍28	03°♓28
As	16°♐27'33"	+00°00'	13°♑32	13°♋32
Mc	28°♍01'09"	+00°00'	01°♈58	01°♎58
⊗	13°♏41	+00°00'	16°♒18	16°♌18

Mars rules the 5th House, and the 5th House is looking rather blocked anyway, with the South Node sitting right at the cusp. So he's not going to be her lover. Saturn doesn't rule the 7th, so she is not going to divorce and then marry him. (Notice that this doesn't speak to whether she would divorce for other reasons.) Saturn is the Almuten of the 11th House, but notice that the sign ruler, Venus is in the 11th House. Also notice that Venus, despite being in Detriment, is actually in better condition than Saturn, since Venus isn't peregrine and Saturn is! Also, Venus is Direct and Saturn is retrograde. Therefore, it is very unlikely that Saturn would be preferred as the 11th House Ruler, so while there might be some possibility of friendship, it's a possibility, not a probability.

The meaning of this horary is that, while there is a chance that they may end up friends, the answer is really: none of the above. And that is what actually happened. He remained the minister of her neighborhood church. And five years later: she was still married!

This chart is also a very good illustration of the importance of the need for both clarity about the question, but also the need for the Querent to ask the question her or his way. Had I badgered her into some variant of the question, will I marry him, the answer would have come out yes – and that was not the case. (Mercury with out of sect Triplicity comes to sextile dignified and fast Jupiter in Sagittarius – a perfection between the rulers of the 1st and 7th Houses.)

Example 87: Door #1 or Door #2?

Sometimes I do conceptualize these questions as being like the television game shows where the contestant has to choose between the unknown items behind the doors! The Querent in this case has an embarrassment of riches: two gentlemen vying for her attention. Which is the better choice?

The Querent supplied me with birth data on the two men, in addition to physical descriptions. Sam was predetermined to be either Jupiter or Saturn (with Capricorn Rising natally, I lean toward Saturn). The reason: salt and pepper hair, and like our last example, older than the Querent. He has a receding hairline and a bit of temper. Saturn in Aries capped the temper part of the description.

I assigned Mitch to Mercury. He has Gemini Rising. He's younger than she is, and while athletic, he's shy, reserved, a computer programmer, and much less social than Sam. Mercury in Taurus – a cud-chewing sign, which I often think of as practically mute – fits the bill – but so does Mars retrograde in shy Virgo!

Once we look at the chart, things become a bit clearer. Since *she* comes out to be Mercury, with Virgo on the 1st House cusp, this shows her identification with Mitch. This is further confirmed by Mitch's other possible Significator Mars being in the 1st House. Since there was a question about which planet to use for Mitch, the attribution of Mercury to the Querent means that we need to switch to Mars for him. Mitch's ruler in the 1st House shows that he has the favored position.

Since I decided that Sam was represented by Saturn, even though I had considered Jupiter, Pisces on the 7th House cusp doesn't change anything.

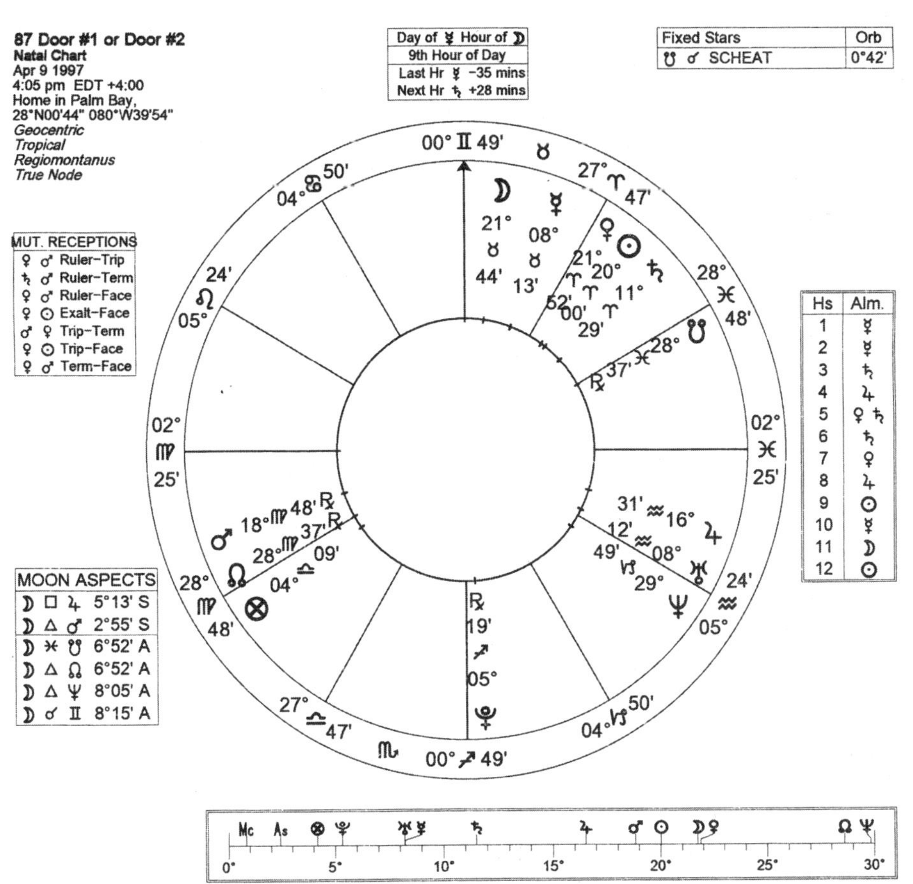

ESSENTIAL DIGNITIES (LEHMAN)								
Pt	Ruler	Exalt	Trip	Term	Face	Detri	Fall	Score
☽	♀	☽ +	♀	♃	♄	♂	--	+4
☉	♂	☉ +	☉ +	☿	♀	♀	♄	+7
☿	♀	☽	♀	☿ +	☿ +	♂	--	+3
♀	♂	☉	☉	♂	♀ +	♀ −	♄	-4
♂	☿	☿	♀	♄	♀	♃	♀	-5 p
♃	♄	--	♄	♀	☿	☉	--	-5 p
♄	♂	☉	☉	♀	☉	♀	♄ −	-9 p
As	☿	☿	♀	☿	☉	♃	♀	--
Mc	☿	☊	♄	☿	♃	♃	☋	--
⊗	♀	♄	♄	♄	☽	♂	☉	--

planets.pts				
Pt	Long.	Travel	Antiscia	C.Ant.
☽	21°♉44'19"	+13°54'	08°♌15	08°♒15
☉	20°♈00'23"	+00°58'	09°♍59	09°♓59
☿	08°♉13	+00°33'	21°♌46	21°♒46
♀	21°♈52	+01°14'	08°♍07	08°♓07
♂	18°♍48 ℞	-00°13'	11°♈11	11°♎11
♃	16°♒31	+00°09'	13°♏28	13°♉28
♄	11°♈29	+00°07'	18°♍30	18°♓30
♅	08°♒12	+00°01'	21°♏47	21°♉47
♆	29°♑49	+00°00'	00°♐10	00°♊10
♇	05°♐19 ℞	-00°01'	24°♑40	24°♋40
☊	28°♍37 ℞	-00°03'	01°♈22	01°♎22
☋	28°♓37 ℞	-00°03'	01°♎22	01°♈22
As	02°♍25'53"	+00°00'	27°♈34	27°♎34
Mc	00°♊49'58"	+00°00'	29°♋10	29°♑10
⊗	04°♎09	+00°00'	25°♓50	25°♍50

Sam is in her 8th House – the death of the relationship with him, at least as far as marriage is concerned!

So Mitch is the chosen one. But I still am not happy with this. Mitch's Significator does not rule the 7th House, so it's almost tempting to throw this aside as a none-of-the-above. It isn't what you would call a strong situation. This fact is further confirmed by the Querent's Significator Mercury having dignity only by Term and Face.

She married Mitch. But three years later, she's still not sure she made the right choice, and she refers to the situation as "complicated."

Example 88: Which job?

In this case, the embarrassment of riches is in terms of jobs: the Querent had had two job offers, and he wanted to know which one to accept. As a practical matter, I have found that it is usually harder for Querents to try to describe jobs with the same kind of color and detail as they would use to describe other people – or, even dwellings. This is especially true, since it is common to interview for jobs of a similar nature, so the differences to an outsider are often subtle.

As a result, when the multiple-choice question involves a job or similar business question, I simply want to know which offer came first. This can still be tricky: what constitutes "first?" I judge this by using the sequence of the last significant event that applies to all options: such as who made a job offer first, who interviewed first, or who contacted the Querent first, whichever is the last complete round. Then, I can use the system of Triplicities to represent the parties. In this case, when I was asked the question, I was told that the first job was in New York, while the second was in Los Angeles.

In this particular chart, I don't have to agonize over whether to use the 6th or the 10th, because both cusps are in Fire signs, so the delineation will be identical. Remember that, since we are using Triplicity Rulers, the Ruler is the same for each member of the same element, so Aries and Sagittarius have the same rulers. And in his case, his real focus was on remuneration from the job, a second house matter, which also has a Fire sign on the cusp.

This does not look like a good situation. He is shown as the fallen Moon in Scorpio, hardly a good starting point. Since this is a day chart, the in-sect Triplicity ruler of the Fire signs is the Sun. The Sun is peregrine and Void of Course, but it is also close to the end of Pisces, and obviously when it enters Aries, the circumstances of this Sun improve dramatically. So I felt that the scenario here would be a cash flow problem for maybe four months, and then a dramatically improved situation.

Job #2 initially looks good: Jupiter in Pisces is the night Triplicity ruler. But it's conjunct the South Node! I judged this to mean that the job would look very strong on paper, but upon arrival, he would discover himself in a snake pit of politics – a good description, I thought, of the Significator of the job conjunct the Dragon's Tail.

This is clearly an easy call: Job #1! Either job entailed relocation, so he was more than happy to take my advice. There was just one problem. Once he moved to New York and started the job, which was at a very prestigious

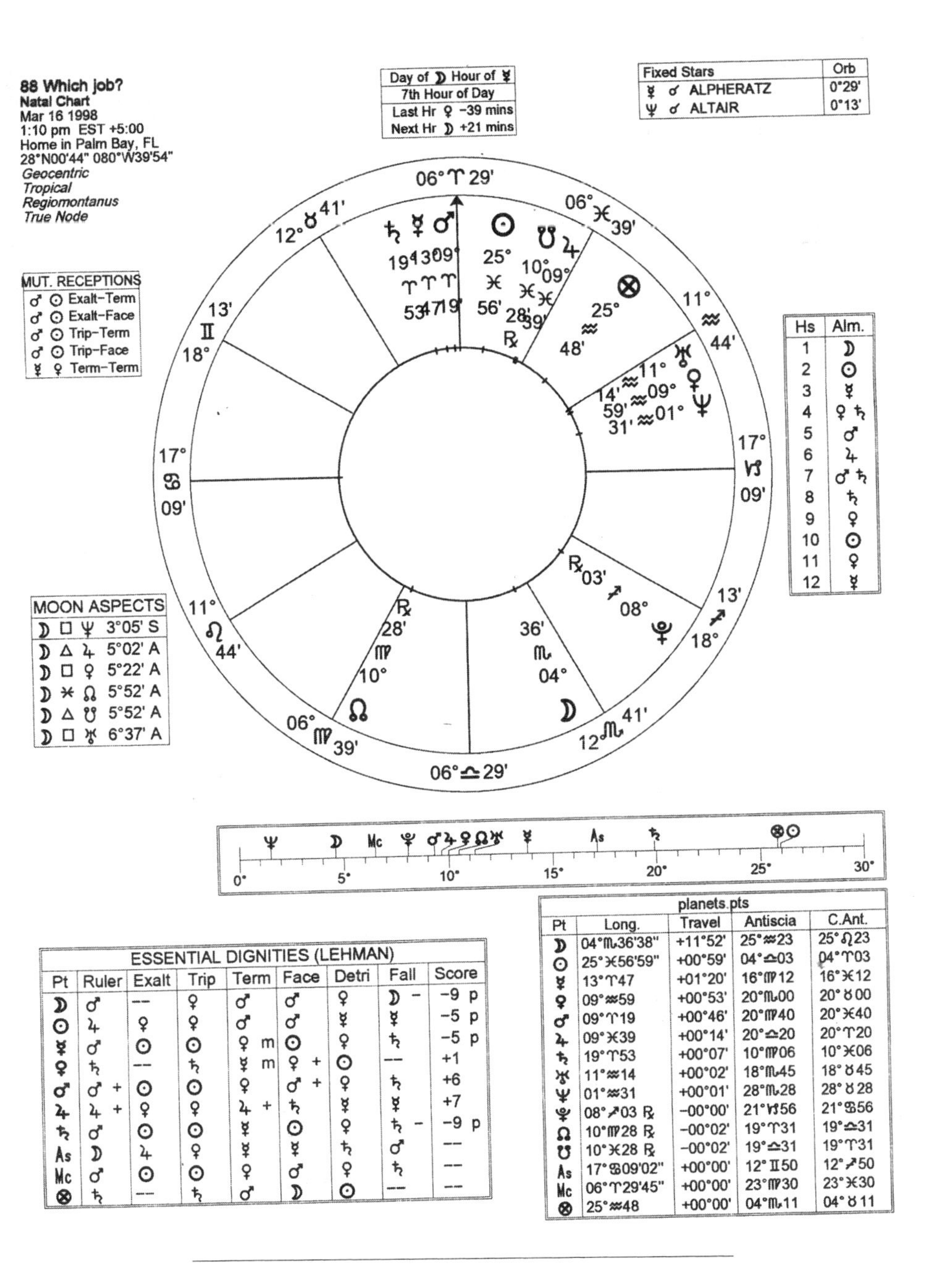

Fixed Stars	Orb
☿ ☌ ALPHERATZ	0°29'
♆ ☌ ALTAIR	0°13'

MUT. RECEPTIONS
♂ ☉ Exalt–Term
♂ ☉ Exalt–Face
♂ ☉ Trip–Term
♂ ☉ Trip–Face
☿ ♀ Term–Term

Hs	Alm.
1	☽
2	☉
3	☿
4	♀ ♄
5	♂
6	♃
7	♂ ♄
8	♄
9	♀
10	☉
11	♀
12	☿

MOON ASPECTS
☽ □ ♆ 3°05' S
☽ △ ♃ 5°02' A
☽ □ ♀ 5°22' A
☽ ⚹ ☊ 5°52' A
☽ △ ☋ 5°52' A
☽ □ ♅ 6°37' A

ESSENTIAL DIGNITIES (LEHMAN)								
Pt	Ruler	Exalt	Trip	Term	Face	Detri	Fall	Score
☽	♂	--	♀	♂	♂	♀	☽ −	−9 p
☉	♃	♀	♀	♂	♂	☿	☿	−5 p
☿	♂	☉	☉	♀ m	☉	♀	♄	−5 p
♀	♄	--	♄	☿ m	♀ +	☉	--	+1
♂	♂ +	☉	☉	♀	♂ +	♀	♄	+6
♃	♃ +	♀	♀	♃ +	♄	☿	☿	+7
♄	♂	☉	☉	☿	☉	♀	♄ −	−9 p
As	☽	♃	♀	☿	☿	♄	♂	--
Mc	♂	☉	☉	♀	♂	♀	♄	--
⊗	♄	---	♄	♂	☽	☉	---	--

planets.pts				
Pt	Long.	Travel	Antiscia	C.Ant.
☽	04°♏36'38"	+11°52'	25°♒23	25°♌23
☉	25°♓56'59"	+00°59'	04°♎03	04°♈03
☿	13°♈47	+01°20'	16°♍12	16°♓12
♀	09°♒59	+00°53'	20°♏00	20°♉00
♂	09°♈19	+00°46'	20°♍40	20°♓40
♃	09°♓39	+00°14'	20°♎20	20°♈20
♄	19°♈53	+00°07'	10°♍06	10°♓06
♅	11°♒14	+00°02'	18°♏45	18°♉45
♆	01°♒31	+00°01'	28°♏28	28°♉28
♇	08°♐03 ℞	−00°00'	21°♑56	21°♋56
☊	10°♍28 ℞	−00°02'	19°♈31	19°♎31
☋	10°♓28 ℞	−00°02'	19°♎31	19°♈31
As	17°♋09'02"	+00°00'	12°♊50	12°♐50
Mc	06°♈29'45"	+00°00'	23°♍30	23°♓30
⊗	25°♒48	+00°00'	04°♏11	04°♉11

firm, he discovered he had landed in a morass of office politics. This swamp continued until he left the job a year later. And what he discovered when he went back to his notes was that the Los Angeles firm had actually called first – so he had inadvertently switched the sequencing of the jobs and landed in the snake pit! So much for the Moon separating from square to Neptune!

Example 89: Which, if any, house?

The Querent was house hunting, and had seen two houses that she liked. Additionally, there was a possibility that she could buy the house that she was presently renting. The question was: which option is the best?

I asked her to describe the houses. Greenmore is a large house, almost what is called a zero-lot line; i.e., the house takes up the bulk of the property, without much surrounding land. It is on a busy corner. Jupiter, I thought.

Longwood is landscaped extensively, the door is purple, and it is clearly overpriced. Venus, I thought.

Her present rental is isolated. Saturn, I thought.

Once I had the rulerships assigned in my mind, I examined the chart. The first thing I noticed was the one degree rising, already suggesting that it's too early to ask the question. Why would that be? Most probably, either one of the three houses is going to undergo a substantial change (like a major price reduction) or she hasn't seen the right house yet.

Saturn rules the 1st, which is certainly appropriate, since she's living in the Saturn house! But Saturn is peregrine and retrograde, showing both her current dwelling's poor condition, and her own inability to change the circumstances surrounding the houses that she has seen. The Moon will square both Venus and Jupiter. Venus would seem to have the edge, since Venus receives the Moon – but Venus is peregrine and cadent, so that will come to naught. This suggests perfection by hassle, if perfection at all. The Moon will also oppose Saturn. If she stays where she is and buys, she will regret it. So what's the problem? With the North Node and Fortuna bracketing the MC, property is more expensive than it is worth!

Synthesizing this information with the early degree rising, I told her that both of the "new" houses are overpriced, not just Longwood, although if she was willing to go through a fair amount of difficulty, she could probably buy either. As for her present situation, no matter how tempting it might be to simply stay and buy, she would regret it if she did.

Therefore, I told her that either she would purchase a house that she hadn't seen yet, or some other circumstance intervening would make her question obsolete – the two obvious delineations for "too early." The next two easy aspects of the Moon are to Mercury in thirteen degrees, or the Sun in seventeen. Seventeen days later she called to say that she had put down an offer on a different house that she had just seen, and that the offer had been accepted. The new house was much less expensive than the other two had been.

Revisiting the 5th & 7th Houses

There really should be no problem distinguishing between the 5th and 7th Houses, but as long as humans want to believe that sexuality is mystical and meaningful, there will be issues of classification. I present here a case study of six interrogations over a period of one and one-half years by a Querent concerning the same relationship. This relationship has all the hallmarks of obsession: the kind that, on the outside, looks absolutely insane. Yet on the

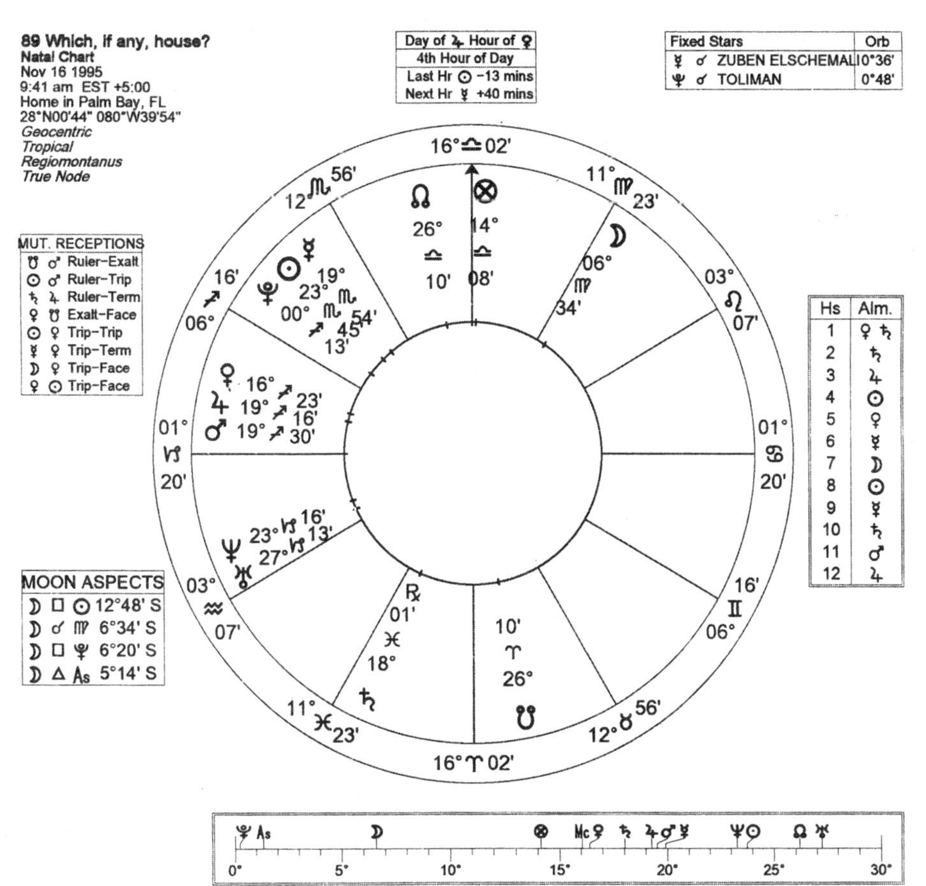

ESSENTIAL DIGNITIES (LEHMAN)								
Pt	Ruler	Exalt	Trip	Term	Face	Detri	Fall	Score
☽	☿	☿	♀	☿	☉	♃	♀	-5 p
☉	♂	--	♀ m	☿	♀	♀	☽	-5 p
☿	♂	--	♀	♀ m	☉	♀	☽	-5 p
♀	♃	☋	☉ m	☿ m	☽	☿	☊	-5 p
♂	♃	☋	☉	♄	☽	☿	☊	-5 p
♃	♃ +	☋	☉	♄	☽	☿	☊	+5
♄	♃	♀	♀	☿	♃	☿	☿	-5 p
As	♄	♂	♀	♀	♃	☽	♃	--
Mc	♀	♄	♄	♃	♄	♂	☉	--
⊗	♀	♄	♄	♃	♄	♂	☉	--

planets.pts				
Pt	Long.	Travel	Antiscia	C.Ant.
☽	06°♍34'27"	+12°33'	23°♈25	23°♎25
☉	23°♏45'39"	+01°00'	06°♒14	06°♌14
☿	19°♏54	+01°36'	10°♒05	10°♌05
♀	16°♐23	+01°14'	13°♑36	13°♋36
♂	19°♐30	+00°44'	10°♑29	10°♋29
♃	19°♐16	+00°12'	10°♑43	10°♋43
♄	18°♓01 ℞	-00°00'	11°♎58	11°♈58
♅	27°♑13	+00°02'	02°♐46	02°♊46
♆	23°♑16	+00°01'	06°♐43	06°♊43
♇	00°♐13	+00°02'	29°♑46	29°♋46
☊	26°♎10	+00°01'	03°♓49	03°♍49
☋	26°♈10	+00°01'	03°♍49	03°♓49
As	01°♑20'02"	+00°00'	28°♐39	28°♊39
Mc	16°♎02'56"	+00°00'	13°♓57	13°♍57
⊗	14°♎08	+00°00'	15°♓51	15°♍51

inside, this woman simply cannot seem to break free of it. What can these horaries teach us?

This woman was referred to me by a natal astrologer who also referred another, similar case to me during this same time period. Both cases were women attempting to engage in relationships which were clearly dysfunctional. In both cases, the men were available sexually, but unavailable emotionally. Both women craved a strong emotional bond, yet were unable to break free, despite continual evidence that matters were not going to change. I suspect that the referring astrologer felt she had done everything she could for these women natally and from the standpoint of synastry. Maybe the more immediate approach of horary would illustrate that, for each "new" event in the series, the same outcome would obtain. Perhaps enough straws would accumulate to finally break the camel's back.

At the beginning of each case, I too examined the nativities and the synastry and reached the same conclusions as the referring astrologer. That these relationships were difficult, obsessive, and hopeless. The men were getting exactly what they wanted (sex/power), and the women wanted more than they had (emotional commitment). The men had absolutely no reason to change, so the women were doomed to continual frustration. Since neither woman viewed her situation as requiring therapy, I was not in a position to refer either to a psychological expert. All I could do was to hope that the repetition of the same themes and issues might eventually allow them to realize that the only change possible was to get out. If anger alternated with compassion on my part, it was merely because I was frustrated at the sacrifice of human potential against a wall of such inexorable circumstance.

In this particular case, the man is an aging rock star, and he is married to someone else. The Querent had been in a financially dependent relationship with him for a number of years, living in an adjacent dwelling to his principal residence, where he could visit her if he chose. He would visit her even when his wife was at home! She and the wife allegedly get along, but who knows what the wife really thinks about this! If this weren't a sufficiently complex lifestyle, the man also has sexual liaisons apart from the two of them, both in the form of additional affairs of varying duration, and also one-night stands.

Over the course of the period from 1995 to 1997, I received a whole series of horaries as this relationship ebbed and flowed.

Example 90a: Event – phone call

This event occurred in the middle of their longest "off" period during the time when I was following the relationship. She had actually moved out and away, and was pursuing a very good job in his absence – she has very bankable job skills when she chooses to apply them.

Here's what happened. She had called him, expecting to get his phone machine, and instead got him directly, and they had talked, and he had mumbled something about the idea that maybe they should get back together again. She wanted to know what to make of the call, and whether it was a good idea to drop her new life and go back with him.

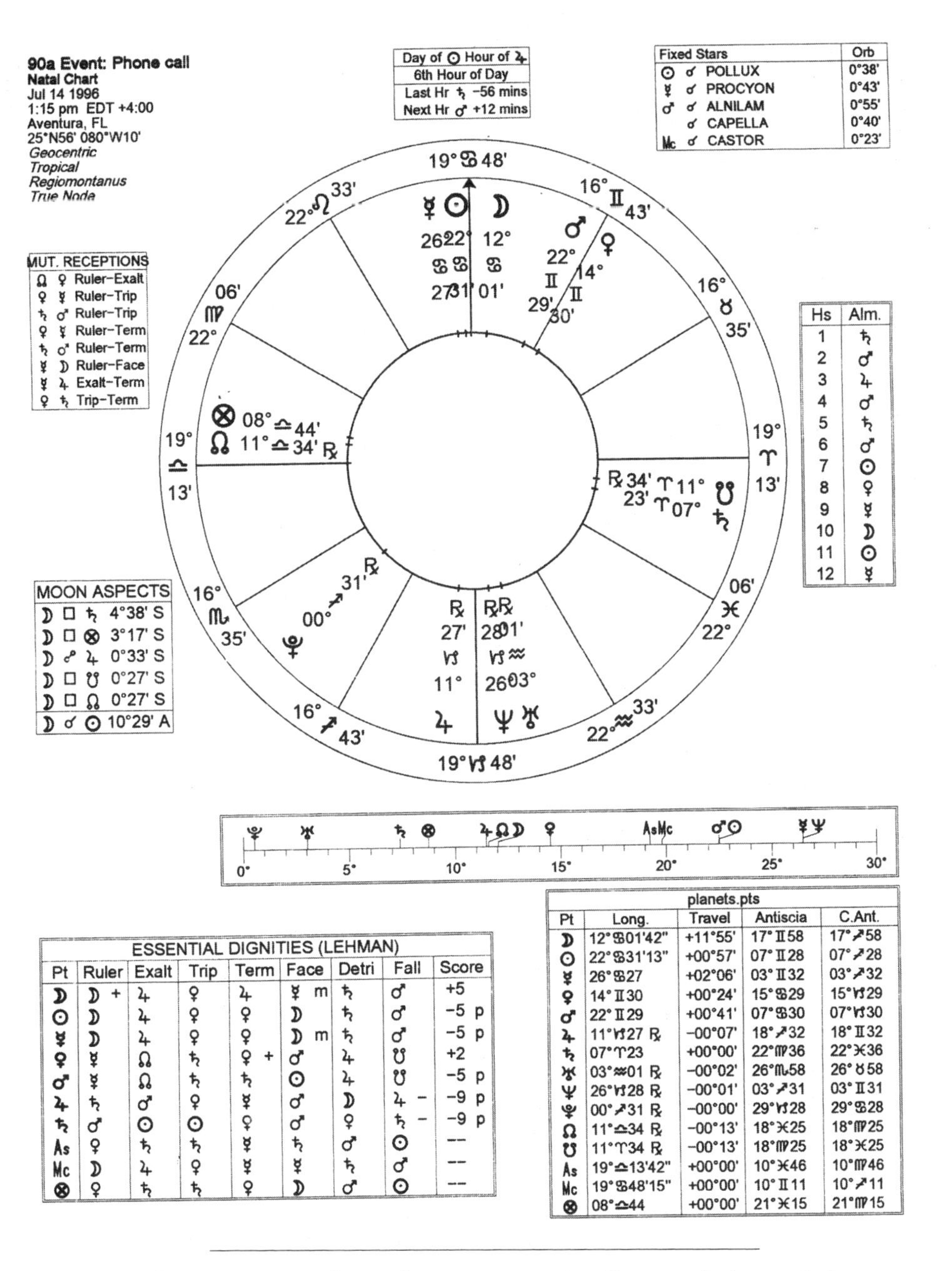

Here's the quandary, from a horary perspective. Because he's married, our Querent is 5th House to him; his wife is unequivocally 7th House. But what is he to her? She was making a point to be absolutely monogamous with him because of her love for him, and she sees him as the major partner of her life. So is he 5th House to her, or 7th? Let's see what the horaries and events tell us.

She made the phone call, so she's the 1st House. She's represented by the slow of course Venus in Gemini: caught between two lives, her current one, and her past one with him. Fair enough! Venus is in Term, so it looks like she is in control of her life. Notice that she could also be Saturn, the Almuten of the 1st, but I rejected that because Venus is more dignified, and certainly described her better.

If he's the 7th House, then he's fast Mars. It appears that Venus is coming to Mars, except that Venus had just recently turned direct, so Venus did not catch up to Mars before Mars went into Cancer. This scenario says: she tries to catch up with him, but she never really gets him back, although for a while it will look like things are improving.

If he's the 5th House, then he's that Saturn in Aries. Venus is past the sextile to Saturn, and she's moving away. The slow of course Moon translates by the square to Saturn, and then the semi-sextile to Venus, but that's not likely to be strong enough to do anything. There is a weak reception here, but that's probably not enough to change the flow of events. She doesn't go back.

But – whichever scenario we pick, the Moon is at the Bendings: a crisis point, or turning point, remember. In a sense, this actually puts her in a position which mandates choice. This was a moment in which she really *could* leave him – if she wanted to. This is the essence of the meaning of a body at the Bendings: it's the moment of choosing between two paths. Remember: this is an event, not a horary. The meaning of the phone call was that she really *could* go either way, but if she decided to stay in her new job, then it really was permanent. There would not be an opportunity to turn back.

She decided to go back to him. She very shortly gave notice at her job, and returned to a life of financial dependency. This chart doesn't really give much insight into whether to use the 5th or the 7th.

Example 90b: What to do?

This question was asked after she had returned to live with him. What was actually occurring at this point was benign neglect. She is Mars, and Mars is in Fall with Triplicity out-of-sect[210] - and late in degree as well.

If this relationship is 7th House, then he's represented by Venus in Cancer, with Triplicity, but at twenty-nine degrees, separating from the conjunction of Mars. He's departing from her. If he's the 5th, then he's Jupiter in Fall. In that scenario, she is way past opposition with him, although the Moon at the Bendings applies to an opposition to Jupiter. So the difference in reading is that in the first case, he's really gone past her, and in the second, there's the moth to the flame temptation with the opposition, with the result of regret!

Once again, the Moon is slow. She stayed. But things really didn't get any better or any closer.

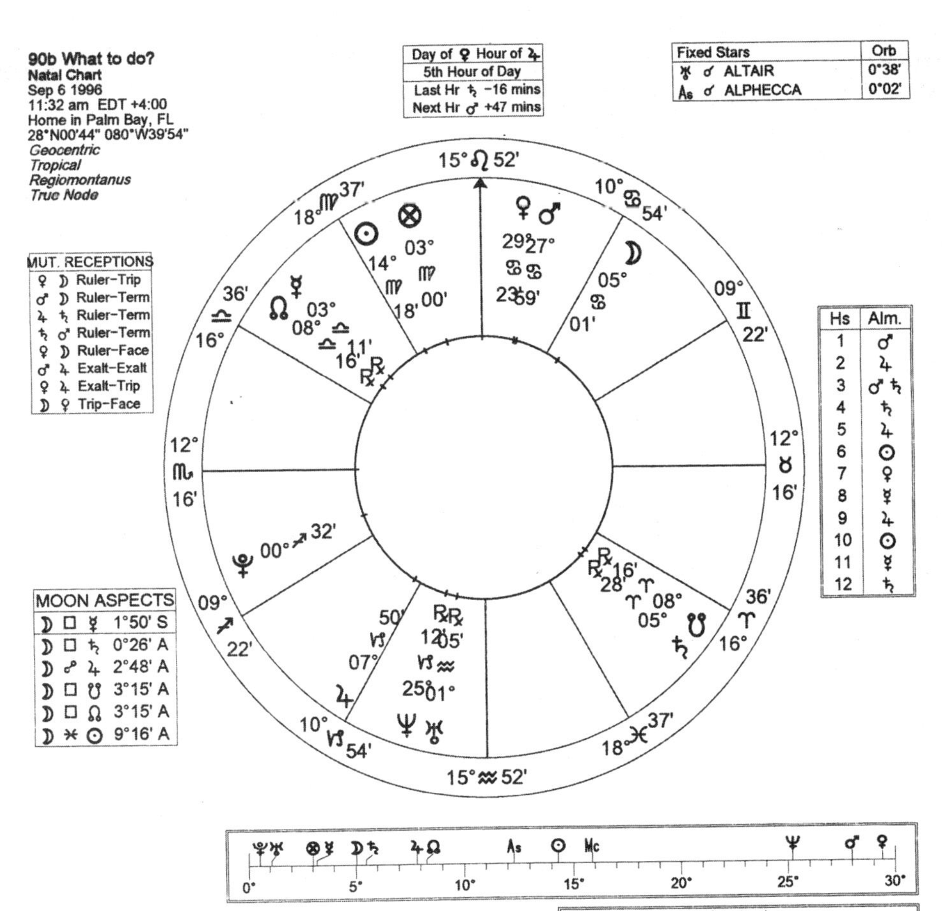

Pt	Ruler	Exalt	Trip	Term	Face	Detri	Fall	Score
ESSENTIAL DIGNITIES (LEHMAN)								
☽	☽ +	♃	♀	♂	♀ m	♄	♂	+5
☉	☿	☿	♀	♃	♀	♃	♀	−5 p
☿	♀	♄	♄	♄	☽	♂	☉	−5 p
♀	☽	♃	♀ +	♄	☽ m	♄	♂	+3
♂	☽	♃ m	♀	♄	☽	♄	♂ −	−9 p
♃	♄	♂ m	♀	☿	♃ +	☽	♃ −	−3
♄	♂	☉	☉	♃	♂	♀	♄ −	−9 p
As	♂	--	♀	♃	☉	♀	☽	--
Mc	☉	--	☉	♀	♃	♄	--	--
⊗	☿	☿	♀	☿	☉	♃	♀	--

Pt	Long.	Travel	Antiscia	C.Ant.
planets.pts				
☽	05°♋01'59"	+11°59'	24°♊58	24°♐58
☉	14°♍18'19"	+00°58'	15°♈41	15°♎41
☿	03°♎11 ℞	−00°14'	26°♓48	26°♍48
♀	29°♋23	+01°03'	00°♊36	00°♐36
♂	27°♋59	+00°37'	02°♊00	02°♐00
♃	07°♑50	+00°00'	22°♐09	22°♊09
♄	05°♈28 ℞	−00°04'	24°♍31	24°♓31
♅	01°♒05 ℞	−00°01'	28°♏54	28°♉54
♆	25°♑12 ℞	−00°00'	04°♐47	04°♊47
♇	00°♐32	+00°00'	29°♑27	29°♋27
☊	08°♎16 ℞	−00°02'	21°♓43	21°♍43
☋	08°♈16 ℞	−00°02'	21°♍43	21°♓43
As	12°♏16'55"	+00°00'	17°♒43	17°♌43
Mc	15°♌52'33"	+00°00'	14°♉07	14°♏07
⊗	03°♍00	+00°00'	26°♈59	26°♎59

Example 90c: Does he want me here?

Things were back to normal. He had acquired yet another girlfriend. This question was: does he even want me here?

The Querent is Mars in this chart, just as in the last one. In this entire set, the Querent is either Venus or Mars: the two planets of passion. This virtually became a signature for her. She would ask the questions either out of a deep emotional place (Venus), or out of the desire to do *something* (Mars). Notice that this is just after sunset: the Sun has set on the possibility of being Almuten. Mars is still in Leo: there's not a whole lot she *can* do. She's stuck.

If he's the 7th, he's Venus in Virgo in the 5th House. What's on his mind?! His New girlfriend is Saturn, Ruler of the 5th from the 7th, appropriately placed in the Querent's 12th House of secret enemies! Venus and Saturn aren't coming to perfection; they're separating from a quincunx. This other relationship isn't even serious.

If he's the 5th House, then he's the Sun, and the Querent's Significator Mars is in his house – she is in his power. Now the new girlfriend would be Jupiter, Ruler of the 9th, which is the 5th from the 5th. Jupiter is in Fall, and his Significator Sun is departing from the square. So the girlfriend's no prize, and she's history anyway.

Either delineation gives the same ultimate answer that the Querent need not worry about the new girlfriend. However, I think the 7th House delineation gives the circumstances a bit more clearly. The 5th House method implies that she and he will reconcile and the relationship will improve, since the Significators (Mars and Sun) are coming together by sextile, but since both are peregrine, it doesn't look overly successful. With the 7th House reading, there isn't even the illusion that things get better.

In either case, she remains powerless, which was to me the most significant thing about the whole question.

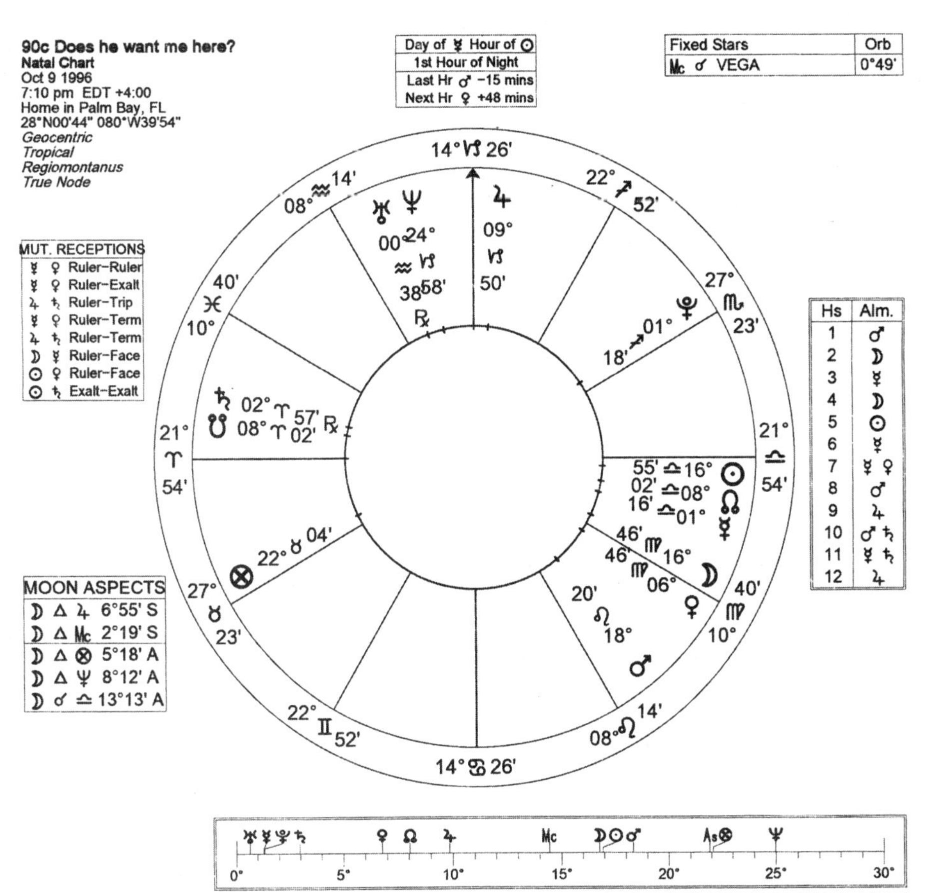

ESSENTIAL DIGNITIES (LEHMAN)								
Pt	Ruler	Exalt	Trip	Term	Face	Detri	Fall	Score
☽	☿	☿	☽ +	♃	♀	♃	♀	+3
☉	♀	♄ m	☿	♃	♄	♂	☉ −	−9 p
☿	♀ m	♄	☿ +	♄	☽	♂	☉	+3
♀	☿ m	☿	☽	☿	☉	♃	♀ −	−9 p
♂	☉	--	♃	♀	♃	♄	--	−5 p
♃	♄	♂	☽	☿	♃ +	☽	♃ −	−3
♄	♂	☉ m	♃	♃	♂	♀	♄ −	−9 p
As	♂	☉	♃	♂	♀	♀	♄	--
Mc	♄	♂	☽	♃	♂	☽	♃	--
⊗	♀	☽	☽	♄	♄	♂	--	--

planets.pts				
Pt	Long.	Travel	Antiscia	C.Ant.
☽	16°♍46'09"	+12°10'	13°♈13	13°♎13
☉	16°♎55'44"	+00°59'	13°♓04	13°♍04
☿	01°♎16	+01°32'	28°♓43	28°♍43
♀	06°♍46	+01°10'	23°♈13	23°♎13
♂	18°♌20	+00°35'	11°♉39	11°♏39
♃	09°♑50	+00°06'	20°♐09	20°♊09
♄	02°♈57 ℞	−00°04'	27°♍02	27°♓02
♅	00°♒38 ℞	−00°00'	29°♏21	29°♉21
♆	24°♑58	+00°00'	05°♐01	05°♊01
♇	01°♐18	+00°01'	28°♑41	28°♋41
☊	08°♎02	+00°00'	21°♓57	21°♍57
☋	08°♈02	+00°00'	21°♍57	21°♓57
As	21°♈54'40"	+00°00'	08°♍05	08°♓05
Mc	14°♑26'18"	+00°00'	15°♐33	15°♊33
⊗	22°♉04	+00°00'	07°♌55	07°♒55

Example 90d: Should I leave him today or tomorrow?

Since she had returned to him several months before, the Querent found him to be mentally abusive, barely paying any attention to her at all. In the midst of total frustration, she asked me the question exactly as I have worded it above. When she put it that way, I asked her if she didn't mean, Would it be in my best interest to leave him, and if so, when? She agreed that my rewording expressed her basic question, although she acknowledged that her original question came out of anger.

The Querent is given by Mars in the 9th House. She has just moved about 1,000 miles to go back with him. And once again, her frustration is peeking through.

If he is the 7th House, he's Venus. Venus has Triplicity by day, as well as Term and Face. However, Venus is also in Fall. Most importantly, Mars and Venus are not in aspect with each other. The Moon *will* sextile Venus, but then square Mars, although she is out of orb for the latter. The Moon is debilitated in Scorpio, so not only is the translation by sextile and square a problem, but this Moon will not perform well.

Judging him by the 5th House, we have to give him the Sun, since that is the only way to separate Scorpio and Aries. In this case, he's the Sun in Detriment. I don't think this describes the situation at all, since in all these questions, he is clearly the one with the power, not her. The symbolism of their Significators being in a partile separating sextile may be poignant. However, two malefics clustering near the 5th House cusp do not look very good for a 5th House relationship in any case.

Given that the Moon, Ascendant *and* Mars are in fixed signs, and that both are weak, the real answer is: *neither* today nor tomorrow. The fixed quality of the Significators argues against any fast movement. While she may feel that she's at the breaking point, the fact is that she isn't ready to go anywhere. But, boy, can she complain about it!

I advised her that the two of them were not in synch at all, and not likely to be for some time. They might as well be on separate planets. She asked me if he would change. I said, possibly in 19 weeks or months (thinking of Venus leaving the sign of Virgo). However, that in no way would guarantee that their relationship would improve. I advised her to get on with her life.

While she may have been angry when she asked the question, she didn't act on it. She stayed.

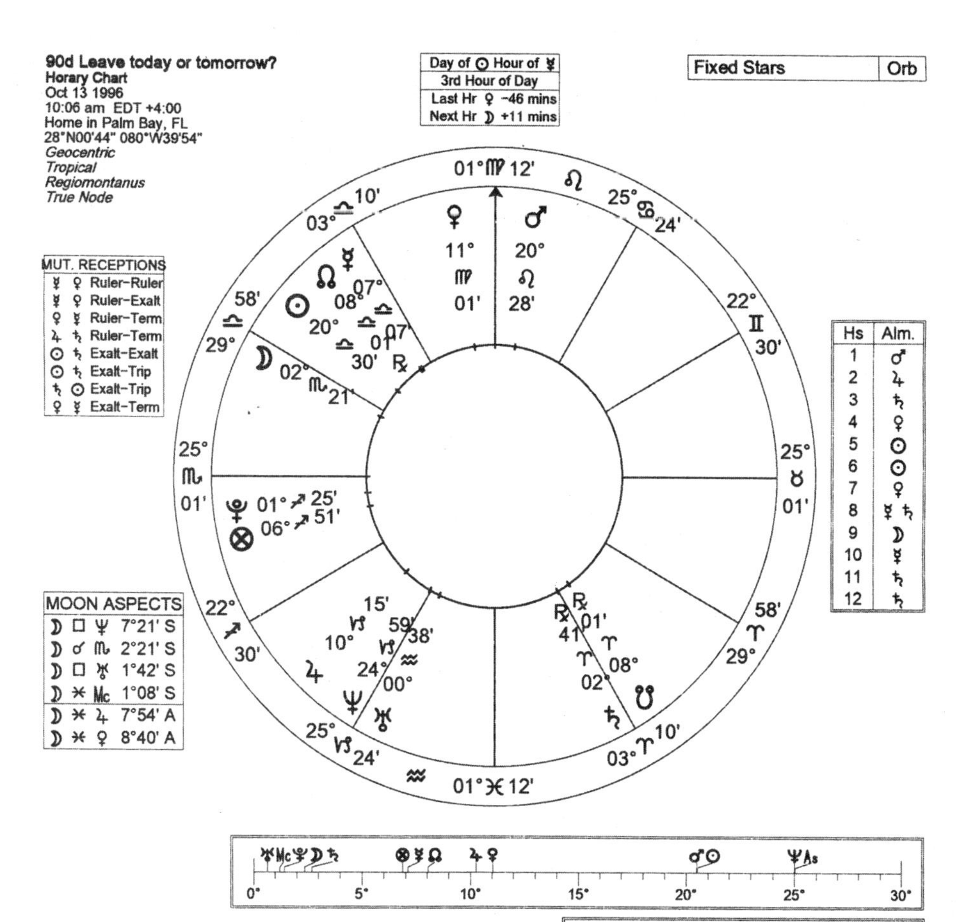

ESSENTIAL DIGNITIES (LEHMAN)								
Pt	Ruler	Exalt	Trip	Term	Face	Detri	Fall	Score
☽	♂	--	♀	♂	♂	♀	☽ −	−9 p
☉	♀	♄ m	♄ m	☿	♃	♂	☉ −	−9 p
☿	♀ m	♄	♄	♀	☽	♂	☉	−5 p
♀	☿ m	☿	♀ +	♀ +	♀ +	♃	♀ −	+2
♂	☉	--	☉	♃	♂ +	♄	--	+1
♃	♄	♂	♀	☿	♂	☽	♃ −	−9 p
♄	♂	☉ m	☉ m	♃	♂	♀	♄ −	−9 p
As	♂	--	♀	☿	♀	♀	☽	--
Mc	☿	☿	♀	☿	☉	♃	♀	--
⊗	♃	☋	☉	♃	☿	☿	☊	--

planets.pts				
Pt	Long.	Travel	Antiscia	C.Ant.
☽	02°♏21'03"	+13°01'	27°♒38	27°♌38
☉	20°♎30'51"	+00°59'	09°♓29	09°♍29
☿	07°♎07	+01°39'	22°♓52	22°♍52
♀	11°♍01	+01°10'	18°♈58	18°♎58
♂	20°♌28	+00°35'	09°♉31	09°♏31
♃	10°♑15	+00°07'	19°♐44	19°♊44
♄	02°♈41 ℞	−00°04'	27°♍18	27°♓18
♅	00°♒38	+00°00'	29°♏21	29°♉21
♆	24°♑59	+00°00'	05°♐00	05°♊00
♇	01°♐25	+00°01'	28°♑34	28°♋34
☊	08°♎01 ℞	−00°01'	21°♓58	21°♍58
☋	08°♈01 ℞	−00°01'	21°♍58	21°♓58
As	25°♏01'36"	+00°00'	04°♒58	04°♌58
Mc	01°♍12'44"	+00°00'	28°♈47	28°♎47
⊗	06°♐51	+00°00'	23°♑08	23°♋08

Example 90e: Should I leave this week?

After she didn't do anything about the last question, it's hardly surprising that a variation on the theme would come up again. Once again, she's Mars, angry at the latest blowup. And once again, she's powerless, Mars having just gone into Libra, its Detriment! And it's slowing down, going retrograde the following month. To add insult to injury, Mars is just about to oppose Saturn, the Almuten of the 7th, although again, I would opt for the 7th House sign Ruler, Venus, which, being merely peregrine in Sagittarius is still in better shape than Saturn in Fall.

Venus will square Mars after leaving Sagittarius for Capricorn. While the square is out of orb, it is suggestive of how things are going!

If he's the 5th House, then he's Moon in Scorpio. Not that this would promise anything better! The Moon in Fall is separating from a semi-sextile, hardly strong enough to do anything, but suggestive of the fact that he's not planning to change in any fundamental way. There's a weak reception between the Significators involving Face: she is afraid of leaving.

Here, the South Node on the Ascendant simply shows her fundamentally destroyed condition. There is nothing that she can do to improve this relationship. Even though this puts her Significator Mars conjunct the North Node, the placement of Mars is conjunct the 7th House cusp, illustrating once again her dependency on him.

In either case, with her weak Mars, she's not likely to do anything drastic anyway. If she hasn't been able to get out with all these other charts, is there any hope that this is the one that makes a difference?

Since I read primarily off the 7th House, I took the impending opposition to Saturn as indicating that things were going to get still worse. The conjunction to the North Node after that could bring something good her way, although I doubted it would mean she would get out. So while I had felt she should have left ages before, I said to her that I doubted that she actually would this time.

She didn't.

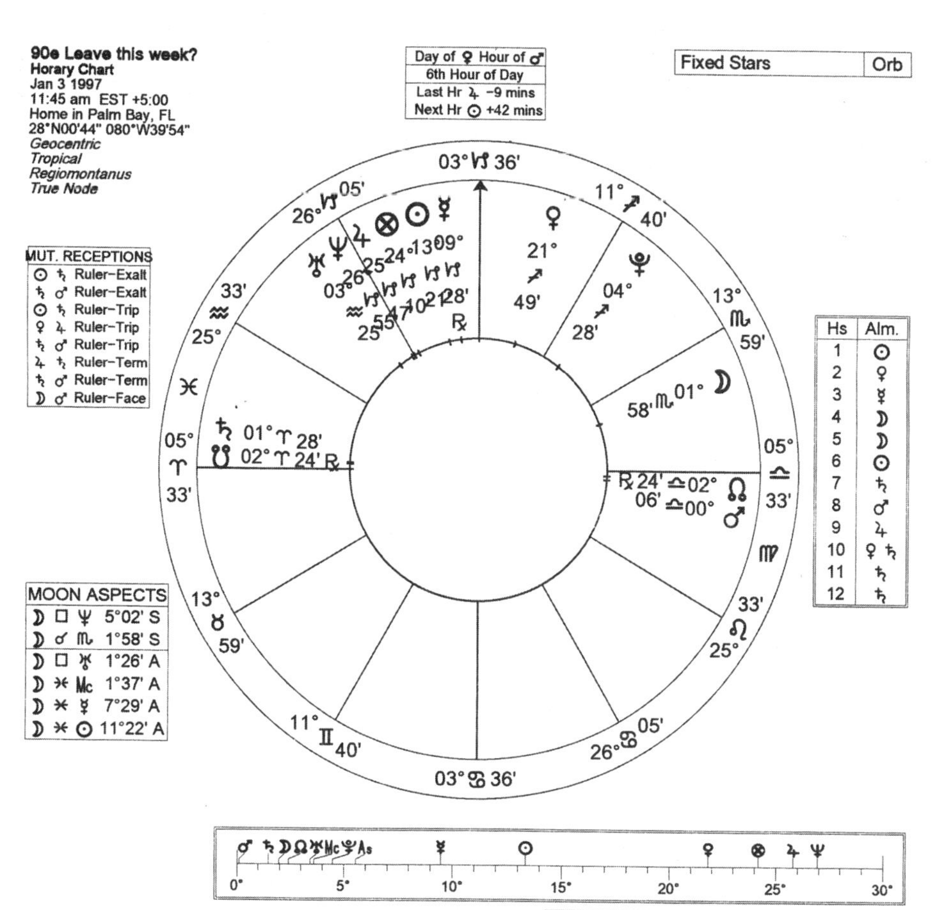

Pt	Ruler	Exalt	Trip	Term	Face	Detri	Fall	Score
ESSENTIAL DIGNITIES (LEHMAN)								
☽	♂	--	♀	♂	♂ m	♀	☽ -	-9 p
☉	♄	♂	♀ m	♃	♂	☽	♃	-5 p
☿	♄	♂	♀	☿ +	♃	☽	♃	+2
♀	♃	☋	☉ m	♄	♄	☿	☊	-5 p
♂	♀	♄	♄	♄	☽ m	♂ -	☉	-10 p
♃	♄	♂	♀	♄ m	☉	☽	♃ -	-9 p
♄	♂	☉	☉	♃ m	♂	♀	♄ -	-9 p
As	♂	☉	☉	♃	♂	♀	♄	--
Mc	♄	♂	♀	♀	♃	☽	♃	--
⊗	♄	♂	♀	♂	☉	☽	♃	--

Pt	Long.	Travel	Antiscia	C.Ant.
planets.pts				
☽	01°♏58'38"	+12°46'	28°♒01	28°♌01
☉	13°♑21'28"	+01°01'	16°♐38	16°♊38
☿	09°♑28 ℞	-01°18'	20°♐31	20°♊31
♀	21°♐49	+01°15'	08°♑10	08°♋10
♂	00°♎06	+00°18'	29°♓53	29°♍53
♃	25°♑47	+00°13'	04°♐12	04°♊12
♄	01°♈28	+00°03'	28°♍31	28°♓31
♅	03°♒25	+00°03'	26°♏34	26°♉34
♆	26°♑55	+00°02'	03°♐04	03°♊04
♇	04°♐28	+00°01'	25°♑31	25°♋31
☊	02°♎24 ℞	-00°02'	27°♓35	27°♍35
☋	02°♈24 ℞	-00°02'	27°♍35	27°♓35
As	05°♈33'34"	+00°00'	24°♍26	24°♓26
Mc	03°♑36'16"	+00°00'	26°♐23	26°♊23
⊗	24°♑10	+00°00'	05°♐49	05°♊49

Example 90f: What can I do about this?

In this last example, she had announced to him that her brother was going to pick her up to take her to the family for Christmas; she had left a note telling him about it, and then, when she hadn't heard from him for a week, she left a second note adding that she assumed it was all right. She found a note written on his desk (but not delivered) to her, telling her to pack all her stuff and leave if she wanted to "go off like that!" So she wanted to know what to do: whether she should compromise, whether it was really the end, or whether he would change his mind before she left.

Once again, she is shown by Mars, although finally she has some dignity and speed – but a major problem. She's Mars in Capricorn, where Mars is exalted, but she is in a partile conjunction to Neptune! "Denial" is a river in Egypt, goes the old pun, and there's no reason to doubt that it's true here.

If he is the 7th House, then he's Venus in early Aquarius, having already separated from the conjunction to Mars and not far from going retrograde. Their relationship is showing in past tense, but that's not the first time!

If he's the 5th House, then he's the Sun in Sagittarius, dignified by Triplicity, but not in relationship to her Significator. There's nothing showing here that argues that she needs to stay in this relationship either.

Notice, however, that she is capable of action, since her Significator is finally dignified. With a relatively late degree rising, things really are too late. So what could I say? Once, again, leave! Did she? That was the last contact I had with her, so I just don't know.

By this time, my question had become: why is she even calling me? Chart after chart shows no relationship, that the relationship was in the past, that she's angry, that things are going nowhere. Why not call someone who could help her get over him, rather than someone who could tell her one more time that it would be a good idea to leave? I would have been delighted to refer her to a psychological astrologer or psychologist in order to examine the kinds of issues and motivations that had allowed her to remain in such an obsessive relationship that seemed more doomed with each successive event or question. However, there's no point making the referral when the client is not seeking help. She saw nothing wrong with this relationship!

All I can surmise is that, while she kept calling, she was making a collection of assessments, and that at some point, the pile would be big enough, and her Significator strong enough, that she would finally act on it.

In examining these charts at the time, I had begun by looking at both the 5th and 7th to try to understand which house the Quesited represented. After the first few charts, I relied on the 7th House exclusively. This became an object lesson that in relationships, what is 7th for one truly can be 5th for the other. This is really the same conclusion that I had already presented for the 3rd House/9th House dilemma when it comes to trips. Distance is in the eye of the beholder. Here, the nature of the relationship is in the eye of the beholder, and the two parties to it may even have separate definitions. Once again, position is relative.

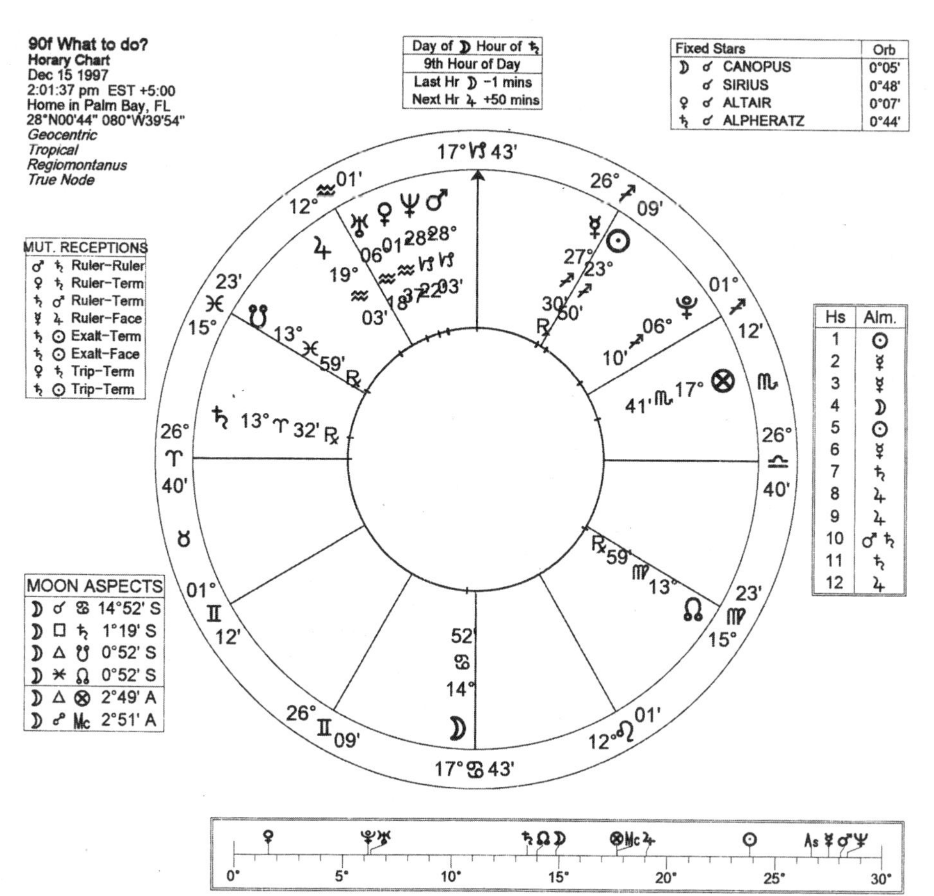

ESSENTIAL DIGNITIES (LEHMAN)								
Pt	Ruler	Exalt	Trip	Term	Face	Detri	Fall	Score
☽	☽ +	♃	♀	☿	☿	♄	♂	+5
☉	♃	☋	☉ +	♄	♄ m	☿	☊	+3
☿	♃	☋	☉	♂	♄	☿ −	☊	−10 p
♀	♄	--	♄	♄ m	♀ +	☉	--	+1
♂	♄ m	♂ +	♀	♄	☉	☽	♃	+4
♃	♄	--	♄	♀	☿	☉	--	−5 p
♄	♂ m	☉	☉	♀ m	☉ m	♀	♄ −	−9 p
As	♂	☉	☉	♄	♀	♀	♄	--
Mc	♄	♂	♀	♃	♂	☽	♃	--
⊗	♂	--	♀	♀	☉	♀	☽	--

planets.pts				
Pt	Long.	Travel	Antiscia	C.Ant.
☽	14°♋52'01"	+13°12'	15°♊07	15°♐07
☉	23°♐50'49"	+01°01'	06°♑09	06°♋09
☿	27°♐30 ℞	−01°19'	02°♑29	02°♋29
♀	01°♒37	+00°23'	28°♏22	28°♉22
♂	28°♑03	+00°46'	01°♐56	01°♊56
♃	19°♒03	+00°11'	10°♏56	10°♉56
♄	13°♈32 ℞	−00°00'	16°♍27	16°♓27
♅	06°♒18	+00°02'	23°♏41	23°♉41
♆	28°♑22	+00°01'	01°♐37	01°♊37
♇	06°♐10	+00°02'	23°♑49	23°♋49
☊	13°♍59 ℞	−00°10'	16°♈00	16°♎00
☋	13°♓59 ℞	−00°10'	16°♎00	16°♈00
As	26°♈40'44"	+00°00'	03°♍19	03°♓19
Mc	17°♑43'39"	+00°00'	12°♐16	12°♊16
⊗	17°♏41	+00°00'	12°♒18	12°♌18

The Consultation Chart

There is actually historical precedent for the consultation chart. We encountered it in Chapter 6 concerning medical horaries. The concept was urine casting – casting a chart for the time of receiving a urine sample from a patient. This chart type is actually the mother of the consultation chart.

It is calculated for the time that a client is scheduled to arrive for an appointment – and then it is adjusted to the actual beginning of the appointment. Many natal astrologers run this chart to get insight into the issues that are likely to be important to the client in a given consultation.

I do not routinely run this chart in my natal work. However, it stands ready to be run at any time – and whenever I run into a problem or a question myself, I do check it.

Example 91: Consultation Chart

Before I became proficient at classical natal astrology, I never would consider doing rectification. Now, I am fairly comfortable at it, provided that I have a fairly small range of time to work with. It is a service I don't generally advertise, and I work mainly by referrals from other astrologers.

One such client had called me up. In addition to asking for the dates and times that are needed for rectification, I asked her what she knew about her birth time. She responded that she was told that it was between 3:00 A.M. and 3:30 A.M. If this seems like a rather narrow range to even bother with rectification, bear in mind that her primary astrologer works with a precise system of prediction. In any case, it was just as well, because she offered only three specific dates, and two general ones.

When I got off the phone with her, something just didn't seem right. I talked to my partner about the whole scenario, and she said: why don't you look at the consultation chart and see if the woman is lying about something! So I ran a chart for the time that the client called me. For consultation charts, I always use my own location.

Here, I don't even have to go through the entire set of rules for whether the rumor is true! The Moon is peregrine, and Mercury has only out-of-sect Triplicity, but more to the point, Mercury is retrograde and conjunct the Sun! Now whether we should consider the cazimi to be dignified – something I have considerable reservations about – in this circumstance my worry is that something is hidden, and here is Mercury completely invisible! So it was pretty obvious to me that she was lying about something.

But then I had to think. What if I consistently checked consultation charts on all my clients! I would probably then find out that a large number of them are lying! What then? I decided that I had to take divination on faith, and simply note that *in this case* I was strongly moved to follow up on this question, whereas most of the time I am not. Routinized questions – like consultation charts on every client – tend to lose their punch. But this was no routine question.

I went ahead and did the rectification. However, after she called me up and got my result, *then* she decided to call an aunt, who told her that actually,

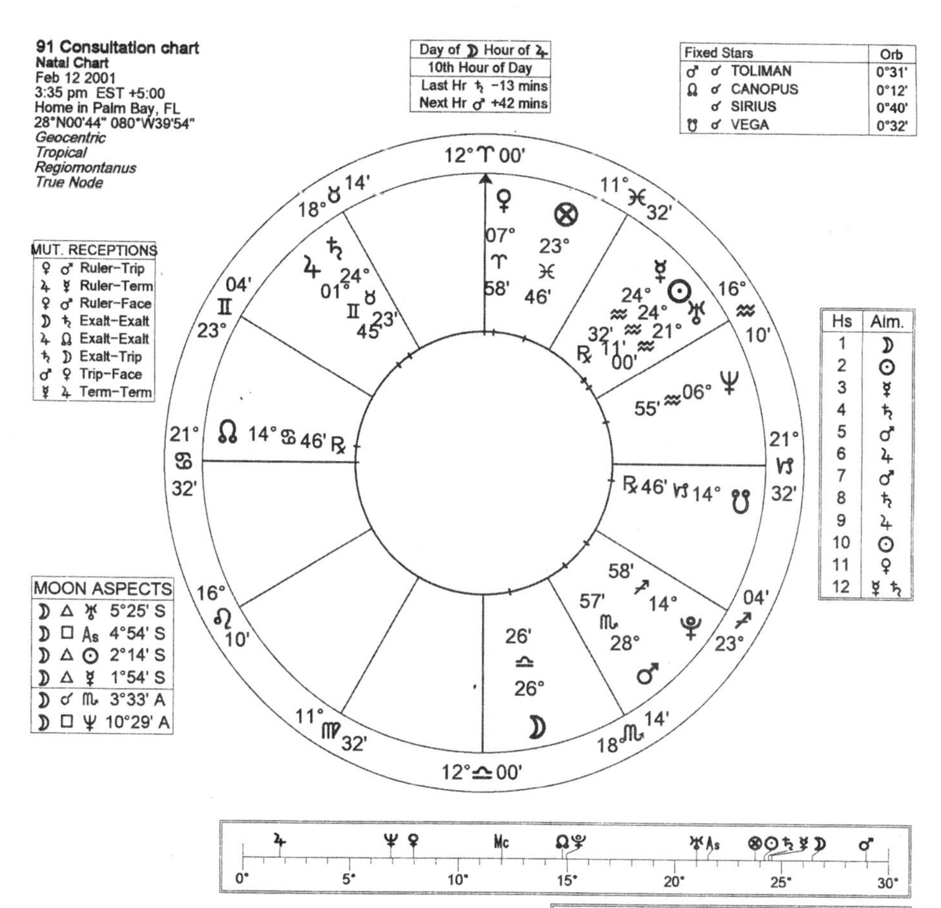

ESSENTIAL DIGNITIES (LEHMAN)								
Pt	Ruler	Exalt	Trip	Term	Face	Detri	Fall	Score
☽	♀	♄ m	♄	♂	♃	♂	☉	−5 p
☉	♄	--	♄	♃	☽	☉ −	--	−10 p
☿	♄	--	♄	♃ m	☽	☉	--	−5 p
♀	♂	☉	☉	♀ +	♂ m	♀ −	♄	−3
♂	♂ +	--	♀	♄	♀ m	♀	☽	+5
♃	☿	☊ m	♄	☿ m	♃ +	♃ −	☋	−4
♄	♀	☽ m	♀	♄ +	♄ +	♂	--	+3
As	☽	♃	♀	♀	☽	♄	♂	--
Mc	♂	☉	☉	♀	☉	♀	♄	--
⊗	♃	♀	♀	♂	♂	☿	☿	--

planets.pts				
Pt	Long.	Travel	Antiscia	C.Ant.
☽	26°♎26'22"	+13°42'	03°♓33	03°♍33
☉	24°♒11'56"	+01°00'	05°♏48	05°♉48
☿	24°♒32 ℞	−01°09'	05°♏27	05°♉27
♀	07°♈58	+00°42'	22°♍01	22°♓01
♂	28°♏57	+00°31'	01°♒02	01°♌02
♃	01°♊45	+00°03'	28°♋14	28°♑14
♄	24°♉23	+00°02'	05°♌36	05°♒36
♅	21°♒00	+00°03'	08°♏59	08°♉59
♆	06°♒55	+00°02'	23°♏04	23°♉04
♇	14°♐58	+00°01'	15°♑01	15°♋01
☊	14°♋46 ℞	−00°03'	15°♊13	15°♐13
☋	14°♑46 ℞	−00°03'	15°♐13	15°♊13
As	21°♋32'09"	+00°00'	08°♊27	08°♐27
Mc	12°♈00'26"	+00°00'	17°♍59	17°♓59
⊗	23°♓46	+00°00'	06°♎13	06°♈13

she had been born around 6:00 A.M. When she called me back with this information, I told her that I had only checked roughly between 3:00 A.M. to 3:30 A.M., actually from 2:44 A.M. to 3:47 A.M., and had given her the best fit for the time range that she had told me, and given the small number of events she had mentioned. She asked me to check again for the period around 6:00 A.M. Interestingly, the consultation chart gave me a very big clue about the subsequent angles in the rectification!

About this time, the referring astrologer called me up to apologize for making the referral. It seems that his wife had taken the call from the client – something quite unusual – and that his wife had had a very bad feeling about this woman from the start. In talking to the woman, the astrologer had decided that she was lying to him, and that she wasn't worth having as a client! He was most amused when I told him about the consultation chart.

This chapter has begun to touch upon some of the advanced applications in horary, the things that don't fall neatly into one house, or that address philosophical issues about our Art. There are more of these areas that I surely could have included. The fact remains, after all these years of doing horaries, it's still possible to surprise me. Not all questions seem to fall neatly into our twelve house system. Horary analysis will continue to challenge the imagination of the practitioner. And occasionally, the Artist simply has to admit to not having any idea how to proceed with the question.

If someone asks me a question I have never received before, and it's a question that Lilly and my other prime sources have not addressed, I tell the Querent that fact. If I have a theory about how to proceed, then I do, but with the proviso that I'm making up the rules as I go along. Usually, it works fine. But whether it does or not, it's a learning experience, and the Querent has a right to know that he or she is at the cutting edge.

Chapter 14

Earning Your Horary Black Belt

A month before testing for my black belt in Tae Kwon Do, I bought a belt rack. A belt rack is a display device that holds the different color belts that a martial arts practitioner earns in the course of moving up the ranks toward black belt. When I unpacked it, I noticed that it had six slots: just perfect to accommodate white, yellow, green, blue, red, and black belts. This rack reminded me of exactly what the problem is in the modern Western concept of Mastery.

Children learn about the black belt early – Bruce Lee movies, action-adventures, and so forth. In all these pop media, the black belt is the awesome or mystical reminder of mastery: you have made it when you have earned it. Clearly, my humble little belt rack was designed for the proud parent who wants to show Johnny or Susie's progress toward Mastery, and finally celebrate it with the installation of the black belt at the top of the rack.

But mastery has nothing to do with mounting a piece of cloth on the wall. When the goal of learning becomes nothing but a colored cloth or a piece of vellum, then mastery is never learned. Any true martial artist will tell you that a black belt is the *beginning* of the long road of learning the lessons of martial art. All it represents is an admission pass to the big tent, but it's a tent already occupied by thousands, maybe even millions.

Achieving mastery means that you work with the skills you have every day. If you take your cloth and hang it on the wall, instead of wearing it around your waist while you continue to train, you've achieved nothing. Mastery is not a single state that, once acquired, never rusts or corrodes.

The only way to become a master of Horary is to do Horary. Yes, you can read this book, and hopefully I can teach you some things you didn't know before. But if you don't go out and apply it, *if you don't go out and find the things I forgot to mention, or didn't know to tell you*, then the study of this work is futile. Horary is meant to be used, enjoyed, laughed at, shouted at, and suffered through. But most of all, the skills are meant to be kept alive, and that means there must be an endless supply of questions to ponder and to answer.

Every practitioner advances the Art. And the Art changes every practitioner. What could be better?

Appendix A

Synopsis of Classical Concepts Necessary to Understand Horary

There are several basic concepts from classical astrology which are absolutely crucial to the understanding of horary. In ***Essential Dignities***[211] and ***Classical Astrology for Modern Living***[212] I described these concepts fully. However, for those new to classical astrology, this can serve as an introduction to these critical components of the classical method.

Essential and Accidental Dignities

Classical Astrology recognizes five essential dignities, and a whole series of accidental ones. The essential dignities are:

- Sign, 5 points of dignity
- Exaltation, 4 points of dignity
- Triplicity, 3 points of dignity
- Term, 2 points of dignity
- Face, 1 point of dignity

Having said that, there are several different methods for the determination of Triplicities and Terms. My preferred Table of Dignities for Horary is shown in Appendix D. This is a synthesis of the traditional sign, exaltation and Face rulers, the Dorothean Triplicities, and the Chaldean Terms. Put another way, this Table differs from Lilly's only in the Triplicities.

The three dignities Sign, Exaltation and Triplicity are called the Major Dignities; Term and Face are the Minor Dignities. This expresses something about the importance of the assessment represented by dignity: it is a method of calculating the strength of a planet, functionally defined as the ability of the planet to get what it wants.

A planet in its own Sign (as Mars in Aries) when it represents a horary Significator, symbolizes a person able to charge out and get what she or he wants. That person is ready and able to do what it takes to accomplish the question. For example, if that Mars in Aries is the Significator of the Querent in a question of marriage, that person will be a go-getter when it comes to whatever is necessary to make the marriage happen: whether asking the Question, or making out the guest list, or calling the florist.

A planet in its own Exaltation (as Sun in Aries) when it represents a horary Significator, shows a person who gets things done by having someone else do it for them: the Sun Significator in our example might hire a wedding consultant to do the job, or have a relative who steps in and does all the work.

A planet in its own Triplicity (as Jupiter in Aries at night) when it represents a horary Significator, gives someone who gets his or her desires by being in the right place at the right time – by luck, in other words. This is the person who remembers at the last minute that nobody ordered the corsages at the florist for the wedding *tomorrow*, and just as the person walks in the door of the florist, the florist gets a cancellation on an order of corsages that were already completed for tomorrow for someone else and our heroine or hero not only gets the flowers, but an incredible deal.

A planet in its own Term (as Mercury at sixteen degrees of Aries) when it represents a horary Significator, gives a person who looks the part, but may not have any skill at all in the matter at hand. Still, having the appearance of competency, the person may yet pull it off. This is someone who walks into the hotel catering office to set up the wedding reception looking completely professional in appearance, that the catering staff treats the person as knowledgeable about the process – whether this is in fact true or not. Because of the air of expertise, the person gets a better deal than she or he might otherwise be capable of negotiating.

A planet in its own Face (as Venus at twenty two degrees of Aries) when it represents a horary Significator, gives someone fearful about the whole process. As a result, while this really isn't much of a dignity, the person's attention is focused! The Querent asking a horary about marriage who has dignity only by Face may be fearful that if he or she doesn't marry the person named, there may never be a marriage at all, or that he or she is too old to have children, or that favorite Aunt Desmerelda will die before she ever sees the Querent married, etc. A planet with dignity only by Face is barely saved from being peregrine.

When a planet has no dignity at all by any of the five means (and this includes both the in-sect and out-of-sect Triplicity rulers), then that planet is ***peregrine***. A peregrine planet in horary represents someone incapable of effecting a result. These people get distracted and wander off the mark. As a result, seldom does an affirmative outcome actually move to fruition if the Significators are peregrine.

A planet in ***Detriment*** or ***Fall*** (also shown in Appendix D) is a planet that is beginning the race several steps behind everyone else. For a planet in this state to get what it wants, the person signified has to come up with a novel solution. Any attempt to accomplish the matter in what would appear to be the most straightforward way will guarantee failure. Because most people are reluctant to actually engage in that level of creativity, the debility frequently stops the person from accomplishing the goal.

Accidental Dignity

The accidental dignities and debilities are shown in Table One. They can be divided into several generic types:

- House placement (i.e., angular, succedent, cadent)
- Motion (swift, slow, direct, retrograde)
- Oriental and Occidental
- Moon increasing or decreasing in Light
- Closeness to the Sun (Under Beams, Combust, Cazimi)
- Aspects to malefic and benefic planets
- Conjunctions with fixed stars and the Nodes of the Moon

Table 1. Accidental Dignities & debilities. Source: Lilly, *Christian Astrology*, p 115.

Accidental Dignities		**Accidental Debilities**	
In the M.C. or Ascendant	5	In the 12th House	-5
In the 7th, 4th & 11th Houses	4	In the 8th & 6th House	-2
In the 2nd & 5th Houses	3	Retrograde	-5
In the 9th House	2	Slow in Motion	-2
In the 3rd House	1	♄ ♃ ♂ Occidental	-2
Direct (except ☉ & ☽)	4	♀ ☿ Oriental	-2
Swift in Motion	2	☽ decreasing in light	-2
♄ ♃ ♂ Oriental	2	Combust of the ☉	-5
♀ ☿ Occidental	2	Under the ☉ Beams	-4
☽ increasing in light, or Occidental	2	Partile ☌ with ♄ or ♂	-5
Free from combustion & ☉ Beams	5	Partile ☌ with ☋	-4
Cazimi	5	Besieged of ♄ or ♂	-5
Partile ☌ with ♃ or ♀	5	Partile ☍ with ♄ or ♂	-4
Partile ☌ with ☊	4	Partile □ with ♄ or ♂	-3
Partile △ with ♃ or ♀	4	In ☌ or within 5° of *Caput Algol*	-5
Partile ⚹ with ♃ or ♀	3		
In ☌ with *Cor Leonis*	6		
In ☌ with *Spica*	5		

The accidental dignities are tallied separately from the essential dignities. One of the frustrations of this system is that it's not entirely clear that all categories of dignity or debility are really equivalent. For example, is being Direct *really* equivalent in strength to being conjunct Spica? I would say, no!

Essential versus Accidental Dignity

The horary beginner often wastes valuable time trying to weigh this conundrum: which of the two is more important? In other words, what do you do when a planet is essentially dignified, but accidentally debilitated, or *vice versa*? The answer is: you cannot make this determination based on the points.

In my experience, having a Significator conjunct one of the especially strong fixed stars, like *Spica* or *Algol,* is sufficient to affect the outcome of the question. It's very rare for a Significator conjunct *Spica* to not succeed; it's very hard for a Significator conjunct *Algol* not to fail.

Each class of accidental dignity rates somewhat differently. An easy aspect to the benefics is probably less helpful than hard aspects to the malefics are harmful. Aid from another or from a circumstance (the fundamental meaning of a sextile or trine to a benefic) is seldom enough to turn a no into a yes, *although if you are reading a horary where the help of another really could be that critical, then this may turn your reading*. For example, if you are asking about a job, and your Significator will trine Jupiter, and Jupiter is not otherwise a Significator in this Question, this could be that Jupiter represents a person with some social standing or authority who comes to your defense. Perhaps the boss you would be working for is a friend of someone who has been a mentor to you, and happens to mention your application. However, this possible boon to your situation is only likely to occur if that benefic is in turn dignified, so essential dignity comes to the fore once more.

The hard aspects to the malefics have somewhat the reverse interpretation. Here, the prospective employer mentions your name to someone who speaks against you, whether from personal knowledge, or simply maliciousness. However, if the malefic is dignified by at least major essential dignity, the effect is much lessened, if not completely eliminated.

Notice that both benefics and malefics essentially debilitated are planets behaving badly: they are unpredictable in their effects.

The house placement of Significators is actually somewhat simpler than the table of accidental dignities implies. The important issue is whether a planet is Cadent, because that may make it more difficult for it to express itself. Angular is best, but there's less of a differential between angular and succedent than either of those two and cadent.

I have not found it necessary to pay attention to whether a planet is oriental or occidental in interpreting Horary charts for my clients.

A planet swift or increasing in Light is significant, but more descriptive of the party involved than what the eventual outcome may be. Similarly, the issue of cazimi, combustion, or beams adds color to the story, although these may affect the outcome as well.

The Part of Fortune

Good comes from the Part of Fortune, if it has dignity through its dispositor(s). Figure 1 shows its method of calculation.

Figure 1. Methods of calculating the Part of Fortune.

Modern:		
Fortuna, Day & Night	=	Ascendant + ☽ - ☉
Spirit, Day & Night	=	Ascendant + ☉ - ☽
Ancient:		
Fortuna, Day	=	Ascendant + ☽ - ☉
Fortuna, Night	=	Ascendant + ☉ - ☽
Spirit, Night	=	Ascendant + ☽ - ☉
Spirit, Day	=	Ascendant + ☉ - ☽

The Part of Fortune, being a calculated point, has no essential dignity, apart from that given to it by its dispositors. When the dispositors are well dignified, then an aspect of a Significator to the Part of Fortune provides a material benefit to that Significator. Points are considered passive; hence, they *do not aspect planets*, although they can receive aspects.

Antiscia and Contra-antiscia

This technique, which goes back to Hellenistic astrology, involves drawing a line between 0 degrees Cancer and 0 degrees Capricorn. We have just split the zodiac along the axis of the Solstices. Now we wish to examine what degrees of the zodiac are symmetrical with respect to this line. But why should we care?

29 degrees Gemini and one degree Cancer are equal in distance to 0 degrees Cancer – they are each one degree away. The day is longest (by definition) when the Sun is at zero Cancer. The Sun at 29 degrees Gemini and one degree Cancer have days of equal length, and nights of equal length. (When I say equal, I mean within the observational capacity of the ancient Greeks.) Both have days just slightly shorter than the longest possible day. This relationship of having days of equal length is referred to as being d***antiscial*** to each other, or as being in ***Antiscion***.

Various pairs of Signs are related to each other by antiscion as shown in Table 2.

Table 2. Antiscial & contra-antiscial signs.

Antiscial signs	Contra-antiscial signs
♈ ♍	♈ ♓
♉ ♌	♉ ♒
♊ ♋	♊ ♑
♎ ♓	♎ ♍
♏ ♒	♏ ♌
♐ ♑	♐ ♋

The sign and degree exactly opposite the antiscial degree of a planet is called its ***Contra-antiscion***.

Planets in antiscial or contra-antiscial relationship were considered to be related to each other as if they were in aspect. A relationship by antiscion was considered analogous to a conjunction. A contra-antiscial relationship was considered analogous to an opposition. The orb to use is unknown, because none of the sources spelled it out. However, omitting Antiscia means that you may miss a possible method for perfection.

Mutual Reception

In an earlier work, I spent an entire chapter on mutual reception.[213] For our purposes here, I want to summarize two concepts; interested readers are referred to my previous work for more detail.

First, the concept that planets in mutual reception somehow "swap positions" (e.g., if the Moon is in Capricorn and Saturn is in Cancer, this can be read as if the Moon were in Cancer and Saturn in Capricorn) can be definitively traced to a modern misunderstanding of an ambiguous translation of Ptolemy. It is simply not true.

Planets in mutual reception retain their own dignities – or lack thereof. What the mutual reception does is guarantee that each of the planets will attempt to come to the aid of the other. How good or how welcome that aid would be is dependent on the intrinsic dignity of the planets involved.

Consider, for example, Mars in Capricorn and Saturn in Cancer in a night chart. This doesn't look quite like a reception at all, but Mars is in Saturn's sign, while Saturn is in Mars' Triplicity. This is a perfectly good reception, but consider the difference from Mars' and Saturn's points of view. Saturn gets help from Mars – Mars in Capricorn is exalted, so this is definitely the kind of help that anyone could value. Saturn has a good ally here. But Mars – the help comes from a Saturn in Detriment. This represents the kind of help that maybe Mars would rather do without! But Mars is stuck with it, so now the help becomes a hindrance.

The second major concept concerning receptions is the difference between strong and weak reception. Strong reception is when the dignities used for the reception are Sign, Exaltation, or Triplicity, as with our example above. Weak reception is when the dignities involved are Term and Face. Weak reception can be virtually ignored, because the link is simply not that strong. This, incidentally, illustrates a weakness in the point system of dignity: a planet with dignities by Term and Face (+2 +1 = +3) is *not* as strong as a planet in Triplicity (+3). There is a bigger gap between the strong and weak dignities, and hence receptions, than there actually is within each of the two groups.

Applying and Separating

It's worth reminding the reader of the importance of distinguishing between applying and separating aspects. This is a concept that can be virtually ignored in Natal, but it is crucial in Horary. A separating aspect represents an event in the past. An applying aspect represents an event in the future. It's that simple.

Appendix B

Who Were Those Guys, Anyway?

There are a lot of names which have been mentioned in this work. Below is a brief synopsis of some of the more important ones.[214]

Al-Biruni, Muhammad ibn Ahmad (973-1048?): al-Biruni's influence was only on Arabic astrology because his works were not among the translations that became available to the Latin West in the Medieval period. In the modern era, his works became available in translation. Most notably, he made lists, so his work is useful as a compendium of what the Arabs and Indians of the time (he studied in India) used as natural rulerships.[215]

Barclay, Olivia (1919-2001): Olivia was my original teacher in Horary. She deserves considerable credit for tirelessly putting forward Lilly as the best horary source at a time when the standard work was Goldstein-Jacobson. Thus, she was one of the early British neoclassicists, although her horary method still incorporated techniques that she derived from modern sources.[216]

Bonatti, Guido (13th Century; dates speculative): Bonatti was of sufficient fame in his own time that Dante placed him in the ***Inferno***. He wrote on all branches of astrology, including natal, horary, electional, mundane, and astro-meteorology. Here we have used portions from his ***Tractatus Sextus*** for the rules of warfare.[217]

Coley, Henry (1633-1707): Coley was Lilly's official successor, and a Latin translator as well, translating works of Bonatti and Cardan into English.[218]

Culpeper, Nicholas (1616-1654): author of the best-known herbal ever published, Culpeper had begun conventional academic training as a physician, when he ran out of money. In those days, that didn't necessarily stop an enterprising person from practicing medicine anyway. Culpeper did, and he used his classical language talent to translate the official pharmacological dispensary into English, making it available to the general public, an act which made him loathed by other physicians.[219]

Dariot, Claude (1533-1594): in addition to publishing a work on horary and electional astrology which was translated into English at the end of the 16th Century, Dariot was a Paracelsan physician. His method was a more complex system than Lilly's, but Lilly acknowledges his debt to Dariot quite extensively.[220]

Dorotheus of Sidon (1st Century C.E.): his work on ***Interrogations*** reads like a modern work on horary and electional, except that so much terminology is archaic. What is clear from his work is that the basic rules for horary were established so early.[221]

Ibn Ezra, Abraham (1089? – 1167): one of the greatest Jewish scholars of the Arabic period, he contributed a number of astrological and astronomical works, building on earlier contributions by Arabic scholars.[222]

Gadbury, John (1627-1704): a one-time student of Lilly, their split was in part political, since Gadbury was a Royalist during the English Civil War. He published a collection of Nativities, as well as his major work ***Genethlialogia***, which we cite here because of its short compendium on horary method.[223]

Goldstein-Jacobson, Ivy (1893-1990): in my early years in astrology, it never occurred to me to go to conventions or meetings, so I never had the privilege to meet this grand old lady of American astrology. Her typescript books were a profound influence for several generations of astrologers, because she wrote on so broad a swath of astrology. Almost every horary astrologer who came of age in the Sixties, Seventies, or early Eighties was profoundly influenced by her work.[224]

Griffin, Anthony (17th Century): little is known of Griffin, but his work on theft was highly praised by Lilly, and we use it here.[225]

Jones, Marc Edmund (1888-1980): in an odd way, I feel a lineage-bearer for this man, because I received the Award given in his name. Dr. Jones had a profound influence on all facets of American astrology, often in ways that now can only be surmised. Working in such diverse fields as degree symbolism and horary, he was systematizer, synthesizer, theoretician, and practitioner.[226]

Lilly, William (1602-1681): Lilly's work on horary remains the most comprehensive book on the subject. In addition to his horary interests, Lilly published an extremely popular almanac, and made prognostications on the side of Parliament during the English Civil War.[227]

Ptolemy (circa 100-178 C.E.): Ptolemy's work, ***Tetrabiblos***, almost single-handedly wiped out much of our knowledge of Hellenistic astrology. Because of its importance. This work was the Bible of subsequent astrologers.[228]

Ramesey, William (17th Century) is mainly known for his work on electional. The preface to his work suggests that he was a Royalist during the English Civil War.[229]

Saunders, Richard (17th Century) wrote one of the major texts on medical astrology during his Century. He was a friend of Lilly's, and he also wrote on chiromancy, as well as mundane and electional astrology.[230]

Watters, Barbara (1907-1984): a major force in the Metro Washington, DC area in her time, Watters wrote a number of highly interesting – and unusual – works. Her horary volume is a common 20th Century reference after Ivy Goldstein-Jacobson for the astrologers of the seventies and early eighties.[231]

Appendix C

Glossary

Accidental Dignity: this is a mix of conditions, all of which relate to the strength of a planet being increased (or decreased, with accidental debility) because of the planet's placement, apart from its tropical zodiacal position. The kinds of factors which are included in the tables of accidental dignity include: house placement, whether oriental or occidental, in conjunction to fixed stars, aspects to benefics or malefics, closeness to the Sun, and speed.

Almuten/Almutem: There are five Essential Dignities for any degree of the zodiac: the rulership (+5), exaltation (+4), triplicity (+3), term (+2), and face (+1). If you take a particular house cusp, find the planet which rules each of the five essential dignities of the position, and assign the points to the planet. That planet with the highest point value is the Almuten. For example: for 8° Aries 15' in a daytime chart: Mars is the ruler (+5), the Sun rules the exaltation (+4), the triplicity (+3) and the face (+1) = +8, and Venus the terms (+2): the Sun is Almuten. Arabic sources give the word as "Almutem," but by the 17th Century, the word was consistently being translated and used as "Almuten."

Antiscion: "Some of the learned in this Art do hold that the Antiscions of the Planets be equivalent unto a Sextile or a Trine-aspect, especially if they were beneficial Planets; and their Contrantiscions to be of the nature of Quadrate or Opposition. How to know the Antiscions is no more than this; first, know the Antiscions of the signs, which is no more but a sign being equally distant with another from Cancer and Capricorn the two Tropicks; as Gemini hath its Antiscion in Cancer, Taurus in Leo, Aries in Virgo, Pisces in Libra, Aquarius in Scorpio, and Capricorn in Sagittary; for when the Sun is in 1° of Gemini, he is as far from the Tropick point of Cancer as when he is in 29° of Cancer; and in the 5° of Taurus, as when the 25° of Leo, &c.... The Contrantiscion is known thus; look in what sign, degree and minute your Antiscion falls, and your contrantiscion will be in the same degree and minute as your opposite sign to your Antiscion. [Ramesey]

Application: "is when two Planets approach each other, either by Body or Aspect; and this may be three several ways:

"First, when both Planets are direct, for example, Jupiter in 11 degrees of Aries, and Mars in 9 degrees of Aries, both of them direct; here Mars applies to a conjunction of Jupiter.

"The second is when two Stars are Retrograde, and apply to each other by a Retrograde motion; thus Jupiter in 9 degrees of Aries. Retrograde, and Mars in 11 degrees of the same Sign Retrograde also, here Mars applies to the body of Jupiter by Retrograde motion.

"Thirdly, when one Planet is Retrograde in more degrees of a Sign, and another direct in fewer; as suppose Mars in 12 degrees of Aries Retrograde, and Venus in 10 degrees of Aries, here Mars applies to Venus and Venus applies to Mars, and this kind of application is of great force and efficacy in all manner of Astrological Resolutions; but this must be remembered also, that a Superior Planet cannot apply to an Inferior one, unless he be Retrograde. "[Partridge]

Beholding: This word has shifted somewhat over time, but it refers to two planets which are either in ptolemaic aspect (conjunction, opposition, trine, square or sextile) or antiscial, or contranticial relationship.

The Bendings: the points square the Nodal axis. If a planet square the Nodes is zodiacally between the North Node and the South Node (i.e., start counting at the North Node), then it is at the Northern Bending; if between the South Node and the North Node, it is at the Southern Bending.

Besieging: "this I think need no Explanation, for every Souldier understands it; as suppose Saturn in 10 deg. Jupiter in 1 deg. and Mars in 13 deg. of Leo; here Jupiter is besieged by Saturn and Mars." [Partridge]

Cazimi: "is when a Planet is in the heart of the Sun; that is, not distant from him above 17 min. as Mars in 10 deg. 30 min. of Aries, the Sun in 10 deg. 15 min. of Aries; here Mars is in Cazimi." [Partridge]

Combustion: "A Planet is Combust when he is not distant from the Sun 8 deg. 30 min. either before or after him; for Example, Jupiter in 10 deg. of Aries, the Sun in 14 deg. and Mars in 18, here both Jupiter and Mars are Combust; and observe that a Planet going to Combustion is more afflicted than when departing from it." [Partridge]

Essential Dignity: Essential dignity is a system for assessing the strength of a planet by its placement in the zodiac alone. There are five essential dignities: by sign, exaltation, triplicity, term, and face. A planet with dignity can act or do as it wants, whereas a planet without dignity has difficulty getting from Point A to Point B except by a very circuitous route.

Face: One of the minor dignities, also called Chaldean decanates. The faces are 10° slices of the signs, marked by planetary rulers falling in the sequence known as the Chaldean order. The Face is given +1 point.

Five degree (5°) rule: Consider the movement of the planets diurnally. For example, the Sun "rises" by going from the 1st House to the 12th House. A planet on the 12th House side of the Ascendant may be said to be angular if it is within 5° of the Ascendant: this is the so-called 5° rule. Depending on the source, this may actually entail anywhere from 2° to 7 or 8°, depending on whether the House moved into is Angular, Succedent, or Cadent (largest for Angular; smallest for Cadent). Generally, Medieval sources give 7° for angular cusps, 5° for succedent cusps, and 3° for cadent cusps.

Joys: This word was used two ways, which can lead to some confusion. One use was as a synonym for "exaltation." The second was an indicator of which house would be the top choice for a given planet. The joys by house are: Mercury = 1st House, Moon = 3rd House, Venus = 5th House, Mars = 6th House, Sun = 9th House, Jupiter = 11th House, and Saturn = 12th House.

Occidental: "is when a Planet or Star sets after the Sun is down." [Partridge]

Oriental: "is when a Planet riseth before the Sun." [Partridge]

Partile: within the same degree number. Notice that this is not an orb size. The Moon at 6 Leo 01 is partile Mars at 6 Leo 59, while the Moon in the same place, and Mars at 5 Leo 59 is within a degree, but not partile. Any aspect may be called either partile, or platic, for those that are not partile.

Peregrine: "a Planet is Peregrine when he is in a Sign and degree where he hath no Essential dignity, as Mars in 26 degrees of Gemini is Peregrine, because he hath no dignity there, &c." [Partridge]

Quality: the Greek system of components that underlaid their elemental and physical systems: the qualities are hot & cold (active), and wet & dry (passive).

Reception "is when two Planets are in each other's dignities, as the Sun in Aries, and Mars in Leo, here is a Reception by House, it may be also by Exaltation, Triplicity, Term and Face." [Partridge]

Sect: whether diurnal or nocturnal. The primary sect of a chart is whether the chart itself is by day or night. A night chart has the Sun posited in the 1st through 6th Houses; a day chart has the Sun in the 12th through 7th Houses: right on the Ascendant-Descendant is anyone's guess! In addition, planets were considered to have intrinsic sect (Sun, Jupiter and Saturn: diurnal; Moon, Venus and Mars: nocturnal; Mercury: mixed); signs had intrinsic sect (Masculine = diurnal, Feminine = nocturnal), and planets had sect placement, according to whether they were diurnally or nocturnally placed in the chart in question.

Sect Light: The Sun, for a day chart; the Moon for a night chart.

Separation: "is when two Planets have been in Conjunction or Aspect and are going from it as Jupiter in 6 degrees of Aries and Mars in 7 degrees; here Mars separates himself from Jupiter; but yet he is not quite separated from him till they are distant from each other 8 degrees 30 minutes, which is the moiety of both their Orbs; what their Orbs and Aspects are." [Partridge]

Temperament: This was a system that Hippocrates used for relating a number of common conditions found in people. He described four temperaments, and each type was characterized by a similar psychology, metabolism, and pattern of illnesses. The four types are given in the following table, taken from ***Classical Astrology for Modern Living***.

Air	Libra, Aquarius, Gemini	Sanguine	Wet, becoming Hot
Fire	Aries, Leo, Sagittarius	Choleric	Hot, becoming Dry
Earth	Capricorn, Taurus, Virgo	Melancholic	Dry, becoming Cold
Water	Cancer, Scorpio, Pisces	Phlegmatic	Cold, becoming Wet

Sanguine types are extroverted social animals; choleric types are quick to anger; melancholics are morose or brooding; and phlegmatics are lethargic.

Term: One of the five essential dignities. The Term ruler was said to be "of the body" of that planet. If the Ascendant is in the Terms of Saturn, it would represent a person serious, older, in a saturnine profession, etc. It is primarily used for physical or outward appearance. The Term was given +2 points, and is considered a minor dignity.

Triplicity: One of the five essential dignities. Triplicities run by element, so there is one set of rulers for the fire signs, another for earth, etc. Triplicity is worth +3 points on the scale of essential dignities. The trick is that there are three different systems. Two of them utilize a day, night, and mixed ruler; the third, which was in common use by English astrologers in the 17th Century, used only day and night. Among the most obvious differences between the two that will be seen in this work is Jupiter being the mixed Triplicity ruler of Air: thus, for a year with Jupiter In Aquarius, Jupiter will often be the most dignified planet, and will virtually always be a contender for use because of the dignity.

Under the Sun's Beams: "a Planet is said to be under the Sun's beams, till he is full 17 degrees distant from him." [Partridge]

Via combusta: zone from 15 Libra to 15 Scorpio. Considered a dangerous area of the sky.

Void of Course: "is when a Planet is separated from one, and doth not apply to any other while he is in that Sign, and it is most observable in the Moon." [Partridge]

Appendix D

Table of Essential Dignities*

	Ruler	Exalt.	Triplicity			Terms					Faces		
			Day	Nght	Mix						0-10	10-20	20-30
♈	♂ D	☉ 19	☉	♃	♄	0 ♃ 6	6 ♀ 14	14 ☿ 21	21 ♂ 26	26 ♄ 30	♂	☉	♀
♉	♀ N	☽ 3	♀	☽	♂	0 ♀ 8	8 ☿ 15	15 ♃ 22	22 ♄ 26	26 ♂ 30	☿	☽	♄
♊	☿ D	☊ 3	♄	☿	♃	0 ☿ 7	7 ♃ 14	14 ♀ 21	21 ♄ 25	25 ♂ 30	♃	♂	☉
♋	☽ DN	♃ 15	♀ **	♂	☽	0 ♂ 6	6 ♃ 13	13 ☿ 20	20 ♀ 27	27 ♄ 30	♀	☿	☽
♌	☉ DN		☉	♃	♄	0 ♄ 6	6 ☿ 13	13 ♀ 19	19 ♃ 25	25 ♂ 30	♄	♃	♂
♍	☿ N	☿ 15	♀	☽	♂	0 ☿ 7	7 ♀ 13	13 ♃ 18	18 ♄ 24	24 ♂ 30	☉	♀	☿
♎	♀ D	♄ 21	♄	☿	♃	0 ♄ 6	6 ♀ 11	11 ♃ 19	19 ☿ 24	24 ♂ 30	☽	♄	♃
♏	♂ N		♀ **	♂	☽	0 ♂ 6	6 ♃ 14	14 ♀ 21	21 ☿ 27	27 ♄ 30	♂	☉	♀
♐	♃ D	☋ 3	☉	♃	♄	0 ♃ 8	8 ♀ 14	14 ☿ 19	19 ♄ 25	25 ♂ 30	☿	☽	♄
♑	♄ N	♂ 28	♀	☽	♂	0 ♀ 6	6 ☿ 12	12 ♃ 19	19 ♂ 25	25 ♄ 30	♃	♂	☉
♒	♄ D		♄	☿	♃	0 ♄ 6	6 ☿ 12	12 ♀ 20	20 ♃ 25	25 ♂ 30	♀	☿	☽
♓	♃ N	♀ 27	♀ **	♂	☽	0 ♀ 8	8 ♃ 14	14 ☿ 20	20 ♂ 26	26 ♄ 30	♄	♃	♂

* Dorothean Triplicities and so-called Ptolemaic or Chaldean Terms.

** Lilly gives both day and night in the water signs to Mars.

Appendix E

Cross Reference List of Methods

The purpose of this section is to list various methods and techniques that you might like to study from chart examples, allowing you to go to those charts that meet your criteria. Under each category, the chart numbers for those charts that match the criterion are given.

Ascendant Early Degrees (Zero Degrees): 62, 63
Ascendant Early Degrees (1-2 Degrees; + denotes Turned Ascendant): 24, 44+, 56, 75, 87, 89
Ascendant Late Degrees (27-29 Degrees): 2, 57, 73
Ascendant Ruler in Azimene Degrees (+ denotes Turned Ascendant): 9, 15, 16, 20, 27, 39, 50, 56, 82, 83+, 85, 87, 90c, 90f
*Ascendant Ruler Combust (8 degrees * means Cazimi):* 32, 45*, 71, 80
*Ascendant Ruler Under Beams (8-17 degrees * means Out of Sign):* 10*, 14, 27*, 41, 64*, 82
Ascendant Ruler Cadent (+ denotes Turned Ascendant): 1, 2, 4, 8, 9, 19, 24, 24+, 28, 29, 32, 34, 35, 41, 44+, 47, 51, 52, 71, 80, 80+, 85, 87, 89, 90b, 90d
Besiegement: 5, 9, 11, 15, 18, 19, 22, 23, 24, 27, 28, 29, 31, 35, 41, 43, 49, 50, 51, 52, 54, 56, 63, 66, 67, 68, 69, 72, 75, 80, 82, 84, 85, 86, 89, 90a, 90b, 90c, 90f
Eclipse near time of Question (i.e., within one week of question): 10, 19, 20, 36, 37, 44, 52, 57, 58, 66, 68, 75, 86, 88, 90c, 90d
Intercepted Sign entirely within the 1st House: 11, 38, 58, 74
Moon in Azimene Degrees: 16, 27, 28, 38, 50, 62, 69, 77, 85, 90a, 90f
Moon at the Bendings (8 degree orb): 20, 56, 57, 60, 69, 71, 76, 77, 90a, 90b
Moon Slow of Course (less than 12 degrees 10 minutes): 2, 6, 7, 14, 16, 22, 30-34, 49, 53, 55, 57, 62, 70, 72, 77, 80, 81, 88, 90a, 90b
Moon Swift of Course (more than 14 degrees 10 minutes): 5, 11, 15, 25-28, 36, 40, 43, 45, 52, 56, 58, 60, 64, 69, 71, 78, 82, 84
Moon Void of Course (means in Cancer, Taurus, Sagittarius or Pisces; ** means in separating partile last aspect):* 9**, 11, 13, 16, 20*, 28, 50*, 51, 56, 62, 83*, 88*, 91
Neptune in the 1st House: 18, 38, 39, 46, 47, 56, 70, 89

Perfection by Antiscia: 39, 58, 61, 68, 70, 81
Perfection by Mutual Reception (means minor reception):* 7*, 15*, 19, 25*, 28, 33, 36, 38*, 40, 41*, 46, 61*, 75, 81, 82*, 84*, 89*, 90a, 90e
Perfection Out-of-Sign: 13, 16, 20, 51, 70, 78, 82
Perfection by Translation (out of orb):* 5, 8, 43*, 44, 54, 55, 64, 75*, 81, 85
Quesited's Ruler in Azimene Degrees: 39, 50, 58, 69, 75, 83, 89
*Quesited's Significator Combust (8 degrees * means Cazimi):* 34, 35, 62, 63, 71, 91*
Quesited's Significator Under Beams (8-17 degrees): 29, 58, 72
Quesited's Ruler Cadent (read back from succedent house):* 1, 2, 9, 15, 19, 22, 24, 25, 26, 27, 28*, 31, 32, 33, 37, 38, 44, 45, 50, 52, 53, 54, 60, 62*, 64, 65, 68, 71, 72, 73, 75, 79, 85, 86, 88, 89, 90a, 90b, 90c, 90e, 90f*
Rendering: 12, 25, 36, 76
Refranation: 28,33,65
Saturn in the 1st House: 9, 11, 12, 38, 53, 61, 62, 74, 75, 82, 84, 85
Significator at the Bendings (8 degree orb): 1, 5, 12, 17, 28, 35, 37, 39, 41, 61, 67, 69, 75, 77, 80
Significator conjunct Fixed Star: 21, 33, 41, 48
Significator read into Previous House (e.g., within 7 degrees of the Ascendant on the 12th House side): 1, 3, 4, 6, 27, 28, 30, 36, 41, 48, 49, 55, 56, 60, 61, 62, 65, 67, 73, 75, 77, 80, 83, 84, 86, 90a, 90c, 90f
Significator Retrograde: 1, 8, 10, 11, 18, 19, 22, 24, 25, 28, 35, 39, 40, 45, 47, 48, 49, 50, 51, 52, 56, 58, 61, 62, 63, 64, 67, 68, 70, 76, 79, 80, 84, 86, 87, 90c, 91
Significator Slow of Course: 10, 15, 21, 31, 32, 43, 57, 65, 67, 77, 90a, 90e, 90f
Significator Swift of Course: 2, 4, 6, 7, 12, 14, 15, 17, 23, 25-30, 34-39, 42, 45, 48, 49, 51, 54, 55, 58, 61, 62, 63, 72-75, 77, 82, 83, 84, 86-89, 90c, 90f
Turned Ascendant: 5, 29, 32, 43, 44, 61, 70, 80, 83

Endnotes

1. For example, Karate, Aikido and Tae Kwon Do were all "invented" in the 20th Century, although they were based on older systems.
2. Gadbury, John. 1658. ***Genethlialogia***, page 235.
3. See the section, "Considerations against Judgment" later in this work.
4. ***Simplified Horary Astrology,*** page 1.
5. From: W. A. Olfdather, Translator. 1928. ***Epictetus II***. Loeb Classical Library: Harvard University Press: Cambridge, MA, page 517.
6. From: Russell Langley. 1970. ***Practical Statistics***. Dover: New York, page 98.
7. Lilly, pages 298-299. Aphorisms 5-8 do not apply to considerations against judgment.
8. Gadbury, page 237.
9. Patrick Curry. 1992. ***A Confusion of Prophets. Victorian and Edwardian Astrology***. Collins & Brown: London, page 10.
10. In ***Classical Astrology for Modern Living***, henceforth referred to as ***CAML***, see page 118.
11. Dorotheus (page 265) refers to it as the equatorial region, but again the meaning and possible significance isn't clear.
12. This is not to imply that Ward is necessarily, or even probably, wrong, at least in Lilly's case. On page 439, Lilly refers to the Moon as *vacua cursus*, a synonym for Void, when it would later square Mars from within the same sign.
13. Pages 122 and 299.
14. Goldstein-Jacobson, pages 76-77.
15. Watters, pages 13-17.
16. This is one of those aphorisms one always finds, but seldom is it defined in a clear enough way to understand its usage. The condition of the Moon is always paramount in most questions, because the Moon is the most frequent means of determining past and future events and actions, not to mention timing of future events. Having said this, the Moon should not be viewed as a means to ignore, negate, or trivialize the primary Significators. As we shall see in subsequent chapters, good delineation requires picking one Significator to represent each subject of the Question.

17. See Lilly, pp 148-150, 155-156.
18. See J. Lee Lehman. 1992. ***The Book of Rulerships*** for a complete listing of body parts by sign.
19. See for example William Ramesey, page 198 for electionals concerning learning any trade or craft being located in the 10th House.
20. I am indebted to Kevin Burk, who discovered the following quotation from the 1927 edition of Alan Leo's ***The Key to Your Own Nativity*** (Fowler: London, reprinted 1969, 1972, page 142):
"Legacies. The Eighth House of each nativity governs legacies, and money coming from others, such as coworkers, partners, etc. It is also concerned with occult affairs, mysterious and secret undertakings; it indicates the sex tendencies."
As Kevin points out, Leo never actually does a delineation using this idea.
21. *The Astrologers Magazine*, Vol. 1, No. 2, page 30.
22. 5th Edition, 1963; reprinted 1971 by Theosophical Publishing House: Wheaton, IL. The 4th Edition, which lacked this statement, was copyright 1952.
23. P. Hawksworth Dix, Volume 5 #2, 1931, page 75; and Lore Brüll Neuda, Volume 7 #2, page 70.
24. He even assigned harlots to the 12th House where they were safely hidden away from the eyes of "normal" society.
25. Ramesey. pp 152-153. He also discusses electing times to improve one's sex life as a matter of the 7th House on page 178.
26. See also Lilly, page 317, "... if a square or opposition be between the *Significators* (and no Reception) the matter will come to nothing."
27. John Gadbury, page 239.
28. This is probably a reference to the concept of emplacement – that some horaries are dependent on where the planets *are* rather than their future movement
29. Henry Coley. 1669. ***Clavis Astrologiae; Or A Key to the whole Art of Astrologie: In Two Parts.*** London: printed for Joseph Coniers. Page 67.
30. Lilly is clear on the latter point not through his definitions but usage: on page 140 he refers to the Moon in Virgo in a day chart as being peregrine.
31. This particular table appeared in Stella Rupertus. 1832. ***An Astrologian's Guide in Horary Astrology.*** London: Simpkin and Marshall. In text format, the idea is much earlier.
32. Lilly, pages 93-99, and 364.
33. Lilly, page 112.
34. Lilly, page 113.
35. Lilly, page 125.
36. Lilly, page 153 uses two different out of sign aspects between the Moon and Saturn and the Sun. On page 386, the Moon applies to the opposition to the Sun out of sign. On page 401, he uses an out of sign sextile to Mars in Cancer. On page 471, it was an out of sign sextile from the Moon in Aquarius to Saturn in Taurus.
37. ***CA***, page 107.

38. Page 440.
39. For more information of the Arabic parts, see Robert Zoller. 1980. ***The Lost Key to Prediction***. Inner Traditions: New York.
40. Blagrave, Joseph. 1671. ***Astrological Practice of Physick***. Obad. Blagrave: London. Available from Ballantrae, page 74.
41. Lilly, page 250.
42. Coley, Henry. 1669. page 63.
43. Pages 262-263.
44. Pages 181, 220.
45. ***CA***, pages 129-167
46. The word "accidents" in Lilly's usage is much broader than our current usage, which we interpret as an event like a car accident: a deleterious event, usually sudden. But to Lilly, an accident was *any* event that was worth considering. Thus, when a Querent asked Lilly about future accidents, it was akin to asking: are there any major upcoming events that I need to know about?"
47. ***DHQ***, page 242.
48. ***CA***, pages 157-166
49. Robert Zoller has found evidence of this activity at ports during US colonial times, and there is little doubt that further work would turn up still more evidence in other places.
50. ***CA***, page 157.
51. ***CA***, page 158-159.
52 ***CA***, page 157.
53. This may in fact bear on the tendency to use the 2nd House in lost object horaries for just about any thing which can be lost: about the only question anyone is likely to ask about these tools is where they are! If there is a question about whether the tool is functional, then that question can be read through the house that would show the functionality. For example, the functionality of medical implements would be shown through the 10th House, which is examined to assess the efficacy of a medical procedure.
54. Remember that generic house designations are always available, such as the 2nd for movable objects, and the 7th for persons to whom one's relations are either too vague or too complex to designate by another house.
55. The Ruler of the 8th House represents Death. In any horary related to health or longevity, this is obviously a possible issue. This idea is extended to the death of functional things; such as the death of a car.
56. These are periods and sub-periods of life ruled by the traditional planets and the Nodes, which depending on the period, may last for months or years.
57. For a fuller explanation of how the Nodes and the points square the Nodes may be understood, see ***CAML***, Chapter 10.
58. ***CA***, pages 167-186.
59. ***Doctrine of Horary Questions***, pages 249-250.
60. Notice, however, that Gadbury is only considering wealth through the 2nd House. There is no mention of inheritance through the 8th House, or gambling or stock profits through the 5th House.
61. *Ibid.*, page 250.

62. As usual, the word "joined" is somewhat ambiguous. Probably the best reading for it is any of the following: conjunct, in aspect to, or in antiscial relationship to. The problem, of course, is that the sources are loose about their definitions, and consistency is by no means guaranteed!
63. Again, the meaning can be ambiguous. Generally, the Fortunes are Venus, Jupiter, the North Node, and the Part of Fortune.
64. i.e., definitely by sign or exaltation; probably by Triplicity.
65. ***CA***, pages 173-177.
66. ***DHQ***, pages 253-258.
67. ***CA***, pages 187-201.
68. ***CA***, page 195
69. Dariot, Claudius. 1653 ***A briefe and most easy Introduction Conducing to the Astrological Judgement of the Stars*** , translated by Fabian Withers. London: Andrew Kemb, page 50.
70. It's criminal cases that require the jury to decide on a standard of "beyond reasonable doubt." Obviously, preponderance of evidence is a lower standard.
71. ***DHQ***, pages 258-263.
72. ***CA***, pages 202-219.
73. ***CA***, page 151.
74. What's an evil placement? This term was never specifically defined, rigorously or otherwise. One would presume that "evil placement" would include combust, conjunct the fixed stars of the nature of Mars or Saturn, in the 6th, 8th, or 12th House, or conjunct the South Node.
75. ***Theft***, pages 4-12.
76. ***CA***, page 394.
77. ***DHQ***, pages 262-263.
78. Griffin gives a similar list, but also adds the Planetary Hour ruler.
79. ***Theft***, pages 49-59.
80. ***CA***, pages 355-359.
81. Griffin, page 4.
82. "The House of the Moon" is the Sign ruler of the Moon.
83. The term "give virtue" can get a little confusing. It's an archaic reference to dispositorship. Saturn gives virtue to Mars by providing Mars with a rulership, in this case by Term. The word can be very confusing until you stop to think that the expression is similarly used with respect to the angles: thus, the construction, "Saturn gives virtue to the Ascendant. Here we finally arrive at a clear meaning, because the Ascendant is not a dispositor itself. An angle can *be* disposed; it cannot dispose something else. So this construction breaks down to mean that Saturn rules the Ascendant by some essential dignity.
84. All of these are from Griffin, pp 11-12.
85. These rules are from Griffin, pp 31-32.
86. *Ibid.*, page 27.
87. *Ibid.*, pp 37-40.
88. *Ibid.*, pp. 34-40.
89. *Ibid.*, page 43.

90. *Ibid.*, page 43.
91. *Ibid.*, pp 49-54
92. Barbara Watters contributed the idea that any planet in the degree of the Nodes is in a fateful location, page 96. Classically, this would be restricted to the hard aspects, as both the conjunction and opposition are actually conjunctions to one Node or the other; and the square point is called the Bendings, after Ptolemy, page 325 – the actual Greek word is *campion*. In this particular case, I think Watters' addition has merit, and should continue to be studied. However, it has also been oversimplified by some people who came after. Watters's "fateful" became "fatal" in other's hands, helped in part by Watters's example of the death of another person than the Querent.
93. Lilly, page 93
94. Lilly discusses this matter on pp. 370 to 371.
95. ***Doctrine of Horary Questions***, pages 263-268.
96. ***CA***, pages 222-242.
97. ***Vade Mecum***, pages 118-199.
98. This is a case where the definition may seem to be a bit like splitting hairs. Mars and Venus actually do come to the trine within the same sign – and in the very degree where Mars made its station. But the aspect isn't even close to being in orb.
99. ***CA***, page 107
100. Lilly, page 236.
101. Gadbury, page 268.
102. Gadbury, page 180, gives this Part as Ascendant + Venus – Mars.
103. ***Carmen Astrologicum***, V 39, 8.
104. ***DHQ***, pages 269-273.
105. ***CA***, pages 243-297.
106. Which themselves have certain problems – like the chemicals necessary to keep the substance in solution, which can themselves provoke an allergic reaction. And increasingly, vaccination-site sarcomas are being observed in pets, who are often subjected to annual vaccination.
107. What's a bio-energetic means? Some technique like acupuncture or massage, color or music therapy, pranic healing, or any other such method that does not rely exclusively on a mechanical approach to the body.
108. I have programmed many of these in Solar Writer/Medicus, available from Esoteric Technologies Pty. Ltd.
109. Please see my ***Book of Rulerships*** for a more comprehensive listing.
110. Culpeper, page 62.
111. Coley, page 183.
112. Culpeper, page 60.
113. Lilly, page 264.
114. Lilly, page 261.
115. Saunders, page 115.
116. Culpeper, page 62.
117. Culpeper, page 60.
118. Culpeper page 62 and Coley page 183.

119. Culpeper page 60.
120. Culpeper, page 62.
121. Culpeper, page 60.
122. Saunders, page 68.
123. Saunders, page 68.
124. Lilly, page 263.
125. Culpeper, page 60.
126. Culpeper, page 60.
127. Saunders, pages 37-38.
128. This is a commercial database that features Lois Rodden's data collection. They can be reached through http://www.astrodatabank.com/.
129. For those astrologers who use the three Triplicity ruler systems, you might think that Jupiter is not peregrine, having participating or mixed Triplicity. I examined this question with my students while Jupiter was transiting Aquarius. Jupiter acted peregrine, so we concluded that, however useful it might be in natal work, the participating Triplicities are ineffective in horary, and to a large extent in electional as well.
130. Qi Jong is a Chinese system of working the energetic system through primarily breathing and slow motion exercise, analogous to the therapeutic effect of Tai Chi. There are many references available to this system. I would recommend Master Shou-Yu Liang and Wen-Ching Wu. 1997. ***Qigong Empowerment***. Dragon Publishing: East Providence, RI.
131. Notice that the Table of Dignities given in the chart examples are constructed in a fashion which only permits the listing of a single Triplicity ruler, namely the "in-sect" one. In my Horary work, I consider Venus as the daytime Triplicity ruler of the Water signs, with Mars out-of-sect.
132. ***CA***, pages 297-404.
133. ***DHQ***, pages 273-283.
134. ***CA***, page 302-303, 317-318.
135. ***CA***, page 307.
136. ***CA***, page 307.
137. ***CA***, page 308.
138. ***CA***, page 309.
139. ***CA***, pages 308-310.
140. Notice that Mars or Saturn only act as malefics if they are not first acting as Significators. For example, if Taurus is rising and Venus applies to Mars, it is an indication of the success of the marriage, rather than an argument that the marriage will be broken off, because Mars acts first as Significator of the 7th, and not as a malefic in this case. So Venus and Mars as Significators can only be afflicted by Saturn, the South Node, or the Outer Planets, and an analogous situation exists from the Sun or Moon as Significator.
141. ***CA***, pages 310-311.
142. ***CA***, pages 311-312.
143. ***CA***, page 312-314.
144. ***CA***, pages 314-316.
145. ***CA***, pages 318-319.

146. ***CA***, pages 302, 303, 305, and 317. Lilly does not say regret, but that has been my interpretation, which has worked stunningly well. Lilly said "With slowness, labor and travail" (page 302), "... the matter be first in despair or suspended..." (page 303), "performance with much adoe" (page 305), or "matter comes to nothing" (page 317).
147. ***CA***, pages 367-368.
148. ***CA***, page 368.
149. Barbara Tuchman.1978. ***A Distant Mirror***. Knopf: New York, page 75.
150. ***CA***, page 380-383.
151. Bonatti, Guido. ***Tractatus Sextus***. Translated by Robert Zoller in successive issues of Astrology Quarterly ***62***(3): 33-38, ***63***(1): 15-25, ***63***(2): 35-45, ***63***(3): 16-22 (1992-1993).
152. ***CA***, pages 379-380.
153. Brady, Bernadette & J. Lee Lehman. 1997. 12th Century Castle Besiegement in Sports. The Results of a Research Project. AA Journal May 1997, or downloadable at: http://www.astrologer.com/aanet/ashes.html
154. ***CA***, page 369.
155. ***CA***, page 373.
156. ***CA***, page 372.
157. ***CA***, pages 373-375.
158. http://home.mpinetnet.net/cmueller/dirty.html
159. ***CA***, pages 55, 373.
160. ***CA***, pages 369-370.
161. ***CA***, pages 371-372.
162. ***CA***, page 377.
163. ***CA***, page 384.
164. ***CA***, pages 404-422.
165. ***CA***, page 411.
166. ***DHQ***, page 285.
167. Page 275
168. Page 278
169. Dorotheus, page 278.
170. ***CA***, page 414
171. ***CA***, pages 422-444.
172. ***CA***, pp 422-423.
173. ***CA***, page 423.
174. ***CA***, page 427.
175. This particular Triplicity was ignored by Lilly and most of the rest of the 17th Century English astrologers.
176. ***CA***, pages 442-444.
177. For further information on this subject, please see Manfred M. Junius. 1979. ***The Practical Handbook of Plant Alchemy***. Healing Arts Press: Rochester, VT; or C.L. Zalewski. 1990. ***Herbs in Magic and Alchemy***. Prism Press: Dorset, England.
178. ***CA***, page 432
179. Partridge, page 12; Ramesey, page 52; ***CA***, page 63.

180. ***CA***, page 139; Dariot 2nd Edition, page 25.
181. ***CA***, page 55; al Biruni, page 276.
182. ***CA***, pages 434-435.
183. ***CA***, pages 613-614.
184. ***Genethlialogia***, pages 155-156.
185. ***Mikropanastron***, page 150.
186. ***CA***, pages 444-457.
187. ***DHQ***, pages 288-290.
188. A thoughtful discussion of these matters as they are likely to apply to the 21st Century is given in Robert D. Kaplan's ***The Coming Anarchy***. Random House: New York, 2000.
189. See, for example, Manly Palmer Hall. 1959. ***Astrological Keywords***. Philosophical Library: New York. Also Rex E. Bills. 1971. ***The Rulership Book***. Macoy Publishing & Masonic Supply Co., Inc.: Richmond, VA.
190. Kaplan, page 81.
191. ***CA***, page 56.
192. ***CA***, page 55.
193. ***CA***, page 444.
194. ***CA***, page 447.
195. ***CA***, pages 450-451.
196. A reference to nineteen degrees Scorpio, but I am not aware of the exact origin of this expression. Nicholas DeVore's ***Encyclopedia of Astrology*** (1947; Philosophical Library: New York) refers to the usage as "ancient," which may be descriptive, but hardly helpful!
197. ***CA***, pages 457-59.
198. Lilly mentions this in the title of the chapter, then never specifically delineates it.
199. ***DHQ***, pages 291-292.
200. ***DHQ***, page 292.
201. ***CA***, pages 460-472.
202. The whole set of Lilly's "on behalf of prisoner" rules are in ***CA***, pages 462-463.
203. ***CA***, pages 463-464.
204. For a fascinating account of this period in England, see Keith Thomas. 1971. ***Religion and the Decline of Magic***. Oxford University Press: New York.
205. ***CA***, pages 464-465.
206. See for example, Abraham ibn Ezra, ***The Beginning of Wisdom***, Levy translation, pages 192-193.
207. That is, Sun in 7th to 12th House.
208. That is, Sun in 1st to 6th House
209. This is easier to do if you know what signs the planets are in.
210. Depending, of course, on whether you want to use Lilly's Triplicities or the Dorothean. I always remember the Lilly ones, but tend to favor the Dorothean ones.
211. 1989. Whitford Press: West Chester, PA.
212. 1996. Whitford Press: West Chester, PA.
213. ***CAML***, Chapter 11.

214. Two good works to have on the history of astrology are:
Jim Tester. 1987. ***A History of Western Astrology***. Boydell: Bury St. Edmunds, and
James Herschel Holden. 1996. ***A History of Horoscopic Astrology***. American Federation of Astrologers: Tempe, AZ.
215. In modern times, his best known works date from 1029. ***The Book of Instruction in the Elements of Astrology***, translated by R. Ramsay Wright, Luzac & Co.: London, 1934. Available from Ballantrae.
216. Her work is 1990. ***Horary Astrology Rediscovered***. Whitford Press: West Chester, PA.
217. ***Tractatus Sextus***. Translated by Robert Zoller in successive issues of Astrology Quarterly ***62***(3): 33-38, ***63***(1): 15-25, ***63***(2): 35-45, ***63***(3): 16-22 (1992-1993).
218. His best known work, in both editions, is: 1669. ***Clavis Astrologiae, or a Key to the whole Art of Astrology. In Two Parts***. Joseph Coniers: London. 1676. ***Clavis Astrologiae, or a Key to the whole Art of Astrology. New Filed and Polished in Three Parts.*** Thomas Sawbridge: London. Available from Ballantrae.
219. His best known astrological work is 1655. ***Astrological Judgment of Diseases from the Decumbiture of the Sick***. American Federation of Astrologers: Tempe, AZ.
220. Three editions worth mentioning:

1583. ***A Brief and Most Easy Introduction to the Astrological Judgement of the Stars. Whereby Every Man May With Small Labor Give Answers to any Question Demanded.*** Translated by Fabian Wither. Reprinted 1992 Just Us & Associates: Issaquah, WA. This version was the one available in Lilly's time.

Dariot, Claude. 1653. ***A Brief Introduction conducing to the Judgment of the Stars, wherein the whole Art of Judiciall Astrologie is briefly and plainly delivered***. Translated by Fabian Withers and enlarged by Nathaniel Spark. London. This was bound with the first English language work on astro-meteorology by Spark, as well as a medical treatise.

There is a modern French edition that has been somewhat cleaned up, I suspect to allow for copyright: 1558/1990. ***Introduction au Jugement des Astres suivie d'un Traité des élections propres pour le commencement des choses***. Adapted to modern French by Chantal Etienne. Pardès: Puiseaux.

221. The version in print is 1976. ***Carmen Astrologicum***, translated by David Pingree. B. G. Teubner Verlagsgesellschaft: Leipzig. Also available: Ascella: Nottsh.
222. One of the most significant of these works was edited by Rachel Levy and Francisco Cantera in 1939: ***The Beginning of Wisdom***. The Johns Hopkins Press: Baltimore, MD.
223. 1658. ***Genethlialogia, or The Doctrine of Nativities Together with The Doctrine of Horarie Questions.*** Printed by J[ohn] C[oniers] for William Larner. In production: Regulus Publishing Co., Ltd.: London.
224. 1960. ***Simplified Horary Astrology***. Frank Severy Publishing: Alhambra, CA.

225. 1665, 1996 ***An Astrological Judgement touching Theft***. Just Us & Associates: Issaquah, WA..
226. In the horary field, the work is 1993. ***Horary Astrology, Practical Techniques for Problem Solving with a Primer of Symbolism***. Aurora Press: Santa Fe, NM.
227. His best-known book is 1647. ***Christian Astrology***. Reprinted in 1985 by Regulus: London. Also available: Just Us & Associates
228. 2nd Century A.D. ***Tetrabiblos***. Translated by F. E. Robbins. Harvard University Press: Cambridge. 1971.
229. 1653. ***Astrologia Restaurata; or Astrology Restored: being an Introduction to the General and Chief part of the Language of the Stars.*** Printed for Robert White: London. Available from Ballantrae.
230. His best known work is: 1677. ***The Astrological Judgment and Practice of Physick, deduced from the Position of the Heavens at the Decumbiture of the Sick Person, &c***. Thomas Sawbridge: London.
231. 1973. ***Horary Astrology and the Judgment of Events***. Valhalla: Washington, DC

Index

About the Author

Lee has a Ph.D. in Botany from Rutgers University. She is author of four previous books with Whitford Press, *The Ultimate Asteroid Book* (1988), *Essential Dignities* (1989), *The Book of Rulerships* (1992), and *Classical Astrology for Modern Living* (1996). In addition she has published a translation from the French of Papus's *Astrology for Initiates*. She originated the Classical Studies course curriculum, which presently includes seven regular courses. She teaches regular classes in Atlanta and Boston, and recurring classes in several other cities. She is on the faculty for Kepler College. In her spare time, she studies herbalism and Chang-Hon style Tae Kwon Do, in which she holds a 1st Dan black belt.

Along with Graham Dawson and Stephanie Johnson of Esoteric Technologies, Lee has created two software report writer programs written specifically for the classical astrologer: Solar Writer/Medicus, for medical questions and decumbitures; and Solar Writer/Classical, for natal delineation in the matter-of-fact style of the Renaissance astrologer. She was the winner of the Marc Edmund Jones Award in 1995.

Lee resides in Florida.